BOOKS BY WALTER KERR

HOW NOT TO WRITE A PLAY
CRITICISM AND CENSORSHIP
PIECES AT EIGHT
THE DECLINE OF PLEASURE
THE THEATER IN SPITE OF ITSELF
TRAGEDY AND COMEDY
THIRTY PLAYS HATH NOVEMBER
GOD ON THE GYMNASIUM FLOOR
THE SILENT CLOWNS

The Silent Clowns

The Silent Clowns

by Walter Kerr

Alfred A. Knopf New York 1979

for Chris, John, Col, Gil, Greg and Kitty, who, like their father before them, "grew up" on silent movies

THIS IS A BORZOI BOOK
PUBLISHED BY ALFRED A. KNOPF, INC.

Published in the United States by Alfred A. Knopf, Inc., New York, and simultaneously in Canada by Random House of Canada Limited, Toronto. Distributed by Random House, Inc., New York.

Library of Congress Cataloging in Publication Data
Kerr, Walter [date]
The silent clowns.
Includes index.
1. Comedy films—History and criticism.
2. Moving-pictures, Silent—History. I. Title.
PN1995.9.C55K4 791.43'0909'17 75-8231
ISBN 0-394-46907-0 Hardcover ISBN 0-394-73450-5 Paperback

Manufactured in the United States of America

Published November 17, 1975
Second Printing December 1975
First Paperback Edition, March 1979

Acknowledgments

With rare exceptions, this is not a book done from memory. My own substantial moviegoing encompassed only the last seven or eight years of silent film's thirty-year reign, and even if I had appeared on the scene sooner I should not for a moment have trusted my personal impressions. The trouble with memory is not that it fails but that it so generously creates. A few years ago I made brief reference in a book to a sequence in which the silent clown Harry Langdon held up a building during a cyclone. Now that I have seen the film again I am stunned to discover what my mind's eye, over the years, had done to it, fusing it with three or four other buildings held up during three or four other cyclones—including one sturdily maintained by the much later Harpo Marx—until I had arrived at a glorious, utterly untrustworthy composite. In approaching the materials freshly, then, I knew I had better see the films freshly—whenever and wherever I could. What follows is a current report on films made forty-six to seventy-eight years ago.

In addition, I had hoped to write a book about the processes of discovery: discovery of the silent camera itself, of its peculiar properties, of the varied uses to which those peculiar properties might best be put, of the highly idiosyncratic relationship each comedian would have to forge for himself with lens, frame, and motion. But this could only be done if I could find the film I *hadn't* seen and try to trace its successive blossomings—its unfolding in general and its separate invitations to quite different clowns—in some sort of coherent sequence.

So the film had to be found—it is still scattered here, there, and everywhere—and looked at twice and thrice again. For indispensable help along the way I am indebted to many institutions and many people. Among them:

Kent D. Eastin of Blackhawk Films in Davenport, Iowa, who loaned me carton upon carton of early short-length and feature material; William K. Everson, who spent hours at his projector showing me materials I might otherwise have missed altogether; James Card of Eastman House in Rochester, New York, who scoured his archives and set up screenings that must have wearied him but gratified me; Pat Sheehan, of the Library of Congress, and Larry Karr of the American Film Institute in Washington, D.C., who provided not only the white gloves for handling ancient nitrate film but the Movieolas to nurse the film through; Charles Silver of the Museum of Modern Art in New York, who gave me a projector and a blank wall and let me run each film as many times as I liked; Peter Robeck of Time-Life, who opened up the cache of Harold Lloyd films the organization has acquired; the British Film Institute in London, and many individuals who helped form scouting parties: Leonard Maltin, Joe Franklin, Gordon Berkow, Spencer Berger, Paul Killiam, Arthur A. Ross, Don Koll, together with—and above all—my good friend Herbert Graff, who searched and searched and found and found and never blinked an eye at the most impossible request.

To all of these I am immensely grateful.

In the matter of illustration—and once again I am indebted to a number of helping hands—it has seemed best to identify sources for photographs at the back of the book. I should like to acknowledge, however, the special courtesies extended to me by George Pratt of Eastman House, Mary Corliss of the Museum of Modern Art, Louise Louvis of the John E. Allen Collection, David Bradley, Roderick Bladel of the Theatre Collection of the New York Public Library, and Sam Gill of the Academy of Motion Picture Arts and Sciences.

And a final, special thanks to George Pratt and William K. Everson, who generously agreed to go over the manuscript, offering correction and advice out of their own vast backgrounds in the field.

The Silent Clowns

Part One The Silent Camera

Part Two Comedy Reborn

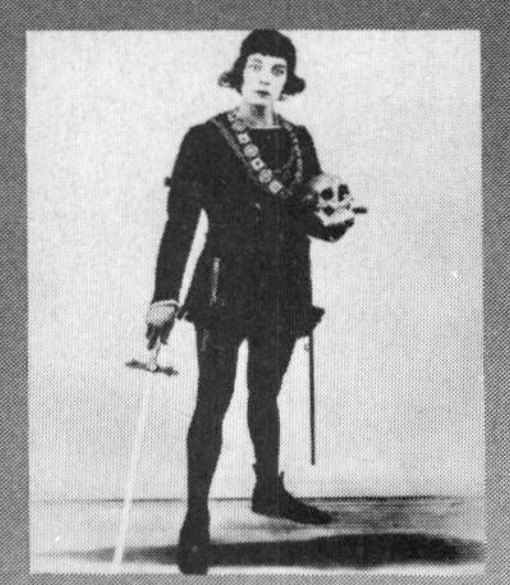

Part Three The Struggle Toward Maturity

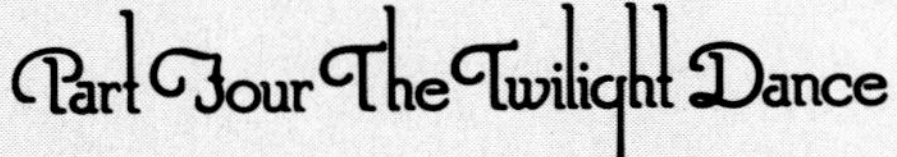

Part Four The Twilight Dance

Part One— The Silent Camera

1. The Pickford Paradox and the Choice of Silence

In casting about for a summary or a signature with which to end his deeply sympathetic salute to silent film, *The Parade's Gone By*, Kevin Brownlow chose what are surely the most mysterious words in his entire book. Too young himself to have experienced silent film at first hand, Mr. Brownlow tracked down everyone he could find who had participated in the birth and growth of this already dead form. Through a collection of interviews with stars, cameramen, producers, and bystanders with long memories he recreated a curious and complete world that not only is no longer with us but was unlike any other while it was. How to say farewell to it? He chose a sentence of Mary Pickford's:

"It would have been more logical if silent pictures had grown out of the talkie instead of the other way round."

The sentence brings us up short. What can the woman have thought she meant? It's easy enough to understand a yearning for the form that had given her a kind of fame almost unimaginable now. But *logical*? Logical to have had it all from the beginning—sound, speech, color, the whole timbre and palette of recognizable life—and then to have stripped it down to a black-and-white dance of mute ghosts?

And yet it is precisely that word *logical*, I think, that snaps us to unexpected attention, teasing us with a truth or a half-truth just out of sight. The woman may sound perverse, but there is something maddeningly accurate buried in her remark. We acknowledge this—as Mr. Brownlow clearly did, placing it in so prominent a position—without being able to isolate our oblique perception. Certainly the process is never going to work Miss Pickford's way. We have had silence, found sound, and are not going back. We know in our bones that there will never again be a time when films, as a general practice and with universal acceptance, show us guns firing, smoke curling from their barrels, without producing any sound at all, or lips moving without issuing audible words. Technology, at least, does not reverse itself.

Why *logical*, then? We may notice in passing that Miss Pickford is expressing a conviction not entirely rooted in personal pride. *Her* career was not destroyed by speech. She won her only Academy Award for her performance in a talking film, *Coquette*. Her career in sound films was shorter and less successful than her literally queenly career in silents—she was growing older, for one thing—but she might easily have claimed success in both forms.

To the end of his days, the silent comedian Harold Lloyd did just that. Lloyd, of course, made a number of talking films—as Keaton did, as Chaplin finally did—and in talking to William Cahn for a sketchy late biography, Lloyd was quick to insist that he had never made a talking film that lost money. When he compiled his old material for theatrical reissue, he carefully included excerpts from sound films—even when they nearly duplicated silent film sequences that were, in fact, better.

I met Mr. Lloyd, a friendly and unpretentious man, only once, at a private screening of a compilation he was still editing. He wanted comments, and I asked him why he had chosen to use the long tangle with a painter's scaffold that was being hauled up the face of an apartment building in *Feet First* rather than the much more celebrated department-store climb, culminating in a battle with a monstrous clock thirteen floors above the street, from *Safety Last*. He hurried past this question, though he was earnestly attentive to most others, murmuring something about the unavailability of legal rights to the latter sequence. I doubted that Mr. Lloyd would have had any real difficulty in acquiring such rights, and I realized at once that I had simply asked a wrong question. Mr. Lloyd wanted to use the passage from *Feet First* because his voice could be heard in it, reminding audiences that his career had spanned the two forms. Any successful performer might be expected to have taken a similar attitude. If Miss Pickford chose not to, if she risked sounding nostalgic at best and preposterous at worst, it was because she had something important in mind.

What I *think* she had in mind was a truism not about silent films in particular but about art in general. Logically, art begins in a taking away. No painter or poet or dramatist in his right mind ever attempts to reproduce the abundance of life *in toto*. He may wish to evoke the *sense* of that abundance, in Brueghel's way or in Shakespeare's, but he doesn't do it by constant addition; he does it by constant subtraction. He limits the frame, sacrifices a dimension, chastens color, looks for absences, refusals, self-imposed limitations that will enable him to suggest more with less. It is the only thing he *can* do. A dramatist may write a play called *Street Scene*, but he cannot have an entire street and all that might happen on it placed on the stage or accounted for in two hours' time. When someone tries this, as David Belasco did in moving an actual boarding-house room onto his stage or borrowing from a Childs restaurant every last bit of silverware necessary to serve stage meals for an evening, it is immediately apparent that it is not worth doing. The more of life, the less of art. The form of a sonnet is arbitrarily restricting, no more representative of the free flow of thought than the severely squared Alexandrine is representative of the free flow of speech. Opportunities are discarded, observation itself is denied, vision and speech are straitjacketed, all in the interests of arriving at an evocative minimum. Stripping down is the preparation for art, a readying for an unencumbered plunge into the depths, as it is to the very end the procedure of art. Every real actor or painter or poet spends more time striking out than wedging in. The deletions take him closer to the core of what he is doing.

They serve another function. They open the door to a second imagination, the viewer's, the listener's. The less complete the canvas, the more there is for the

A fiddler stays close to the recording apparatus while his colleagues dance in one of Edison's earliest attempts to add a moving image to his phonograph. Prior to 1895.

viewer to contribute. He must work with hints, and the more he must do for himself, the more deeply engaged he becomes in the work. Audiences are rarely aware of how active they become in the presence of work that is created by nuance, by incomplete statement. With their own imaginations forcibly alerted, they move forward to *meet* the imagination of the man who has composed what they are watching. There is a journey and a greeting, an exchange of experience, a handshake on truth. The two make the image together.

I am anticipating here, but it is in fact much more tiring to watch a silent film than a sound film, as I discovered in a screening room recently. I had spent some days running through early short comedies made before moviegoing had become a regular occupation of mine. Though I was rarely bored, each day I found myself getting hungry after an hour or two. I suddenly realized that I was working harder to attend to the screen than I normally did, despite my intense interest. And that, having been so long accustomed to sound, I *wanted* sound. I didn't want it for the film, which was complete on its own terms. I wanted it for *me*, as something to lean on, something to support me, something to make attention automatic. I had grown lazy. Silence is not a softer form; it is a more demanding one.

When the artist, in whatever medium, provides *all* the stimuli necessary to keep his audience awake and fully informed, the audience, having nothing to do, goes limp. This is not to say that audiences at today's sound films, which blaze with color and screech with car-skids, are limp. But there was a time when they were. In the late 1940's and early 1950's, audience attendance at films dropped so spectacularly that thousands of film houses closed and the studio system itself was destroyed. The decline is normally attributed to television. But in certain Rocky Mountain states where television was not yet available, the falloff was exactly as precipitous. Filmmakers had put their audiences to sleep. They had done it by taking care of everything—smoothing the way with slow dissolves that made transitions plain, firmly ending sequences with fade-outs followed by a few seconds of blankness to indicate the passage of time, beginning new sequences with fade-ins that made adjustment easy, *always* indicating shifts of time and place with calendar leaves slipping from the wall, candles burning down, railroad wheels racing. Movement within a scene, no matter how many shifts of position the camera might record, was complete: long establishing shot in which we could identify the room and see a character entering it, pickup shot from the doorway as the character moved deeper into the room, reaction shot from another character watching him come closer—the whole clock accounted for moment by moment. Of course there were graceful elisions, interesting camera-made metaphors, as there always had been. But if film had nearly, and too literally, ground to a halt, it was partly because it had learned to be too helpful.

The problem was solved, more or less, with a scissors. Directors and editors began leaving things out: indications of time, place, advancing steps in the story. Suddenly we were hurtled from room to room, country to country, year to year, event to event—and left to account for the spaces between jumps for ourselves. The new game was to see if one could *follow* the film, so swift were its leaps, so wide it gaps. The audience, now put to work again, promptly woke up.

It should be clear from our most recent experience of film that if art tends to become livelier as it learns to leave things out, artists are not always astute enough to remember this. Artists, whole schools of them, do indeed nod; and nodding seems to invite total recall. Audiences too can grow sluggish for reasons that have little to do with art, more to do with ebbs of energy in the body politic. There are times—long times—when audiences prefer being coddled to being challenged; they are weary at the moment and look for a form of waking sleep. Menander, the

Opposite, above: Coquelin in a sound film excerpt from *Cyrano de Bergerac*, with amplifying horn plainly visible. Paris, 1902.

Below: "I am the queen of fairies" announces this sprite before dancing in *Nursery Favorites*, one of Edison's 1913 efforts to make sound film commercial.

Greek writer of Middle Comedy, came *after* the spare, vertical practices of the great Greek dramatists; he introduced a great deal more realism, a richer abundance of homely detail, than his predecessors had cared to bother with. Apparently his audiences loved him for it. But these audiences were no longer confident Greeks on the move; they were Greeks in a state of submission to military and political defeat. Menander made things easier for them, more palatable with his profusion of small things observed; he did not necessarily advance the quality of theater. It would take—somewhere, sometime—a new courage to do that.

The history of art, then, has not been a record of uninterrupted, ever-increasing selectivity, moving from an initial and quite childish love for superabundant detail to an ultimate, exquisitely chaste refusal of detail. It has, rather, been a seesaw affair, with periods of relative severity giving way to a new taste for opulence, periods of opulence being shattered by fresh calls to severity. Of the two, however, the taste for opulence is more nearly a giving-in, more likely to end in somnolence. The revolution that shatters the somnolence, whether it is an Armory Show or a *Citizen Kane*, is almost always a call to part with something we thought we could not do without. See how Samuel Beckett and Harold Pinter are trying to strip us down today: Pinter will not even tell us what his story is. The bent of art, when it is attempting to renew itself as art, is toward reduction.

In which case it is not *illogical* to say, with Miss Pickford, that sound and speech and color might very well have been voluntarily abandoned—down the years much more radical divestitures have taken place in the arts—in favor of the more austere, more imaginatively demanding pleasures of silence. The art of music, after the feasts it has had, is flirting with silence right now.

As it happens, though, there is no need to defend Miss Pickford's remark. Something suprisingly like what she envisioned actually happened in the first place. The original moviegoing audience could have had sound but didn't want it. It *chose* silence. It chose silence for at least fifteen years, the fifteen years in which all the major treasures of the silent form were created.

We never think of silent films as having represented a choice on the part of the public, and of course there was no one early moment in which fully developed sound was placed side by side with silence and a vote taken, though the situation came very close to that many times before 1928. We think of silent films as having been silent from necessity, because they *couldn't* speak, didn't know how to—critics have written that films spoke the minute they were able to. We imagine motion pictures as developing directly out of the necessarily mute photograph, waiting for the day when engineers would devise means of rescuing the form and making it whole.

None of these casual suppositions is true. Motion pictures were not devised as an extension of the photograph, though they were that. They came into being as a proposed extension of the phonograph. When Thomas Edison went into his laboratory to devise a means of unspooling a succession of still pictures rapidly enough to create the illusion of movement, he wasn't interested in the illusion of movement for its own sake. That had existed, in various forms of zoötrope, for a long time: a disc like a carousel turned, and the eye looked at successive images through a slit. The effect could be combined with a magic lantern and projected on a screen as early as 1853. Children can still flip a prepared picture-book and achieve the illusion. Edison was, rather, looking for a way to make his phonograph records *visible*. He wasn't trying to make pictures that moved; he was trying to make sound that could be seen. The sound was ready, and he owned the patents on it; if he could tie a moving image to it, he would have the form whole.

He did find a way to make the pictures. And the first films he made were

Opposite, top to bottom: Weber and Fields, DeWolfe Hopper, Ben Bard and Jack Pearl in stage routines photographed by Lee DeForest with his highly sophisticated sound-on-film system. 1922.

sound films. One of the earliest filmed records we have of Edison in production—inside the celebrated Black Maria, little more than a tar-paper shack geared to move with the sun—shows a violinist merrily piping his tune into a phonograph horn while the camera turns. But there were problems—of accurate synchronization and adequate amplification for public places.

While Edison was still searching for a satisfactory means of adding his new invention to the dominant phonograph, something unexpected happened. Large numbers of people became avidly interested in the pictures as pictures, whether they could talk or not. Queues formed in penny arcades before machines with peep-hole slots in them. It was enough just to watch, for a mere thirty seconds or so, the image of a man sneezing, a woman dancing, an ocean roller breaking on the beach. Curiously, when Edison added earphones to the machines—now called Kinetophones—so that sight and sound might be simultaneous, public preference was for the purely silent pictures. Edison dismissed this preference as a fad, bound to diminish in time, and continued work—as did his competitors abroad—toward the real objective.

With considerable success. As early as 1900, in Paris, it was possible to go to the Phono Cinema Theater to see *and hear* both Bernhardt and Coquelin perform on a screen. A 1902 film, recorded on discs, of Coquelin's rhymed duel from *Cyrano de Bergerac* exists and can still be seen and heard today. The sound fidelity is no worse than that of phonograph records of the period, which means that it would have seemed quite "natural" to audiences at the time.

In England the Gaumont Company was exhibiting its own form of sound film by 1904, not only in major cities but across the countryside. The press was very often enthusiastic, and the sheer novelty of the exhibitions drew crowds, temporarily. London's *Morning Post* reported in February of 1907 that "the operatic items are a great advance on anything of the kind hitherto seen, the voices coming through clear and strong, while the synchronization of the sound with the picture is most precise." But mechanical success did not mean that the public had been truly converted. No wave of enthusiasm swept silence away.

There seems to have been very little, if any, interchange of information between inventors in France, Britain, and America, presumably because patents were valuable and each man wished to call perfected sound film his own. Edison, for instance, did not make another commercial attempt at exhibition until 1913, this time with theatrical amplification. When he did—sung passages from *La Bohème* were among the attractions—the reaction was cool. *Talkers Flop* was the message of a *Variety* headline that year.

If there were still any leftover difficulties in making sound film thoroughly viable in America, they were resolved by the development of the telephone repeater in 1914.

Nineteen fourteen. Everything vital was available in America the year before the appearance of *The Birth of a Nation*. Only the indifference of the public stilled further effort. Dedicated engineers continued their work in private, and to no profit. By 1922 the American inventor Lee De Forest had mastered the highly sophisticated technique of recording sound not on discs but on the film itself and was exhibiting his short subjects—Eddie Cantor singing, Weber and Fields performing their traditional vaudeville act—in the few theaters that could be persuaded to wire for sound. The American Film Institute in Washington has recently projected a number of these films at festivals: they are technically most acceptable and in some cases charming. I remember the theater in which they played in Chicago when I was a boy, and of course I could have seen them then. I didn't bother. Buster Keaton was starring in his first feature film that year.

The Pickford Paradox and the Choice of Silence

If the audience had given any real indication from, say, 1904 onward that it cared about seeing the transformation completed, the silent feature film would simply never have existed. Historians would be left today with a handful of primitive short films, developed only as far as *The Great Train Robbery, The New York Hat*, and *The Battle at Elderbush Gulch* were developed. If audiences had cared to see and hear Eddie Cantor on a screen in 1922—and Mr. Cantor comes through most engagingly today—and had decided then that it preferred talking films, Harold Lloyd's silent career would have been cut off before *Why Worry?;* Chaplin—who as yet had only one feature to his credit and was not as firmly entrenched as he would be in 1929—might not have made *The Pilgrim, The Gold Rush*, or *City Lights*; and a silent Harry Langdon would never have appeared at all. There were five or six more years of silence to come after Mr. De Forest's foolproof method was available and exhibited. In those five or six years *The Covered Wagon, The Hunchback of Notre Dame, The White Sister, Merry-Go-Round, The Thief of Bagdad, The Big Parade, The Last Laugh, The Unholy Three, Ben-Hur, Variety, Beau Geste, Potemkin, The Way of All Flesh, Wings, Seventh Heaven, Underworld,* and *The Crowd* were made. However one may regard this group of films today, it is a substantial body of a certain kind of work. The audience chose it. Sound now existed in its entirety and was put aside in favor of a continuing loyalty to a form audiences had done more than grow accustomed to: they had learned to understand and to cooperate with a *style*. Silent film was an experience not readily surrendered.

Nineteen twenty-eight was the transitional year, with silence still predominating—for the last time. When the *New York Times* ran its annual list of "Best Films" on January 1, 1929, all ten of those chosen were silents. It was simply assumed that silence was the "art" form, sound film a commercial novelty. Sound films are in fact acknowledged in the report. Of seventeen additional "worthy" films, fifteen were silent, two sound. A kind of footnote is added acknowledging four more sound films. A total of twenty-five distinguished silents ranked well above the six talking films—and this in the year when the rush was on, when sound would take over forever.

It had been possible for many of us to attend silence and sound side by side for a year or more before the cataclysm of 1928. The management of the principal movie house in the town in which I grew up had installed the Warner Brothers' Vitaphone process early, spurred by the rumored success—it seemed a freak at the time—of Al Jolson's *The Jazz Singer*. Week after week we would sit through three Vitaphone short subjects: Marion Talley or Giovanni Martinelli singing an aria, Smith and Dale or Van and Schenck doing a vaudeville turn. But we simply sat through them while we waited for the serious business of the evening, the silent feature: perhaps Josef von Sternberg's *The Last Command* or Buster Keaton's *Steamboat Bill Jr.* The short subjects caused no excitement of any kind, brought in no new patronage. They were simply regarded as mechanical—and hence inferior—versions of the same vaudeville acts that had always appeared in film theaters by way of prologue to the silent feature. Excitement about sound waited on something else. Continued at this level, sound film might have failed again.

The audience knew what it had come for, and the surrender to sound was very gradual. It had long ago done, first by inference and then in fact, what Mary Pickford suggests: expressed a preference for a severely limited form over a busy and superabundant one. For much of silent film history the decision to cling to spareness may be taken as deliberate. The audience was in love and meant to stay that way.

Little Miss Muffett and a seagoing swain sing and dance in Edison's 1913 *Nursery Favorites*.

2. The Unique Experience

Audiences were loath to part with silence because they knew the experience they were having was unique. No earlier generation had ever been offered it. No later generation, once sound had come, would be able to put its pieces together again. Once surrendered, it would be surrendered for good. Today many people find it difficult to understand, let alone enjoy.

Nostalgia can do little for it now, which may be as well. There are of course many people alive who once loved it and have fond memories. But those feelings were in part dependent on a dawnlike freshness about the form that cannot be felt these long years later, looking at prints now frozen in time, prints that remain exactly as they were though *we* have changed. We look at silent films now through our own aging, our own altered senses, our own vivid and restless acquaintance with sound. Their sheen, even when the camera-work glows with an unspoiled ardor, even when we are fortunate enough to see an almost blindingly brilliant tinted print on its original stock, is dulled, dulled by the absence of all the things we once carried into darkened, organ-swept theaters. The smells of tile and leather and nitrate and buttered popcorn were all part of the experience. The curtain that did not pull back until the projectionist had flashed the title on the screen was part of it. Our sense of having been born at the right moment—think of it! to have been born fifty years earlier would have meant being denied Douglas Fairbanks, denied Tom Mix, denied the very sight of a man climbing the drawbridge-chain of a medieval castle, of a cowboy jumping his horse directly through a plate-glass window—was an exhilarating part of it. Never mind the telephone or the radio: Every time we entered the cheapest of motion-picture theaters, we were ushered, awe-struck, into Avalon.

Though I shifted my own allegiance to the legitimate theater when I was in my early twenties—ironically, the coming of sound may have had something to do with that shift, leading me from words to more and better words—I did for a long time have a nostalgic pull toward certain quivering memories of my youth. For I had begun seeing silent films with some freedom and consistency in 1920, the year my mother gave me permission, at last, to go to the movies alone—though of course only on weekends. I was then seven. I remember that I was first taken to a movie house by my father some three or four years earlier, no doubt to see a William S. Hart film, and I am told that I spent most of my time crawling under the seats, seriously distracting my father. I remember nothing of the occasion except a glass slide: the black silhouette of Charlie Chaplin against a red background with lettering indicating, my father explained to me, that Mr. Chaplin was to be seen next week. Sometime after that, it must have been very soon, I stopped crawling under the seats. I became so enamored of the giant, ghostly moving images that I became an irresistible nuisance to my maiden aunts, who could be counted on to take me to the movies so long as I didn't stop begging. Permission to go alone came finally, I think, to free my aunts for other duties.

I was just in time to see Harold Lloyd's first tentative spreading of his agile wings beyond short comedies in a forty-minute "feature" called *A Sailor-Made Man*, just in time to see Douglas Fairbanks begin his costume films by cheerfully dueling with a dozen opponents while sitting cross-legged on a table in *The Mark of Zorro*, just in time to watch caveman Buster Keaton drag his mate by the hair across a prehistoric skyline in *his* first feature, *The Three Ages*. On Saturday afternoons the mirror of the world opened up and let me through. If Fairbanks was a genie loosed to spirit himself onto churchtops, high among the mission bells, the clowns were no less magical: outsized, omnipotent creatures emerged from some Druidical forest to cast spells on a pliable universe. If, in *The Navigator*, Keaton slowly emerged from the water at ocean's edge encaged in the monstrous helmet and inflated body of a deep-sea diver to seem an avenging god to hundreds of cannibals who had captured his girl, it was no happenstance of plotting. Gods are what they were, more than men.

Because I felt passion for many of these figures—when I first saw Keaton I didn't simply laugh at him, I fused with him, psyche locked to psyche; I recognized him as something known before birth, whatever that says about me—I have, as I say, yearned in what may be called a nostalgic way to see their films again. I will tell you what happens when that wish is granted. The first time you renew acquaintance with such a film, vagrant smoke-curls of nostalgia hover somewhere just beyond vision, just beyond smell, just beyond touching. They are almost there, you can almost remember. But the film, unreeling, is already asserting itself for the thing it is—without you. It is in the process of killing nostalgia. Nostalgia depends on the absence of what is longed for, survives only as recollection. Sometimes some of its values can be reconstructed as pastiche: in the legitimate theater, Sandy Wilson's *The Boy Friend* and the so-called revival of *No, No, Nanette* have served as variant examples. But one was an entirely new work, mocking a dead style as it drew on some of its pleasures, and the other was an inventive approximation and blending of half a dozen styles: the libretto of *No, No, Nanette* was entirely rewritten for "revival" because, I am told, the original text would have proved much too cynical in tone for contemporary audiences to wax nostalgic about. If you remember the twenties at all, or have studied them, you will realize that that is probably so.

The second time you see an old film—which is precisely itself and neither reconstruction nor approximation—not a trace of sentimental memory remains. You may fight to get it back, but you will lose. You will see your old film, in one important sense, dead. Silent film is a dead form, as Latin is a dead language. Neither corresponds to our day-to-day patterns of seeing or hearing. Neither is current coin, neither is going to be helpful in that part of our lives that is changing and growing.

But a dead form can have its own special pleasure. Its virtue is that it can be seen whole. No contemporary film or novel or painting—let alone a piece of music—can be known in this way, in its ultimate fullness, with all boundaries drawn and filled. Whatever is contemporary, sharing our living, is still fluid, unfinished, working its way toward a destination that cannot yet be described or even imagined. Judgments—even responses—must be temporary, tentative, in part inhibited. Where is the form going? Wait and see. What value can be assigned this particular step in the dark? Someone will say, sometime.

A dead form, by its termination, relaxes inhibition. There it all is, beginning, middle, and end, inspiration and achievement, known limitation and compensation, false starts and sidetracks and successful defiances. A closed book, yes. But with the last page written, not maddeningly missing just as we have grown interested in the story. The boundaries are visible, established, permanent now. Being established, they free us to play inside them, aware of where we are the whole time—which is why many men have always relished playing inside the completed worlds of Latin and Greek. Such a world can be seen more clearly, possessed more fully, explored less fearfully, perhaps loved more disinterestedly. In coming to an end, silent film did become an absolute, which means that it can be absolutely known.

What do we see as we look back now with a detachment that cannot be subverted? We see that all silent film, serious or comic, was fantasy—fantasy of a previously unknown, partly accidental, highly original, peculiarly literal kind. I am not speaking of the subjective fantasies that it did indeed engender in many willing hearts, of the raptures of matrons persuaded that it was they Valentino held in his arms, of the wish-fulfillment boys and men found in imagining themselves as lithe as Fairbanks and as suavely persuasive as Ronald Colman. When I was thirteen I made friends with a projectionist in our town; he often let me come up into the booth while he was showing or even cutting film. Cutting was necessary because our town, like many towns then, had a censor: the censor would view the film in the morning, order deletions, and the projectionist would "purify" the film before the first afternoon run. The cut film was never restored to the prints, which in part accounts for the astonishingly mutilated form in which many films—copied from prints rather than the vanished negatives—survive today. Conceive of the condition of a print after the censors of a hundred towns had had their say! The excised film went into the wastebasket, from which, with the projectionist's genial connivance, I was free to retrieve it. After a while, in a nice little pile at home, I had what must unquestionably have been the most extensive collection of shots of Vilma Banky's décolletage existing anywhere in America. I had a tiny Keystone hand-cranked projector, too, of course. I know what it is to fantasize.

Certainly films encouraged this sort of private rhapsody, often enough deliberately; Hollywood wasn't constantly called a "dream factory" for nothing. And silence provided a better womb for it than sound does: the still auditorium grazed only by music, the fortunate wordlessness of the Talmadges and then a Garbo who could not talk back when secretly approached or make difficult verbal demands on the dreamer. It was easier to *be* Milton Sills or Agnes Ayres in the circumstances.

But this sort of subjective fantasizing is a natural tendency of all film, whether silent or sound. The French film critic André Bazin has made the point that film—rather than the stage—is the medium with which we identify. We do so because there is nothing else we can do. There is no performer present in the flesh, as there is on the stage, no one we can challenge, interrupt, catch in a human flaw; the figure on a screen is already so remote that we scarcely dare doubt him.

Caveman Buster Keaton carrying his love-prize home in *Three Ages*, 1923.

The Unique Experience

Because the actor we seem to be watching is already off in Africa making yet another film, quite out of earshot, we cannot contend with him as we constantly contend with an actor on the stage, believing, disbelieving, withdrawing and assenting from moment to moment, sending up signals of our present pleasure or displeasure by our applause, our silence, our restlessness, our very breathing. In films, with the actor absent and only his shadow remaining, there is nothing for an audience to do but attach itself firmly to the phantom and go for the ride. Perversely, we care more for the actor because he can care nothing for us; he doesn't know us, isn't aware that we are there. Instead of becoming companions or even combatants, we become faithful dogs and follow adoringly at heel.

Though silence aided such identification in certain obvious ways, this kind of fantasizing is a property of film as such and so has survived into sound. Marlene Dietrich, lighted by von Sternberg and moving through his myriad gauzes, became a cult-object almost as readily as Garbo had earlier, though all of Miss Dietrich's successes were in talking films. The special quality of silent film fantasy rested on another, much firmer, base.

It was fantasy objectively, abstractly, of the essence, bred in the bone. The fantasy was not in the viewers' heads but in the film, locked there, the necessary result of the diverse and in fact contradictory elements that had come together to create it. Consider how casually the elements of built-in fantasy play across the screen—working minor miracles in passing—and how naturally they are accepted in a commonplace short comedy of the 1920's, Lloyd Hamilton's *Move Along*. I have called Mr. Hamilton's comedy commonplace, though it is not quite that; much of his work was superior to that of dozens of other amiable clowns who never quite made the jump into feature films. But a more or less regulation short comedy, one of the thousands made in the decade as support for feature films, may serve better than an important one to help us see clearly what was simply taken for granted.

In *Move Along*, Mr. Hamilton is having an exceedingly difficult time trying to tie his shoelace. He is on a public street, and you know how that is: where do you put your foot while you do it? Mr. Hamilton—a plumpish man with dainty fingers, a waddle for a walk, and a pancake hat set horizontally on the prim, doughy moon of his face—seizes every reasonable opportunity.

He spies a wooden box, but the box collapses at the touch of his foot. There is an ashcan ahead. Hastening toward it, and with his toe poised for the lift, he is forced to hesitate briefly and politely while several passers-by cross his path. The moment they are gone, he resumes his forward rhythm only to see the ashcan hoisted away from him into the air. A pickup man is emptying it.

Moving along, as both the title and an omnipresent policeman are constantly urging him to do, he becomes a bit more desperate. An elderly frock-coated gentleman is bent nearly double attempting to remove a bit of mud from a woman's shoe. Mr. Hamilton promptly places his own foot on the gentleman's backside, more or less doubling the image like acrobats ascending one another, only to have the gentleman turn on him violently.

Fortunately, just along the curb there stands a water-wagon, its rear wheel exposed, inviting, and of suitable height. Going to it with some dignity, Mr. Hamilton begins his operation only to receive the full spray of the wagon, which has been instantly turned on.

Without further ado, he marches directly into the center of the street and hails a streetcar. The streetcar stops. Mr. Hamilton puts his foot on the streetcar's running board and ties his shoelace. He then waves the streetcar away.

I am deeply enamored of that streetcar, not to mention the use to which it

Lloyd Hamilton summons a streetcar for his own special needs in *Move Along*.

Opposite: Lloyd Hamilton unaware that the dinner he yearns for is resting on top of his head. *Move Along*.

is put. For, in this tiny fragment of film, all the essential ingredients of silent film comedy are fully present. The streetcar is a real streetcar. It moves. And it moves without a sound.

Each of these ingredients is vitally important. Before trying to say why, let me complete the record of Mr. Hamilton's difficult day.

Hungry, he passes a restaurant and is able to see, through the plate glass, a wealthy customer putting down a gourmet's meal. While he is standing there, yearning, a waiter from the restaurant leaves by the street door carrying a full dinner on a tray. The takeout order is balanced on the waiter's flat palm at exactly Mr. Hamilton's head-height. We see the waiter pass so closely that the tray slides imperceptibly onto the top of Mr. Hamilton's head, where it remains as the waiter vanishes from view. Mr. Hamilton continues to yearn, not knowing what treasures crown him. The tray is retrieved before he can discover and take advantage of his good fortune.

Nudged along once again by the policeman who seems to be his guardian devil, he returns to his rooming house. A milk bottle stands outside a neighbor's door. As he reaches for it, it is taken in. In his room, his landlady stands ready to evict him. Out he goes, taking his bed and trunk with him—there is a ride down a stairway on the bed here—to do what he can to make a home for himself on the streets. He settles for lodgings under a store awning, opening his trunk to hang a picture, using one large hat as a shade for the lamppost, a smaller one stuck on a stick for an ashtray. The alarm clock is wound and placed on a fireplug, and Mr. Hamilton snuggles into bed under the awning. It begins to rain. It rains hard enough to fill the awning like a canvas tub and then to make it overflow, dumping some gallons of water down onto Mr. Hamilton's bide-a-wee. Later, the rain turns to snow and a new inventiveness is required.

Now at first sight the style of the little film, the inspiration for this last sequence, and even some of its particular sight-gags, may seem closely related to—even identical with—a sequence that Fred and Adele Astaire once performed in a P. G. Wodehouse-Guy Bolton Broadway musical. The Astaires also were evicted. They also set up light housekeeping on the street. A picture was hung, the coffee percolator was plugged into lamppost and hydrant. And it did begin to rain. They danced in the rain.

Yet there is a world of difference between the two sequences. Both, to be sure, are fantasies. They are impertinently offered improbabilities which are perfectly willing, with a wink, to become impossibilities. It is not really possible to cook by street lamp, at least not in the time allotted. Nor is it really possible for a man to support a full tray on his head without knowing that *something* is there. The underlying assumption of both improvisations is that they are not to be believed. They offer false worlds to be entered, as one would enter a conspiracy. Enter, and you will see how much fun it is.

But stage fantasy and film fantasy are radically different things. Stage fantasy is fantasy all of a piece. Everything is false at once, making for an easy consistency. The backdrop is false: the rooming house from which the Astaires are evicted is only, and plainly, paint. The props are false: no real street lamps, no real fireplugs. The street is false: it is simply the stage floor; in a moment it will be a ballroom. The rain is false: it is created by a pinwheel of light and not even a thin sheet of water carried off in a trough; though this last trick can in fact be performed on stage, it would not have been done in this case lest the dancers slip on the overspray. The whole brightly colored, brilliantly and arbitrarily lighted environment in which the Astaires worked is candidly unreal to begin with; the performers are surrounded, bounded, by artifice. It is not so difficult to smile and behave preposterously, to do unreal things in an enchantingly artificial way, in a universe ready-made for the prank.

But film? The streets are real, the streetcars are real, the trashcans, the trays, the water-wagons and the water in them are all real. When the cameraman called "Cut!"—if he did anything so conventional—once the awning had loosed the deluge upon Mr. Hamilton, Mr. Hamilton was *wet.*

Film was, to begin with, fact, not fancy. That was its first appeal. For a long time it was its only appeal. To the end of its days it will never escape the consequences, or the obligations, of being permanently bound to fact, of being indebted to fact for its excitement and dependent upon it for its integrity. A cardboard streetcar would not have done. The cardboard train on which Jack Oakie arrives to meet Charlie Chaplin in *The Great Dictator* is readily detectable, and it spoils what would otherwise have been an extremely funny sequence. Our steady expectation of the camera is that it will give us actuality, not artifice.

How much more difficult and unlikely for it, then, to have arrived at even so simple a fantastic improvisation as the brief *Move Along.* That a medium committed to actuality should have embroiled itself in fantasy at all—putting perfectly real objects to such very odd uses—was scarcely to have been expected. That it should have made fantasy its principal product for something like twenty-six years is now, even in retrospect, astonishing. For so strange a thing to have happened, film would have had to invent—by hook or crook or happenstance—fantasy of an absolutely unprecedented kind, unrelated to anything the stage had done before it. That is what it did do. It invented a fantasy of fact.

Roscoe Arbuckle working on a roped-off public street.

3. The Fact in the Fantasy

The fact came from the nature of the camera. The camera is not of itself an imaginative instrument. It is a machine, a scientific tool devised to record data actually present to it while its aperture is open, and to record that data with impersonal fidelity. As has often been said of it, and as often forgotten, it cannot lie. The only lying that is ever done occurs either behind or before the camera, by men manipulating the instrument or manipulating the objects to be photographed. When the shutter snaps, the film noncommittally reproduces what is there. Film, in its essence, is a document.

All of the first excitement it engendered came from this documentary quality, this capacity to reproduce the real world with utter fidelity. The people who spent their pennies and nickels to stare into the slots provided by amusement-arcade Vitascope machines, like the people who saw film enlarged on screens in vaudeville houses or in the suddenly flourishing storefront nickelodeons, were looking—in the beginning, and for a longer time than we now care to recall—at little more than a Staten Island ferryboat discharging its passengers, steam engines roaring past or perhaps head-on at the viewer, a nurse bathing a baby, policemen parading past on St. Patrick's Day.

The excitement depended on the incontestable reality of the image. Once those oncoming locomotives had been increased to lifelike, or greater than lifelike, proportions on a screen, they loomed quite literally as a threat. Audiences are known to have stampeded, flying from their seats in terror, as a locomotive bore down. At one early exhibition, according to filmmaker Albert E. Smith in his memoir, *Two Reels and a Crank*, the theater manager rushed to the projection booth screaming, "Shut the goddam thing off! A lady's fainted!"

People had, of course, seen still photographs of all these things long before, without terror or even any particular sense of presence; but they had been looked at from a distance in space and time. Motion changed all that. If the camera guaranteed authenticity, motion made it *now*. Here we were, suddenly, skimming the edge of the Grand Canyon, charting the snakelike course of a river far below.

Here we were, at a fire, with the flames visibly, progressively eating parts of the building away. Here we were, at a prizefight, with the real Johnson and the real Jeffries offering and parrying and receiving blows. Change went forward in our presence; it made us present.

"I have seen Niagara thunder over her gorge in the noblest frenzy ever beheld by man," rhapsodized Frederick Starr in a piece for the Chicago *Tribune* in 1909, recovered for us now by Stanley Kauffmann and Bruce Henstell in their fine anthology, *American Film Criticism*; "I have watched an English railroad train draw into a station, take on its passengers, and then chug away with its stubby little engine through the Yorkshire Dells, past old Norman Abbeys silhouetted against the skyline, while a cluster of century-aged cottages loomed up in the valley below. . . . I have looked upon weird dances and outlandish frolics in every quarter of the globe, and I didn't have to leave Chicago for a moment."

The sensation of coping with real objects in the present tense was out of all proportion to its cause; film was still a record, even though it moved. But it was a kind of record no one had ever seen before, and its impact, even when the report was of something ordinary and familiar, was overwhelming. Had no one seen a kiss before? Not in this way. One of the relatively few surviving films that almost everyone has come across in museum showings or in commercial compilations is the still-celebrated May Irwin–John Rice *The Kiss*. The film runs less than a minute. Though both Miss Irwin and Mr. Rice were professional performers, we do not look at them as actors here. We simply see a rather large, coarsely grained, agreeably puckish woman heartily embrace and kiss a sportive gentleman with a formidable beard. But, for the first time, we see it monumentally close up, we see it all from beginning to end, and we see it with none of life's discreet need to turn away. We are permitted to be *fully* present.

If the combined intimacy and authenticity of the camera made familiar things astonishing, it could do even more for the unfamiliar. The world was full of objects and events that were known or rumored to be real, that could be observed, but that were not normally open to casual eyes. Much—no doubt most—early film has disappeared. Those filmmakers who wished to copyright or otherwise preserve their work were permitted to do so by filing with the Library of Congress in Washington paper rolls on which each frame was printed separately. There was no provision at the time for copyrighting material on inflammable celluloid. The process was clumsy, but it has left us with a few treasures. Among the paper rolls which have now been restored to celluloid is a two-minute subject called *Electrocuting an Elephant*. That, precisely, is what we are offered.

We are permitted to see an elephant whose hooves are chained to stakes in the ground. The elephant weaves about; we see that it is a real elephant. Suddenly four puffs of smoke blossom from the chains at its hooves. The elephant shudders, topples over, shudders again, lies still. Men move about in the background waiting for the throes to stop. That is all. The film was separately titled, separately sold, probably exhibited on a bill with eight or ten other such pryings into events normally hidden. The camera could go where the surprising secrets were, generously taking us with it.

The flexibility of the camera at once provided audiences with another, and very important, aspect of reality hitherto denied to earthbound eyes: scale. It was now possible to see Niagara Falls not only through the spray at its base but from overhead. The camera's range of vision was wider than man's; its power of focus was greater; and it was footloose. Without effort we could chart—with our own eyes—the breaking up of ice floes, the massive inundation of river banks, the meeting of planes in midair, virtually anything we thought might thrill us. The

Opposite: The event has to have been arranged, but the train crash is real.

Above: Atlantic City Fire Department on the run in 1897, subsequent frames indicating that the horses knocked the camera over; San Francisco Earthquake, 1906; Squires vs. Burns prizefight, 1907; Great Toronto Fire, 1904.

world itself expanded under our moving wings as scale, courtesy of the camera, became an *open sesame* to an Arabian Nights of fact. In due time comedians would be straddling the naked girders of uncompleted skyscrapers, manipulating ocean liners, climbing giant balloons in midair. In the meantime the Vitagraph Company was off to Cuba to record the actual assault by Theodore Roosevelt on San Juan Hill.

Magical as the camera might be, it was expected to exercise its magic on fact, to bring back verification, not invention. When a cameraman was through with the Spanish-American War he went off to the Boer; he scouted the San Francisco earthquake and the Galveston Flood. On one occasion a cameraman even sat waiting for the Brooklyn Bridge to fall; an ill-founded rumor had promised the event, and no maker of documents would have cared to miss *that.*

The original identification of film with document was so natural and so complete that it was not until seven long years after its first large-scale public exhibition that anyone thought to make entire fiction of it. Thomas Edison's first Vitascope program was presented at Koster and Bial's Music Hall, as an adjunct to vaudeville, in 1896. But it wasn't until 1903 that Edwin S. Porter succeeded in persuading an audience to attend to a ten-minute film, *The Great Train Robbery*, that was candidly and without apology sheer play-acting, unabashed story-telling.

There had of course been a bit of cheating along the way. During those seven years, some "fact" had been fabricated. Albert E. Smith, the man with the Vitagraph camera, confesses that when he came back from San Juan Hill with his precious, and authentic, footage, he discovered that the gunship battle in Santiago Bay had been fought while he was sailing home and had completely superseded in the public mind the earlier glories he had photographed. Rather than seem to be reporting stale news, he provided his own battle of Santiago Bay, placing cutout miniatures of battleships in an improvised tub and using cigar smoke not only to suggest cannon-fire but to help obscure the crudeness of what he was up to. The film was successful and, thanks to the cigar smoke, accepted as fact.

I find even more curious a kind of "simulated" event that was apparently intended to satisfy the newly developed craving for sights previously unseen. In the Library of Congress collection there are several separate one-minute films detailing the removal of a condemned woman from her death cell, apparently the same woman's death by hanging, the execution of a spy, and *The Finding of Bodies*, though the last film doesn't say what bodies are being found. All are obviously staged, though they are not acted. That is to say, the figures involved make no least gesture toward characterization or even emotion; they move stonily through the duties assigned them, as though serving as neutral illustration. It doesn't seem possible that any audience could have believed it was actually looking at the execution of a spy: the stone wall against which the victim stands is plainly painted, his executioners stand so close to him and the wall—no doubt to get all of the figures into one frame of film—that the blast must have demolished both, rather devastatingly, on the instant. Yet the look of the films remains documentary, as their titles suggest that we are at last seeing the real thing. Perhaps in some mentally evasive and wish-fulfilling way, they were half believed in.

Impulses toward storytelling also kept cropping up during the seven-year insistence on, and exhilaration in, fact. An episode might be arranged for the camera, comic or serious: a small boy turning over his mother's washtub, a burglar apprehended at a rooftop skylight. The impulse, however, was always oddly aborted, almost as though the audience might cease believing in the reality of what it saw if the boy went on to other pranks, culminating in a sort of Our Gang

Opposite, above: A Georges Méliès explosion, all paint and canvas.

Below: The real thing, as film learned to do it, in a Sennett comedy.

RUB
AUSAGE

comedy, or if the burglar was shown to have a past or a future. A glimpse of moving life was all that was offered; the fact that it was life caught in motion was what was important.

Outright fantasy—in effect, stage fantasy—also came early. In France a professional magician named Georges Méliès became interested in the camera precisely because it could be made to *seem* to lie. It could, for instance, be stopped at a certain frame until an object—a chair, a bed, a man—was removed from its range and then started up again. Between the two frames the chair, bed, or man would seem to disappear. Using painted sets in a studio, Méliès went on with his magic—transforming rods into snakes and sending rockets head-on into the grimacing face of the moon.

Méliès's work was popular for a time, as illusionistic tricks so often are, and his methods were imitated. But the vogue abruptly ceased, as I think it was bound to do, leaving no major film tradition behind except that of the frankly animated cartoon. The visual tricks were possible; to some minds they were inviting. But they bore no relation to the fundamental purpose of the camera. Indeed, they violated it. Could a factual instrument, and an audience ready to believe in it, be outwitted? Yes, and there was some fun in the outwitting, the violation. But this was a temporary sort of fun, a taking apart of a walking doll's mechanism to see what makes it work, and in short order it created as much distaste as delight in the audience.

Documentation was what was demanded of the camera, and even after film had found its way to the excitements of storytelling, it was expected that, though the narratives might be fictitious, the photography would be true. When, years later, Harold Lloyd was to be seen dangling from the face of a clock high above the street, the busy street below him and his precise relationship to that street were accepted as—and in fact were—authentic. That was the special thrill, the unique pleasure, of *this* kind of storytelling—as opposed to that of the stage or printed page—and the thrill and the pleasure lasted just so long as the camera could be trusted.

The freshness that films possessed while they respected the camera's demand for truth can still be felt today when one is running a fragment of film from an early Douglas Fairbanks romantic comedy or a Tom Mix western. In the one, Fairbanks, leather-jacketed and wearing a coonskin frontiersman's cap, lifts his girl over a stile in an open field; in the other, Mix strolls with *his* girl through what seems acres of daisies. A breeze blows through both scenes, a breeze that makes curls fly and budding boughs wave everywhere, a breeze with the scent of film's dawn in it. The stile is a real one, the daisies are growing. The performers had taken the trouble to go where the backgrounds were and to join them in an entirely moving universe.

"Location" shooting wasn't called that then; it was taken for granted, and later, after many middle years spent almost entirely inside studios where papier-mâché tree trunks and non-running brooks fooled almost no one, it had to be rediscovered. The vitality of film depends in part—a very great part—on the honor that is paid the camera, the respect shown to its eye; the narrative action itself is certified by the truth of what otherwise fills the frame. The celebrated remark of an early filmmaker, "A tree is a tree," was meant to be cynical. A director wanted to go some distance on location, where the trees were right for the story; the producer told him to shoot it next door in Griffith Park, adding the laconic phrase. But it can also be read Gertrude Stein's way. A rose is a *rose*. A tree, even in Griffith Park, is a true tree, and it helped persuade audiences that some of the exceedingly strange things that went on before, in, and around it were

Opposite: Buster Keaton and Natalie Talmadge strolling through the natural backgrounds for *Our Hospitality*.

Above: The stylized "theater" magic of Georges Méliès.

demonstrably, delightfully real.

As storytelling crept into film, the plain document continued alongside it; sometimes the two met in an insane, yet not unrelated, dance. The first short comedy in which Charlie Chaplin wore his improvised "tramp" costume—it was the second film he made and a very short one indeed, running no more than five minutes—was released on what was called a "split" reel. Chaplin's antics took up half the reel. The other half consisted of a fact-film called *Olives and Their Oil*. The reel was released in 1914, eleven years after the firm establishment of pure narrative with *The Great Train Robbery*. Outright fact had not yet surrendered to narrative. It would take still another year before American storytelling exploded into the awesome complexity of *The Birth of a Nation*. First, seven years of sheer fact, or near fact; then, twelve years of toe-dancing, lightly skipping back and forth between fact and fancy that was rooted in fact.

The toe-dancing can be seen, most literally, in the Chaplin film itself, *Kid Auto Races at Venice*. The title is explicit, the camera is wholly honest. Bona fide children's automobile races were being held in Venice, California, and Mack Sennett sent his crew out to photograph them, tossing in his perplexing new comedian—whose first film had not been good—to see if any incidental humor could be incorporated into the record. Chaplin's instinct for the camera, along with his essential and ultimate relationship to it, here asserted itself for the first time. What he did, and all he did, was to pretend to be a bystander at the races hoping to get his picture taken.

He strolls into camera range with elaborate nonchalance, affecting not to notice that he is being photographed while very carefully exposing himself to full and insistent view. Ordered out of range by the cameraman's assistants, who now and then emerge halfway into the film to shoo him off, he is most apologetic, tipping his hat and discreetly retreating. As soon as the camera takes up a new position, he is back, quite obscuring the children who are heading homemade cars down a runway to the track. He is elbowing his way into immortality, both as a "character" in the film and as a professional comedian to be remembered. And he is doing it by calling attention to the camera as camera.

He would do this throughout his career, using the instrument as a means of establishing a direct and openly acknowledged relationship between himself and his audience. In fact, he is, with this film, establishing himself as *one among the audience*, one among those who are astonished by this new mechanical marvel, one among those who would like to be photographed by it, and—he would make the most of the implication later—one among those who are invariably chased away. He looked at the camera and went through it, joining the rest of us. The seeds of his subsequent hold on the public, the mysterious and almost inexplicable bond between this performer and everyman, were there. Interestingly, they were put there by pointing a finger at the actuality of what was happening, at the fact that some men were taking a picture of something real.

The storytelling feature film took over in volume after 1915, as the audience became enraptured with an evolving form of narrative fantasy that was like nothing it had imagined before, and straight fact was pared down to the newsreel—one on every bill. But throughout the great days of silent screen fiction, there remained some men—directors, photographers—to insist that film in its purest form would always be essentially if not wholly "documentary." From time to time they made their point vivid. In 1921, Robert Allerton Parker was praising the work of filmmakers Sheeler and Strand in these words, reprinted in George C. Pratt's valuable compilation *Spellbound in Darkness*: "There was no heroine, no villain, no plot," only the "docking of the *Aquitania*, surrounded by those busy Lilliputian

tugs; the pencil-like office buildings stretching upwards for a place in the sun.... Yet it was all thrilling, exciting, dramatic—but dramatic in the language of plasticity. It was honestly, gloriously photographic, devoid of trickery and imitation."

In 1922, while Valentino was making love to Nita Naldi and Douglas Fairbanks was meeting his musketeers behind the Luxembourg and Lillian and Dorothy Gish were wandering through Griffith's French Revolution and Richard Barthelmess was somehow thrashing the daylights out of Ernest Torrence, a director named Robert Flaherty made and succeeded in releasing a simple, factual camera record of day-to-day Eskimo life, *Nanook of the North*. The film was an enormous success; audiences found it neither difficult nor odd to turn away from their cherished fantasies and renew an earlier passion that had not died.

The "documentary" and its claims have never been wholly neglected. Deep into the sound era, Pare Lorentz would create a considerable stir with *The River* and *The Plough that Broke the Plains*; and in 1972 a good many of us were unnecessarily astonished to discover that we could sit still for four and one half hours while Marcel Ophuls' *The Sorrow and the Pity* took us painstakingly, and painfully, through recorded interviews with men and women who had joined or avoided joining the French underground during World War II. The camera reasserts its nature and primary function often: it was built so that we might confidently believe.

The power of the camera to report with absolute, or near-absolute, accuracy continued to have implications for every silent film made, of whatever kind. No matter how reality might be combined with narrative improvisation, no matter what conspiracies the camera might engage in with the most fertile of imaginations, no matter what Mack Sennett or Harold Lloyd or the D. W. Griffith of *Intolerance* might do to it, the camera was forced—if it was to remain itself—to keep a foothold on fact. Fact was its mainspring, the link to fact its lifeline. The power to record actuality became an obligation to do so—one that could not, or should not, ever be dishonored.

Above: Robert Flaherty's documentary *Nanook of the North*.

Below: Chaplin establishing his intimacy with the camera during the filming of an actual event, *Kid Auto Races at Venice*.

4. The Fantasy in the Fact

Given the nature of the camera, it is really surprising that it should ever have turned to fiction, narrative, "art" at all—let alone to that rather rarefied form of art called fantasy. Much more surprising, in fact, than that it should have dallied with documentation for so long.

But from the beginning there were aspects of the image produced by the camera that opened the doors to some kind of playfulness, that actually cried out for the type of inventiveness and conscious formalization we associate with art. We said earlier that art begins in a taking away. Certain things *had* been taken away, automatically and simply as part of the machine's operation, from the total reality of the camera image. Each of them was an invitation to the exercise of imagination.

The picture, for instance, lacked depth. It was flat, two-dimensional; it did not record the planes of space in which the tumbling action took place. Two people might pass one another on the screen; they did so on *exactly* the same level. That was a reduction, and it called for some imaginative compensation. The audience had to supply two levels while it was actually looking at only one. It did so quickly and without complaint, bringing to films something of the same cooperation it had always brought to painting.

At the same time, flatness brought into play another imagination, that of the cameraman. Where three dimensions exist but only two can be photographed, the placement of the camera itself becomes vitally important. Place it ineptly and you will get unbearable distortion. It is possible—we have all seen such shots—to place a moving camera in a head-on relation to moving horses so that the horses, though their legs are pounding up and down with piston force, seem to be standing still in space.

Conversely, discerning placement of the camera can actually use the inevitable distortion to suggest a dimension that isn't there. It can also do what the cameraman did who photographed a passing waiter's tray sliding unnoticed onto Lloyd Hamilton's head. It can suspend space. In the Hamilton film we are to believe, simultaneously, in two planes and one. The waiter and Mr. Hamilton clearly occupy two separate planes. Otherwise they would bump. But the tray in the waiter's hand and Mr. Hamilton's head occupy a single plane. Otherwise it would not be possible for the tray to transfer itself from the waiter's palm to Hamilton's head. The simultaneous expansion and compression of plane function perfectly. The unbelievable gag is not only funny, it is believable. We see it happen, and there is no arguing with that. A cameraman has done his work well. In any case, in every case, a judgment is involved. It is an imaginative one.

It was also swiftly discovered that the camera—perhaps photographing various phases of the advance of a supply train during a real war—could change position abruptly without the intervention of a title to announce the change of place, angle, or even time. The freedom of the camera to overleap time and place was in fact one of its obvious virtues and constituted one of the audience's greatest satisfactions. Whatever mental shorthand might be required by the jumps could be easily managed.

But such freedom submitted the factual record to the interposition of yet another imagination, that of the man who pieced the shots together. His was necessary work, not a gratuitous seeking to make art of a document. The camera could not afford to stand still; it had to move where the movement was. And the separate records it made with each imposed movement had later to be assembled in some sort of intelligible order, perhaps even into an order with a rhythmic impact. Inevitably, editing was born, editing that would lead all the way to Eisenstein's Odessa steps sequence in *Potemkin*: parasols in the sun, booted feet descending, a baby carriage broken loose, booted feet descending, smashed eyeglasses streaked with blood, booted feet descending, a woman carrying her child upward into gunfire, feet descending forever. A primitive requirement of motion-picture photography, and in fact a limitation on its claim to record the whole of reality, proved an escape hatch into art.

Furthermore, this "true" record appeared in black and white, which meant that once again it was not altogether true. There were no flesh tones, fires burned white, nights were black rather than blue—until the practice began of tinting all night scenes blue, at which point the actors' faces turned blue as well. The absence of color *accented* the absence of plane—hues produce gradations and suggest depth—so that silent film photography at its cleanest tended to take on the sharply conventionalized outlines of a line-drawing rather than the suggestiveness of a wash and thereby engaged the audience still more deeply in a cooperative activity, an eager "filling-in."

The audience clung to this last convention far longer than it did to that of silence. Like sound, some form of color had been available from the outset, even though in its most primitive stages the color had to be painted onto individual prints by hand. But Technicolor, a process which produces and mixes two or three tones mechanically, was already in existence in 1915, and throughout the twenties various isolated sequences in feature films made use of it. Technicolor was applied to complete feature films in 1917, 1922, and 1924; Douglas Fairbanks seized on its continuing improvements for *The Black Pirate* in 1926. None of these excursions into color created an eagerness for more, and even with the coming of sound, when one might have expected the demand for "naturalness" to become total, color was for years confined to musicals and to animated cartoons. It wasn't until the 1960's that color became omnipresent, so enamored was the audience of a limitation it seems to have found productive.

Each limitation on the camera's power to reproduce reality with total fidelity did pave the way to an exercise of art, each taking away called for and got an

Real racing cars take wing in Sennett's *Lizzies of the Field.*

imaginative response; arbitrary boundaries proved quickly fertile, as they always had. Playful fiction could escape through the loopholes in fact, and film—that sworn truth-teller—could be made to tell a story.

But there was one taking away that did more than invite degrees of artistry. It was so massive and unlifelike a limitation that it froze the newly possible art form into a single, rather narrow, altogether unexpected channel, confining the thrust toward art to a highly specialized strand of art—to fantasy, to what I have called a fantasy of fact.

The limitation that sealed the form was silence itself, that accident Edison had never intended. The other limitations we have spoken of may be regarded as inherent in the nature of film; this one was gratuitous, unplanned, a denial of possibility and of probability as well. The camera had given us reality. Silence took it away again. Silence contradicted the camera.

Here we were, with a railroad train roaring down a track at us, and we heard no roar. The real train was suddenly an immaterial train. Here we were, with a masked bandit firing a revolver directly into our faces—at the end of *The Great Train Robbery*—and we no more heard the shot than we felt any bullet enter our breasts. Here was Buster Keaton, on the coal car of his locomotive, passing *two* entire armies without noticing them, because neither he nor we could hear them. A universe had been halved and went on as though nothing had happened.

Fantasy is always born of contradiction. It comes of putting together identifiably real elements that—once they are placed in tandem—promptly lose their claim to being real. We know well enough what a horse looks like. We know what the wings of a large bird look like. When we join the two to make, for our idle pleasure, a winged horse, we rather suppose that we have made an improvement on nature. What we tend to forget in the process is that, while we are having such fun contradicting both horse and bird, we are also robbing each of something vital. The horse is in fact a poorer horse for having wings; he has lost—or begun to lose—his identity. A mule that can talk may be something of a marvel and may amuse us; but he is no true mule. A boy named Peter Pan who can fly is, *because* he can fly, something less than a boy. Perhaps that is why he is always played by a girl. I am not suggesting, mind you, that girls are less than boys—not in this day and age. I am simply saying that when a boy is provided with qualities that are quite alien to his existential being he is at once deprived of that being and must cast about, ambiguously, for another form to contain him. The new form will be, for him, less real. Every such addition is a subtraction.

Silence was the subtraction that guaranteed films would be, so long as they remained mute, flights of fancy. Flights of a new kind of fancy: *fact* robbed of its weight and made impertinently, defiantly airborne. A speaking man who could not be heard was precisely as fantastic an object as a talking mule. If he lost something of his powers as a man in the enforced hush, the loss freed him to behave as improbably as the mule. Suddenly comedians were released to run at an opponent on the second or third floor of a building, miss the opponent and go headlong through a window, dive the two or three stories to land on their heads below, get up and saunter jauntily away. All of it authenticated by the camera.

"In the cinema," Elie Faure wrote in 1920, "the whole drama unrolls in absolute silence, from which not only words, but the noise of feet, the sound of the wind and the crowds, all the murmurs, all the tones of nature are absent." What was liberated by the absence? Lloyd Hamilton's streetcar, for one thing. Mr. Hamilton's insouciant gag would not really have been possible if the world had intruded with its badgering sound. His nonchalant jaunt to the tracks would have lost effortlessness and line if it had been inundated with the threatening dimension of noise, with the real world's familiar and harrowing hazard of rumbling truck wheels and shattering horns. His graceful, rather imperious, signal to the streetcar to stop might pass muster today as comic inflection; streetcars, where they still exist, *do* stop. But that the car should have paused just long enough for him to tie his shoe and then have serenely sailed on is film fantasy through and through. Here a chariot from heaven—an entirely tangible one—seems to have swung low for Mr. Hamilton, made its obeisance, and gone on without a sound.

Silent films were constantly assuming that what the audience couldn't hear, the performers needn't. Every comedian, sooner or later, dangled precariously high over a precipice. In his first feature, *Tramp, Tramp, Tramp*, Harry Langdon is attempting to disentangle himself from a flock of sheep out to pasture. Spying a high board fence, he climbs it and swings over. As he reaches the other side, his sweater catches on a nail. In a hurry to get on with his business, he pulls frantically at the sweater to release it. What he hasn't noticed is that he is now suspended hundreds of feet directly above a highway teeming with traffic. He goes right on working to free himself for the fall. The sequence is a very funny one. But its existence depends on Mr. Langdon having no ears. Highways are noisy.

In silent films a performer's hearing was often highly selective. If he could hear at all, he heard what the narrative wanted him to hear. That, and no more. In the three-reel *Never Weaken*, one of Harold Lloyd's earlier experiments with stunting, the comedian believes he has killed himself. Despondent over the loss of his girl, he blindfolds himself, pulls the trigger of a revolver, and instantly slumps over his office desk. As he does so, a huge girder glides through the window behind him and locks itself between the rungs of his chair. Construction work is going on next door. The girder lifts the blindfolded Lloyd through the window and out above the street, stories below, without his knowledge. Across the way, through a window, *we* see a girl playing a harp. Lloyd is at once deeply gratified, concluding that he has died and gone to heaven. A few moments later he is somewhat bewildered: there is a Dixieland jazz band playing raucously nearby. Shortly he loses his blindfold *and* his composure; his slippery struggle among swaying girders—one of the most frighteningly real ever put on film—begins. But his successive stages of discovery are all arbitrary, because we can hear nothing and he can choose what he will hear. The harp, the jazz, the riveting, and the city noises would all have occurred simultaneously, cacophonously.

This arbitrary, and frequently total, dismissal of sound as an aspect of reality became so much second nature to audiences that when E. A. Dupont, directing the German film *Variety*, wished to insist that a man waiting inside a hotel room could hear a woman's footsteps in the corridor, he dollied his camera forward until the screen contained nothing but an intense, curiously monstrous close-up of the man's ear. The audience needed reminding, during the film, that hearing was *possible*.

One of the strangest consequences of silence was that it destroyed consequences. A thing might be seen to happen, but no logical aftereffects necessarily flowed from it. Not only could a clown land on his head after a spectacular two-story dive and get up whole, but a comedian could be shot in the seat of the pants and never be wounded. The comedian taking the shot presumably felt it; he jumped. But we did not feel him feeling the shot; we simply laughed and asked no questions when he came down intact and begging for more.

The fantasy of silence suspended our obligation to feel, whenever we wished to suspend it. The look of life remained; the sensations associated with it disappeared. We were freed to stare at sights we might, but shouldn't, enjoy without penalty, without any unpleasant exercise of our own sympathies or any concern

Plunging headlong through walls or dangling precariously from cliffs, no one is going to get hurt.

for the performer's well-being. During Mack Sennett's reign, millions of cartridges must have been fired as comedians whipped out revolvers and let fly in all directions. No bullet ever dropped a clown. These men were immortal.

There is a sense in which the immortality conferred by silence must be taken seriously. The men and women on a silent screen, whether in comic or serious films, were real men and women, and yet they were not. The camera said they were; silence denied it. What were they, then? They have often been called dream figures, and occasionally a director of surrealistic bent has been willing to compose whole films as though these were in fact dreams—*The Cabinet of Dr. Caligari* is a case in point—though this has never become the cinematic mainstream. I should say, rather, that silent films are more nearly *waking* fantasies, those projections of our conscious minds in which we place ourselves in situations amatory, vengeful, triumphant, or whatever. When we are actually asleep and dreaming, the figures present often do speak to us; we hear—and often remember—what they say. You may have noticed, however, that when we are merely daydreaming, we do all the talking. The imagined people on whom we are projecting our desires or expectations are normally mute, pliant, mere audiences for our fantastications. If they do speak, they say what we make them say.

There is something more than that to it, though, more than a wishful and even wistful self-assertion. Figures on a silent screen, though tongue-tied, are not quite so pliant. They do not offer a submissive gratification. They engender—or did once engender—something closer to awe. When I went, as a youngster, to see—let's take something unexceptional—Thomas Meighan in *The Bachelor Daddy*, a story whose implications are all contained in its title, I believed that Mr. Meighan was some kind of a man. Not a man I could ever meet. In fact, when I met his brother some forty years later, I was still capable of a sense of dislocation; I had not expected to come in contact with any Meighan of flesh and blood. The figure on the screen was enormous, without color, free as ectoplasm to materialize wherever and whenever he wished, weightless, extraordinarily graceful in his capacity to usher thought through a perpetual hush. His very speechlessness was part of that grace, ease, and power. I could watch Mr. Meighan play a perfectly ordinary man in a perfectly ordinary domestic situation; I could sentimentalize over his embarrassed and then solicitous relationship with a child; I could be amused by the wry quirk of his eyebrows. But I could not accept him as *mere* man; he was more than that. He was both the shadow and the sum of all men of a certain kind and I was accepting him not as an actor who might pick up his salary but as an archetype to whom offerings might be *given*.

Archetype alone is too abstract a word. The figure was not an abstraction, not an emptied out symbol, though Elie Faure did think that films, as they progressed after 1920, might best end by turning their "cinemimics" into mobile plastic objects. There was the testament of Mr. Meighan's kinky hair, his smile displaying good teeth and many of them, his lanky height.

He was—as all performers able to exercise this authority over a silent camera were—the nearest the world had ever come to realizing, visually, a Platonic essence, that *idea* of man in the mind of God which served as matrix for individual, tangible men. The figures in a silent film occupied a sort of halfway house along this road back to God's mind. They were not altogether immaterial, not altogether universal, of course: John Gilbert had feverish eyes, uniquely his; Douglas Fairbanks had a double chin. Yet they had not altogether materialized, either. We know individuals best by the idiosyncratic nature of their thought processes, which are normally conveyed to us by words. Wordless, these figures had not quite yet reached earth; they were still a distance away from and above

Opposite: The drop is a long one, but we're free to enjoy it.

Love among the archetypes: Rudolph Valentino and Vilma Banky in *The Son of the Sheik*.

Opposite: Douglas Fairbanks and his dancing companions in *Robin Hood*.

us, caught in the process of coming down from the celestial matrix. It is very easy, at the end of *The Iron Mask*, to accept Douglas Fairbanks leaping from a terrace to a cloud, marching back with his fellow musketeers to where he came from.

The archetype half-fleshed. That was the sense of it, lost now, and it accounted for various phenomena of the time. One of these, a small but charming one, was the habit films had of labeling everything *The*. Halfway through a film a title might appear: "The storm." Why not "A storm?" What is *the* storm that it should be so familiarly referred to, so swiftly accepted, as absolute? Silent film, with its archetypal overtones, tended to make everything absolute. *The* meeting, *the* betrayal, *the* elder brother, *the* shipwreck. As though we had known long beforehand that these things were coming, and had to be.

The shipwreck. Albert Smith tells us that Alan Dale, a well-known drama critic, condescended to review a film in 1914 and was much taken with it, above all with its climax:

"The little yacht's cabin is smashed into smithereens. The millionaire is seen dead, floating in the water. The evil mother-in-law is shown in her cabin, the water gradually rising—to her knees, to her waist, until she is submerged. They are revealed floundering in the dismal waters, a hopeless and awe-struck lot, until rescue, in the shape of an ocean steamer, arrives. No 'drama' could give one such an idea of the terrors of a wreck. The agony and anguish of it were rushed home to us. We palpitated at the silence of it—that seemed part of the tragedy. Not a word—not a sound—as the terrible catastrophe was pictured for us. We realized every newspaper description of shipwreck's misery as these films greeted us."

How had the silence become part of the tragedy? By making this shipwreck both a particular shipwreck and *every* shipwreck, subtly elevating it to the status of iconography and myth, an essence written on air.

The phenomenon was extended, varied, and sometimes made painful as the *the* quality became attached to the performers themselves, rapidly turning them—even after their names were known and widely advertised—into *the* vamp, *the* tramp, *the* orchid lady, *the* baby, *the* fat man, *the* great lover, *the* great stone face; it was necessary for Douglas Fairbanks and Mary Pickford to become *the* king and queen of films in the public mind. And stars in their private lives were unable to resist assuming the shimmering halations that accompanied their images on a screen. Both Gloria Swanson and Pola Negri *became* royalty, one by marrying a marquis, the other by marrying a prince, possibly to reduce the disparity between themselves and their on-screen presences. Small wonder. Whenever such performers appeared in public, they carried with them the proportions of their screen images and generated a response in proportion to *that*. When Mary Pickford and Douglas Fairbanks went to Europe together for the first time—and, later, when Chaplin followed suit—hundreds of thousands of people massed in the squares outside the hotels in which they stayed, waiting for a chance appearance, a royal wave, from a balcony. These people, known in some way to be real but essentially inaccessible, treated as near-gods in the sense that gods exist but do not speak to us, were forced to live their otherworldliness. Francis X. Bushman was not allowed to reveal the fact that he had a wife and many children: archetypes do not have children. When *the* fat man, Roscoe Arbuckle, was charged with manslaughter, it was no longer possible for him to remain on the screen: immaterial objects do not engage in sex-play. Valentino, dead early, provoked a hysteria of mourning so in excess of all reason that it remains legendary, legendary and not a little disgraceful in its savagery: People clawed one another to get near the bier, indifferently—almost vengefully—destroying the trappings of the occasion. Can some of the savagery have come from a sense that Valentino wasn't supposed to

die until the public was through with him? Archetypes, being immaterial, are by definition immortal; sheiks should be no more vulnerable than clowns.

We continue to admire and even to love stars; it is hard to imagine worshiping them. But as late as 1931, after sound had begun to rob silent performers of their semi-mythological status, a gentleman escorting four or five of us through the studios—my high-school graduation present was a trip to Hollywood—felt himself bound to caution us at the outset: "Now, you've got to stop and remember this—they are only human beings."

Silence made them less and more than that. I began by mentioning *The Bachelor Daddy* because it was a simple, domestic film. No matter how simple, how domestic, how prosaic, how "realistic" a film might be, the figures that moved through it and the familiar objects they touched were made transcendent by silence. Films that meant to be more than mere "program" pictures took greater advantage of the insubstantiality that freed attested fact to become buoyant fantasy. Romances of every kind filled the screen: *The Sea Hawk, Beau Geste, Scaramouche, Seventh Heaven, The Mark of Zorro, Captain Blood, Ben-Hur, Janice Meredith, Monsieur Beaucaire, Orphans of the Storm, The White Sister, The Hunchback of Notre Dame, Beau Brummel, Little Old New York*. None of these was what I have called "stage" fantasy, formal make-believe. All, whether their fantasizing was sentimental or grotesque, took place—or were accepted as taking place—in the camera's certified world. But the sound that most often accompanied them was that of organ music, an instrument previously associated with another world altogether. And the new buildings built to house the films were called either "palaces" or "cathedrals." When we set out to go to one of them, we were on our way to the Granada or the Paradise.

Not even the most earnest attempts to make earthy, lifelike serious films about commonplace, recognizable people ever escaped—or wished to escape—the quasi-fairy-tale quality silence permitted. *Broken Blossoms* is D. W. Griffith's most brutally naturalistic genre study: London's Limehouse in all its squalor and despair. It is a fine film. But its heroine is as virginally ethereal as the dawn mists on the street, her father is an ogre drawn to the scale of the Brothers Grimm, her young Chinese savior and then avenger is lotus-blossom to the core. Naturalism itself has arrived at a new, infinitely more rarefied, nature. King Vidor's *The Crowd* is an honest attempt to record the very ordinary meetings, matings, and estrangements of underpaid office workers, the nameless and faceless who throng city sidewalks at five in the afternoon. But the office in which the struggling non-hero slaves is an office composed of what seems one hundred identical desks, manned by identical non-identities performing mechanically stylized tasks. Inevitably, the soberest attempts to come to grips with "real life" take on the mysterious overtones of silent iconography, breathe the same air as their more openly romantic fellows.

The joy of film began in fact. "Thanks to the movie camera," René Clair exclaimed in 1922, "real people in real fields were finally going to become a work of art. At last, no more canvas trees, no more painted skies!" And where did silence take this fact? Mr. Clair in 1923:

"Judge *Robin Hood* as you would judge a ballet or a fairy pantomime. Look at it for just a moment with simple eyes. Pay attention only to the perfection of the motions, of the motion; the cinema was created to record it. *Robin Hood* is an army of banners on the march, steel-clad horses galloping, free men dancing in a forest, sprints through a castle built for giants, leaps that traverse space, streams, forests, countrysides. . . ."

5. Fantasy Intensified: Music and the Dancing Image

This fairy tale of fact, this balletic reality, was reinforced in its effect by two factors. One of them was the mantle of music which did not so much accompany the film as swathe it in an all-encompassing richness that could be felt, surrounding the viewer and shutting him off from worldly intrusion. The other was the speed at which silent film was projected, a speed that had the effect of further stylizing the real.

When recordings of silent film music are made today they are most often made on pianos alone and, if the recording means to be funny, on tinny pianos at that. Nothing could be less representative of the experience audiences had, once the day of the primitive nickelodeon was past. Early storefront theaters did make do with pianos; but by the time I was seven, there was just one theater piano left in our town, in a shabby ten-cent house condemned to fifth-run showings and revivals. The "best" of the houses available to me—and it was not in the metropolitan center but on the very edge of the suburbs—maintained a full pit-orchestra for all evening performances, an orchestra capable of managing its own showy, if obvious, "overture" before the performance proper began and of doing ample justice to the most ambitious films then being made. During the musicians' rest periods, an elaborate organ took over. Because the organ did full-time duty at matinees, and because the middle-grade houses which could not afford orchestras relied on it alone, the deep-throated swells of Wurlitzer or Kimballs became the sounds most often associated with silent film: a degree of nostalgia *can* be recovered if one can get his hands on a Gaylord Carter tape made, say, during a retrospective showing of *Robin Hood*.

In 1915 *The Birth of a Nation*, first shown in a legitimate theater at a two-dollar top, inaugurated the practice of arranging full-orchestra scores carefully cued to particular films; thereafter audiences understood that if they were to see a film at its most complete they would go where the orchestras were. But to the end of the silent period, the smallest houses with the feeblest organs were provided with carefully conceived, often evocative, "cue-sheets."

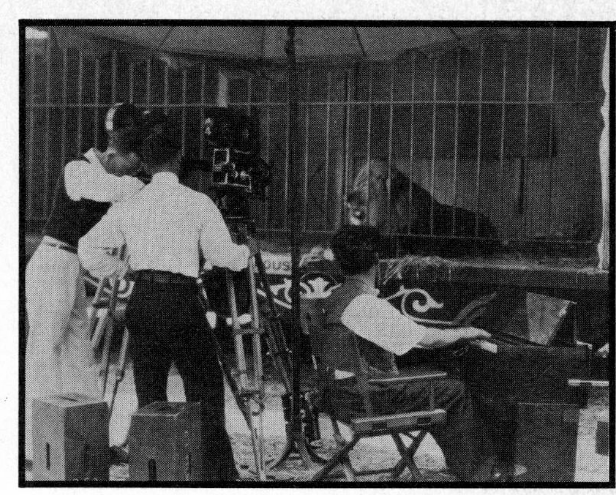

Music was not an accessory to silent film; it was an integral part of it. The scores on the soundtracks of films today *are* accessories, very much second fiddles. They must get out of the way, dive down under, whenever dialogue begins. Silent film music was under no such interdict. It was, in itself, an uninterrupted whole, full partner to the visual image—free, sustained, assertive. To take music from a silent film is to take half its life away.

I was very much surprised, on visiting Henri Langlois's Cinémathèque Française in Paris—possibly the most extensive repository of old film now available to us—to find myself watching the film in what was in fact dead silence. I turned to the pleasant young filmmaker who had escorted me through the building and asked him if he knew why no score of any kind—piano, organ, tape—had been provided. He wasn't certain, but he ventured the thought that the cutting-rhythms of the film might be better seen and appreciated without the presence of other rhythms.

Nothing could be wider of the mark. One of the functions of music, beyond providing a cradle for the whole, is to create smaller pocket-rhythms, rhythms for scenes, varying moods. Films are cut to a rhythm, to be sure; the director-cutter always has something in mind. But cuts are cuts, and they are sharp, jagged, potentially dislocating. A scene of a single mood may contain thirty or forty of them. Music acts as a seal on these, binding into a unit what are actually fragments. In silent film, with the additional disjunction of titles frequently threatening to interrupt the flow, the overarching authority of musical rhythms is all but imperative. Music safely gathers together elements that are actually radically contentious—in the case of titles, we must suddenly stop seeing backgrounds and see black, we must stop looking at people and objects and hurriedly begin to read—and holds them, with its own compelling structure, in its arms.

But music does much more than that. It releases a silent film to its audience, carries the film forward by means of its own accents into the auditorium, makes the film emotionally intelligible in something of the same way that words and realistic sounds make current films intelligible. Without music, a silent film can lose both intellectual and emotional focus, can become a series of equal quantities gliding by. Music detains and projects those quantities one by one, drawing them from the screen as though there were a magnet at our backs. The matter is easily tested. Project any silent film with no score or with a random, inappropriate one. It will retain some of its qualities, but it will seem to pass at a considerable distance, its remoteness in time intensified, its *presence* shrouded. Run the same film with a score that has been made with sympathetic attention to the rhythms it does possess and it will, if it is at all a good film, leap from the screen. I have repeatedly experimented with certain early Chaplin films which, run silently, seem now and again amusing. Appropriately scored, the laughs triple. There is a reason why Chaplin's movements have so often been called balletic; an internal relationship exists between music and the very concept of silent motion.

This relationship was recognized very early. Because no speaking actor was directly present to the audience, and because the camera was serving as a ghostly intermediary, cinema, as Elie Faure found, was immediately established "as further away from the theater than from music." Once one began to admit the nonlogical rhythms of camera positioning and editing, Faure continued, it was plain that "the interpenetration, the crossing and association of movements and cadences . . . give us the impression that even the most mediocre films unroll in *musical space*."

Music was of course often played during actual filming. Gestures could be made to a beat as cutters could cut, with their heads and fingers, to a beat. King Vidor has discussed in some detail his use of music during the filming, and prior

Even a lion seems responsive to an organist's "mood" music on the set of Chaplin's *The Circus*.

to the showing, of *The Big Parade*. "The thought struck me," he writes in his autobiography, *A Tree is a Tree*, "that if I could [create a] slow, measured cadence as my American troops approached the front line, I could illustrate the proximity of death with a telling and powerful effect. I was in the realm of my private obsession, experimenting with the possibilities of 'silent music.'

"I took a metronome into the projection room and set the tempo. . . . When we filmed the March through Belleau Wood in a small forest near Los Angeles, I used the same metronome, and a drummer with a bass drum amplified the metronomic ticks so that all in a range of several hundred yards could hear. I instructed the men that each step must be taken on a drum beat, each turn of the head, lift of a rifle, pull of a trigger, in short, every physical movement must occur on the beat of the drum. Those extras who were veterans of the AEF and had served time in France thought I had gone completely daft and expressed their ridicule most volubly. One British veteran wanted to know if he were performing in 'some bloody ballet.' I did not say so at the time, but that is exactly what it was—a bloody ballet, a ballet of death."

When Darryl Zanuck remarked that there never was such a thing as a silent picture, he simply meant that each person working on a film worked with music in mind, adapting himself—consciously or not—to an eventual fusion he could *hear*. No editor in the cutting room assembled a fast chase without anticipating the "hurry music" that would later double its tension. If one clown hit another on the head with a mallet he knew that the accompanying sound heard in the theater would not be literal. Today's sound-effects are literal; a thud must be a thud, except in animated cartoons. But the theater organist's screech when the mallet struck in a silent film was—in spite of the camera's visual reality—much nearer the piercing harmonic stab heard in animated cartoons today. The sting was a musical sting, not the sound of the mallet's thump. Because silence and its blood brother, music, had destroyed the literalness of the effect, the clown did not have to be literal in creating it. He was liberated by the two formalities that guaranteed him immunity to fantasize in his own way—adopting extravagant positions, executing majestically insane windups, striking as though his colleague's head offered the resistance of Vulcan's forge.

Because music was nonliteral, it supported fantasy handsomely. Bathed in it, Norma Talmadge could reign over Graustark yet one more time; supported by it, Douglas Fairbanks could clasp his girl's hands, leap to a wall, and swing the girl over it in one breath-taking lift that had no home outside dance; irrationally propelled by it, Buster Keaton could drop the receiver during a telephone conversation with *his* girl and race twenty city blocks to arrive at her home before she had hung up.

The speed at which Keaton ran constituted another pressure toward fantasy that came about partly by accident and then by design. Whether it was Keaton running for comic effect or John Gilbert, in a completely serious film, alighting from a train to greet his mother, movement in silent film became a kind of winged horse of its own. Men and women might seem to fly, or at least to elide with great grace the more cumbersome movements of earthbound bodies, because portions of their movements were simply not photographed. A dancer on a stage may *seem* to spin faster and leap higher than normal human musculature and the laws of gravity permit, but that is an illusion, created by his skill. In the case of silent films, the in-between movements—those in which gravity might be felt asserting itself or the sluggish body sensed to be straining through space—were not there to be seen. They had been bypassed, flexibly and at will, by the hand of the man cranking the camera. He had taken fewer pictures than the eye requires to see movement at a lifelike rate. As a result, if the performers did not actually dance, the viewer's eye did.

I am not now speaking of that obviously speeded-up motion that is familiar to all of us as a comic device and is deliberately intended as absurd: Ben Turpin, one foot tied to a car, hopping toward the horizon like a marionette jerked to eternity; Albert Finney, in those portions of the sound film *Tom Jones* that were constructed as silent film parody, whipping up and down staircases in jagged lightning-streak rhythm. These are intramural jokes, acknowledgments that film is film and can be played with to give us either mechanically accelerated action or its converse, "slow-motion." We always know when this is happening and are meant to know.

I am speaking of a lesser but very marked acceleration that was used in *all* silent film and was accepted as normal for the form. When Harold Lloyd, running from a policeman, dropped down one manhole only to pop up immediately from another, just in time to kick the policeman—who was now peering down into the first—he did so neither at a preposterously exaggerated rate that was meant to be detected as such nor at a lifelike rate that would allow for the time and physical exertion the action would actually consume. The movement was recorded at a telescoped rate somewhere between the two, a rate that took the labor out of life and gave its gestures a new and delightful buoyancy, a watch-spring precision. What was customary for the form was in fact rhythmically unfaithful to life.

Uniform rhythmic fidelity did not appear on the screen until sound came in, and then it was enforced. In order to capture the tones of the human voice without distortion, it was necessary to establish a camera rate of twenty-four frames of film per second, which may be taken as the rate at which we normally hear and see. Camera speed was now locked, motor-driven, inflexible. Before speech rhythms and tones mattered, however, the camera *and* the projector that showed the film were both relatively free agents, flexible tools in the hands of the fantasists—the virtual musicians—who operated them.

Camera and projection speed could have been standardized much earlier, if there had been any good reason for doing so. Thomas Edison is said to have exposed his first film at a rate of forty-eight frames per second, which would have produced a slow-motion effect of truly ectoplasmic quality unless projectors were built to run at wildly clattering speed. During the silent era, with cameras hand-cranked for the most part, every sort of speed was employed; all were available. Undoubtedly the equivalent of sound speed was occasionally made use of, especially after 1925: when a scenarist wished the action slowed down briefly to establish a mood or to make a subtle psychological point, he would simply indicate to the cameraman that he wanted more frames per second during the shooting. Over-all, however, the practice developed of shooting film at approximately sixteen or eighteen frames per second—which means that, by sound speed or "normal" standards, some stages of the movement had been omitted—and then projecting it at a rate very close to the more rapid sound-projection rate. Thus the camera made elisions and the projector took up the slack by running the film fast enough to avoid "flicker." The result was not only faster than life, it was cleaner, less effortful, more dynamic.

Because it is difficult to be exact about these matters now, certain misconceptions have grown up and some controversy has been stirred. It is difficult to be exact because of the variables involved. Each cameraman cranked at his own rate, was proud of his particular "cadence." But no two cameramen's cadences can ever have been the same. Each was further under instruction from his director and sometimes his scenarist to vary his cadence from shot to shot. Within a

Both Chaplin and Keaton missed the rhythm of the hand-cranked silent camer when it gave way to the mechanizatior of sound.

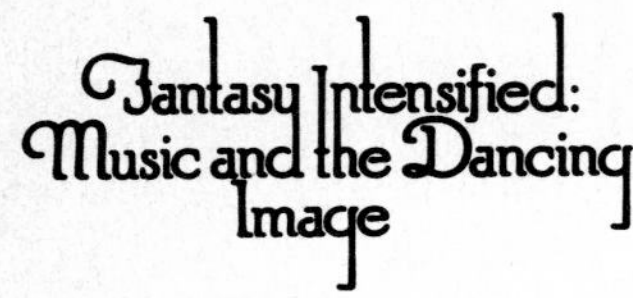

single completed film a wide range of speeds may appear. And when the film was projected in a theater, it was subject to the ministrations of yet another free agent, an operator who could put his finger to an unmarked rheostat and alter the film speed from shot to shot, reel to reel, hour to hour. Good projectionists prided themselves on their sensitivity. James Card, director of the film department at the Eastman House archives in Rochester, New York, has unearthed a bit of advice given by a projectionist to his colleagues in a 1911 issue of *Moving Picture World*: "The operator 'renders' a film, if he is a real operator, exactly as does the musician render a piece of music, in that, within limits, the action of the scene being portrayed depends entirely on his judgment. . . . Watch the scene closely and by variation of speed bring out everything there is in it. No set rule applies. Only the application of brains to the matter of speed can properly render a film. I have often changed speed half a dozen times on one film of 1000 feet." There was also an unhappy corollary to this particular freedom. If the manager of the theater had a long line of patrons waiting to get in for the next showing, he might instruct the operator to hurry the film unmercifully.

With so many intangibles involved, it is dangerous to be dogmatic about what was and is proper silent film speed. What *should* you be seeing as you visit a museum showing, or glance at television, today? Unfortunately, one misconception has been built directly into the contemporary projectors on which most silent film is shown, sadly confusing any discussion almost before it can begin. Most silent film is now run on sixteen-millimeter projectors, and the manufacturers of these machines, eager to make them adaptable to both sound and silence, have equipped them not with flexible rheostats but with a speed-control switch that can be turned to just two positions. Turn it to "Sound" and the machine will run at twenty-four frames per second, which is correct. Turn it to "Silent" and the machine will run at sixteen-to-eighteen frames per second, which is a howling blunder. Silent films were *shot* at that rate, much of the time. But they were never shown at that rate. In fact, as James Card has pointed out, a projectionist running the nitrate film of the period past his carbon arcs at the sluggish rate of sixteen frames per second would be openly courting fire.

What has obviously happened is that contemporary manufacturers, working mainly from an experience of sound film and its wholly natural rhythms, have assumed that the purpose of a "silent" speed is to make silent films appear to move as "naturally" as sound films do. That they were never so intended has been amply demonstrated both by Mr. Card and by David Shepard writing for the American Film Institute in Washington, D.C.

Mr. Card uses Douglas Fairbanks's *Robin Hood* as illustration. Instructions regarding the speed at which a given film was to be shown usually came with the music cue-sheets of the period. They were given in terms of minutes per reel rather than frames per second. The producers asked that *Robin Hood* be shown at the rate of twelve minutes per reel. Current sound film runs at a little better than eleven and one half minutes per reel, or very close to the rate specified for the Fairbanks silent film. On the other hand, the arbitrary and misleading "silent" projection speed puts film through the machine at the rate of nearly seventeen minutes per reel. At this rate, a film intended to run for two hours and eight minutes extends itself, altogether artificially, to a full three hours, leaving poor Robin, in Mr. Card's words, "painfully limping through the forest." Run at sound speed, *Robin Hood* misses its original full timing by only seven minutes.

Mr. Shepard adds that Fairbanks's *The Thief of Bagdad* would run an hour overtime if dragged through the projector at so-called "silent" speed, and that instructions for Chaplin's *The Gold Rush* indicate approximately sound speed. Sometimes these instructions were incorporated into the film itself, appearing on the "leader"—those few feet of mainly blank film which are used for threading the projector. The leader for *Down to the Sea in Ships*, a film in which a hoydenish ingenue named Clara Bow made an early appearance, specifies that the reel is to be run not at a preposterous "silent" speed of seventeen minutes, and not even at the eleven-and-a-half-minute speed of contemporary sound film, but in eleven minutes exactly, which means that the action would have moved more rapidly than *any* household projector can now show us. Buster Keaton's *Sherlock Jr.* and *Seven Chances* were meant to be projected at that rate too.

There were variations—Lon Chaney's *The Phantom of the Opera* was timed for fourteen minutes to the reel, so that it does race a bit at sound speed—but there would seem to be no escaping the conclusion that given only two choices, as we are today, sound speed is infinitely preferable. As Mr. Card concludes, "Examination of thousands of cue-sheets for silent films has failed to turn up a single one which indicates that a film should be projected at sixteen and one half minutes per reel or sixteen frames per second." The films *did* move rapidly.

When they are shown on television there is no choice of speeds, a circumstance which has helped give rise to the illusion that the films are in some way being betrayed. Television—this must be one of its few virtues—is incapable of reproducing the slower "silent" rate: the electronic scanning rate prohibits it. And, seen at sound speed, certain primitive or at least relatively early films do project rather breathlessly. Because several of D. W. Griffith's important films fall into this category, a quarrel has ensued with sound speed identified as the villain.

Actually, the defects are most often in the films themselves. Although Billy Bitzer, Griffith's principal cameraman, was as much a genius as his master, he did sometimes crank his camera erratically, leaving us with patches of action that are dizzying to watch and gone before they can be grasped. And though Griffith was a great innovator, he was sometimes an inexplicably careless editor, splicing between scenes shot at an intelligible speed inchoate fragments shot at an unworkable rate. Various efforts have been made through the years to compensate for his oversights: some sequences have been "stretched" by reprinting every other frame to ease the frantic flow of the action. Unfortunately, this produces a stop-and-start effect that is almost as bothersome as the racehorse tempo it is meant to correct.

Griffith and Bitzer were of course not alone in putting together early films without sufficient regard for a tolerable optical rhythm: among Buster Keaton's short comedies, there is one—*The Haunted House*—that contains sequences too slowly cranked; and I don't think Chaplin's second Mutual comedy, *The Fireman*, can be followed at sound speed. The number of films that suffer severely from interior dislocations of this kind, however, is limited, and only a return to rheostat control—with an affectionate hand constantly on the dial—can properly salvage them. Their loss is a real loss. But it should not be allowed to falsify a general truth: silent film *chose*, by control of the camera and through instructions to projectionists, to move at an unreal, stylized, in effect fantasized rate.

There was every reason why it should have done so. For one thing, silent film was entirely aware that it lacked speech, though the figures on the screen were very often seen speaking. To have photographed the actors speaking at a "normal" rate would have been excruciatingly laborious, indeed would have called emphatic attention to what was missing. Much more sensible to accelerate silent speech, so long as it did not race beyond the conventionally believable. If one actually watches John Gilbert's lips as he is so swiftly greeting his mother and friends in *The Flesh and the Devil*, one realizes that, if recorded, the sound

'DOWN TO THE SEA IN SHIPS"

REEL FOUR

Operator: Please run eleven minutes for 1,000 feet.

This frame of "leader" from an important feature of 1922 instructs the projectionist to run the film at a rate even faster than sound speed.

must have been nearly a gabble. But the stylization was quickly accepted; there was an eminently sensible logic behind it.

Directors and performers discovered early that the severity of line and lightness of motion created by the acceleration were virtues that could be exploited. Keaton's celebrated stop-on-a-dime reversals of direction and Chaplin's even more celebrated one-foot skid for a corner turn were obvious products of close study by the comedians of their intensified rates on the screen. Either device, done at a "natural" tempo, would lose its specific humor, its capacity to make us laugh with a gasp. We should see the run being braked, almost painfully so, and the clown's struggle for control as he hoisted his body another way. We should feel the weight of it. Chaplin was agile and Keaton a trained acrobat; personal equipment helped create the effect. But it was the omission of intermediary frames that made the effect nearly magical. "Keaton once told me," Penelope Gilliatt has written in *The New Yorker*, "that he and Chaplin missed the sound of the cameras cranking after they stopped making silent films. Because of the rhythm."

To sense the precise difference between the rhythm to which sound has accustomed us and the much more blithely animated rhythm of silent film—and, really, to end the argument—it is only necessary to look at the last two silent films Chaplin made, *City Lights* and *Modern Times*. Both have, and from the beginning were meant to have, soundtracks: music by Chaplin, occasional whistles, bells, and even lip-synch speech as the manager of the factory in *Modern Times* relays instructions to harried workers via remote-control television. Both films were therefore *required* to be projected at sound speed. But they were photographed at the old silent speed. The least glance at *Modern Times* reveals instantly that all of Chaplin's work in the film—his losing battle with a moving conveyor-belt, his entrapment in and regurgitation by the giant cogs of the machinery, his insane dance with an oilcan—has been filmed at a rate that puts springs on his heels and makes unleashed jackknives of his elbows. This was the standard practice during silence; this is how the films looked when they were projected as their creators intended; this was still Chaplin's method a full seven years after sound had been established and he was making use of sound.

For those who like sharp contrasts, there is an interesting moment late in *Modern Times*. Chaplin has been working as a waiter in a café, and he has been persuaded—all of this still in the birdlike busyness of silent rhythm—to become part of the floor show by singing a song. He is nervous, and so are we: Chaplin's actual voice is about to be heard for the first time. He receives a last good-luck hug from Paulette Goddard in the dressing room, at the old silent speed that makes the hug snap like a bear trap. But as the film cuts to the café floor and Chaplin enters to perform, one rhythm must be exchanged for another, a new and slower world must be entered. Chaplin is canny about the matter: he begins not by singing but by doing a few vaudeville backslides designed to conceal the transition. Then, at the center of the floor, the moment comes. The shooting rate has been altered so that his words will be properly recorded. Suddenly the very air is heavier, the universe slows down, the man on the floor is an actual man and no sprite. The song, composed of nonsense syllables, is completed—it feels odd throughout, as though a motor were losing power—and Chaplin moves away to the dressing room. This time he throws caution to the winds, makes no transition at all. On the split-second, as he bursts into the dressing room and back into the world of silence as well, there is a leap of film and a leap of heart. In one cut, we have taken off again, abandoned strict reality for a light agitation that makes a pirouetting puppet of Miss Goddard and a near-dervish of Mr. Chaplin. We have agreed on fantasy once more, on movement with the power of flight, and are happy enough with our bargain.

16. Serious Film: The Disadvantages of Silence

Serious film lost nothing with the coming of sound. Comedy lost, or changed, its character completely. As René Clair has recently written, "The golden age of American comedy ended with the coming of the talking picture." Why was that?

Fundamentally, things turned out as they did because fantasy is inimical to seriousness and can only diminish its pretensions to weight, while comedy is utterly at home with it. This has always been so, but it became devastatingly clear once more when sound and silence finally met head-on.

Al Jolson is credited with having brought about the sound revolution, and he did in fact turn the tide. He did it, however, in a surprising way. One's first assumption is that the excitement of hearing Jolson sing was the excitement that tumbled down one form and gave rise to another. It wasn't quite like that. If anyone goes back to Jolson's first film, *The Jazz Singer*, today, he does go back to hear the songs; and the restless, penetrating, ebullient bleat of the man who called himself "the world's greatest entertainer"—so far as I am concerned, he was every bit of that—is still an enormous pleasure to listen to. But the songs themselves, and the peculiar form in which the film was cast, might have succeeded and then passed away as a "special event," a novelty, the visit of a great man of the theater to a medium that would show him hospitality and then return to its main business. Cantor, singing, changed nothing in 1922. Van and Schenck, singing, were going to change nothing in 1927. Jolson might have done better and still not have shattered a style: *The Jazz Singer* was widely regarded as a fluke in 1927, and it was a year or more before studios other than Warner Brothers were frantically buying sound equipment.

What destroyed a habit and reversed a preference was something else. It was the sound of Jolson speaking. Jolson spoke very little in the film. *The Jazz Singer*, like the even more successful *The Singing Fool* that followed, was for the most part a silent film. The entire narrative of *The Jazz Singer*, four fifths of its length,

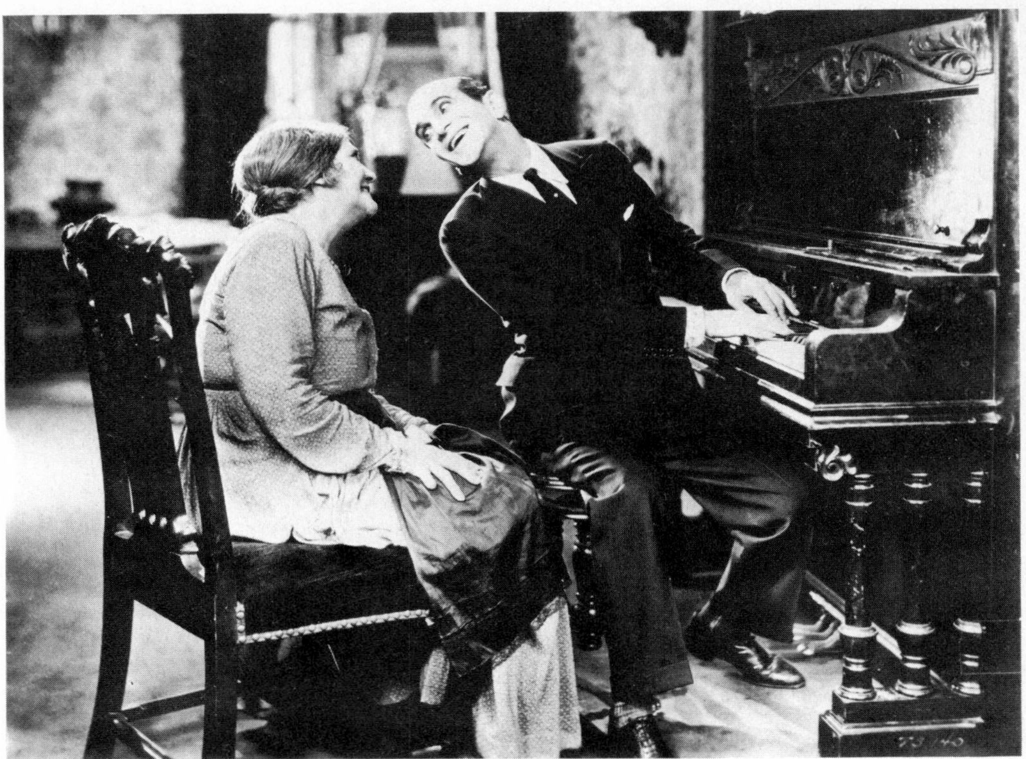

As Jolson finishes this song, he turns to his mother and speaks intimately. *The Jazz Singer*.

is mute, with titles. The songs are simply recorded interludes, nightclub or theater turns, and the bastard form thus created might possibly have been preserved indefinitely for those performers who could make reasonable use of it. The stage entertainers might have done their specialties, intermittently, while all else remained silent. Indeed, the "part-talking" film did continue for quite a long while.

But Jolson had done one thing, unpredictably, that made the changeover inevitable. He had talked, for a few moments, not in the stylized vaudeville patter of Weber and Fields, but like a human being. Finishing one of his songs at the piano, he turned to the actress who played his mother and chatted with her, asking her how she had liked the song, reassuring her of his devotion. The monologue was brief, and expendable; in fact, it was a violation of the film's form. Legend has it that the moment had not been planned, that Jolson spontaneously turned from the piano and, brimming over with energy, improvised the passage on the spot. Legend also has it that Warner Brothers considered deleting the few spoken words. The words changed everything. Suddenly the audience wanted to hear men and women speaking like men and women.

There was a reason why they should have done so. Serious silent film had always labored at an actual disadvantage. Comedy might thrive on silence, wrest from it a distinctive character. But seriousness was dependent on thought, on the complex mental operations governing the behavior of men and women, and thought has always been best conveyed by words. Thought can of course be conveyed by other means: by the lift of an eyebrow, the curl of a lip, the withdrawal of a hand. But the thoughts conveyed by these means must be readily recognizable to a vast audience, which means that they must be close to elementary. Required to express intense psychological states through visual means alone, performers are forced to do more, and more, with their entire bodies. The more is both too much and not enough. While it is certainly not true that silent film acting was as exaggerated as parodists have so often tried to make us believe, exaggeration was necessary as emotion reached a certain temperature with no words available to release heat. Ramon Novarro is personable and perfectly plausible for most of the silent *Ben-Hur*; driven to extremes of anguish, however, he must writhe

embarrassingly. So must Greta Garbo in *The Flesh and the Devil.* Douglas Fairbanks had a habit of quickly cloaking his face whenever he was required to express an interior state of any intensity. Given a narrative of some psychological complexity, and one that means to keep moving the while, words are wanted. They do the job more rapidly, more clearly, and with infinitely greater penetration.

Handsome solutions—even if they were only partial solutions—to the problem were devised by gifted directors. Spectacle was not only natural fodder for the camera, it was excellent compensation for what was lacking: no one needed dialogue to understand a race across an ice-floe, the Johnstown flood, chariots colliding in the Circus Maximus, infantrymen advancing through Belleau Wood. The Civil War battle scenes directed by Griffith and photographed by Bitzer for *The Birth of a Nation* continue to represent the serious silent film at its most expressive. The canvas is large, the issues are plain, the editing is breath-taking. The serious silent film is doing one of the things it can do, most powerfully: with all complexity reduced to a head-on clash between two clearly defined contestants, it is hurtling us through that clash with both intimacy and sweep. Now we are above the battle, seeing its thrusting and yielding patterns whole; now we are inside it, locked in close-up to a bayoneted man falling. It is still possible to sense the shock that must have run through audiences when the techniques were astonishingly new. The film, of course, cannot maintain its stature as it turns—as it *must* turn—to the ideological intricacies that brought about, accompanied, and followed the battles. Suddenly a great piece of filmmaking becomes an appalling film. It is appalling mainly because of its racial bias. But the ideological underpinnings of the film suffer from something more than bias: they suffer, inevitably, from simplism. Ready-made motives must be given to "scalawag" politicians if the story is to hurry on to the melodrama of its hooded night rides, its ambushed cabins, its attempted rapes. The film is complex, but its complexity is one of event rather than thought. The film is capable of nuance, but not of depth.

Spectacle is what we *can* have. It can exist, within silence, at a very high level of sophistication. When the director is a wizard with both a camera and a

The magnified passions of silence: Greta Garbo and John Gilbert, *The Flesh and the Devil*; Vilma Banky and Montagu Love, *One Night of Love*.

Overleaf: Spectacle; *The Birth of a Nation*.

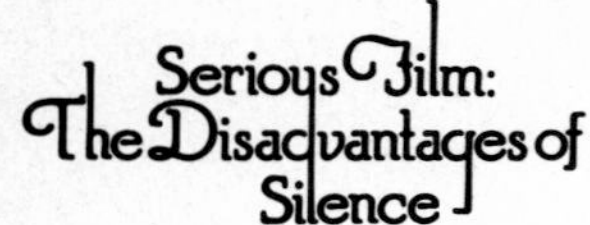

scissors, as Eisenstein was in his distinctive kind of montage, film can arrive at a purely visual intensity that seems to embroil us fiercely in the rhythm of the event. The Odessa steps sequence mentioned earlier, as stunning today as when it was made, reports its clash in a savage assault of whipped-away images, torn from our eyes almost before we have taken them in. But again the dizzying immediate structure rests upon an exceedingly simple base. Those are Cossacks coming down the steps. We know nothing of what they are thinking, nor do we ask.

When, in *Ten Days That Shook the World* and after the massed struggle at a rising drawbridge is over, Eisenstein must account at length for the subtle political maneuverings that have achieved a revolution, he is as handicapped as Griffith was. The film slackens; debating figures elude us. We can only look, and guess. No matter, up to a point. The films, for the visual greatness of their best passages, are masterpieces.

Spectacle, whether penny-plain or highly sophisticated, was not serious film's only weapon. Directors learned the value of understatement too, though it had to be used sparingly if pace was to be maintained. I said that *The Birth of a Nation* was capable of nuance. When Henry B. Walthall, a Southern colonel during the war, returns at its end to his ruined homestead, we know that his impoverished mother and little sister are waiting for him inside the charred house. Unable to contain her joy, the sister bursts onto the porch, hugs him, subsides in mute embarrassment as he fingers the tiny patches of cotton she has fixed to her dress in lieu of ermine. He then moves toward the doorway. As he reaches it, his mother's arms are thrust through it to him. We see no more than that. The half-hidden embrace that follows is all the more touching for what it omits; synecdoche has proved a weapon even here. In Clarence Brown's *The Flesh and the Devil,* Greta Garbo and John Gilbert are discovered in guilty embrace by Miss Garbo's husband. A duel between husband and lover is arranged. The duel, at dawn, is photographed entirely in silhouette: five or six shadowy figures on a hillside wreathed in mist. The duelists take their traditional stances, back to back, and, when the signal is given, measure off the paces to their respective firing positions. As they do, both leave the screen at opposite sides. After a moment, two curls of smoke from their pistols drift in at the edges of the screen. The seconds now run off, each to his man, as the scene fades. We do not know what has happened. We fade in to Miss Garbo seated before a mirror. As she completes her dressing, a couturier's hands appear in the frame, gently placing Miss Garbo's hat and veil on her head. The hat and veil are black.

And, of course, silent film did have words to help carry its thought forward. There were "captions" in quotation marks meant to indicate dialogue exchanges. And there were "titles," often lengthy paragraphs meant to establish background, to bridge gaps in the narrative, even to provide motivation when motivation could not be—or had not been—adequately conveyed in gesture.

Unfortunately for serious films, dialogue captions proved a trap. They not only called attention to the thinness of thought imposed by silent fantasy, they made the thinness thinner. Obviously, captions could not account for all that two or more people were saying as their lips moved so swiftly. The form would have stopped dead in its tracks—it sometimes did—if it had attempted to record so much as a fifth or even a tenth of any given conversation; the audience had not come to read lines but to see faces, motion. But this meant two things: an enormous amount of what the characters were actually thinking and feeling would have to be dismissed entirely; and the few words intended to summarize all of this would have to be close to primer level. It was necessary to reduce verbally expressed thought to something like its lowest common denominator if the film was

Opposite: Spectacle—the Odessa steps sequence, *Potemkin*. Nuance—the homecoming embrace in *The Birth of a Nation*.

to remain a film and predominantly visual.

The caption generally did this, making what virtue it could of an enforced simplicity. Over the years screen-writers—the best were in great demand—became skilled at their peculiar kind of shorthand: there were witty captions, there were affecting captions, there were captions that seemed truly to belong to the personalities of the people moving their lips. But to the end, and at its best, serious silent film was condemned to doing its writing in broad strokes. Josef von Sternberg's *The Last Command* remains an exceptionally interesting film, engrossing today in its narrative turns and psychological inflections. It was released at the very close of the era, in 1928, and must be accepted as more or less representative of the form at its maturity. Its captions were written by Herman J. Mankiewicz, crown prince of the craft. Yet when it is time to introduce Evelyn Brent and establish her importance in the narrative, an aide must say to his commanding officer—who is examining her passport—that "She is the most dangerous revolutionary in Russia!" One knew that she was a revolutionary; one had not quite thought she was out of a Dick Tracy cartoon.

Nor did the longer and more "literary" titles that provided us with information between scenes in any way increase the intellectual content of a serious film. Instead, they created new invitations to trouble. They could, in certain circumstances, prove valuable to a film, reinforcing its atmosphere and very nearly providing it with its texture. Kevin Brownlow has cited examples from James Cruze's *The Covered Wagon*, this among them:

"Month after month, over the Western Rockies, Northwest across the thirsty land of the Shoshones and the mighty Snake, the Men of the Plow held to their purpose."

That *is* attractive, in a Henry Wadsworth Longfellow–Boys' Guide to the West sort of way; faded in and out between long-shots of caravans snaking through gulleys and close-ups of wagon wheels plunging into mud, it helps to create the dogged rhythm of the film. But the literary subtitle was at best a confession that silent film could not do its work alone—it had to borrow from the novelist to move its narrative through time and space—and at worst an invitation not to do the work at all.

For instance, no one used, or abused, the subtitle more than the man who established silent film in all its power, D. W. Griffith. *Intolerance*, still called a masterwork by some though it seems to me a complete failure on its own terms, would be psychologically unintelligible if it were not for verbal signposts slapped in our faces every minute or oftener explaining just what is in the minds of certain ancient priests of Babylon, of a mountain girl who loves Belshazzar, of a Rhapsode who loves the mountain girl. We never do understand the intent of the conniving priests from anything they do on the screen; in fact, we scarcely recognize them from scene to scene. Here psychology has not been filmed, it has been interpolated.

That excessive titling represented a betrayal of the form was recognized early. Thoughtful directors learned to pride themselves on keeping titles and captions to the indispensable minimum, though this was more readily achieved in comedies than in serious films. A dream did grow up among makers of serious films of a titleless form, one that would tell its story and generate its emotions through mime alone. The dream was fully realized, or almost fully realized, just once. In F. W. Murnau's *The Last Laugh*, Emil Jannings plays an elderly hotel doorman, pompous, proud of his uniform, proud of the status it gives him in his tenement community. One day Mr. Jannings reports to work as usual only to find a new man in his place, his uniform usurped. His world collapses: the hotel literally seems to be

A characteristic posture of silence, permitted its stylization by its very speechlessness: Rudolph Valentino in *Monsieur Beaucaire*.

Opposite: Emil Jannings as the dismissed hotel doorman in *The Last Laugh*, F. W. Murnau's experiment with the titleless film.

toppling over on him.

Murnau was able to describe the man, his sense of position, his fatigue, his stunned incomprehension, and the nightmare that followed clearly enough without titles—though a few helpful words appeared along the way in letters, on calendars, on the icing of a cake. The film is still down in all the books as a milestone in silent film history. Oddly, it had no successors. Seen today, it is possible to guess why: the film must move so slowly and so patiently in order to establish its wordless points that it is obliged to do with fewer of them. Content has been reduced once again.

For all the blessings that skilled pantomime, spectacle, montage, and evocative camera placement had bestowed on it, serious silent film lacked something vital to true seriousness: that last plunge into psychic depths that language takes, the thickness that comes of knowing a man in his thoughts. Whenever two or more people were seen conversing for too long a time without a caption appearing, audiences grew restive: they wanted to know what these serious people were saying. Thus the caption became self-propagating; and the caption was inadequate.

This restiveness is reinforced today, after our long experience of sound, when we go back to the major films of the silent period. The best comedies present no problem; we ask for nothing more. But to see a film like von Sternberg's *Underworld* now is almost to scream for language. The essence of the film, apart from the thrashing shoot-out at its climax, lies in the relationships that exist and change between a boss gangster, his paramour, and her once-derelict lover. Here are not only passions but minds at work, some coarse, some subtle. To eavesdrop on them from far corners, missing transitions, missing inflections, is frustrating, no matter how imaginatively the camera is guided. We grow hungry for intimacy and are fended off. That is more or less the case with any serious silent film revisited today. We can still be filled with admiration for what was in fact accomplished; we can, in some cases, still be truly moved. But it is difficult, at serious films, to escape a feeling of incompleteness.

It was just this experience of psychological completion, of sudden intimacy with thought, of having ceased moving on a parallel track to the people on the screen and swerved to move toward them, that Jolson hinted at in a few words and that finally brought a demand for thousands more. A serious talking film is richer than its silent equivalent: it has lost nothing of spectacle, of camera mobility, of fluid editing, or of sensitive performance; and it has added a dimension proper to seriousness in letting us know more of its characters' psyches.

The serious silent films that endure best are those that did not strain after a depth sealed away from them but that adapted themselves comfortably to the level romantic fantasy had imposed. If a "serious" film could be made almost entirely of spectacle and a persuasive love story—as *The Big Parade* was— it might do its work honestly; I confess that *The Big Parade* still leaves me in tears. Perhaps the difference between what could be accepted as "serious" under silence and what became markedly more dimensional, more realistically demanding, with sound can be glimpsed in the unhappy fate of John Gilbert, whose extraordinarily animated and attractive work in *The Big Parade* made a star of him. Gilbert had subsequently been teamed with Garbo in a series of near-Ruritanian romances: ancient chateaux, orchids in the garden, military brass bands, fevered sex, passion whispered but never heard. Legend has it that his voice, in his first talking film, proved too high-pitched and reedy to survive the demands of sound. Not so: his voice was neither better nor worse than the voices of a dozen other stars whose careers continued, and in his few later appearances on the sound screen no one bothered to mention it.

Serious Film: The Disadvantages of Silence

What happened to Gilbert was that his studio obtusely decided to introduce him to sound in a film *exactly like* the films in which he had sinned glamorously with Garbo. The film was called *His Glorious Night*, a new blonde beauty was provided as prey, and the ardent wooing that had been so seductive was translated into speech. Instantly, the audience laughed. What the audience had been so willing to fantasize for itself by way of lovemaking under silence could not be believed for a moment in a world made more dimensional by words.

By contrast, Ronald Colman's studio behaved intelligently. Colman had been playing opposite Vilma Banky in a series of moonlit struggles with the *droit du seigneur* that were virtually identical with the Gilbert-Garbo films. No attempt was made to pursue the tradition into sound. Instead, Colman was given a swift change of clothes and style, he was cast as a contemporary adventurer in an urbane thriller called *Bulldog Drummond*, playwright Sidney Howard was summoned from New York to provide him with witty, entirely plausible speech. The new look and sound were entirely successful, and a career was salvaged to last for more than another twenty years. Colman's speaking voice was in fact a superior one. But it had not made the crucial difference. One kind of credulity created by silence had ended; another had to be, and was, established.

Fantasy and seriousness do not walk hand in hand. By definition fantasy is incapable of complete sobriety: it is too playful, it respects reality too little, for that. And deep seriousness, in turn, wants no part of fantasy. Serious drama—at its most intense, tragedy—must refuse the escape clauses, the easy outs, the evasions and contradictions of reality that fantasy so invitingly offers.

It is otherwise with comedy. Comedy and fantasy have been jolly conspirators from the beginning. Almost the first comic figures on Aristophanes' stage were talking frogs and bird-men. Shakespeare's Puck can circle the globe in the twinkling of an eye and Molière's Don Juan—to take an example less extravagant—can make love to two women simultaneously, one on each arm. The bond of comedy with fantasy—it is not exclusive, just an easy mating at will—comes from comedy's impatience with the real. Comedy does not much care for the real world: that world is cold and wet and hot and slippery and infested with bees at all the wrong times. The world puts a man to work just trying to cope with it, and work, in the clown's view, is at all costs to be avoided. Daydreaming is better. What daydreaming won't do, perhaps fantastic trickery will. Evasion is of the essence.

None of the limitations of the silent screen, then, seemed limitations to its comedians. Rather, they seemed opportunities for slipping ever more elaborately through the cogs of the cosmic machinery, escaping the indignities of a dimensional, hostile universe. Fly through the transom when a policeman locks the door? Why not?

The fantasy born of silence was simply one more gift dropped into the laps of men determined to outwit reality. A portion of that unpleasant universe had already been destroyed, thank you. How much easier to get around! Their imaginations were released along with their limbs, and no voice could be heard to say them nay. I don't know—I don't believe—that anyone ever cared whether comedy found a voice. Those of us who were there at the time literally dreaded hearing Chaplin or Keaton or Lloyd speak; for these figures speech would not only be an excrescence, it would betray something we knew of them.

A form had been created that cradled clowns perfectly—all desires, all impulses indulged.

Serious silent film tended inevitably toward romantic fantasy: Lewis Stone and Ramon Novarro, *The Prisoner of Zenda*.

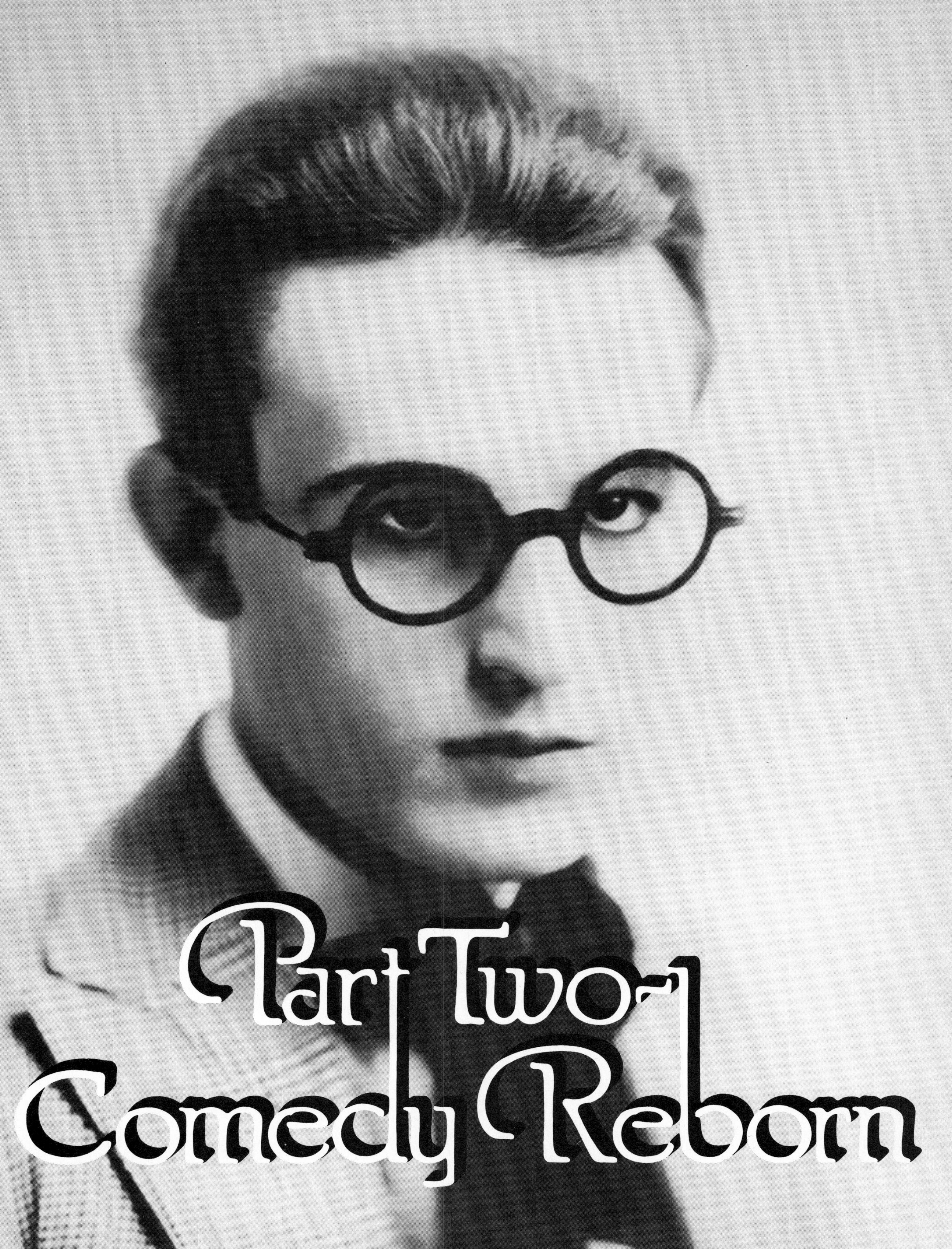

Part Two— Comedy Reborn

7. Comedy in Search of Its Freedom

It took time to find the form. The first film comedies, once the possibility and the pleasures of narrative had been established, were mainly stage derivations, ten-minute domestic sketches that might have played equally well in vaudeville. In a way, this is odd. When Edwin S. Porter firmly established a narrative form for films—hinting at it strongly in a simulated documentary called *The Life of an American Fireman* and realizing it in the outright fiction of *The Great Train Robbery*—he did so by using the fantasy-scale film permitted: horse-drawn fire engines belching smoke as they raced out on call, locomotives halted by masked bandits who later fired guns in our faces. And, for the purposes of comedy, fantasy had been more than strongly intimated in the work of Méliès and in Porter's own *The Dream of a Rarebit Fiend*; in this last film, a man floating in his bed high above the city was tumbled out of it to land on the weathervane of a steeple, where he was spun round and round until he was dropped once again through the roof of his own bedroom. In a Vitagraph film of 1906, *And the Villain Still Pursued Her*, the hero was seen clambering about on the surface of a giant balloon in midair, anticipating Buster Keaton by a good fifteen years. But these were "magic" or "dream" films, *too* fantastic for film's purposes: they violated too transparently the other half of film's promise, that the camera's report would be real. Film comedy swung the other way, and marked time.

The hold of the legitimate stage was at first strong, in any case. If films were going to tell a story, they were going to be doing what the stage had always done, and the impulse to do it the stage's way was reflexive. Actors were in the beginning always photographed at full length and deployed about painted interiors in stage compositions. When Griffith wanted to move closer for a three-quarter shot or a close-up, the opposition he met from his backers was instinctive: actors were stage people, and stage people were seen whole; audiences would not pay to see half of what the stage showed them. When films eventually became longer—"feature" films of the period tended to run just short of an hour—the impetus toward length came from Adolph Zukor's determination to photograph Famous

Players in Famous Plays. The stage was raided, though film was rarely advanced.

Early film comedy took much the same tack. In France, in 1906, a dapper comedian named Max Linder, who was equally at home on stage or screen, began making the slight situation comedies that had their origins in polite boulevard farce. *Max Pedicure* finds him pursuing a woman to her drawing room, where he is being well enough received until her husband comes home. She explains that Max is simply there to give her her weekly pedicure, whereupon the husband decides that he wants one too, settling down to his newspaper and offering a foot. Linder—noted for his dark, confiding eyes as much as for his impeccable dress—stares long and perplexedly at the husband's shoe, wondering precisely what to do with it, then removes it and swiftly lathers the man's foot as though he were going to shave it, grinning directly into the camera as he pursues his imposture. There is not much more to the film than that, but it was one of nearly a hundred—*Max Takes a Bath, Max Is Jealous, Max's Mother-In-Law*—that made Linder the most admired comedian in films until Chaplin appeared. Indeed, Chaplin later acknowledged his debt to him, though it is not easy now to see precisely what that debt may have been.

Perhaps we can catch a glimpse. In one of his finest short films, Chaplin would go to a costume ball dressed in a suit of armor, armor that would have to be pried loose with a can opener. In *City Lights* he would be discovered cradled and asleep in the arms of a statue being unveiled, a situation that had already been used—in wild variation—by Keaton. Much earlier than either of these is a Linder one-reeler, *Max and the Statue*, in which both devices appear in embryo.

Max goes to a costume ball in a suit of armor, drinks all night long, stumbles sodden onto the street at daybreak, passes out on the sidewalk. Meantime, two thieves have invaded the Louvre and stolen a suit of armor, or a statue of a man in a suit of armor—it is difficult to say which—that is apparently new and to be unveiled the following day. Police discover the theft, take to the streets, come upon Max still stretched out on the sidewalk, assume him to be the lost treasure, and restore him to the pedestal in the Louvre, draped. A committee appears for the unveiling, which now takes place. Linder makes no particular comedy of the unveiling: it remained for Keaton and Chaplin to do that. His head simply tilts very slightly in dazed weariness, so that we shall be reminded it is he; the committee does not notice and departs. Once again the thieves invade the room; this time they seize Linder, hurrying their new prize to an underground lair where they attempt to open the armor with tools, though not with a can opener. Under the effort, Max revives, frightens them off, then strolls into the frame at film's end, still in armor, strumming a guitar.

While it is unlikely that either Chaplin or Keaton borrowed directly at such long distance from Linder, it is clear enough that Linder intuited—in however limited a way—certain of the stranger gestures silent comedy might make. There is a tantalizing sense of Keaton, though not a literal anticipation, in that last image: armor and a guitar. If Linder establishes for himself no particular identity in the film, if he finds little that is funny *within* the situation he has imagined, he has nonetheless begun his imaginings in a right place: the matter-of-fact grotesque. In *Max Takes a Bath*, he buys a tub, carries it home to his apartment house, attempts to fill it one water glass at a time, decides that only the hallway tap in the building will do the job, fills the tub in the hallway, and takes his bath there, submerging himself considerately whenever a neighboring tenant passes by. In *Max Is Jealous*, suspecting his wife of infidelity, he trains a dog to stand guard, to tiptoe toward doors and listen for surreptitious lovemaking, even to telephone him at the office when a paramour is present. Linder splits his screen inventively for

Max Linder setting about his domestic work in a 1908 short comedy, *Troubles of a Grass Widower.*

the warning telephone call: in three separate panels we see the dog phoning, the city streets between, Max being alerted at the other end. This brief jest ends with the wife gone and Max facing the dog across his breakfast table, offering it sugar for its coffee and giving it a farewell kiss as he briskly sets off to work.

Jack Spears, in an informed and sympathetic tribute to Linder in *Hollywood: The Golden Era*, further credits the comedian with having anticipated the more robust outdoor antics of the clowns who would follow him; and Linder did indeed present himself, from time to time, on ice skates or as an Alpine climber. The credit requires this modification: as athlete or acrobat, Max is a dub, unable to remain erect on his ice skates, trying to retrieve his toppled hat and falling on it, dissolving into tears as *Max Wants to Skate* comes to a close. Mr. Spears goes on to describe a pleasantly ingenious, and I would think more characteristic, Linder situation: accidentally intoxicated, Max has quarreled with a general over a taxicab, been challenged to a duel, accepted the general's card, and offered his own. In a subsequent contretemps resulting in a second challenge, he exchanges the general's card for that of his new adversary. Challenges multiply, each produces yet another wrong card, and soon half the men of Paris are dueling one another while Max, scot free, finds comfort with the general's wife.

But we are back to the boudoir again. Linder was essentially an indoor man, a trimly turned out *bon vivant*, insisting on restraint in his gagging, thoroughly disliking chases, refusing or failing to drain from his initial extravagances the vast logical absurdity that was in them. Thrown into a physical situation, he seems to have found his comedy in evading it.

As Linder's early fame increased both in France and abroad, he was swiftly surrounded by comedians who varied his patterns without extending them greatly. A fellow Parisian named André Deed appeared in French films as Boireau, in Italian films as Cretinetti; for American showings, he was redubbed Foolshead. Originally a Folies-Bergères dancer and acrobat with an unruly shock of hair, an assertive nose, and a puckered lower lip not unlike that of the later Fernandel, he was as apt as not to appear as a boyish hellion in a sailor suit, perhaps wiring the equipment in his father's laboratory to everything else in the house, so that cooks, neighbors, and hastily summoned gendarmes were sent into a St. Vitus dance of electrical shock before they could lay hands on him.

Ferdinand Guillaume took as one of his screen names Polidor, wandering down a country road in long frock coat, straw hat, and collar gaping wide at the neck to steal a goose, tuck it beneath his jacket, and go to a dinner-party with his prize huddled against him; the unruly goose of course disrupts the festivities. But *Polidor and the Goose* is not a "road" film; its disruptions are those of dinner table and bedroom. As Tontolini, Guillaume was everlastingly stealing dress suits to make his way into fashionable soirées, where, drinking too much, he managed to bring ferocious dowagers down upon him. In *Tontolini and the Suffragettes* he succeeds in disrupting a meeting of the campaigning women by depositing a box of rats in their midst. The comedian Mauritz Schwartz, better known as Little Moritz, made humor of his height by presenting himself to his beloved's father only to be turned away because of his diminutive stature, whereupon he returned on concealed stilts to amaze one and all with his sudden growth.

Each of these secondary, but productive and popular, buffoons toyed now and again with the freedoms open to film, though most often in the magician's manner of Méliès. Boireau forced his pursuers to walk on the ceiling in order to get near him; Tontolini, rolling downstairs after being evicted from a party, curled himself up in a carpet, spun out into the street and straight up the side of a building. But these are "special effects," incidental tricks to provide endings for material

Opposite: The immaculate Linder.

Above: Linder being made immaculate by Essanay colleagues during his American work in 1917.

Overleaf: Max Linder broadening his style for his first American film, *Max Comes Across.*

Comedy in Search of Its Freedom

substantially interior and domestic; the four walls of the stage were very hard to shake.

In America the best loved of the period's comedians was a cheerful, grizzled Toby jug of a man, John Bunny, a British-born stage actor who was passionate about films and literally begged his way into them. Teamed most often with a spindly virago named Flora Finch, he made more than one hundred and fifty short comedies before his sudden death in 1915; still enormously popular, he had worn himself out playing Bottom in a stage tour of *A Midsummer Night's Dream.*

The Bunny-Finch comedies were cut to the familiar vaudeville cloth and could have been toured as readily as the *Dream*. In *Stenographer Wanted*, made about 1910, Mr. Bunny and his business partner have placed an ad for a new stenographer and are prepared to inspect the applicants with great pleasure. They do so, peering through the keyhole to their inner office at the girls waiting outside, one arguing for a blonde, the other for a brunette. While they are tossing a coin to decide the issue, Miss Finch appears in the anteroom, a stork's body capped by the head and beak of a withered owl. The partners nearly faint at the sight of her, quickly hire the winner of the toss, then, in the course of a vehement business argument, lose her. Meanwhile, their wives have arrived, taken a good look at the all too tasty applicants, and promptly hired Miss Finch for them. The film ends with Miss Finch erect and piously chewing gum at the typewriter while Bunny, already shaped like a keg in a wine cellar, pantomimes to his partner that they'd better slip out for a drink. All of the action takes place in the office.

The tradition was continued, most successfully, by Mr. and Mrs. Sidney Drew, whose work began before the Mack Sennett-Keystone explosion of 1912 and remained popular alongside it until Mr. Drew died in 1919. The basic shape of the work can be seen in a two-reeler of 1912 called *The Professional Patient*, a thing of essentially stage interiors and rhythms in which Mr. Drew is hired by a dentist to pose as a cheerful client. His duty is to emerge—as many times a day as necessary—from the dental torture chamber with an exalted expression on his face, thus reassuring those who are apprehensively waiting their turns.

Drew, a tall man with gnomish features and a marionette's carved mouth, given to making flip "stage" exits with one hand perched high on the doorframe before the whiplash turn, sensed in a small way the pleasant liberties film might take. In *The Professional Patient* he doesn't want to waste a freshly lighted cigarette while making his brief tour of the outer office. He places the cigarette deftly between a ready pair of false teeth. As other films, notably the Keystones, changed character, Drew became aware of the change without abandoning his personal style. *Goodness Gracious*, made in 1914, means to be a burlesque of *stage* melodrama: as a villain pursuing the heroine on a painted canvas street, he moves a prop tree with him whenever he wishes to hide. But at one point the satirical object changes. He throws the heroine from a second-story window, races down the stairs, catches her before she lands: obviously he is now satirizing other men's films. Later in the same film he goes outdoors for a streetcar chase, using speeded-up and reversed action. But though he made certain adaptations to the free-fantasy that was then developing, throughout his career he clung to his origins: one of his last films, *The Amateur Liar* of 1919, finds him telling one white lie and then watching a dozen others snowball from it—the kind of situation on which stage comedy thrives and which in fact depends on words. The Drews' domestic style continued to be admired and sometimes preferred to what went on around it. Praising *Romance and Rings* in 1919, an anonymous *New York Times* reviewer couldn't resist remarking that "screen comedies are usually so coarse, clumsy, or stupid that the notable exceptions are highly desired . . . as a re-

John Bunny and Flora Finch in *A Cure for Pokeritis.*

lief." The popular Mr. and Mrs. Carter de Haven helped maintain the style.

Mack Sennett himself did not at once sense film's potential freedom from an inherited stage formula. After he had been working under Griffith at the Biograph studios for about two years, Sennett was given his first opportunity to direct: the man originally assigned to the job had had a nervous breakdown. In *Comrades*, made in 1911, he not only appears as a tramp—Sennett, stocky and coarse-featured, never would escape looking like a rube—but tries out such theories of film comedy as he then held. He does, temporarily, take the action out of doors. Two tramps read in a newspaper that a distinguished visitor is expected at a certain house. Sennett steals a suit of clothes; his buddy—played by Dell Henderson—puts them on and successfully passes himself off at the house as the visitor. At night, he is ceremoniously put to bed. Sennett, left outside and cold, wants in. Henderson, enjoying his new luxury, ignores his friend altogether. Sennett climbs into the room by a ladder but is refused bed space; he must sleep on the floor. Soon the ruse is discovered, and there is a limited chase.

The film moves very slowly and without particular comic invention. More surprisingly, its materials remain those of routine stage farce: impersonation, betrayal, discovery. These are pursued with a heavy-handed literalness; no buoyancy appears even in the handling of the ladder. Once more there is nothing that could not be done, or had not been done, on a stage. The interiors belong to social comedy. The exteriors are perfunctory.

Social comedy of an essentially realistic sort continued to play a part, though a decidedly secondary one, in silent film comedy to the end. Perhaps the man who sustained the Linder-Drew tradition—or something close to it—longest in short comedies was a sleekly pompadoured householder and occasional *bon vivant* named Charley Chase. Chase, with his trim mustache, twitching nose, readily displayed teeth and contracting shoulder blades, fussed his way through scores of short comedies, taking his children to the movies or impersonating a visiting nobleman in a plot-line not far removed from that of *Comrades*.

Chase has his fans today, understandably: he was likeable, and he was precise. But the work he did, upper-middle-class in texture and decently plausible in execution, kept him just outside the mainstream that his zanier friends and colleagues Stan Laurel and Oliver Hardy were entering during the last years of silence. No attempt was ever made to move him into feature-length films.

Max Linder had made the attempt at feature films, with ultimately tragic results. He had been engaged in one of his stage performances at the outbreak of World War I; although given to deep depressions and already scarred by abdominal surgery, he attempted to volunteer for service, was rejected, and compensated by using his own car to deliver military dispatches to the battlefields. He suffered further damage to his health when his car was struck by a shell. At the close of the war he came to the United States because, by the time the Armistice was reached, American-made films completely dominated the international screen.

That had not always been the case. Earlier, European filmmakers had been both more innovative and more ambitious than their American competitors. Linder himself had been the first film comedian of worldwide stature, and his fellow comedians were working out comic "chases" long before the device took root in the United States. Feature-length films, resisted by American financiers, blossomed in France with Sarah Bernhardt's *Queen Elizabeth*: Adolph Zukor's successful importation of the film in its full four-reel length was needed to convince American entrepreneurs that audiences would sit still for so long. The Italians pioneered in developing even longer "spectacles," issuing the two-hour *Quo Vadis* in 1913. But with the outbreak of the war, European film pro-

Mr. and Mrs. Sidney Drew.

duction came to a halt, American films leapt into the breach, and by 1918 the faces known around the world—there was no language barrier, of course—were American faces, faces that had become synonymous with the word *screen*. If this book is almost exclusively concerned with American comedians, it is because the reign of silence *was* an American reign.

The longer films Linder made during his two visits to the United States have their points. The first, *Max Comes Across*, was favorably reviewed: in one sequence, Linder, accompanist at a shipboard concert during rough weather, pursued and was pursued by a grand piano rolling with the waves. In *Seven Years' Bad Luck* he repeated a bit of business he is said to have introduced to films during his earlier work in France. A servant breaks Linder's cheval glass at the very moment he wants to shave. The servant thereupon impersonates Linder, standing opposite him in the empty frame, duplicating his shaving gestures meticulously. Chaplin may be the only comedian not indebted to Linder for this particular "turn." In *The Three Must-Get-Theres*, Linder's limply titled parody of the recently released Fairbanks film, the comedian made stunning use of an overhead shot he seems to have been devoted to. He had opened an earlier film with the camera looking down on a circle of bachelors offering a toast to the groom, but had found no gag to go with it. Now he found the gag. D'Artagnan is completely encircled by his enemies, the Cardinal's guards, and their rapiers are drawn, converging like spokes on his throat. As they lunge, he ducks, and they all kill each other.

But these films are victims of an overriding problem. Silent comedy had already taken its turn toward irrepressible fantasy, toward clowns unabashed by the demonstrable instability of the universe. What was this eminently polite, even well-manicured man doing in a world that would no longer stand still while he adjusted his boutonniere? Linder went to desperate lengths to adapt himself to the new visual liberties. He pulled a silk stocking over his head to pose as a Negro, he popped a pipe into his face and spectacles over his eyes to pose as a station master, mixing himself up in a gluepot the while. He opened *The Three Must-Get-Theres* with seventeenth-century court ladies playing trombones, and, when it was time for D'Artagnan to get from Calais to Dover, he attached sails to his horse to make it a nonstop trip across the water—and did it rather awkwardly. The *New York Times* reviewer in 1922 pointed out that "the spirit of the original Fairbanks film is too gay, it is too exultantly free from the weight of an assumed every-day reality, for it to be touched by any burlesque." But something more important is wrong: the comedian himself is not sufficiently open in outline to avail himself of the "exultantly free" spirit of a Fairbanks, let alone a Keaton or Chaplin. The very polish of his image—its unmistakable boulevard-bourgeois character—binds him to a kind of comedy that will from this time on, in silent film, always be second best. Only one man, Raymond Griffith, ever found a way to take his top hat and opera cape into the eerie outer space of invention rampant, and we shall have to speak of him later.

Linder went home to France, where, ill and discouraged by the relative unpopularity of his American films, he killed himself. A form in which he had excelled had inexplicably changed its tune and danced heartlessly away from him, requiring a new breed of clown to make the most of its invitations. The revolution is normally identified with Mack Sennett, and it was indeed Sennett who finally took hold of the form by the scruff of the neck, stood it on its head, and shook the gold from its pockets.

But Sennett did not give the form its quintessential American shape. So far as I can determine, D. W. Griffith did. This must sound strange: Griffith made very few comedies; his sense of humor was so undeveloped that even the rustic high-jinks of *Way Down East* were beyond him; and he hated slapstick and all of its relatives, wishing to rid the Fine Arts lot of that "jack-rabbit," Fairbanks, for leaping about so much. Yet in at least one of his rare comedies he laid out the master plan for what would ultimately become "pure" silent film comedy, offering its architecture and even its details for an entire generation to copy.

He directed *The Curtain Pole*, in 1908, himself. The ten-minute film seems to begin as regulation social comedy: A top-hatted fop—prototype of all the "Counts" that would turn up in the first year of Sennett comedies—with a nose slightly built up to suggest the grotesquerie tc come, enters a drawing room where a girl is attempting to hang a drape. Out of ardor for the girl and in eagerness to help, he officiously takes over, promptly breaking the pole. Unruffled, he assures everyone that he will be back with a new pole almost instantly. Out he goes, and the realistic fantasia that will dominate both the film and the future begins.

Immediately Griffith introduces a grace note that will be borrowed, in one way or another, by every major comedian. En route to the draper's shop, the fop passes a saloon and decides to stop in and fortify himself. The camera is in long-shot position, across the street from the saloon. As the fop disappears through the doors, the camera simply holds on the empty façade, holds for what seems at first an inexplicable and then finally a funny length of time. After this entirely static shot, the fop reappears, drunk. The camera has fantasized time by telescoping it outrageously; and it has made comedy of its own altogether deadpan behavior. A neutral screen can create humor by implication. Chaplin, in *City Lights*, simply refines the device. With his boxing gloves securely tied on for the night's match, he remembers something he must do and quickly whispers a request for information into a fellow boxer's ear. Because he whispers, we assume he wants to know where the bathroom is. He leaves the screen, and the camera holds. In a moment or two he is back, wrists extended. Would the boxer please untie his gloves? The joke, subsequently followed by quite another one, is born of what we assume while we are permitted to see nothing, has been created while we wait and of our waiting. But, as I say, that is only a grace note.

Drunk, and having picked up an amiable companion at the bar, the fop goes to a shop, buys the pole he needs, summons a carriage to take him back to the house. The pole, however, is much too long to be safely tucked into the carriage; nothing for it but to let half its length stretch out the window and into the street. Now the journey and the havoc take over. Careering along the crowded city streets, the carriage veers near enough to the curb for the pole to trip, tumble, and batter all passers-by within range, to overturn a baby buggy, to make a holocaust of a vegetable bin, to crack into a lamppost and clip it in half. The outraged victims are quickly in full hue and cry, an ever-swelling mob pursuing the juggernaut at top speed. Griffith cuts back and forth between the marauding vehicle and the infuriated citizenry in what was probably his first—possibly his only—*comic* chase. Eventually, and with maximum damage done, the fop returns breathlessly to the drawing room, only to find that someone else has restored the drape.

If Griffith did not bother to repeat his own comic formula, it was because he lacked a real taste for it; he was not temperamentally light-minded. And this is already evident in *The Curtain Pole*. The mob that fills the streets in angry pursuit is not truly a comic mob; there is nothing in its attitude or behavior to distinguish it from a mob in *The Birth of a Nation*. In these images there is no interior lift, no manic ebullience, nothing of the savage *esprit* that Harold Lloyd would bring to a mob doing battle over a streetcar in *Speedy*.

Charley Chase is already a natty figure in his early work for Sennett: with Mabel Normand in *Mabel's New Job*.

Yet, intellectually, the vision is sound and the die is cast. Understanding film as he did, Griffith plainly foresaw what its comic patterns might be or ought to be, grasped at the outset silent comedy's freedom to make a spectacular hash of reality without in the least compromising the camera's insistence on reality. The streets, the people, the baby buggies, the vegetable bins are all real. So are the forces that ride over them—the fop, the carriage, the curtain pole. No "stage" fantasy, no Méliès magic here. But, thanks to the scale of film and the permissiveness of silence, a relationship that was sheer nightmare could be established between these realities—the subconscious unleashed on public streets, the surreal derived from incontestable fact. The whole world could be knocked over in one great swoop, while audiences cheered the verification of their wildest dreams.

I have been told that Mack Sennett appears in the film, as the fop, though I do not recognize him. If it is indeed he, it is curious that he made no use of Griffith's formula when given an opportunity to direct *Comrades* three years later—doubly curious, considering that *The Curtain Pole*, when looked at today, quite obviously establishes the premises for everything Sennett did thereafter. Perhaps he had to rediscover these for himself. However it may have come about, when the man who would soon come to be called the King of Comedy set up shop on his own by forming Keystone in 1912, he built his "fun factory" firmly on a blueprint Griffith had laid out. From thenceforward, automobiles would knock over fire hydrants so that the men working on the hydrants could be sprayed into the air by the fury of the water, motorcycles and cars would plunge in great arcs from the ends of piers into the ocean, an amorous aviatrix would rescue her lover by plane from the top of a dynamited and already crumbling smokestack, an unlucky escapee would dive from a twentieth-story window to have his fall broken by a series of awnings and then arrive at the street just as the last awning had been pulled up. As James Agee said of the clowns who made the world their toboggan, "Words can hardly suggest how energetically they collided and bounced apart, meeting in full gallop around the corner of a house; how hard and how often they fell on their backsides; or with what fantastically adroit clumsiness they got themselves fouled up in folding ladders, garden hoses, tethered animals and each other's headlong cross-purposes."

The matrix had been set, in all of its madness; and from it would derive whatever greatness silent film comedy was ultimately to know.

Douglas Fairbanks as an exuberant D'Artagnan in *The Three Musketeers*; Max Linder doing a close parody in his *The Three Must-Get-Theres.*

8. Sennett: The Insensitive Master Carpenter

What was a Sennett film like?

Let's be as objective as we can. In *The Knockout*, made in 1914, the second year of Keystone's operation and the year that Chaplin joined the company, a boyish Fatty Arbuckle is seen sharing his hamburger with his dog. His girl comes by and gives him a kiss on the ear. Arbuckle grins, puts his fingertip to his ear and then into his mouth, as though appropriating the kiss and savoring it. Al St. John, a man with thyroid eyes whose ankles seemed to extend to his shoulder blades, shuffles past and pauses to flirt with the girl. Arbuckle is instantly furious, and a knockabout, casually brutal fight ensues. At one point Arbuckle advances grimacing so that his contorted, here almost bull-like, features fill the screen.

When it is suggested that he enter the prize ring that night to compete for a purse, he is at once cowardly; cowardice and belligerence alternate with indifferent logic through the balance of the twenty-minute film. Agreeing to the battle and planning to change into boxers' trunks, Arbuckle begins to unbutton his trousers, then looks directly into the camera and makes a gesture for it to go up a little. The camera raises its angle obligingly so that we can see no more than his head. When he has completed the change, he motions it down again.

What had been presented to him as an easy victory in the ring becomes complicated by the arrival of a genuine fighter, Edgar Kennedy. The fight takes place nonetheless, with Chaplin doing a three-minute bit as the referee, taking some of the fighters' wild blows by accident, collapsing against the ring-post, pulling himself along the ropes as though he were groggily boating. Sheriff Mack Swain is on hand to make sure the fight is an honest one. When Kennedy wins it, Arbuckle, in a rage, seizes the sheriff's gun and begins firing, first at Kennedy and then at random. A melee ensues in which Kennedy escapes from the hall while the onlookers scramble to get out of Arbuckle's range. The chase takes to the streets.

The Keystone Kops are called in, and when chief Ford Sterling blows his whistle five or six of them hurtle through the door of the station-house waiting room, topple his desk, and pile on top of one another. Meanwhile, Kennedy has managed to climb to a rooftop, pursued by Arbuckle and—once they have bolted through the crowd—the Kops. We now watch the entire menagerie running, leaping, sliding, and diving from roof to roof, much of the chase shot so that the tumblebug figures are silhouetted against the skyline.

Kennedy plunges down a skylight into a fashionable soirée, followed closely by Arbuckle, who is still firing in all directions. The Kops, hot on their heels, are now shooting too, bowling over ladies and liveried servants as they come. So much for social comedy. Out on the streets again, and having lost Kennedy, Arbuckle begins a gun duel with the Kops, who produce a lariat and succeed in roping him. The subsequent tug-of-war goes Arbuckle's way. Running down the road, he hauls them after him on their stomachs, "cracks the whip" with them, and then, when they refuse to let go, lugs them to a pier, where he leaps into the water carrying the lot of them with him. The End.

It is probable that, except for an innovative detail here and there, the substance of this "plot" doesn't strike you as particularly funny. My point is that it isn't, not through today's eyes. I have, in the past months, sat through dozens of Keystones and later Sennetts—the Keystone trademark disappeared after five years—without once being trapped into laughter. And so I must confess that Sennett seems to me not so much the King as the Carpenter of Comedy. He built the house. It is hard now to believe that he ever entertained friends in it.

Why isn't this film, which is actually a good bit better than the standard Keystone product of the time, truly funny today? Obviously the pattern is a right one: Chaplin, Keaton, Lloyd, and Langdon not only grew out of it but clung to its values till the end of their careers—Chaplin dangling from a cabin teetering on the edge of a cliff, Langdon hanging by his sweater-thread, Keaton riding an uprooted tree through a hurricane, Lloyd smashing his horse-drawn streetcar into elevated girders on his wild drive through the intersections of town. And the pattern did work. These early films were enormously popular. Of the people in *The Knockout*, Arbuckle and Chaplin became feature-film stars, St. John and Swain each starred in their own short-comedy series, and Edgar Kennedy went on to develop his celebrated "slow burn," lasting as long as any and longer than most.

It is no secret that all but the finest comedy dates after a while: there are humors in the everyday air that are blown away with the next morning's winds. But these were the humors of not so very long ago; they should be reasonably fresh to our minds because their premises remain familiar through the best work of Keaton and Chaplin. Approached sympathetically and with a minimal exercise of historical imagination, they ought to yield more than they do, considering the excitement and even the adoration they once engendered.

But neither time nor the survival of echoes is a good measure of distance. We are farther from these films than our gray hairs show. The films are, I think, victims of what may be a curious law. Whenever an entirely new form is let loose on the world, it must begin at the very beginning. Silent film comedy began as though comedy had never existed, as though Aristophanes had never existed, as though sophistication of the same materials had never been achieved. A completely new form seems to take man back to his dawn, to revive and repeat an entire cycle of race-memories picked up along the evolutionary path, to start as primitively as if the Neanderthals were still a threat, and to probe toward the future with the weapons and level of wit of cavemen.

In fact, the most apt description I know of these first screen comedies appears in a book about chimpanzees, Jane Van Lawick-Goodall's *In the Shadow of Man*. "Young chimps," the author comments, "like to play with each other, chasing round a tree trunk, leaping one after the other through the treetops, dangling, each from one hand, while they spar and hit each other. . . . [The chimp] learns during play which type of branch is safe to jump onto and which will break, and he practices gymnastic skills, such as leaping down from one branch and catching another far below. . . . He discovers which of his playmates can be intimidated by a show of strength and which of them will in a similar context turn around and call his bluff." In other words, he is learning by rude and random and utterly amoral behavior what the universe and his fellow creatures will tolerate.

Chaplin, actually in a bearskin, swinging a spiked club and swatting Mack Swain on the head for no other reason than to see what response the exercise will bring; Chaplin and Marie Dressler conducting their wooing by throwing bricks at each other; country girl Mabel Normand beating a city girl around a tree trunk with a stick; villainous Ford Sterling never handing anything to anyone but hurling it at him with enough force to knock him down a flight of stairs; Louise Fazenda removing Mack Swain's hat and smoothing his few hairs down, preparatory to hitting him on the head with a baseball bat; Mack Swain running Chester Conklin off a cliff and rescuing him by roping him around the neck and hauling him all the way back up again; Chester Conklin, active but characterless, loading balls into a cannon and blowing up everything in sight; Chaplin, without malice, lifting his left foot to kick a woman through a doorway.

Here are genuine primitives at play, before laws were, before emotion was. The form is iconoclastic to the bone, its gestures are as gratuitous as they are extravagant, the conduct of all involved is utterly heartless. Yet to say that the conduct is heartless is not to say that it is cruel. Not quite. There was an unspoken law of silent comedy under which no one ever got hurt. When someone is seen to be hurt—as Chaplin is, briefly, floating unconscious in a bay during *The Adventurer*—the image is immediately false and unattractive, a violation of the form's promise. These comedies are pre-emotional; we are never to be disturbed or even concerned. Indeed, they do their work at a level in the development of comedy that is earlier than the earliest rule-of-thumb known. It is a rule-of-thumb that comic figures—people who make you laugh—are automatically sympathetic. But Ford Sterling is neither sympathetic nor unsympathetic as he steals a bag of money, loses it, and spends the rest of the film violently trying to get it back; Chaplin isn't worrying about whether or not you like him as he taps his cigarette ash into the open palm of a girl's hand. All of the characters, as Gilbert Seldes has said, are "scamps, scoundrels, shysters, fakers, tramps," and they behave just as spontaneously and as callously as scamps and scoundrels do.

This *is* play, but it is primeval play, play in the treetops before *mores* were heard of, play without cause or consequence or social feeling. It erupted volcanically, as though from the bowels of the earth; long-buried impulses in man simply shot to the surface at incredible speed to splatter wantonly over the landscape. The eruption took place *after* comedy as such had known the sophistication of Aristophanes' lyrics, of Shakespeare's Beatrice and Benedick, of Oscar Wilde's *The Importance of Being Earnest*. But what had gone before did not matter to this conscienceless rebirth. The world had become new through the medium of the camera. Man became new with it.

It is this state of mind, and its reported pleasures, that we are no longer able to re-enter. We have since become sophisticated *in the very form* that was then so rambunctiously, so casually, so unself-consciously chimp-like; we no longer see the world or the camera's view of it as they were seen then. Perhaps we might have laughed too in 1914. At least we would have felt excitement.

Chaplin plays a bit part as referee while Arbuckle and Edgar Kennedy do battle in *The Knockout*. Later, the Keystone Kops take to the rooftops for a climactic chase.

I say "perhaps" we might have laughed, because I'm not entirely sure—

Sennett: The Insensitive Master Carpenter

though I'm certain we'd have felt the excitement. There is very little in the Sennett films, for all their breakneck pace and bizarre manhandling of the universe, that one would care to call humor under analytic examination. Normally it is possible to understand a joke that has faded, to recapture the principle that once provoked laughter while being unable to recapture the laughter itself. Most of Aristophanes' "lost" jokes, for instance, can be deciphered and grasped or approximated as comic *ideas*. Not so with Sennett, for the most part. The jokes, as jokes, are rarely there, any more than chimps make true jokes in the treetops; activity is all, and the activity is so headlong that there is scarcely time to pause for the "constructed" quality of a jest. "Once we stop to let anybody analyze us, we're sunk," Gene Fowler reports Sennett as having said. The films are successful agitations, successful explorations of elaborate visual possibilities; if laughter once accompanied them, it has to have been the laughter of breathlessness, not the laughter of perception. I am somewhat relieved to discover that in the collected *The New York Times Film Reviews*, a man writing in 1921 could speak of Mack Sennett's "alleged" comedies as being very often "utterly dull."

Sennett was capable of invention and innovation. He knew how to create expectation and then to defeat it—just as his comedians learned to understand what they were doing sufficiently to mock it. In *The Waiter's Ball* Arbuckle and St. John are whacking away at one another with brooms. One broom breaks. The fight stops completely while another broom is procured. It then begins exactly where it has left off. Here the clowns grasp their activity as routine, mechanical, essentially meaningless, and make sport of the fact. This is Bergson's "automated" comedy, and it suggests the dim beginnings of an intellectual maturity. Chaplin would make delectable use of it in *Easy Street* during a chase around a bed: having become accustomed to the pattern of the chase, he is unable to reverse it when his opponent does, and so is nearly caught.

Sennett was conscious of film as film and able to view its properties ironically. In *Mabel's Dramatic Career* of 1914, Sennett himself, appearing as a rube who has loved, betrayed, and then lost Mabel Normand to the big city, passes a movie house one day and discovers that she is in the current film. He goes inside to see what kind of movie star she has become, sitting next to Arbuckle, a city chap who plainly loves movies and is hysterically over-responsive to them. We now attend to the film-within-a-film, contrasting screen life with audience life, Sennett's responses with Arbuckle's. Sennett, yokel that he is, takes the screen narrative seriously, is infuriated that villain Ford Sterling should be maltreating Miss Normand so. Determined to avenge her, he leaves the theater, whips out the customary pistol, discovers where she lives, and creeps up to the window. Looking in, he finds Mabel and Sterling happily married and the parents of a brood. For the period, these formal and psychological complexities were relatively subtle.

But Sennett was not a subtle man. Indeed, he was astonishingly insensitive in at least three important ways. He was first of all insensitive to the interior tensions of the very form he was exploiting. A tension did exist, in this fantasy of fact, between the reality guaranteed by the camera and the freedom from reality bestowed by silence. The two contraries met and fused at a thin, delicate line deep in the heart of the form, and while the breadth of the line is impossible to measure, it can be trod over, even stomped over in either direction. The action can become too real for the fantasy of silence, as happened whenever anyone seemed hurt. And the action can become too fantastic for the camera's promise of authenticity, violating the integrity of the instrument. Contending forces have to be kept in balance or the form breaks apart.

Mack Sennett himself, ready to attack the film-within-a-film but being restrained by Roscoe Arbuckle. *Mabel's Dramatic Career.*

Sennett was certainly aware of this duality. Many of his early films were what

might be called quasi-documentary comedies, mainly dependent on factual backgrounds or props for their interest. Even before he formed Keystone and was still directing at Biograph, he had made a ten-minute short with Mabel Normand called *A Dash Through the Clouds*, in which Miss Normand was seen actually going up in an open-wing, box-kite airplane. The story-line makes a stab at pretending that she is in love with the pilot, but if the pilot is decidedly undemonstrative it is because he is an actual pilot and a nonprofessional. There are no built sets for the film, Sennett simply shot it where he could, and its value for audiences can have lain only in seeing pretty Miss Normand really go up in one of those dangerous things.

At Keystone he often did what he had done for *Kid Auto Races in Venice*: send a company out with a camera to improvise as best they could during an actual event—a GAR parade, for instance. The real Barney Oldfield was corralled for a racing film, Fatty Arbuckle and Mabel Normand spent time romping through the San Diego Exposition and the San Francisco World's Fair. The public's thirst for the real, and the camera's capacity for satisfying it, were known quantities to Sennett.

But the gifts bestowed by the camera did not stir in Sennett any sense of reciprocal obligation. When he erred, he erred on the side of fantasification, pressing the liberties made possible by silence not only to that shimmering center-line but well past it into transparent fraud. It was perfectly all right for Billy Bevan to drive a crowded circus wagon over a cliff and then, at the bottom, have everyone emerge unscathed and hopping. Silence granted that. It was *almost* all right for Hank Mann to whip a restaurant tablecloth away with such adroitness that the silverware and ketchup bottles remained firmly in place and then—by means of reversing the film—have him whip the tablecloth right back again, all appurtenances intact. It is quite another thing, however, to have an extremely fat man dive into a swimming pool with such force that all the other bathers are seen—by reverse film—to dive backward out of it. It is not simply that the image is unamusing in itself; our sense of form is being insulted. We understand trickery as well as the next fellow and do not like it served cold. Sennett exercised no taste in such matters, literally lacked a comic-fantasy conscience. He might show us a newspaper photographer attempting to follow a moving subject; when the subject turned the corner of a fence, the photographer's lens stretched itself like a snake and turned too. Or a janitor vacuuming at random, sucking the stockings from a girl's leg and the hair from a poodle. Or poor Hank Mann hiding in a barrel, only

Poor Hank Mann, in tree trunk, has not yet been stretched double his length but is soon likely to be.

Overleaf: Bobby Vernon with the Bathing Beauties.

OTL-

Sennett: The Insensitive Master Carpenter

Arbuckle in Kop uniform making matters difficult for Al St. John; Arbuckle and girl friend stranded on telephone wires.

Opposite: Unidentified comedian on unguided Sennett missile; St. John stunting high over an amusement park; the Kops in some danger of making contact with a plane.

to have both his head and feet tugged at until he is stretched double his length. In *Lizzies of the Field* an automobile is stretched double as well. These *are* stretches, by any standard; they seemed offensive to me when I first saw them, and they are formally vulgar now, dishonoring the composite nature of silent comedy. The camera, in its essential function, has been negated; in a sense, it is scarcely necessary any longer: the car-stretch and the photographer's lens-stretch could be done on a stage with trick props. Silent comedy wanted more integrity than this, and would get it from the major comedians.

In addition, Sennett was just as insensitive to the matter of comic tone. It is often difficult to tell, especially when watching one of his so-called "parody" films, just when comedy is intended and just when the presumably parodied melodrama is actually being played straight. *Teddy at the Throttle*, for instance, begins as social comedy, with Wallace Beery as Gloria Swanson's guardian, plotting to marry her for her inheritance. More than half the twenty-minute film takes place in potted-palm drawing rooms and ballrooms, with domestic intrigue the order of the day and broad comedy suddenly and unpredictably introduced only when diminutive Bobby Vernon is hoisted into the air, courtesy of a concealed wire, by his oversized dancing partner. As a conventionally dramatic storm comes up, Gloria is locked in a cloakroom, from which she frees herself by smashing the door-paneling; phoning her lawyer for help, she takes off into the storm after her true love, Vernon, while Beery takes to the wind and the rain as well. After various mishaps, few explicitly funny, Beery succeeds in chaining Miss Swanson to the railroad tracks, while the train, with her lawyer on it, bears down upon her. There are obvious echoes of nineteenth-century melodrama here, and one does not accept with an entirely straight face the image of Miss Swanson chained to the tracks. But the emotions and the manipulations that have led her there are virtually straight; and Sennett is counting on a "thrill," not a comic, finish. The finish is given a faint dash of humor by having Miss Swanson rescued by her dog, Teddy; Teddy manages to dive from a second-story window, leap onto the train while it is moving rapidly, and alert the engineer in time to stop the train just short of Miss Swanson's demise. Miss Swanson's demise, incidentally, has been further prevented by the presence of a sizable ditch immediately beneath her—the

ditch does not appear until the very last shot—and she is clearly seen burrowing her way into it as the train slows, just in case. All motivations in the film are contained in titles, explanations lacking any specific comic edge: "A Desperate Plot to Put Gloria Away, to Save Himself from Prison."

There is no knowing, from moment to moment, just what sort of film we are looking at: call it overplotted social intrigue capped by a dramatic chase, *disguised* as satirical melodrama. But the disguise is thin indeed: satirical inflection is at an absolute minimum, and Sennett is counting—for his climax—on precisely the sort of excitement he pretends to be burlesquing. This sort of sleight of hand, or simple uncertainty, reappears again and again: in *Her Torpedoed Love* the ship on which Louise Fazenda's husband works is blown apart at sea, and Ford Sterling is busy enticing her into a false marriage for her money when the rescued husband returns; in *A Small Town Idol*, Ben Turpin, as a celebrated movie star, returns home only to be accused, with complete seriousness, of murdering Phyllis Haver's father; in *Barney Oldfield's Race for Life*—the title itself is almost unambiguously serious—it is Mabel Normand who is tied to the railroad tracks, with Ford Sterling doing the dirty work and Oldfield himself racing to the spot. In all of Sennett's advertised "parodies" that I have been able to see, only once does a "joke" proclaim itself forthrightly: Sheriff Mack Swain, in *His Bitter Pill*, is in utter despair because his girl has deserted him, but he cannot shoot himself because he is the sheriff.

Many films which begin plainly enough as comedies turn melodramatically sentimental in an apparent effort to extricate themselves from the continuing need to be funny. Sam Bernard, a roly-poly figure with waxen mustaches, is trying very hard to poison an enemy in *Because He Loved Her*. Being a bakery cook, he puts poison into a pie. The pie is accidentally bought and is being fed to a little girl as the ultimate dash-to-the-rescue takes place. *Call a Cop* shifts gears by locking a little boy into a safe and having a fire break out. Such apprehension as audiences may have felt in these instances could scarcely be called comic. In fact, it is uncertain that Sennett ever defined for himself what *he* meant by comic. Anything disruptive that moved rapidly was, in all probability, the simple, largely unquestioned formula.

Sennett: The Insensitive Master Carpenter

Finally, Sennett hurt himself most, and most surprisingly, by his insensitivity to quality in the performers he had discovered. Beyond question, he had an instinct for talent. He signed Chaplin on the strength of having seen him in a vaudeville act once—if we are to believe his version of the event. Much later, close to the end of the silent era, he insisted that the odd, slow-moving, already slightly over-age Harry Langdon was likely material, though his staff could not see how, and assigned two of his best men—Harry Edwards and Frank Capra—the task of finding him a screen character. Between Chaplin in his second year and Langdon toward the end, Sennett gathered about him a remarkable assembly of animated buffoons, attractive girls, and—behind the cameras—editors and gagmen like Capra and Raymond Griffith. The legend that every major silent film comedian learned his trade under Sennett is not entirely true. Keaton was never on the lot; he began his work with Arbuckle after Arbuckle had left Sennett. Lloyd was there, but only for a few months, during which he went unnoticed: he can still be seen, in an Arbuckle female-impersonation called *Miss Fatty's Seaside Lovers*, agitatedly trying to call attention to himself in the background, overeager, callow, as dogged and as transparently decent as the figure he was later to play.

But Sennett invariably lost his people as they began to find themselves. Chaplin was gone after a single year, during which he had made thirty-five films, including the feature-length *Tillie's Punctured Romance*. Though his popularity was already enormous, and though Sennett was given an opportunity to match the larger and thoroughly justified salaries being offered Chaplin, he let the new star go. No doubt he felt that a Ford Sterling or a Roscoe Arbuckle would serve his purposes as well as Chaplin—and so, once we understand the limitations of those purposes, he would. Arbuckle stayed on for four years, then considered himself ready for independent production. Langdon stayed until his screen character had been fully developed by Edwards and Capra, then went elsewhere into features, taking the two men with him. Nearly all of the more or less interchangeable secondary clowns—Ford Sterling, Hank Mann, Chester Conklin, Billy Bevan, Mack Swain—departed to make their own two-reel films; some of them, defeated, later returned to the fold. Gloria Swanson and, later, Carole Lombard took on stature only after leaving; Mabel Normand, who was in love with Sennett, might have stayed on indefinitely—especially after the success of her feature film *Mickey*—but left for emotional rather than creative reasons. For most, the problem was creative.

Though Sennett could detect talent, it was enormously difficult for that talent to ripen under him in any personal, idiosyncratic way. The films did not allow pauses for individual identification. The clowns were, in effect, masked blurs racing from entrance to exit, knocking over indoor tables and outdoor pedestrians along the way. The masks came with the mustaches. Not all early silent comedy insisted on the copious bearding, the drooping handlebars, the fungus-like eyebrows we tend to associate with the form. Lloyd, beginning anew with Hal Roach, did at first use a mustache but one so slender as to be often invisible. The more domestic comedians—John Bunny, Sidney Drew—used none at all. Even on the Sennett lot, if the man himself was large enough to establish his outline swiftly and unmistakably while keeping on the run—like the rubber-ball Arbuckle or the portly Mack Swain—no cascades of crepe-hair were thought necessary. Slim Summerville was so tall that he could always be found on the screen, unadorned; he was easy to see as he kept one enemy at bay with his long left leg while drubbing another with his fists. For most of the others—of unexceptional size and unremarkable features—the masks were the devices that made them

Arbuckle and Mabel Normand became Sennett's mainstays after Chaplin's departure. Above: Fatty, in a dream, is being inventive about disposing of wife Mabel.

Opposite: A touching domestic scene.

WCK-101

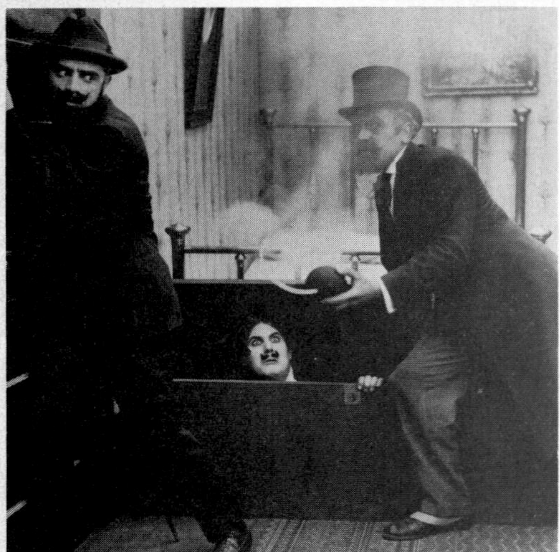

Among the troubled: Charlie Murray with baby, Slim Summerville in blazing loft, the Kops in their best-known photograph, Syd Chaplin hiding where it will do him no good at all.

visible while racing.

The masks could, in sensitive hands, be valuable. Chaplin, whether by accident or intuition, chose a trim and modest "toothbrush" that would lift when his nose lifted, then added nothing but heavily lined eyebrows. The two points of marked reference ended in defining him: both accented whatever expression he might choose to use. It is commonplace now to see caricatures of Chaplin consisting of nothing but these outlines. Even so, their importance may be underestimated. To know precisely how important they were in creating a flexible underscoring for everything the comedian wished to convey, it is only necessary to look at a rehearsal shot that has survived from *City Lights*. In ordinary street clothes and with no makeup at all, Chaplin goes through his delectable routine with the nude statuette in a store window: pretending to examine the window's art objects with a connoisseur's finesse, he is actually stealing looks at the statuette. Though the rehearsal shot anticipates the scene as it appears in the completed film in every detail—except that the nude has been transferred from left to right—nothing of the final comic effect is there. We cannot *see* Chaplin, cannot follow the shifts from disinterested appreciation to guilty glances, without the trademarks. They are really birthmarks. And whenever, in one of his Sennett films, Chaplin does a female impersonation, the effect is the same: the comedian's face simply vanishes.

Ford Sterling, coming early enough to films to preempt the standard Dutch-comic's chin whiskers of vaudeville, was a bit more fortunate than some. But most of the lesser lights remained lesser because they were essentially hidden by their masks, their massive whiskerings: Hank Mann could replace Chester Conklin who could replace Billy Bevan in any Sennett film almost at will. These gentlemen acquired hints of personality over the years, often in their own subsequent short comedies or as supporting players in feature films: Chester Conklin's querulous squint at last made its way past the walrus mustache, so absolute under Sennett that in one film the calling card he presented to an employer read simply "A. C. Walrus"; Billy Bevan could always be identified from behind because his head was shaped like a wigmaker's wood block—though when I ran one of his early Sennetts recently, a child watching it sharply complained, "His mustache is too long"; Hank Mann's eyes, upraised ethereally beneath his bowl-trimmed bangs, suggested a man of potential style—and even feeling—if he had ever been permitted to stand still. Mann is probably best remembered now as the prize-fighter in *City Lights* who is highly suspicious of Chaplin's virility, and the waste of his comic gifts seems to me the sorriest of the lot.

The celebrated Keystone Kops were even less than masks. They were flailing tailcoats and inverted-spittoon helmets lurching past the camera so swiftly and so interchangeably that it can become something of a game trying to guess which members of the stock company are Kops each time around. Not much of a game, I am sorry to say, because the phantoms are gone before a guess can be verified—gone spilling out of the ends of paddy wagons, gone racing in rowboats that sink with all hands. And, surprisingly, they were not used very often. If there is one legend associated with Sennett more than another, it is that of the Kops; the one name instantly summons up the other. And we have an image of the Kops—acquired mainly through compilations of films, sentimental testaments to the frenzy of silent comedy—that tends to assign to them an effervescent omnipresence they never had.

As I worked my way through the films, I kept expecting to find, sooner or later, at least one in which they would either predominate or at least carry a large enough role to satisfy the appetite legend had created in me. Wondering what

I'd missed, I wrote to Kent D. Eastin, whose loving labors at Blackhawk Films in Davenport, Iowa, have probably preserved and made available more early screen material than any other contemporary source. Mr. Eastin replied: "The dominance of the Keystone Kops in the various films in which they appeared is, I believe, a myth. I think I have now seen, in the last few years, at least a third of all the Keystones that were made [more than five hundred and twenty comedies appeared under the Keystone trademark] and in none of them does the story seem to be built around the Kops. Rather, they . . . usually come to the fore in the whirlwind climax. The Keystone image has, of course, been enhanced by the tying together for television of climaxes from many of the Keystone films . . . but an original of that magnitude has yet to be seen by me." The Kops are an occasional fillip, hurled into someone else's free-for-all, not really more than that.

On the Force or advanced from it to leading roles, a Keystone comedian could be forgiven if he failed to develop a distinct character for himself. There is a characteristic Sennett sequence in which Billy Bevan, blindfolded, is about to dive from a high springboard into a tank of water. In the few seconds before he dives, a thirsty elephant miraculously drains the tank. Bevan dives, crashes through the cement flooring of the tank and, momentum unspent, explodes through the earth a few yards away. The comedian has nothing to do with whatever joke there is; the joke is all in the mechanics. Not only are close-ups relatively rare in Sennett—except for those of Mabel Normand—but the camera is generally kept far enough away from the action to make certain that *all* the action, however broad its outlines, is seen. Faces are not of the essence. It wasn't that Sennett lacked respect for his comedians as persons; it was that he left them little or no breathing space in which to become individualized.

The problem vexed Chaplin, as he tells us in his autobiography, during the early part of his year with Sennett. He had come as a novice and at first floundered badly. He had hit, luckily, upon his new costume and manner in time to keep himself from being fired. But he still had to work the way others in the company did. If, for instance, he had improvised a gag that required him to pause, for a moment, in the center of the screen in order to establish its premises, he invariably discovered later in the screening room that the gag had been cut. He devised a tentative solution to the dilemma. He did all his best bits of business while entering a doorway or leaving the screen, knowing that Sennett at least had to keep the entrances and exits if the film was to be coherent. Sennett was not really much interested in what might happen between coming and going, and when Chaplin abandoned the studio it was undoubtedly for more money, but not for more money alone; it was for room.

Sennett's films continued to be profitable throughout the 1920's, long after the best of his earlier discoveries had gone; his name alone continued to assure his films of bookings. But in 1926, with silent screen comedy fully mature, he would still be making *The Prince of Pilsener* with Ben Turpin. Here again, the presumed parody. Turpin is got up to look like Erich von Stroheim: glistening military uniform, close-cropped hair, monocle, overlong cigarette holder. But parody, comment, does not extend beyond Mr. Turpin's appearance. By way of a "joke," he is given an ice-cream cone to lick. The girl he is making love to absently runs her fingertip along the rim of a stove; when she puts her finger to her lip, it provides her with a mustache. When Turpin takes his bride in his arms, he sits on a pin-cushion.

Little has changed.

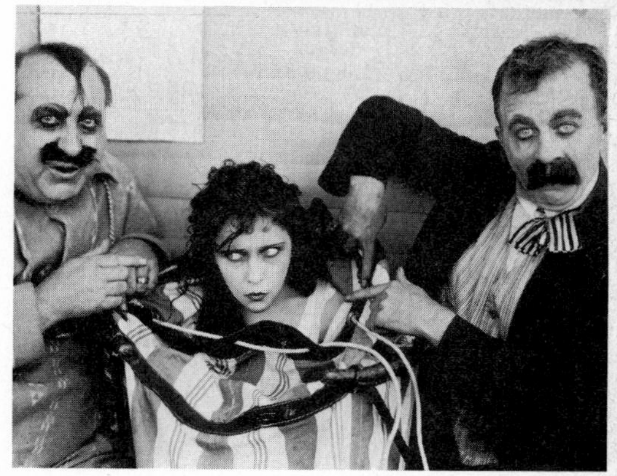

Into a wall, hard; Mabel Normand's turn to be chained to the tracks; cliffhanging again; mother and tot afloat in a flooded basement; Mack Swain and Chester Conklin bag Gloria Swanson.

9. Chaplin: An Outline Becomes a Character

When, in an early Keystone comedy, Chaplin kicks Mack Swain in the stomach, it isn't particularly funny. When, in a later feature-length film called *The Pilgrim*, he kicks a small boy in the stomach, it is marvelously funny. The similarity and the difference are instructive. Both acts are outrageous, in the original Sennett manner. If anything, the second is a great deal more outrageous—closer to our private but suppressed fantasies of dealing with children—than the first. But the second is funny for a reason that goes deeper than the bizarre physicality of the act. Chaplin has taken great pains earlier in the film to make us thoroughly detest the little monster, to make certain that we shall be immensely gratified when he gets exactly what is coming to him. We not only laugh at the deed, we applaud it. Chaplin has justified whatever is fantastic about the gesture, made it conform to an emotional reality. Violence has been rooted in sanity.

At Keystone, no kick ever needed to be justified. The invitation of an available backside was motivation enough. If one man had a pitchfork in his hand and another man, entirely unoffending, was observed bending over, there was just one thing to do: use the pitchfork. Chaplin, whose first task was to call attention to himself by behaving, if possible, even more outrageously than those about him, moved to the assault with a will. Having knocked someone down, he promptly used him as a doormat. Wanting a kiss from a girl, he seized her nose with a pair of dental pliers and drew her to him. He tossed his own baby about as though it were a rag doll, pushed his wife in the face and tumbled her over. No matter if he swung at a man and, when the man ducked, hit a girl full in the face; he would leap on Marie Dressler's back and ride her like a horse rather than let her escape his villainous intentions. In *Tillie's Punctured Romance* he was in fact the villain. In a film about making films, he offered the director who had just fired him his hand to show that there were no hard feelings; when the director put out *his* hand, Chaplin hit him hard with a suitcase. Having stolen another man's doughnut, he wiped his fingers on the man's beard. He used his flexible bamboo cane not only to clean his fingernails and then his ears, he drilled it into another man's navel and revolved it like a corkscrew before giving it a final, devastating thrust. Willing to administer undeserved punishment, he was also willing to take it, permitting himself to be kicked head first into a trashbasket, pulled out by the hair, then hurled backward to jackknife into the basket again. Swaggering, flexing his body in eternal readiness, twitching upper lip and mustache in cold contemplation of future mayhem to come, he sought excuse neither for his aggressive extravagances nor for incidental bits of business introduced quite at random. Preparing to move a piano, he oiled the elbow of his jacket. Tripping over a doormat, he picked it up and blew his nose on it. In all of this he was very little funnier than the other frenzied acrobats about him. He was simply neater and more efficient in his malice, in his irrelevance. He was noticed for his economy in doing what didn't need doing at all.

Yet there has to have been something more than that, even in the Keystones. Audiences loved Chaplin on sight, though he had given them nothing to love in any sentimental sense; within a very few months he was the most popular comedian in films. It is easy to make one of two mistakes in looking at his earliest comedies now. Because we are so enamored of the later Chaplin, because we know what he *did* become, we can read our affection and knowledge back into these often flailing exercises and see more than is actually there. Or, conversely, we can throw up our hands in bewilderment and ask how anything so coarse, frantic, unconstructed, and comically incomplete can have been accepted as even mildly amusing, in which case we shall see less than is there. What was happening, I think, during this first experimental year was that Chaplin, while doing his Keystone duty and doing it with might and main, was in effect making his audience a promise. The promise wasn't clear, but it was tantalizing. The audience intuitively clung to it.

With patience, the promise can be felt even in Chaplin's very first film, admittedly a failure. In *Making a Living*, the comedian is, on our terms, virtually unrecognizable: he wears a top hat, a long, narrow frock coat, an ascot, a monocle, and a handlebar mustache. "Dude" that he is, we first see him making a touch. He is unattractively belligerent about it. But, a bit later in the film, he is in a newspaper office trying to persuade an editor to give him an assignment. As he presses his cause, he keeps slapping the editor on the knee, for emphasis. The editor, annoyed but making nothing of it, shifts his knee to a less accessible position. Chaplin, without interrupting his sales talk or even seeming to pay attention to what he is doing, automatically pulls the knee back so that he can continue to pound it. In a few seconds of film he has established what would become a permanent, immensely productive pattern: he is adjusting the rest of the universe to his merely reflexive needs. Keaton would never have done it. Keaton accepted the universe as it was, then turned it against itself. Chaplin made it malleable, made it suit his convenience even when that convenience was most temporary and inconsequential. A man must be comfortable.

Rebuffed, and taking an indignant stance in the doorway, Chaplin strikes his cane against the floor. His celluloid shirtcuff slides down the cane from the impact. Later still—let us skip the plotting—the editor approves of something he has done. Impulsively, Chaplin leaps forward and kisses him on the forehead. The business with the shirtcuff is simply a vaudeville trick, though it is immaculately executed. But the kiss is new. It is not Keystone; when Keystone was irrational it was irrational with bricks. It is a first sign of something uncontrollable in Chaplin, uncontrollable and forever unrequited.

Chaplin waiting for a handout in his first film and first costume. *Making a Living.*

Overall, and while Chaplin was learning to turn corners at right angles with a skip-step, to flick his cigarette behind him and kick it high with his foot, to roll

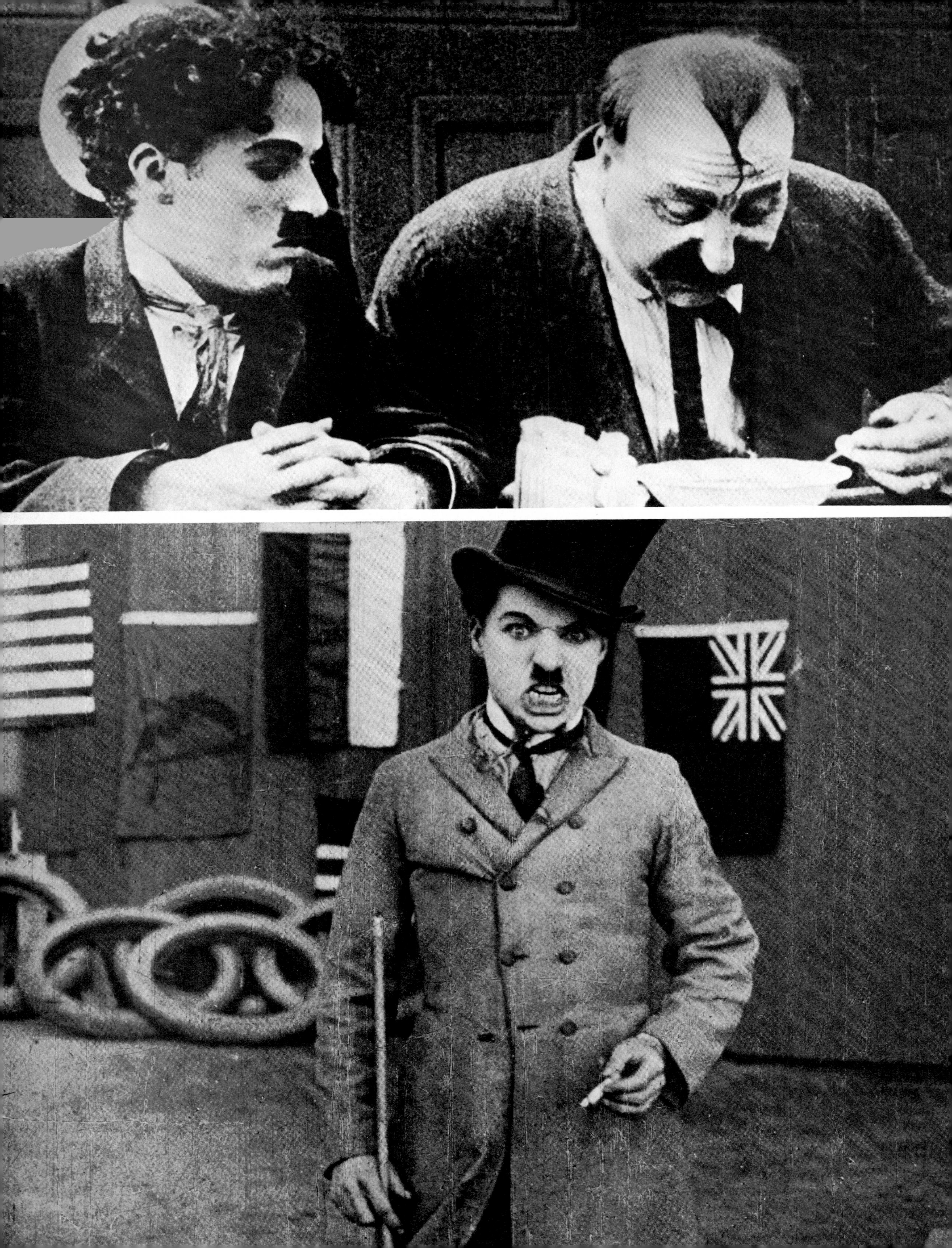

his hat along his arm and hook his cane into his vest pocket for future reference, the year at Keystone found him developing two profitable personal strains. One was the power to confide in the audience directly. The other was the insistence—perhaps it was the first realization—that the best comedy would always be played seriously.

I have mentioned Chaplin's double invasion of the camera in *Kid Auto Races at Venice*: his attempts, as a character, to get into the photographer's range, and his identification not with the figures on screen but with those in the audience who are constantly denied the same opportunity. Chaplin liked this intimate arrangement; he would always use it. He did not wish to be known in the third person, or as a figure in another world. He wished to communicate with his audience in the first person, and to belong to its world—not to the world of the characters. Essentially, Chaplin established himself as one of us, not one of them, whoever they might be. The seeds of his ultimate estrangement lie in this and are to become terribly important.

Every successful film star had to learn to appropriate the camera. No one can simply be photographed in passing, however interesting the work he may be doing, and still establish himself in the audience eye and mind. Confrontation is necessary; the man or woman must be able to turn front and control—not simply fill—the space. For most performers, including the clowns, this did not mean winking mischievously into the camera: it meant creating a tension, when photographed full-face and alone, that defied the camera to move away. The camera, for all practical purposes, was stared down, became obedient, attentive. Keaton, Lloyd, and Langdon used it in this way, without other intimacy.

But some others, a very few, went further—though further was dangerous and might end in the destruction of the objective image. Douglas Fairbanks literally winked at us, in the very heart of the action, often; the gesture was a joke shared between us. As a result, even his best costume films, for all their massive pageantry, sustained themselves joyously at a light-comedy level. Chaplin did not normally bother to wink, he did more: he shared everything with us, delight and distress both. By the time he had been nine months with Sennett, he had become popular enough to begin to do things his own way. Permitted at last to devise and direct his own short films, he was free to pause, just a little bit, to move the camera up closer, to experiment with an eye-to-eye relationship between the otherwise busy figure and ourselves.

In *His Trysting Place* he is seated at a lunch counter next to Mack Swain. Swain is noisily slurping his soup. Now, Chaplin is no higher in the social scale than Mack Swain; he has shown us very little gentlemanly behavior of his own. In a moment, inevitably, he is going to be hurling that bowl of soup into Swain's face. That is what we are waiting for. While we are waiting, however, with the camera close up on the heads of the two men, Chaplin spends his time looking directly at us, lifting his eyebrows and sniffishly twitching that mustached lip, asking us with his whole being whether Swain's manners aren't appalling. He doesn't ask anyone else. He doesn't show us anyone else being appalled. The camera functions not simply as an instrument for photographing one man's reactions but also as an instrument for drawing us into a *tête-à-tête* with him and enabling us to nod assent to his question.

He isn't begging for sympathy; there is no plea for approval of what he may be going to do next. He is just gossiping with us, silently but intimately; it is as though we were clucking together over the back fence. The pause for a private comparing of notes is gratifying, more gratifying than the regulation violence that follows. The comedian has breathed, the very camera seems to have sighed.

Opposite: Charlie soberly attends to Mack Swain's eating habits before turning to us for an intimate sharing of disapproval. *His Trysting Place*. The Chaplin costume had still not become entirely stable at the time of his tenth Keystone. *Mabel at the Wheel*.

Above: A drunken Charlie in earnest conversation with a dummy. *Mabel's Married Life*.

Chaplin has begun to link himself to us not as a love object but as a casual, ever-so-knowing neighbor whose trials are ours and can be conveyed, over tea, at a glance.

Even when he is not asking us questions so directly, much of what he does is for us alone. In *Getting Acquainted*, while he just happens to be holding his cane upside down, the hook of the cane accidentally lifts Mabel Normand's skirt. Wishing to show Mabel both his innocence and his penitence, he spanks the cane, speaks to it in earnest fatherly rebuke. Then, for us and not really for himself at all, he kisses it.

The business of speaking to the cane would be merely coy if it were not done in utter earnest. But Chaplin was already formulating in practice a credo he would put into words later: "If what you're doing is funny, you don't have to be funny doing it." The prescription may sound obvious enough in the abstract, but for many beginning silent comedians it was elusive. In his early solo work, Stan Laurel had a thoroughly destructive habit of giggling into the camera all the time he was acting out a joke, sometimes slapping his knees to make certain we knew he knew the joke was funny. Even Keaton, in one of his first supporting roles with Arbuckle, can be seen laughing—unthinkable later on—and grimacing wildly in an effort to create comedy where there was none. Chaplin, as early as his fourth month at Keystone in *Mabel's Married Life*, had discovered the comic value of believing with intense seriousness in whatever he might be doing. What he is doing in that film is having a conversation with a dummy. He has come home drunk. In the living room there is a boxer's training dummy that wife Mabel has just bought for him, hoping that he will use it to get back in trim; the dummy has a rounded base so that, given the slightest tap, it will bob about. Charlie, foggy from his evening out, mistakes it for an intruder. He attempts to persuade it to leave, to order it to leave, to cajole and to threaten and to make manly demands upon its honor, touching it familiarly and then more roughly as he does. As the dummy rebounds variously from the varied degrees of manhandling, Charlie mistakes each movement for an intelligent or argumentative response. He *listens*, gives consideration to each response, offers reasonable riposte. Because he believes so entirely in the reality of the dummy, we begin to believe too: at the very least we now see the dummy's movements as Charlie does; we detect flexible, almost rational, life in them. Our double knowledge—sharing Charlie's vision, retaining our own knowledge that the dummy is only a dummy—makes the sequence quite funny; the comedy depends entirely on the drunken Chaplin's behaving so soberly. In passing, it should be noticed that the sequence would not be possible without its silence: in a talking film, the dummy's failure to speak would destroy the impression that it is responding. But for Chaplin, the importance of the moment lies in the total absorption he has brought to it, one that brushes aside by-the-way gags and gambles everything on sustained concentration.

When Chaplin left Keystone for Essanay in 1915, he began to have a little more time to think about his craft. His new contract specified that during his second year in films he would have to make no more than fourteen short comedies of ten to twenty minutes each, which meant that instead of completing a largely improvised film in two or three days—as he often had done at Keystone—he might spend as much as three weeks on a single subject. His new freedom would by no means lead him to discard the basic Keystone outline: as a paperhanger he would still make a mess of the walls; as a rowdy in a theater gallery he would cap the evening by unwinding a fire hose and unleashing gallons of water on the entire house.

Neither would he surrender the matter-of-fact callousness, the amoral opportunism of all Keystone comedians. Not entirely, certainly not immediately. Holding his seductive leading lady in a Theda Bara "vampire" position with one arm, he would use the other arm to dig his elbow into her midriff so that he might have a prop for his chin. He would jump high enough to kick a policeman in the shoulders, toppling him over backward; he would stand on his hands in order to kick another policeman in the face. His love affair with matches continued. At Keystone, he had struck a match to light his cigarette on the bald head of a restaurant patron; at Essanay he used the bald head of a tuba-player in a theater orchestra, then the bare feet of a lady snake charmer. In one Essanay film, which he did not intend to release, he struck a match against the exposed bare feet of a drunk in a flophouse, then, having lighted his cigar, left the burning match propped between the sleeping man's toes.

But almost at once he began to make things less gratuitous, working his way slowly toward that ultimate kick in *The Pilgrim* that would delight audiences with its *appropriateness*. He began to feel a need to justify—emotionally or rationally—the violence, even the randomness, with which he would not part. He found himself looking for the other half of the joke.

At Sennett, half a joke had always been good enough: make a stab at it, and get on with the chase. But a "joke," properly speaking, is always composed of two parts. One image is superimposed on another, to which it is not at all related, in order to make an apparent—but wildly incongruous—fit. At Keystone, for instance, Chaplin had almost reflexively taken everyone's pulse. It seemed something to do when nothing else was going on. In *Laughing Gas*, as a dental assistant, he had taken a patient's pulse at the wrist and then again on the sole of his shoe. But this extension, this search for a second step that would end in a true joke, is merely random. There is no real fit, and the business isn't funny. At Essanay, however, Chaplin, as the janitor in *The Bank*, paused in his labors to glance at a waiting customer, then—gratuitously as ever—took his pulse. Showing concern over the pulse, he asked the man to stick out his tongue. The man complied, whereupon Chaplin promptly used the man's tongue to lick a stamp, which he immediately affixed to a letter he wished to mail. The joke has been completed, come whole, its two unrelated parts perfectly juxtaposed in time and space.

The doubleness takes longer, because its two images must be established separately; but when the mismates come together, there is a real chance for a laugh, even a laugh that might last. Chaplin takes his time about opening the giant vault in *The Bank* before safely depositing his shabby coat and hat in it for the day. And such incongruous juxtaposition of values can, once the trick has been learned, be slyly and ironically implied rather than violently stated. In *Work*, made at Essanay, Charlie and a fellow paperhanger are preparing for their unskilled assault on the walls when the lady of the house appears, studies them for a moment, then scoops up her available silverware and locks it in a safe. The gesture is not lost upon Charlie and companion. They at once, and not too ostentatiously, gather together their own wallets and watches and padlock them with a large safety-pin into one of Charlie's pockets. The gag may be outrageous, but it has a purpose.

And something else was happening. Chaplin, without abandoning his instinct for lunging headlong at the nearest object before it could behave just as badly toward him, was becoming fastidious in his violence. He would now help a woman out of a pool if he had inadvertently knocked her into it; of course, if she proceeded to berate him for having bumped her in the first place, he would knock her back in again. Before going into the ring in *The Champion*—with a

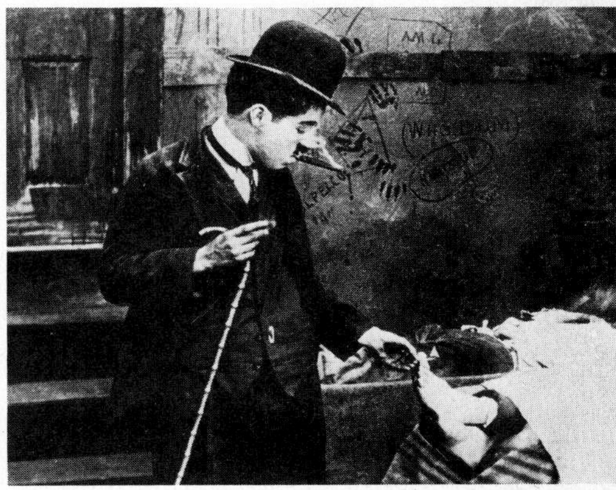

Charlie, as Don José, using his true love as a prop. *Carmen*. In a flophouse, he discards his lighted match by placing it between a sleeping man's toes. *Triple Trouble*. In *The Bank*, he once more takes a customer's pulse, then goes on to find the other half of the joke.

horseshoe helpfully tucked into one boxing glove—he takes care that nothing about him will be personally offensive: he thoughtfully dabs beer behind his earlobes and on the soles of his feet. He is most courteous to an elderly drunk in a flophouse. He first makes up the man's bed, then hits him on the head with a mallet to ensure sleep, then kisses him goodnight. The kiss and the blow are merging.

The presence of Edna Purviance may have had something to do with an emerging gentility. Miss Purviance, who joined him for his second film at Essanay and stayed on as leading lady for thirty-four more, was a new kind of foil for Chaplin. Mabel Normand, most often his sparring partner at Keystone, had been a near-clown in her own right, an attractive hoyden with a swiftly outraged mouth and a swiftly upraised fist. It had been tit for tat, umbrella-spoke for umbrella-spoke, between them. Miss Purviance, however, was blonde and placid; though she wasn't, she seemed rather larger than Chaplin, a trace matronly. It was more natural for her to play the mother in *The Kid* than a gate-crasher in boys' clothes—fetching as she looks in the boys' clothes—in *Behind the Screen*. In general, one felt that she was trying to do Chaplin good—a fact that both attracted him and made him wary.

He would never be able to do to her what he had done casually to Mabel Normand. In *The Bank*, as janitor, he carries a mop loosely over his shoulder. Quite a few bank officials and customers get the mop full in the face. Mabel Normand would have got it. Not Edna—ever. Indeed, in this film Charlie is so dreamily enamored of her that, when the mop swings, it swings back into his own face: the association of adoration with immediate mishap was to remain with him, ever more brilliantly, through *City Lights*. Still, adoration of Edna is only an occasional note at Essanay. If she has some influence on his behavior, it is of a maternal, and not altogether successful, nature.

In *Police* the two are seated at a dining-room table. The lady of the house has caught Charlie, a thief, ransacking the place. She makes a deeply impassioned speech, pleading with him to reform. He is attentive, and it is his turn to be touched. In the course of her little sermon, and thinking only of his good, she moves the beer he has been drinking away from him. Without taking his eyes off her or ceasing to seem an utterly rapt penitent, he gets the beer back. There is a new refinement in this man; he is genteelly untrustworthy.

Who and what was he, really? This was a question that plainly began to intrigue, if not trouble, Chaplin during his year at Essanay. At Keystone he had developed a comic image, an extraordinarily popular one. He still had to develop a character. We think of him now simply as "the tramp": that is his character, and we accept it even when we do not understand it. But he had as yet arrived at no such identity; neither did he arrive at it simply by making an Essanay comedy called *The Tramp*.

He was certainly in search of a character when he made *The Tramp*, as he was when he began a feature he planned to call *Life*. The feature was never finished: the constant pressure to get his popular short comedies into theaters on time kept him away from it. We happen to know something about the film now only because, after Chaplin's departure from Essanay at the end of his specified year, the studio gathered up its fragments and incorporated them into a hodgepodge called *Triple Trouble*, filled out by further snippets from *Work* and borrowings from *Police*.

The resulting film is worthless, except for what it can tell us about the vein Chaplin was tempted to explore in imagining his own kind of feature. What is most clear is that it was to take place in a shabbier than usual environment, with

Chaplin an underdog among underdogs. What there is of *Life* is set in a flophouse, with Charlie ambiguously ministering to drunks and thieves before trying to get to sleep himself. He not only kisses the man he has lulled to sleep with a mallet, he taps his cigar ash into the man's open mouth before dropping alongside his own cot to pray. He says his prayers in a fast two seconds, exactly as Jackie Coogan would do in *The Kid* six years later. He hunches under the bedclothes as he would do to conceal Coogan in that same film. He reverses himself under the blankets, putting his head where his shoes are, the better to keep a watch on marauders, as he would do with Mack Swain in *The Gold Rush.* The few feet of rescued film seethe with inventive business he would not know how to use properly until later. But even though the pusillanimity and the quick prayer are growing closer together in this film, the character is still an in-and-out business, two contrary impulses trying to find a psychic solution that will hold them in equilibrium.

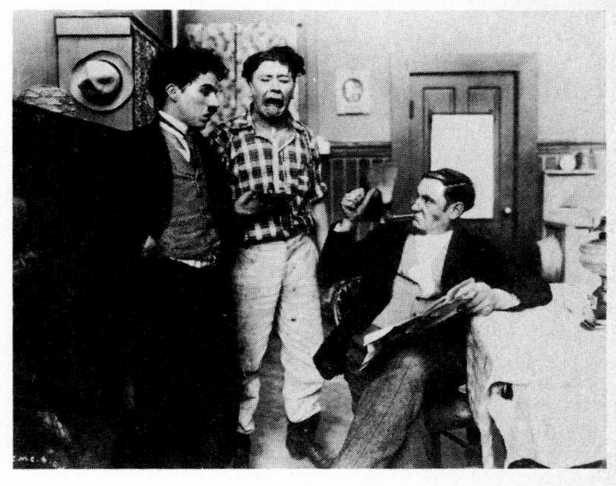

When he made *The Tramp*, exactly halfway through his year at Essanay, he was obviously conducting an experiment, though there is nothing to say that he meant the film to be in any way definitive. Because we know him as "the tramp" now, we are inclined to view the film as a firm first statement of his ultimate intentions, as *the* seminal Chaplin film. The deliberate introduction of pathos and the fact that the comedy closes with a shot of Chaplin trudging down the road alone seem to confirm the view.

But the film is much more nearly a curio, a puzzle, a mysterious misstep than it is a declaration of style. It is, in fact, a failure: it solves none of its own problems of tone, answers none of the questions it raises. But we mustn't place a greater burden on the film than Chaplin intended it to carry. When he appeared in *The Tramp*, he wasn't making an announcement. He was simply playing a tramp in the same way he had earlier, in comparable films, played a waiter, a dentist, a husband, a wife, a cook, a caveman, a film actor, a star boarder, a *bon vivant.* That he did not in the least regard *The Tramp* as a watershed film is plain from what he did after it: he went right on adopting new disguises, appearing as a paperhanger, a floorwalker, a fireman, a studio property man, a policeman, an escaped convict, a wealthy drunk, even Don José in *Carmen*. With a possible single exception, he would not explicitly be a tramp again until twenty more films had been made and he was at last ready, in *A Dog's Life*, to say precisely who he was.

The tramp is at this point a convenience for something else, perhaps an intuitively sensed convenience that Chaplin knew would somehow serve him well later but one that was needed just now to help him try for a specific effect. Could the audience be persuaded to do anything but laugh at Chaplin? Might it briefly take him seriously, even feel sorry for him? He wanted to know, and the film is constructed, quite awkwardly, with that objective in mind. An unemployed man—by far the greater number of Chaplin's short comedies find him gainfully employed when we meet him—who could be taken on and then abandoned again was a logical choice for the film's purposes.

In *The Tramp*, Charlie appears from the dusty road, sits beside a tree to eat his lunch, has his lunch stolen by lurking thieves, contents himself with grass, then hears the thieves molesting Edna, whom he promptly and acrobatically rescues. In gratitude, she takes him home to her farmhouse, where her father gives him a job. If the film has been regulation Essanay comedy until now, here it reverts to Keystone. Charlie, on a ladder to the hayloft, dumps sack after sack of grain on those unfortunate enough to work below him. Those who are spared the grain bags get the pitchfork. Charlie sets fire to his own pants, then to the news-

Managing the police in *Police*, Chaplin's last and best Essanay and a considerable advance over the final Keystone, *His Prehistoric Past*. In *The Tramp*, broad comedy and attempted pathos are at odds with each other.

paper the girl's father is reading. He tries and fails—as every silent comedian after him would—to milk a cow.

In all of this there is one lovely shot, the first of what I think of as the Chaplin master-images. Charlie is in an orange grove, seen in long-shot, simply watering the trees with a sprinkling can as though they were delicate spring flowers. Hopping from one row to the next, crossing his own trail diagonally until he has spun a spiderlike human web among inanimate objects, he seems to place himself temporarily in a sympathetic, productive universe, where he is enormously happy. The shot directly anticipates the rare happy ending of *A Dog's Life*, with a straw-hatted Chaplin taking adroit care of his bean rows before returning to his charming cottage, his picture-book wife.

In *The Tramp* the thieves return, planning to rob the house. At an upstairs window, Charlie, mallet in hand, succeeds in disposing of them, one by one, blow by blow. Chasing after them, however, he comes within range of the farmer's rifle-fire and is shot in the leg. That is our first shock. The form, this fantasia of unfelt violence, does not quite allow for it. He is taken in by Edna, nursed, fed, coddled. He basks in her care, is obviously falling in love, tends to assume that she loves him. Then her fiancé arrives. Charlie, stunned, looks on.

Now, alone in the farmhouse, Chaplin mourns. He writes a farewell note. Turning his back to us, he cries. His love has not been the conventional comic love that is either casually reciprocated or, failing that, shrugged off with a joke. It has, much to our surprise, been more elemental than that. Readying himself to go, and trying not to lose touch with a comic vein altogether, Chaplin wipes his tears first on the farmer's hat and then on a dishtowel. He takes his leave, lingeringly, then shuffles down the road, his cane curving under the weight of his sorrow. Before the image can iris out, however, he suddenly shrugs, shakes himself, does a little kick-step, and moves along more rapidly, perhaps with a lighter heart.

But the second shock has been too much for us, and for the film. From the time that Chaplin is wounded seriously and then just as seriously attended, falling seriously in love, we are, formally, bewildered. This is no longer the world of Keystone or of Essanay; it is another world altogether, one that does not yet quite exist. Our expectations have been violated, and we are all at sea. *Should* we have taken the man more seriously when he was thumping about with sacks of wheat, when he was pumping the tail of the cow to produce milk? There is no way to go back; and to go forward—with his tears—we should have to start all over. The film simply breaks, and there is no unifying response we can find to make. We see that Chaplin can play a "straight" scene effectively, as we do again—just as bafflingly—at the end of his burlesque of *Carmen*, with Edna dying in his arms. But the single character whose silhouette embraces both sentiment and comedy, and both *at the same time*, has not yet been born.

I cannot pretend to know when Chaplin discovered for himself what his true, all-embracing, ultimate, and indivisible comic character was. I only know when *I* see it for the first time—fleetingly, but with the force of a thunderbolt. The moment comes toward the end of his last film for Essanay, *Police*.

Police is a particularly good comedy—for this stage of the game—on other counts. It opens as Charlie is released from jail, an image of second birth—for this man who seemed never to have had a first—that would recur obsessively in later comedies until in *Modern Times* it becomes the rhythmic structure of the film: clapped into jail, let out, clapped in, let out, over and over again. Bent on reform, he refuses an opportunity to relieve a man of his watch and wallet, only to see a bogus preacher lift both a moment later. When a gunman robs

Opposite: In *Police*, to save Charlie from the law, Edna introduces him as her husband, whereupon he becomes even more confidently the man of the house than he would seem to be, eighteen months later, in *The Adventurer*.

Charlie, going hurriedly through his pockets, Charlie simultaneously goes through the gunman's, coming out even: the interplay is so expert that he fools us as readily as he does the gunman. Deciding to burglarize a house and working to pry open a porch window, he is approached quietly, knowingly, by a policeman from behind. Becoming aware of the policeman, Charlie politely asks him to hand him the mallet for his chisel. The policeman, willing to bide his time, does so. Charlie hits him with the mallet. Politeness pays. The film's business is casual, ironic. The policemen themselves are deliberate inversions of everything Sennett had done: so far from behaving like struck ninepins in a frantic anxiety to get to the scene of the crime, the officers at the station house casually finish their tea before answering the call from Edna informing them of a burglar in the house, thoroughly enjoy their cigars on a leisurely drive to the premises.

Indeed, they dally so along the way that Edna has time to catch Charlie herself, decide that he is no more than a strayed sheep, sit him down and reason with him about his future. By the time the police do arrive, she is persuaded of his penitence, and—to save him—she introduces him not as a thief but as her husband.

It is at this point that a virtual miracle takes place. With no transition at all, Charlie *becomes* Edna's husband. Affable, outgoing, utterly at home, digging his hands into his pockets and flexing his knees as though he were master of his own domain and ready to get out the humidor, he is all bourgeois bonhomie, the host par excellence, eager to show his guests about and have them back soon again. No one has ever been more completely the confident man of the house.

The impersonation lasts for only a moment or two, but, for me, its implications are immense. It is entirely clear that Charlie could have been this man at any time he chose to adopt the role. He is no born underdog, deprived of opportunity by an unfeeling society. He is not inept, uneducated, uninformed, socially unacceptable. There is nothing in his natural equipment or in his background, nothing cruelly unjust in the society around him to keep him from most acceptably playing for a full twenty-four hours a day the part he is playing now. He might have married Edna, might have run a house, might have had children, might have gone to church, might have worked and become rich, might have done anything he cared to put his mind to. The competence is there, in plain view. The posture is believed in, even by the police. No barrier stands between his talents and the assumption of a role in which they might be exercised. *He is no natural tramp.*

Suddenly we realize that this has always been so—and, looking into the future, see that it always will be. The moment he wishes to become a boxer, he becomes an extraordinarily deft one. The moment he wishes to put on roller skates, he becomes Nijinsky on wheels. The moment he wishes to become a rich man, he becomes a rich man, though when he does he tends to drink. If he wishes to marry, he marries, takes his children on outings; if he wishes to rescue a woman from a burning building, his skill and bravery are unexampled; if he wishes to walk a high-wire, he walks a high-wire superbly; if he wishes to set a table for dinner, he sets it with Cordon Bleu finesse; if he wishes to gamble, he is at once a shark; if he proclaims himself count or ambassador, his manners are impeccable; if he is asked to deliver a sermon, he can do it on the instant and do it so well that he feels justified in coming back for three bows; if he is asked to lay bricks, he can do *that* with unparalleled speed and expertise; if he is inducted as a soldier, he can capture the Kaiser. He can farm, play a violin, cope with bullies, duel as Fairbanks dueled. He can be a woman, seductively.

In a film he made the following year, *The Floorwalker*, there is a startling, abruptly and almost inexplicably funny, passage. The manager of the department

store is about to make off with a bagful of money. Charlie walks into the office at this moment, also carrying a bag. The two come face to face. Suddenly we—and they—realize that they look alike. They go into a "mirror" routine, as though there were actually a looking-glass between them, with Charlie duplicating each of the manager's movements precisely. Groping, they touch fingers. The manager, illusion destroyed by the touch, now clears his head and reaches out his hands, holding Charlie's face between them to study the resemblance, staring directly into his eyes. Charlie apparently mistakes what the man is doing for a homosexual gesture. With prompt compliance he bobs forward to kiss him full on the mouth. Ask him to be a homosexual, he will be a homosexual.

For *A Night in the Show*, made at Essanay, Chaplin decided to adapt a routine he had earlier performed in vaudeville, but to adapt it in a way only film could make possible. He would play two parts: a white-tie "swell" in the orchestra and a lowbrow nuisance in the gallery. Characteristically, he took no advantage of the camera's openness to trickery; Chaplin's use of the camera would always be chaste, even static, confined largely to patient waiting while he reached through it to make contact with us. He made no effort whatever to do what other film-makers were doing and what was easily possible: to bring the two figures together in a single frame through double exposure. He merely cut back and forth between them. The only thing that interests him, obviously, is the opportunity to be two entirely different men at the same time.

The secret of Chaplin, as a character, is that he can be anyone.

That is his problem. The secret is a devastating one. For the man who can, with the flick of a finger or the blink of an eyelash, instantly transform himself into absolutely anyone is a man who must, in his heart, remain no one. To be able to play a role, to know the role as a role, is to see through it. To be able to play them all is to see through them all. But that leaves nothing, no way of life, no permanent commitment in which such a man can possibly believe. Just as Don Juan, loving everyone, can love no one, so Chaplin, impersonating everyone, can have no person. With every posture exposed as an artifice that can be adopted on the instant and just as instantly dropped, the door to the world in which less perceptive, less malleable people *do* accept postures and pursue them to blind profit is effectively sealed off. Who would wish to be part of a world that can so easily be faked? And how would you go about it? You can't believe in what you know better than, in what you can *do* without believing. Infinitely adaptable but universally a fraud, Chaplin now has no one identity to embrace, to enter whole-heartedly, to feel secure about, to find rest in. He can only come out of nowhere, open his bag of tricks on demand, pretend to be what is asked of him for a moment or so, and go away again.

Perhaps that is why he is so eager to be with *us*. As we come into the theater we put our roles behind us—we are no longer separately teachers or bankers or janitors or wives—to accept the anonymity of the mass. Temporarily we are nobodies too, unengaged in the artifices we are watching. He belongs beside us, looking on. Of course, when the artifice is over, he can't go home with us. So he goes down the road.

The tramp is a philosophical, not a social, statement. And it was a conclusion to which Chaplin came, not a choice he imposed from the outset. The tramp is the residue of all the bricklayers and householders and *bon vivants* and women and fiddlers and floorwalkers and drunks and ministers Chaplin had played so well, too well. The tramp was all that was left. Sometimes the dark pain filling Chaplin's eyes is in excess of the situation at hand. It comes from the hopeless limitation of having no limitations.

Charlie as a scowling "swell," one half of his dual role in *A Night at the Show*.

10. Chaplin: Playfulness Unleashed

The discovery that he could not be anyone because it was too easy to be everyone unleashed a number of things in Chaplin. To begin with, it resolved the problem posed by *The Tramp*. He no longer had to alternate between comedy and pathos, developing each tone separately. He could be funny and sad at the same time, now that the news about himself was clear.

Why? Because the comedy came *in* the impersonation, in the incredible skill of it, for just as long as it lasted; and the pathos came in the knowledge that it could not last. I have mentioned how deeply Chaplin came to believe in whatever comic business he might be doing. But that is the only thing he believes in. He can believe in a dummy, in the content of a sermon, in his conduct as a fraudulent count. He gives himself totally to the unreality of the moment. But he knows, all the while, that the unreality is unreal and that the moment will soon be over. This certainty underlies, and is simultaneous with, the intensity of his assumption of any role. We shall often see him collapse inwardly with regret the moment an imposture has ended, or is about to end; there is no way of sustaining it, of committing himself to it indefinitely, and he must now return to his nothingness. The coming nothingness haunts him even as he is being his most brilliantly accomplished. The pretense to commitment is, literally, achingly funny. It is marvelous that he can enter so wholeheartedly into the activity that briefly engages him, shattering to realize that his heart is not in it at all.

Chaplin did not immediately make the most of this new simultaneity as he left Essanay to spend his third year in films with Mutual, a company that had offered him ten times his Essanay salary to make twelve films in twelve months. While he was making the films—the twelve months actually stretched into eighteen—he was busy exploring certain other consequences of his discovery. But he did pause to crystallize the new and more intimate relationship between pathos and comedy in his third Mutual film, *The Vagabond*.

The vagabond Chaplin gives us is, by the way, not precisely what we mean by a "tramp." A tramp, in the American experience, is someone who wanders

the world's byways in order to live on handouts. When, much later, Harry Langdon briefly adopts a "tramp" character, he is seen emerging rebuffed from a back doorway and scrawling a chalked "No" on the gatepost, which is what, as children, we always heard that tramps did. There is no such shot in all of Chaplin. Why would Chaplin beg when he is such an expert glazier, jeweler, barber, mixer of cocktails? When he wants a meal he will get it through his own skills, whether they are those of a rogue or a master craftsman. In *The Vagabond,* he is a violinist—from the look of things, a wildly accomplished one.

We first see Chaplin's feet shuffling forward, beneath the swing-doors of a saloon, quite as though those splayed and battered shoes had—even for him—begun to take on iconographic status. He means to play his violin for coins at the street corner but is driven away by a German band. Going into the country, he comes upon an unkempt slavey, Edna, doing the washing for a gypsy caravan. He knocks on the fence rail before disturbing her. Performing on the violin for her, he is a dashing virtuoso, taking many bows; but his performance brings the savage gypsies—the film has a fairy-tale texture throughout—down on them both. Leaping to it, Charlie handily disposes of the entire tribe, commandeers a wagon, and carries Edna away. Once they have safely set up light housekeeping along the road, Charlie delouses Edna, giving her face a thorough soaping, cleaning out her ears and her nostrils, as he would Jackie Coogan's a few years later. He does up her hair with a safety pin that had been holding his trousers together.

Then he sets the table for dinner, quite unaware that Edna is falling in love with a painter she has met in the woods. He is meticulous about the dinner appointments, as precise and as thorough as he has been about Edna's toilet. An inverted tub serves as a table. A checkered shirt, neatly draped, becomes the tablecloth. The arms of the shirt are now rolled up into professionally folded napkins, standing regal on the table. The sequence is delightful in its sheer invention; but our delight is permanently compromised. All the while we are laughing at the caterer's finesse with which the vagabond turns shirt-sleeves into perfect pyramids of linen, we are aware that the table is a tub, the tablecloth a torn shirt, the napkins an illusion that will be shattered the instant anyone tries to use them. There is no disentangling the contrasted elements here: what is funny is rooted in the shabbiness of the equipment, the forlorn state of affairs. In addition, a warning hovers over us. We know what is happening to Edna.

So, to be sure, does Charlie, a moment later. The painter is brought to dinner, and, though Charlie is polite enough to bob a little curtsy in greeting, the jealousy in his eyes as Edna devotes all of her table-talk to her lover is—for the first time—genuinely painful. Seething and preoccupied, Charlie sits on a hot stove: the moment of pathos must also always be a moment of comic insult. Charlie tries to compete, doing his own drawings on the side of the caravan. But neither the idyll nor the awkward triangle can last. Who, including Charlie, ever supposed it would? Edna's identity is soon discovered through a portrait her lover has painted of her—naturally, she'd been stolen by the gypsies as a child—and her mother arrives to take her home in a limousine. There is a second master-image: Chaplin alone by the wagon, one arm upraised to rest against it, watching the committed world roar away in the dust.

Though the fusion of tones is perfectly realized during the body of this short film, its ending gave Chaplin trouble. What next step for the vagabond? Originally, Chaplin had him commit suicide, or attempt to commit suicide, by plunging headlong into a pond. But the sequence was wrong and had to be replaced. What was wrong with it? The despair. Only the truly hopeful can truly despair, and, in all honesty, Charlie hadn't hoped that much. His love for Edna in the film isn't

Charlie, violinist, serenades gypsy-slavey Edna in *The Vagabond.*

the direct and purposeful love that sees, in ardent eye-to-eye encounter, a productive future, though we shall get just that from Chaplin a bit later in at least one Mutual film. It is, rather, a reflexive, almost paternal love: love is what you feel for girls who look like Edna, and you promptly go through all the appropriate motions; but you count on nothing. It is over very quickly—and unsurprisingly.

Another ending, utterly ambiguous, was devised. Edna, though she is delighted to be in the car with her mother and lover, can't leave the man who has been so good to her. The car turns around and, stirring up just as much dust, comes back; Charlie is whisked into it bodily, and it roars away again. The film ends. What is Charlie doing in the car? There is no answering that question, any more than there is as we watch Edna open the door of her mansion at the end of *The Kid*, admit Charlie, then close the door and the film together. The vagabond, the tramp, can be taken in. But there is no "in," really—not for him. The ambiguous ending, with emotion going one way and logic another, becomes the only valid ending for a Chaplin film in which his double effect—pathos and comedy inextricably joined—has played a continuing part. *City Lights* must end with an enormous close-up of Chaplin—hopeful, hopeless—that tells us not a thing about tomorrow. Of course, we know. We understand the man by this time and can no longer be baffled either by his competence or his position as outcast.

The Vagabond, though successful in fusing its opposites and establishing Chaplin's over-all identity, is a loner among the Mutual comedies. In the others, Chaplin is busy as can be, sounding out a whole series of alternate inflections suggested by the character he has fully come to understand. A few, *The Fireman* and *The Count* in particular, are uninspired films, scarcely more than echoes of Essanay and even Keystone. *One A.M.*, a solo film for Chaplin and as such a bit of a stunt, contains a fine routine with a folding bed, though it is the kind of routine other comedians could and would perform. But most of the Mutuals leap with a new life, make new and exhilarating discoveries.

It was obvious, for instance, that if Chaplin could seem to be anyone he chose on the spur of the moment, a lot of other seeming must be going on too. What about those people on the "inside" who go so confidently about their roles? Are they play-acting as well? Are they even greater frauds than the "tramp" for pretending not to be? The trim and righteous manager in *The Floorwalker* is the fellow who gets not only his finger but his whole fist into the till. In *The Pawnshop* an elderly, heartsore man comes by to part with the last memento of his beloved wife, their wedding ring. His tale brings Chaplin to tears. Charlie does the best he can for him by way of an exchange. Taking the money, the old man adds it to a wad of bills in his pocket thick enough to plug a breached dike. Charlie hits *himself* on the head with a hammer for having been taken in.

In a later film, *The Pilgrim*, Charlie would discover—not too much to his surprise—that a pious elder of the church not only kept a pint of whiskey in his back pocket but had once even kept a woman. This view of personality as something unstable was not a jaundiced one, not wholly negative. In the same film a sheriff who pursues Charlie, shoots at him, nabs him, and forcibly takes him away from Edna proves, before the fade-out, to be an exceedingly kindly chap. No doubt the ultimate image of character instability in Chaplin is that of the wealthy drunk in *City Lights*, frigidly standoffish when sober, bosom friend in his cups. If each man was not a hundred men—as Chaplin seemed to his sorrow to be—he was at least two.

Nor could public ideals be trusted. In *The Immigrant*, Charlie and his fellow aliens are at last to be admitted to the Land of the Free. At the very moment the Statue of Liberty comes into view, they are one and all roped off like cattle,

prisoners of officialdom. Many commentators have liked to read this scene as an early indication of Chaplin's social conscience, as some have chosen to see in it an anti-American bias. The fact that he repeated the device in a much later and decidedly bitter talking film, *The King in New York*, tends to support these ideas by hindsight. But there is no need to attribute specific political significance to the incident in *The Immigrant*. Commentators never seem to notice, for instance, that in the various Chaplin films in which strikes occur, Charlie, so far from adopting any sort of liberal position, immediately leaps into the role of eager strikebreaker. When the union walks out, he takes over. So far as I can see, there is nothing socially or politically schematic in any of Chaplin's early or middle films; when, in a few later ones, he did turn to social attitudinizing, he probably did so because he had been reading his commentators and felt it was expected of him. What interested him, what delighted him, was instability itself, the fact that things are certainly not what they seem; and *that* conviction can take off in any direction at all.

He took special delight, during this period, not only in the instability of roles, of personality, of public ideals, but in the instability of inanimate objects. He developed a passion for visual metaphor—for any one physical object that could be substituted for a quite different object and *seem* to become it, however temporarily. The beginnings of this happy flirtation with impossibly related "properties" can be seen in the later Essanay films, above all in his burlesque of *Carmen*.

Carmen is now a tedious botch of a film because Essanay, after Chaplin had departed, expanded it from an intended twenty minutes to forty, restoring material that Chaplin had abandoned and adding a gruelingly unfunny Ben Turpin subplot in the hope that audiences wouldn't notice that Chaplin's and Turpin's paths never cross. Turpin—with crossed eyes and the permanently stunned expression of a haddock on ice—became popular because his affliction defined him immediately; like fat comics, like tall comics, he could be detected at any point in a chase. No camera had to pause for him. When it did pause—he wound up at Sennett, which is surely where he belonged—he offered it very little. I am sorry to say that I have never at any time seen him do anything that made me laugh. But *requiescat*.

In *Carmen*, Chaplin began to play extensively and improbably with all the props that came to hand. He used Don José's dagger as a toothpick, as a knife to eat with. Escamillo's plate was so clean by the time *he* had finished eating that Chaplin was able to use it as a mirror. He played a game of billiards with scallions as balls and his dueling sword as a cue.

Comedians have always made use of props, though most often to mismanage them. W. C. Fields played an extremely funny game of billiards, but he played it with billiard balls. On stage, Bobby Clark might notice a showgirl enter in a vivid red gown and ask, "Who ordered lobster?" but there was no further effort to make the verbal metaphor operate visually. Mr. Clark never tried to put a knife and fork to the girl. Harpo Marx played with visual puns, maliciously. When Chico needed a flashlight and asked in his hurried Italian accent, "Where's da flash?" Harpo would promptly produce a fish. But the comparison was meant to be outrageously inappropriate; it is essentially verbal, not visual, and, in any case, no attempt was made to employ the fish *as* flashlight.

I can think of no stage comedian who made use of swift, evocative substitutions, who fell in love with the interchangeability of things, in the way that Chaplin did. There may have been such a clown, somewhere, sometime; after all, the kind of moments we are talking about are often spontaneous additions to the text and don't get written down.

Above: Dice in his hand, Charlie winds up for a fast ball. *The Immigrant*.

Overleaf, left—Top: In the slums of *Easy Street*; under the folding bed of the solo film *One A.M.*

Middle: In the mission house, *Easy Street*; dancing into a rescued Edna's arms, *Easy Street*.

Bottom: The female impersonation of *A Woman*; entering the promised land, *The Immigrant*.

Right, top: Escaped-convict Charlie alarmed by his new pajamas in *The Adventurer*.

Bottom: Living-statue Charlie in the dressing room of *The Cure*.

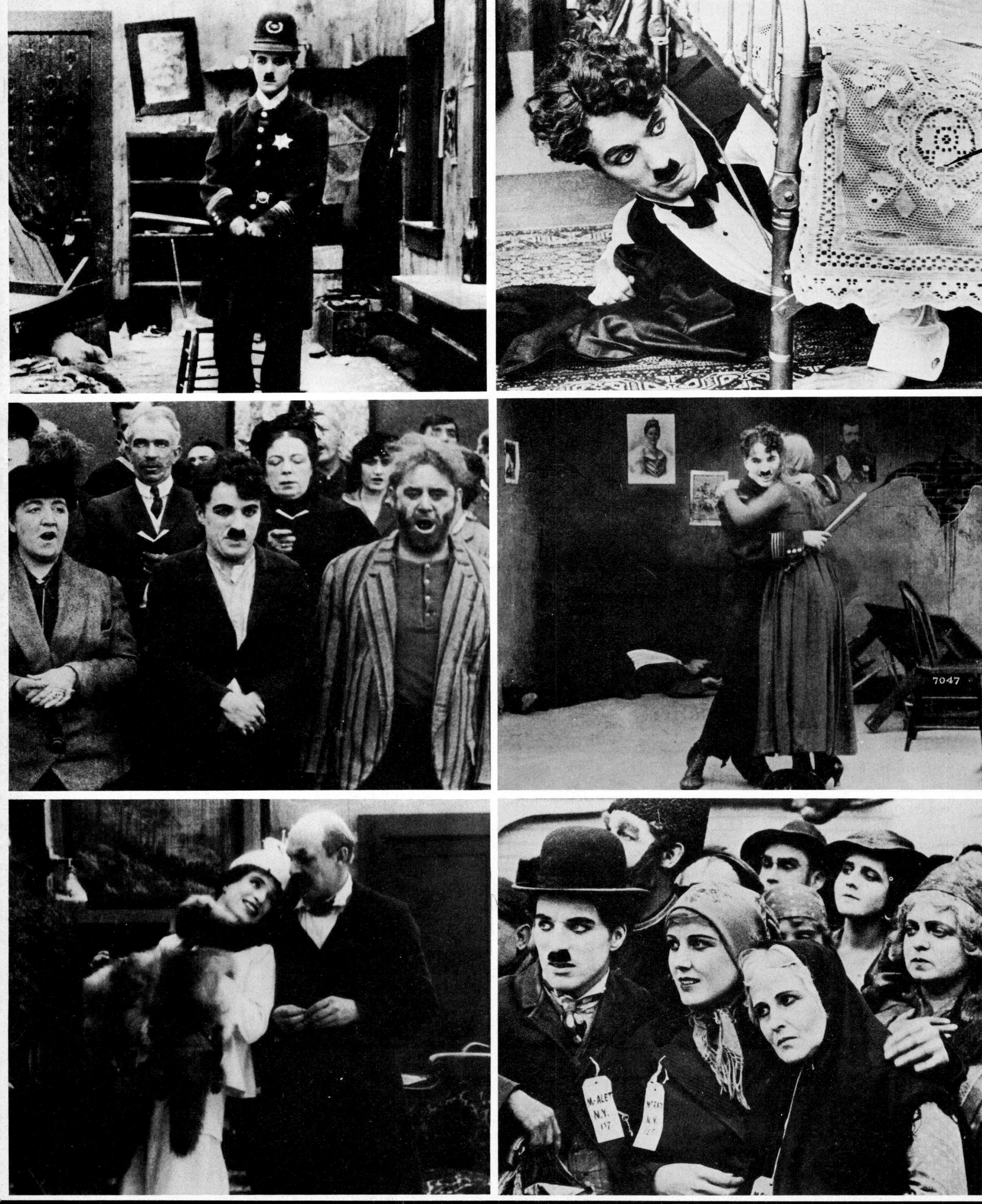
7047

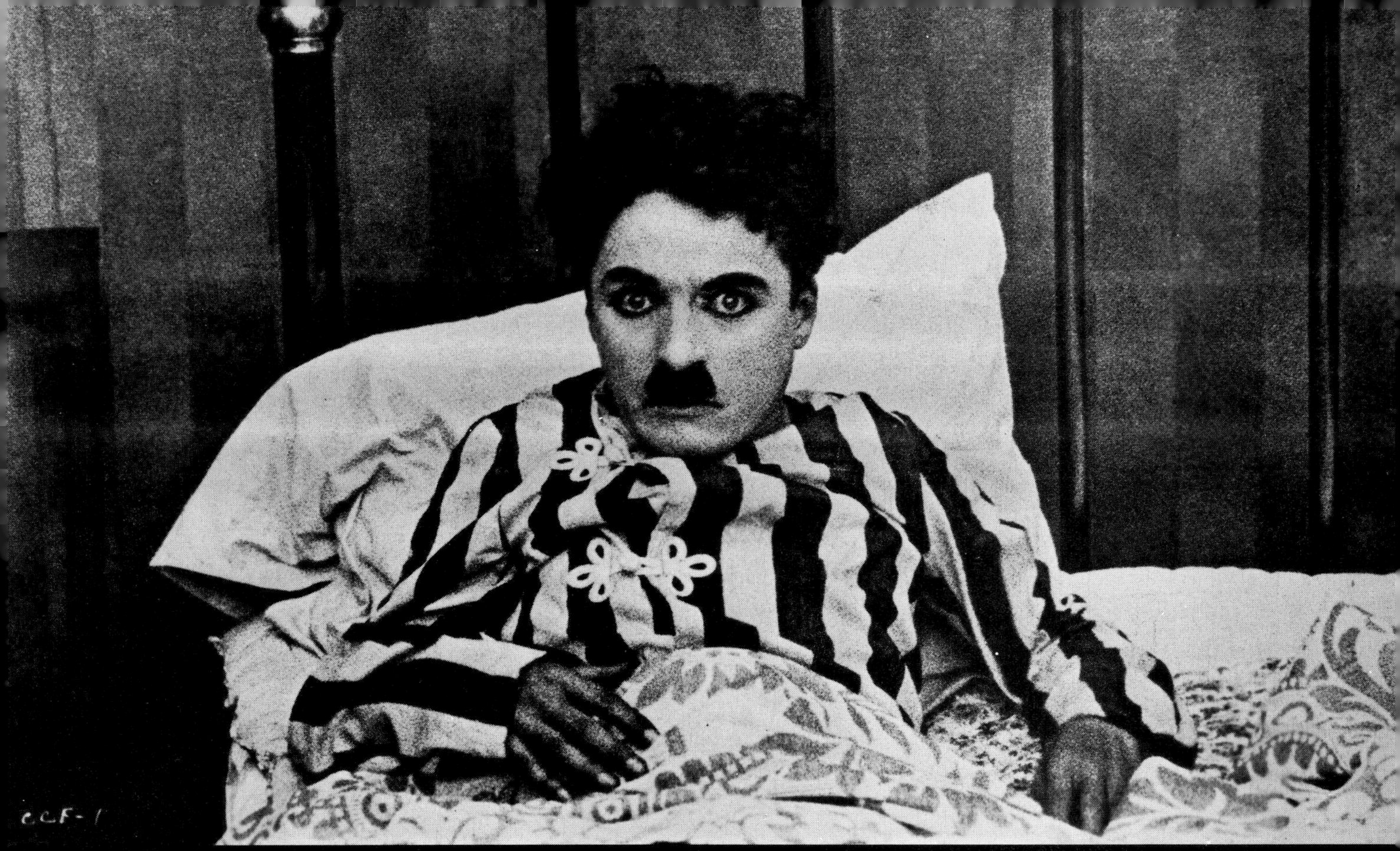

CCF-1

CCF-13

But the camera itself had created a new opportunity. It could range at will, picking up any prop it liked; and it could bring props together in an intimate focus forever denied to the stage. The fantasy of silence added to the invitation: with sound gone, we could be made to attend to the visual relationships *exclusively*, reducing the threat of improbability. In *Behind the Screen*, Chaplin plays a remarkable xylophone made up, on the instant, of emptied pie tins and a pair of hambones left over from lunch.

But *Behind the Screen* is a virtual explosion of such metaphor. In this seventh Mutual film, Chaplin not only dives behind a barricade to use a pair of beer bottles as binoculars, he spends a fascinating amount of time lathering, toweling, currying, manicuring, and otherwise grooming the head and paws of a bearskin rug. No more satisfied customer can ever have visited a salon. In *The Fireman* he issues dinner plates as though he were dealing a pack of cards, in *The Immigrant* he shoots dice as though he were a pitcher winding up for an especially terrifying curve-ball, in *The Pawnshop* he decides that a long piece of string he can't sweep up from the floor is an aerialist's high-wire and promptly goes into a deeply concentrated balancing act; later in that film he serenades Edna in the kitchen, Hawaiian-style, with a roll of dough slung around his neck for a lei and a cooking spoon serving as ukulele.

The metaphor becomes, on occasion, very quiet. In *The Adventurer*, Charlie is an escaped convict who has been rescued from drowning and put to bed, unconscious, in a pair of borrowed striped pajamas. In the morning, he wakes, yawns, stretches. Stretching, his hands grip the bars of the iron bedstead behind him. They are at once prison bars. At the same moment he notices the black-and-white striped pajamas.

And the metaphor itself can become notoriously unstable, changing its terms without warning. There is a justly celebrated sequence in *The Pawnshop*—composed of the two longest sustained "takes" Chaplin had yet permitted himself—in which he is asked by a customer to examine a clock. What will Charlie give him for it? Charlie must test the reliability of the clock. He applies a stethoscope to it, turning it into a sick baby. Failing to get to its insides with an auger, he turns it into a can of tuna fish and cuts away its lid with an opener. It does not have a very hopeful odor. The insides are attacked with a jeweler's eyeglass; it is delicate Swiss-work now. But its teeth are bad and a dentist's forceps must be applied. Defective plumbing too; a hammer will help. Its inner mechanisms begin to uncoil. He measures and snips them off like yardgoods. When its minor parts begin to squiggle about on the counter like larvae, he uses an oil can as exterminator. He gathers the parts together into the man's hat and gives them back. No deal. A clock—unlikely object—can be a baby, a can of fish, an open mouth, a bolt of cotton—*anything*. Chaplin has gone beyond mere look-alikes. The identity of an object lies only in the attitude one takes toward it. The man of all attitudes makes the universe his helpless plaything.

I have suggested that Chaplin's awareness of instability in some way exhilarated him. It did more than that. It taught him to dance.

We think quite casually of Chaplin as part-dancer now—having heard so endlessly about the Pan in him—but we rarely ask where it came from. He wasn't trained as a dancer. He showed no particular flair for it in his thirty-five Keystone or even his fourteen Essanay films. He became world-famous without having declared it as part of his natural equipment. Apparently he didn't finally begin to dance just because he *could* dance. He needed a better reason.

The reason came with the character he had finally created, as a necessary consequence of the man he found himself to be. In a sense, dance was forced on

Opposite: Instability and metaphor; a clock becomes anything Charlie wants it to be in *The Pawnshop*.

him. I think it happened this way. I've suggested that this man of all attitudes, skilled at all roles, found it so easy to adopt any of them that he could give complete credence to none. But that meant he could not really give credence to the narratives in which he and all those other strange people were embroiled, either. He could not wholly participate in their "plots." He might help them out here and there, play a part now and then. But even while he was doing so he must remain forever detached. It was the detachment that was danced.

Look at the ending of *The Pawnshop*. Charlie is both coward and hero of the occasion. A burly thief has broken loose in the pawnshop, and a battle has been raging. Charlie has swiftly taken refuge in a trunk, slamming the lid down over him. With the others still in full cry, the thief emerges from the vault, arms loaded with loot, a pistol at the ready. Backing toward the door, he keeps the others at bay. Charlie pops up out of the trunk behind him, brains him with a rolling pin. As the villain drops to the floor and the others begin to raise their hands in joy, Charlie hops from the trunk, turns directly to us, and goes into a cross-ankled, spread-eagled dancer's applause-finish, quite as though the orchestra were now blaring out a sign-off "Ta-taa!"

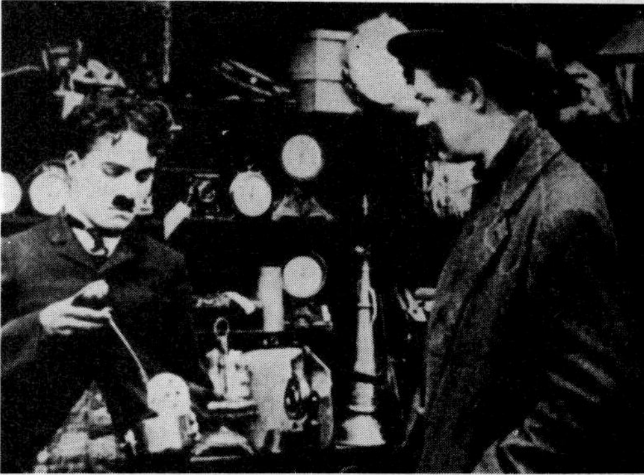

He has done it all—stopped the villain, saved the money, earned the gratitude of his employer, delighted Edna—and he hasn't believed a minute of it. The entire structure of the final scene, directed by Chaplin, is arranged to support this effect: The chasers and the chased move in darting one-two-three patterns that must be called balletic. There is no time for melodrama or even incidental comedy. Everything is geared to a single declaration: do not believe, it has all been a game. The film claps shut like a curtain. What does Charlie care about congratulations from those he has rescued, gratitude from his employer? What, even, does he care about Edna? These things are wiped away in a final flourish: we are pretending, to a metronome beat. Bows, please.

Charlie is happy enough taking his bow, pleased with himself. But the bow is something he shares with us, not with those other people. He has forgotten all about *them*. He never belonged to them, anyway. Chaplin's very playfulness comes of his inability to participate.

The detachment released him. Having no commitments, unable to make any, he was at least free to skip where he would, with a shrug. Chaplin's dances always do begin with a shrug: the shoulders lift first, then the feet gambol away. And the dances always say the same thing: You may believe, if you wish, in the events I have been passing through, but do not make the mistake of thinking I have done more than pass through. Ta-*taa*!

Earlier in *The Pawnshop*, Charlie and a fellow worker seem to make fighting a part-time occupation. It is what they *do* whenever they are together. When they carry a ladder outside the store to wash windows, Charlie promptly locks his opponent between two rungs of the horizontal ladder, gets a boy to hold it still, and proceeds to pummel his prisoner. But as he feints and jabs, the thrusts become more a boxer's warm-up than an attempt to strike his victim, eliding gently into near-dance. Charlie is no longer interested in the fight, or in winning. Going through the motions, he declares himself free of them. When a policeman approaches, he does not have to alter his rhythm or his attitude to skip away gaily, like a ten-year-old child. If, like other comedians, Charlie had *believed* in the policeman, if the policeman had truly frightened him, he would have done what other comedians always did: break stride and run. Instead, he remains above such things because he is not really part of them.

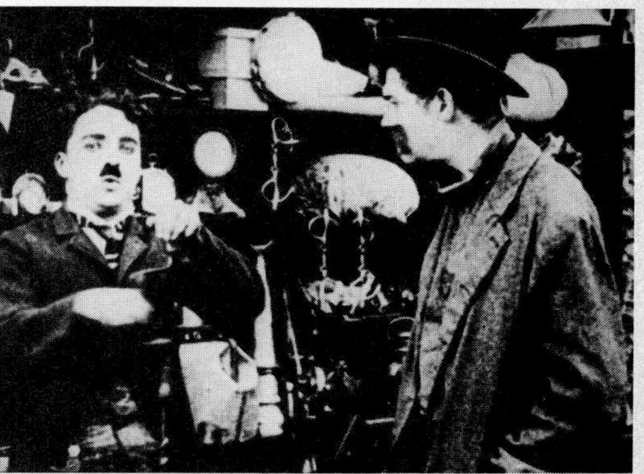

In no Mutual film does Chaplin dance simply to dance. He would do that later, after he had become self-conscious about the Pan image—in *Sunnyside*,

where he would openly play Pan, as though by popular demand, and sportively gambol among girls in a glade. For all that you may have heard about the sequence, a glance at the film now will at once reveal the dance as aimless, shapeless, unfocused. It is not truly effective because it has no function in the comedy other than to let Chaplin display a talent with which he has been credited.

But that is not enough, and dance never appears in such isolation while Chaplin is in the process of developing it. Even the very earliest hints of it in the Mutual comedies are used as crowbars to detach Chaplin from the action. When the German band in *The Vagabond* is chasing him in and out of the saloon, he takes time en route to tip his hat to the barflies along the way. In effect, he is acknowledging their applause, establishing the chase as pure artifice, sheer design. When the bulky and ferocious Eric Campbell, who served as his villain at Mutual, strikes at him again and again in *The Floorwalker*, each time Charlie succeeds in ducking the blow he goes into his spread-eagle bow for us. Of course, he can't always be as detached as he might like: once, Eric succeeds in hitting him while he is bowing.

The ballet stance appears as soon as he has coasted, on roller skates, onto the floor in *The Rink*. Chaplin's gifts as a skater *are* natural gifts, of an extraordinary sort; and again, they are used in part simply as display. But as soon as he has completed his first gaudy arabesques, he begins to choreograph the skating to mock the situation: he and the furious Eric Campbell engage in a hypnotic series of rhythmic stomach-bumps.

In *The Cure* he goes to the locker room to undress, retiring behind a drawn curtain. Far from sober, he begins to throw his clothing, as he sheds it, over the top of the enclosure. It first strikes Eric, then another inhabitant of the locker room. Each assumes the other has assaulted him, and a brouhaha is quickly under way. As the two men fight, the last of Charlie's belongings comes sailing over the bar. Both see it and realize what has happened. They approach the curtain, murder in their hearts. As they whip it open, Charlie, in a bathing suit, goes into a "living statue" posture, a most graceful one. He whips the curtains closed and then quickly open again and again to reveal a series of modeled studies, each more artistic than the last. The situation has vanished in the danced transformation.

Easy Street is an exquisite short comedy, humor encapsulated in the regular rhythms of light verse. Its patterns of movement are as candidly stylized as a *pas de deux*, detailing the narrative while begging leave to doubt its reality except as pure form. The film, incidentally, is the single Mutual comedy in which Chaplin first appears as a true "tramp," penniless, hungry, but not wanting a job. He would rather steal the collection box at a neighborhood mission house than work. Edna, the missionary's daughter, nonetheless inspires him to reform, and he accepts the role of policeman, rapping his captain's knuckles with his nightstick when the captain cordially slaps him on the back. He moves into a Hogarthian slum street, where Eric is already at work balletically beating up the entire populace. Having kissed Eric's hand by way of supplication, having temporarily gassed him and taken his pulse, the two men engage, inevitably, in a chase.

Chaplin's chases, now that he is designing them for sport rather than for suspense, have become compressed in space. He wants us to see the patterning, its repetitions and variations, all at once, rather than spread out over the landscape and the rooftops in slapstick's conventional manner. Here Charlie and Eric race up and down a single staircase, in and out of a single upstairs room, bolt through a first-story window to the street, and then in and up and out again. The pattern, swift and devious as it is, becomes habit; Charlie begins to dogtrot as though he had been programmed to staircase, room, window, street by a computer. He lets

Opposite: Detachment through dancing.

Top: The stance that ends *The Pawnshop*; the plot-defying solo flights in *The Floorwalker*.

Bottom: Off and away in *The Rink*.

Above: In the unstable environment of *One A.M.*

us know precisely how he feels about it all. He is loving it. So far from being fearful, he breaks into a quick grin for us as he makes one more tour of the stairs. Of course, this is the overconfident instant in which Eric nearly catches him.

The rhythmic exercise is brought to an end when Charlie drops an iron stove onto Eric's head from the upper room. Charlie is king of the street now, for a while, and he does what Eric has done before him: he saunters down its coarsely paved center while denizens of the area creep from their cellar lodgings to stare at him in awe, making undulating waves at the edge of the gutter; then he spins, his coattails flying, and all vanish like blown leaves.

His command of the weaving pattern is temporary, however. Edna has been kidnapped and is locked in a basement room with a rape-minded dope addict. Charlie arrives through the ceiling, accidentally sits on the addict's needle, and immediately flings himself into a precisely conceived and articulated battle *mécanique* that sees him delivering his final blow to the addict in a rhythm that will directly turn him into Edna's arms. The fight and the embrace are all one, beats in a completed tune. What is left that is real? Only the visual syncopation.

The Mutuals are the gayest of all the Chaplin films. There is no danger anymore. What can happen to a man who has no stake in things? No danger, at least, that cannot be danced away from, or even into. The dance will draw the plot's fangs—and its pleasures too. The best thing to do with thin ice is to skim over it, without weight. Chaplin continues to develop every sort of incidental gag—working as a waiter in *The Rink* he is asked by a customer for the bill and is able to establish what the gentleman has had for dinner by inspecting his tie, lapel, and ears. But at Mutual his main thrust was toward the hop, skip, and jump that brought him through the climactic mayhem unscathed, because disbelieving—in *The Adventurer*, in *Behind the Screen*. The latter film, in the new playfulness of its violence, offers us yet another master-image. Charlie is manning a huge lever that controls a trapdoor in the studio floor. As he gaily flings the lever this way and that, resting his head on it and kicking one heel high in air, dropping half the studio through the trap and catching emerging victims by the throat, his joy is entirely without malice. He doesn't even know what is happening to the destroyed world about him. He is in love with his toy, and with his own carefree relationship to it, just as he would be—destructively, and in the throes of a nervous breakdown that completely isolated him from his fellow workers—years later in *Modern Times*.

Just once at Mutual did he open himself to a wholehearted relationship with another person, with Edna. The event occurs in *The Immigrant*, a charming and ingeniously constructed film, and the change is instantly detectable. When he meets Edna on shipboard, before their arrival in America, his eyes behave differently. They don't fill with the automatic adoration or instant mooning that has marked the other films and has defeat already written on it; instead, he meets her gaze fully, smiles warmly, invites a return. He is offering her, for the first time, an unmistakable invitation. They are in the ship's dining room, such as it is: benches on either side of a planked table. The sea is rough, and the soup dishes have been sliding from one side of the table to the other, so that Charlie and the chap opposite him have had to take alternate sips. When Edna enters, Charlie gives her his place, then stays to stare at her. The stare is a plain promise that he is interested and available. Suddenly he becomes not a funny icon but familiar flesh. He may be as poor as she, he may make his stake as a gambler, he may be down to his last fifty-cent piece the next time they meet, but he is offering her one stability: if she will return his love, she may have it.

The film follows through on its premise. The two do meet again, in a beanery;

there is a brilliantly funny and complex pursuit of the nearly lost fifty-cent piece; the two are hired by a passing painter to pose for him. With work available, Chaplin wants marriage, drags Edna through the rain to get a license. Outside the bureau, she has a fit of shyness, starts to run away. Charlie catches her with his cane, kisses her, carries her kicking into the building. The rain keeps pouring down outside.

Chaplin would, it turns out, make one commitment. He would commit himself to a woman who could commit herself to him, as he was. That is still something of an ambiguity: the woman would be committing herself to, and accepting the commitment of, a man who could not commit himself. Plainly, Chaplin did not expect to find very many such women. He begins his romances with that knowledge on his face.

In subsequent films, he will again experiment with apparently completed romances. They are all, I think, brushed lightly with question marks. When, at the end of *A Dog's Life*, he comes in from his fairy-tale bean rows to pick up his Gretel and spin her around in his arms, the two turn their attention to a cradle nearby, stoop to it. In it are his faithful dog's newborn pups. The joke suggests that that is all we are to expect of this family. The ending of *The Gold Rush* tells us, in a single sequence, that Charlie gets the girl and—by means of a candid subtitle—that the picture should not end in this way. At the end of *Modern Times*, Charlie and his gamine go down the road as a pair. But she is under-age and on the run from the authorities. We may make what we will of each of these waivers.

In *The Immigrant*, there is no waiver at all. Chaplin seems able to accept without qualification Edna's acceptance of him. I am not certain that he ever again looked at one of his loves with the openness of feeling he showers on this motherless but fully mature girl. The surrender is simply uncharacteristic.

What can the exception have meant to Chaplin? I can only suppose he wishes to show us, at least once, that behind the dancing façade he has erected as a shield against the world's instabilities, there is—potentially at least—a whole man. He has met no whole man. He would still like to be one.

Above: Edna Purviance is the charming boy who so puzzles Charlie in *Behind the Screen*.

Left: One of Chaplin's very few appearances as a true tramp; the opening sequence of *Easy Street*.

11. Harold Lloyd: Hard Work

In attempting to trace the interior logic of Chaplin's growing character, I haven't meant to suggest that Chaplin himself pursued it in a rigidly systematic way, step by step, implication by implication. Artists, including great clowns, rarely work in so linear a fashion. They are apt to make their advances in intuitive leaps, *seeing* an image just ahead of them and going after it headlong rather than constructing it rationally. After all, Chaplin hit upon his basic costume in the second film he made and rarely altered its essential outlines thereafter; he simply had to find out, by trial and error and sudden inspiration, what was inside the outline. In the end, there *would* be subterranean connections, logical relationships, between all the inflections, the variations, the unforeseen consequences that went to fill up the costume. But the process of filling up, while it is still under way, is often subconscious.

Buster Keaton, for instance, protested to the end of his days that he had no notion of what his admirers were talking about when they spoke, as Andrew Sarris did, of his "cerebral" qualities, or when they detected a pervasive surrealism in his films that—considering the period in which the films were made—virtually placed him in the avant-garde. "I was just trying to get laughs" was his constant and stubborn answer to questions. Keaton was, in fact, a brilliant analyst of film, as his dazzling film-within-a-film in *Sherlock Jr.* plainly indicates: the sequence illustrates basic theories of continuity and cutting more vividly and with greater precision than theorists themselves have ever been able to do. But the analysis is not in Keaton's head. It is in the film. He went past cerebration and worked only with the thing itself, creating what amounts to theory out of his body, his camera, his fingers, a pair of scissors. Art is often something done before it is something thought; Keaton's impulses were not only stronger but more accurate than any verbal formulation he might have chosen to offer for them. Nor can Harry Langdon have arrived by any rational means at his "baby" image: a full-grown man actually chasing girls with the sweet, yearning awkwardness of a five-year-old. An image so preposterous could not be consciously constructed. It can only

have "come" to him, out of living tissue already on the move, in rehearsal, in performance—a gesture made instinctively before its significance could be grasped.

Among the principal clowns of the silent screen, Harold Lloyd was the exception. He had to think it all out. No impulsively assembled costume that was forever right, no gravely iconographic mask and stance that would mark him as almost from Mars, no infantile failure of motor-control that would abort all of his gestures in mid-flight. Lloyd was an ordinary man, like the rest of us: ungrotesque, uninspired. If he wanted to be a successful film comedian he would have to *learn* how to be one, and learn the hard way.

That was what took him so long. "Long" is a relative term in this context. After all, only seven years elapsed between the time that his friend and producer, Hal Roach, told him that he had to become the comedian of the company and the full realization of his character and his appeal in the feature-length *Grandma's Boy*. But Chaplin had defined himself in three years. Keaton managed it in not more than fifteen short films. Lloyd literally floundered through eighty to a hundred ten- or twenty-minute comedies before he even so much as glimpsed what he might honestly be about.

At least seventy of these were made without the horn-rimmed spectacles by which the comedian is now recognized, and though the films somehow managed to become successful enough to keep production going, Lloyd knew that he didn't know what he was doing and detested himself for it. In fact, he had more or less decided to give up comedy altogether and go into dramatic films when he stumbled upon the glasses. Even with the glasses, there was five more years' work to do: the early "glass" comedies—as Lloyd called them—had provided him with a distinctive visual image but an image that was still without purpose. In due time, Lloyd acquired skills that were superb of their kind. But they were acquired skills. He got no gift from the gods.

Actually, Lloyd appeared in a film before Chaplin did: in 1913, fresh from high school, he was paid three dollars one day by the Edison Company to cover himself with makeup and do extra work as a Yaqui Indian. In high school he had been as close to the All-American boy as stage-struck boys ever get: he was not only a good debater, he was a good boxer. He wanted to act but he wanted to act on the stage, and he did a great deal of work with stock companies touring the West Coast both before and after his voice broke. It was only when he could not get work in the legitimate theater that he turned, temporarily he hoped, to films.

The device by which he managed to get inside a studio—most directors had their favorite extras, and admission wasn't all that easy—reads like a partial scenario for one of his later films. Employed extras needed passes to get through the studio gate in the morning. Lloyd had none. But he noticed that when they went out at lunch-time in full makeup, the makeup alone was enough to get them past the gatekeeper at one o'clock. He thereupon dawdled away his mornings, made himself up lavishly during the noon hour, and joined the returning throng, with a casual wave to the gateman, for the afternoon's shooting. Lloyd was dogged, inventive, self-made. It hadn't occurred to him that he might someday play himself.

He met another young man, Hal Roach, in the extras' waiting room. In 1915 Roach acquired enough money to take a fling at production and invited Lloyd to come along, capacity undefined. When Roach's regular comedian departed after four quick failures, Roach—according to Harold Lloyd's *An American Comedy*, written in collaboration with Wesley W. Stout—turned to Lloyd and said, "Harold, you've got to be the low comedian. Think up some funny get-up and let's get busy." The funny get-up seems to have been an amalgam of all of Mack

Harold and Bebe Daniels in a 1917 "glass" film. Lloyd did not pursue the "glass" character exclusively for the first year or so, protecting himself by alternating his new image with the more familiar, and temporarily more profitable, Lonesome Luke films.

Sennett's bewhiskered, battered-hat gentlemen; the "character" was named Willie Work, and the two films that were made were unsuccessful. Lloyd learned just one thing in the process: the camera could be treacherous. After he had taken a bruising downhill fall between the tracks of a cable car, it was discovered that the camera had been so placed as to make the hill an utterly level road. The information would be helpful later.

Lloyd left Roach, did his brief stint at Sennett, then returned to see if between them they mightn't work out a more salable comic commodity. Lloyd's method of going about this perfectly describes his habit of mind. After he had acquired a pair of English shoes and a black-and-white vertically striped shirt, he added "the coat of a woman's tailored suit, a pair of very tight and short trousers, a vest too short, a cut-down collar, a cut-down hat, and two dots of a mustache." As he tells us in *An American Comedy*, "The cunning thought behind all this, you will observe, was to reverse the Chaplin outfit. All his clothes were too large, mine all too small."

What is of interest here is neither the admitted imitativeness nor the rather attractive candor but the entirely rational process itself. Lloyd invented nothing spontaneously. He had to figure out a "get-up," and he *figured* it out.

With the reverse-Chaplin costume, and with nothing more than that, he plunged into the long series of pre-glasses films in which he was known as Lonesome Luke. The physical image itself, lacking a core, was never very stable. The "two dots of a mustache" sometimes—as in *Movie Muddle*—turn into two faint trailing lines, almost Oriental in appearance, that are so far from meeting on his upper lip that in some shots he appears to have no mustache at all. *Movie Muddle* has only a beginning joke with which to make its way: Luke is simultaneously ticket-seller, ticket-taker, and usher in the theater in which he works. Apart from flirting with a pretty customer, the teenage Bebe Daniels, he has nothing more comic to do than fight reflexively and compulsively with the theater's projectionist, Harry "Snub" Pollard, who winds up entangled in thousands of feet of film. It would be difficult to say, as the film is fading out, which of the two—Pollard or Lloyd—is meant to be the comedian of the occasion.

The indebtedness to Chaplin was not merely a matter of an inverted costume, stable or unstable. In *Just "Nuts"* Lloyd uses a shuffling walk, shrugging his shoulders and handling his cigarette in Chaplin's manner. Even his normally "straight-American" hair has suddenly been marceled to a Chaplin bushiness. When he is knocked backward into an ashcan, he folds up like a deck chair precisely as Chaplin so often had done. When, at a drinking fountain, he succeeds in soaking the man next to him, he tips his hat. The one borrowed device he shows signs of absorbing naturally is the unbroken rhythm-shift: coming out of a door and seeing a cop, he immediately circles back in, without a sharp break of pace. Where this serves as a detaching, then a dancing, force for Chaplin, with Lloyd it is simply an isolated bit of business that says nothing about the "character."

He often misunderstood what he borrowed. In *Pipe the Whiskers* he ostentatiously removes his coat and hat from his private storage space, a grandfather clock. Chaplin, of course, had constantly stored things in unlikely places: in *The Pawnshop* he had kept his lunch locked away in the shop's vault; in *The Rink* he had gone into the kitchen of the restaurant in which he worked and removed *his* coat and hat from the stove. Both incongruities function as comedy because they contain implications our minds can play with: the lunch in the vault suggests that Charlie trusts *nobody*, and the stove-heated hat and coat may at least keep him warm, at some risk to the clothes. A grandfather clock, though, lacks both unsuitability and overtone. The shape of the clock is as close as anything can be to the

Opposite, above: The triple-play involves Harold, Noah Young, and Snub Pollard and leads, at right, to the rescue of Mildred Davis. *From Hand to Mouth.*

Below: Before the "glass" films, Lloyd appeared as Lonesome Luke, most often with Bebe Daniels.

shape of a closet. The clothes will be well-kept there; the choice is truly logical. And only logical. The "joke" is arbitrary, without dimension.

Nor would the later assumption of the "glass" character automatically change things. In *All Aboard* he would go to his furnished room, remove the meat for his dinner from a locked cashbox, dust it off, and put it in a frying pan. Keeping meat in a cashbox does not make us laugh. Substitutions of this kind, if they are to strike us as funny, must have an inappropriate appropriateness: the right job must be done by the wrong object. Here object *and* job are wrong: if we react at all to the sight of the unrefrigerated meat, we shudder. Lloyd was still following the blueprint of a joke without having grasped what it was meant to house.

William K. Everson, in his monograph on Hal Roach written for the Museum of Modern Art, has pointed out how closely the settings for Lloyd's films followed Chaplin's. As soon as Chaplin had made *The Fireman*, Lloyd made *Fireman, Save My Child.* As soon as Chaplin had made *The Cure*, laid in a health resort complete with medicinal well and gymnasium, Lloyd made *Pipe the Whiskers*, well and gymnasium intact. "The most blatant copy of all," Mr. Everson adds, "was perhaps *Lonesome Luke on Tin Can Alley*, which was released a scant two months after *Easy Street.*" The physical backgrounds were less stylized, and less attractive, than Chaplin's; but they plainly attempted to echo the back-alley mood.

Lloyd was by no means as conscienceless as he may seem from these instances. Aping Chaplin was common practice among comedians: Chaplin had become so popular and, by this time, so utterly in command of his character that he seemed not so much *a* funny man as *the* funny man, the comic font itself, an absolute from which all other work in the vein must necessarily be derived. Comedy was in effect defined as what Chaplin did, and Chaplinesque traits, bits of business, flourished everywhere. In at least one case, that of Billy West, an attempt was made not to imitate Chaplin but to *duplicate* him—by adopting every detail of costume and mannerism that Chaplin had developed. Harold Lloyd was simply struggling to make what he could of himself inside a prevailing and calmly accepted tradition.

It is possible, here and there in the Lonesome Luke films that survive, to see traces of a playfulness and a capacity for compounding gags that would become Lloyd's own. When a sheriff tucks his thumbs into his suspenders and flexes his knees in rhythmic contentment, Lloyd adopts the posture and seems happy rocking in rhythm with him. The business accomplishes nothing in particular, but it does foreshadow the half-cocky, half-wistful willingness to go along with the other fellow—up to a point—that marked the beginning of many of Lloyd's later gags. When he steps on the bandaged foot of a gouty patient and the patient throws up his hands in protest, Lloyd promptly begins a game of clap-hands with him. He is being no more unfeeling than any other clown of the period here; and he is beginning to make childlike metaphors.

In *Luke and the Bangtails* he rolls up his sleeves to announce a fight. The other fellow rolls up *his* sleeves. Lloyd rolls his down again. He is now on the track of something: the aggressive young fellow who has second thoughts. We get a glimpse of the Lloyd face in dismayed repose after he has lost his money gambling in *Tin Can Alley*. This image of rueful dejection, of a nice chap distressed that he is no more than he is, will become basic to the later Lloyd, mouth almost squared in pain, head bent slightly to one shoulder. But one must look quickly for it here: the *Lonesome Lukes*, having nowhere to go, go fast—entropy at full gallop. There is nothing personal enough to cry pause for close-ups.

In the main, the action of these early comedies is swift, brutal, and meaning-

less. Sometimes Lloyd disappears from a film for long stretches, almost as though it hadn't been built around him—a confession, no doubt, that he had been unable to invent business for himself in certain sequences and simply turned them over, in desperation, to his support. Sometimes he engages in business that shows him inept alongside competing clowns. In *his* spa, there are many elderly gentlemen in wheelchairs constantly on the go. He acquires a whistle and directs the wheelchair traffic. That is *almost* a joke; but it is uncomfortably close to what is merely reasonable. Buster Keaton, pursued in *The Haunted House* by dozens of sheeted figures, finally finds the place so congested that, with a sigh, he becomes a traffic cop for ghosts, turning this way and that with his arms extended so that the ectoplasmic parade will be orderly. That, I scarcely need say, is better.

And sometimes one can see Lloyd's inexperience turning into experience on the spot. In *Bangtails* a bale of hay has fallen on a stable-keeper, pinning him helplessly. Lloyd first stands on top of the bale of hay in order to try to pull it off the victim, a weak and irritating version of a standard ploy: the business of pulling a rug out from under oneself. But he has a second idea. He goes to the stables, gets a horse, brings him to the bale, and waits until the horse has eaten all the hay. He is beginning—it is very important—to develop patience in humor, and with it. The kind of parlay at which he would have no equal is on the verge of being born: Don't throw away the situation, follow a broad joke with a broader but at the same time more plausible one.

The discovery of the glasses did not quickly make Lloyd over. Nor did the discovery come out of *him*, out of a growing realization of who and what he might be. Dissatisfied as he was with what he had been doing, no flash of inspiration rescued him. He simply went to the movies one night, saw a pattern laid out before him, and adopted it. In his own words again:

"I saw a dramatic picture at a downtown theater. . . .The central character was a fighting parson, tolerant and peaceful until riled, then a tartar. Glasses emphasized his placidity. The heavy had stolen the girl, carrying her away on horseback. The parson leaped on another horse, pursued, overtook the villain, dragged him from his horse and the two were lost in a cloud of dust. When the dust cleared, the heavy lay prone and still, while the parson dusted his clothes with careless flecks of his handkerchief, replaced his glasses and resumed his ministerial calm."

That, of course, is an excellent description of the comic formula Lloyd would use in his maturity. It even contains an entire scene from one of his later silent features. *The Kid Brother* ends with just such a battle obscured entirely by its own dust, and it is a tribute to what Lloyd became that it seems fresh and even original in his final handling of it.

For the moment, however, he had acquired only the glasses, using them for the first time in the 1917 *Over the Fence*. They did not at once make him placid, or shy, or "peaceful until riled." Getting aboard ship, he would freely kick a tiny steward about. He would chase a little girl for blocks to snatch her cookie away, follow a man in quick-step for just as long waiting for the right moment to clout him with a block of wood. In a skating rink—even with the glasses, he continued to lean on Chaplin's locales—he would beat an elderly man on the head with his cane by way of applauding a contestant. The Sennett callousness died hard in everyone, and though a title might refer to Lloyd as "that rice pudding in pants," it was bumptiousness that drove the thirty-odd films he made during his first year in hornrims.

Lloyd, the thinking man, was shrewd. Keaton was helpless in the hands of the man who financed him. Chaplin, shrewd enough, had a still cannier half-

Harold spanking a pirate in *Captain Kidd's Kids.*

brother, Sydney, to do much of his planning. But Lloyd plotted his own course, with the expertise of a trained public-relations man, the moment he decided on the glasses—and before he had any clear vision of what the glasses might mean as "character." He had earlier advanced the Lonesome Luke films from one to two reels, and prestige might have demanded that he start off the "glass" comedies at that length. Instead, Lloyd insisted on returning to the simpler and less profitable ten-minute formula—for a reason. He knew that he could turn out a one-reeler each week, whereas the double length was somewhat unpredictable, as Chaplin was already learning. He wanted the "glasses" on the screen every week of the year and was determined to saturate the country with the image. The trademark came first; its contents would have to come along as they could. His calculation was successful. At the end of a year and a half, he was not only able to expand the "glass" films to twenty minutes each, he was able to get nearly ten times the rental fees for them.

But exposure alone wouldn't do the trick. Something in this agile, agitated, overeager young man would have to catch the fancy of the country other than his brashness. It *was* the brashness, and the breathless pace it generated, that helped to endear him to me as a child, I'm sure. A last-run movie house in my home town adopted the practice of running a short Lloyd comedy every Saturday afternoon, and faithful attendance became the ritual Lloyd had hoped it would be. Those of us who so delighted in him did not really think of him as an isolated star: he was one of a trio of maddened puppets—Lloyd, Bebe Daniels, Snub Pollard—whose wires were invisible but whose freedom to skim the landscape without any sort of friction left us gasping. A gasp is sometimes a substitute for laughter, and it sometimes becomes laughter as sheer release. It is evident now that Lloyd used it both ways, whether he had a joke to tell or not. We did respond in some exhilarated way to the marionettes' indifference to gravity and all other inhibitions as they proceeded to take staterooms, lunch counters, pool halls apart. The response, a relatively primitive one, is no longer there as the films rocket by today, though a faint memory of it returns in a sequence from *All Aboard*. Harold, stowed away in a trunk in order to pursue Bebe to Europe, is sliding from stateroom to stateroom as the ship rolls. The trunk rolls into Bebe's room just in time for him to pop up and kiss her good night, then rolls back again to the cabin in which an enemy awaits him. The business is over in a few seconds, but every few seconds contain just as much precisely-timed movement. Sleight-of-foot, sleight-of-props, kept the carousel revolving—while Lloyd went on struggling to find something richer.

There is a suggestion of something richer in an unexpectedly charming one-reel film, *Spring Fever*. Suddenly Lloyd has given over falling into bass drums and walking around in them to offer himself instead as a quite ordinary office clerk who can't keep his mind on his bookkeeping. The weather, coming in the window, is far too nice. He keeps straying to the window, watching children running around trees and lovers boating on the river, thoughtlessly tearing up his account sheets as he yearns for the outdoors. His employer and fellow clerks constantly return him to his desk. Unable to control the urge inside him, he grabs his straw hat from the office rack and tries to escape. He is caught, his hat returned to its proper place. He tries again with the same results. The third time he has the foresight to pluck two identical hats from the rack so that when the one he is wearing is snatched from him on his way out he is able to replace it instantly and move on without a rhythm-break.

Once outside, Harold's spirits erupt. He skips across the grass, links arms with a courting couple, tries to settle arguments on park benches, eventually

Opposite: Harold at bay in *Bumping into Broadway*.

engages in a spontaneous pursuit of Bebe Daniels—who is running from suitor Snub Pollard—around an enormous bush. His exuberance often misfires and sends the beneficiaries of his ardor toppling into ashcans, and the film finally is as physical as any other Lloyd film. But the impulse behind it is one of irresistible high spirits. Lloyd skipping innocently is a happier man than Lloyd thrashing wantonly.

Though his interest in Bebe Daniels is a spur-of-the-moment thing in *Spring Fever* and comes to an emotionally routine conclusion—it is the weather, not the girl, that moves him—Lloyd gradually, in other films, was finding some use for his heroine, beginning to look at her with greater curiosity, occasionally letting us see him twisting his fingers awkwardly and a shade ruefully as he stared from a doorway. But Miss Daniels, like Chaplin's Mabel Normand, was a comedienne in her own right: a spirited creature well able to answer for herself. It wasn't until she finally left Roach to make features for Cecil B. De Mille that Lloyd acquired—in Mildred Davis, whom he later married—the kind of Nell Brinkley girl, soft ringlets framing her dimples, who would have enough delicacy to slow him down. The minister's daughter down the block, which is what Miss Davis seemed to be, had to be taken care of.

At first he took care of her with his customary aplomb, often in top hat, at least once in a prince's regalia, becoming so engrossed in her that he quite forgot to order an honor guard to stop marching until it had marched, unhesitatingly, into a pool. But by this time a much more fundamental change was taking place in Lloyd. From his extended apprenticeship he was learning one crucial thing: for his kind of comedy, if he was going to have any kind of his own, it was best not to be *too* accomplished, best for triumph not to come easily.

Chaplin could be an instant expert at everything and triumph so effortlessly that his climaxes could be danced; that was all right because there was an interior shadow haunting him the whole time. But Lloyd possessed no such shadow, no such intimation of ultimate distress. He was unmistakably young, he was now neatly dressed, he was eminently marriageable, he was obviously destined for the ranks of solid citizenry. Given his transparent normality, he would have to emphasize not the ease but the difficulty he encountered in managing any situation at all. This may seem an obvious prescription: clowns usually have difficulties. But Chaplin had become the new norm, had set a mold difficult for competitors to break. And Lloyd had his own extravagant energies to contend with.

If he was going to emphasize difficulty, he would still need an outlet for those energies. He would also still need the brickbat, the chase and the pace, expected of silent film comedy. He learned, gradually, how to let the difficulty lead to the delirium, how to get into trouble backward. In *Don't Shove* he begins a sequence with a reversal that does not immediately involve himself. Noah Young, an oversized bully, is attacked by a medium-sized rival; Young immediately bursts into tears and threatens to tell his "little brother Willie" on his assailant. Little Brother Willie, a mere child, comes along, and, with a few quick rabbit-punches, disposes of the offender. Harold, who has been observing the situation at a safe distance, promptly asks Little Willie to teach him to box. Willie is willing, and the lesson begins. A policeman strolls by. Swinging wild, Harold clouts the policeman. The chase is on. But it has begun in Harold's confessed incompetence, not in his aggressiveness or his skill. We are much more amused than we were when he was mauling pint-sized bellhops.

In *From Hand to Mouth* he works out what would become a classic reversal. For all of his screen life he has been running from policemen, as have his fellow clowns: policemen automatically chase comedians, with or without cause. This time he cannot get a policeman to chase him. He is desperately in need of one. Miss Davis has been kidnapped and is being held in a shack. He expostulates with a corner cop, pleads with him to come. The cop, deep in casual conversation with a friend, simply brushes him away. So do others. He is frantic. A thought overtakes him. He sticks out his tongue at one, who *does* start after him. Beginning to run and passing other policemen, Lloyd whacks one, trips another, turns a hose on a third, throws rocks, eventually smashes the plate-glass window of the police station itself as he races by. By this time he has the entire force in action against him, pursuing him directly to the shack, where of course Mildred is rescued. He has done all the damage he used to do out of unadulterated cockiness, but he has now done it from dire need—indeed, out of utter helplessness.

Where in earlier films he was able to manage the unlikeliest situations with a snap of his fingers—in *Fireman, Save My Child* he saved a building that was being ravaged by fire simply by blowing the fire out—he now begins to have trouble with the most elementary tasks. His new incompetence leads him into highly conventional comedy, unfunny today: he makes a mess of the kitchen trying to put a nipple on a baby's bottle; his hair frizzes upward to stand on end in fright when he is confronted by ghosts. It also leads him into something much less conventional by the standards of the day. He has enormous difficulty, for instance, in committing suicide. Just why Lloyd uses the suicide motif more often than other clowns is difficult to say. He employs it in at least three of his short "glass" films. In one he is first seen with a pistol at his temple; the weapon turns out, rather feebly from a comic or any other point of view, to be a water pistol. He then goes to a bridge and climbs over the railing. A passer-by stops, not to plead with him but to ask for a light. He supplies the match, readies himself to jump again. Another passer-by asks him for the time. He supplies that too, letting the ironies fall where they may. Then he jumps. He lands upright in a canoe and is carried away, frustrated and safe.

In another he repeats the opening business with the pistol almost exactly, extending it by placing himself directly in front of an oncoming streetcar which curves to a side-track just before it can accommodate him. He then goes to the bridge, where he takes care to put cotton in his ears against possibly dirty water. This time, however, he arrives at what may be called a Lloyd master-shot, one involving perfect placement of the camera. When he leaps from the bridge, he lands upright and just ankle-deep in water. The effect is as startling as it is funny. For we have totally believed, through the camera's eye, in the water's depth. The shot is a long one, embracing the span of the bridge and a considerable body of water; there are no telltale ripples to suggest shallowness or shore anywhere; the very scope of the image implies depth. The camera has not for a moment lied; we see all that is there to see; and we share Lloyd's shock at his discovery. The truth itself can be deceptive, and laughter is born of the news. In his feature "thrill" films, Lloyd's use of the camera would be masterly in much the same way.

The third suicide attempt comes in one of the short "thrill" films, *Never Weaken*. Harold is in the process of shooting himself, indirectly, by means of a complicated apparatus involving a doorknob, a telephone, and string tied to a trigger. Suicide remains difficult, requires ingenuity. While he is waiting for death, an even more elaborate promise of death overtakes him as he is inadvertently swung out on a girder over a high building under construction.

Conceivably, the threats of death by suicide and death by stunting were linked in Lloyd's mind, one leading to the other. The effort at suicide would, happily, always fail; that was the comedy of it. What about death by stunting? A tingle of possibility stirs. The brash man is hideously vulnerable.

Bebe Daniels with Harold at the well in a 1918 "glass" film.

12. The Roach Lot: A Bit More Method in the Madness

Hal Roach, in a conversation with William K. Everson, said of Lloyd that "of course he wasn't funny in himself; he needed his writers and a constant stream of gags. I remember in our early days together he was always so concerned about being a comedian all the time. A transition shot might just call for him to walk out of a door and across a room. Midway he'd stop in his tracks, turn to me and say, 'What do I do to be funny?'"

The gags and the situations that triggered them were provided by a stable of idea-men, not so much writers as split-second improvisers who could match wits with one another in an office or on the set before the comedians came to work for the day. Lloyd needed such a stable more than the other major comedians and eventually put together an extraordinarily capable one which would never abandon a joke without at least tripling its effect. But all studios producing comedies had staffs of this sort: Sennett sat in his oversized bathtub in a glassed-in penthouse accepting and discarding his team's improvisations for the dozen or more films in production, then watched the work in progress from his windows. Frank Capra has told us in *The Name Above the Title* what it was like for a gag-man to feel Sennett's lash.

Hal Roach, who comes across a bland man in most film histories, seems not to have used a lash. Though he often functioned as a director himself, he was either quickly bored by the task or felt inadequate to it: doing a two-reeler with Lloyd he might throw up his hands midway in the second reel, urging the clowns to "wrap it up" themselves or providing someone else to guide them. He needed, or wanted, help as much as Lloyd did. He got it by making the studio the most relaxed and friendliest in the business. Instead of creating an atmosphere of intense competitive pressure, he encouraged his hirelings to doodle, to invent by amusing one another, to lend a hand in any capacity that offered itself. As a result, the Roach studio matured more first-rate directors than any other—Leo McCarey, George Stevens, and George Marshall among them. More importantly, work at the studio was casually cooperative: Stan Laurel, generally held to be the swiftest improviser after Chaplin, would answer a call to Charley Chase's set to help construct an elusive gag; Chase, joining Roach after some years of straight slapstick at Sennett, would reply in kind by directing Laurel or any of their other companions on the lot.

Roach has always stood second to Sennett in the public imagination, partly because Sennett established the formula which Roach was willing enough to borrow, partly because Sennett the man was decidedly the more assertive figure. Roach had no personal flamboyance to contribute to legend; he remains an "enigma" to Mr. Everson and no more than a title-credit to most others. A glance at the short comedies made at his studio in the late teens and early twenties, however, at once suggests that the work Roach coddled into being is in fact more inventive and more flexible than Sennett's. In the end it was Roach who had the greater staying power. Roach had no notion whatever of abandoning the original Sennett impulse, but he did have some interesting variations to play upon it.

The Sennett outline is virtually intact, for instance, in a 1923 Roach comedy starring Snub Pollard and Jimmy Finlayson called *Sold at Auction*. Pollard, with his upside-down Kaiser Wilhelm mustache and eyes that seemed constantly about to brim with tears, had been dropped from the Lloyd comedies as Lloyd's character grew more "normal." Finlayson, whose mustache seemed electrified as it leapt from his lip in two bristling straight lines, was a Scotsman with a gift for squinting one eye while irising open the other until it seemed to possess the warning power of a lighthouse.

The outline? While Finlayson and his family are on vacation, Pollard mistakenly auctions off the entire contents of their home. With Finlayson's return, every last item must be recovered, not only the grand piano—at present on a runaway slide downhill—but a pair of false teeth. The teeth themselves generate a chase of spectacular proportions. They have been bought by an airplane pilot. Pollard takes off after him in a second plane, demolishes a barn in the process, acquires a pig on one wing, climbs out to rescue it, then falls from the wing to an oil derrick where his foot is entangled in a rope that swings him in a great arc directly into the plane he is pursuing. The teeth, thanks to everything that Keystone bequeathed Roach, are recovered.

But within the film are signs of a slightly different mind at work. When Finlayson goes on vacation, he goes on a motorcycle. The motorcycle has four sidecars in a row, one for each member of the family. Naturally, it occupies the entire street. Eventually, during a chase, it picks up four marching policemen, carrying on with its new cargo at top speed. Sennett would have built a trick car of some sort, one that perhaps could be stretched like rubber to make room for additional riders. Roach is a shade more strict. Many motorcycles have sidecars. Why not keep adding sidecars to the sidecars? The notion is nearly feasible. There is really only one thing wrong with it: in order to get it through traffic, traffic will have to be destroyed. Roach arrives at as much destruction as Sennett could conceivably have desired, but he does it with a point of logic carried farther than logic will go. The preposterous is always funnier for having been sanely thought out.

Roach's short comedies dip straight to the bottom of Sennett's bag of tricks, occasionally employing one of the cheapest. Whenever an incidental effect was wanted that could not easily be photographed—the buzzing of a bee around a comedian's face, for instance—Sennett and his fellows thought nothing of adding pen-and-ink animation to the photographed human image. A comedian might take

The Sennett influence carries over: Clyde Cook and friend dangling from a precariously moored train. *Wandering Papas.*

a bottle of whiskey from the shelf, the label might—courtesy of animation—turn into a death's head, the death's head might wink at him. The technique is, obviously, a violation of form. The camera has photographed one thing, cartoonists have superimposed another. Straight animation is a field of its own, a specifically limited one: the camera helps naked lines to move. If I have chosen not to treat animation in this book—despite the ingenuity and genuine imagination that went into Max Fleischer's *Out of the Inkwell* cartoons or into Disney's happy pre-sound experiments with *Oswald the Lucky Rabbit*—it is because animation does its work, in brief spurts, outside the realm of factual fantasy that was silent film comedy's distinctive vein.

When Roach employed pen-and-ink superimposition on a photographed shot, however, there was often a second step to help justify the invasion. In *Sold at Auction* we see wasps congregating on Jimmy Finlayson's shirt collar, and the wasps are inked in. But Roach at least pauses over the business long enough to call attention to what is going on, to develop a gag-within-the-gag. The wasps engage in a precise military drill, forming in ranks and advancing smartly, before attacking. The joke is as much *on* the film as in it.

The film—not at all an important one but reasonably representative of what may be done on one lot rather than another—contains other pleasantries. Snub Pollard manages to get aboard that grand piano as it rolls dizzyingly downhill, heading for an intersection. He stops it just in time by pressing the soft pedal. At the end of the film, Pollard is prepared to hang himself from a lamppost. A policeman strolls by and watches with interest but without concern as the would-be suicide strings himself up. As luck would have it, Pollard doesn't kill himself; he breaks the lamppost. The policeman becomes furious and immediately gives chase.

This last is an obvious echo of those disinterested passers-by who saw Lloyd poised on a bridge and casually asked the time of day. It is also a forerunner of all those policemen and bystanders who would watch while Laurel and Hardy began their wilder depredations, staring with curiosity and only a little disbelief, intervening not at all until personally attacked or until shocked by the failure to observe some small social nicety. On the Roach lot it was thought funny—and it was funny—to let the workaday world take outrage quite for granted, temporarily at least. Of *course* people killed themselves and wantonly whitewashed automobile after automobile along the street. Madness was the norm. But in Sennett's comedies, where madness was also the norm, no one ever held still long enough to say so. At Sennett all present leapt to the attack on the instant, giving the films a single dimension. At Roach the background was filled in: here were ordinary people seeing nothing at all extraordinary in the unusual things going on about them. Their passivity made the world insane on the double. It also, unpredictably, made it more human: there was a psychological truth inside the inertia. Further, it established a new and more profitable rhythm for slapstick without taking anything away from the ultimate slapstick itself. The work, destructive or self-destructive, could begin in an infinite calm, with great deliberateness. It could pursue its course without interference for quite a long while; no hurry. Then, when it was time, acceleration could come gradually, having so unruffled a rhythm to rest on. Once it did get going, it could go anywhere at all—faster for the contrast with what had gone before.

We are in part anticipating here, with the late-silent images of Laurel and Hardy so fresh in our minds; but the seeds of the style were studio seeds and can be seen sending up first shoots in the work of so minor a comedian as Snub Pollard. Roach continued to star Pollard in two-reelers for a considerable time in the twenties, though never with anything like the success he was having with Lloyd or would have with Laurel and Hardy. Two things worked against Pollard, one personal, the other a matter of the basic drift of the lot itself.

Pollard, like so many other of the likeable secondary buffoons who tumbled to near-fame in the company of the major stars, lacked the comic discretion that great clowning wants. There is a Pollard film called *At the Ringside* that might almost be used as a final examination in a school for comedians-in-training. A moment arrives when Pollard is in the ring with Noah Young, battling for the hundred-dollar purse that gave rise to so many screen comedies. Pollard's girl at ringside, eager to help her hero, has just blown pepper in Young's direction, and he, with a mighty expansion of his chest, is about to sneeze. Question for a beginning comedian: At just what point in the sneeze—on the rising "Ahhh" or the descending "Choo!"—do you hit him? In the film Pollard hits him on the uptake, halfway through the sneeze. The timing could not be more wrong. Seeing him do it, we don't *like* him. A sneeze is a convulsive thing, painful until completed. Obviously the right timing for the blow is one beat *after* the "Choo!," giving Young his satisfaction just before he is given his comeuppance and allowing for a one-two-three progression inside the gag. Pollard's own comic instincts were unreliable.

And his heavily mustached-and-eyebrowed image, derived from Sennett, was no longer the fundamental image of the Roach lot. Roach did keep mustached and bearded comedians about him—Jimmy Finlayson and Andy Clyde, appearing in supporting roles after their individual series had failed, the Jewish comedian Max Davidson with his natural beard—but, whether consciously or not, he seemed to want to move in another direction. He wanted to take off the masks.

Possibly he thought the human face was funny enough as it was. Certainly Laurel's and Hardy's turned out to be. But Roach, like Sennett, had begun making films with a half-formed vision of what he one day might do. Sennett had projected, however vaguely at the outset, a series of comedies about cops. Roach had always wanted to make a series about children. There may have been more than that to it. In speaking to Mr. Everson about comedy in general he said, "One of the big secrets of successful comedy is in relating it all to childhood. Laurel and Hardy built their whole routine around that."

He got his series about children in the enormously successful Our Gang comedies. But even as he was developing these, he was beginning to turn his adult comedians into something close to their equivalents. In fact, the real children and the overage children turn up together in a Charley Chase comedy called *Fraidy Cat*. The trimly mustached Chase, a timid young man in a suit as neat as Lloyd's, has visited his doctor and been told to "diet a week." Mistaking the doctor's phrase for the information that he will "die in a week," he promptly overcomes his natural cowardice. He beats up the first passers-by he meets, who just happen to be the small children of Our Gang. That is not good comic business, but no matter.

Elsewhere in the film, during one of his reversions to cowardice, Chase simply stands frozen while a tormentor snaps his bow tie against his Adam's apple, grips the lapels of his coat and tears them slowly downward, turns him around and rips apart the tails of his jacket. Once again we are looking at material that will be extensively, even ritualistically, developed by Laurel and Hardy, quite possibly with Chase's connivance. But the thought does occur: Only children—whether out of obedience or fear—permit this sort of systematic insult and despoliation. In the Chase film his childlike impotence is immediately underscored when his tormentor is beaten away with a broom by his aged mother. The image is virtually

Rooftop decapitation: Clyde Cook at the mercy of James Finlayson's scimitar. *Moonlight and Noses.*

identical with one in Lloyd's *Grandma's Boy*: a bully gets the broom from grandma. Indeed, the image gives birth to one of Roach's most frequently used plots: the weakling hero made brave by a kindly old lady.

The appearance of some members of Our Gang in this film, by the way, reflects a minor but charming and entirely characteristic practice of the Roach studio. Comedians often dropped briefly into one another's films with an air of real spontaneity. In one Our Gang comedy the Gang manages to break into a movie studio by inserting themselves quite satisfactorily among prop dummies being trucked into the lot. Once in, they are discovered and chased. The chase takes them past Harold Lloyd working against a South American background. They appeal to Lloyd for help. He obliges by hiding them under a variety of sombreros that are scattered about on the ground. The episode is visually amusing; it becomes a little something more than that because Lloyd enters so wholeheartedly into the game, quite as though he were an eager and unself-conscious bit player again. Will Rogers appears just as casually with the Gang in *Jubilo, Jr.*

The Our Gang comedies themselves were, for all their domestic orientation toward home, birthday parties, and mock bullfights in the backyard, gauged to an attractive level of fantasy. The Gang—fat Joe Cobb, curly-headed Mary Kornman, freckled Mickey Daniels, tiny black Farina and the rest—are capable of considerable invention, constructing their own locomotive from abandoned boilers, washtubs, and orange crates, with a dog-drawn taxi awaiting the engine as it chugs into its own private station. Devising their own amusement park, they keep shooting-gallery targets moving by using guinea-pig power, turn a goat into a camel by strapping two derbies to its back. In one film Mickey Daniels, a child with an extraordinarily sensitive face, succeeds in escaping piano practice by rigging an ingenious set of pulleys connected on one end to the keys and on the other to a half-dozen kittens, while relieving his younger brother of saxophone practice by attaching a bellows to the mouthpiece and connecting *that* to their father's rocking chair. Sometimes the gagging is routine or forced: Joe Cobb, neglected by his mother, bakes his own birthday cake, inadvertently filling it with tacks, soap, and so many other unassimilable elements that it bulges out of the oven in Mack Sennett excess. But in their more ambitious moments the youngsters walk a delicate but secure line between what is possible for children to accomplish and what the dream-silence of film invited.

The *Our Gang* personnel varied somewhat from season to season but fat Joe Cobb and little black Farina were stalwarts.

The comedies are also somewhat advanced for the period in their matter-of-

fact acceptance of Farina as a full-fledged member of the group. Racial stereotypes were everywhere in silent film, and Farina may have simply fitted into the waiver that acknowledged all "pickaninnies" to be "cute." Comedians used blacks and, slightly less often, Jews as readily available quick-jokes. Blacks gambled, shook their knees in fright when a cat stirred under a sheet, avoided work. Chaplin used racial humor much less often than his colleagues: when his street-peddlers were unmistakably Jewish, he did not mock them for it, but played them straight; when, in *City Lights*, a black prizefighter anointed himself with a rabbit's foot before entering the ring, Chaplin was at the very least as superstitious as he. Keaton would often use a much more unpleasant device. In search of a woman to marry, he would trail one on the street—only to discover on coming level with her that she was black and promptly reverse his steps. Lloyd would enter a burning building to rescue the heroine and emerge, blinded by smoke, with a black. I suppose we can be grateful that he did not throw her back in. And, bargaining in a pawnshop with the hand-wringing Jewish proprietor, Lloyd would unconsciously wind up wringing his own hands in the stereotype's rhythm.

If most of these usages are offensive now, they were simply unconsidered then. There was no public movement to call attention to what was discriminatory or demeaning; the black and Jewish performers were to all appearances perfectly willing to play along; the American air was simply being thoughtlessly inhaled. The fault was not in the films but in the society; the images were learned signals producing an automatic response.

Farina, however, moved about socially without question. If there was a birthday party at a white child's home, Farina would of course be invited, would of course bring a gift, would of course be made welcome. More curiously, if the Gang formed its own secret society patently modeled on the Ku Klux Klan, called it the Cluck Cluck Clams and wore white sheets to meetings, Farina and his black brother would not only be routinely accepted as members but would appear—without any apparent awareness of ambiguity—wearing the white sheets. The mind reels from time to time, but the films sail on, having it both ways—or, in Farina's case, no troubled way at all.

At the same time there is a sequence that leaves me gasping and confused. I do not know the name of the film in which it appears; I have been able to see it only in fragments. But a chimpanzee—Roach made a series of films called *The Dippy Doo-Dads* starring animals—enters the frame and sits on a curbstone.

Shortly, Farina appears and sits beside him. There is no real business between them. They are simply placed side by side, and one can only be shocked to think that the camera is doing nothing but comparing them. Then a grown black man comes by—he may or may not be Farina's father—to see the two sitting side by side, yank Farina to his feet, and haul him away, scolding furiously. The psychological implications of the sequence and their possible function as comedy baffle me altogether.

In the process of removing the masks, Roach drew to the studio performers known for their faces. He tried to make short-comedy stars of stage and screen performers whose luck had at least temporarily run out—Priscilla Dean, Theda Bara, and Lionel Barrymore among them. Roach had no luck with this venture: the performers hadn't been clowns and no longer had youth enough or doggedness enough to set about learning as Lloyd was learning. It is merely embarrassing now to watch Lionel Barrymore try to light a cigarette by unthinkingly putting the match in his mouth or to see him staggering under the burden of a drunken Gertrude Astor until both have toppled backward into a pool.

Roach had only slightly better luck with Will Rogers, who had been on the Broadway stage and had made feature films but was now "between" careers. Rogers made two reasonably successful shorts, *Uncensored Movies* and *Big Moments from Little Pictures*, in which he kidded other men's films: as Valentino he flourished his cape at a bull until a propman carelessly removed the bull's horns; as Douglas Fairbanks he shot an arrow into an arrow; as Ford Sterling of the Keystone Kops he let loose a gaggle of driverless autos that spread out over a field and then turned in demonic unison to advance upon *him*. In comedies in which he played a cowpoke yearned after by spinsters, he kept the kidding alive in titles: one title in *The Cake Eater* interrupts the horseplay to announce that someday someone will make a film showing cowboys at work, "but the public isn't ready for it yet." A second exclaims: "Another novelty! A girl comes to a ranch who isn't a school teacher." The credits read "Titles by Will Rogers," as indeed they should; whatever humor is in these films is both interpolated and verbal, and Rogers and Roach finally gave up the effort, with Rogers remarking, "All I do is run around barns and lose my pants."

While Roach was branching out in a number of directions, some swiftly unprofitable but most converging to create a distinctive style, Lloyd—now pretty much in charge of his own corner of the lot—was beginning to intersperse his marriage-and-chase comedies with the "thrill" films that were to become his single most distinctive contribution to silent film comedy. Stunt men had been at work all along—*Love, Speed, and Thrills* was a typical Mack Sennett title. But the stunting had been bravura or trick stuff: successful leaps from trains to autos, from trees to horseback, from tower to airplane, from bridge to steamer. Somehow, no one had discovered the skin-prickling excitement of simply climbing.

Lloyd had begun to climb: girders, window ledges, later on whole buildings. He did not present himself as a competent climber, or a confident one. He presented himself as awkward and terrified. The concept of difficulty, of vulnerability, had by this time taken firm hold. More than that, it was now ready to reach out for ultimates: no matter how much spunk a man had, he couldn't be very sure of himself hanging from an unmoored girder nine or ten stories up.

The first short "thrill" film was a one-reeler called *Look Out Below*, in which Lloyd performed on a structure of girders built directly over a railway tunnel. The notion was "original with us as far as I know," Lloyd tells us, adding that "neither it nor any of its three descendants contained any doubling, double exposure, or trick photography."

The second placed the heroine in as much danger as himself. In *High and Dizzy*, directed by Roach, Mildred Davis appears as a sleepwalker, straying onto the window ledge of her hotel room in her wanderings, passing Harold's window and thus luring him to the rescue. He is, unfortunately, tipsy. On the outside of the building, he grabs at a rain spout that promptly bends him well over the street; then, slipping on a bar of soap, he winds up clinging to the ledge by his fingernails. While he is kicking at a window in the floor below, hoping for help, the minister who inhabits the lower apartment appears to reprove him for "disturbing my study." At least the minister is available a few moments later to marry Harold and Mildred, all leaning out of their respective windows and using the cord-ring of a window shade to complete the ceremony before Mildred's father can break down the apartment door and call halt.

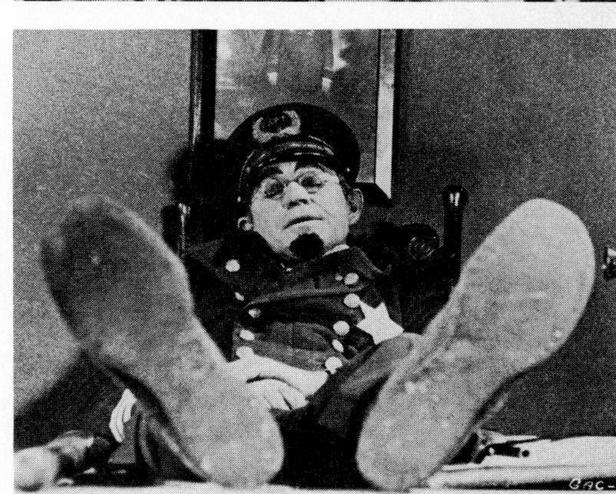

The first half of *Never Weaken*, made in 1921, is standard Lloyd of the period. Mildred is about to lose her job as secretary to a chiropractor—no patients. Harold, thoroughly resourceful at the outset, hires an acrobat to take falls in the street and pretend injury so that he can manipulate him back to health on the spot and then pass out cards recommending Mildred's employer. Spying a water-wagon, he scatters soap-flakes about the street in its trail so that the whole world will be upended and have to resort to medical help. These are thought-out gags, products of the conference room, glib and functional and coolly impersonal. Lloyd almost seems a traveling salesman with a line of merchandisable jokes, rather strained ones.

But the atmosphere, and the quality of the comedy, change abruptly once Harold has wound up astride a swinging beam hundreds of feet in the air. Now everything eludes him. If he grabs at a fixed stanchion in the open network, one foot becomes hopelessly caught on a girder being swung away. If he climbs a ladder, the ladder is climbing too, leaving him dangling from its last rung and rising higher in the void. If he leaps from contact with a hot rivet to an upright ahead, the upright glides out into space at his touch. If he huddles on hands and knees on a girder that seems permanent, another girder moves inexorably forward to brush him off. If, dropping, he lands on a catwalk plank, the plank becomes a teeter-totter, spilling him toward the street again. The invention is staggering, the surprises breath-taking; I know people who still find the film painful to watch. The scramble at skyscraper height is resolved by what became a characteristic Lloyd inversion: having closed his eyes tight against the lost future, he arrives at a construction elevator that carries him to the ground. Unaware of what has happened, he continues to grope his way forward, making contact with an as yet unused beam and inching along it at snail's pace in full view of puzzled workmen. Eventually he touches a policeman's leg, grips it for security, cocks his head, opens his eyes, blinks, tests the earth to make certain that is what it is, then sighs and grips the workman's leg tighter. He is human after all. Pressing his vulnerability to human-fly proportions, Lloyd has come very close to establishing a "character" for his bespectacled image, a fusion of the contradictory strains he had so labored to develop.

Aggressiveness, both native to him and inherited from the film comedy tradition, was clearly not enough in itself to give Lloyd any real distinction; it doesn't in the first half of *Never Weaken*. But if the aggression could be made inadvertent, if it could be provoked by sheer helplessness, if it could be drawn upon under the pressure of absolute necessity and imminent peril of death, *then* it would be consistent with the look of the nice young man. Let everything be horrendously difficult for the nice young man; then call upon his grit.

Will Rogers appeared most often as a cowpoke but occasionally, as below, he liked impersonating other clowns in parodies of their films. That is he, not Ford Sterling, in *Big Moments from Little Pictures*.

Overleaf: Lloyd's toying with "thrill" films was still tentative in *High and Dizzy*, much more thorough as he tangled with the girders of *Never Weaken*.

The Roach Lot: A Bit More Method in the Madness

Harold Lloyd wound up playing himself. Starting off with no true gift for inventing any other *persona*, no lucky insight that would give him instant mythological status; straining this way and that to ape or approximate or invert other men's work; putting his intelligence to the task of learning, and keeping at it even when he was himself filled with dismay, he arrived at the one character he was qualified to play, the one image he could adopt with complete integrity: his own.

How close the screen figure is to the man may be better realized when we remember that all the climbing he did, after the first brief experiment, was done with a sadly damaged right hand. In 1919, while he was making a two-reel "glass" picture called *Haunted Spooks*, he was asked to pose for still photographs. Someone brought him a prop bomb: for a gag shot, he was to use its already sputtering fuse to light his cigarette. The bomb, inexplicably, turned out to be a real one. It detonated with enough force to tear out the roof of the studio. In the hospital, Lloyd's sight was at first thought lost. He despaired of ever acting again. Typically, he cheered himself up by telling himself that acting wasn't necessary to him, he could direct: there was undoubtedly both courage *and* truth in the thought. His sight was saved, his extensive facial scars were successfully treated. In the end, he came away with only one impairment: the bomb had blown away the thumb and index finger of his right hand. Interestingly, in his 1926 *An American Comedy*, he describes the explosion, and its possible implications for his future, in great detail—without mentioning that anything had happened to his hand. Undoubtedly he did not want this information to linger with the audience as it watched him stunting: that would create *too* much apprehension, too much sympathy, for comedy. In any event, he put on gloves over rubber fingers and went on doing what he had been doing.

Lloyd climbing was Lloyd climbing.

13. An Inquisitive Keaton and a Generous Arbuckle

Buster Keaton was the man who entered the shooting gallery in which he worked, picked up a paintpot and brush, painted a hook on the wall, and hung his hat on the hook. Buster Keaton was the man who, chased by thugs and trapped in a room offering no available exit, spied a seascape on the wall and dived into it. Buster Keaton was the man who sat, a prisoner on shipboard, morosely looking at the world through a porthole, only to have his captor enter the cabin and remove the porthole. Buster Keaton was the man for whom the physical universe was exactly as flat, as falsely dimensional, as the screen on which film was shown.

On entering films, Keaton literally entered the screen—slipped into it sidewise, there being no third dimension—and welded himself fast to its illusionistic properties. He became indistinguishable from the screen and the film projected on it, inseparable from the contracted backgrounds in which he was placed, spawn of the camera eye, plaything of the projector's sprockets. He was strict about the world he inhabited, strict about his place in it. Though he often spoke of "camera tricks," he played no tricks *on* the camera; Sennett's rigged props, Sennett's evasions of the possible, did not interest him. What interested him—almost to mania—was the form into which he had stumbled, its natural peculiarities which could be embraced to the point where he dissolved into them but which must never be violated by an excess of reality *or* of fantasy. The camera and screen together had, in some measure, falsified reality; Keaton would be that false and no more. Camera and screen together had also in some measure "improved" on reality, offered it certain escape hatches; Keaton would capitalize on all the open ends with a placid confidence. He did not so much use the camera as join it on its journey. This involved a high degree of surrender on his part, as though he were putting out his hands to the handcuffs and saying, "All right, I'll go quietly." Quietly, he went. He was the most silent, as well as the most cinematic, of silent screen comedians.

His "surrealism," then, was nothing like a conscious—or even unconscious—

borrowing from other art forms then coming into vogue; neither was it a response to a philosophical stirring in the general air. It was, very simply and very purely, an exhaustive investigation of a medium that had just been born, that had never been tested to its extremities before, and that was—when carefully examined—very odd. Chaplin was using his otherwise neglected camera to establish intimacy and focus. Lloyd was finally playing with camera positioning to create thrills. Keaton, in effect, started over, pulled back, said, "Hey, wait a minute! What *is* this thing?" As fast as he could discover its properties, he showed them to us: not as theory but as graven image. Without him, we might have regarded the camera contentedly as a mere means of photographing funny people, as we were later—for a time—content to regard it as a mere means of photographing talking people. Keaton was more *curious* than that: he wanted to know how everything—man-made, God-made, or a conjunction of the two—worked. Uncovering the camera's workings, he made it master in its own house, established its identity.

A corollary: Keaton's growth would not be a matter of finding a character for himself; it would be a matter of finding a character for the film in which he was to be seen. The film as independent, self-defining object became his goal; though he was everlastingly present in the film, he was present as possessed rather than possessing. As a performer, a personality, he was sharply defined, more rigidly so than most. Plain bones, Egyptian eyes, tight skin, nose carved of shale. But how little he asks of us, as a person! He asks for no emotional response whatever: no fears, no tears, no satisfaction in triumph. No intimacy: he will not confide in us, not tell us what he is thinking, not even smile. We are not related to him because we are not inside the screen, as he is. Try to touch him and he will dissolve like a brown leaf. Keaton is a part of the backdrop even when he is going through it. Do not look for him on the other side of the backdrop; it has no other side.

Because Keaton's curiosity was insatiable, and because he would not drop a dry fire hose, a bottomless wicker basket, or a camera until he had satisfied it, he arrived with astonishing speed at the kind of film that would house his understanding of the new medium. No more than fifteen short comedies made in tandem with Roscoe Arbuckle and he was ready. Chaplin, swift as he was, had taken forty-nine to arrive at the full freedom of the Mutuals. Lloyd, as we have seen, labored on well past one hundred. But the very first film Keaton released as a star, once his association with Arbuckle had ended, was, breath-takingly, an explosion of style. To sit through dozens and dozens of short comedies of the period and then to come upon *One Week* is to see the one thing no man ever sees: a garden at the moment of blooming. There had been all that desperate effort at becoming; now self-possessed life has arrived, matter of fact about its beauty.

I mentioned a dry fire hose. There is a moment—one that I am surprised was not cut—in a late Arbuckle-Keaton comedy, *The Garage*, that may give us as strong a sense of the twenty-four-year-old Keaton as any we can now have. Fatty and Buster have hurried the town's fire equipment to a blazing building, but the hose has sprung a leak. Fatty sits on the leak, temporarily letting the water flow. Then a streetcar cuts the hose in two. Buster, standing before the fire with the nozzle in his hand, notices that nothing is coming out of it. That is interesting. Not disturbing, just interesting. Buster does not, as another comedian would, immediately jump up and down in anxiety over the perishing building, race about looking for alternatives. Instead, he studies the nozzle. You can see him asking: what became of the water that was here just a moment ago; if there are pressures involved, where precisely did they go; what after all makes water flow? If this were one of Keaton's own films, you know that there would now be a quick fade-out and fade-in with the physics of the situation resolved and a highly improbable pumping system fully at work. But this is an Arbuckle, still mainly in the Keystone tradition, and it is going to race off after something else. I am surprised that the image wasn't clipped sooner, because there is no gag to it, only something characteristic of this particular, soberly dedicated man. Yet, if you can catch it before it is gone, there is something funny about the spectacle: one lone figure attending to the *cause* of things while everyone about him frantically deals with effects. Of course, the house will burn down at this rate. But what is more important—to save the house or to understand physics? Keaton is interested in facts, especially while they are still invisible.

It was with just such open-mindedness that Keaton must have examined and then "climbed inside" the camera on his first day in a studio. "Climbed inside" is biographer Rudi Blesh's phrase for what happened when Keaton met instrument: in *Keaton,* he goes on to describe Buster fanatically "inspecting the intricate gears and threading sprockets, and, in particular, the alternating shutter, that basic invention that made moving pictures possible by photographing and stopping a swift series of separate images . . . then screening them in the same stop-and-go way." Keaton himself, in an interview with Herbert Feinstein, said that on being invited into a studio by Arbuckle "the first thing I did was make a friend with the cameraman and get in the cutting room and tear a camera to pieces and find out . . . things I could do with a camera that I couldn't do on stage." The man fell in love with a *way* of duplicating, and not duplicating, reality.

As a child, touring the country in a vaudeville act with his parents, Keaton had instinctively developed a passion for gadgetry, on stage and off. At the age of fourteen, according to Blesh, he spent part of his summer holiday perfecting an insanely complicated device that would wake up a friend who chronically slept through all alarms. He also rigged an outhouse whose walls fell outward, leaving only a rather unconcealing roof intact. Once Keaton began making his own films, this gadgetry sometimes turned up as part of the narrative. The strain was a minor one in Keaton and is not to be confused with his essentially philosophic interest in form, but it did recur, with offhand charm, through the whole body of his work. In the two-reel *The Scarecrow,* for instance, Buster and his big brother sit down to breakfast. Sugar bowl and salt and pepper shakers hang above them on flexible strings, ready to be pulled down for instant use or "passed" in a graceful arc above the table. A tiny table-wagon, wound on a trolley wire, runs buns back and forth. The tug of yet another string releases the lid of the icebox and flips out a ketchup bottle, which is returned automatically once each man has had his will of it. When the table has been cleared, there is a flipboard in its center that restores a pleasant bowl of flowers into an upright position.

But these are byproducts of Keaton's uncontrollable itch to ferret out the function of things, an itch that went much deeper than holiday tinkering. Given a camera, he knew that he had in his hands something more than a toy, even a toy that would permit him to photograph himself playing nine roles in the same frame of film. He had a mirror of the universe that altered the universe in certain subtle but important ways, which meant that between the record and the fact there was an exhilarating no-man's-land in which extraordinary but not necessarily untrue events might take place. There was a gap there; he meant to live in it.

Not at once of course. For the most part, during his two years with Arbuckle, he was simply biding his time, content to learn. He had come accidentally to a studio. The family vaudeville act, which he had crawled into at the age of nine months and which he had entered for good when he was two, had reached the point of dissolution. Buster came to New York, alone, to accept a Broadway role in *The Passing Show of 1917.* While he was waiting for rehearsals to begin—

Buster Keaton prays for guidance as he gambles with Roscoe Arbuckle and Sybil Seely.

An Inquisitive Keaton and a Generous Arbuckle

and, as it happens, working out an entirely silent act for a turn in a legitimate revue—he met an old friend who was on his way to the East Side loft in which Arbuckle was beginning to make his own two-reelers. Having nothing else to do for the day, Keaton went along.

Arbuckle, once Chaplin had left Keystone, had become Sennett's principal comedian, co-starring often with Mabel Normand. After three years his popularity had grown to the point at which the producer Joseph Schenck, already shaping film destinies, was able to establish an independent company for him, the Comique. Arbuckle was introduced to Keaton, no doubt recognized him from vaudeville, promptly suggested he jump into a scene with them. Keaton hesitated until he had spent several hours with the camera, the cutting room, the previous day's "rushes," then jumped. The sequence, as Keaton describes it in his collaboration with Charles Samuels, *My Wonderful World of Slapstick*, "called for me to buy a quarter's worth of molasses. But after it was ladled out I discovered that I had dropped the quarter into the molasses. Roscoe, Al St. John, and myself all took turns at trying to get the quarter. The three of us were smeared with molasses from head to foot before we were finished." Keaton took particular pride, later on, in the fact that the entire melee was filmed without retakes, "the only movie-comedy scene ever made with a newcomer that was photographed only once."

The Butcher Boy is, of course, comedy firmly in the Sennett tradition; Arbuckle would never have the inventiveness to create another. And though Buster Keaton re-enacted the passage for various television shows toward the end of his life, there is nothing—apart from the somber flag of his face, instantly arresting—particularly Keatonish about it. Or, if there is, it is not in the sticky free-for-all but in the stray-dog gesture with which he makes the whole thing plausible. Actually he does not drop the quarter in the molasses. As he prepares to put the empty bucket down on the counter, he flips the coin in the air, kisses it goodbye, pops it into the can as payment, and then pushes both toward Arbuckle. Arbuckle, inattentive, doesn't notice the quarter and fills the can. But it is necessary for Keaton to be inattentive as well, and that would not only multiply improbabilities coarsely but would, for Keaton as we have come to know him, be out of character. What Keaton does is distract himself by interesting himself. He becomes wholly absorbed in a game of checkers that is being played by a couple of elderly country-store hangers-on. We will always believe in Keaton's compulsive concentration on the next thing set before him. The distraction itself is not thumpingly funny; it merely permits the molasses to be poured. But the habit of mind is intensely promising.

By the end of this first day's work Keaton knew where his future lay. Without so much as asking how much his salary might be if he stayed on—it turned out to be less than one sixth of what he would then have earned on Broadway—he arranged to have his contract for *The Passing Show* torn up and dove headlong into supporting work for Arbuckle, taking falls from piers and flour sacks full in the face as the presumably routine labor of any company's third banana. Al St. John, Arbuckle's goblin-faced nephew, had come from Sennett with him and would, in the beginning but not for long, take precedence as the supporting players chased Fatty through girls' dormitories and bathing houses, swung on trapezes and trotted along the tops of moving trains.

The early Arbuckle-Keaton films find Keaton quite content to tag along. In *The Butcher Boy* he is invariably the third man to tumble through a window, though his falls are much better composed than St. John's: St. John flails, letting his spindly legs thrash where they will; Keaton's sprawls have spine to them. In *Fatty at Coney Island*, St. John steals Buster's girl from him when Buster's pock-

Opposite, above: Arbuckle and Keaton at less than swords' points in *Good Night, Nurse*. As bartender and dude in *Out West*.

Below: Keaton, tugging at Arbuckle's trousers, in his first film appearance. *The Butcher Boy*.

A7008-17

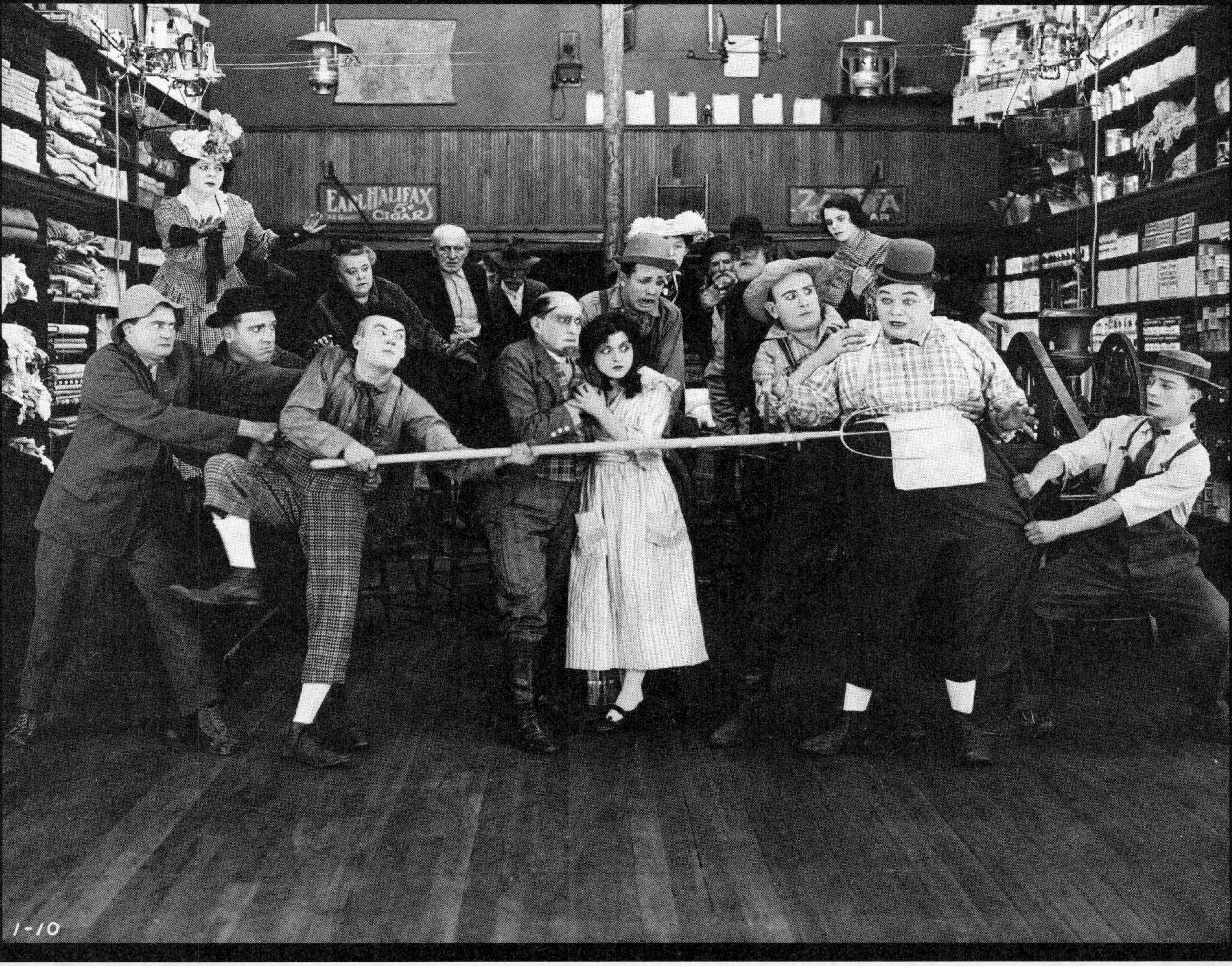

ets prove empty; thereafter Keaton is virtually a loner, picked up by the camera now and then when he is prepared to do a backflip simply to show that he can do a backflip but otherwise unengaged in the multiple flirtations that are going on.

He does, by the way, cry when his girl is taken away from him, as he cries again later when he helps Arbuckle out of the water only to be hurled in himself. He also laughs, laughs when he discovers that he has accidentally hit Arbuckle with an amusement-park mallet, laughs when he recognizes Arbuckle decked out in skirt and curls. The stone face has not yet set; he is as animated, and as characterless in the animation, as St. John. There is a legend that Keaton learned as a small child never to so much as smile if he wished to achieve his particular comic effect. His father, in their vigorously acrobatic vaudeville act, had made a pitched ball of him, hurling him high against a backdrop and letting him slide down it head first, righting himself with a somersault just inches from the floor. His father had also often tossed him into the orchestra pit's bass drum. The story has it that Buster tried coming up smiling, to show that he wasn't the least bit hurt, but that when he emerged smiling from the drum the audience sat unmoved. When he came up deadpan, the audience roared. Hence his specific gravity. The story may be true for the vaudeville act. If so, Keaton lost sight of its implications during his apprenticeship with Arbuckle—he is still to be seen laughing in one of their last films together—and only resumed the uncompromised mask when he began producing films of his own.

Deep interest, however, is a sober state of mind, and the essential sobriety is there. It stems from an awareness that the world about one is intensely present and has tricks up its sleeve. Keaton falling is still Keaton paying attention. He will never fall the same way twice, because in falling the first time he has taken the measure of all the natural properties that entered into the act—the hardness or resilience of surfaces, the precise rhythm of objects moving at or away from him, the lay of the knowable land. At Coney Island, he is still in the process of noticing: he steps into a whirling crazy-cart and promptly spills over its edge onto a rising and dipping floor. When two carts collide, he is bounced from the one he is driving into the one that has crashed into it, whereupon he flips backward once again onto that undulating open track. Even as you watch him doing it, you know in your bones what he will do next time—though next time is not in the film. Next time he will arc perfectly from one car to the other, land precisely in the driver's seat, and sail away confidently. What matter which car? The issue is one of serene adaptation to invisible forces that work.

In the films with Arbuckle, Keaton does not arrive at his full mastery of matter, does not even assert himself as iconographic occupant of the frame. The films are too raggle-taggle for that, impatient of any thoughtfulness that does not trigger immediate violence, apt to break off in the middle and race away to new materials more easily tapped. Arbuckle, the Sennett man, was still in a hurry, fearful of empty spaces; Keaton would have to wait for a free hand in order to make comedy of just those spaces.

But there was another reason for the contrast between the self-effacing work Keaton would do for Arbuckle and the completely assured, staggeringly original work he would do the moment he was loosed on his own. The two men were extraordinarily generous companions. They were also very much alike.

Neither was professionally aggressive. Though Keaton came to films with a name and an already long career as youthful headliner behind him, he neither fought for more footage nor yearned for his freedom. He liked Arbuckle and was content to learn from him. After being drafted during World War I and spending eleven months away from the studio, Keaton returned in 1919 to find that he had indeed been noticed in the Arbuckle films. Warner Brothers offered him a thousand dollars a week to star on his own. He stayed with Arbuckle at a fourth of the salary. He did not engineer his own eventual entry into independent production. When, in 1920, Joseph Schenck decided to move Arbuckle into feature-film production at Paramount, he appointed Keaton to take over the Comique studio. *Given* the situation, Keaton rose to it like a rocket; but he had to be given it. When, in the late twenties and not too long before sound came in, Schenck announced that he was dismantling the independent studio and handing Keaton over to Metro-Goldwyn-Mayer's assembly line, the comedian was stunned but went docilely. The assembly line destroyed him. He was a man who required total independence to do his characteristic work, but he would not fight for it.

Keaton smiles along with Arbuckle in a playful pose from *Moonshine*.

Arbuckle's role in the relationship was, in a way, even stranger. Arbuckle was the star. Yet he thought nothing of keeping a supporting comedian in his company who was plainly more imaginative than he. Indeed, as the later films show, he thought nothing of submitting himself to the dictates of that imagination, surrendering his right to preeminence, joining Keaton as partner in gags Keaton had unmistakably devised. He let his hireling—and friend—determine his style.

"The longer I worked with Roscoe the more I liked him," Keaton said. "Arbuckle was that rarity, a truly jolly fat man. He had no meanness, malice, or jealousy in him. Everything seemed to amuse and delight him. He was free with his advice and too free in lending and spending money. I could not have found a better-natured man to teach me the movie business, or a more knowledgeable one. We never had an argument."

Two men who wouldn't argue, except about one thing. Arbuckle, apparently, liked to repeat—and work by—the already standard cliché that the average mental age of members of the movie audience was twelve. Keaton brooded, then announced that anyone who truly believed that wouldn't be in pictures for long. Though Keaton was not what would be called an intellectual, he knew that intuition went deeper than test-scores, and that the universe, in its orderly disorder, was on the side of intuition. Ordinary reasoning could be outguessed, and the audience was quick enough to understand what was happening.

Whatever limited concepts Arbuckle held to, he listened to Keaton. Keaton, following the camera, early developed an insistence on the integrity of the frame. Of course a film could cut from frame to frame during a single event, its separate stages photographed separately and then pieced together. It was the easiest thing in the world to do. One shot could show a man throwing a pie; another shot—taken quite independently and even, as occasionally happened, a year or two later—could show the pie splattering in another man's face. One shot could show a dog getting a hose between its teeth; the next, without the dog, could show a stream of water knocking a man down. This kind of manipulation was omnipresent and reached such absurdly detailed heights that in a Sennett-made Sydney Chaplin film called *Gussle Rivals Jonah*, three separate shots were used to account for a flung fish. One showed the fish being thrown; a second caught the fish passing in midair; a third reported its landing in the face of the victim. This is something more than overdetailed, unduly literal exposition. It is a refusal on the part of comedian and cameraman to provide the precise pleasure the audience has come for: to see an actual thing happen. What the audience has seen is two or three partial things happen. It was Keaton's notion that cutting, valuable as it was in a thousand ways, must not replace the recording function of the camera, must not *create* the happening. The happening must happen, be photographed intact, then be related by cutting to other happenings. The event itself must not be falsified.

Keaton would make this a first principle of his later work, where we would see him in long-shot acting in full relationship to the bears or bridges that confronted him; but it was already more than a glimmer as he worked with Arbuckle on *A Desert Hero*. Mr. Blesh describes the scene called for: Arbuckle was to be kicked off a freight train, "roll down a steep railroad embankment, across a dusty street, and on in through the swinging doors of a western saloon." Following standard procedure, Arbuckle planned the sequence as separate shots: tumble from the car, roll down the hill, crash into the saloon. It was scarcely safe for Arbuckle, at two hundred and eighty pounds and most of that muscle, to attempt the entire fall-and-roll without interim rest and careful shot-by-shot camera placement. Keaton objected. "For a real effect and to convince people that it's on the level," he said, "*do* it on the level. No faking. Move the camera back and take it all in one shot. Don't cut until he disappears through the doors." To make his point, and to keep Arbuckle from injury, Keaton padded himself to Arbuckle's proportions and performed the stunt himself, as he invariably would whenever his stubbornness about premises threatened others with risk. He doubled for a girl flying out of a shoot-the-chutes in *Coney Island*, as he would later double for a chap bumped off a racing motorcycle in *Sherlock Jr.* Strictly speaking, integrity has not been wholly preserved. That isn't Arbuckle going through the saloon doors. But Keaton could rectify that when he made his own films.

Tentatively, in the Arbuckle films, Keaton begins to experiment with two other preoccupations: the collapsed dimensionality of the screen and the geometric fidelity of matter. In *Backstage* he appears to be walking down a flight of stairs, returning, walking down again. We discover, when he wants us to, that there is no flight of stairs. The banister behind which he so plausibly descends is nothing more than a backstage flat, thin lath and canvas, and what he is really doing is getting to his knees now and then to nail something to the floor. In the same film he gives to Arbuckle what would in time—and on a much greater scale—become one of his trademarks. A stage wall—once again a flat—falls over, disturbing Arbuckle not at all because he is standing, most conveniently, in a window.

These are first probings, unpursued in detail or in scale. Keaton would have to be alone in his no-man's-land before he could display its full geography. The strongest impression the later Arbuckle-Keaton films give is of ever closer collaboration, of a doubleness in which it is Arbuckle who obliges his partner. There are two bits of togetherness in *The Garage* that have obviously been patterned by Keaton—they are in his strict, easy rhythm—and then learned, almost as dance steps, by Roscoe. In the first, Buster is walking in time-step behind the fat man as they pass a policeman, so that the policeman will not notice that Buster is temporarily without trousers. They turn a corner, which will of course expose Buster's rear. As they do, and seconds before the curious policeman can put his head around the corner, Fatty executes a smart boxlike turn, never missing a step, that will place him behind Buster and so save the day. They continue in rhythm down the street. The bit is neat drill-mastering, and it is Arbuckle who is the trainee.

A moment later, still walking in tandem, they pass a clothing store that has trousers piled on an outdoor ledge. Again without altering pace, Buster snatches up a pair, shoots his legs forward as Arbuckle hoists him into the air, slips into the trousers and has his feet back on the ground exactly in time to accommodate Arbuckle's stride. They are choreographic companions, though not quite what one would wish to call a comedy team. They are almost *too* well-related for that.

Arbuckle's popularity seems to have been not at all threatened by his increasing obeisance to his fellow performer, nor did it abate when the two were separated and Arbuckle made feature films alone. At least eight of these were successful before scandal erased his career overnight. What happened was grossly unjust. Following a weekend drinking-and-sex party thrown by Arbuckle and some friends in San Francisco, a woman who had been present died of peritonitis. Immediately, rumor—and a good bit of hysterical false evidence—went to work: charges of "rape" and "murder" filled the air, the image of Arbuckle as an exceptionally heavy man ravishing a woman fastened itself upon the public imagination, and though there never was any valid evidence that Arbuckle had been responsible for her death, the practical verdict was reached before the case came to court. His films were banned across the country; religious groups attacked him, glad at last to have a case to make against sin-ridden Hollywood; producers, panicked, agreed to withhold two completed but unreleased features from the screen and to make no effort to salvage the man, however innocent he might be. All of this before the first of three trials had begun. There were two hung juries. A third jury cleared him in six minutes, issuing a remarkably strong statement in his defense. A week after his acquittal the Hays Office, newly formed watchdog of Hollywood morals, barred him from ever working on the screen again.

It is difficult even now for us to judge Arbuckle's work as a comedian, given the lurid associations of the three trials and the vague after-image they have stamped over his face. And if we do get past those associations, we are confronted with something equally blinding: an appalled sympathy for this living figure who was told at the age of thirty-four that he could never work again. One way or another, we are looking not at what he does but at *him*.

I am certainly not going to pretend to an impossible detachment. But we might take a look at what he does. He behaves very much like a child, a somewhat petulant one. Watched over by his dragon-wife at the seashore, he plays with a shovel and a bucket of sand, pouting the while. Seeing a dog dig a hole for himself in the sand, he follows suit, burying himself completely. He now sends up a periscope—where did he get it?—to keep tabs on his wife's movements. Freed at last to roam an amusement park, he sticks his tongue out at a fortune-telling machine that has not been kind to him.

I have been able to see one of his unreleased features, *Leap Year*. In it he is given to tantrums, jumping up and down in his riding boots like an infant refusing to do his mother's bidding, puffing out his cheeks in rapid exasperation like a blowfish. His smile is pleasant, but he scowls as much as he smiles. He checks the camera often, looking first at one adversary, then at us, then at a second assailant, and when it is time for a duel with one of them he arranges—implausibly, and simply to compound the difficulties of the duel—to fight his opponent with ashtrays balanced on both heads. He is often coy, ducking his head shyly as one girl after another proposes marriage to him. The film, which presents him as a stammering young socialite whose every aborted utterance to a girl is instantly accepted as an offer of marriage, could probably not have been released even if there had been an early acquittal. Too much of its content—women pursuing him, backflips into boudoirs—would have stirred precisely the overtones that had to be quieted if anyone was to laugh.

He often appeared as a woman, sometimes because the narrative called for a temporary disguise, sometimes on the premise, then taken for granted, that a man might play a woman whenever he chose. The practice was common. Wallace Beery began his work in films as a female impersonator in the Essanay *Sweedie* comedies, performing as a muscular housemaid. Chaplin made *A Woman*, though his face lacked accent with the mustache and eyebrows gone; and he often cast his supporting comedian, friend, and devoted admirer, Henry Bergman, as Mrs.

Above: Loyal bit-player Henry Bergman was apt to turn up as a woman whenever heavy falls lay ahead.

Below, Wallace Beery, as the housemaid Sweedie, looks down on Leo White.

Flirty whenever the melee required a woman to take a heavy fall. Arbuckle employed the device more often than any, though, and tended to make the most of its peeping-Tom possibilities. Sent, in his curls, to a women's dressing room at the seashore, he would sit himself down comfortably and enjoy the surrounding view, letting the situation speak for itself without further gagging. He might then thoughtlessly betray himself by removing his wig, giving rise to the next chase. His forgetfulness is hard to believe, considering his quite conscious enjoyment of his temporary advantage; but Arbuckle's moves were often arbitrary.

He had a reputation among fellow professionals for being quickly inventive, able to conjure up on-the-spot business to keep a film going. His inventiveness, however, seems to have been largely of the Sennett brand, a way of hurling bodies together or into telephone poles that would send them careering in odd directions. Genuine slyness, or original use of the medium, is rare. It is true that in *The Rough House*, he not only slices salami by applying it directly to an electric fan but impales two breakfast rolls on forks and performs a bun-dance that anticipates Chaplin's in *The Gold Rush*. In *Moonshine* he rescues Buster from a rockslide, washes him off in a mountain stream, hangs him on a tree limb to dry; but whose gag was it? I had long credited him with an original piece of business that appears in *The Garage*: he is inside an automobile polishing one of its windows, and when he has completed the job to his satisfaction he reaches through the nonexistent window to pick up a fresh rag. In the process of tracking down the two men's films, however, I discovered that Keaton had already used the gag in *The Bellboy* a full year earlier. Arbuckle's own repertory was not extensive.

He was, I think, one of the "lucky" ones whose simple physical outlines established him swiftly and archetypically in the public mind when films were new and the identities of those appearing in them dreamlike and godlike. He was loved not so much for what he did as for what he looked like. The amiable, bouncing fat man, capable of cloddishness and even of cruelty but eternally forgiven because of the resilience and gaiety with which he bears the cross of his shape, has always been part of the dramatic *mythos*, easy to respond to: it gives us Toby Belches as well as John Bunnys. Arbuckle was its ready-made incarnation at a time when neither insight nor subtlety was asked of the image. He had only to appear, as curved as a ball and as unmalicious as a baby, to be accepted as a natural resident of the new pantheon. I do not find in the work proper much that is salvageable. The best things in *Leap Year*, for instance, are the titles, which are filled with a playful candor about filmmaking: "Cutting inside, we find . . . " and "Closeup of Roscoe Arbuckle as. . . ."

Keaton, missing the fatal San Francisco party by chance, did all he could privately to help. But he was already deep in his own filmmaking, calling attention to film as film not in the titles but in the moving frames themselves. He paused, briefly, before plunging into his own starring two-reelers, to appear in a feature-length comedy melodrama, *The Saphead*, for Metro. The role—that of an exceedingly rich young man who assumes responsibility for the amorous misbehavior of his brother-in-law—was not at all tailored to his talents, but he made his way honorably through the film, biding his time, doing what the narrative required of him, modestly appropriating any opportunity to inflect a situation *his* way. At one point the plot requires that he buy a seat on the stock exchange for a hundred thousand dollars. The sum impresses him. When he finally enters the stock exchange, he looks about for a chair that can possibly cost so much, finding one near the door, sitting in it, testing it, satisfying himself that it offers a hundred thousand dollars worth of sturdiness and comfort. The moment is delicious; but he was ready for more than passing moments now.

14. The Keaton "No"

As a star in his own right, Buster Keaton comes all at once and all of a piece. From the moment he began making short comedies independently in 1920, the whole repertoire—rich, bizarre, unindebted to others, and inimitable in itself—is there. The porkpie hat sits evenly astride his head, a companion so faithful that it floats patiently on the water long after Buster is presumed drowned, knowing that when he does surface he will surface directly under it. The girl stands beside him, stupid as can be, ready to help move a house that has been built on the wrong lot by propping it up with an automobile jack. The elements with which he is at odds and in which he is so much at home—wind, water, the natural geometry of a universe God made and washed His hands of—already swirl, pivot, fold and unfold about him, defying his efforts to nail them together with a hammer and then, as the hammer flies from his hand, politely fusing them for him. The brush he needs, if he is going to paint a hook on which to hang his hat, is available. So is a subway to take him directly to the North Pole. Peculiar as he is, Keaton arrives on the scene so placidly intact that it is impossible to chart him as a process, he can only be pored over as a map.

And because the topography *is* peculiar, it can be misleading. We can become so fascinated by what is odd in Keaton that we quite forget what is commonplace about Keaton. Keaton is a comedian like other comedians, a clown making use of the standard vocabulary of clowns. He tells stories that are meant to be both stories and funny; he uses gags because they are gags. He hurls himself ardently into a Romeo and Juliet love affair, devoting his best energies to circumventing the fence and the families that would keep boy and girl apart. He may be a bit more interested in the challenge than he is in the girl, but he is out to marry her nonetheless. He begins a film by marrying the girl and *then* goes on to cope with her family, or with the prefabricated house they have been given for a wedding present on which the numbers that identify the pieces to be put together have all been incorrectly marked. He needs a job and gets one, in a shooting gallery where

the Mafia will find and make use of him. He builds a boat in the family basement and then has a little difficulty getting it out. There is always some sort of narrative nonsense going forward.

His plots are generally of two kinds: they are either like knots in a string that is tied to nothing in particular, or they are like nests of boxes, each box growing smaller as it fits snugly into its rectangular bed.

The former are essentially improvisations, like *The Balloonatic* or *Day-dreams*. In the one he goes ballooning, fishing, boating, bear- and girl-hunting; in the other he plays doctor, Wall Street operator, Hamlet, and unhappy resident of a ferry boat's paddle wheel. Each episode accounts for itself, more or less fatally, more or less fortunately; what holds them together may be scarcely more than the inquisitive serenity of his stroll. Call them charm-bracelet films.

The others are more complex, though the principle of compression—of concentric shapes slipping inside one another—may be as simple as it is in *One Week*, the first film released by his own company. On Monday Buster is married, on Tuesday he begins to assemble the mismarked house he has inherited, on Wednesday he studies the structure that now looks like a dragon's mouth filled with wayward teeth, on Thursday he tries to provide it on the outside with a chimney and on the inside with a piano, on Friday there is a disastrous house-warming in a windstorm, on Saturday he discovers that the house has been built on the wrong side of the railroad tracks, on Sunday he manages to move it as far as the railroad tracks. The days of the week close down to make a noose. *The Goat* is trickier. Buster is photographed, by accident. The photograph is circulated, virtually countrywide, as that of a wanted criminal. Buster is surrounded—in newspapers, on billboards, in the horrified eyes of total strangers—by his own face. He carries his nemesis with him, Keaton closing in on Keaton. His plots may be stranger than other men's, and more provocative. They are still plots.

Moving through them, whether they are ambling outward or coiling in, Keaton will use incidental comic business not far removed from that employed daily by his colleagues. Emerging from the church, once he has been married in *One Week*, he is inundated by rice and old shoes. He pauses in his husbandly stride just long enough to compare a pair of shoes that has been thrown at him with the pair he is wearing, decides to keep the flung pair. Almost anyone might have done that, though not so solemnly. Working in a shooting gallery in *The High Sign*, he is asked by a customer for a rifle, which he promptly provides. The customer holds him up with it. I am surprised that Lloyd did not beat him to this one, though I am more pleased by Keaton's matter-of-fact submission as his hands go directly up—Keaton always appreciates the intelligence of the other fellow—than I would have been by Lloyd's startled gape and italicizing shudder. In *The Balloonatic* he is steadily plucking fish out of the water by hand and just as steadily losing them: the basket into which he pops them has lost its bottom. He never does notice that the bottom is gone, but he recognizes the expression on the face of one of the fish as it comes around again, leading him to investigate

Keaton goes upstream. Keaton goes downstream. *The Boat.*

Opposite: The prefabricated house that Keaton built. *One Week.*

the situation. Could anyone else have done that? Perhaps.

If Keaton does have an edge where regulation gags are concerned, it is in his gift for the "aftergag." Everybody made messes with gluepots. In *The Haunted House*, Buster, working as a bank teller, makes a mess with a gluepot, managing to get all the money he is trying to count out irretrievably stuck together, struggling ever so manfully to pry firmly affixed dollar bills from the palms of his hands and the soles of his feet. Discouraged—Keaton could become discouraged—he plunges his hands into his pockets as if to forget about the whole thing. At this moment the bank is held up. He cannot, of course, get his hands up on demand: they are now stuck in his pockets. Eventually, under the prodding of a gun, he does. The hands come up with the pockets attached to them, like mittens. In *The Paleface*, with Indians on the rampage in a white man's land office, you *know* that some white man is going to be wearing a toupee and that he is going to be very easily "scalped," much to some Indian's surprise. Except that it doesn't happen that way. It is Buster, friend of the Indians though momentarily distrusted by them, who crawls on hands and knees, tomahawk in hand, after a scalawag official who is himself creeping away from the office. Seeing that he is trapped, the official, with a deep sigh, removes his toupee and *hands* it to Buster. Buster at once takes it to the Indian chief, who commends him for his heroism and reinstates him in the tribe's good graces. When Keaton is doing familiar business, it is always wise to wait to see what *else* he is going to do with it.

But these are his obeisances to what may be called the literary traditions of a form: narrative, situation, incident. He is deeply interested in them all, wants his laughs. Yet he wants something else even more, and he wants it in strict relation to the laughs. When he first began tinkering with a camera to see what it could produce that the stage couldn't, he was indeed interested in scale and spectacle—locomotives, ocean liners, whole houses built askew—but not in scale and spectacle alone. He was interested in the exceedingly strange relationship that existed between these things and the instrument that photographed them. Keaton wanted—however he may have phrased it in his own mind—a specifically cinematic comedy, wanted *all* of the comedy that could be derived from the camera's unique properties, wanted the native, idiosyncratic, *necessary* humor of this unprecedented world of film. How do you go about getting that?

He began by calling direct attention to the camera—to its lens, to its frame, to the flat screen on which its images would be projected.

Curiously, and stubbornly, he called attention to the camera's presence as a barrier. We can look at him all we like, we are free to see that what he does is often beautiful, but we are forever cut off from him by a solid piece of glass, a lens. He insists on it. Chaplin might pretend there was no lens and so leap through it; Keaton would reach out and rap his knuckles on the glass to show how hard it was. There is an otherwise inexplicable moment in his short comedy *The Goat*, a moment that has nothing to do with the story-line of that ingeniously complex little film and nothing to do with paving the way for a gag. It exists on principle and to illustrate one.

The camera is planted between two railroad tracks. A speeding train is headed—a long way off—directly toward us. It keeps coming at savage speed. The speed continues without slackening until the engine is directly against the camera lens. The train stops abruptly, impossibly. Keaton is sitting on the front of the engine, staring fixedly—transfixingly—at us, his eyes the glaring painted eyes of a mummy just removed from a sarcophagus, his arms folded implacably, locked. He has come headlong at us precisely as far as he can go—and no further. The relationship stops here. Keaton lives in a flatland bordering on the lens, one

The Keaton "No"

our senses have no power to invade; neither can he share our thickness; what separates us is invisible, though its very function is to make things visible. He has thrust himself at us to show us where "No" is.

He flirted with the camera once, and worried about it. In *The High Sign* a man has dropped a banana peel on the sidewalk. Keaton comes round the corner. Our expectation, overtrained by exposure to hundreds of banana peels in hundreds of short comedies, is clear. But Keaton does not slip. He passes the peel safely and swerves left out of frame. Just as he swerves, he turns his head halfway toward us and makes the "high sign" of the film—hands crossed beneath his nose, fingers wriggling—at us. The gesture is so glancing we almost lose it. It is, of course, mocking us, calling attention to the irony of our defeated expectations.

He didn't have to do it—I don't think he ever did it again—and the stress, together with the intimacy, bothered him. It was, he says in his autobiography, "like thumbing my nose at the audience, and saying, 'Fooled you that time, didn't I?' " In the end, he continues, "I decided that I had made the mistake of outsmarting the audience a little too much. But instead of cutting this scene out I added a shot. In this, after passing the camera and giving the sign, I slipped on a second banana peel somebody had dropped." In effect, he apologized for what he had done. The apology was mainly for having been *above* the audience in the gag. But it was the violation of a mutual privacy—the grimace of "I fooled you"—that was most offensive, by his standards. There is no "you" in Keaton films, only "he" and "it," which is why the two could merge so easily into the surreal "he-it" we shall speak of shortly.

For Keaton the camera frame was an absolute, as the camera lens was an absolute barrier. Almost all silent film comedians had called attention to the frame at one time or another, in one way or another. We remember Arbuckle doing it whenever he wished to undo his trousers: the frame could be raised or lowered to accommodate him. Harold Lloyd made a stab at it, though an uncomprehending one: surrounded by a dozen onlookers and wishing to kiss Bebe Daniels in private, he gave a signal to the cameraman to lower the lens while he and Bebe ducked to the ground. The use lacks ordinary logic: though we drop with the lens to see nothing but the couple kissing, it is perfectly apparent that the onlookers can still see them kissing, too. The camera has been identified as a camera to no real purpose.

But these are in any case self-conscious adjustments of the aperture, altering what we may look at from moment to moment but not alerting us to the fact that we may be—and in a sense always are—shut out entirely. Keaton wants the shut-out, every so often, to keep our wits awake, to intensify our awareness of what we are doing in this experience of motion pictures. Thus, when wife Sybil Seely in *One Week* is taking a bath and loses the bar of soap over the side of the tub, the frame does not discreetly look away until she can rise to retrieve the soap. Instead, a man's hand—symbolically, Keaton's—comes up from nowhere to blot out the image by covering the lens. Keaton ends *The Blacksmith* by pulling down a window-blind right in our faces with "The End" written on it.

Even when the action is taking place some distance from the lens, Keaton often prefers to perform it on an assumed straight line that is exactly parallel to the lens, echoing its absoluteness. In many of his very best gags he confines the comic business to a lateral plane as flat as the screen it is to be shown on.

He goes a-hunting in *The Balloonatic*, shotgun over his shoulder. He does not realize that a great grizzly bear is waddling immediately behind him. He approaches a log. There is a squirrel on it. Fine game. Crouching, he approaches the log stealthily until it seems that he must be able to see the whites of the

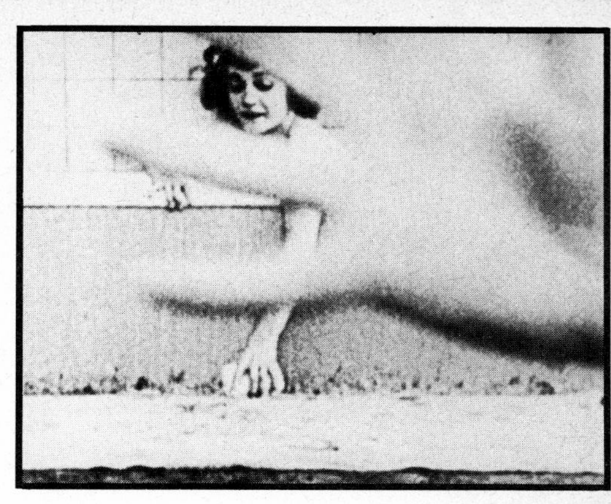

Opposite, side panel: Buster ejected and pursued in *Daydreams*; humiliated in *My Wife's Relations*; at rest, with bear, in *The Balloonatic*.

Right: The Keaton "No" charges at us, top-speed, and freezes abruptly at the lens. *The Goat*.

Above: Blotting out the lens for privacy. *One Week*.

squirrel's eyes. He takes aim. Before he can fire, alas, a *second* great grizzly bear rises toweringly from behind the log.

Buster, quick in crises, grips the barrel of his shotgun between both hands, raises the butt end high, and brings it down mightily on the grizzly's head, with the barrel of the shotgun slipping between his legs as he does. The impact of the blow fires the shotgun. The shot, from between his legs, kills the first grizzly behind him. All in one mighty, split-second arc. He doesn't know he has killed the first, because he never did know it was there. He finds out when, relieved at having disposed of the second, he sits on it.

The episode is representative of Keaton in a half-dozen ways, including his insistence on no trickery. We see the whole happening at once, and, seeing it without the help of convenient cutting, take a special delight in its precision. But, for the moment, suppose we pay attention to just one thing: the strict linear assumption on which the gag is based. The gag depends on the first bear, the second bear, Buster and the gun all inhabiting a single, severely narrow plane. Let the bear behind Buster be ever so slightly off this straight line, wandering around in the space that is presumably available, and the event won't take place. In life, with depth to work and wander in, so adventitious a lineup would rarely fall into position. On a flat screen, and with Keaton, it is matter of fact.

It is much the same with Buster's startlingly funny escape from a locked apartment, and a detective who is about to do him in, in *The Goat*. Buster has been invited to dinner by the girl, whom he has just met. The detective, who has been chasing Keaton all day and getting by far the worst of it, returns home. He is the girl's father. Looking up from grace before the meal, Buster and the detective recognize each other across the table. While Buster sits stunned, the detective orders wife and daughter out of the room, locks the door, bends the key into unusable shape. No escape. With the camera menacingly recording his expanding outlines, the detective advances upon Buster. It is time for the flat shot.

Buster's legs retract upward so that his heels grip the edge of the chair he is sitting on. Then he leaps forward, using the table as a springboard, and goes straight through the transom over the otherwise barred door—*and* over the monster approaching him. Chair, table, transom constitute the shortest distance between two points; Keaton traverses the space—which we didn't even recognize as a possible escape hatch—as cleanly as a bullet. He doesn't, by the way, bother to show us how he lands on the other side. When we pick him up, he is already in the hallway racing for a phone booth. The laugh is in the line; it is more than a laugh, it is a joy, the joy of an arrow going straight. Lucky that, on this surface, tables and chairs exist only in direct relation to transoms.

In *The Boat* he has put together a magnificently malleable small ship. Because, going up and down river, he will be passing under bridges, everything on the ship that projects upward has been made readily retractable: masts, funnel, radio antennae. Come to a bridge and the whole lot will bend backward, in graceful deference to powers best not met head-on. The turn of a lever will do the trick—and does do it, to Buster's order, several times. Unfortunately, as yet one more bridge approaches, Buster is momentarily preoccupied with a flag that needs adjusting at the rear of the vessel. Ship meets bridge and, one by one, the flexible uprights are *mowed* backward. Mast hits funnel, funnel hits spar, spar hits Buster on the head just as he is turning from the flag. Buster goes into the water. He wouldn't have if he'd been half an inch upstage or downstage. But we aren't on a stage anymore, as Keaton so excitedly noticed on his first day in a studio. No up or down here, just a uniform surface on which all moves are made.

Of course, there is still an up and down—laterally. I spoke of the boat going

Opposite, above: The distractible Keaton is really hunting bear. Notice the walk, a relic of his vaudeville slapshoe days. *The Balloonatic.*

Below: Buster and wife Sybil Seely not quite prepared for a formal launching. *The Boat.*

K-N-3-2

The multiple Keatons of *The Playhouse* include half the orchestra, a couple in a loge, and a song-and-dance team onstage. As if that weren't enough, he multiplies leading ladies, falling in love [illegible] a twin—but which?

up- and down-river, and that is exactly what it does in the film. Headed up-river, it sails loyally on an incline steep enough to scale Alps. Headed down-river, vice versa: the boat's nose pursues a plunging course that promises to take it out of the frame in the lower right-hand corner. The images are not prepared for. We simply come to them, and delight in what we recognize as a visual pun.

Keaton had no qualms about manipulating the camera lens itself. To get the uphill and downhill shots all he had to do was tilt the camera. That, in his understanding of the game, was cricket. He would be against cheating through unfair cutting. He would, most of the time, be against faking the thing photographed. If he was going to play with the camera, he would play with *it*—not with the world it recorded, not with the resulting film in a laboratory. The distinction may seem a subtle one, and Keaton did occasionally violate it; but he had a strong sense of honor about what he showed to his audiences.

The Playhouse carries the point about as far as it will go. Here Buster strolls into a vaudeville theater, alone. He remains alone and not alone. When the conductor emerges from the orchestra pit, it is Keaton. When he brings his baton down for the overture, the three musicians on his right sawing away at the strings are all Keaton, side by side. The brass section, on his left, is composed of three more Keatons. Backstage a stagehand grips ropes to get the curtain up. Keaton, of course. There is a minstrel show going on, interlocutor and eight end men. Keaton straight across the screen. In a box, watching the show, sit husband and wife, the wife fanning herself assiduously. Two Keatons. Above them, in another box, mother and child, child sucking on a lollipop. Two more. When the boy drops his lollipop, it lands on the lap of a dowager who inadvertently uses it as a lorgnette. She and her drowsy husband: Keaton. And more to come.

Laboratory work? No. Double exposures are made in laboratories: one completed film image superimposed upon another, or two halved images carefully juxtaposed. In the case of superimpositions, the doubling is obvious and is usually meant to be, as in dream sequences or reminiscences. In the case of split images—Douglas Fairbanks, as both father and son dueling beside each other in *Don Q, Son of Zorro*—the line at which the halves mesh is, at this stage of laboratory work, either noticeably fuzzy or patently defined by a prop. There is no fuzziness, no least hint of a join, in *The Playhouse*, early as it is. It was all recorded on a single piece of film.

Keaton later explained how he had managed the minstrel show. He had simply taped off eight ninths of the camera lens, permitting one ninth of the film to be exposed as he went through his routine at, say, extreme stage left. He then rewound the film, returning it to its starting point, retaped the lens to obliterate the area just used and to open up a second area, repeated his onstage routine in a new position. After the camera-eye had been separately bandaged nine times he had a continuous record with no evident "joins"—the camera had remained immobile throughout—and with no real duplicity. The fact had been photographed, piece by piece.

He would do still more ingenious things in his feature films, some so stunning as to remain bewildering today. But the principle is established here: you mustn't falsify what is in front of the camera; but you are free to select what is to be photographed, and to decide how it is to be photographed. The camera is an eye, and you are at liberty to squint or blink or do whatever you might do with your own eye. Just don't lie about what you finally see.

Keaton begins in a series of creative refusals. But what is all this strictness leading to?

15. Keaton: Exploring the Gap Between Life and Lens

You will notice that Keaton is strict about two things. He is strict about the fact of the camera: it is there, standing between us. And he is strict about the factual nature of what is photographed: it too is there, untampered with. But, however much these two strictures may say for a man's integrity as a filmmaker, do they—taken together—actually create comedy? Comedy of a special kind?

There are those who scarcely care whether Keaton is funny or not, he is so brilliant a technician, so uncompromising a natural theorist. An exceptionally perceptive young critic, writing under a pseudonym in the *New York Times*, has gone back to the films that were made before he was born and returned with a report:

"Pure visual comedy has been dead for forty years in the cinema, although people often talk about it as if it were still here, at least as a standard. And it certainly isn't. Visual comedy, in the hands of its greatest practitioners, Chaplin and Keaton, was closer to the poetry of dreams than to humor. Chaplin was funnier than Keaton because his movies were visually less perfect. Chaplin himself was the sole transformer of the images in his films; his presence was their primary beauty. There was always a little visual dullness there to put an edge on a laugh. He made great movies simply by stepping into the frame often enough. . . .

"Keaton, on the other hand, made a few perfect visual movies, whose corny themes became actual filmed myths. He realized, from shot to shot, dreamlike entities from the American and universal subconscious, with a subtlety and power equaled in American films only by Griffith and Welles. Dreams, like the movies of the great silent comedians, are like humor stripped of its formulas and restraints, but at their best and deepest they are not funny."

It is perfectly true that Keaton need not be funny to be admired. I often find myself not caring whether I laugh so long as I can simply remain in the presence of such otherworldly, unconcerned authority. One can say that Keaton is stunning in the sense that he truly stuns: one is reduced to a silence as firm as his own by

the rectitude—mathematical, spiritual—with which he enters a gate, paddles a canoe, appears in a window. Keaton does not have to clown to lay claim to the space he occupies. It is his by daimonic right.

But let's not surrender comedy too readily. Even at his "best and deepest," Keaton did want those laughs. It is inconceivable that he should have worked out his ever-so-pure first premises without a glimmer in his eye that saw absurdity coming of them. Absurdity did come of them.

I have mentioned Keaton painting a hook on which to hang his hat. This bit of business occurs in *The High Sign*, the first film he made after separating from Arbuckle, though not the first he released. The business, obviously, goes beyond what we have been talking about: factual use of the camera, fidelity to the photographed world. It is also, once we have got the hang of the man and his mind, funny. But there is another bit of business in *The High Sign*—also having to do with his hat—that goes beyond *that*.

Later in the day Buster returns to the shooting gallery in which he works and simply places his hat against a spot on the wall where there is no hook. The hat slides down until it finds one.

But that is impossible—except in a world that contradicts itself. Let's say that there *is* a nail or a hook somewhere beneath the hat. It must project from the wall in order to catch the hat. But if it projects from the wall it is going to catch the lower brim of the hat first and probably topple the hat off onto the floor. It doesn't. It permits the lower brim to glide past without obstruction, *then* projects in time to catch the inside of the upper brim. In short, it both projects and does not project at the same time.

Keaton, ever the explorer, scans the horizon wherever he may be, with dog-team in *The Frozen North* (above) or among Southwest Indian friends in *The Paleface* (opposite, left). Having arrived in *The Frozen North* by subway, he begins by parodying the westerns of William S. Hart (opposite, right).

Which is what film does. I have been placing great stress—along with Keaton—on the flatness of the image as recorded by the camera. But the world which the camera records is itself not flat: it has depth, projects into space. Does the camera record *that*? Yes, it does, deceptively. Dimension is photographed without dimension, but both exist. We are dealing with solid geometry pro-

jected on a perfectly flat page. Keaton lives and works *inside* the projection, which means that he can use either property—depth, no depth—when and as he wishes and can even use them against each other should his fancy so choose. He is only following the laws of the medium he inhabits.

Thus, in *The Paleface*, wishing to escape the Indian tribe that has suddenly turned so hostile, he spies a horse standing ready in the shrubbery. He hastens to it, goes around behind, and swings himself up into a saddle that the shrubbery happens to conceal from our view. He now rides out, backward, leaving the horse exactly as we have seen it. He has mounted a second horse, waiting directly behind the first though facing in the opposite direction.

Literally, the world seems to pull apart. We *saw* him mount the horse, we *see* him being carried away on a horse with his noble profile facing its rump, we are still staring at the first horse as though it had produced the second by parthenogenesis.

The cross-eyed image is both dizzying and suddenly side-splitting. It is also entirely plausible, Keaton having taken such pains to arrange the shrubbery naturally. Many comedians tended to telegraph their illusionistic effects by arranging the concealing devices so narrowly that they covered *only* the area to be hidden. The camouflage was too precise. One look and our suspicions were aroused. Keaton, who had known Houdini from childhood and may even have been given his nickname by the magician, had a hand for teasing the eye in wrong directions.

But pay attention to what he is saying. Dimension—depth enough to contain two horses—exists. The camera, however, records this dimension in such a way that, as Buster swings over the second horse in depth, we see him—or seem to see him—mounting the first on the only plane available to us. The joke consists in laying bare the simultaneity.

How does Keaton get us past the one open end in the image's irrefutable logic—the fact that he himself, moving inside the simultaneity, does not notice that there are two horses? By his competence. A trained horseman, going about his business nonchalantly, does not have to look as he swings a leg over a saddle. His mind, a very busy one, is on other matters.

And, of course, he is helped immensely by our own straying habits of mind, our dependence on a certain amount of illusion as we go about the daily conduct of our affairs. How often do we really look? Not always, or we'd never miss a stair. In *The Goat*, Buster has just dived through the transom to escape his nemesis. A telephone booth and an elevator stand side by side in the hallway. Buster pops into the telephone booth, plainly visible behind its glassed-in upper portion. His pursuer erupts from the apartment, charges down the hallway, sees Buster slowly go downward until his face vanishes from view. Immediately he heads for the stairs, racing to catch Buster at another floor. Obviously—to him—Buster has taken the elevator. But of course he hasn't. He has simply lowered himself inside the phone booth. The human eye is a kind of camera too, susceptible to false impressions when it isn't attending properly.

The fact is that *all* the time we are looking at the screen we are uncertain of what we are seeing, enmeshed in an instability. There is a world up there that can contract or expand without warning. If Buster Keaton wishes to walk into a bank carrying a cane and, in passing, hang the cane upside down on the wall, there is nothing to forbid his doing it. The cane, mind you, is hanging by its shaft, which means that it is hanging by nothing at all—except the adhesiveness of an image so flat that everything in it must inevitably become stuck together. There is no dimension to detach cane from wall, and so it stays there.

On the other hand, what seems dimensionless can create room for itself at will. There is a magnificently composed shot at the end of *One Week* in which Buster and his wife, having moved their house onto the railroad tracks and got stuck there, clasp each other in terror and shut their eyes tight because a roaring locomotive is bearing down on them. At what should be the moment of impact, the train bypasses them entirely. It is on another track. We are as startled as they, the path of the locomotive has seemed so certain. We have been warned that depth exists, somewhere, in the image, because the train has come into view on a sweeping curve; curves suggest breathing space. Yet the flat composition—house, Buster, wife, advancing train—so compresses our expectation that we can, for the moment, imagine nothing more than the trajectory we see. And we are fooled, thunderingly fooled. The fact that another locomotive, coming from the opposite direction, does plow into Buster's house and turn it into a sea-spray of splinters just as the couple are congratulating themselves on their narrow escape is good additional comedy but not of the essence. The essential comedy has been made of our terrible uncertainty of vision in this elusive form.

Indeed, our uncertainty is at all times so great that the universe itself is in

Immobile or about his chores, Buster is forlorn in *The Love Nest*. Joe Roberts, with his ax ready, was Keaton's standard "heavy."

Opposite: Joining the inanimate. Above: The balloon man of *The Balloonatic*. Below: The canoe man of the same film.

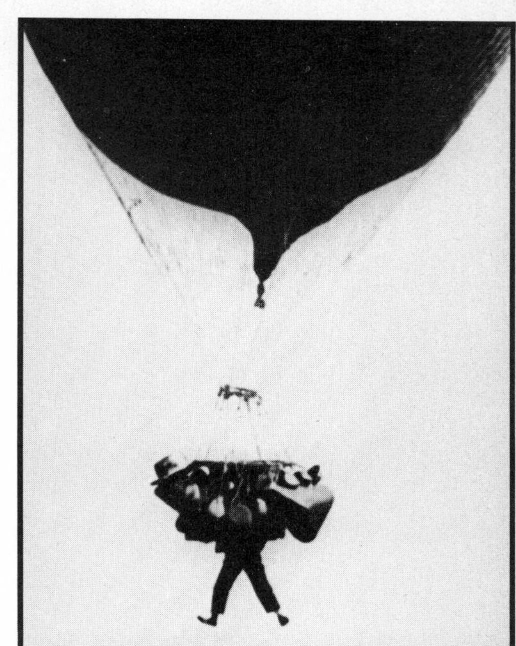

constant danger of dissolution. What we are seeing is not what we are seeing is what we are seeing. By the time Keaton has finished impersonating the entire audience, orchestra, and vaudeville show in *The Playhouse*, we are ready to move on. We dissolve to find Buster asleep in a bedroom; he has dreamed the whole thing. A hefty fellow with a mustache appears and rudely awakens him. The moment Buster *is* awake, the entire room dissolves about him: walls pull apart, doors vanish. Being awake is no guarantee of stability, of solidity. As it happens, Buster has been sleeping in a stage set, which is now being struck. But the implications are clear. When you don't know where dimension is, or when it will next appear, you can count on nothing holding firm. Watch the bottoms drop out in Keaton films: the bottom of a trunk, the bottom of a trash can, the bottom of a balloon basket, the bottom of a fishing pouch, the bottom of a wicker container that is supposed to house a cat. Neither bottom nor back wall can ever be considered a constant when depth itself is optional, arbitrary.

Keaton played with his options. Playing with them, he made a further astonishing discovery. Since both objects and people inhabited the same plane, there was nothing to keep people and objects from fusing, from turning into one another.

Buster goes up in an ascension balloon. He is not supposed to do so, he is merely rubbernecking while top-hatted officials say farewell to an aeronaut. To get rid of him, one of the ground crew hands Buster a pennant and motions him to affix it to the balloon. Buster climbs the netting to the very top, where he is still busy trying to tack the pennant in place when the bottom of the aeronaut's basket gives way, leaving the aeronaut quite grounded while the balloon—and Buster—float free, high in air. In due time, Buster decides to crawl down the netting and take up residence in the basket. He slips from the ropes into the basket. He also slips right through the basket, its bottom having been left behind, saving himself at the last minute by gripping its rim. His legs are spread open, in full view, below. What we are now looking at, in long-shot, is that surreal "he-it" that carries Keaton deepest into nightmare. We are looking at a monstrous man-balloon: Keaton's legs, the basket as torso, the balloon itself as head. The image could be Bosch, all too easily Dali; it is simply Keaton behaving normally in his very special milieu, availing himself of the probable absurdities of a form in which men and matter merge.

In the same film, not long after, Buster is boating. We see him paddling his canoe efficiently, rhythmically, down an ample stream. The motion is like music. Then he spies something on the bank: a rabbit. Ever in search of game, he puts down his paddle and takes up his shotgun. But he is too far from the bank for steady aim. He and the canoe therefore walk toward the bank into shallower water. The canoe does walk: Buster's legs have been in the water, thrust through the bottom of the boat, the whole time. When the rabbit runs away before Buster

can fire, Buster turns placidly back to the water, walks himself and the suspended canoe into it, paddles away again. There is an amphibious creature here. Which is it: man or canoe?

Inanimate objects become animate, men become things. Buster can become so completely a thing that it is impossible to isolate him from the rigid material object we see. He is running, as usual, from the police. He passes a clothing store, one that has half-dummies on poles outside it, dressed in Inverness capes and caps. In a trice, Buster is such a dummy, feet vanished altogether, his plaster of Paris face locked in immobility between cape and cap. He doesn't look like a man in disguise; he looks the gelid product of a mold.

If merging with inanimate objects can reduce him almost to rigor mortis, the reverse is equally true. He can invest the inanimate with life, by implication, whether he is joining it at the moment or not. On the run, he passes a cigar-store Indian, pausing long enough to strike a match for his cigarette on its presumably wooden arm. The Indian, tomahawk in air, turns on him. We become so accustomed to this kind of transposition that in *The Paleface* we need only to see a gate to see Keaton. This time the Indians are real Indians, and they are angry: white men have cheated them out of their lands. The Indian chief, on his reservation, points to the gate in the picket fence that marks off their present territory and announces solemnly that the first white man to walk through that gate must be killed. We are certain, of course, that before very long Buster will come through it. But at the moment we do not see him. There is only a close-up of the gate. Just that. The close-up is held for a few seconds longer than would be normal. In those few seconds, somehow, we see that the gate *looks* like Keaton. And we laugh at nothing more than our habit, Keaton-inculcated, of equating matter and man.

In *The Goat*, Buster is chased past a ceremony: a new statue is about to be unveiled. He arrives on the scene a beat or two earlier than his pursuers and has time to notice the artist and the city officials who are gathering about the concealing sheet. He vanishes behind the sheet. When the unveiling takes place, his pursuers having now reached the spot, Buster is seated astride a newly sculpted horse. Though the artist shows some astonishment, no one else sees anything amiss: Buster is as much a carving as the horse, quite belongs to the composition. Except that the horse, as it happens, is not a carving; it is something closer to plaster, and plaster not yet dry. It begins to buckle, ever so slowly, ever so hauntingly, under Buster's weight. As it does, it begins to seem a live thing dying. The sag in the center forces the head erect, the knees lock forward as though the beast were trying to rise, the blood of the torso turns watery as bones melt to a tangle. For as long as he can, and though he now seems to be sinking into a nest of writhing snakes, Buster holds his position: he and the dissolving horse remain one, share a fate. This is, in effect, Keaton's Laocoön. He is master until the other half of him rolls over and expires.

Keaton is at home with the inanimate. The camera has joined them together. That is why the most mysterious of Keaton's effects seem inevitable, predestined, indivisible, final. I know of no image more ghost-ridden, or more inexplicably *just*, than the one that climaxes *The Love Nest*. We have for some minutes been baffled as to what is going on. Keaton has set himself adrift from a larger ship in a small rowboat. The sea is endless. The rowboat is sinking. Then, in the middle of nowhere, his craft drifts aimlessly against the rear of a structure that seems odd to begin with: it looks as though someone had erected an advertising billboard in the middle of the ocean and Keaton were coming up behind it, becoming entangled with its supports. He climbs onto the puzzling structure—

Above: Buster astride, and a part of, the dying statue. *The Goat*.

Opposite: Before inspiration strikes in *The Love Nest*.

VE NEST

This isn't the perch Buster arrives at in *The Love Nest*, but perches of any sort become him. *Cops.*

we are puzzled, he is merely methodical, making the best of whatever is available—just in time to save himself as his craft founders. When we next see him he has crawled to the top of the towering flat surface, got out his rod and bait, and is nonchalantly fishing from it. Obviously he hasn't bothered to ask himself what this unlikely perch may be; it suits his present purposes, he is at one with it. We now find out what it is. We cut to a row of battleships out for target practice, sailors manning their guns. Keaton is sitting atop an enormous target, towed to sea and left there for the fusillade that is to come—that is coming right now. But as the ships prepare to fire, Keaton is wholly at peace, perfectly in place, entirely attuned to sea and sky and the great rectangle on which he rests like one cocked ear. He belongs to the thing he has joined; he *is* the target. When Keaton joins an object, one has no wish to pry him loose from it, no matter what shellfire may be in store. Harmony has been achieved; we can accept its consequences.

When, having failed at all his efforts to prove himself capable of supporting a wife in *Daydreams* and having been reduced to a battered hulk in the process, Keaton is delivered home by parcel post—a tag attached to him for identification—to be hauled out of the van like any other sack of mail, slung over the postman's shoulder, and dumped down inside the door as his girl's father signs a receipt, he is not stretching fantasy beyond the boundaries he has firmly established. He exists in a world in which inert matter can be given animation and in which animated man can return the compliment by playing dead. The visual properties of the screen, so carefully defined by and in the films, make the interchange a casual one, an honorable one, and a funny one.

The premises of this kind of comedy are, in the end, quite simple. The camera is a stable factor, doing its work with integrity. The universe being photographed is a stable factor, possessed of an integrity of its own. But the relationship between them is unstable—hopelessly, hilariously unstable. Two absolutes come together at a point that cannot be absolutely detected. Not by the human eye. We cannot say with assurance where the lens ends and life begins, or vice versa.

The instability renders the form subject to fits. Fits of expansion and contraction. Fits of simultaneity. Fits of fusion. Fits of inattention and of expectation foiled and of all the elisions of focus that the conjunction of camera and universe just naturally falls heir to. A gap has opened wide, and the clown can topple into it or escape through it. Specifically cinematic comedy never apologizes for this gap. Neither does it attempt to conceal it. Rather, it thrives on it. All the comedian has to do is remain alert to the everlasting slipperiness of the only environment he knows.

It's no accident that what is probably our most familiar image of Keaton is of him scanning the horizon, hand at his brow to keep the sun from his eyes, body arched forward, feet hooked perilously into the rigging of a ship. He doesn't have to be at sea, or have rigging available, to adopt the posture. He does it all the time—on the backs of horses, on the tops of balloons. It is, in fact, his essential posture: he is an explorer. He explores the universe exactly as he explores film: with a view to measuring the immeasurable before he enters it, so that he will know how to behave when he is there. No matter that there is nothing at all to be seen on the horizon: the boundaries of this world are invisible, anyway. The rigging beneath his feet will give way. He understands that. The horse will move. He expects that too. He will be propelled into the indeterminate, the mockingly inscrutable. But he will be prepared to cooperate with it the moment he arrives.

16. The Keaton Curve: A Study in Cooperation

Keaton did cooperate with the universe, a trait that continues to distinguish him from his fellow comedians. Most clowns regarded the physical world as an obstacle to be overcome or evaded, by ingenuity or by grit. Keaton felt otherwise. He knew all about obstacles, of course. But treacherous as the universe might be, Keaton trusted it.

It is tempting to think that he arrived at his attitude because of the way the physical world treated him one day in his childhood, when he was not yet three. As an infant, he'd been kept in a trunk backstage while his mother and father performed the family act. That hadn't worked out too well: once he was accidentally locked into the trunk, kept company only by a ventriloquist's dummy, until he nearly smothered; very often, as soon as he could free himself from the trunk, he strolled on stage and interrupted the proceedings. In desperation, his mother started leaving him at the local boarding house, with the housekeeper presumably watching over him. While he was there, on the day in question, a cyclone blew up. Warned, his parents raced home from the theater and up the boarding house stairs, only to find that air pressure from the cyclone—which had just carried the roof of the house away—had sealed the door against them. When they did succeed in forcing the door, Buster was gone.

Alerted by the winds, Buster had wandered to the window to see what was brewing and had been immediately sucked through it by the eye of the storm. "Before Joe and Myra were halfway up the stairs," Rudi Blesh writes, "their son was sailing high over trees and houses, too amazed to be afraid, and then coasting down a slow-relaxing ramp of air to land gently in the very center of an empty street." The spot at which he landed was four blocks away.

The child to whom that happened might well place a little confidence in wind and height, in the tricks natural forces play as they romp through space. Naturally, one doesn't wish to become an amateur analyst and derive all of Keaton's later emotional attitudes from a single freakish, yet benevolent, event.

But Keaton has more or less told us to do so, not only through his conversations with Mr. Blesh but through one of his later feature films. In *Steamboat Bill Jr.* three of his childhood associations appear in a closely locked pattern, one that is surely deliberate: there is a cyclone that picks him up clinging to a tree and deposits him, still with tree, in a raging river very near the side-wheeler he has been desperately trying to reach; the same cyclone, a few moments earlier in its fury, has hurled him high against a theater backdrop so that he can slide down it, neck-first, as he always had done in the family vaudeville act; and at one point it puts him in close conjunction with a curiously ominous ventriloquist's dummy. No real gag is achieved with the dummy; it is apparently there simply to complete the trio of childhood memories. Keaton does seem to be calling clear attention to the sources of his odd compact with the ominous.

Such a compact exists in all of the films, even the early ones. It is not a firm truce, not a gullible man's handshake with powers unpredictable enough to flip him on his ear, using the handshake as lever. It is nearer a wary cease-fire, a watching and waiting with some confidence in the opposition's intentions. The physical universe is violent, no question about that. It *may* do a man in. Then again, just as violently, it may do him a favor. What Keaton understands—and what he bases his bargain on—is the essential *neutrality* of its behavior. Perhaps the best thing to do in the circumstances is to try to match its indifference: when worst comes to worst, stand still. The building falling over on you may leave you a window. Patience is wanted: if you can last it out, there will be another roll of the dice, or the spheres. If you are watching a ball game through a forbidden peephole in a fence and a cop comes along and collars you, don't resist. Submit and prepare to accompany him. Before you have moved two feet a pop-fly from the ball park may arc over the fence and obligingly drop the cop for you.

Of course, patience comes hard to all men, and Keaton is a human being. He does resist, sometimes. It is then that he makes his biggest mistakes. When the newly built house of *One Week* begins to spin on its axis during a windstorm, it unceremoniously whirls him out the front door and into the drenching rain. He is determined to get back in, no matter how fast the vulnerable structure is now revolving. He races the house, trying to keep pace with the front door, losing ground all the time as he leaps over the porch rails and slides through mud. He tries another way, standing still till the front door comes dizzyingly around again, trying to gauge its aperture in the brief second it is available, diving at it headlong. Naturally, he misses it, the acceleration being so great, his head ramming into the side wall time after time. In due time he seems to succeed, making his spurt just enough ahead of the door's rotating appearance to mesh with it. In he goes, and then—in a staggeringly sustained single shot—he is whipped through every room in the house, toppling furniture as he flies, until he has been hurled out the front door once more. Grit will get you nowhere, except back where you started.

He is constantly trying to nail things down, with as little success. In *The Boat* he nails the steering wheel in place, hoping to keep the ship on course long enough to attend to other matters. The fixed course sends the ship cavorting in circles. When winds—again—turn the boat over and over in the water while he is desperately trying to telegraph his position to the Coast Guard, he nails his shoes to the floor in an effort to keep upright at the instrument whether the ship is topsy-turvy or not. The shoes hold him in place for at least one loop-the-loop, then stay fixed to the floor—now the ceiling—while his feet pull out of them and drop him headlong to the boards. When the hull of the ship springs a leak the size of a water-faucet, he nails a breakfast pancake—we are already aware that his wife cooks pancakes of solid oak—over the incoming jet of water.

The pancake, now moistened for the first time, gives way, whereupon he takes further frantic steps. Noting precisely where the arched stream hits the bottom of the boat, he drills a hole in the bottom to let the incoming water out. Needless to say, the action taken is unsatisfactory. The gag is, for Keaton, not even a good gag. Keaton is rarely persuasive when he is behaving stupidly. We know that he knows better than that—we have watched him make judgments all along and respect his canny eye—and we don't want to see him wasting his time making jokes that are not practical jokes. When Keaton's gags don't work—when he installs a trapdoor himself and then forgetfully walks into it, or when he puts an oversized vase in a suitcase and closes the suitcase with his knee though it is clear that the pressure must break the vase—it is usually because he is underestimating the intelligence we attribute to him. He is working too hard in a new sense: fighting against what *is* instead of rolling with it.

We can see his intelligence at work even *when* he is taking up arms futilely, laboring to do what cannot be done by sheer labor. In film after film, we watch him learn. In an uncharacteristically Sennettish ploy, his enemy has been bounced, trampoline-style, so high in a house that his head has broken through the roof. Buster happens to be working on the roof at the time and sees that the fellow's head is hopelessly stuck there. Having nothing but a crowbar at hand, he tries to pry it loose with that. Not, in itself, very good or original business. He doesn't succeed. With a snappish sigh of despair, he gives up, tossing the crowbar aside. The crowbar hits his enemy's head with such uncalculated force that it not only loosens the stranglehold but drops the man a couple of flights. Accident is more reliable than effort. A few minutes later Buster is astride the peak of the roof, struggling with a ready-made chimney that is exceedingly awkward to handle and wondering how he is ever going to get it down to its prepared hole on the steep slant. He slips, loses balance, slides directly down to the hole and through it, leaving the chimney behind him perfectly in place. Things will work out provided you plan nothing, resist nothing; we can see Keaton's eye grasping this information every time matters are, rather literally, taken out of his hands.

They are taken out of his hands altogether by what I think of as the Keaton Curve. Keaton realized, in double-quick time, that the universe played ball with a curve, that it was itself curved. And he knew that the course of the Curve, whether great or small, was precisely as fortuitous, as uncontrollable, as the minor inadvertencies I've been describing. In *Neighbors* he is wooing the girl who lives in the house just across the fence. The families are feuding, and the fence is a barrier. Buster does manage to slip through its gate, though, and up into the girl's third-floor room, where he is discovered. Before her father can do him violence, Buster leaps to the window, seizes the pulley of a clothesline that crosses both yards, rides the pulley at accelerating speed into a window of his own house. The momentum of the ride, however, is such that it hurls him forward and head first onto a banister that carries him zooming down a flight, shoots him out another window and across the yard on a lower clothesline, back into the house he has just come from—and the waiting grasp of that wrathful father. He might as well never have fled. That's the Curve, stood on end so that we can see it flat, like a circus hoop.

He could also loop it loose as a lariat, stretching it through time to become the shape of his plotting. The Curve, mind you, is like the universe that begets it: neutral. It can be helpful or harmful without caring. In *The High Sign* he needs a newspaper; he wants to read the "Help Wanted" ads. Straying by an amusement-park carousel, he simply puts one hand out toward the riders and comes away with a newspaper that must have been sticking out of some fellow's

Natural balances may or may not work out in Buster's favor, but a confident surrender to their laws is the best way to play it. *Cops.*

Overleaf: Buster is a rather noticeable stage extra in *Daydreams.*

pocket. He sits on a park bench, unfolds the newspaper—it just so happens that when he has opened it full to its center fold it opens again downward and then upward and then outward again, so that he has as much infinity on his hands as he cares to manage—and does find a job available in a shooting gallery. The newspaper is neatly refolded and is being held carelessly in Keaton's hand when a man comes along, takes the paper, and pays him for it. Though it hadn't occurred to us, Keaton *could* have been mistaken for a news-vendor. Of one thing we are certain. The man who buys the paper is the man who lost it on the carousel. The Circle complete, Buster is ahead one job plus five cents.

In *The Goat* the Curve unemotionally works the other way around. Outracing a dozen or so cops, Buster dives into an enormous moving van whose rear ramp is down, plunges through the driver's window up front, climbs over the cab onto the roof—just as the cops are all piling into the van after him. The moment the last cop is aboard, Buster, from his godlike perch on the roof, hauls up the rear ramp and locks the lot of them in. He walks away, dusting his hands, satisfied; the van drives off. Later, after various other brushes with the law from which he has just as ingeniously extricated himself, he is walking along a street empty enough to promise peace. Smack in the middle of the block the van backs to the curb, having reached its natural destination, to discharge directly before Buster the enraged police he has bottled up. Set something in motion away from you and you can count on meeting it face to face.

Though the universe might be unemotional, and Keaton himself nearly so in his effort to adapt to it, the man did have feelings—though, I think, only two sets of them. The spectacle of the Curve rounding upon one, willy-nilly, bringing relief or disaster with equal detachment, must breed in a man a certain fatalism, with faintly dour overtones. A man is helpless unless he can help himself to the universe's own laws and habits, taking advantage of them by tucking himself into them. But that is hard. You can't always think quickly enough, and often there is no time to wait. The eternal effort wearies Keaton. The one thing he will permit himself when adaptation has failed is a quick grunt of exasperation, his mouth dropping open to take in just enough air to say, "Oh, shoot!", his shoulders lifting and then falling sharply as his lungs expel a justified dismay.

There is some jaundice in the man, and it extends to people as well as planets. It extends, among other things, to his heroines. The girls in Keaton films are never very important: they are merely there to be rescued and as likely to foul up the rescue as do anything else; they are there to go for the ride; they are there to sit at home reading letters while he does the work of the film. He never did choose to identify himself with a permanent or semi-permanent leading lady, as other comedians did, and it is doubtful that many actresses would have cared to take on so generally suspect a job. Interchangeable faces known as Sybil Seely and Virginia Fox stayed on longest, more or less sharing the first twelve short comedies; whenever they were temporarily replaced, it would be by yet another characterless substitute; only Phyllis Haver and Renée Adorée went on to some sort of later distinction, and it is doubtful that their single appearances in Keaton films contributed much to their rise.

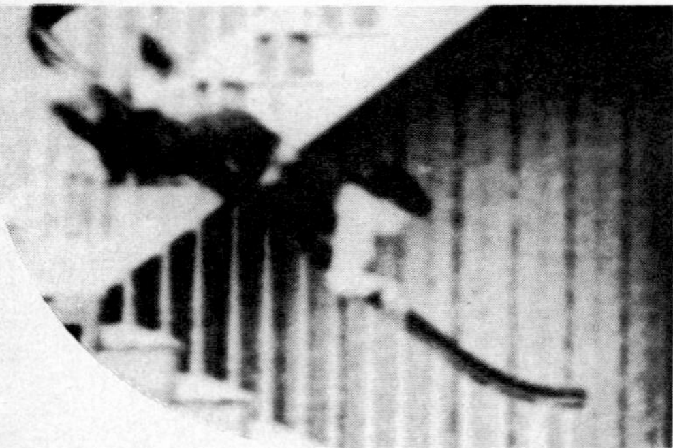

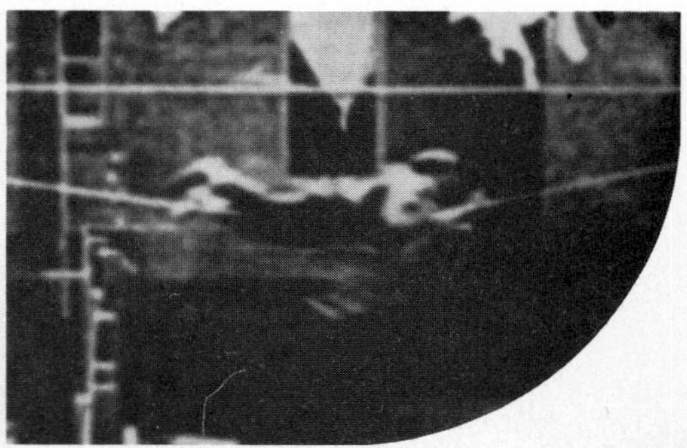

Keaton liked girls, needed girls, married girls, doubted the competence of girls, was afraid of girls. A girl was not only someone who cooked pancakes that could not possibly be eaten; she was someone on a river bank who saw you drowning and, moved to help, picked up a rope and threw both ends of it at you. If she was not battering you black and blue during an unfortunate ride in The Tunnel of Love, she was someone who, having waited too long for you to rescue her from a menacing long-horned steer, simply sighed her own exasperated sigh, took the steer by the horns, and wrangled him to a fall. The theme is much more developed in his features, but all of Keaton's rescues are complicated by the fact that the girl being rescued invariably gets her clawing hands into Keaton's mouth, Keaton's hair, around Keaton's neck; the likelihood is that she will kill him before he can save her.

Marriage, desirable as it may be, is a dubious proposition as well. When the young couple of *Neighbors* are finally to be married, one of the wedding gifts is a book, *How to Box*. When the couple of *The Blacksmith* are married, a title reads, "Many a honeymoon express has ended thusly," followed by a shot of toy trains on a trestle crashing head-on and tumbling from the rails. Of course, if the girl was a heartless snob and would *not* marry you, matters were just as bad. At the end of *Cops*, Keaton has succeeded in locking his pursuers into their own police station, dropping the key into a wastebasket. The girl comes by and turns him down forever. Buster retrieves the key, unlocks the station door, and stands there—a willing victim—until he is seized by dozens of hands and yanked inside. As "The End" fades onto the screen, we see that the title is decorated by a drawing of a gravestone, with Keaton's porkpie hat aslant it. One way or another, this is where all man's hopes are heading. Sooner may be better than later.

But the somber strain in Keaton is only one half of his root response. The other is a superb serenity. It is not a cheerful serenity; that would be too much. It is simply the other side of resignation, the unruffled calm that comes of having accepted whatever is. Keaton is always showing us, in little ways, how ready he is to accept the unthinkable as normal. No matter where he is caught just now—atop an unguided balloon, inside the churning paddle wheel of a ferry boat, on deck during a storm that is carrying mast and antennae away—the first thing he does is go for an evening stroll. He locks his hands behind his back, sets his eyes straight forward, and begins to walk as casually as the environment permits. More casually. His feeling, clearly, is that if he treats the circumstances as routine, they will become routine, falling into place around him. They don't always, but that doesn't deter him or limit his confidence. When he has climbed down the balloon and found himself alone in a bottomless basket, he promptly sets up light housekeeping, with a tub and a washboard and his socks hanging out to dry.

He himself is not only casually adaptable, he is most casually prepared to adapt to his purposes all things that come to hand—in a way that is quite different from Chaplin's use of metaphor. When Chaplin plays billiards with scallions or makes a xylophone out of pie tins, he is simply being playful. Keaton touches nothing unless he can make it instantly functional. In need of a ladder to climb to the roof, he removes the porch railing and stands it on end. In need of two grills to encase a fish he means to fry over a campfire, he makes do with two tennis rackets. In lieu of snowshoes, two guitars. When the orchestra pit is accidentally flooded in *The Playhouse* and he must escape from the stage manager who wishes to throttle him, he uses the bass viol as a canoe and a fiddle for a paddle as he sails placidly out of reach.

There are other ways of keeping one's eyes open to natural physical alter-

Having found temporary lodgings in a paddle-wheel, Buster goes for an evening stroll. *Daydreams*.

Opposite: The Keaton curve in its simplest form: across the yard on a pulley, down and around on a banister, back where he came from on a revolving clothesline. *Neighbors*.

Light housekeeping, complete with decoys, in *The Balloonatic.*

natives, sometimes much bigger and more complicated ways. He is running from an Indian tribe and comes to a rotted suspension bridge over a chasm. Only a few feeble slats still remain on the wires, remnants of the walkway that once was there. Even these are nearly out of reach, and if he does reach them there is nothing beyond them but empty air. He is not perturbed. He dives for the first slat, and makes it—just as the Indians appear at cliff's edge and the leader prepares to try his own leap. Buster is already busy. He removes the first slat and places it beyond the last—when the Indian does leap, he grabs empty air and goes down—and then proceeds to remove pieces one by one, reconstructing the bridge ahead of him as he crawls across the gorge on a handful of shifting supports. A small matter of mathematics, and the whole thing is managed. Sometimes alternatives are simpler, though not at all obvious. He has come to one side of a river bank in his rush, preparing to cross. Directly opposite him, on the other bank, appears an Indian, who immediately dives deep into the water to get at him. Buster, unflurried, at once dives into the river himself, *toward* his pursuer, certain that he will pass him invisibly underwater. Such an escape route has not in the least occurred to us; but Keaton is very perceptive about these things.

His confidence increases in scale until it achieves a kind of geometric majesty. How is he to rescue his girl from that house across the fence in *Neighbors*? Think in terms of physics and you will see that there are practical means. We look at the three stories of Buster's house, one window above another. As one of Buster's brothers steps out of the first-story opening, another steps onto his shoulders from the second story while Buster steps onto *his* shoulders from the third. The three-man totem pole now crosses the yard to the girl's third-story window, makes one trip back with her luggage, returns for her. To make certain that we don't miss the opportunities a logically built universe lays open to us, Keaton carries totem pole and girl into a chase. Almost the first thing they run into is a three-story scaffold, which accepts them easily, one structure matches another so perfectly. There is no break in rhythm as they scurry from shoulder to scaffolding and back again. The world has holes in it. Just find them.

Keaton trusts, accepts, adapts, takes advantage of the regular behavior of forces greater than he. Is he being burned at the stake? The fire will at least light his cigarette. Occasionally a kind of logical rage seems to overtake him, a weariness of waiting that verges almost on madness. He is held captive on a fair-sized ship and cannot escape. He is hungry and has nothing to eat. Without further ado, his face at last truly turned to stone, he marches down a gangway fixed to the outside of the hull straight into and under the water, a shotgun over his shoulder. After a moment, a faint puff of smoke blows up from the waves. He returns, stolidly, stubbornly, carrying a fish he has just shot. Physical laws or no physical laws, he is going to have something to *eat*.

But mostly—and most profitably—he waits. There is, after all, a way to escape that ship, provided physical laws are once more acknowledged and embraced. Held in reserve on the upper deck is a smallish lifeboat. Keaton cannot, however, lift and launch it alone. What to do? Bring the inexorably neutral into play. Buster gashes a hole in the hull of the large ship so that water will pour in. Enough water and the large ship will sink. Buster establishes himself in the lifeboat, biding his time until the main vessel goes down and his own cozy craft drifts off onto the open sea. What could be more reasonable?

The sinking takes time, of course. Buster whiles away the hours playing solitaire—unconcerned, essentially comfortable with fire and flood if not famine, at peace with himself and all powers. He is, at heart and at his best, a man waiting for a favorable hurricane.

17. Some Imperfect Tools

One Sunday afternoon when I was eleven or so, I had what was for me, at the time, a shattering experience. I had been looking forward all week to the arrival, at the best of our neighborhood film houses, of Larry Semon's feature-length version of *The Wizard of Oz*. In addition to being hopelessly movie-struck I was Oz-struck, having long since been through all the books in the series. And I had not yet begun to question Larry Semon's standing in the pantheon of mute and dazzling clowns.

Having rechecked the Sunday newspaper to make certain the film was showing and having enjoyed the streetcar ride to the theater in anticipation of things to come, I turned the corner to glance up at the familiar, always glamorous, marquee. No Larry Semon, no *Wizard of Oz*. Inexplicably, some other film in which I had no interest at all—probably something with Elliott Dexter and Rosemary Theby, or what we called a "grown-up" film, all tuxedos and leers over tea—had usurped its place without warning. I stopped in my tracks, disbelieving; I walked to the other side of the lettered marquee to see if some miracle might put things right on that side; I asked at the box office. It was all true. My Sunday pleasure in ashes, I pursued my inquiries all the way to the assistant manager, who was taking tickets at the moment and whom I had talked to before. He shook his head. "We couldn't get the film," he said. "The company that made it went bankrupt yesterday."

The prospect of disaster overtaking anything so magical as a film company, the notion that the very ground on which my favorites stood might be in some mysterious way insecure, appalled me. Another manager with whom I often chatted in the lobby had once locked his hands behind his back, cocked his head at me, and announced, "You like movies *too* much." I had promptly dismissed his own proud detachment as crass and commercial; he had no *love* for what he bought and sold. But I was, truthfully enough, enamored to the point of blindness, uncritically the slave of enchanted images. How could one not be blinded by the light from that screen? How not be shocked to think of film, vivid film, moldering in an unclaimed can? It so happens that Larry Semon's version of *The Wizard of Oz* is still around, ironically more accessible now than then. It is a film that ought to have bankrupted everyone associated with it.

Larry Semon looked like a silent film comedian, walked like a silent film comedian, *was* a successful silent film comedian for a considerable time. He had no hesitation in starring himself in a comedy called *The Perfect Clown*, and he made his way—however precariously—from two-reelers into features. But, like so many of the other satellites that revolved about Chaplin, Keaton, and Lloyd and even seemed their equals at the turn of the 1920's, he was a man headed for eventual failure, a face and a walk without an idea to see him home.

Clown faces, clown bodies, were quite enough for near-instant stardom during the years when Chaplin's constantly quadrupling salary sent filmmakers scurrying about frantically for possible duplicates. Some of the also-rans possessed genuine skills, many had had successful careers in vaudeville, almost all were sufficiently bizarre in appearance to hint at laughter before they had done much of anything. Semon might have been, and in fact was, a cartoon. The performer had spent time drawing a newspaper comic strip before he was taken on by the Vitagraph studios in New York as a director. Later, after he had managed to get himself in front of the camera, he attempted to prop up his screen career by syndicating a strip on the side, reproducing himself as his chief pen-and-ink figure.

All the external qualifications were present, enticingly. He painted his face a pasty white, letting the line where the makeup ended show at the back of his neck. His mouth turned upward in a V-shaped simper, his eyelids were creased downward so that all his features seemed to converge in a squeeze-play about his enormous curved nose. The ears that framed his lemony look might have been an elephant's. There was no mistaking the invitation: laugh.

He moved with distinctive style, most often on tiptoe. Wearing balloon-baggy trousers hiked up so high that they covered his chest and left his deft ankles thoroughly visible, he worked with a dainty lift-step, as though testing the earth before him to make certain it wasn't too hot. In *The Wizard of Oz* there is a time when it *is* too hot: each tentative probe of his toe brings a lightning-bolt down on the spot, forcing him to retract into a foetal huddle, hands knuckled together like a suppliant mouse.

When warned to reverse direction, he could reverse with the about-face yank of a moving object in a shooting gallery, one elbow back, the other forward, a discus-throwing posture turned solid as wood. There was a trace of the eccentric dancer about him: when he ran, he ran dapper in his spats; when he moved more cautiously, his feet seemed as webbed as a duck's.

Once in a while, though rarely, traces of imagination turn up in his more elaborate visual jokes. In a two-reeler, *Her Boy Friend*, we are on a pier looking at an enormous, neatly stacked pile of packing crates, all shapes and sizes, all interlocked. Slowly out of the solid wall of packaging emerge two robotlike figures, creatures made of suitcase-sized cartons, leaving their outlines carved precisely in the tower of crating behind them. They are, it turns out, Semon and his girl's father, in effective disguise. The fantastic possibility is persuasive.

Semon's relatively early death in 1928, after he had been forced to abandon his own films and had shifted gears slightly by appearing as a supporting player in Josef von Sternberg's *Underworld*, is most often attributed to his chronic anxiety. Throughout his career he had been known as a worrier, someone who fretted endlessly whether a film seemed to be going well or badly, someone so fearful of drying up prematurely that he crammed a notebook full of gags against

Opposite: In the accordion-pleated car, Larry Semon and his actress-wife, Dorothy Dwan.

Below: Lupino Lane and his scissor legs in *Swords' Points*, yet another spinoff of *The Three Musketeers*.

the future. Some commentators have chosen to respect him for his fearful conscientiousness.

But it is just this quality that destroys the films. They are frantic—in the end, only frantic. Semon is so terrified that a moment of footage won't move, that there will be a pause during which the audience will catch its breath and not laugh, that he allows himself no field of grace in which to establish a personality or prepare for a joke requiring minimal thought. Flour sacks begin to fly through the air in the very first frame; if the last frame is to be "funnier" the objects hurtling through space must be magnified and multiplied. Lured into ruinously costly spectacle that eventually led to a break with his backers, Semon blew up buildings, toppled silos, made hash of giant sawmills, sent autos plunging into houses with a prodigality Sennett wouldn't have attempted.

His impatience kept him from ever finishing a story he had started to tell, or from finding enough substance in it to sustain a film for twenty mintues. *A Simple Sap* seems to begin as a comedy about Larry's pet airplane; he hurries his girl, Dorothy Dwan, into it for a ride. We discover that it is pulled by a donkey. The matter, outsized and merely puzzling as it is, is not pursued. The film detours for some laboratory trickery: an egg develops two legs and an inexplicable tail, becomes stuck in flypaper as it attempts to walk about, becomes, just as inexplicably, a lizard when the shell is fully broken. The plot next seems to have something to do with selling Dorothy's uncle's store, whereupon a cavalierly unmotivated free-for-all takes place, with a dislodged smokestack tumbling down near an electric fan to blow soot all over the man who might have bought the grocery. Semon begins as a child in *School Days*, then, after a rushed nine minutes, jumps the film twenty years ahead so that he can resume toppling fat men off ladders into vast mudbaths—mudbaths were rather an obsession of his—and plunging missiles and people through roofs and walls.

The anxiety led Semon into excessive stunting, and the stunting led him into fakery. The great arched falls that were often taken in Semon's films—from the top of a silo to a haystack far below, from high in a ship's rigging far out over the ship and sea—were undeniably impressive. They were, however, taken by stunt men, not by the star. Entire chase sequences for his films were often shot while he was away from the studio on business or vacation. Close-ups could be added later, after doubles had done the principal work.

Where Semon was more directly concerned, the cheating continued—in the camera-work, in the cutting, in the often slovenly matching of shots. I had always remembered from my childhood what I considered Semon's "signature," a bit of business in which he would discover a girl imprisoned behind a locked door, rush away from the door to gather up steam, brace his shoulders manfully, rush at the door to crack it open, and then find himself sailing through the suddenly opened door straight across the room and out the window on his head. I supposed that he did this often, and he may have done so. But in the films I've been able to look at recently I find only one example of it, a poor one. Semon's fall from window to street in *Her Boy Friend* is an almost classic example of easy evasion. It is in three shots. In the first he plunges through the window, though the shot does not say how high the window is. In the second we see him falling, against an utterly blank skydrop. In the third we see him hit the street, from a low enough camera angle to have permitted him simply to leap to the position.

As we know, Semon was by no means alone in faking business through opportunistic cutting. Nor was he alone in making use of another kind of rigged fall. It was common practice to combine the use of a dummy with the use of stop-motion photography. But there are two hitches to this second method, and they arè always apparent. A dummy is recognizable as a dummy, no matter how well shaped or weighted. And, inevitably, there is a sickening little lurch, a split second of contradiction, as the dummy—courtesy of stop-motion—turns into the real clown on the street. Life seems to lose a beat; the universe twitches.

The moment this happens—and it happens a great deal in lesser silent film comedy—the form itself is denied. One premise of the form is that a clown falling from a second-story window never gets hurt; that is a condition of the essential fantasy. But if we are aware that it is *not* the clown who is not getting hurt, but a shabby substitute instead, the fantasy is just as damaged. For it must be a fantasy of fact.

To make the form work perfectly, the comedian has got to do the stunt. Naturally, most comedians were willing, from time to time, to let the form *be* imperfect so long as they could get the laugh without undue danger or expense. Even Keaton, strictest of them all, surrendered occasionally. In *Cops*, for instance, he permits himself the use of a wire. He has just done a brilliant bit of geometric fooling: running from a horde of policemen he has come upon a long ladder perched against a fence, just parallel to the camera lens; he has climbed it midway so that it balances precariously on the edge of the fence and can be tilted either way on its fulcrum; and he has shown us delectable variations of counterweight and poise as he contends with police who are grabbing at both ends of the teeter-totter. But he must, finally, get out of there, and to do it he perches himself at an extreme end of the ladder so that a cop forcibly lowering the opposite end turns it into a catapult, sending Keaton flying over all heads and across the city street. But the wire that helps him fly gives us a visible untruth: the trajectory of the flight is slack, its rhythm is no more a human rhythm than the wire Chaplin uses to hurry him up a cliff-face in *The Adventurer.*

We are doubly sorry to see Keaton surrender now and then, because it is Keaton who has taught us, more than anyone, what to demand of the form. Most of the time—almost all of it—Keaton is doing what he seems to be doing. He takes his falls, we see them intact, we see him rise intact afterward. In *One Week* he inadvertently walks out of an open door that has no staircase attached to it and plunges two stories to land on his back. It can be done, we are there when it is done, a standard is set. With Keaton we would rather skip a gag than have him fake it.

With Semon it scarcely matters, because everything is faked—the flour sack that sails at a dead level across a room, the woodpecker that lights on the comedian's head and squirts water in his eye, the rowboat that leaves the lake and keeps going over rocks, the block of wood that is chopped out of a stump to fly in an impossible arc through a roof and interrupt a wedding. Semon cheats to keep going; he has, really, nothing to stop for. He has the clear outlines of a clown's face and feet, but no clown's innards; he is a man without material. Typically, after he had long fought for the right to make a feature film of *The Wizard of Oz*, he began by instantly jettisoning the material he was given. Apart from a Kansas cyclone and his own eventual appearance as a scarecrow—visually, he makes an excellent scarecrow—there is nothing in the film to differentiate it from his short comedies. In Kansas there are falls from trees, falls from silos; Semon repeats, from *School Days* of five years before, the business of waking up from a hen-house nap with eggs splattering down into his eyes. In Oz there are omnipresent trapdoors so that one and all can be plunged into mudbaths. The vein, in the end, is narrow and desperately reworked.

In a sense, it was possible to be too *much* of a clown for the factual nature of silent film fantasy. If a performer relied entirely on his face and his body—as

Opposite: Lupino Lane was close enough to a circus clown to be drawn as one. Larry Semon came nearly as close *au naturel.* Keaton, with his nose and mouth smudged, smudged his identity, too—disturbingly.

circus clowns do—to create comedy on the instant and very much in passing, it was likely that his *persona* would be too thin for a medium that insisted on a degree of recognizable reality. Genuine circus clowns, for instance, were quickly signed and starred by eager producers—Toto, Joe Jackson, the lot of them—but never with success. A film or two and the pure zany would be back with Barnum and Bailey, using his extravagant makeup and his breakaway props to stir fleeting—but no more than fleeting—laughter as he incessantly strolled the ring.

For silent comedy purposes, a man might be—even needed to be—something of a grotesque; but not so much a grotesque that he could not plausibly hail a taxi. Passing him on the street, we should certainly think him odd; but we should still think him an odd human being. Keaton's mask is interesting in this respect. It *is* a mask, impermeable bone structure. And it could very readily become a clown's mask. Every once in a while in a Keaton film there is a reason for him to appear with a smudged nose. A faint touch of soot and the face turns storybook-stylized, a depersonalized thing of paint. Interesting as Keaton looks under these circumstances, we are always relieved when the smudge is wiped away, as we are relieved when he *stops* being a perfect chimpanzee in *The Playhouse*. We want the man back; he will still be called a clown but he will now be a clown of substance. Indeed, Keaton's face could be called the archetypal clown-face stripped naked, the pale flesh that is left when all the paintpots are thrown away. It is a negative rather than a positive. But the nakedness makes him vulnerable, immediate, dimensional enough to stand still for a moment and interest us in his thoughtful occupation of space.

The more closely a silent film comedian resembled an actual circus clown—Semon came close—the more certain he was to be condemned to second rank. Lupino Lane, for instance, never did escape from two-reelers into starring features, though his equipment was superior to Semon's: a more pensively amusing face, a body capable of infinitely greater virtuosity. Lane did not come from a circus but from its blood brother, the British music hall, where the Lupino family had been taking skilled falls and executing standing somersaults for generations. Chaplin, bred on the same ground, escaped early; Lane seems to have stayed long enough to have become rigidly fixed in its intricate patterns of stunting: no clown in the world knows better than a British music-hall clown how to trap his foot in a bucket or engage himself disastrously with a passing ladder. And Lane, in all probability, really preferred the music-hall stage to the screen.

He looked rather like a lemur, enormous oval eyes dominating a face that narrowed swiftly to a tucked-in chin, the mouth between a bit repressed as though he had just said something unfortunate and hoped never to repeat it. The face rarely expressed anything, certainly not thought; an irrelevant spitcurl on the right temple, however, made it seem vaguely cheerful.

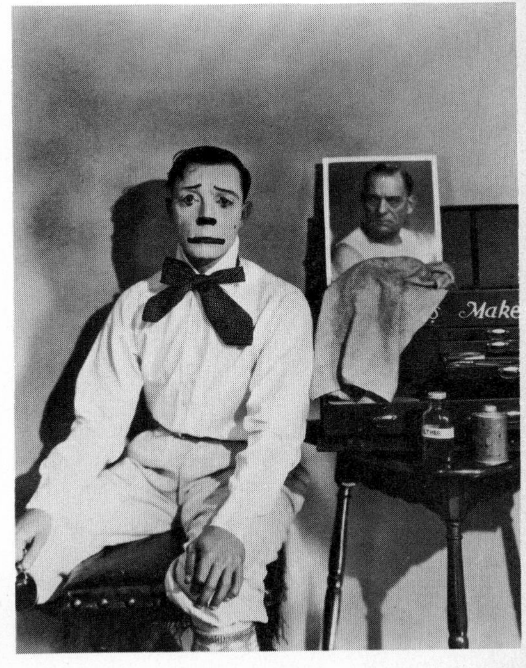

The body was extraordinary, as flexible as a paper doll whose joints are eyelets that permit legs to jackknife any old way. Seated on the floor, he could grab one ankle and hoist it over him in a spin that would bring him into instant standing position, confounding an unready opponent. Or, again seated on the floor, he might swiftly spread his legs wide into a dancer's "split" position and force himself upward like a scissors being closed. Wishing to threaten someone with a leap, he could bring both legs off the floor, high, one straight forward, the other straight back, covering all options. To somersault from table to floor, *or* from floor to table, was nothing.

He could be inventive with props. In *Swords' Points*, yet another variation on *The Three Musketeers*, he is sent to a tavern cellar to bring up six mugs of wine. He runs his rapier through six mug handles and carries them that way. He deposits the mugs beneath six wine casks, withdraws the rapier to flash it in air and bring it down across the six corks that seal the casks. Instantly wine flows from six casks into six cups. Unfortunately, the flow gets out of hand and inundates the cellar. No matter. He swims to a tray, deposits six fresh—and empty—mugs upon it, submerges himself *and* the tray in order to fill up the containers, rises and makes for the stairs. Later, he is honorable in a duel. Whenever he happens to slice off a bit of his opponent's rapier, he stops to shorten his own to the same length. Fair is fair. Eventually both are dueling with hilts.

But, attractive as Lane can be, there are self-imposed, or clown-imposed, limits to his vocabulary. When he isn't actually executing a gag, he isn't anybody. He is only the sum of his "turns." This leads, as with Semon, to leaning on trick devices; "turns" cannot be repeated indefinitely, and the space between them must be filled up. Lane's particular reliance was upon reverse photography. In England his early films had made extensive use of distorting mirrors, amusement-park variety. Now, in the later Hollywood comedies, he took to perfecting quite long sequences in which he would seem to rise from a flattened position without bothering to grip an ankle or perhaps to slither snakelike on his belly backward down a flight of steps into a waiting car. Some ingenuity, of course, must go into this sort of illusion. To perform forward what will be shown backward involves a degree of grace if the image is not to come out awkward. But constantly relying upon this kind of trickery is, in the end, a confession: the clown, faced with a camera, makes *it* do the work, his own resources having run out.

Clowns of the second rank can also be spotted in the quality of their borrowing. I am not speaking of outright imitation now—as Lloyd for so long aped Chaplin directly—but of the quite casual interchange of bits of business and workable backgrounds among men who had already arrived at their identities. This kind of borrowing was open, a tacit agreement to share the common wealth. Sooner or later Chaplin, Keaton, and Langdon all turned up as streetcleaners in white jackets. Chaplin and Keaton both launched ships that sank instantly. Langdon and Chaplin made use of blind heroines. Keaton, Lloyd, and Langdon all went to college. Chaplin, Keaton, and Langdon spent time in the prize ring. Among the master comedians it didn't really matter who did what first. It was understood that the number of playing cards was limited, the deck was promptly shuffled, one used the cards that came to hand.

But the master comedians borrowed—paradoxically—as a means of defining themselves. The device that was being appropriated might be entirely familiar. But if it could be made, for the moment, to seem appropriate to Keaton rather than Langdon, if it could fit snugly under Lloyd's arm or quite naturally provoke Chaplin's sniff, if it could conform without effort to the dip, shuffle, or retard of this or that man's private syncopation, then it would not only be rejuvenated as a device but would most specifically call our attention to what was unique about *this* performer.

Not so with those whose identities were less firmly held, less assertively developed. Thus, when Lupino Lane, trapped by cannibals and tied to a stake, discovers that the stake is not securely imbedded and that he can in fact walk around with it at will—confusing his captors no end—we do not find ourselves imaginatively challenged, and then captivated, by his appropriation of a gag used earlier by Keaton. We do not wait, in some suspense, to see what fresh stylistic mark he will leave on it. We scarcely see *him* doing the gag at all. We simply see the gag, isolated in space, as torn from its moorings as the stake is. And we realize that it still belongs to Keaton: the earlier imprint is stronger than the one being made now. We even remember why. There is nothing so character-

Opposite: Joe Jackson, in the ship's rigging, was one of the real circus clowns who tried films and failed. *A Modern Enoch Arden*, made by Keystone in 1916.

Below: Lloyd Hamilton, much admired, still a mystery.

istic here as Keaton's bowing his head in greeting to an approaching, menacing Indian in such a way that the nod will bring the stake tied to his back directly down on the Indian's skull.

It is doubly disheartening to see Lloyd Hamilton, in a two-reeler made relatively late in the 1920's, making use of business with a vacuum cleaner—sucking drapes from the walls, clothes from men's backs, hair from a dog—that the undistinguished Billy Bevan had exhausted, to no particular effect, some three or four years earlier. Doubly disheartening because, of all the satellite figures who remained bound to short comedies in the period, Hamilton was very probably the best.

"Lloyd [Hamilton] was one of the funniest men in silent pictures," Keaton told Herbert Feinstein in an interview for *The Massachusetts Review*, and most other professional comedians of the period tended to echo this view. Hamilton was not only popular with audiences but admired by his colleagues, possibly because he had worked out a costume *and* a cast of mind that owed nothing to anyone else. The working-out was a long time delayed. Hamilton had almost inadvertently become successful as early as 1914 as half of an impromptu comedy team known as Ham and Bud, thrown together on the Kalem lot and held together for something like two hundred one-reel films. The Ham of Ham and Bud, however, bears no resemblance to the Lloyd Hamilton we spoke of in an earlier chapter, the overgrown chap with his baby fat still about him who inventively hails a streetcar to help him lace a shoe. In a Kalem film like *Blundering Blacksmiths* he is almost invisible behind caterpillar eyebrows and mustache-sprays that seem horsetails; he is presented as ferociously muscular and given to bending iron bars with his bare hands; his companion, Bud Duncan, is merely a pint-sized foil for Ham's massiveness, without comic interest of his own.

The transformation of this whiskered behemoth into the faintly effeminate "overgrown boy" Keaton called him was an astonishing one, and fair proof of the comedian's originality. Effeminate mannerisms, by the way, did not imply homosexuality in this period; homosexuality was acknowledged and kidded, but it was more likely to be indicated by a man wearing a wristwatch than by his walking from the hips or delicately retracting his fingers when surprised. Hamilton waddled, and his use of his hands was prim indeed; but as often as not he was presented as married and the father of children. A comic style did not have to account for itself in realistic terms.

I am not going to dally over Hamilton here, partly because we have already spoken of his presumably representative *Move Along* in some detail, partly because so many of his films have been lost—a fire in the Educational Films warehouse is thought to have destroyed most of his negatives—that it is difficult to be certain now just what *is* representative of the man. I have been able to find nothing else as good as *Move Along*, but he can still be seen, pancake cap aslant on sleekly flattened-down hair, taking a whisk broom to his threadbare topcoat and brushing it to ribbons with the barest whisk. Straightening the lapel of his jacket, he loses the lapel. When, with a sigh, he tosses the lapel away, the sleeve of his jacket goes with it. Meeting a friend on the street, he shakes hands with him; the rest of the jacket attaches itself to the handshake. The shredding is unforced, and even a bit touching.

Among secondary comedians, Hamilton had the strongest sense of the conjuction of fantasy and reality that silent film had unwittingly spawned. In *In the Movies* he is taking leave of his aged parents in their vine-covered country cottage, promising to heed their warnings to be careful on his trip to the "big city" and on no account to go anywhere "near the movies." With a parting sigh, he turns from the gate, takes one step away, and is *in* the big city. The big city, with its bustling sidewalks and traffic-cluttered streets, comes directly to the door of the cottage, rather as though God had drawn an invisible line that instantly turned greenery into town. When, at the film's ending, after a rather unfortunate fling at acting in the movies, he returns to the cottage again, it is just that step away. Hamilton is casual about offering no explanation. You can see that it's so, can't you?

Hamilton's face, his walk, and his cool command of the improbable entered that necessary middle-ground between the overstylized shapes of the circus and the underaccented gestures of ordinary residents of the planet. Real enough to have a mother—though in one film his mother is cross-eyed—he is still enough out of touch with things to fail to notice that in taking his coat from a coat rack he has not made the separation complete, so that the entire rack strolls with him as he imperiously patrols the street. He belongs to the world of the plausibly bizarre, the "too much" that can still be photographed, and why he should have been reduced in the later twenties to unvaried borrowings of material short on quality in the first place is a mystery that can be resolved only by the recovery of more of his films. There is always hope: whatever may have happened to negatives, isolated prints turn up in the unlikeliest places.

Part Three– The Struggle Toward Maturity

18. The Risks of Length and Complexity: Chaplin Takes the Plunge

But a marked change was already taking place in the contours of silent film comedy and the status of the comedians who worked in it. Until the turn of the 1920's the two-reel, twenty-minute short was not simply *a* short subject but *the* comedy on every motion-picture bill. The bill would be composed of a feature film—at first normally five reels long, then more or less standardized at seven—together with a newsreel, a cartoon or travelogue, and the comedy. The comedy, then in the hands of men like Chaplin, Keaton, and Lloyd, was not only an essential part of every program, it was often the most important item in the evening's grab bag. Short comedies were often billed above the features; managers were well aware that Chaplin's name on the marquee meant more to audiences than Shirley Mason's or Lew Cody's, and if a Keaton two-reeler was available the theater owner might take the opportunity to combine it with the weakest feature he was under contract to play, counting on Keaton to fill the house. Comedy was still something that occupied twenty minutes, though those twenty minutes might be extraordinarily valuable.

By the time that someone like Lupino Lane—let alone Billy Dooley, a tall and eel-like creature in a sailor suit whose chief claim to humor was the ability to twist his mouth into a figure-eight—came along, matters were quite different. The major comedians had inched themselves into features, cautiously expanding to three or four reels before plunging into seven, which meant that comedy itself occupied a new and even dominant place in the film hierarchy, leaving the twenty-minute prank little more than an also-ran. The two-reeler might still be regarded as a training school for features, and a comedian *might* make it to the big time—Harry Langdon managed it—but it no longer occupied a very special place in the hearts and loyalties of audiences. With major comedians making features, the minors were likely to be treated as mere filler; production values became routinized and even careless. Work as shabby as that turned out by the Christie Brothers—flimsy sets, frantic and repetitive plots, personnel drawn from clowns who had

worn out their welcomes at Sennett and elsewhere—was one result. Sennett himself continued, tiredly but still profitably, to go through the motions of having the flowers on Louise Fazenda's hats pop straight into the air to show how frightened the poor girl was. With the important stars gone from the field, the field itself became mechanized—and all the harder to escape.

The major stars had not moved to features out of any sense of self-importance. Very often their first extensions to three and four reels were inadvertent: in the course of developing an idea, they found they had shot so many funny sequences that it would have been insane to abandon any of them. They simply let the new comedy run overlength. Keaton's *Daydreams*, intended as a two-reeler, slipped over into three, as Lloyd's *A Sailor-Made Man* did to four. The story-line of Chaplin's *The Kid* "demanded more than the planned footage," Theodore Huff tells us, and Harold Lloyd himself describes the gradual growth of what was to become a phenomenal success, *Grandma's Boy*: "I had carried the idea of *Grandma's Boy* in my head for three years and tried to fit it into one- and two-reel lengths, but it would not be squeezed in. Finally I concluded to make it in whatever length it might work out. When it was finished and cut we had five reels, and five good ones, but it had cost us more than $100,000."

The cost squeeze was the second factor that pushed the principal comedians into features. As they tried to improve their films, reshooting more often and placing themselves in more elaborate and varied locales, they discovered that their expenses were running higher than any rental income they could hope to demand for a mere twenty minutes of film. Film rentals still depended mainly on length: it often happened that an exhibitor would pay more for the weak five-reel feature that was being rescued by a two-reel Lloyd than he paid for the popular Lloyd. And the only way to increase rentals was to increase length. In effect, the stars were forced into features—that or cut back on quality, returning to their ramshackle beginnings.

Even so, they moved tentatively, uncertain as to just how long their highly specialized styles could be sustained at a single sitting. They were none of them romantic figures, able to slip into "straight" features and simply bring their playfulness along as a dividend. Lloyd, indeed, looked more or less normal, and one could assume he would get the girl. He wouldn't get her, however, until he had won a war single-handedly with no military equipment whatsoever or until he had swung like a pendulum on a rope fourteen stories in air. Chaplin and Keaton were plainly eccentrics, unlikely candidates for the kind of complex narrative in which either genuine emotion or plausible storytelling would engage an audience's attention for an hour or more. There *had* been one early feature built around acknowledged grotesques—Sennett's *Tillie's Punctured Romance*—but, successful as the film was, it seemed to defy repetition. There was doubt that these extravagant strays, mutations in the species, could go for more than the length of a vaudeville "turn" without exhausting their extremely odd mannerisms. Even the speed at which they normally worked might count against them at greater length; pace palls when it isn't relieved by the quieter passages permitted "normal" folk. Pushed to it, each major comedian had to solve the problem in his own way.

Chaplin's was the most difficult, in large part because he demanded so much of himself, no doubt sensing that somewhere ahead—if he could find it—lay a richer lode, an untapped dimension. He might have been easier on himself. When he completed his Mutual contract in 1917, he was offered another: one million dollars for twelve more short films, with the Mutual company responsible for all production costs. He took another course, chose another contract. First National, a company formed by theater exhibitors to fight the rental demands

Although Sennett put Marie Dressler, Chaplin, and Mabel Normand together in a highly successful feature-length comedy during Chaplin's first year in pictures, the formula seemed unrepeatable and major comedians were slow to abandon the shorter forms. *Tillie's Punctured Romance.*

The Risks of Length and Complexity: Chaplin Takes the Plunge

being made by the studio monopolies, offered him a million dollars for eight films to be completed in eighteen months—with the comedian paying his own production costs. Though he was to do four fewer films for the million, he was taking—and knew he was taking—the poorer offer. If production costs got out of hand, there might be little left for himself. But he wanted the independence of being his own producer, and he wanted it for a purpose.

From the beginning he had obviously yearned for a kind of comedy that would, without ceasing to be comedy, look life in the eye with a bit more candor, and perhaps at greater length. He knew, from his own harrowing childhood and from the seedy poverty that had inspired the very creation of his costume, that what was funny wasn't *funny*; laughter was an evasion of despair. Behind the business of staring hungrily through restaurant windows, sitting huddled in rain-swept doorways, lacking ten dollars for the rent or a dime for a bed in a flophouse—all standard comic plights—lurked genuine anguish, a pain that could be felt. Comedy, once thought about, sobered a man up. But how to catch the underlying seriousness without damaging the dance of the comedy?

He had made tentative stabs in this direction earlier, as we know. The flophouse sequence from *Life*—all that is left of the uncompleted feature he attempted at Essanay—has, for all the knockabout comedy that is in it, a darker, dingier air about it than anything Chaplin had appeared in up to that time. The title itself suggests what he was after. *The Tramp*, also for Essanay, took a step toward hinting that Charlie had a heart and could be hurt; but the hint was forced into a film that wasn't built to house it. *The Vagabond*, his third film for Mutual, did solve the problem in miniature: if he could be funny pretending to elegance while using materials that were shamefully shabby, then the comedy and the truth beneath would be fused. But he hadn't pursued the vein: it involved him in further complications, including an ending for *The Vagabond* he couldn't get right, and for the remaining nine comedies of that contract he was content to skip youthfully through a world that wouldn't have him but couldn't resist him.

But skylarking can't go on forever, happy and beloved as the truant may be. There is no way to make comedy richer by making it funnier—and funnier and funnier. There is only one way of making comedy richer—and, paradoxically, funnier—and that is by making it more serious. Chaplin's intuitions were right, firmly rooted in the nature and the known history of comedy. Comedy isn't an independent form, a world of its own or a law unto itself. It is a parasite on tragedy, parodying it by calling attention to what is foolish about all that earnestness. The tragic hero, the first to be born, is a man who places himself apart from society in order to achieve a goal—stealing fire from heaven, bringing justice to Athens, setting Denmark right—that society itself is either too corrupt or too fearful to seek. Though the tragic hero will suffer and even die in his struggle against the status quo, he will—for the most part—realize his aspiration, bring about change. He is thus both an outcast and in some sense a savior, or at least an advance scout.

Chaplin wasn't after tragedy as such, obviously, though the character he had already fashioned for himself embraced, by accident and instinct, certain of the tragic hero's qualities. He was an outcast by temperament, and he had aspirations of a sort. What Chaplin wanted to do was to dig for the seriousness of comedy's origins, knowing perfectly well that such seriousness was there and was intimately related to the prankish nose-thumbing it had provoked. He wanted to come close enough to seriousness to be able to tickle it with his cane directly, pointing out its earnestness and its absurdities at one and the same time.

The danger was that, in coming so close, the seriousness might swallow the comedy. Chaplin was now the funniest man in the world. To be funnier, he had to risk seriousness. Seriousness, too deeply entered, might destroy what he had become. The situation was delicate, and he had to deal with it under two conflicting pressures: the pressure of his popularity, and the pressure of his ambition. The eight First National films were to be made in eighteen months. It took him five years to make them.

The crunch—much of his own making—was horrendous, and it would take the confidence and indefatigability of genius to survive it, meeting its dual demands day by day. Once he had made his decision, its implications were clear to him. On the day his brother Sydney, who had negotiated the First National contract, excitedly told him the news, Chaplin was only ambiguously pleased: "I suppose that's wonderful," he said. Pressed by Sydney to show more enthusiasm, he pointed out one side of the bind he had got himself into: "The money had to be earned." It had to be earned—by Chaplin's being just as funny as he always had been—not simply to satisfy First National and the vast audiences that now awaited each new film in high expectation, but also to pay for the studio he would have to build for himself. As he moved most deeply into seriousness with his fourth film, *The Kid*, he outlined what he was trying to do in conversation with a well-known writer of the period, Gouverneur Morris. Morris, normally a "charming, sympathetic fellow," dismissed the effort out of hand: "It won't work. The form must be pure, either slapstick or drama; you cannot mix them, otherwise one element of your story will fail." Throughout the First National period, and even up to the later *The Gold Rush*, both audiences and critics were to be heard crying that Chaplin was trying to take their comedy away from them; they continued to go to his films, though.

Realistic as he might be about economic and audience pressures, Chaplin would not be dissuaded. He also knew that the change—whatever it was he might be able to discover beneath the buffoonery—could not be radical. He would have to move not so much fearfully as thoughtfully, introducing one or two elements at a time of the solider, grayer "real" world without disrupting the surface texture, the fantasia of hop, skip, and kick he had so joyously mastered. He would also alternate styles, sometimes following up a thrust toward faint melancholy with a film bursting with slapstick alone. The main strain—the strain that was to end in the much more complex figure we now know—is developed in the first, third, fifth, and eighth films of the First National series: *A Dog's Life, Sunnyside, The Kid*, and *The Pilgrim*. I'd like to speak of them in that order, reserving the "relief" films for briefer discussion.

The thirty-minute *A Dog's Life*, as delightful a romp as any the comedian had capered through, and still generally regarded as Chaplin's first "masterpiece," makes only three unstressed moves to alter the atmosphere. The dust beneath the comedian's feet is dustier. The dancing that formerly served to express the comedian's disbelief in the plot is now incorporated into the plot and made to involve other people. And a slight structural frame, something to enclose the fun and games, begins to appear: Chaplin's relationship with, and even identification with, a dog serves to open, complicate, and conclude the action.

None of this is permitted to interfere with the fun and games. *A Dog's Life* is actually composed of six balletically conceived and executed "turns," incredibly inventive, one following so quickly upon the other's barely disappeared heels that we are left breathless with the spontaneity and precision of it all. The first finds Charlie, wakened from sleep in a vacant lot by the tantalizing odor of a frankfurter, rolling back and forth beneath a board fence to filch a hot dog—returning for mustard, since he never does anything by halves—and then continuing the back-and-forth roll in coy flirtation with a cop who has spotted his misdeed and is futilely

Charlie and brother Syd engage in an I-spy routine over a plate of muffins. *A Dog's Life*.

rounding the fence on foot in an effort to waylay him.

The second takes place in an employment office. Though Charlie is plainly a vagabond, sleeping in the open, he is still no professional tramp: the first thing he does after breakfast is to go look for work. At the head of the line of those waiting for assignments, Charlie moves quickly forward the moment the two employment clerks open their windows for the day. Not quickly enough. Without in any way seeming to race, another applicant arrives at the first window one rhythmic beat before Charlie. Charlie moves to the second window, only to be anticipated, on the same stroke of the unhurried metronome, again. He begins to move more rapidly from window to window, always arriving just in time to find himself staring at an interloper's back. The pattern goes on, mathematically immaculate, faster and faster without for a moment turning frantic, ending in Charlie's double skid to windows being slapped shut in his face. Not only Charlie's movements, but those of a dozen burly plug-uglies, have been choreographed.

The third is a game played, for the first time, with brother Sydney, who had now joined his company in addition to managing his affairs. Syd, in apron and derby and Dutch-comic mustache, is behind the counter of an open-air lunch wagon. Charlie, strolling by, leans his elbow on the counter as though he had nothing else in the world to do. Each time Syd turns his attention to a frying pan, Charlie stuffs a muffin into his mouth. Syd knows what is happening, for the plate of muffins is rapidly disappearing. But he cannot catch Charlie at it. The prolonged game of "I-spy," most of it in a sustained shot so that Charlie's mouth must be truly crammed without giving the secret away, is so exquisitely timed that you know that each of its participants—as character and as performer—is enjoying the hide-and-seek pattern too much to bother with the simple reality of the situation. The reality of the situation is that the plate is now virtually empty and only Charlie could have emptied it. On the evidence, Syd could—and certainly should—shoo him out of there. He doesn't. He wants to *catch* him.

This is followed by a routine that will be imitated until doomsday, less sensitively; God knows when it was born. Charlie must recover a stolen wallet from two thugs seated over a table in a tavern booth; the side curtains at their backs are drawn. Charlie steps into the next booth, picks up a mallet, tests the curtain for the shape of one thug's head. Before striking, he remembers something. Us. Considerately, he steps forward to draw the front curtain over *his* booth, so that we shall not have to witness the distasteful blow. Now, looking in on the thugs, we see the one nearest Charlie acquire a stunned glaze in his eyes while his arms drop limp; we see Charlie's hands snuggled in from behind to replace his victim's; and we watch the expressive but ever so matter-of-fact hands do all of the things the thug, if he were conscious, might do—take a sip of beer, wipe his mouth afterward, rub his palms together in satisfaction, straighten his tie, shake hands with his partner in crime, beckon him closer with the crook of a finger, slug him with a bottle the moment he is close enough. Charlie has, by the way, managed to steal a sip of beer for himself, by way of a small refresher, during the routine.

He now has the wallet and is on his way out of the tavern, crawling on hands and knees behind the bar. Trapped between the bartender's legs, he is hauled upward by the hair, the wallet is seized for inspection, and the thugs, recovered, arrive at the very moment it is being displayed. At once a four-way snatch at the wallet, from hand to hand and back again, becomes a dizzying shell-game, a virtual dance of sticky fingers functioning at breathtaking speed. Thereafter Charlie races for safety to the lunch wagon, losing the wallet along the way, while the thugs pursue with guns blazing. We are into the last game: Charlie and Syd popping up alternately from behind the counter like mechanized targets in a shooting gallery

Opposite: Charlie and Scraps begin a less-than-well-fed day. *A Dog's Life.*

The Risks of Length and Complexity: Chaplin Takes the Plunge

Above: Charlie plugs the knothole that is causing such a draft.

Opposite: Companions for the night, and a threesome for the future. *A Dog's Life.*

while cups and saucers explode about them and the plate Charlie is using as a shield has two holes blasted into it, turning it into an excellent view-finder for the bobbing man behind it.

These dervish-like displays of dexterity, blissfully executed not only by Chaplin but by the men he was deftly drawing into his whiplash style, constitute the comic body of the film, the guarantee that laughter will be virtually uninterrupted. But why a "masterpiece" and not simply an extension and a rhythmic refinement of the Mutual abandon?

The dirt floor of the vacant lot on which Charlie is discovered sleeping is now real dirt, hard, soiling, transparently uncomfortable. He will make nothing of this, or, rather, he will deflect attention from it with a gag without denying its presence. The board fence beside him is aged, rickety, uneven at ground level, obviously no shelter from wind. The wind bothers him, a bit. He studies its cause. There is a small knothole in one board. He stuffs that with a piece of cloth and curls up to sleep again, reassured. The joke has had a double face: it is funny because closing off the least source of wind is preposterous in the circumstances; it also accents the circumstances. The comedy and a certain harshness of fact are being welded.

When he goes to the tavern, The Green Lantern, the paint is peeling from the cement walls that frame its entrance, the sign promising *Beer 5¢* is weathered almost to obliteration. The curbstone on which he sits is littered: there is garbage for him to probe in search of possible food. Compare the environment in which all of the spirited gagging takes place with that of the earlier *Easy Street* and the new texture becomes plain. Easy Street is a slum street, populated by bullies, drug addicts, impoverished women who must steal. But it is as clean as a drawing for a fairy tale. *A Dog's Life* is not a *picture* of a place but a *place*. The "setting," as a fancifully arranged background for a comedian's antics, is disappearing and something closer to unblinking documentation is taking its place.

The comedian himself is faintly altered in appearance. Though he has lost none of his resilience, he has lost some color in his cheeks. The cheeks are noticeably hollow, hollower than they will ever be again until the final moments of *City Lights*. Entering The Green Lantern and pausing to hand-roll a cigarette, he doesn't hesitate to turn to let us see the harsh lines in his face, the momentary mean resentment in his eyes. This last image may have been intended, in part, as parody: he *does* look a little like William S. Hart grimly dominating a saloon. But it is not quite specific parody, and it lets us see Chaplin as potentially haggard, as someone whose way of life creates physical changes in a free spirit. We're seeing *more* of him, between laughs, even during laughs.

The incorporation of others into the balletic sequences alters their significance in the film. When Chaplin dances alone, he is casting doubt on the story. When others dance with him, they are encouraging belief in it. The mockery of the gratuitous "Ta-taa!" has become the urgency of men looking for work. And the parallelism developed between Charlie's days and a dog's leads not so much to opportunistic symbolism as to a cohesive structure for the film, another advance—toward a modest seriousness—over unfettered improvisation.

Though the symbolism is there, it is neither underscored nor established for its own sake. Charlie wakes in a vacant lot; the dog, Scraps, wakes in an abandoned washtub. Scraps must fight for his food, as Charlie does. After Charlie rescues Scraps from a marauding pack that would deprive him of his food, he attempts to take him into The Green Lantern. Since dogs, like penniless men, are forbidden entry, Charlie stuffs him into his trousers, though—as Charlie now saunters into the tavern as nonchalantly as possible—the dog's tail protrudes, wagging happily, through a hole in the seat of Charlie's trousers. The dog and Charlie are one.

Two thugs are about to interfere with the trio's new-found affluence. *A Dog's Life.*

Below: Charlie admires Edna in *Sunnyside.*

They are also nearly one when they curl up together in Charlie's lot for the next night's sleep. Charlie uses Scraps for a pillow, at least until he becomes aware that Scraps is bounteous host to fleas. The identification does not escape us.

But the dog shapes the plot. While Charlie is idly going through garbage, Scraps is fighting for his own share of the neighborhood's leavings and must be rescued. Taking Scraps into the tavern in search of sustenance, Charlie meets Edna. Waking the second morning, it is the dog who first discovers the wallet, which has been temporarily buried a few inches underground by the thugs. Since Scraps has made him affluent, Charlie is free to return to Edna and propose marriage, not to mention children. During the melee that follows, in which Charlie loses the wallet, it is Scraps who recovers it. Scraps thus creates the film's happy ending: Charlie and Edna can have a cottage in the country, surviving cozily on Charlie's skills as farmer. And it is Scraps' puppies who fill the cradle inside the cottage. The fun and games, abundant as they are, have not had to keep the picture going. There has been a small narrative motor working inside it all the while, a realistic relationship giving rise to the fantastification, prodding it, profiting by it, fusing ever so easily with it.

The increased reality—if not yet deep seriousness—of the grime, the absorbed choreography, and the controlling companionship with Scraps is, in a way, forced upon our attention by the film's Hansel-and-Gretel ending. Suddenly nothing is real: not the immaculately arranged bean rows Charlie is so happily tending, not the quaintly beamed, lace-curtained cottage with its picturesque fireplace, not the Dutch cap and hausfrau cleanliness of Edna's out-of-period costume. When Charlie comes into the house to embrace his bride and swing her about childlike on his back, we are, unmistakably, in never-never land. The ending is not a dream sequence, as it might have been in another film. It is a deliberate reversal of everything we have been looking at: an impossible picture-book ending that, by being so patently unlikely, forcibly reminds us of the day Charlie, Edna, and Scraps spent earlier, the ugly tangible world that forced them into all the escapades we have laughed at. The film's essential texture is accented in retrospect.

For his third film, following the success of *A Dog's Life* and the even greater commercial rewards of the straightforward gagging of *Shoulder Arms*, Chaplin chose to try once more what he had not brought off in *The Tramp*. And once more he did not bring it off, for much the same reasons. In the three-reel *Sunnyside* he placed himself in a rural setting, became strangely submissive to a world that showed him little more than contempt, wooed Edna at first with some success and then forlornly, stood crumpled in the garden while she strolled away with another man, dreamed of dancing with nymphs only to end in a cactus patch. He strove to make us feel directly sorry for a figure incapable of fending for himself. But the bid for pathos, if that is what we must now call it, is a cheat; he cannot find a frame that will contain it honestly. And the wistful dreaming of nymphs leads him equally astray: he is dancing in Elysian fields not because the dance has a purpose—either of mockery or of integration—but because his balletic qualities have been noticed by critics and he has taken their remarks a bit too seriously.

The flaws—they were fatal, and the film was a failure—are of course softened by a degree of humor. Pursuing his new sense of the earth-earthy even in Arcadia—the film opens with shots of a church spire, geese wandering the dirt roads, leafless trees—Charlie rises to his chores in the decrepit hotel in which he works and attends to the lobby. The lobby floor is cracked; grass is sprouting through it. Dutifully, Charlie waters the grass. Driving a herd of cattle to pasture, he keeps them on the move by using his cane as a bandmaster's baton. When a motorist's car is wrecked and the unconscious victim brought in, Charlie automatically snatches up pen and ledger and invites him to register.

But the comedy itself is, for the most part, either muted or routine. The hotel proprietor has a habit of kicking Charlie. When he misses one kick, banging his toe against a bedpost, Charlie docilely returns for the kick, accepting his due. That is mildly funny, but not a Chaplin we know. Mopping up the hotel lobby, he manages to swing the mop in the faces of various patrons, as though he were still back at Essanay, or even Keystone; unsure of what kind of comedy might best accompany the more sober effect he is after, he ceases to invent, merely repeats.

And some of the comedy is forced. Sure that he is losing Edna to the fashionable motorist, who has now recovered and is sporting a walking-stick with a cigarette lighter in its ivory tip, Charlie pathetically apes him, using unraveling footless socks for spats and a candle built into his cane for lighter. The extravagance neither amuses us very much nor elicits the sympathy he is after.

The comedy is erratic because his mind is elsewhere: on the moment when he can look through a flowered window and see Edna chatting happily with his rival, on the moment when he can let his body sag all too suddenly in sorrow as he stands deserted by the pair, head down, spirit crippled. From the relative, scarcely more than intimated, realistic grubbiness of *A Dog's Life*, he has tried to move toward tears—his, perhaps ours—without yet having found a firm way of letting them spring from, and lead effortlessly back into, laughter. They are isolates here, as he has become alien to himself.

I have called the bid a cheat because the pathos occurs in a dream sequence, reversing all reason. Normally Charlie dreams of happiness and wakes to the gutter. That is something like truth. Here he is actually happy—Edna hasn't deserted him at all—but dreams of misery. The misery, then, is gratuitous, a posture Chaplin wishes to display for its own sake. We are left bewildered and unhappy ourselves on two counts: we haven't been moved by the fabrication, and we don't find its needless introduction in any way funny.

The romp with the nymphs in the field—also a dream sequence—is not only similarly gratuitous but a shattering disappointment in quite another way. We discover that Chaplin isn't really a dancer after all. So long as he was taking mock ballet stances to show his indifference to the narrative or using surprisingly choreographic patterns to elude enemies and contend with fellow job-seekers, the flexibility of his body and the flawless timing of his movements suggested the Pan he was so often called. But he was not truly Pan, or even the Pierrot he called himself at this time—not someone who could divert us with rhythmic skills in a void. He was a comedian who needed to attach himself to something—to a situation he could mock, to a dilemma calling for escape—in order to bring his grace, his artful shifts of tempo, into play. Given a nondancing function to perform, he seemed a dancer. Cast into the open fields with a half-dozen girls, he merely skips and prances without design. The effect is loose, aimless, less airborne than when he is trapped in rooms, pursued by narrative. Suddenly we see his footwork as shapeless, unpatterned; there is no external pressure to demand or contain it. He never made this particular mistake again.

If *Sunnyside* was, over-all, a mistake, it is probably one he had to make if he was to continue his search for a comic base that would acknowledge the emotional desperation underlying and unleashing so much of our laughter. After the great success of his two previous films, he undoubtedly felt entitled to the try. Two films later he would try again—and this time discover, once and for all, the flick of the wrist that would make the combination work.

Dream-sequences all: Charlie literally playing Pan and dancing with nymphs, Charlie feeling sorry for himself. *Sunnyside*.

19. The Chaplin Breakthrough: Making Seriousness Funny

The Kid has often been described as a sentimental film—and it is that, though only in a most circumscribed way. What sentimentality it contains is lavished on an adult world that has nothing to do with Charlie, or even with his rearing a child he has inherited. Indeed, the sentimentality is almost exclusively confined to a single figure, who is seen with Chaplin only late in the film and then in passages that can be counted in seconds: Edna, unwed mother, eventual opera star, regretful and guilt-ridden social worker. Charlie and his charge, played by Jackie Coogan with a face that is as hauntingly open and as subtly expressive now as it seemed in 1921, escape the charge entirely, miraculously, intelligently.

This time Chaplin made no bones about what he was up to. "A comedy with a smile—and perhaps a tear" is the first title we read. To get the first tear Chaplin indulges his taste for bathos—a taste he indulged when he took *others* seriously—shamelessly. Edna is being released from a maternity hospital with her fatherless infant in her arms. "Her only crime—that she is a mother," a further title informs us. As nurse and gatekeeper watch her go, the figure of Christ carrying His cross is superimposed upon her. She passes a church and stands before one of its stained-glass windows to watch a wedding party leave. Edna looks on at a happiness she will never have. And yet a wedding is no guarantee of happiness. The bride is in the bloom of youth, a sacrifice. The groom is elderly, rich, no doubt heartless. A flower falls from the bride's bouquet. The groom, unseeing, crushes it with his foot as he descends the church stairs. As the party moves away, we focus on the forlorn Edna: behind her the stained-glass window lights up in such a way as to provide her with a halo. Later in the film, after she has abandoned her baby and gone on to a successful career, she once more meets the man who seduced her. As they stand on a balcony morosely retracing the past, a large, flowered volume is superimposed upon them: the page that is being turned reads, in lavish script, "Regrets."

Sentimental indeed; ominously so. Yet the moment Chaplin appears—and

without in any way destroying the story that has already been established—everything changes. Though Charlie is going to find that abandoned baby and care for that abandoned baby and love that abandoned baby and be reduced to despair when it is taken from him, no further trace of bathos will mark the film. The comedian has hit upon the trick—it is more than a trick, it is a philosophical premise for dimensional comedy—of permitting us to see and to feel what is realistically distressing about life through the magnifying glass, and *only* through the magnifying glass, of humor. The two are not to be alternated, not even closely alternated. And seriousness is not to have priority. That belongs to comedy if it is going to *be* comedy. Chaplin has at last created a landscape with figures. The two are one, though the elements are different. The landscape is serious. The figures are comic. Our attention is on the figures; we will sense the landscape soon enough.

The solution is at once apparent in the film's first gag, a very small, very celebrated one. Edna has abandoned the baby in a limousine that seems to promise the infant the attention of wealth, the limousine has been stolen by thieves, the thieves have discovered themselves inadvertent kidnappers and have deposited the baby hastily on the ground in a slum back alley. Almost at once, in the distance, we meet Charlie ambling along, taking the air with a degree of assumed elegance, finding himself constantly showered with trash that is being dumped from tenement porches above. He is aware of the trash and casts an occasional reproving glance upward; it does not diminish his composure and, no matter what rains down on him, he continues his stroll. He pauses, now that he is close to us, to extract a butt from the sardine can that serves as his cigarette case, fastidiously removing his fingerless gloves as he does so. Glancing at the gloves, he at first tucks them into his jacket pocket, then reconsiders and tosses them away, disposing of a little trash of his own. The baby near his feet cries. He hears it, sees it. He immediately glances upward to see what porch it has been thrown from.

The gag—fleeting as it is—is a superb one. But it is important to notice what Chaplin is doing. He has not created a gag for the sake of the gag. He has done it to protect, and even to conceal momentarily, the seriousness of the situation. For the comedian has been placed in a situation utterly serious, one with which he is presumably unequipped to deal but with which he *must* deal. He is confronted with a living, breathing infant for whom he must assume some responsibility. The narrative moment calls for a deeply human response—he cannot simply run away and leave the baby to die of starvation, exposure, or rat-bite—and he is, in this narrative, going to make an appropriate response, accept a serious burden seriously. But before doing so, before giving it so much as a thought, he has destroyed the sentiment—let alone the possible sentimentality—of the meeting. He has, for one startlingly hilarious moment, identified the baby with casual debris.

The pattern is followed, flawlessly, throughout. Of course he makes efforts to pass the baby on to other hands—comic efforts—only to take a beating with an umbrella for his pains. The mother in whose carriage he attempts to deposit the infant is a monster. His various efforts defeated, he slumps to a curbstone and stares at his unwanted bundle. There is a sewer drain in the street beside him. He studies it, even lifts its lid tentatively. But he decides against the sewer as the answer to his dilemma. He will have to accept this burden—this serious burden—but he has done his extravagantly funny, even harshly fantastic, best to avoid it. He discovers a note pinned to the infant's blanket, a note which will ask the finder to love and care for the child. He pricks his thumb badly trying to unpin the note. Resigned, he rises, though the camera does not. We simply see his feet shuffle away, a trace heavier for what he is carrying, perhaps, but still the splayed feet

With a cop already at hand, there's going to be no ditching this bundle for Charlie. *The Kid.*

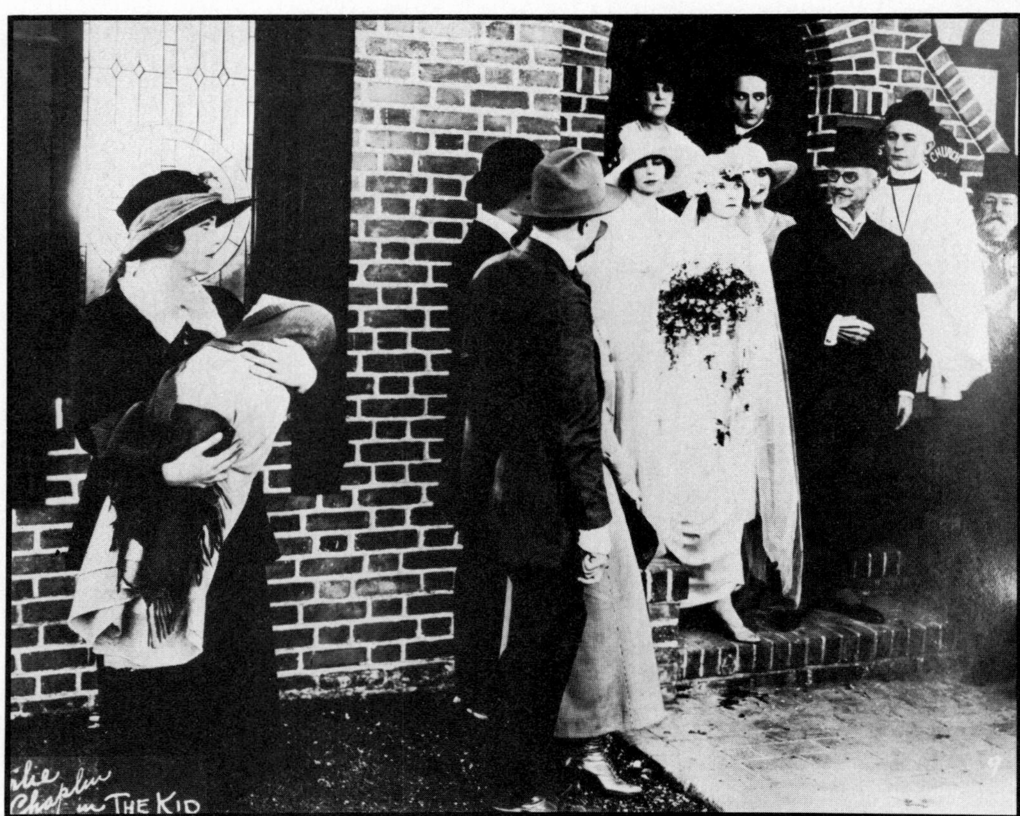

that spell Chaplin, comic. There is no shot of him carrying his accepted burden alone.

Arriving at the courtyard door that leads to his attic quarters—he rents a room and has a trade, it would appear—he must explain to the slatterns lounging on the stoop where the blanketed infant has come from. "It's mine," he says in a title. "I found it." The slatterns make nothing of the matter, no doubt supposing the child *his*, all right, and accepting the apologetic explanation cynically; these slatterns have taken on the background reality of *A Dog's Life*.

In the attic room above—dingy beneath the skylight, a haven for broken-legged chairs—he sets about meeting his quite sober responsibilities with the chameleon-like expertise he has hitherto lavished on casual comic impersonations. He must be a father now, so he becomes one, deftly scissoring diapers out of old clothing, stringing a coffee pot with a nipple on it from a rafter beside the infant's improvised hammock, cutting a circle into the bottom of a cane chair so that it can be placed over a cuspidor for toilet-training when the time comes. The devices are all funny; even the baby seems to think so, responding delightedly to the shoulder-wriggles and twitching headshakes Charlie offers by way of passing entertainment. He is loving and caring for the child, gag by gag.

The structural underpinnings of the film will grow increasingly serious. They begin lightly enough—after five years have passed and Jackie Coogan has appeared in ragamuffin cap and baggy trousers—with the trade to which Charlie has apprenticed his charge. Charlie is a glazier, strolling the streets with panes of glass strapped to his back, soliciting window-repair jobs. Jackie's job is to break the windows. On a certain morning, while Jackie is displaying his own expertise with rocks, a policeman's suspicions are aroused and Jackie is trailed. He immediately runs to Charlie on the street, making certain conclusions inescapable. The policeman follows them, somewhat increasing his speed. Charlie, not himself under suspicion but aware that Jackie has been spied, keeps kicking the child away as they retreat. Once again the double effect works superbly. To kick a trusting

Above, left: Having rejected the sewer as a possible "out," Charlie resigns himself to his burden. *The Kid.*

Above, right: In a moment the stained-glass halo behind Edna's head will light up, accenting *The Kid's* only area of sentimentality.

Opposite, left: Charlie the glazier warily teaching an apprentice his trade.

Right: The eternal trio, before the next chase begins. *The Kid.*

child away is—if taken seriously, and this relationship *is* a serious one—a bewildering and painful thing for the child. Jackie's "father" is denying him, at least thrice. But we look at the betrayal and laugh uproariously. Our focus is entirely on Charlie's predicament, on the increasing pace of their leavetaking and the obvious rhythmic promise of a coming chase. There is even a saving sense in which Charlie is trying to protect Jackie from the danger of being identified with *him*. But all threads are one, and the thread is—in its absolute need to disassociate rock-throwing from window-mending—uncorruptedly funny.

The process can be described as one of undercutting the seriousness with comedy the instant seriousness threatens to become dominant. The gag must get the jump. And so it does, always. Jackie becomes seriously ill. When the incompetent doctor arrives, Charlie manages to get the thermometer in *his* mouth; does the child's breathing in and breathing out for him, nobly; shouts into the doctor's stethoscope when the forgetful doctor is unable to hear him because of those plugs in his ears. Coogan's face, in repose against the bedstead, is inattentive, glazed, worrisome. Against it, before it, we are playing out the mutual incomprehension of doctor and Charlie.

When the doctor asks how Chaplin happened to come by the child, Charlie shows him Edna's note; he has kept it carefully stored in an ancient copy of the *Police Gazette*. When the case is reported to the local authorities and an orphanage truck is sent to carry Jackie away, Charlie and the child fight their oppressors with every kitchen utensil, including the flour-bowl, they can lay hands on. When the child *is* overpowered and taken to the waiting truck, Charlie eludes the policeman in charge by escaping through the skylight and doing a balancing act across the neighborhood rooftops, at one point climbing the steep pitch of a roof only to come face to face with a cop who has just climbed the other side.

Once Charlie has retrieved the child, the situation is more serious than before. He has, in effect, kidnapped him, is now beyond the law. The two dare not return home; they venture to spend the night in a flophouse. Charlie has a

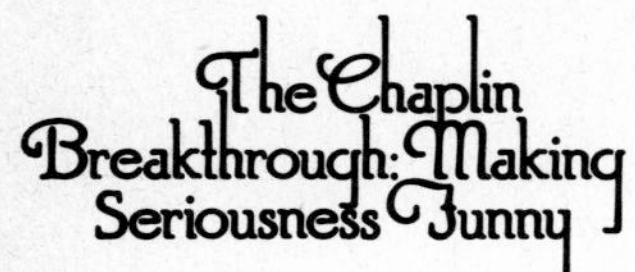

dime for one admission. Jackie lurks just outside a window so that as Charlie stretches to prepare for sleep, he can slip open the window to permit Jackie a dive in and under the bedclothes. But Jackie must come out to kneel for his nightly prayers. With a suspicious proprietor on the prowl, Jackie hastily reenters the bedclothes by the foot of the bed, where he poses as Charlie's upraised knees.

The two are in dire and constant danger of discovery; in fact, the proprietor is just now reading a newspaper offering a reward for the return of the child, whose presence he has discovered. During these moments of tension, Charlie is performing an enchanting routine. On entering the flophouse, he was at first unable to find a dime for his own admission, let alone a second for Jackie's. But he did find the one and resorted to the bit of deception at the window to provide a night's sleep for Jackie. Now, as he begins to undress, a presumably sleeping pickpocket in the bed just beside theirs is furtively running his fingers through Charlie's pockets. *He* finds a second dime, quite astonishing Charlie. Naturally, Charlie snatches the dime and slaps the slippery hand away. Then he thinks better of it. He draws the pickpocket's talented hand back into his clothing to see if, perhaps, he may not uncover more.

Even as the proprietor is stealthily turning down the gaslights and preparing to spirit Jackie away for the reward, the comedy continues: Jackie and Charlie asleep are both subject to spasmodic leg-twitches, and a kind of unconscious infighting is going on steadily, even reaching to the next bed. When, in the morning and after discovering Jackie gone, Charlie returns to his own stoop to sit lonely and defeated, he is prepared to summarize the new method with a last and perfect joke. After he has dreamed awhile, a policeman shakes him awake, orders him to come along. Having no longer any reason to resist, Charlie struggles to his feet, docilely lets the cop collar him, and starts to move down the alleyway with him. But there are two low hitching posts in the alley; in passing, the policeman and Charlie let one come between them. That is unthinkable. Charlie quickly reverses direction to swing back around the post and rejoin the policeman on *his* side. It is bad luck to let an inanimate object separate two strolling friends.

The key to the trick of keeping comedy alive and accented while matters of real moment are taking place had already been hinted at in *A Dog's Life*: the dog, furiously digging up the wallet that would change Charlie's fortunes completely, sends most of the dirt flying directly into Charlie's face. It would achieve its ultimate precision and beauty in the much later *City Lights*: Charlie has seen and instantly been smitten by a girl selling flowers on a street corner; he has discovered, watching her grope for some dropped coins, that she is blind; he has pretended to leave, then slipped back to sit along a fence, unabashedly staring at her as she moves to the corner fountain to change the water for her flowers. Blind, she throws the dirty water into his adoring face. Everything is legitimate: as love is established, love gets it straight in the eye.

But it was in *The Kid* that Chaplin seemed to realize, at last, precisely what was required. Here the method, with its instant ironies and overlaid moods, was opened to its fullness, employed at every turn, made a wholly conscious and forever-after available staple of his repertoire. It was the answer to the question that had plagued him: how to cope with life honestly without throwing away his extraordinary skills as a comic fantasist. He would now be able to employ it, if he chose, in larger and more emotional structures.

I do not much like the word pathos, though it is the term commonly used to describe Chaplin's secondary effect. It is a little too close to bathos—though their meanings need not blur—and it suggests the dangers of self-pity. Chaplin did not really indulge himself in self-pity. Seriousness, just enough seriousness to

Opposite, above: Easy rapport with an alter ego. Chaplin and Coogan on the set of *The Kid.*

Below: Having airily denied himself emotion for so long, Charlie is at last honestly free to display it. *The Kid.*

allow for a degree of emotion on screen and a corresponding emotional response from the audience, is more nearly what he was after. And *The Kid* achieves it in delicate balance. There is open emotional display at the dramatic climax of the film. Jackie, torn from Charlie and penned in the orphanage truck, sobs uncontrollably, his outstretched arms begging for rescue. When Charlie, after the rooftop chase and a leap into the passing truck, has efficiently disposed of the guard and been reunited with the child, he embraces the boy passionately, kissing him again and again full on the lips. The moment is not in the least mawkish; it is what we expect to see, what we wish to see, a taken-for-granted love between the two finally and fully expressed in crisis.

But that kiss has been skillfully prepared for, by negation. Charlie has denied himself and the child this sort of demonstrative affection from the outset, making it plain—even if playfully—that he wants none of it. Early in the film, after Charlie has inspected Jackie's hands, hair, ears, and nose, and has given him a bit of a barber's toweling to make certain his neck is clean, Jackie, on his way out, attempts to give Charlie a peck. Charlie not only ducks it, he gives him a back-kick by way of fending off such nonsense. Later, Jackie is given a toy dog as he sits on the stoop outside; Edna, as volunteer social worker, has come by and unknowingly spoken a few words with her own child. In the attic room with Charlie, Jackie wants Charlie to kiss the dog. Charlie, feeling a fool, tries to avoid it, as grown men do. Jackie insists and Charlie finally gives in, as perfunctorily as possible. By first denying a kiss and by later allowing one—but only under preposterous circumstances—a kind of dike has been built and then just slightly breached. It is the holding back that helps us finally to open the floodgates. We have been sensible all along; it is sensible now to admit to what is true. Emotion has been legitimatized by the refusal to indulge it callowly.

Nor is the debatable "heaven" sequence—one in which Charlie, having lost Jackie, dreams that the shabby courtyard has become celestially bowered with flowers and peopled by friends and enemies with wings—specifically sentimental. The sequence has always aroused controversy: some First National executives wanted it cut before the film was released, many critics have argued that it is out of tone with what has gone before and is in itself muddled. It *is* muddled, displaying an inferior aspect of Chaplin's mind at work. Crammed into the short passage are pompous symbols of Innocence and Temptation—relayed to us mainly through titles and propelled by a Devil-figure who appears and vanishes courtesy of trick photography—that have nothing to do with the narrative and are hopelessly simplistic as philosophic statement of any sort. Paulette Goddard is reported to have said of Chaplin, "Oh, Charlie sometimes thinks he thinks." He is thinking here, and the thought is as intrusive as it is naïve. It need not have been. If, for instance, the sequence had shown us Charlie's quite normal interest in sex leading him somehow to betray the boy, it might easily have made dramatic sense, reinforcing the psychological guilt he feels at having lost Jackie. Charlie's interest in sex has been established earlier in a prolonged flirtation with a woman whose window he is mending; and we probably do want to know, in these circumstances, that Charlie's heterosexual instincts are functioning routinely. Instead of pursuing what has been established, however, Charlie is prompted by the Devil-figure to toy with a woman-angel we have never met before, and the new flirtation is worked out gratuitously, without reference to the boy. All that happens is arbitrary, though it is in part fun to watch. Once its defects have been granted, however, and supposing the film to have been completed and edited, it was probably essential that Chaplin retain it. The narrative needs a passage of rhythmic relief—*light* relief—at this point. Otherwise, we should be forced to

Above: The fraudulent minister of *The Pilgrim*.

Opposite: Delivering the David-and-Goliath sermon in *The Pilgrim*, and taking danced bows for it afterward.

move directly from Charlie's dismay at the disappearance of the child to his rediscovery of the child, robbing that rediscovery of interim tension and delayed, hence doubled, delight.

The film's ending is ambiguous, as it ought to be. Jackie has been restored to Edna, and Edna has sent a policeman not to arrest Charlie but to bring him to Jackie at her home. The door opens, Charlie is astonished, Charlie and Jackie are reunited. On what terms, for how long? There is no way of saying. Chaplin had taken an enormous risk to his own image in making the film at all, engaging himself in a role and a relationship that seemed to promise some sort of permanence. The fact that the relationship was with a child, and its social function highly dubious, helped to keep Chaplin's psychological isolation reasonably inviolate. But at the end of the film he is faced with a structured society again: mother, child, home. Even as he is admitted into the house, he is out of place. The door closes, and the film ends. To go one foot further, into the house with Charlie, would be to raise *exclusively* serious questions, and that is the one thing that the film and its exquisitely balanced method will not allow. Call it no ending, if you will. That is what Chaplin is always saying: no ending, no permanence, for him.

I have mentioned that Charlie's relationship with the child was, socially, highly dubious, and a word is in order on that. One of the film's most fascinating, and in a subterranean way most delectable, ambiguities lies in the doubleness of Charlie's "love and care" for the child. On the one hand, he preaches not only cleanliness but proper table manners: catching Jackie eating his morning pancakes with a knife, he rebukes him sternly for bringing the sharp, rather than the dull, edge to his mouth. An education in fastidiousness is very much part of each day's program. On the other hand, he is training Jackie to cheat the gas meter by recovering any coins deposited, to break windows as part of an honest day's work, to sneak into flophouses, and to fight well: there is an hilarious incidental sequence in which Charlie, seeing that Jackie can whip an opponent twice his size, takes over his training as a fight-manager would, watering and toweling him and showing him precisely where his opponent is vulnerable. He is rearing the boy to behave socially as *he* does: with impeccable manners and an eye out for the main clout.

In working with Coogan, who responded with astonishing adroitness to his direction, Chaplin was in reality—and in a multiplicity of ways—studying himself. Obviously *The Kid* derives from Chaplin's own childhood: even the brick courtyard is a London courtyard, as the gas meter is a London gas meter, calling for a shilling rather than a quarter. Chaplin is looking back. But he is also, through the child performer, observing the mature performer he himself now is. The child's mannerisms are all Chaplin's. If the child, about to throw a rock, finds himself watched by a policeman, he begins to toss the rock idly about, whistling the while, just as Chaplin had done when caught with a brick in *A Dog's Life*. If Jackie is at the stove cooking the morning pancakes, he snips off a small piece of one, tastes it critically, nods his satisfaction with the most matter-of-fact and least emphatic of nods precisely as Chaplin would sample the almost-done shoe in *The Gold Rush*. There is even a reversal of roles in the film: it is Jackie who must scold Charlie out of bed mornings, ordering him with fatherly authority to get into his dressing gown—the dressing gown is the bedspread he has slept under with a convenient center hole for his head—and get to table while things are still hot. It is not so much a matter of Jackie imitating Charlie as it is of transplanted identities, a give-and-take of personality. Chaplin is able, through an alter ego and at this central stage in his career, to stand back and study what he is and what he does. It may have been this detachment—this opportunity of seeing himself—that enabled him to resolve the esthetic problems he had posed for himself when he set out to make seriousness funny.

The fourth film in our sequence—the eighth and last for First National—made no such all-out effort at putting emotion at the command of comedy frame by frame. There was no need for all-out effort now: Chaplin had mastered the fusion and could employ it when and where he would. *The Pilgrim*, a charming and relatively neglected film today, is only four reels long, though technically a feature; *The Kid* had finally grown to six. And *The Pilgrim* protects its occasional double tone and Chaplin's essential image, without risk, from the outset. Charlie is an escaped convict who has purloined a minister's black frock coat and saucer-shaped hat while the minister is swimming. Hurrying by train to any outpost sufficiently remote from Sing Sing, he is mistaken by a rural welcoming committee for a new pastor all are awaiting; the actual pastor has been detained. Of course he will play the role of minister, with increasing aptitude: giving the day's sermon, supervising the collection, participating in afternoon tea at Edna's house, carving the Sunday dinner, rescuing the family's savings when they are stolen.

Yet the more he is at home in the role, the less he can ever hope to be. There is no possibility of establishing a permanent relationship with the Edna he becomes devoted to—not for a convict fraudulently garbed as a minister. The issue is closed before it can be opened. An actual minister will one day arrive, a sheriff will see his "Wanted" photograph in a newspaper, *something* will happen, and no doubt very quickly, to send him on his way again.

The seeds of an ultimate parting, at whatever emotional temperature, are inherent in the convict-pastor image itself: when the time comes, separation is inevitable. With this established so early, the film is at once free to play whatever pranks it likes, to unleash in Charlie all those impulses toward impersonation and improvisation that constitute his limited delight in life. What is remarkable about the film is that, given the freedom to behave as broadly as he likes, Chaplin opts for understatement. The very best gags in *The Pilgrim* are so small in design and so fleeting in execution that, at a first viewing, they are very often missed. Early in the film, Charlie, in a railroad station waiting for the agent to make out his ticket, places his hands on the bars of the ticket window as he would the bars of a jail cell. It is very thoughtless of him, and he catches himself instantly; nonetheless, his hands inadvertently stray back to the bars when the agent asks him a question. With a ticket purchased, he hurries directly to the train and crawls into its understructure, ready out of habit to ride the rods, ticket or no. The conductor comes by. Charlie promptly, and without any sense of incongruity, hands him his ticket. The conductor, of course, escorts him to a coach. Arriving at his random destination, he steps from the coach to find a sheriff reaching a hand toward him. Without further ado Charlie surrenders, offering his wrists to the expected handcuffs. The sheriff, who is part of the welcoming committee for the new pastor, shakes hands with him. Charlie's adaptation to the handshake is as swift and natural as his impulse to give up.

Escorted to the church by deacon Mack Swain and handed a hymnal with which to begin the service, Charlie reflexively places his right hand on the book and raises the left to swear. While Swain and another vestryman are taking up the collection on the two sides of the congregation, Charlie keeps a sharp eye on the proceedings, though he forgets himself enough to whistle as he does. Swain seems to have missed a contributor. Charlie quietly but firmly signals him to get the box back to the bypassed, possibly recalcitrant, parishioner. Forced to wait at the lectern while a hymn is sung, his left foot inevitably strays to its base as though there were a bar-rail there. None of these things is sharply focused on or extended until

a sluggish audience can catch up. All are simply there, a form of shorthand now; either we have achieved an entente with Charlie so swiftly perceptive and mutually respectful that we see what he is doing even when he seems forgetfully casual about it, or we are lost. "Don't sell it," he would increasingly tell his actors. "Remember they're peeking at you." Intimacy with this strange figure had matured to the point where explanations were unnecessary and the barest nod could summon up associations, even histories, grasped long ago.

The David and Goliath sermon that follows is perhaps the one passage by which *The Pilgrim* is identified today, though in itself it seems to me the least inventive, least nuanced of Chaplin's gambits in the film. Charlie plays both David and Goliath, pretending to a menacing height on the one hand and a diminutive apprehension on the other. But this is an obvious vaudeville pattern, refreshed only by the sight of Charlie, once he has severed Goliath's head, hurriedly counting the giant out, ringside-style. More delightful, to me, is what happens when the contest is done. Finished, and plainly exhilarated by his accomplishment, Charlie throws his arms open to acknowledge the nonexistent applause of the congregation, bobbing up and down in deep curtsies, accepting adulation by blowing kisses, skipping off into the vestry and hurrying back for encores. Here he is totally himself: the performer who can *only* be a performer, but who expects the performance to be appreciated.

The film has its fair share—oh, more than that—of fun and games, this time plot-danced in tandem with Charles "Chuck" Reisner, who had joined Chaplin's company as the street bully in *The Kid* and appears here as a former cellmate. Reisner recognizes the clerically dressed Charlie on the street, trails him to Edna's home, and immediately proceeds to rob everyone in sight—the deacon of his wallet, Edna's mother of her mortgage money. Charlie, though a pal, must foil his efforts. Sometimes he does it athletically, as in a wonderfully designed sequence with Charlie on Reisner's back using his quick feet to slam shut a money-drawer each time Reisner rips it open. And sometimes slyly: the moment Reisner has actually purloined the deacon's wallet, Charlie becomes a professional magician, using his demonstrably empty handkerchief to spirit the wallet from one pocket to the other and so back to its rightful owner. These passages are capped by an exquisitely timed upstairs sequence, with Charlie standing guard over bedroom doors closed for the night and managing to intercept Reisner's stealthy attempts to return below. Opening and closing doors function to a musical beat, with Charlie as concertmeister mastering the flow of events meticulously.

While all of this is going on, the cloud—hovering by implication from the beginning—remains. It is given brief exposure midway. In the early evening Charlie and Edna stand chatting by the garden gate. There are no titles and we don't know precisely what Charlie is telling Edna. There is no mistaking his ruefulness, though; no doubt he is intimating something of his past. The mood is one of confessional regret. Typically, it is confounded as Charlie gets his hand caught between fence pickets.

But the money *is* finally stolen, Charlie hastens to a saloon to retrieve it from Reisner, the sheriff arrives at Edna's to express doubt that Charlie will ever return: his identity as a convict has been established. When Charlie does return with the money and places it in Edna's hands, he finds the sheriff's gun at his back. Though Edna earnestly points out that Charlie has behaved honestly, the sheriff—politely enough—insists that the law is the law and that he must do his duty. He leads Charlie away.

The two or three minutes that follow seem to me the most beautiful in all of Chaplin. Instead of carting Charlie to the local jail, the sheriff leads him—the

If the sheriff wants flowers, he shall have flowers wherever he goes. *The Pilgrim*.

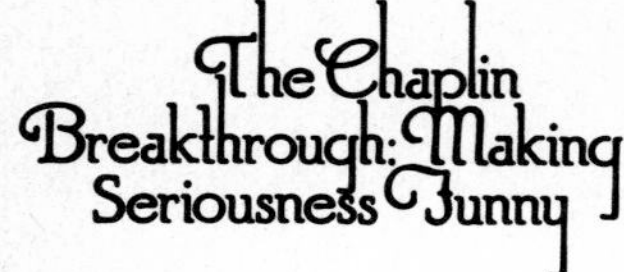

sheriff on horseback, Charlie shuffling alongside—to the Mexican border. Charlie, simply awaiting further instructions, leans on the roadsign that points one way to Mexico, the other to the United States. The sheriff lights a cigarette. Glancing at Charlie speculatively, he suggests that Charlie go pick him some flowers. Charlie, ever willing and no one to question the orders of an unfathomable authority, quickly gathers a bunch from the ground near his feet. No, no, the sheriff orders; he wants flowers that are farther away—over there in Mexico. Charlie understands nothing, but dutifully crosses the border to his task. Once Charlie is gone, the sheriff smiles a smile of mild sympathy and just as mild contempt, throws away the flowers he's been given, and rides away.

The camera now positions itself for a long-shot: the curved desert road along which the sheriff is departing. As the sheriff on horseback comes closer to us, there is a sudden flurry of dust in the background: it is Charlie racing with all his heart along that curved road to catch up with the sheriff and present him with the particular blooms he has asked for. With the camera holding position, the sheriff, exasperated, simply seizes Charlie by the scruff of the neck and rides him rapidly, Charlie's feet scrambling to keep pace, back along the whole dusty curve until both are out of frame.

At the border, the sheriff quickly gives Charlie a healthy kick into Mexico and rides off. Some people are so uncomprehending that they must be booted into freedom. But now—and at last—Charlie understands. His face lights up in disbelieving gratitude, he clasps his hands above his head in a salute of thanks and farewell, he blows kisses with his hand, with his whole twitching body. The sheriff glances back scowling, waves him off in disgust. With one more parting wave, Charlie expands to his freedom, arms extended, inhaling joyously, the Count of Monte Cristo discovering that the world is his. He looks about at the clean air, the unbroken promise of the landscape before him, moves into it. Instantly bandits hidden behind sagebrush rise and begin shooting at one another. Charlie retreats in panic—but where to go? Immediately he is on his way, fast, straight down the borderline, one foot in Mexico, the other in the United States. The man who is too much of everyone to be anyone can only live everywhere and nowhere.

A free man, most temporarily. *The Pilgrim.*

20. Chaplin Betwixt and Between

The pressure toward a dimension that would include a degree of emotion and some intimation of the seriousness hidden deep in all comedy came from within Chaplin. While he was responding to this interior pressure in the films of which we have been speaking, he was under other pressures that increased radically as he worked to turn out the interim "merely funny" films, the four others he needed to fulfill his contract.

Money was the first pressure, and it asserted itself almost immediately. As popular as the initial film for First National, *A Dog's Life*, had been, its costs had run well over budget and the additional burden was Chaplin's. Even so, he at once envisioned a much more ambitious project, a war film—eventually *Shoulder Arms*—that would run to five reels, or feature-length. He began shooting with that in mind, very much against the advice of industry mentors who thought that World War I could not be kidded while it was still being fought. There had also been unjustified public criticism of Chaplin for not being in the army himself—in fact, he did not meet the army's physical requirements—and his appearance as a soldier on film might only increase the resentment. But he had done what he could to display his patriotism, first by touring for two months with Pickford and Fairbanks on a Liberty Bond campaign and then by making a short propaganda film, *The Bond*, which he released to theaters without charge.

At the same time, he was going ahead with the projected feature-length war comedy and had actually filmed certain early sequences in which his wretched home life, involving a tyrannical wife and four children, was intimated, driving him to an induction-into-the-army sequence in which he was stripped for examination and then left to wander nude in a maze of cubicles populated by stenographers.

But he began to worry as he worked. In spite of all that had been shot, Chaplin decided to open *Shoulder Arms* with Charlie already in boot camp—trying to teach his outgoing feet to turn inward as he marched—then whisked him quickly to the mud and lice of the German front lines. The film, when completed, was released as a three-reel short, which is what *A Dog's Life* had been.

Changing plans as he went, and abandoning so much that had been shot, Chaplin not only took longer to make the film than his schedule and money warranted but became deeply discouraged with it. He claims, in his autobiography, to have been ready to scrap it when he showed it to his friend Douglas Fairbanks one day. "Sweet Douglas, he was my greatest audience," Chaplin reports. Fairbanks had roared with laughter, and the film was released—at what may conceivably have been the most propitious time for it, three weeks before the Armistice was signed. With their worries ended, audiences could openly enjoy what had appalled them for so long.

Shoulder Arms was one of Chaplin's greatest commercial successes, and for a long time both audiences and critics would measure subsequent films by its standards. Its standards were those of straight gag comedy. The film is actually scrappy in its structure and editing, fading in and out of brief incidental routines with the help of more titles than Chaplin was generally inclined to use. It is also heavily dependent on wartime associations very much in the public mind: wet trenches with street signs marked "Broadway and Rotten Row," omnipresent cooties, gift packages, the new taboo of three-on-a-match, the French nation pictured as a woman with head bowed low before her shattered home, fat Germans and pint-sized ones all equipped with spiked mustaches, leering enemy officers apt to do anything at all to available women, the Kaiser himself, Limburger cheese.

If the film no longer seems the masterwork it did to its idolators of 1918, it is partly because its concerns are so much those of 1918: for the only time during his silent career Chaplin had made use of materials dirrectly linked to the news of the day; the news of any day cannot help dating somewhat. And it is partly because of a certain mechanical coolness in the gagging, as though Chaplin had decided that in going into the unfamiliar trenches—whose mud is as real as the dirt in *A Dog's Life*—he had better bring some reliable formula fooling along. His tin helmet flips about on his head with the burst of each nearby bomb, a basic Sennett trick. When a package arrives for him, it contains dog biscuits. His identity tag is #13; when he flips a coin for luck it comes up tails; when he strikes his chest to reassure himself, he breaks the pocket mirror in his jacket. He does things that are too easy and things that are not cinematic. Too easy: when he wants to uncap a beer bottle or to light a cigarette, he lifts it out of frame above his head, bringing each back with the work done by presumed flying bullets. Uncinematic: he and Syd sight an enemy plane overhead, fire at it, watch it curve downward and crash—all mimed in a single take with the camera held uninterruptedly on their faces. That is "stage" humor. When Charlie is disguised as a German officer and Syd is brought in as captive, Charlie alternately slaps him around and embraces him, depending on who's looking. Syd ultimately makes a gesture of "Enough of that, now," as though he'd rather be shot than go on with the routine, and we are a little bit inclined to agree with him.

But there are lovely things in the film, and Charlie and Syd display a rapport in feeling as well as comic timing that was never so well realized again. With the first shot of Syd in a dugout, playing a harmonica while his seal-like eyes seem to graze over oceans of loneliness, one realizes that he is something more than simply Charlie's brother with a bigger mustache. After Charlie has politely knocked at the dugout doorpost—in a pouring rain—and entered to discover that they are sharing quarters rapidly filling with water, he settles bunkside to his dinner. He has none. He resorts to eating the cheese in a mousetrap he carries. Syd, gnawing at a sizable loaf of bread, offers him some. Charlie gratefully declines, patting his stomach. All full. Going to sleep in a lower bunk now completely covered with water—Charlie pauses to fluff the sodden pillow nonetheless—Charlie and Syd

Above: Domestic Chaplin footage the audience never saw. From the abandoned opening sequences of *Shoulder Arms*.

Opposite: The completed *Shoulder Arms* begins with Charlie in boot camp, having difficulty with his wayward feet, then whisks him quickly to a World War I dugout, hungry. Brother Syd is at right.

Below: Charlie triumphant as a building conveniently subsides onto his pursuers.

engage in inventive byplay over Syd's snoring, then wake in the morning to find only their heads above sea level. Charlie reaches under for his bare foot, hoists it out of the water, tries to slap some life into it. He can feel none at all. But Syd can, with a howl. It is his foot. Lunching in the trench outside, Syd casts Charlie a morose sideways look, as if to commiserate with him on the boredom of it all; the shells that are exploding about them leave them unmoved as they munch.

Charlie, on his own, arrives at three unforgettable bits of business. Receiving no mail at all, he stands in the rain over another doughboy's shoulder, reading his letter with him, his face responding as sensitively to each succeeding line as the doughboy's does. Together, in immaculate and touching unison, they smile, express sudden apprehension, almost expire with relief. The earnestness, the complete concentration, Chaplin brings to the moment is dazzling. Later, he employs a device that would be endlessly imitated and, for that matter, may not have been invented by him; there is no record, however, of anyone else doing it half so well. Alone on the second story of Edna's bombed-out house—the upper brickwork is entirely gone, the panes of the windows have been blasted away—he carefully opens the glassless window to look out. Satisfied that there is no enemy to be seen, he not only closes the window but pulls down the shade so that he can nap on the bed in a room without walls or ceiling.

And the degree to which fantasy remained matter of fact, even in the intensified realism of Chaplin's comedies of the period, is demonstrated, delightfully, when he is sent on a spying mission disguised as a tree. Legs encased in barklike sheathing, face showing through a hole in the trunk that would have invited wintering raccoons, arms extended as branches until they dwindle into twigs, Charlie takes up his open-field stance wherever the exigencies of his task suggest, stationing himself close at one point to German officers making a campfire. The officers naturally need wood and one is sent to axe down a tree. The care with which Chaplin invariably prepared for his fantasy by rooting it in probability is at once indicated: the officer does not immediately approach Charlie, though naturally we are expecting to see the tree-Charlie chopped down, but first has a whack at a larger, sturdier trunk. But the officer is lazy and looks about for easier kindling. Now it is Charlie's turn, *after* the situation has been made real. With his extended branch-arms Charlie is able to dispose of the woodsman who is whacking at him in little more than a single blow, taking care of several others similarly before one German becomes too curious and the chase begins. The chase takes us into a densely wooded forest, with Charlie's ferocious pursuer bayoneting every tree in sight while Charlie, perhaps invisibly perched on a stump just behind him, leaps gracefully away. Aware as we are throughout that Charlie's "tree" is nothing more than papier-mâché camouflage, we are—in at least one stunning moment—as deceived as the German, unable to spot Charlie in the tangle of trees until he has been bypassed and allowed to scurry to safety. The fantasy—extended as it is and photographed in an actual location rather than in a studio setting where disguise might have been made easier by having *all* of the trees faked—functions handsomely indeed: real and outrageously unreal mesh without difficulty. We scarcely pause to wonder at the oddity of the form we are dancing through.

With *Shoulder Arms* far and away the most commercially successful film Chaplin had made to date, and with Chaplin himself eager to devote more money and time to pursuing his ultimate, more serious, goal, the actor went to First National executives to ask for a not unreasonable revision of his contract terms. Though *Shoulder Arms* was returning millions of dollars and attracting other stars to the company by virtue of his prestige, Chaplin was received coldly and told that he must abide by the contract he'd signed. There were still six pictures to go. "I could deliver the six pictures in a couple of months, if you want that kind of pictures," Chaplin tells us he replied. He got nowhere, a result that led in a roundabout way to his agreement to join Douglas Fairbanks and Mary Pickford in a company of their own, United Artists, a move which would permit them to retain the profits of their work. Ironically, this promise of freedom became one more burden upon Chaplin: he couldn't join his friends until he'd completed six pictures, and they would become impatient while he worked more and more slowly.

Not only more slowly, but more daringly. It was at this juncture that he took his chances with the attempted lyricism and relative sobriety of *Sunnyside*, perhaps on the theory that he was entitled to a step in his own envisioned direction after the phenomenal success he'd just delivered. But *Sunnyside* was both an artistic and a commercial failure, making matters a great deal worse. He hadn't made a "funny" film, and he hadn't found the emotional base he was after either. At this point, he may not have panicked but he did do what many others—Harry Langdon among them, most disastrously—would do: attempt to recoup his comic standing by reverting to an earlier formula that no longer contained its own inspiration. Chaplin turned out a two-reeler he might have made with Mabel Normand at Keystone, *A Day's Pleasure*, and turned it out without energy or invention. He goes through the motions: taking his wife and two children on an outing, he has trouble starting the family car, trouble with traffic cops at an intersection, trouble saving a seat for himself on an excursion steamer, trouble trying to dance on a deck that is rocking him toward nausea, trouble with a trombone that a member of the jazz band on board is sliding directly under his nose, trouble with a deck chair.

I suppose the measure of Chaplin's listless return to this kind of random improvisation can best be taken by his evident inability to find endings for gags half-heartedly begun. When the Negro trombone-player—who has turned white as he becomes seasick—slides his instrument again and again directly across Charlie's mustache, Charlie finds no variant, no reversal, no sudden metaphor to cap the business. In the end, he simply throws the instrument overboard. Tackling a deck chair that needs to be folded into position, he arrives at none of the interesting but nonfunctional geometric shapes Keaton would shortly achieve; he simply makes a visually flat mess of it. He throws the deck chair overboard too. It is a get-rid-of-it film, seemingly dismissed by Chaplin in the making, dismissible now. The presumed antidote to *Sunnyside* had failed, too.

Aware that the return to "safe" gagging was anything but safe, Chaplin made what was probably the most important decision of his career. He would pursue his own strongest instinct, no matter what pressures dogged him, and spend an entire year making *The Kid*. By the end of the year, and with the film still not edited, he was in a critical position. His cash reserves were almost nonexistent. His first wife, Mildred Harris, was suing him for divorce; with no cash readily available, there was a strong likelihood that Miss Harris's lawyers would make an attempt to attach the negative of *The Kid*. Such an attempt was eventually made. Forewarned, Chaplin spirited the uncut film—in what he describes as some fifty reels of variant "takes"—across the California border and into Utah, where California community-property laws did not apply. He completed the editing of the film in his hotel room, previewed it once without announcement in Salt Lake City to wildly enthusiastic response, then hurried to New York to confer with First National. He was now confident that the six-reel feature was his finest work to date, and when First National, feigning indifference, offered to pay him for it as though it were no more than three two-reel shorts—which would have returned him less than he had spent making it—he simply refused to give them the film until they agreed to new and better terms. First National surrendered, *The*

Kid was sensationally successful, everybody made money.

Buoyed up by the knowledge that he had solved the creative problem that most obsessed him, he now turned with some élan to two short "funny" films, the first of which, *The Idle Class*, seems to have been made with dispatch. The second, *Pay Day*, was ready for shooting—sets built, company assembled—when Chaplin abruptly called a halt and, virtually without explanation, sailed for Europe. It would seem that the accumulated tensions of his divorce, his financial uncertainties, the demands he made on himself in his work, and the ever-increasing urgency with which Pickford and Fairbanks prodded him to hurry his schedule and join them at United Artists had brought him close to nervous, perhaps creative, exhaustion. The Pickford-Fairbanks anxiety was understandable enough: they were having to carry the new company virtually alone and it was taking Chaplin, who had helped form it, three years to arrive on its doorstep. But Chaplin resented the nagging: instead of hastening his work, he tells us, it had the effect of slowing him down. In any event, the stay in Europe was a long one.

Both *The Idle Class* and *Pay Day* are fine Chaplin short comedies, profiting in minor details and here-and-there intimations from the more complex Charlie that *The Kid* had established. There is nothing at all serious about *Pay Day*, but Charlie does appear for work—late—through an opening in a board fence with a lily in his hand. Having inhaled its aroma to his own satisfaction, he presents it to his foreman by way of compensation for his tardiness. The lily is something new: the very fact that it requires no explanation indicates that a playful esthete has emerged in Charlie, that there simply are no boundaries to the potential absurdities, the flexibility, of this image.

Much later, once Charlie and his cronies have spent the evening on the town and become thoroughly drunk, Charlie attempts to get into his topcoat in the rain only to find that he has thrust one arm into another fellow's coat. Since the other fellow departs immediately, Charlie is dragged after him along the wet pavement, much too weary to protest. They pass a policeman, who is merely puzzled by the spectacle. Charlie tips his hat to him, not only maintaining the social decencies in the circumstances but accepting the circumstances themselves as entirely normal as he rides out of view on his back. Hereafter, Charlie would invariably tip his hat when observance of the amenities was least called for—in *The Circus* he and a fellow suspect whom he has not met are racing side by side from a policeman; he tips his hat to the fellow suspect, at top speed—as though to remind us that *all* situations, no matter how extraordinary, are, after all, ordinary for him.

His fondness for metaphor was taking more elaborate, less antic forms. Still far from sober after his evening out and having missed the last streetcar, he spies another—except that it isn't. He enters a lunch wagon, uses a suspended roll of salami to straphang, picks up a newspaper on the counter and reads absently as he rides. When the baffled proprietor approaches him, he dutifully pays his fare. When the proprietor begins to expostulate, Charlie waves him aside gratefully and graciously: no, this isn't his stop, thank you, not yet.

And in *Pay Day*, Chaplin did something most unusual for him: he experimented, in a lengthy gag, with trick-photography. He is on a second-story scaffold, and Syd and another workman are tossing bricks up to him to be stored in neat piles. Foreman Mack Swain orders them to work faster. They do, sending the bricks curving upward like swallows in wild flight, with Charlie forced to catch them any which way: between his knees, beneath his chin, one on heel, one on toe, astride his rump. The perfect catches are of course miraculous, and the miracle is nothing more than reverse photography. Chaplin has achieved the perfection of the sequence by flipping the bricks down rather than attracting them,

Charlie soberly counts his weekly salary before his dragon-wife can relieve him of it. *Payday*.

magnetlike, in midair. A possible justification for this "cheating" may be found in the enormous inventiveness of its design. The passage, run forward or backward, has been choreographed; planning its rhythm and its physical variations must have been nearly as difficult as actually doing the stunt—if the stunt could be done at all. In any case, Charlie lets us know exactly what he is going to do before he begins doing it: he first whips out a handkerchief, dries the palms of his hands as acrobats do, and takes the vaudeville-balletic stance that announces a stunt in the offing. He understands that we will understand, introducing the trickery by taking bows for it first.

The Idle Class is better again, considerably so. *Pay Day* has its conventional two-reel-comedy images: the dragon-wife with a rolling pin, yet another exposure to Limburger cheese, Charlie adding up four "twos" to get "nine" as he had in a lesser moment at Mutual. *The Idle Class*, on the other hand, has not only an extraordinarily fertile feel to it—it moves almost breathlessly from one surprise to another—but a density of incident and ambivalence of image rich enough to have sustained a much longer film.

When *The Idle Class* is remembered today, two things are generally said or thought of it. The title suggests that Chaplin's social conscience is at work, and those who like to read tendentiousness into his films suppose that it is an attack, of however light a sort, on the rich. But the film is more ambiguous than that and all the more tantalizing for it. There *are* idle rich in the film: we meet Charlie, mustache trimmed a bit, in top hat, adjusting his boutonniere in a mirror before mixing the additional cocktail that will keep him from meeting his wife on time. But there are two Charlies in the film: the other, shabby as ever, is at the same time extricating himself from the underside of a freight car, carrying his golf clubs with him. In playing a dual role, Chaplin is plainly leaving a question open: *which* is the idle class?

The other thing that is most often said about the film is that it is, at root, a reversion to Keystone formula: improvisation on a golf course, shabby Charlie's invasion of a costume ball, a chase and a slapstick fight. Certainly these things appear, and in quite rapid sequence. But there is a doubleness about all of them, and an interaction between them, that produces overtones—teasing speculations—that likely would not have appeared in a comedy made earlier than *The Kid.*

It should be stressed that the film is funny, one of the funniest short comedies Chaplin ever made: Charlie teeing up and preparing a demonic swing only to discover he has no golf ball; Charlie nonchalantly strolling the course while kicking another man's ball away until he can pocket it; Charlie, too cagey to let himself be knocked down a second time, dropping flat on his back before the blow can be delivered.

More arresting is the fact that Edna is deeply interested in both Charlies but that neither can ever bring her happiness. It comes about this way. She is married to the rich one, the perennial drunk who completes his toilet before the mirror to stroll into the hotel lobby without trousers, and she is constantly threatening to divorce him. She promises to withdraw her latest threat if he will come to the evening's costume ball and behave well. Doing his indifferent best to oblige her, he decides to dress himself in a full suit of armor: as he sips a last cocktail before leaving his room, the visor slips down over his face and locks. When he does stumble into the ball, a hazardous halberd in his hand, he is both blinded and unrecognizable.

The shabby Charlie, meanwhile, has by happenstance also found his way to the ball. He is immediately accepted by Edna as her husband, as his clothes are accepted as a costume. He is immensely surprised—and then delighted—to

Opposite: After a night's revel with cronies, Charlie straphangs his way home in a lunch wagon.

At home, below, the conventional dragon-wife with rolling pin denies him his much-needed sleep. *Payday.*

be summoned to her side, bewildered but warmed by the hand she tenderly places over his. A hint of possibility—the possibility of a *serious* relationship if only the two Charlies were really one—hovers over the moment, stirring echoes of those more recent films in which emotion somehow asserted itself. Edna seems genuinely drawn to the man, he to her.

The farce of the situation soon explodes, there is a chase ending in the rich Charlie's hotel suite, a fight between ragged Charlie and the Charlie encased in armor: among other things, ragged Charlie severely hurts his hand punching the visor, then swiftly resolves the problem by holding a pillow over the visor with his left hand while he pounds away at it with his right. In due time, identities are unscrambled: ragged Charlie is able to open the visor with a can opener to reveal rich Charlie inside it, courtesy of a double. Edna's father orders ragged Charlie to leave. Charlie, as though he had not heard and suddenly very much the man of manners, glances at his watch, seems horrified at the lateness of the hour, apologizes for having to go. Throughout the melee Edna, when we see her, is somewhat torn: will her real husband turn out to be the man she rather likes or the man she despises? As ragged Charlie is leaving, Edna turns from him coolly: if he *is* as ragged as he looks, he cannot be for her, either. When he has gone, though, she relents, ambiguously begging her father to bring him back. On the street outside, Charlie gracefully accepts the father's apology, kicks him, and moves on.

The two Charlies of *The Idle Class*: above, Edna's rich, inebriated husband; opposite: the vagabond she rather likes but must dismiss.

There are too many Charlies for Edna to have the one she wants, just as there are too many Charlies for Charlie ever to find a place for himself, in ballroom, boudoir, pulpit, or opera star's home. In a sense, Chaplin has here dramatized his own character by dividing it; he is always, at the very least, two people, each aware

of and in contest with the other, each denied the social root and the emotional rewards a committed identity might give him.

If the film is slapstick, the slapstick is haunted. One may come away from it with vivid memories of its rush of gags—Chaplin's brilliantly executed evasion of the fact that he has no trousers, Chaplin turning his back on us apparently to sob over Edna's divorce threat and then turning front to reveal that he is in fact shaking a cocktail—but it has a slightly longer reach than that: thinking about it the next day may push into the foreground the immediate intimacy between Edna and Charlie while he is being mistaken for a reformed husband, the odd upward look he casts while he is getting a can opener out of his pocket to unveil his rival. The upward look has no special emotion built into it, no apprehension, no regret; it is a look one often sees on Chaplin's face when he is concentrating simultaneously on what he is doing and on what he must do next. He will always do whatever is expected of him, whatever its consequences. His attention is upon the immediately necessary; it is also upon the road he knows will follow. He will use his best talents both ways, in a spirit of pure detachment. It is, after all, the detachment that defines him.

With the successful *The Idle Class* and *Pay Day* completed, Chaplin had only *The Pilgrim* to go. *The Pilgrim* done with—he still took his time over it and expanded it to four reels—he was finally free of First National, free of financial stresses, free of short films for good, free to join his friends in a studio they owned jointly, free to make films precisely as he wished to make them. He would continue to run into creative blocks; but he could now afford to wait these out, even—as happened some six or seven years later—to wait out talking pictures.

21. Lloyd: The Virtuous Filmmaking of the Virtuous American

The temptation in writing about Harold Lloyd's feature films is to try to explain why he isn't Chaplin or Keaton. But that, right off, leaves something out of account. The fact is that, in one strict sense, he was more popular than either of them in the twenties. To make the statement stick, popularity must be measured in terms of audience attendance at the films the three men made and the money that rolled in as a consequence. But that is what popularity is normally thought to be about.

I think it would be safe to say that Chaplin's most successful films, taken one by one, earned more money than Lloyd's most successful. But during the 1920's Chaplin, working ever more slowly, made four features. Lloyd made eleven. Which meant that, year after year, without interruption, people were lining up to see Lloyd, talk about him, love him in a way not entirely communicable today, enrich him. Any trade journal keeping track of the annual earnings of comedians—for themselves and for exhibitors—would have had to name Lloyd champion. Lloyd *always* outgrossed Keaton.

Why? What had happened to this tenacious, at first imitative, relatively uninspired young man to land him at the top of the heap? Laboring mightily, borrowing even his glasses, dropping the search for a comic image larger and stranger than himself to offer his own dogged ambition as image enough, Lloyd at last ran into luck. Unable to create for himself an outsized figure sufficiently bizarre and ambivalent to function as myth, he fell, almost without thinking, and because of who and what he was, into a myth that already existed: the myth of the good American.

The good American, still devoutly believed in during the 1920's, was two things: he was aggressive, and he was innocent. Americans could not have tamed a continent if they had not been aggressive; they would not be able to make America "the greatest nation on earth" unless they remained so. "Up-and-at-'em," "do-or-die" were still the mottoes of the day. But whatever had been done aggressively, or was being done aggressively, had been and was being done

from the noblest motives, motives that had just recently helped make the world safe for democracy. The American's energy was a virtuous energy, spent always in the cause of good. A vigor that extended to brashness on the one hand; a clear conscience on the other.

And there was Harold Lloyd. A boy whom nothing could defeat, or even deter. Grit, sand, spunk—the whole lot. A boy who could wipe out a military dictatorship with the help of a faithful friend and the girl next door, a boy who could devise an advertising campaign that would put his department store on the map, a boy who could save a trolley owner's franchise from the monopolists who would swallow it, a boy who could herd roughnecks into church.

And all the while a shy and awkward boy, one who might cry in his room at night, a boy whose very naïveté stemmed from an excess of good will. The glasses were, after all, the saving grace. They masked, and justified, the nakedness of the aggression. America did understand, in the 1920's, that it was both callously ambitious *and* naïve. It had already begun to sense that, in making the world safe for democracy, it had fumbled the beautiful dream at the conference table, had been no match for wilier men. But its intentions had been pure, hadn't they? Which was worse, naïveté or old-world craftiness? Naïveté, after all, went arm in arm with innocence. Defensively or no, America began to take pride in its decency. Decency might make mistakes but at least they would not be indecent mistakes. Better to be naïve than nasty. There was some glory in it. And, perhaps, if the aggressiveness could be kept up until the nation possessed unchallengeable power, and if the innocence could be kept unsullied so that the power would then be generously used, an ideal balance might be achieved. Guts and goodness in tandem. It was there already in every American boy who rose from shoe clerk to national hero.

Harold, as his own courageous grandfather, is decorated for his Civil War heroism in *Grandma's Boy*.

Harold Lloyd slipped into that boy's shoes with his first five-reel film, *Grandma's Boy*, and stayed there. In *Grandma's Boy*, Harold—he is always called Harold in the films, only the surname changes—is a well-meaning young fellow who is more than willing to crank away at the ice-cream freezer for Mildred Davis's mother. He doesn't *like* to fight. When a bully interposes himself between Harold and Mildred, going so far as to dump Harold down a well before he appropriates the ice cream and presents it as *his* gift to Mildred's mother, Harold does nothing. His clean boyish face, with its squared mouth that could melt away at the edges in dismay, does not so much register frustration as regret. He wishes he knew what to do short of fighting.

In due time, he comes to wonder if he isn't a coward. But granny, with whom he lives, knows better than that. What the lad needs is faith in himself and the moral permission to fight. So granny cooks up a little story about Harold's Civil War grandfather—grandfather's portrait on the wall shows us Harold again, this time with rectangular eyeglasses and sideburns—who thought himself cowardly until given a talisman by a gypsy hag to whom he had been kind. With the talisman in his fist, Harold's grandfather became a terror, disposing of the entire enemy high command as he purloined military secrets. Granny gives Harold the talisman—really a carved umbrella handle—and when a local posse proves too cautious to take on an armed tramp who has murdered a storekeeper, Harold leaps to the fore, teeth set and eyes ablaze, recklessly braving the tramp's fire. He is, as it happens, afraid of a black cat that crosses his path while he is boldly walking into bullets, but avoiding the cat is precisely what enables him to take the tramp by surprise; a battle-*cum*-chase follows in which Harold and tramp exchange roles of conqueror and conquered across the countryside. The tramp is finally reduced to exhaustion by Harold's sheer persistence and Harold winds up the fray by trundling the tramp to the courthouse in a baby buggy.

Having disposed of the tramp, he turns to the bully. During one of the longest, most resolute comic fights ever filmed, Harold temporarily loses his talisman and is temporarily unsure of himself again. Informed by granny that the whole thing is a hoax and that all he has really needed is some confidence in himself, he turns manly on the instant, not only ridding himself of the bully once and for all but becoming lordly with Mildred as well. He *informs* her that they are going to be married—"RIGHT NOW," the title tells us in capital letters—before whisking her into his arms and carrying her, via stepping-stones, across a brook toward a fade-out. That he falls into the brook, taking her with him, just before that fade-out is only a reminder of the essential image. The nice young man, when aroused, is a tiger. But remember, all he wanted was to be a nice young man, and he will be one again—with all of his awkwardness intact—as soon as the job is done.

Grandma's Boy was enormously successful from the moment of its release, and the formula was repeated almost verbatim in *The Freshman, The Kid Brother, Girl Shy*, and *Safety Last*. In finally using his own "normal" qualities to define himself on screen, Lloyd had also defined Americans, most agreeably, for themselves. This is what they really were, always had been; and they liked the look of it. If the films were almost equally successful in Europe—though in Europe Chaplin and Keaton have always been the true demigods—it was because the Old World had very recently had a quite personal experience of this chap: he'd pulled that world's chestnuts out of the fire, chewing gum the while, during World War I. Lloyd could call one film *Speedy*, and insist that friends call him Speedy in yet another film, because that is what he was, once the wraps were off. He could call a third *For Heaven's Sake*—the title is a conscious pun—because

that is what the energy was unleashed for, heaven's sake. It is in the last-named film that he kicks, trips, and otherwise assaults an entire neighborhood of hoodlums in order to make them chase him into a Bowery-type mission, where, under certain circumstances, they will listen raptly to a sermon. Lloyd deliberately perpetuated the image in his personal life, remaining married to the same woman until she died, devoting much of his free time to benevolent activities sponsored by fraternal organizations. No reason not to call his autobiography *An American Comedy.*

Interestingly, the formula was open to what must now seem a surprising variation—without loss of its essential meaning. Lloyd himself insisted on a policy of change: no two "shy" pictures in a row. What was the variation? At first sight, it seems rather a radical one. Instead of the timid and flailing poor boy who must make good at all costs, Lloyd appears in at least three of his features as a cocky, exceedingly rich young wastrel.

On meeting him in *For Heaven's Sake*, we are told that he has just bought a new car to match his white trousers. Wrecking the car more or less instantly, he strolls to an automobile showroom, selects another car, dashes off a check for it while nattily juggling his long cigarette holder between his teeth, and drives it directly from shop to street. When this car is commandeered by police in urgent pursuit of thieves, it is first thoroughly shot up and then, stalling on railroad tracks, ground to smoking rubble by a locomotive. Harold, without a care in the world, lights his cigarette from the smoking rubble.

In *A Sailor-Made Man*, the transitional four-reeler with which Lloyd eased himself from shorts into features, the jaunty step, white ducks, and the cigarette

Cock-of-the-walk Harold, doing the Navy a favor by deigning to enlist. *A Sailor-Made Man.*

Overleaf: In *For Heaven's Sake*, what's one more wrecked car to cavalier Harold?

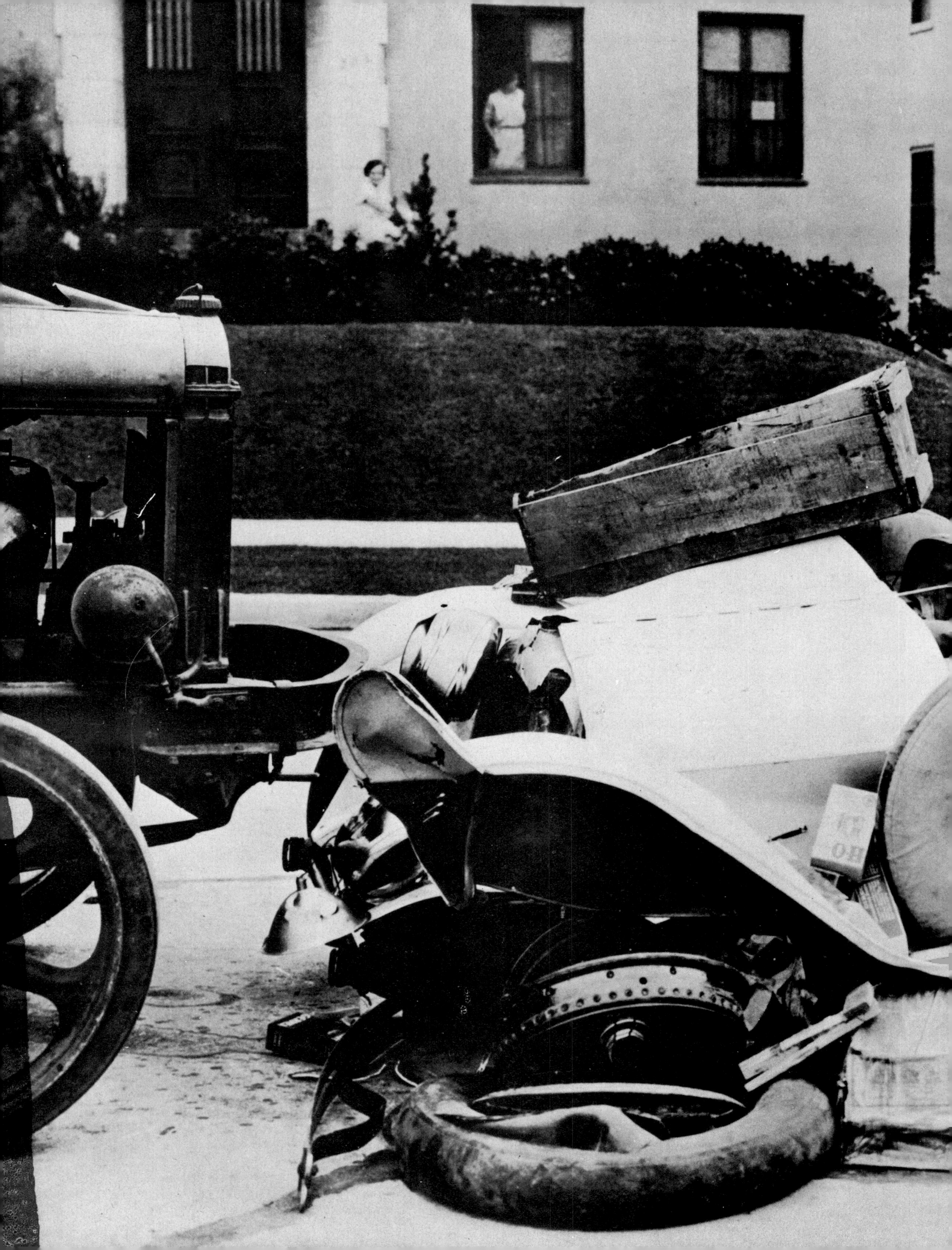

holder so cavalierly used are already present. When he decides to join the Marines, he enters the recruiting office swinging his cane nonchalantly, makes himself at home at the sergeant's desk while the stunned sergeant looks on, pours himself a refreshing glass of water, announces his intentions as though bestowing a favor on the forces, and tips the presiding officer as he saunters away.

And in *Why Worry?*, one of his most charming films, he begins as a well-to-do hypochondriac, coddled by a lovely nurse whose loveliness he never deigns to notice, escorted aboard a cruise ship in a wheelchair, deposited for peace and quiet in a tiny Latin-American country. He does notice, as he takes the air in the public streets, that there seems to be some shooting going on, here and there. Informed that a revolution has broken out, he simply replies, imperiously, "Well, tell them to stop it." Cock of the walk in these films.

This must seem a far cry from the fumbling lad without a dime for dinner who ultimately must risk his neck to make his name. It's not, though, for two reasons somewhat peculiar to the period. In the 1920's, Americans *liked* rich people. The people who lived in the best house in town were the best people in town, cherished for having—by hard work and virtuous living—set an example for everyone else. It was good of them simply to have settled in this community. To be invited through the gates, as occasionally did happen, was an honor; to see the occupants of the house riding the local streets in their limousines—the older dowagers still drove electric cars, slowly, ever so slowly—provoked a thrill of pride. There was nothing prejudicial, then, in coming from a house or a family set apart. After all, everybody was going to get rich sooner or later—probably, before 1929.

And, by one of those complex simultaneities so persistent in human nature, everybody felt sorry for rich people. Or pretended to feel sorry for them, above all for their children. The children of the rich were felt to be underprivileged, denied the character-building that comes of having to do for oneself, denied the friendly contacts of ordinary rough-and-tumble street life, denied experience and challenge. They were not so much spoiled as sheltered—and, in the sheltering, weakened. One could always shed a tear for the golden-haired rich child, alone among expensive dolls or toy trains, pressing its nose against the window pane, yearning for the liveliness beyond the great grilled fence. Mary Pickford had one of her greatest successes with a film called *The Poor Little Rich Girl.*

Harold Lloyd could draw upon the same reservoir of sympathy, or at least ready tolerance, as a poor little rich boy incapable, for all his cockiness, of fending for himself. Thrown into a revolution, surrounded by thugs, beset by wicked rajas eager to kidnap Mildred, he was forced to learn how to cope, drop his insouciant air of privilege, forget his checkbook and his hypochondria, and dig in.

In the end, it all came to the same thing: the rich boy, like the poor boy, had to make a man of himself. "Make a man of yourself," is what Mildred's father tells rich young Harold in the first reel of his first demi-feature, and the pattern remains firm whether we meet the lad shy or suave. In a few films—*Dr. Jack* and *Speedy*—he strikes a kind of middle ground between his two options, letting the gangling youngster serve as everyone's friend, eager to help. In *Hot Water* he is already married and condemned to conventional in-law problems. Significantly, *Dr. Jack* and *Hot Water* were his least successful films of the period: the poverty-to-manhood or riches-to-manhood outline wasn't sharp enough to see these films through their extended length; both might better have been made as shorts. But in *Dr. Jack* he keeps the formula half alive by switching it from himself to Mildred, presented, in an early title, as "The Sick Little Well Girl"—a girl so coddled by wealthy parents that she has become an enforced invalid, waiting for rescue at Harold's hands. Harold rescues her by teaching her to enjoy a natural taste for danger. In general, the films suggest that the rich can be as unlucky as the poor, and that rich American or poor American can overcome his beginning handicaps by nerving himself to the impossible. Each is innately virtuous, born good; each must learn to use the gumption God gave him.

Of course the gags continued. The black cat, simple as it is, is among the better ones in *Grandma's Boy*. But it should be evident from even a brief outline of that film, or from the underlying Horatio Alger mythos itself, that gagging—for Lloyd—was far from the heart of the matter. He would scatter gags profusely throughout his films; but he was confronted, always, with one special bit of knowledge: *he* was no joke.

Chaplin was a joke, Keaton was a joke. Both carried their incongruities with them. The fastidiousness of Chaplin's manner and the shabbiness of his clothes denied each other on the spot. Keaton's rigidity of face and stance was contradicted by the quicksilver of his brain.

But there was nothing inappropriate about Lloyd. The glasses did not contradict the spunk; they complemented it, at least in the eyes of Americans who shared his dual belief in vigor and virtue. There is no mystery in Lloyd, no wondering how this unprecedented fusion of odd parts came about, no command that we believe in what we must acknowledge as absurd. Lloyd fitted himself; and that left him with nothing intrinsically funny.

He knew that, had always known it; his early cry, "What do I do to be funny?" must have echoed through the studio until the end of his career. If he was to become a major comedian—and he was determined on that—he would have to do more than scatter comic bits in and around a rapidly moving narrative line. He would have to involve himself in values powerful enough to justify his own presence in the film, his dominance of the film. He would have to find a way or ways of earning a deep audience commitment to him that would be compatible both with the national archetype he had fallen heir to and the comedy that would decorate it.

Fortunately, the archetype itself suggested two qualities that might be developed to the point where gagging could well be secondary. The aggressiveness suggested "thrill" comedy, in which laughter depends not so much on the quality of the joke as on the fact that it occurs when an audience's nerves are so titillatingly ravaged that response comes on the double. If the man in danger isn't funny, the danger itself will seek an outlet in laughter, given the least cue. And the innocence, the moral earnestness, suggested a vast reservoir of sympathy to be tapped, sympathy so binding that it would carry the central figure from comic crisis to comic crisis without anyone noticing, or caring, that the comedy was all happening to him, not emanating from him.

Lloyd became a master of both substitutes. "Thrill" comedy had been born with the form; it had been Sennett's principal mainstay when humor was hard to come by; Lloyd himself had been experimenting with it in his two-reelers. But could it be amplified, intensified, sustained over a long enough time and on a large enough scale to serve as a sort of summary of the genre, becoming virtually mythic in itself? Lloyd wanted an important film, not a conventional one. His thrills would have to be more thrilling than anyone else's.

They were, in *Safety Last*. What is astonishing about *Safety Last*, in which Harold unwillingly climbs the face of a department store until he has survived twelve or thirteen stories, is that virtually every shot in it keeps the street below in view. Harold may be having trouble with pigeons that are flapping on his shoulders while he hangs by his fingernails; the street, the streetcars, the tumblebug

A lonely Mary Pickford in *The Poor Little Rich Girl*.

Harold nearing the top of his climb in *Safety Last*. Clinging to a runaway bus in *For Heaven's Sake*. Dangling from a loose trolley in *Girl Shy*.

Opposite: One silent comedy image that has never lost its power as myth. *Safety Last.*

autos, the pedestrians scurrying on their own errands are there, a sickening drop away. Harold may grab the minute-hand of a huge clock as he falls from a window, and his weight may be slowly but horrendously pulling the entire clock-face from the wall: we see all of this from slightly above him, and to his left, with the busy canyon in view. Even close-ups of Harold's terror-stricken face as he clutches at a rope that is swiftly slipping through his hands are angled to show us exactly where he is and what may happen to him. And it *may* happen to him.

Lloyd is giving the "thrill" film its ultimate authenticity, an authenticity so firm that, though *Safety Last* has neither been re-released nor excerpted for compilations in more than forty years, the spectacle of Harold hanging from that clock-face persists in the public mind like a race-memory. Made today, its effectiveness would be destroyed by "process" shooting: actors working, altogether safely, before previously photographed backgrounds projected on a second screen behind them. In a contemporary pastiche of the 1920's called *Thoroughly Modern Millie*, actors may once more clamber about high windowsills and dangle from flagpoles, but our eyes tell us throughout that we are looking either at painted buildings or separately shot backgrounds, or both at once. We cannot respond *against* our own clear knowledge. And so we don't; the thrill vanishes. There are no screams in the auditorium now, only indifference and, worse yet, irritation.

Lloyd wanted screams and got them honestly. Working before "process" had been invented and scorning paint, he went up an actual building, hand hold by hand hold. He did take what steps he could to minimize the danger. The department store he climbed was situated on a hill, which made the drop to the street beneath seem, at certain camera angles, a great deal steeper than it was. But what the camera recorded, at these angles, was factual recording; the instrument may have been carefully placed, but what it saw it truly saw. There was, in addition and out of range, a platform beneath him. Lloyd said, in conversation, that it was two stories beneath, not very wide, and covered with a mattress; the greatest danger was that, in hitting the mattress, he might bounce and go over the side. In *An American Comedy* he places it as much as three stories below; no doubt for certain shots it was lifted a great deal closer.

One long-shot in the film, photographed from a structure cater-cornered to the building Lloyd is climbing, indicates that the platform is at least three floors below. Another, shot from the top of the department store, shows Lloyd midway and coming up with no platform at all beneath him. Lloyd constantly insisted that he had used no doubles in the film. One is inclined to doubt him, given these few shots. Yet if the climber is not Lloyd, it is also pretty plainly not Bill Strothers, the professional human fly he hired to instruct him and to play his friend in the film; Strothers is short and stocky. If any genuine deception was practiced, as it had to have been for Lloyd to swing pendulum-like from the top of the building secured by nothing more than a rope knotted about one ankle, it was minimal; Lloyd reported throwing his shoulder out of joint in his lunge at the clock's hands.

In fact, he demanded more of himself than he need have. Very often we are close up on his face, his shoulders, his clawed fingers, as he struggles to free himself from a net that has dropped on him, as he spreadeagles himself against a window that tilts on a fulcrum rather than riding up and down on a sash, as he wrestles himself over a projecting cornice. Dozens of such shots might have been made in a studio or at ground level. No filmmaker is *obliged* to include a vast background in every frame of film, and if our attention is for the moment entirely centered on Harold's problem with a tilting window there is no reason for not setting up the window elsewhere and shooting it head-on. Lloyd *chose* to do his close-shots from an angle that kept the drop eternally visible. If he was going to do

MAJESTIC
MAJESTIC

a "thrill" film, he would keep the thrill in every foot of it.

Intent on learning where he could not originate, he had come to understand thoroughly the special nature of the medium in which he worked. He hadn't Keaton's obsessive curiosity about it. On his own, he developed only one small trademark out of the form's dimensional contradictions. He did like the deceptive "pullback" shot, and used it well. In *Grandma's Boy* we seem to see him cranking a car. We pull back to discover that what he is so assiduously cranking is an ice-cream freezer. In *A Sailor-Made Man* we seem to see him painting a picture, hand poised with the brush and darting in for an occasional stroke, head cocked in judicious criticism of each tentative dab. We pull back to discover that he is standing over the painter's shoulder and that the hand is not his at all. In *For Heaven's Sake*, he and the girl seem to be spending the evening on a moonlit beach, sand running through their fingers, water rippling at their feet. We pull back to discover that they are relaxing on a construction site, the sand and water mere materials; the gently curved moon behind them is a sign for the Crescent Laundry.

But if Lloyd's interest in the odd compression of film did not extend beyond such pleasantries, his respect for its integrity was almost total. Lloyd made no further "climbing" pictures during the silent period. But as he carried the "thrill" principle into a half-dozen other backgrounds, he took his insistence on authenticity with him. *Girl Shy*, for instance, is virtually one long chase. The girl is on her way to the altar, about to marry the wrong man; Harold is miles away. In his feverish rush to the rescue, he chases a train in an automobile while fighting off a woman's scarf that has blown about his head; he drives a motorcycle through a grocery store and then into a ditch from which the diggers fly one by one; he commandeers a streetcar that runs wild through the streets when its trolley swings free. Straddling the roof to fix the trolley, he is swung out over city traffic until he is at last able to drop directly into the front seat of a passing car. The action is reported with total fidelity: real streetcar, real traffic, real drop.

There is one shot in the film that perhaps ought to have been cut. Having lost all his other vehicles, Harold appropriates a two-horse cart, whipping it through the city as though the city were the Circus Maximus. One of the cart's wheels becomes loose and spins away—business Lloyd would repeat in *Speedy*. Loosing the traces, Harold climbs onto the back of one horse, the other still racing in tandem beside him, the jiggling camera ferociously recording every inch of the derring-do. At this point in the film's making Lloyd and horses took what was obviously a very nasty and unrehearsed spill; the camera, however, kept on turning as Lloyd hurriedly remounted the struggling horses and dashed away. The moment is suddenly chilling, we have such a strong sense of being present at a true accident, of seeing beyond the camera's reality to yet another reality. The permissiveness of fantasy is shaken, momentarily. But no matter. Harold makes it to the church on time.

This may be as good a time as any to acknowledge a debt we felt as children to one of Lloyd's practices. He often gave us something no one else would: the double climax. Children are quick to recognize structural rhythms. When we went to see a western, we knew what to expect: a short introductory passage, an initial fight or thrill of fair proportions, a sizable lull to develop romantic and other plot complications, then a final, substantial chase and battle. But when the chase and battle were over, they were over, and there was always—when we were first going to the movies—a terrible feeling of letdown as we sensed the fade-out to come. We wanted the battle to go on forever.

Harold to the rescue, poultry or no poultry, by motorcycle, streetcar, or horse cart. *Girl Shy*.

Lloyd virtually gave us that. In *Grandma's Boy* he has really done enough

The pullback shot: Harold and Jobyna Ralston's moonlit beach proves, rather quickly, to be a construction site. *For Heaven's Sake.*

for one film in single-handedly besting a murderer and delivering him to the authorities. But no. There is still that local bully to taunt Harold on his way home to Mildred. Harold strips off his jacket for action and is promptly knocked down. Up from the dust, he is knocked down again. Defeated half a dozen times, he groggily, gamely rises to dive after his tormentor until they have fought through the farmyard, high up in the loft, back on the ground again after a joint tumble onto a haystack, on and on and on. This was the bonus we had always yearned for and never dared count on, the climax we had waited for stretched to satiety at last. Lloyd knew where his strengths lay, and used them.

For all his reputation as a man who could invent and compound gags indefinitely so long as they did not have to originate in his character, the strength was never in the gagging. Occasionally there is a nice surprise. In *Girl Shy*, as he is snatching vehicle after vehicle in his race to the altar, he leaps into an empty automobile which is immediately towed away backward. The image is independently amusing, original and self-contained, even if something of its force comes from our knowledge that the last thing in the world Harold wants is to go *backward.* More often, the gags are trivial, Sennett-shopworn, even strained. Among the things that happen to Harold while he is climbing in *Safety Last*: a boy in a window spills popcorn on his head, attracting the pigeons; a mouse runs up his trouser-leg, leading to a frantic dance on a ledge. In themselves, uninventive hand-me-downs.

Lloyd did develop a knack for giving the hand-me-down a new shape. In *Hot Water* some small boys have released a spider on a streetcar, and we know that somehow it is going to get into Harold's trousers. But it does not crawl up his leg. Harold is seated, and the spider drops onto his lap without his noticing; a moment later a woman passenger happens to drop a handkerchief over the spider. Harold sees the square of white on his lap, assumes it is his shirttail just come out, and in a frenzy of embarrassment tucks it under his belt. *He* puts the spider in his trousers. Perhaps he has done a lot of work getting it there, but the twist is his own.

Sometimes too much work is involved. As he is marrying the girl at the end of *For Heaven's Sake*, he is so worshipfully engrossed in her that he doesn't look down to see where he is putting the ring. Instead of putting it on her finger he slips it onto the tail of a dog that has somehow been maneuvered between them. The maneuvering is more than the joke ever could have been worth. Approaching yet another high window in *Safety Last*, he comes upon a photographer's studio at the very moment a man posing as a gunman is having his picture taken, pistol at the ready; when the photographer's flash goes off, Harold is sure he has been shot and makes haste to start climbing again. The rigged gag wouldn't amuse us much—we should scarcely believe it—if it weren't for that ever-present street far below.

The thrills acted as a pressure cooker for the gags, keeping them so restlessly on the bubble and under such a high emotional temperature that it no longer mattered whether they were small or ordinary or familiar. Keaton once wondered aloud whether Lloyd was trying to become a comedian or an acrobat. The remark may sound odd coming from Keaton, himself a trained acrobat. But the point is well enough taken.

Lloyd, climbing to the top as all good Americans were expected to do, became an acrobat who could frighten people into laughing. Because he made the fright legitimate, the laughter could be accepted as legitimate too.

22. Lloyd: Architect of Sympathy

Even more important to Lloyd, as the 1920's galloped along, was his ever-increasing ability to create sympathy for his game kid, a sympathy that did not simply depend on the fact that the boy doing stunts for us might be dropped to his death at any moment but that belonged, rather, to the other half of his composite image: his niceness.

Obvious enough. We like nice boys. But for Lloyd it was never that easy; the matter had to be worked on, built up. Curiously, the sympathy we feel for Lloyd is not a personal one. The mere sight of him on a screen does not generate it, any more than it suggests instant comedy. Come upon him laboring over a butter churn or buying an automobile or studying a picture that is being painted, and our response, until something else happens, is apt to be neutral. We don't even know that he is nice, the glasses notwithstanding, until we've thoroughly investigated the circumstances in which he's been placed.

The sympathy Lloyd learned to earn for himself was a narrative sympathy: it came from organizing the events of a film so adroitly that we had, in the end, no way of resisting what the structure was doing to us. Lloyd became so expert at tipping narrative in his favor that he could do it backward, sidewise, or head-on.

Backward was easiest. We first see the bully in *Grandma's Boy* coming along a country lane. He pauses and, altogether gratuitously, shies a stick at a cat. Well, we're certainly not going to like *him*. That leaves us Harold to like. In *Why Worry?*, while Harold is beginning to realize that the earthly paradise in which he'd hoped to soothe his nerves is actually a hotbed of revolution, we see the rebels horsewhipping peasant women. Even though Harold still hasn't chosen sides, we're on his. He may be rich, hypochondriacal, and bossy; but surely he would never whip women. Sympathy by default, or refraction, is rather primitive gamesmanship; but it does its own small share of the film's emotional work and, surprisingly, seems an inoffensive tactic—belonging to the period—when the films are looked at again today.

Harold, unawed, meets a giant in a jail cell. Harold helps the giant pull a tooth.

Opposite: The giant helps Harold bombard bridges and gunboats. *Why Worry?*

Sidewise was slyer, often subtler. One curious trait Lloyd exhibited was an ability to strike up friendships with figures who ought to have qualified as bullies. Sometimes the bully is just a bully, and Lloyd has to whip him, at whatever cost. But a surprising number of the films begin with Harold at the actual or potential mercy of a roughneck bigger than he and end with Harold and the thug-like menace bosom pals. In *A Sailor-Made Man*, for instance, the spindly Harold is at first tossed about like a rag doll by the burly Noah Young, playing his bunkmate on board ship. When Young gets himself into trouble with the commanding officer—a crate he has hurled at Harold hits the wrong man—Harold promptly and politely takes the blame. He is put to work swabbing decks in consequence. Young is baffled. What kind of patsy takes the blame? Confronted with a phenomenon he has never run into before, he hesitantly joins Harold at work, trying to figure him out. In no time Young is offering him a healthy chaw at his tobacco. As the film proceeds, they become inseparable buddies.

In *For Heaven's Sake*, Harold torments a townful of gamblers, thieves, and con men into chasing him into the mission house run by the girl's father. Before they can dismember Harold on the premises, a cop enters; they must behave, temporarily. They do not behave perfectly: one of the group steals the cop's watch. The moment the theft is discovered, the men are lined up to be searched. Swiftly, Harold goes into action. He will take up the mission collection. And so he passes among the wide-eyed hoodlums, just ahead of the searching cop, collecting not only the stolen watch in his basket but anything else the vulnerable men might not wish to have found in their pockets, including the plot jewels. They now vastly admire their savior and are willing to attend the mission, singing hymns and listening to sermons, regularly.

That is to say, because thugs like Harold, we like him. Cannily, Lloyd recognized and used a law of the street, one that all children know. For a nice boy to win the friendship of the toughest kid on the block is an accolade, a sign that he is possessed of powers we hadn't quite guessed at. It's not a matter of the mild fellow attaching himself to the strong one for protection; obviously, the strong one, if he were really a roughneck, would have no reason to tolerate that. The stronger must have seen something to admire in the weaker; we take his word for it, and admire the weaker too.

Lloyd stretched the principle to engagingly fantastic limits in *Why Worry?*, which may be my own favorite among the films: he became buddies with a giant.

Harold is captured by the island's revolutionary party and thrown into prison. Immediately he looks about for means of escape. In fact, he is so preoccupied with the problem that he doesn't notice the two enormous feet that protrude from a recessed bed in the cell—at least not until the man who belongs to the feet slowly rises to full height. Harold's nose comes to his elbow.

The giant, by the way, is a real one, as he had to be if the comedy's fantasy was to be valid. Lloyd searched far and wide to find a man of heroic proportions and, as it happens, found two: the first died before production work could begin; the second—a Minnesotan named John Aasen—roams through the film carrying, without sign of effort, five or six women in his arms at will.

Harold is not in the least awed by his cellmate. He is, rather, instantly imperious, taking his own authority for granted, accepting the giant's bulk and strength as just what he needs for his present purposes. Using the giant as a human ladder, he reaches a high window; the giant boosts him out of it, onto his head in a courtyard. We do see that the giant himself is going to have trouble getting through the smallish window. Indeed, we never see him get through it; in a pleasantly backhanded ellipsis, we simply notice, via a casual later shot, the enormous gap in the

prison wall the giant has made in lunging through.

The giant, it turns out, is suffering from a violent toothache, and Harold, the hypochondriac who is medically oriented anyway, will matter-of-factly help him pull the tooth. He fails, any number of times: if he attaches the tooth to the rope of a saddle horse and sends the horse racing away, the rope simply uncoils; if he ties the free end of the rope to himself and runs as fast as he can, he is only jerked to a violent stop in the dust. In a remarkably well-executed trick shot, he tries climbing the giant, all of his weight on the rope; he goes up the great body at a right angle to it, his own back parallel to the ground as he plants his feet on knees, thighs, midriff. The other end of rope has to have been anchored to something other than the giant's neck, probably to something behind him, courtesy of split-screen. But one must see the sequence some five or six times before detecting even the faintest instability between the two halves of the image, and in this case the originality and quite plausible absurdity of the joke seem to justify the mild cheating. Engrossed as we now are in the joint efforts of Harold and giant, we scarcely remember that any cheating is needed.

Eventually, and after Harold has taken a variety of falls, the tooth is extracted. The giant is now so grateful that he drops to his knees to salaam before Harold, even places Harold's nattily shod foot on his head. He is Harold's man forevermore, and he will not only uproot trees for him, he will carry the barrel of a cannon strapped to his back so that he need only bend over for Harold to pull a string that will send balls crashing into river barges and demolishing enemy bridges.

The puppy-dog fidelity of this Goliath to a bespectacled and benevolent David does more than endear the giant to us; it endears the object of his affections to us as well. When power kneels, it is to the deserving; ergo, Harold deserves. He even deserves what the giant, called Colosso in the film, does for him in the film's most extravagant venture into practical fantasy. The villain of the piece is manhandling the girl on a second-floor balcony. Harold, racing to help, has wound up on a similar balcony directly across the street. There is no way of leaping from one to the other. The giant, as inventive as he is loyal, hurries to Harold's balcony, rips it from the wall, and carries it above his head across the street to the other building, so that Harold can bounce from his to hers in time to do the villain in.

Lloyd can use the girl to make us like *him*. In the same film, Jobyna Ralston plays the pretty young nurse who feeds Harold his pills, takes his pulse, and is otherwise ignored by him. *Why Worry?* was Miss Ralston's first film with Lloyd; she stayed with him for five more, virtually until the end of the silent period. She had been doing leads in two-reel comedies on the Roach lot when Mildred Davis, having completed four features with Lloyd, decided to accept another studio's offer to do straight roles. She never did do them; Lloyd promptly married her, and she retired from the screen. But Miss Ralston was an even better companion for Lloyd than Miss Davis had been. Miss Davis had been blonde, ringleted, smiling, bland. Miss Ralston was at once more vulnerable—her mouth seemed to tremble before an impending injury, her brunette hair softly framed even softer features—and more self-assertive. Behind the delicacy lurked a bit of the gamine, and whenever Harold needed to be roused to action or scolded out of his rich boy's assumptions, she could turn on him with spitfire animation. She blended something of Bebe Daniels's tomboyishness with Mildred Davis's Goldilocks sweetness, and the odd combination offered Lloyd one more opportunity of slipping sympathy in through a side door.

At long last, in *Why Worry?*, she does turn on him, giving him a thorough, thoroughly unexpected, tongue-lashing for his airs, his hypochondria, and his

Jobyna and Harold (left to right): Hat-check girl at the prom; apparition in a dusty mirror; comfort in a time of humiliation; helpmeet and adored adviser. *The Freshman.*

neglect. The camera holds on her in a sustained close-up, waiting until the temperature is quite high. If we wonder how Harold is reacting to all of this, we suppose it must be with astonishment and dismay. Then we cut to Harold. He is staring at her, for the first time, with the most adoring smile imaginable. He *likes* her for what she is saying. And, as planned, we like him for liking it.

During the latter half of the 1920's—Lloyd left the Roach lot to produce independently in 1924—Jobyna Ralston played an increasing role in what was to become, for Lloyd, a new kind of gagging—gagging that had as much to do with romantic sympathy and sensitive placement of the camera as with rigged embarrassment or surprise. Where Mildred Davis's function had most often been to stand by in apprehension while Harold captured an outlaw or got to the top of a building, Jobyna began to turn up at the center of the gag itself. The gag mellows in consequence, as Lloyd himself seemed to do.

The Kid Brother, made in 1927, is a consciously "beautiful" film, perhaps self-consciously so. Lloyd, who did not take a directorial credit on his films, had until now used Fred Newmeyer and Sam Taylor to guide him through his adventures; for *The Kid Brother* he employed Ted Wilde and J. A. Howe, who may have had something to do with the ever-so-carefully framed compositions, the glistening sunlight through trees and the smokily stirred dust, that give the venture a sheen uncommon to Lloyd. One doesn't expect this comedian's films to open with a panoramic shot of a curved beach at sunset, a circus wagon trundling along a path near us, an abandoned ship lying aslant in the bay. Using the circus wagon to begin the film, and the abandoned ship to end it, Lloyd and his collaborators

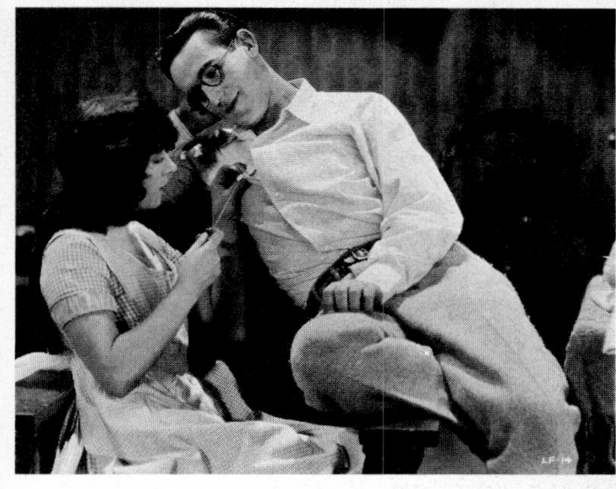

have in effect bounded the complete narrative in a single shot.

But the gags themselves are softer, lighter, much more directly related to the film's sentiment now—with Jobyna very much in evidence. Jobyna earns her precarious living as a dancer with a traveling medicine-show. Harold has been deputized by his father, the sheriff, to shut the show down. He sets about his task reluctantly, and ineptly. In part because of his incompetence, the portable stage and canvas scenery catch fire. Flames leap into the night; everything is destroyed. Jobyna, surveying the smoldering ruins, is distraught; Harold, pretty miserable himself, puts his arm around her. As they stand together, a few drops fall onto the back of his hand. It occurs to him that it is raining, and he checks the night sky. No rain. Realizing at last that these are tears, he draws her closer, sympathizing deeply. Gradually there are more drops, then a torrent. Terrified that any woman should be capable of such grief, Harold is on the verge of panic himself until he thinks to look upward again. It *has* begun to rain. He is very much relieved. Lloyd is now getting his laughs while comforting the girl.

The first meeting between Harold and Jobyna in *The Kid Brother*—or, to be more precise, their first parting—involves the young couple and the camera in an ingenious parlay, one of the choicest combinations of angle, sentiment, and gag that I know. Harold just happens to have rescued Jobyna from the unwelcome attentions of a prowling roustabout and she is grateful. They chat for a moment, stroll shyly through the woodland. Then it is time for farewells, and Jobyna disappears down a hillside. Harold is all agog, can't really pursue her, can't let her go. There is a tree handy. If he can climb it to a certain height, perhaps he'll be able

Overleaf: Lloyd teaching his audiences to care. Counterclockwise: Unwelcomed at college; allowed to think himself on the team; urged to address his "admiring" classmates; rehearsing the gestures that will make him popular. Dogged on the field, downed on the field. Up and off again, benched, bedraggled, brutalized. *The Freshman.*

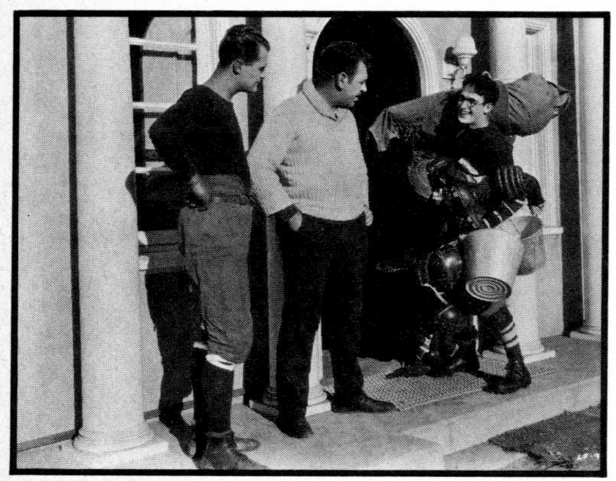

to see her below the hill. He climbs, the camera climbs with him, gradually Jobyna's retreating figure comes into view again. He hails her, calls out a question: what's her name? She turns in surprise, calls back: Mary. Then she vanishes into the landscape again. Urgently inspired, Harold climbs higher. Yes, he can see her again. Where does she live? Her reply comes up from the valley: with the medicine-show. She disappears for a third time, and Harold climbs for a third time. He still has to say goodbye. Jobyna, tiny in the distance, turns again to wave her own goodbye, then slips out of sight altogether.

The use of camera and girl to create both sympathy and surprise is nicely illustrated in the tremendously popular *The Freshman*, made two years earlier. Harold has arrived at college with glorious visions dancing through his head only to find himself, almost at once, virtually penniless. He is reduced to taking an attic room in a boarding house, where we know he is bound to be lonely. Shown the room by the matron who runs the place, he is dismayed but resigned. It's not what he ever dreamed of, but it can, after all, be smartened up. Left alone, he sets about tidying it, comes eventually to a mirror that is entirely clouded over by accumulated grime. He gets a rag and goes to work on the mirror, circling outward from its center. As he completes the central oval, he stops and stares at what he has wrought. There, in the mirror, is Jobyna.

This *is* what he has dreamed of, and it is quite as though she had materialized by a magic wave of the hand. He is relieved to turn and find her, altogether substantial, behind him. It is her mother who operates the boarding house, and she has come to help with the cleaning. But as we laugh at his discovery, we realize that the laughter has certain dimensions to it. We are responding not only to Harold's simple shock but to the utterly unforced camera placement that has made his shock possible and to the fact that he has summoned a friend out of thin air

as well.

But *The Freshman* is, in its entirety, Lloyd's most emphatic and extensive exercise in creating sympathy head-on. No bones about it: we are going to feel keenly for this boy whether he is ever funny or not. The narrative crunch is going to leave us helpless.

We are forewarned. Before setting foot on campus, Harold has built up naïve daydreams. As a way of preparing himself for the rituals of an unfamiliar life, he has seen his favorite college movie six times and learned to imitate every one of its preposterously romantic postures. He has trained himself to do a tricky little jig-step that ends in an outstretched hand by way of greeting and has memorized the greeting itself: "I'm just a regular fellow, step right up and call me Speedy." He has mooned over the college yearbook, imagined himself captain of the football team, president of his class. He is utterly confident that, being so knowing about campus ways, he will make a great hit. His mother and father, listening to him rehearse in his room, hope he won't have his heart broken.

Stepping from the train into a crowd of upperclassmen gleefully reuniting, he is the only boy on the platform carrying golf clubs and a ukulele. The crowd dissolves, splitting into back-slapping twos and fours, leaving him alone. But not quite. The campus bully catches a glimpse of him, points him out to some friends. They find him hilarious. But they do not ridicule him openly. Instead, they pretend admiration, beg him to teach them his jig-step, even lure him into addressing the entire student body in the auditorium before the dean can arrive. Uneasily, he complies, then gets his wind, launches into the sort of uplifting rhetoric he has learned from the movies. The crowd in the auditorium, quickly catching on to the fact that this boy is a fool, applauds him wildly. Mocking him the while, the whole campus persuades him that he is just what Tate College ordered.

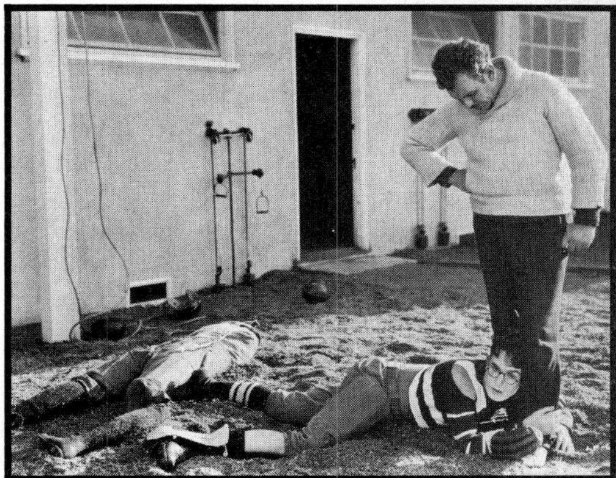

Once again, in *The Kid Brother*, Harold loses every battle on the way to winning the war.

Photographs of Harold appear in the college magazine, with captions remarking on his swift rise to popularity. The photographs and captions are inside jokes, giggled over at soda fountains. Harold carefully cuts them out and pins them proudly to his wall. Though Harold is so inept at football practice that he is used as tackling dummy when the sandbag dummy comes apart, the coach lets him think he has made the team; he is really water boy. When it is time for someone to proclaim himself host at the Fall Frolic—footing the bills as well—Harold, given his standing, feels it is his obligation to do so. The students spend a gala night dancing and drinking at his expense, keeping their secret to themselves.

At last the secret breaks. At the height of the party, the campus bully forces himself on Jobyna, who has been operating the hat-check concession. Coming upon them, Harold, in a stunned rage, knocks the bully down, whereupon he is venomously told that he is not the campus hero, he is the campus joke. Harold cannot believe his ears. But he sees that Jobyna knows, has known all along. To stop her tears, he pretends not to care, forces a shaken grin, gives the most indifferent shrug he can. Then, unable to help himself, he clings to the portieres, sobbing. Now it is Jobyna who is candid with him. There is only one thing wrong with him: he has never been himself. Fiercely fired by her faith in him, he sets his teeth and vows to show them what he's made of in tomorrow's climactic football game. At the football game he is kept sitting on the bench until the last substitute is carried off the field on a stretcher. Once in, of course, he wins the game.

Are there no gags along the way? Dozens, including a celebrated sequence at the Frolic in which his hastily basted-together new tuxedo comes apart seam by seam. All the while Harold is giving his address in the auditorium, a kitten is clawing its way out of his turtleneck sweater. During the big game, as he scans the skies for a football coming his way, he seems to see a dozen balls bobbing in air; someone has let balloons loose during the play. The quality of the gags is as variable as ever. It matters no more here than it does in the "thrill" films; these gags are not functioning as gags alone, they are functioning as humiliation. They may be mechanical, and they may be familiar; all that counts is that they hurt Harold.

Without transparent self-pity, Lloyd became an architect of pity, teaching an audience to ache over what was happening—or what might happen—to this decent, if overeager, kid. The narrative pressure is still there today, even if we have come to recognize much of the comedy as less than original. The last time I saw *The Freshman* I saw it in the company of two nine-year-old girls, both experienced moviegoers. Halfway through the film one of them turned to me in alarm. "Did this really happen?" she asked, demanding an answer. The structure remains intensely persuasive.

Lloyd's compensations for the lack of a true comic *persona* were powerful enough to make the problem seem irrelevant to an entire generation; even now, when we speak of silent film comedy we speak instantly of three names—Chaplin, Lloyd, Keaton, perhaps with the pecking-order changed. Today we admire Lloyd, admire his so painfully acquired craft and, for that matter, his integrity as a filmmaker. If we cannot love him with the passion felt by those who shared his time and his assumptions, it isn't because the thrills are no longer thrilling or because the architectural sympathy has been drained of effect. It is because we don't share the interlocked time and assumptions. What was lucky for Lloyd—his falling heir to a national archetype—is unlucky for us and for the full force of the films. The myth of the good American has lately slipped away from us; we look about for other, much more complicated, icons to show us back to ourselves.

23. The Keaton Quiet

Buster Keaton's films were sorely neglected for twenty-five years. In the recent excitement that has come of their rediscovery, there has been a tendency toward overcorrection: he has been hailed, here and there, not only as Chaplin's equal but as Chaplin's superior. This, I think, is waste effort, a misreading of Keaton's very values. Chaplin is likely to retain his preeminence among silent film comedians in part because he is so instantly accessible—no need to introduce or explain him, just run one of his films for a child or a thirty-year-old who has never seen him and response will come like a geyser—and in part because his comedy is contained entirely in his *persona*, a *persona* so multi-layered that it cannot be exhausted.

Keaton wants more study because he was himself a student: quizzical, cryptic, dispassionate, a man whose work could never be finished because there was always another corner to be turned. I confess that *I* find his work fascinating above that of all others. But that is a matter of temperament: Keaton was compulsively analytical, a trait that no doubt speaks directly to my own sorry habits of mind. Temperaments can lock in love and stay sane: Let Chaplin be king, and Keaton court jester. The king effectively rules, the jester tells the truth.

Chaplin appropriated film to his own image. Lloyd manipulated it with an architect's knowledgeability. Keaton preferred to function as its conscience. While others were using film to point at themselves or their daredeviltries, Keaton pointed in the opposite direction: at the thing itself. He insisted that film was film. He insisted that silent film was silent. Whatever was idiosyncratic about him—clothes, stance, emotional makeup—would have to find expression in and about these two prime facts.

I have called Keaton the most silent of silent film comedians without quite explaining why. The silence was related to another deeply rooted quality—that immobility, the sense of alert repose, we have so often seen in him. Keaton could run like a jackrabbit, and, in almost every feature film, he did. He could stunt like

In almost every film, Keaton took flight. This happens to be *Seven Chances*.

Lloyd, as honestly and even more dangerously. His pictures are motion pictures. Yet, though there is a hurricane eternally raging about him, and though he is often fully caught up in it, Keaton's constant drift is toward the quiet at the hurricane's eye.

Keaton ran so often during the twelve features he made in the 1920's that the sprint became a trademark: audiences waited for the cue that would, once in every five or seven reels, send him flying. He raced through city streets, outpacing police and traffic; he leapt, at top speed, the hedges that turned into hurdles on a vast college campus; ponds and streams could not break his stride, even though they sometimes left him with a snapping-turtle locked to his tie; mountain gorges were made to be bridged in a single, spread-legged, continuum. The camera makes a tracer bullet of him as he goes; his course leaves an after-image against the sky.

His stunting was so taken for granted and so dangerous that he broke his neck. He broke it during the making of his third feature film, *Sherlock Jr.*, and the shot in which he did it is still in the film. Buster is running pell-mell along the tops of a string of boxcars, thoughtlessly heading for the rear of the train. The last car comes, speeds by beneath him. Lost in midair he dives for the only object available, the spout of a railroad water tower projecting over the tracks. His weight lowers the spout just enough to release its water supply: a cascade hits him with Niagara-like force, hurtling him to the tracks below. In filming, his neck hit one of the tracks and snapped. Because he didn't realize what had happened, the scene plunges on: two men on a handcar whom he has also drenched take after him. Buster hops up and hares off across the fields.

Keaton suffered blinding headaches for a time after the mishap, but because he wasn't otherwise incapacitated he went right on working. It wasn't until several years later, when he was being given a routine insurance examination, that a doctor pointed the break out to him and remarked on how well it had healed.

There are hair-raising moments in *Sherlock Jr.*'s ultimate chase. Buster is on a motorcycle, plunging headlong across a high, narrow aqueduct. In a long-shot we see that ahead of him there is a sizable gap in the structure, perhaps twenty feet wide, one more drop into empty air. A truck on the road beneath is slowly approaching the gap. Just as Buster nears the appalling precipice, a second truck appears from the opposite direction. The two trucks pass each other, inside the gap, exactly in time to provide the winged Buster with a continuing roadway: he whips across their tops to connect directly with the resumed aqueduct. Then, astonishingly, the entire aqueduct begins to fall toward us. Buster rides straight on down with it, meeting the ground with grace and no diminution of speed, tearing off on his thoroughly reckless journey.

A few moments later that journey brings him into obvious collision course with an advancing train. Buster and motorcycle are in the foreground; the camera is close on them, moving at their violent rate. We see plainly enough that it is Buster on the machine. In the background, just as plainly, is the onrushing locomotive, curving inexorably toward the camera. Buster—and camera—whip across the tracks directly in front of the locomotive, clearing it by what seems inches.

It should perhaps be mentioned that Buster is seated on the handlebars of the motorcycle, and that the machine is driverless. Buster supposes that a friend is doing the driving, but a bump in the road has long since dismissed the friend. In fact, during the shooting of the sequence, the actor playing Buster's friend had been unwilling to take the fall from the driver's seat. Keaton promptly placed another actor, dressed as himself, on the handlebars, put on the friend's costume, and took the bump himself. He then resumed his own lone place on the unguided bars.

With one known exception—he could not do the pole-vault into a high second-story window in *College* and hired an Olympic star to do it for him—Keaton used no doubles. The people who worked with him were forever trying to persuade him not to do what he planned to do. He couldn't be talked out of taking an enormous drop, tied to another man, from a cliff into a swirling river for *Our Hospitality*. And when it came time to tumble a massive building façade on him during the hurricane in *Steamboat Bill Jr.*, everyone rebelled. Keaton was using a gag he'd experimented with twice before, though never on this scale: he would stand utterly still beneath the falling structure so that when it landed he would emerge unscathed in the small opening provided by an attic window. "The clearance of that window," Rudi Blesh quotes Keaton as saying, "was exactly three inches over my head and past each shoulder. And the front of the building—I'm not kidding—weighed two tons. It had to be built heavy and rigid in order not to bend or twist in that wind."

Keaton goes on to remember "the whole gang" begging him to forego the stunt. His story editor threatened to quit, his director simply absented himself from the set, and, when Keaton stubbornly persisted in having the collapse photographed, the cameramen operated their cameras while looking the other way. The shot, in the completed film, is stunning.

But it is stunning in a special way, Keaton's way. It is not, for instance, frightening, as a similar shot of Lloyd's might have been frightening. When Lloyd stunted, he meant to terrify; and he increased the audience's agitation by letting us see how agitated *he* was in the situation. Nothing of the sort here. Buster is placid. The wall falls impassively. When it has fallen, wall and Buster have arrived at an entirely equitable relationship. There is nothing to scream about.

That is, in part, what I mean by Keaton's silence, a stillness of emotion as

Keaton, on motorcycle, approaches the gap in the trestle, a gap providentially filled by two trucks just in time to create a continuing roadway. *Sherlock Jr.*

Overleaf: The universal stillness. *Go West.*

well as body, a universal stillness that comes of things functioning well, of having achieved occult harmony. But there are more ways of being silent than that.

One can, for instance, keep one's counsel about what is happening outside the frame, intimating that life is still going on out there but making no noise at all in the process. *Our Hospitality* was Keaton's second feature film, and it is filled with reticences. Buster is riding in the last coach of an early nineteenth-century railroad train; a coachman with a horn sits atop it; the roadbed is decidedly bumpy. The rear wheels of the coach come off. The jolt unseats the coachman, toppling him onto the tracks. The carriage drags on a bit till halted. Buster, quite naturally, hops from his seat to help the fallen coachman. He is getting the poor fellow to his feet and dusting him off when something entirely unexpected happens. The rear wheels of the coach roll into the frame to send both men somersaulting into the air.

The wheels, which disappeared from view as the camera followed the train to a stop, have not vanished from the universe. Had we thought that? They have been leading a life of their own all the while out there, remaining in motion because they *were* in motion, following natural law with an unemotional rectitude until they quite properly upend two men who are in their way. But how silent they have been in coming. In Keaton's films we do not hear what we cannot see.

In effect, he could have made us "hear" the onrushing wheels very simply. All he had to do was interpolate a shot of the isolated wheels still rolling along. We should then have expected them, supplying our own additional dimension, and what we might lose in surprise we would gain in heightened anticipation of the coming tumble. Most other comedians chose to show the looming threat and so gain suspense. Keaton steadfastly does it his way. Keep it a secret till it's happened, let no word of warning be heard.

An identifying close-up in a film always functions as a shout. If a man is reaching for a box of pancake batter on a shelf high above him and, distracted, plucks off a box of popcorn instead—so that the pancakes, when cooked, will flip about like maddened powder puffs—the customary practice of silent film was to intercut a tight view of the wrong box. Every such shot is a weakness, certainly in Keaton's view: an unnecessary headline has been permitted to scream at us, an exclamation point has been inserted directly into the middle of a sentence.

Buster unperturbed by a rapidly developing hurricane in *Steamboat Bill Jr.* Buster swinging out over falls prior to rescuing his girl from the tumbling rapids of *Our Hospitality*.

Keaton disliked exclamation points: too noisy. If the joke is a reasonable one, there is no need to fire a starting gun. The joke will explain itself, in mute majesty, to those who can see.

Take the Case of the Slithering Rope, also from *Our Hospitality*. Buster is trapped on a ledge halfway up—or halfway down—a precipitous cliff-face. There is a man at the top of the cliff who wishes to shoot Buster, though Buster does not know that. The man throws down a rope, tying it about his own waist, calling to Buster to do the same, which he does. The man is actually hoping to lure Buster into an exposed position, so that he can draw a decent bead on him. Buster tests a few of the projecting rocks about him, finds one firm enough, glances up. The man's pistol is aimed directly at him. Buster grasps the situation instantly and hastily retreats to shelter, inadvertently giving the rope a small tug as he does so. His attention is now called to the rope. It has been taut before. Now it is rapidly slithering downward, dribbling away before his eyes. Buster is much taken with the phenomenon simply because it *is* a phenomenon. As he watches it with such interest, the man's body flashes past him, heading for the river far below. That, it turns out, is quite interesting too. Buster contemplates the matter, attentively alert, until the rope goes taut again, this time from below, and *he* is yanked from his perch to plunge down with the man he is tied to.

Essentially, the comedy is compressed into one sustained frame. There is no cut to the man above to show him being jerked from the clifftop. Buster's face observing a body hurtling by is quite enough. There is a brief cut to the fallen man temporarily caught in a tree and thrashing loose, which means that the rope will go taut again. But the sequence is almost completely silent about critical matters happening off-frame, preferring to focus on Keaton's repose at the dead center of things, a man studying a rope that is behaving oddly. Keaton's quiet, together with the refusal to *explain* everything, becomes a marvel of implication.

The silences are sometimes quite literal, tongue-tied on the double. Buster, about to leave town in *Steamboat Bill Jr.*, sees the girl with whom he has been tiffing coming toward him on the road. He at once puts his bag down, hangs his head sheepishly, and begins to stammer out some sort of explanation for his recent conduct. Instead of pausing to hear what he might have to say, the girl circles behind him in continuing hauteur and vanishes into a public building. When Buster looks up to face her, there is no one anywhere on the street. After a moment's bafflement, Buster accepts her disappearance forlornly—a mirage, perhaps?—and, picking up his bag, wanders on down the road. The girl, meantime, has had second thoughts, or something like one-and-three-quarter thoughts. She reappears from the building, biting her lip, and begins to follow Buster tentatively, unsure of what she means to do. When he pauses, she pauses. When he moves on again, so does she. She is not getting much closer. Then Buster stops altogether. He has seen his father being thrown into jail: he will have to remain in town and save him. His dead stop has not, this time, stopped the girl; she is within a few feet of him now. Squaring his shoulders with this new task before him, Buster hikes his valise and turns to go home. In the same instant, the girl has turned. There she is, walking away from him. Where in the hell did she come from? There is no answer; she has gone into the building again. Nor has his question been put into words. The whole little dance of indecision, with its exquisite counterpoint, has been made up of visual thrusts and parries alone. The joke is in the rhythm of what we see; our ears, if we had any, would get us nowhere. Keaton's comedies are unheard chords, harmonies struck in space and time and requiring no other form of amplification.

Keaton could chord his cosmos when he was alone on the screen—and he

Buster, in search of a bride, arrives alone in church, later awakening from a short nap to find himself less than alone and rather oversupplied with brides. *Seven Chances.*

was often alone. In *Seven Chances* he enters a church to be married. There is no one else there. In a shot from the altar-rail toward the arch of the open door, we see his slender, methodical, top-hatted figure rise from the exterior steps, then—without change of pace—march with sure resolution down the center aisle, the glistening curves of the pews seeming to lap gently beside him like sea-spray. At the front of the church he pauses and then, without hesitation, selects a place for himself, very slightly in from the aisle. I do not know why this one place is exactly the right place for Keaton to sit in all of that vacant church. I only know that as he sits the lines and masses of the church go as still as he, grow quiet, freeze. He has placed his weight just where it will counterbalance the contending tensions about him, seated himself in the one spot that will halt the earth's busyness.

Keaton would often open up spaces and leave them there until he entered. Entering, he would change them not at all. He does not disturb their proportions; he fulfills them. In *Battling Butler* there is a very long camera "hold" on the door of a prize-ring dressing room. We simply stare at the emptiness for a time. Then, scarcely moving at all, Keaton melts through it. He is no fighter; he is a fop being forced to fight. He enters in the clothes that belong to him: top hat, tails, walking stick. A dejected snail, he stops. He carries a horseshoe in his limp free hand. What had been the emptiness of the room is now the emptiness of the room plus Keaton. Zero.

Keaton was called Zero—or something like it—when his short films were first released in France. Outside America, in the early days, comedians were often given local names, tags that familiarly described them: even now it is possible to buy Laurel and Hardy dolls in Italy that are not called Laurel and Hardy but Crich e Croch. Keaton's French alias was Malec. Ask a Frenchman who remembers what the name might have signified, idiomatically and with affection, and he will grope for a bit with a smile on his face and finally come up with something like "the hole in the doughnut."

The cipher was not simply a matter of Keaton's composed countenance, though of course there is an emotional Zero to contend with there. It has also to do with the cancellation of masses and stresses, horizontals and verticals, by the equalizing solemnity of his presence: when the façade falls during the hurricane, three inches equal two tons. More than that, Zero works its way into the stories he tells and the gags he makes use of. In *Sherlock Jr.* he is a small-town film projectionist who is studying to be a detective. Unfortunately, on his very first try at detective work he ends up branded the culprit: he is banished from his girl's house forever. While he is falling asleep in his projection booth and dreaming of the great sleuth he hopes to become, the girl—in about two minutes of quick thinking—tracks down the real criminal. The film is no more than a third over, but a simple reversal of role has canceled the film's entire narrative base. All the time he is dreaming of solutions, everything has been solved.

Our Hospitality is the story of a Southern blood-feud, and Buster finds himself trapped in the home of the family that means to exterminate him. In anybody else's narrative the problem would be to get out of there as quickly as possible. In Keaton's the problem is to stay *in* the house. He is only safe so long as he remains under his sworn enemy's roof. Southern gentlemanliness forbids killing a man while he is your guest. Stalemate—for just as long as Buster does *not* move. At the closest conceivable quarters, bloodlust is at its most quiet.

Individual gags arrive at nothingness again and again and again. He is undersea repairing a leak in a ship's hull, a phantom in a diving-suit performing a slow-motion dance. His hands become dirty. He picks up a pail from the ocean floor, drags it through the encompassing water to fill it, washes his hands in *its* water, then—ever so thoughtfully—empties the pail again. One disposes of what is dirty. And water equals water, with nothing left over.

He is on the run, desperate to reach his girl's house by seven o'clock. Time is of the essence, and what time is it now? At last he passes a clock shop. Salvation. He scans the window eagerly. Dozens and dozens of animated clock faces. Each tells a different time. Universal negation seems to leer at him.

He is waiting on tables at college and has got his thumb in the soup. He is told to bring something he *can't* get his thumb into. He brings coffee. The cup is upside down on the saucer, its rim unavailable. The cup is perfectly centered, the saucer perfectly dry. Deftly, he removes the cup. The saucer at once fills with coffee. Who suspended gravity while Keaton was turning the full cup upside down?

Each of these zeroes breeds its own odd silence, takes on something of the quiet and weightlessness of outer space. Keaton is working *in* space, of course: there are the hulls and clocks and coffee cups to prove it. But he is capable, when he wishes, of turning visible space itself into a momentary void. Faceless, he moves through the nameless. In fact, it wouldn't be stretching things a bit to call Keaton not so much silent comedy's first surrealist as silent comedy's first existentialist. Existentialism posits that existence precedes essence, which means that no man is born into the world with an essential nature already given him, with an identity on tap and an instinctive set of rules to guide him. He is born more

Opposite: In *Sherlock Jr.* a reluctant Kathryn McGuire returns Buster's ring.

Above: A quiet tryst at the pianoforte in *Our Hospitality*.

Overleaf: Buster enjoys a tranquil dinner with the family that means to kill him the moment he leaves, in the same film.

nearly a blank—Keaton's face will do as an image—and with no established relationship to any other thing on this planet. But he may be able to make an identity for himself out of those relationships he *does* establish as he puts a first foot down in an unfamiliar universe that is, for him, a void.

The foot goes out and touches something. What is it? It may glide out from under; it may hold. Either way, why? The foot may touch, mysteriously, another foot. Whose? No one else has a sure identity yet, either. Is the spot to be contested or surrendered? Find out. Try the other foot. The whole body may slip dizzily into the abyss, or it may, seraphically, be borne aloft by unexpected headwinds, hidden hands. It is not so much a matter of danger or safety—the void is unpredictably dangerous and unpredictably safe—as it is of gaining necessary knowledge. And see what haunting parabolas the discoveries make!

In *Our Hospitality* Buster is straddling the engine and the coal car of a runaway train. As the train speeds along a river bank, engine and coal car become uncoupled and begin to separate. Buster has one foot on each, and the gap between them is widening. Just before he can be dropped beneath the wheels or perhaps rent in two, the coal car derails and goes tumbling down the bank into the rapids, Buster with it. As the coal car hits the water, it instantly becomes a canoe; without reflection, without transition, Buster calmly paddles it with a coal shovel. He has made his adaptation to the existentially unforeseeable without comment, in perfect silence.

Keaton was not only still when he was doing nothing, he was still *in motion*. Existential man must move in a universe that moves perpetually; unidentified man making his way through the unknowable void is, Jean-Paul Sartre says, *condemned* to action. Buster, the condemned man, maintains his reserve no matter what is happening. A moment or two later in the same film he has been tumbled out of his improvised canoe and is being carried helplessly along through the rock-strewn rapids to a waterfall. En route, he passes his girl standing on the river bank. With nothing but his head above water and that moving swiftly with the current, he simply looks at her. No cry for help, no struggle to reach her, just mute acceptance of the fact that people in motion tend to pass people standing still. He could be driftwood. Or, perhaps, something a little more knowing than that. I keep forgetting that there is a dog in the picture, and I keep cursing myself for forgetting. The dog, Buster's pet, is firmly established and repeatedly reintroduced. Why does he vanish for me? I think because Keaton effectively usurps his identity: they are too much of a kind to be differentiated. The look in Buster's eyes as he is swept so noncommittally past the girl he dearly loves is the alert yet unprotesting, wounded yet comprehending look of a puzzled spaniel—a spaniel being taken he knows not where, acknowledging necessity without speech. I think there is no more penetrating shot in the film—it goes straight to Keaton's docility—and few funnier.

Keaton's passivity while he was in fact active, his reluctance to insist upon a clamoring identity as he submitted to the rush of the void, his willingness to concede the void an intelligence with which he did not care to quarrel cannot have come from formal philosophizing, certainly not from having read Kierkegaard or solemnly anticipated Sartre. Where, then, did so tight a fit originate, unless we are to say—as we very well may—that Keaton's simple intuitions about the nature of man in the universe were as breathtakingly perceptive as they were, in fact, simple? It is just possible that they came from film itself, from the frame held up to light in the hand.

Opposite: After rescuing the heroine, Kathryn McGuire, in *Sherlock Jr.*, Buster's getaway car takes a wrong route. No matter. Buster will have the craft seaworthy in a minute.

Film *is* stillness in motion. There is no such thing as a moving picture. All pictures are still pictures. The illusion of movement in film comes from passing a

succession of perfectly frozen images before a lens so rapidly, with a convenient eyeblink between them, that we are deceived into thinking that stillness is action. Take the film out of the projector and look at any one frame—as you now must, if you wish to see it at all—and you will see what Keaton may have seen all his life: rigidity at the heart of things, rigidity as the very condition of apparent activity. Keaton may have taken his esthetic—even his attitude toward life—from the knowledge he derived every time he fingered a strip of celluloid. What was printed on the celluloid was immobile, silent as the tomb, an extract and an abstract from the void. It was also, at the same time, part of a continuum, and when the continuum was seen whole—miracle of miracles that this should be possible—what had been indisputably dead leapt to unreal, yet mysteriously persuasive, life. Now Zero moves, has being, joins the tangible—without ceasing to be Zero. Whether he arrived at his identity consciously or not, Keaton became what film is.

Keaton examining the world he lives in.
Sherlock Jr.

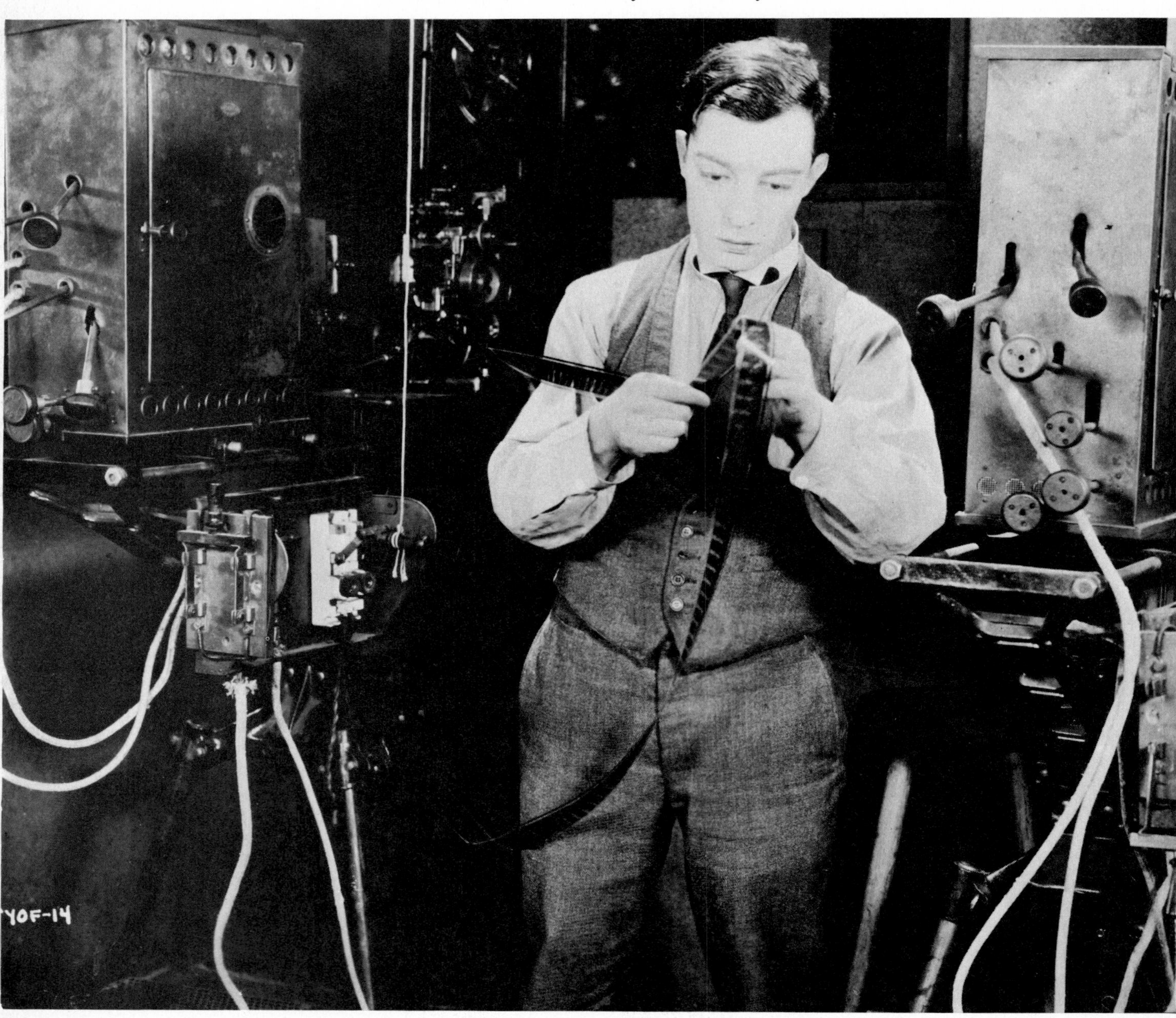

24. Keaton as Film

Keaton made twelve feature films in six years. In all of them he kept right on having nightmares. He saw things that were there.

He saw boulders breaking loose from a mountainside in apparently personal malice, roaring down on him in all sizes, by tumbling twos and threes, fives and tens. He saw hundreds of cattle roaming the city streets, invading Turkish baths and crowded department stores, creating monstrous traffic jams that were half-animal, half-automobile. And in transplanting his visions onto film, he saw film, compounding the unreality.

Some of his more extravagant hallucinations helped him as a filmmaker, some unexpectedly double-crossed him. He hadn't really wanted to make *Seven Chances*, based on a stage play, but someone on his staff had bought it and he felt obliged to go ahead. He did his best to escape its four-wall limitations and finish it off with a rousing chase. The chase was almost rousing enough—not yet a world-beater—when he previewed the film. Then he noticed something. As he cleared a hilltop flying from his pursuers, a few pebbles were dislodged and trickled downhill after him. The audience laughed. Inspired on the spot, Keaton took the film back to the studio and invented the boulders, giving himself not only a hilarious finish for the film but one of his most representative toe-dances with the animated inanimate.

With the herd of cattle in *Go West* he was less lucky. The basic image is insanely inviting, and the sight of Buster leading the herd from a railway platform into the city streets like a placid Pied Piper who has got his instructions wrong is enchanting. But at this point another kind of nightmare took over. The film, at its climax, had to move, and move fast. Cattle just don't move that fast, especially when faced with the very obstructions meant to make their presence in midtown grotesque. In the end Buster is patently perspiring trying to create the impression that there is a stampede going on; we are all too aware that it is only he who is doing the running. For all its incidental charms, the film arrives at a climax that is

a mere patch of gags devised to conceal the fact that no true chase is in progress, and Keaton was happy to wash his hands of livestock once shooting was done.

Even his passion for film, and his close personal identification with it, eventually posed a problem for him. It was clear that he still had a great deal to say on the subject, a great deal to show us about the arbitrary nature of the form we were so happy with, and it looked—for a moment—as if he were about to say and show it all in his first starring feature, the delightful *The Three Ages* of 1923.

The Three Ages seems to set itself up as a parody of another man's film, D.W. Griffith's *Intolerance*. Griffith, fully as carried away with the flexibility of film as Keaton was, had taken four distinct narrative lines and intercut them, so that Babylonian chariots jostled model-T Fords and Huguenot France rubbed shoulders with Christ's Jerusalem. Back and forth in time the film leapt, at first with gentle transition, at last with brutal abruptness.

There was fun to be found here, surely. Keaton picked up the gauntlet by presenting himself, in rhythmic alternation, as a caveman pacing a dinosaur's back and propelling himself by catapult toward the girl he must save; as the least noble Roman of them all, thrown to lions approximately as indifferent as he; and as a completely contemporary swain who, when ignored in a restaurant by the girl at the next table, watches her apply powder, lipstick, rouge, and mascara in public and then—fair is fair—appropriates her mirror to shave himself.

But Keaton, though he might enjoy the flight through time and space that film permitted, was not by nature a parodist. He had tried his hand at the vein at least once before, in the two-reel *The Frozen North*, mocking the western star William S. Hart by rolling a cigarette as Hart did—or, rather, as he didn't—and whipping pistol out of holster to shoot down the wrong woman. Yet even in that short film he hadn't been able to keep his mind on the mark: there was probably too little malice in him for that. In *The Frozen North* Keaton is clearly happiest when he forgets all about parody and simply continues his close inspection of the unreliable properties of nature. He tilts his chair, for relaxation, against the wall of an igloo—and promptly disappears through the wall. Snow is exceedingly insubstantial stuff.

In *The Three Ages* parody once again goes swiftly by the boards. The format becomes no more than an excuse—a very happy one—to improvise as impertinently as he had in his two-reelers. The film *is* three two-reelers, antically interlocked, and was even made with a secret proviso in mind. Suppose audiences didn't want Keaton at feature length, and the film showed signs of failing? Outside a frame of film, Keaton was often a hesitant man. If failure threatened, he could always re-edit *The Three Ages* into separate short comedies and release them one by one. Griffith, after all, had done just that when *Intolerance* proved unprofitable at the box office, reissuing two of the four stories as isolated features.

Keaton's fears were groundless and the improvisation held, even when multiplied by three. Indeed, with no single sustained narrative to pay obeisance to, Keaton's invention goes calmly berserk. On the day of the great chariot race in ancient Rome, it just happens to be snowing. The gates of the arena are thrown open, majestically, to admit a Buster in toga who has already made his characteristic pact with a shifty universe. His chariot is on ski runners and is drawn not by horses but by huskies. When, during the race, one of the huskies is disabled, Buster is unruffled. He frees the dog from the traces and replaces him with a spare huskie from the trunk at the rear of his vehicle.

In the lion's den, he remembers vaguely that there is always something a man can do to make a ravening beast his friend. He thinks about it. It has something to do with paws, doesn't it? He seats himself beside the beast and manicures its nails.

The cattle Keaton couldn't move fast enough in *Go West*.

In the lion's den of *Three Ages*, Buster contemplative, lion uncommunicative. From the same film, Buster ready for the great chariot race and Buster dramatically at odds with rival driver Wallace Beery.

Delectable as all this is, though, it makes little comment on film as such, and Keaton was obsessively driven toward further probing of the form's innards. Thus, a year later, he turned his attention to *Sherlock Jr.*, the film in which he broke his neck and also all the ground rules he had ever laid down, issuing his most exhaustive—and his last—invitation to audiences to join him in analyzing the peculiar representation/misrepresentation of life the silent screen had embroiled them in.

Sherlock Jr. is, plainly and simply, a film about film. It pretends to be about a boy who wants to be a detective while actually earning his living as a film projectionist, but it eludes its human outline early and turns into an almost abstract—though uninterruptedly funny—statement of shocking first principles. In it, Keaton takes us where he has never taken us before: inside the film.

Always he had held up his hand against the lens, shut us out, showed us where "Halt!" was. And, in fact, he begins *Sherlock Jr.* by dramatizing this same rejection once again—in a sequence that is simultaneously brilliant film comedy and brilliant film criticism.

Buster has been driven from his girl's house back to his lonely perch in a movie theater's projection booth. He threads a reel into the machine, then falls asleep. As he sleeps, a second Buster emerges from the cocoon, one body giving silent birth to another. The ghostly Buster chances to look through the operator's peephole toward the screen. Various actors are playing a melodrama, something to do with stolen pearls. One by one the actors turn their backs to the camera briefly, and—in entirely transparent double exposure—turn once more to us with their identities changed. The girl of the film is now the real girl he has lost; the villain of the film is now the local chap he has lost her to; the father of the film is now the father who has just forbidden him the house. But look. The new screen villain is maltreating his girl.

Something must be done. The ghostly Buster moves toward the doorway of the booth, thoughtlessly plucking a ghostly porkpie hat from the wall, leaving the real hat still hanging there. He will go down into the theater.

There is a curious technical mystery here. The double exposures or dissolves that lift Buster's second body from his first, Buster's second hat from his first, are utter perfection. The double exposures on the screen below are all too obviously

Left to right: Having been ejected from the screen in *Sherlock Jr.*, projectionist Buster considers another try. Whereupon he finally makes it, arriving inside the film in full dress. Once inside the film, Buster can defy dimension and penetrate anything. He is about to step through the mirror he has dressed by, and then pop through an assistant's midriff, reversing the business as it is actually seen in *Sherlock Jr.*

fakes. Why? It is clear that Keaton could have made the dissolves on the screen as precisely dovetailed, as undetectable to the eye, as he has the dissolves in the booth. What does he mean by the contrast? Is he carefully pointing a finger at one illusionistic trick, exposing it, at the same time he lulls us into accepting another as though it were no trick at all? Our relationship with the screen is apparently a double one. With one part of our minds we know that the camera is playing a trick on us; with another we take delight in refusing to see through the trick. It is as though we were recording fact with the left eye, fancy with the right, but were still forced to use both eyes to see anything at all. As I say, curious.

Down Buster goes—into the center aisle, then gradually to a seat up front. Now the villain is *really* maltreating his girl. Unable to restrain himself, or preserve his identity, Buster clambers over the piano and leaps into the screen, interrupting the sequence and spinning the villain toward him. The villain collars him and throws him out of the screen, into the pit. Without thinking, Buster has invaded the screen, the one thing he has told us no man can do. He has, however, been firmly ejected—this time.

As the threat to the girl continues, Buster tries strategy, slowly creeping up the few stairs at the side of the frame as though he might sneak into it laterally. He leaps once more. As he leaps, the film betrays him. It cuts. Instead of landing in the room in which his girl is being molested, he lands quite outside the house. The father emerges from the front door, seems to have forgotten something, does not seem to be aware of Buster, goes back into the house.

At least Buster has not been thrown out. A step has been taken. Buster will try the door himself. When there is no response to his knock, he means to lean against the doorframe and wait. But the film cuts again and there is no frame to support him. He finds himself tumbling over a bench in a park. Needing to think things through, he decides to sit on the bench. He sits, however, in the middle of a city street's busy traffic: another cut. Taking a step to the right to escape being run down by a car, he finds he has taken a step to the edge of a rocky precipice. Peering over, he finds himself in a forest staring directly into the jaws of a lion. Retreating from the beast, he walks into the path of an express train on a desert. Sitting on a sand mound, he is instantly sitting on a reef in mid-ocean. He dives, but not into water; a cut makes it a snow bank, and he is stuck in it head first. Extricating himself and reaching toward a tree trunk for support, he is back in the garden, falling over that bench again. A real man's first experience *in* a film has ended.

It has been disastrous. Real men are no more equipped to inhabit the dynamics of film than they are to survive outer space under *its* laws. To survive outer

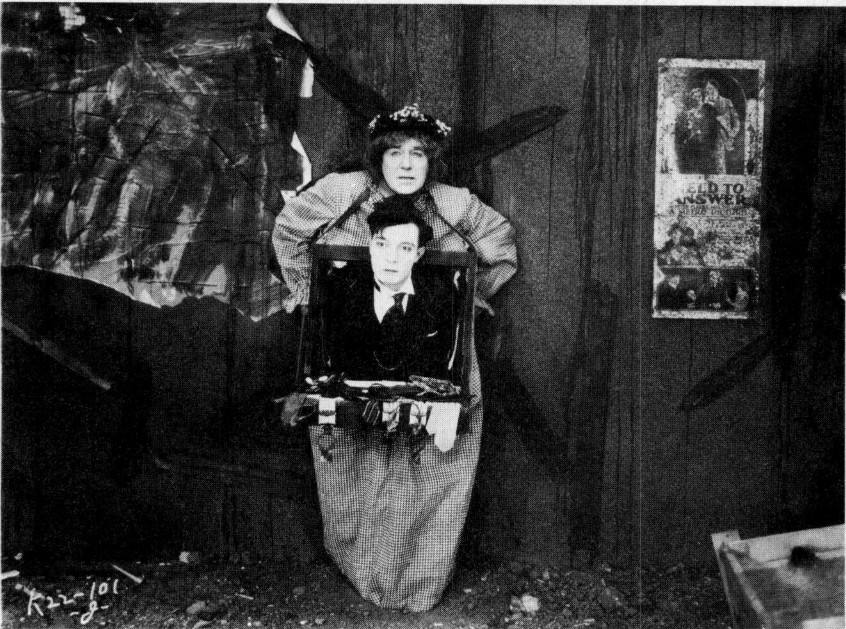

space a man must take his environment with him. But he cannot do that in film because film's properties and man's properties are of contrary orders altogether. Man's presence in the universe, so long as he is still in the universe, is a sustained one, continuous in time and space; film is discontinuous. Man's presence on earth, so long as he is on the earth, is organic, all of a piece; film is all pieces, broken, fragmented. Man's knowledge of himself is in great part a logical knowledge, moving in linear fashion from cause to effect, from one to two, from A to B; film is arbitrary on all counts.

Had we not known all that before? Known it and not known it. Certainly we had not *seen* it. Keaton showed us the impossible to show us that it was impossible. Distinguishing absolutely between life on the screen and life in nature—and, for that matter, between screen life and *stage* life—Keaton defined the new form as no analyst before him had done, marking out its liberties and its limitations precisely. But not as theory. He made the contradiction visible. Before Buster penetrates the screen in *Sherlock Jr.* he must step onto the stage in front of it. So long as he is on the stage, he remains himself, a whole man in command of his behavior, his environment. It is only when he enters the screen that he skids into indeterminate time and space. The stage, then, is a medium which explores life on life's terms. Film explores life on *film's* terms, which is quite a different, indeed a devastatingly different, matter. It may do some of the things other forms do. But it does them uniquely, requires unique forms of perception, has untranslatable habits.

How did Keaton film the impossible? The success with which he cut from background to background while sustaining the perfectly continuous presence of his own person was so great that it baffled not only audiences but his colleagues as well. When *Sherlock Jr.* was first being shown in Los Angeles, cameramen and directors tended to boast of the number of times they'd been to see the film—and not discovered its secret. Keaton had remained Keaton throughout the lightning-flash changes, with no telltale shifts of bodily outline or hints of not-quite-right dissolves. But there was no ready-made way of doing that.

Long afterward, Keaton explained how he'd done it. Obviously, he'd measured the distance between the camera and himself in the first shot and maintained it meticulously thereafter. But posture is something else: no man can reproduce the folds and tensions of his body, inch by inch, once he has moved it to another location. What Keaton did was to complete his first shot and develop it in the laboratory; he then clipped the last frame of film from the developed positive and placed it inside the camera's viewfinder; the cameraman, watching through the viewfinder, could now coax Keaton into placing himself so that he coincided in

Overleaf: You may not find the first two shots in *Seven Chances*, the third in *Our Hospitality*, or the fourth in *Go West*, the films to which they are credited. Yet, even as "posed" shots, they are spiritually right, Keaton in iconographic summary. And he did use the sun-dial gag, with Roman numerals, in several films.

every way with what the cameraman was looking at; the frame was then removed and the next excerpt shot. With the pieces spliced together, Keaton is blithely uninterrupted.

But if *Sherlock Jr.* has thus far given audiences and professionals a stunning lesson in what film is, it has by no means completed its work. In more elaborated form, and with contradiction actually photographed, it has only repeated Keaton's original "No!" There is no footing for a real man inside the screen. At this point the film changes its attitude. As if yielding to an audience's demand *still* to be let in, and having outlined the dangers most fairly, it opens itself wide to admit us all. The screen seems to move forward gradually to encompass us, the frame passing over our heads and well past our ears. We are going to share the comedian's world.

Once we are inside we make a sharp discovery: *we* now have even less stability than Buster had when he was playing interloper. While we were watching *him* being cut against, we still had a measuring rod, a link to our reality: his own sustained presence. Now we have lost that, lost our objective view of what film life is like, and are completely at the mercy of transformations we cannot grasp because we have been absorbed into them.

Keaton let go at this juncture even of some of his most cherished principles. Strictness was no longer relevant if there was no detached observer to demand or appreciate it. What is there to be strict about if we are one and all lost in an eternal dissolve, an eternal transformation, equally at the mercy of an unknown hand wielding a scissors or adjusting the lens that has captured us? The film quickly becomes a series of transformations that grow stranger and stranger, more and more arbitrary.

Keaton, now that we have gone through the screen to share his world, can himself go through nearly anything. All barriers are down. The business of "going through" becomes the visual keynote of the balance of the film. Buster stands before his mirror, adjusts his top hat and tie, then steps jauntily through the mirror. He approaches a huge wall safe, dials the combination that will unlock it, swings its door open, and walks directly through it onto a city street.

Pursuing the jewel thieves to an isolated cabin, he removes a circus hoop from his car and places it carefully against a cabin window. He then enters the cabin, taunts the thieves, snatches the jewels, and dives for the window. We cut to the outside of the cabin; the wall dissolves to let *us* see through it. Buster is running toward the window, plunging through. The plunge takes him through the circus hoop as well, from which he emerges transformed into a little old lady. He patters his way along the road as the thieves burst from the cabin in pursuit; penetrating his disguise, they give chase.

The chase eventually finds him boxed into an alleyway from which there is no exit: two side walls of solid brick, a tall fence at the rear, enemies approaching from both sides at the front. Standing against the fence, however, is his assistant, also now dressed as an old lady. As the thieves round the corners, Buster turns toward the fence, sprints, and dives directly through the old lady's stomach, disappearing entirely.

Some of the film's penetrations, its plunges through a dissolving material world, are legitimate by Keaton's normal standards. Riding the motorcycle's handlebars down a curving road, he sees a monstrous machine, a solid rectangle on wheels, approaching him around the bend. He keeps on going, sure to collide. The machine turns the bend and proves not solid at all: it is a platform on giant legs, with nothing but open space between. Buster sails through with aplomb, his constant trust justified.

But the headlong dive through a man-woman's stomach is something else

Opposite: Keaton the unfathomable.
Go West.

again, by strict standards a Sennettish cheat. Why has the perfectionist permitted himself that here? Because, I suppose, we must still be taught that our logic is not film's logic, and that if we are going to invade the screen we must leave *that* logic behind. In prying, we have lost ourselves, lost our touchstones. See what happens. Reference points vanish here, we cannot insist upon the rectitude we demanded when we were safely, so judiciously, in our seats. We aren't in life any longer. We inhabit the deception and so become illusions ourselves. Illusions are in no position to make demands on reality.

The film, which makes room for a great many other things, including a masterly game of impossible pool, has not quite finished attending to film. After Buster has eluded the thieves by transforming the chassis of an automobile into a slightly less than seaworthy sailboat, we are released at last from the film's interior, taken back to the projection booth. Buster is awake now, the girl has just hurried in to tell him that she has long since solved the mystery and all is well.

He is terribly relieved, she terribly compliant. He doesn't quite know what to do with her compliance, however. He glances through the aperture toward the screen. On screen, the restored hero is taking the girl's hands in his. Buster makes note of the fact and manages to do the same thing. His girl expects more, plainly. He checks the screen again, sees that the hero is kissing the girl's hands, jumps a bit, then follows the film's lead. He checks again. The hero is giving the girl a ring. Buster does the same; his girl is deeply pleased. Another sly glance through the aperture. The screen lovers are kissing. Good enough. He will do that as well, and he does. One last look for guidance. On screen there is a dissolve to the now married couple, a multiplicity of babies on both laps. Buster scratches his head, staring, as both films end.

It is all very well to take instruction from the screen—as audiences were then doing in so many ways—but can you trust it to tell the truth, even when you are outside it? Is *this* the inevitable next step, and is it altogether desirable? Buster's scratch and stare are somewhat ambiguous, unfinished. He is no innocent: it is impossible to think him baffled as to how this last dissolve has come about. But, unfaithful to life as film is, does it *always* lie? Real life may not be an entirely safe proposition, either.

No doubt Keaton had now investigated the boundaries of his medium, including a foray into forbidden territory, to his own satisfaction and would have turned away from the formal preoccupations of *Sherlock Jr.* in any case. But there were more practical reasons for doing so. Though *Sherlock Jr.* was a successful film—Keaton's features normally cost just over two hundred thousand dollars to make and normally grossed more than a million—it was noticeably less profitable than his first two features had been. Though it might have earned him the undying admiration of professionals, it had—for all the brilliance of its gags and the authenticity of its stunting—seemed a shade too "special" for the folks out front. Structurally, the film *is* loose, as it was more or less bound to be once all law had been suspended. But Keaton would have to look elsewhere for a vital center of interest, slipping in his private trysts with the camera where and when he could.

He did continue to slip these in. In *Seven Chances*, which is not about film at all, he presents us with two dissolves that are quite as mysterious, and quite as dazzling, as anything in *Sherlock Jr.* He is going from the country club to his girl's home; his car is parked at the curb. He strolls down the country club lawn, climbs into his car, grasps the steering wheel, and both he and car remain entirely immobile while the background dissolves to the girl's house. Now that he is there, he climbs out of the car and strolls up the *girl's* lawn. He has never moved, only the background has dissolved, yet the background is not film: he can walk on it. The effect is repeated once the girl has turned him down and he must go back to the club. The sense of being able to step on what is patently intangible is overwhelming. The trick has to have been done, of course, exactly as it was done in *Sherlock Jr.* If it is even more breath-taking here, it is probably because Keaton was closer to the camera and could reposition himself more precisely still. And in *The Cameraman*, a late feature, he once more directly involves himself with film, carrying his tripod over his shoulder as he scurries from Tong war to regatta in pursuit of newsreel material. He also makes film triumphant over people in one of the most genuinely surprising comic climaxes any silent comedian ever devised. But there is no use of film here in any role other than that of factual recorder; it belongs to the plot, not to Keaton's playfulness.

What did the public demand of Keaton above and beyond his idiosyncratic interests? By the time he had completed his next feature, the superb *The Navigator*, he knew. As he explained in his autobiography, he had a curious experience with one elaborate gag in that film. For an underwater sequence, he constructed some fifteen hundred rubber fish which kept rotating past the camera, completely blocking other traffic on the ocean floor. If a larger fish wanted to get through the steady stream that the school created, it simply couldn't. Buster, in diving helmet and at work on the hull of his ship, took notice of the unsuitable jam-up. Always interested in maintaining an orderly universe, he left his work, pinned a starfish to his breast, and functioned as a traffic cop for the underwater population.

He shot the gag, at considerable expense, and included it not only in the completed film but in the short "trailer" intended for advertising purposes. He was stunned at what then happened. During a series of previews, whenever the "trailer" was run separately, the audience laughed uproariously. But whenever the complete feature was run, the gag was greeted with stony silence.

"I threw the gag out," Keaton reported. "There was nothing else to do." Why had it succeeded in isolation and failed as part of a narrative? At this point in *The Navigator*'s narrative, Buster is working so hard on the ocean floor because the ship on which he and his girl have been adrift is in danger of being invaded by cannibals. The girl, at the moment, is on deck maintaining Buster's air supply. The cannibals, in their outriggers, are approaching ship and girl rapidly. "The other gags," Keaton concluded, "were accepted by audiences who saw the whole picture because they did not interfere with my job of saving the girl. But when I directed the submarine traffic I was interrupting the rescue to do something else that couldn't help us out of the jam."

Gags, then, could no longer take precedence over "the girl." As we have seen, in his short films "the girl" had been for the most part a handy prop: someone to wait at home while he went to the big city to make good, someone to keep the children huddled about her while Buster tried to right a ship in a storm. At feature length, however, audiences would not tolerate such blithe dismissal while Buster monopolized the camera eye. "The girl" must be as present as he, and "the girl" stands for much more than the girl: she stands for narrative underpinnings complex enough to keep audience interest alive over a considerable span, for suspense that will tie gags together, for the emotional satisfaction an audience gets from watching a relationship work itself out.

Keaton's films, in short, would have to become more like those of other comedians. Occasionally, under this pressure, they did, too much so: *College* is weak Keaton because—for the most part—it could have been just as well done by Harold Lloyd.

Here was the situation. What was he going to do about it? Keaton preserved his uniqueness by the highly original attitude he took toward "the girl."

Buster gives thought to marrying a hat-check girl in *Seven Chances.* The girl remains unidentified, but she played several short scenes with Keaton more skillfully than his heroines were in the habit of doing.

Below: The highly unusual pool game in *Sherlock Jr.*

25. Keaton: The Girl and the Grave

Keaton was no misogynist. He did not dislike girls. On the contrary, he thought they were the prettiest little things imaginable. In *Battling Butler*, in a forest, he has just met his Mountain Girl, who is ferociously angry because both he and his valet have unintentionally fired buckshot at her. She flies at the two of them, gives them a tongue-lashing that seems to spit hailstones, then, for good measure, pelts them with rocks. Though he is very much at the center of the storm, Buster seeks no shelter; he is simply unfailingly attentive. When she has finally stalked away, having hurled another rock or two in farewell, Buster looks at his valet. "Isn't she pretty?" he says.

Keaton's captions are generally as terse as that, just a step shy of his infinitely preferred silence. But they mean what they say. Indeed Buster is so captivated by The Mountain Girl's prettiness that at their very next meeting he invites her to a formal dinner in the forest, served in chafing dish by his valet on a perfectly appointed cardtable. The legs of the cardtable sink slowly into the ground under the weight of Buster's elbows as he stares rapturously at his find.

He also understood—or at least agreed—that girls were necessary. One should even marry them. In *The Navigator*, after he has breakfasted in his silk bathrobe, he stares out the window of his mansion to see a "Just Married" couple going festively by in a car. He turns to his valet, deeply reflective, and speaks, briefly. "I think I'll get married," he says. There is a pause to allow for his expression not to change. "Today," he adds. He is next seen in top hat entering his limousine to be driven to his girl's house. His girl lives across the street. The car makes a perfect U-turn. In this instance, he is rejected. He accepts his dismissal as matter-of-factly as he has accepted the desirability of marriage.

He is always proposing, whether forced to or not. In *Seven Chances* he is forced to: he will lose seven million dollars if he isn't married by seven o'clock. Most often he proposes by choice, and *very* often his offer is snapped up before he can quite get it out. Never mind. Once accepted, he leaps to the kiss, ecstatically. We recognize the ecstasy by his promptness.

For all their swiftness in having him, Keaton does not see girls as fundamentally aggressive. He may have a spot of trouble with an old hag who is being throttled by her husband: stepping up to save her, he finds himself being roundly beaten by her. But she is a hag, and something seems to have gone wrong somewhere. Girls, including young wives, are not like that. After Buster has married the Mountain Girl in *Battling Butler*, his new wife is suddenly introduced to another woman who also seems to be Buster's wife. Quite naturally, a quarrel ensues. But it is a restrained quarrel, no rocks. Where another director might well have leapt at the opportunity of pitching the two women into each other's hair—there would be pleasant irony in it, because Buster is supposed to be the fighter—Keaton, directing the film, refuses the battle. *He* will do the fighting, thank you.

He is thus respectful, honorable, and adoring. There is just one terrible hitch. The pact that Keaton has long since made with the not entirely sane universe—his plea of *nolo contendere*, his willingness to go along and let it ride—is a pact that no girl, no woman, can ever comprehend or agree to. Women take up arms against a sea of troubles, and so double them. Women are activists, highly rational creatures who would not think for a moment of going fishing while trouble was afoot, certainly not of standing still until a falling building fell. Instead, they *do* things, and the doing, alas, completely upsets the ever-so-tentative, ever-so-delicate harmony Keaton's watchful waiting has achieved.

The comedian had this all worked out by the time he'd finished *The Navigator* and found himself bound to the girl as permanent companion. What he had done, in his mind's eye, was to reverse exactly the traditional concept of the two sexes: *he* was the passive plaything of nature, the intuitive creature who acted—when he acted—on instinct; she was the eternal busybody with ideas bubbling in her head. No other comedian ever saw the girl in just that light. Perhaps they were unobservant; maybe they lied. Keaton himself hadn't quite defined the issue earlier. In his first feature he was still doing the free-hand exercises that had made his short comedies such fun, in his third feature he had been totally preoccupied with film, and in the one that came between, *Our Hospitality*, the heroine had been played by Natalie Talmadge, his wife in real life. A man probably wouldn't make the point when his wife was the woman in question.

But with *The Navigator* all is clear—very quietly clear. Keaton never stresses, never points a finger at, the troublesome vision he has arrived at. The most gallant of all his silences is his silence about the girl. He tells us nothing directly. He simply puts himself to work, and lets *her* go to work, and permits us to observe for ourselves—if only we will—the catastrophe that comes of admitting an alien element to an equation.

Whatever goes wrong in *The Navigator* goes wrong because the girl is thinking. Her thinking does not have to be unintelligent; it need only be inopportune. In a world composed of matter—a world that Keaton has mastered by surrendering to its laws until they are ready to turn in his favor—a kind of anti-matter has been unleashed. Buster and the girl, here played by Kathryn McGuire, have been cast adrift at sea on an otherwise uninhabited ocean liner. After a day or so another ship appears on the horizon. Rescue! They must run up a flag for help. Buster is busy getting one into place. She does not like that one. Try the "bright one." Much prettier. Buster obliges, and the rescue ship instantly reverses course and steams away. They have run up the quarantine flag. It *was* prettier, though.

They must somehow chase the rescue ship. The girl insists. We next see Buster in a tiny rowboat trying to pull the great liner after him in hot pursuit of their vanishing visitor. It is one of the most sublimely impractical shots in all of

Buster valiantly faces the breakfast The Girl has prepared for them as they drift on the open seas of *The Navigator*.

Below, The Girl makes her own choice of a rescue flag.

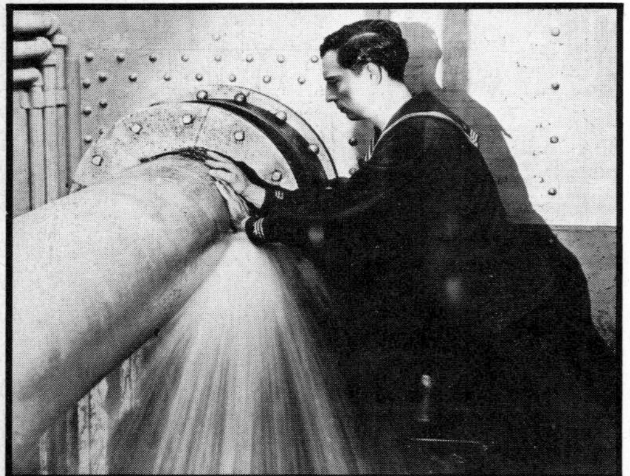

Above: Left to his own devices, Buster takes a forgetful bath, discovers the dangers and advantages of a toy cannon, attempts to stop an unstoppable leak, and prepares a fireworks assault on cannibals. *The Navigator*.

Opposite: Buster surrenders to The Girl's insistence that he become a deep-sea diver; Below: The Buster-god emerges from the sea, frightening off the cannibals who hold The Girl captive. The Girl uses the god as her seagoing doormat. *The Navigator*.

Keaton, this image of minnow tugging whale, and its balance of miniature and mass is exquisitely characteristic of the man. Yet he would never have done this on his own. Never.

Returning defeated to the liner, and losing his rowboat in the process, Buster is thrown a life-preserver by the girl on the deck high above. It hits him on the head. Throwing him a double line rigged to a pulley and holding it firm in her fists, she promptly descends into the water as Buster rides up to the deck. Locating her after some bafflement, he dives from the deck into the sea and succeeds in getting her to the foot of a ladder against the hull. They will now start up. The girl, making quick note of the height she must climb and an even quicker check of her relative safety in Buster's arms, instantly faints. The stricken look in Buster's eyes as he realizes that he must carry her the long way up conveys more than resignation. There is deathly knowledge in it, knowledge that things will always be this way, knowledge that women can faint guiltlessly, on cue. Intelligent creatures.

On deck he has great difficulty with a recalcitrant deck chair. Chaplin had once muffed this business. But Chaplin had not thought to do it as Keaton is doing it: with the unconscious girl already stretched out on the chair. It is more difficult, and God knows funnier, this way. Once the girl has been blanketed into the deck chair for a good night's rest, the ship begins to rock rhythmically. The deck chair rolls with it, a pendulum inching ever closer to the unrailed side of the ship. Buster notices just in time, dives to embrace the girl and hold her safe as the chair goes over. He gets his face slapped for such undue familiarity. Then, when the girl realizes fully what has happened, he gets his face clawed, as he would in half a dozen films, while the girl wraps her arms about him in mortal terror.

It rains, pours, while they are sleeping on deck, and they struggle into the ship's saloon, there to while away the hours playing cards. Buster tries to shuffle the cards. They are wet. The vain shuffle, one of the most inspired two minutes in the silent comedy pantheon, is hilarious because it is methodical: Buster continues to treat the limp, curling, matted cards as though they were in prime condition and needed only firmness in the managing. But we have skipped a detail. It is water lodged in the brim of the girl's sailor cap that has sloshed all over the cards as she sits in the banquette. Of course Buster *could* have got them wet. He didn't.

Sighting land only to discover that it is a cannibal isle and the cannibals are coming, Buster collapses onto a bench, wretchedly disturbed but ready for fate. The ship has struck a sand bar, sprung a leak. Nothing to be done about it. Buster has in fact noticed that there is a diving suit, complete with helmet, hung against the deck wall, but he is not a deep-sea diver and has given it no further thought. He then becomes alert, fearfully alert. He is aware that the girl *is* thinking of it, that she is studying a manual of instruction for work on the ocean floor, that nothing he can ever say or do will prevent her from screwing that helmet onto his head and sending him down to do the repair job. And that without even waving him farewell. His eyes inside the helmet yearn for a word, a gesture, as he climbs over the side; she is too taken up with the machinery that will supply his air.

Once the cannibals have invaded the ship, cut Buster's air hose, and spirited the girl away to the beach, Buster must do something about the fact that he cannot breathe. We see him making his somnambulistic way underwater, pausing only to give battle to an octopus. Then, from the beach, where the girl lies surrounded by her captors, we look toward the vast ocean. Out of it, slowly, arms extended, legs wide apart, emerges the inflated, helmeted Buster. There is no question of what we are looking at: Proteus rising from the sea, the god come. Keaton's own kind of intelligence, his intuitive sense of opportunity given, comes into play here: we know that he knows how he looks. From the first parting of

the waters he is plainly playing the god.

The cannibals flee, the girl picks up a paddle, and she and Buster immediately make for the water again. In a sustained shot—to let us see that what is happening *can* happen—the girl turns the inflated Buster over on his back, climbs astride him and paddles him as she would a raft back to the liner. The god is her seagoing doormat.

Even her kiss is fatal. Buster, with the cannibals attacking the ship again, has spirited her down a lifeline to an outrigger canoe. As he is following her down, she succeeds in falling into the water and losing the outrigger. They are alone in an ocean, cannibals coming from everywhere, and Buster's resignation takes over again. With their arms about one another, they will simply drown. Slowly they disappear beneath the water. And now the rewards of Buster's resignation proclaim themselves as well. Slowly the two heads reappear, rising from the water. They have "drowned" directly above a surfacing submarine and are at present standing on its hatch. Inside the submarine, at long last rescued, the girl kisses Buster. The experience so stuns him, is so little what he *ever* expected, that he collapses against the ship's control lever and sends them all tumbling against the ceiling as the submarine spins over and over in the water. Where the girl is concerned, one must even beware of success.

The Navigator is one of Keaton's two perfect films—the other, *The General*, requires discussion in another connection—and it has many other things on its mind: Buster on a listing deck at midnight, with all of the cabin doors swinging open and shut, ectoplasmically, behind him; Buster desperately trying to escape a small cannon, fuse already lit, that has become attached to his ankle; Buster leaping in panic into a lounge chair that instantly develops additional arms and legs, the arms and legs of the girl he has sat on. But if it establishes one thing more than another that will from this time forward set him apart from his fellow comedians, and from the "normal" world at large, it is his realization of what the girl could and would do to him.

She would deprive him of the only security he knew, the security of rolling with the universal punch. He couldn't have *his* universe and the girl both. They weren't on speaking terms. He chose the girl, knowing exactly what he was getting into. He chose her with love, with docility. How polite he is in *The Navigator* after she has served him coffee made of whole beans and salt water, and he has had to go to the ship's rail rather quickly! Returning, he pantomimes that he has had to make a telephone call. A girl's feelings must be spared.

The cost was high, and it would show now and then. Yes, a man would marry this creature, and be glad of it. But what if—think of it, *what if*—two hundred of them wanted to marry you at once? He let the question pop, it would seem, from his subconscious in *Seven Chances*. Although he is pursuing a perfectly nice, ordinary girl, two hundred brides in their veils are pursuing him, on roller skates, on bicycles, on horseback, on stolen trolley cars, greed in their hearts and bricks in their hands. They will have him or kill him, dropping him from cranes in front of locomotives, cutting him off at mountain passes, new Furies from an old underworld that live on in our nightmares. They can only be routed, finally, by a downrush of giant boulders that may themselves kill Buster while saving him. But he is more at home with boulders.

Would he have been more at home with calves? He raised the question in *Go West*. There *is* a girl in *Go West*, and he walks twice around a well to get a better look at her. But his real devotion is reserved for Brown Eyes, a stray in the herd that so attaches itself to him he cannot let it spend the night alone. It must not be bothered by bulls, either; Buster steals a pair of elk's antlers and ties them

to Brown Eyes's noble forehead as a means of forestalling improper amorous pursuits. At the end of the film Buster has saved the girl's father from bankruptcy by leading an entire herd of cattle through the business district of a large city in order to get it to the yards on time. As a reward, the father offers him anything he wants. "I want her," Buster replies, making a gesture behind him. It so happens that both Brown Eyes and the girl are standing somewhere behind him, and the father naturally assumes he is about to lose a daughter. Not so. Buster wants Brown Eyes, and gets her. The girl is a trifle humiliated, but Buster is clear about *that.* Even so, as all four drive away in the family car, Buster and Brown Eyes in the rear seat, father and daughter up front, Buster is at least leaning over the seat to chat with the girl. Perhaps a man can afford to chance a second love.

It's a risk, though, if you dare to look the matter right in the eye. Comedians had always used the girl as a subtext for their films: girls to drive them on. Keaton, accepting the necessity of the girl, used her in a way that slightly altered, and complicated, the subtext: he used her to drive him on and drive him crazy. *College* is a relatively routine film, and no particular use is made of the girl's capacity for unsettling cosmic harmonies. Then, at the very end of the film, a strange and savage thing happens. Keaton has gone for six reels playing it everybody else's way, the conventionally romantic way: a pleasant girl, and Buster will rescue her, marry her. In fact, he is in such a hurry to get married that he hustles her to the altar while he is still in his college track suit. The two emerge from the church, yearn-

Buster and Brown Eyes, his first love in *Go West.*

ingly searching each other's eyes. Fast dissolve. The couple with too many children. Fast dissolve. The couple aged, alone, and snarling bitterly at each other. Fast dissolve. Two gravestones side by side.

What is this abrupt slap in the face doing at the end of an otherwise unquestioning love story? It takes no more than eleven seconds of playing time to deliver its chill, and yet it undoes on the spot all of the yearning, the struggle and the victory, of the narrative.

The bitter candor—and it *is* bitter—is not prepared for; it not only takes us by surprise, it seems to take Keaton by surprise, as though a truth too long suppressed had turned to bile and erupted with volcanic force. It's still funny, because there is truth in it; but it is bleak indeed.

The bleak streak in Keaton had always been there, and it is not wholly the result of his experience with "the girl"—though it is she who most often makes it surface. It would be easy—much too easy, I think—to read into this bleakness Keaton's private marital difficulties, which were constant and real. He had married into a matriarchy, one peopled with powers either greater or more assertive than he. His wife's sisters, Norma and Constance Talmadge, were both important stars; mother Peg Talmadge governed the clan; Norma was married to Joe Schenck, the man who financed Keaton's films and guaranteed—until a fatal day—his independence. The atmosphere was both heady and claustrophobic, Keaton the mere clown of the tribe. His home was scarcely his own, he was banished from the master bedroom early, he was financially dependent on a brother-in-law. In the end, after that brother-in-law had taken away his independence and his career had disintegrated, his unstable marriage came shatteringly apart. He was himself slipping into alcoholism, and, since we have heard the story only from Keaton's point of view, there is no real possibility of assessing responsibility fairly. The upshot, however, was blood-curdling. Natalie Talmadge stripped him of his house, his fortune, and his children, going so far as to legally change the children's names so that there would be no trace of Keaton to linger after him. He had often played what he was now reduced to: Zero.

He was not a fatalist about his marriage and fought to preserve it: Natalie Talmadge's appearance in *Our Hospitality* came about because Keaton thought that an extended time on location in the mountains, with their infant son, might help solidify a relationship that had seemed unsteady from the beginning. Neither did he surrender to Zero when Zero engulfed him. He fought his way out of alcoholism at a terrible cost to his nervous system, remarried, and stubbornly accepted whatever odd jobs might be given him. I trailed him to Hoboken, New Jersey, in 1949, where he was appearing in a shabby stock company production of *Three Men on a Horse*. There he was, idly sauntering into an onstage bar to casually throw one leg over it, forgetfully throw the other over it a minute or two later, and of course take a thumping five-foot fall on his back. Struggling to get a drunken girl into bed by wrapping her in a blanket and lugging the blanket over his shoulder, he made the business more vigorously funny than it had been when he first used it in the film *Spite Marriage*. I went backstage to chat with him afterward and had rather a long wait. The man who came from the shower was in a state close to total physical exhaustion: his second wife pummeled him, toweled him, back into condition as a fighter's trainer might. The next day he would do a matinee as well as evening performance. He continued to work at anything and everything—in circuses, on television, as a bit player in films—until the end of his life. Fortunately, he lived long enough to find a retrospective showing of his films the surprise hit of the Venice Film Festival in 1965 and to receive a standing ovation. He might be willing to drown in his films; he wasn't like that offscreen.

Yet the melancholy, together with a hint of savage rebellion, was there, and it crops up surprisingly. Watching the climax of *Battling Butler* we can only wonder in astonishment whatever prompted him to do the film's final fight utterly straight. We have seen him be extraordinarily funny in a boxing ring earlier, during a session with sparring partners. Now, in the film's closing reel, he suddenly seems no comedian at all. In a training room above the arena he lets himself be battered brutally by his rival for an excruciating length of time, trying to cover himself, putting up the feeblest of defenses. Then, without warning, he can take no more. He turns on his assailant and proceeds to give him an even more merciless thrashing, pounding him bloody against the walls of the small room, picking him up off the floor to batter him senseless again.

We have been expecting comedy, and expecting it in some scale: perhaps there will be a wild and inappropriate give-and-take throughout the aisles and seats of the deserted arena, a fight fought everywhere but in the center ring. Not at all. Instead, at intolerably close quarters, we are given a slugging-match that is all venom and sting. It is the only time in his films that Keaton permitted comedy to give way to a greater urgency, whatever that urgency may have meant to him. What it is most reminiscent of, I would say, is Rudi Blesh's description of what had happened between Keaton and his father before the breakup of their vaudeville act. The father, Joe Keaton, had grown intensely bitter as he felt himself aging, resentful of his diminishing physical abilities. The vaudeville act was a roughhouse one, and Buster began to find himself being genuinely manhandled, the victim of "lickings onstage for things that had happened before." At one perform-

The boxing stance is comic, but the final fight is savage. *Battling Butler*. The moment with the girl near the end of *College* seems tender enough. Within eleven seconds it will have become thoroughly chilling.

ance Joe kicked Buster in the back of the neck and knocked him out for twenty-two hours. "Mad most of the time," Buster described him, "and could look at you as if he didn't know you. . . . When I smelled whiskey across the stage, I got braced." To stop it, Buster could only respond in kind. "Finally I'd get sore, and we'd start trading." At nineteen, he'd had to whip his own father to keep from being whipped.

Keaton held no grudges and, once he'd become a star, used his father—importantly, in *Sherlock Jr.*—in several of his films. Joe's high-kick knocks a man's hat off in *Our Hospitality*. Did Buster inherit a strain from Joe, or was he still battling Joe, as he exposed the underside of the mask in *Battling Butler*? And how much did the strain shape the character he played throughout his career? We marvel at his patience on film; but patience is often bought at the price of great pain.

Be that as it may, the patience, together with a sad certainty that it will come to no good in the end, is most often reflected in Buster's copings with The Girl. Keaton changed his leading ladies constantly, perhaps because Natalie Talmadge pretended or felt jealousy. But he would have had to change them in any case, for the simple reason that there can be no such thing as a "perfect" leading lady for Keaton. How can a girl be perfect when she is the wrong note in the melody? The last we see of Buster in *Steamboat Bill Jr.* is his gasping, splashing form as he rescues another man from the river. The girl is waiting on a nearby ship. Who is it that Buster has dived in to rescue? A minister, to marry them. As Buster brings the minister toward the ship, dutifully, energetically, his eyes are filled with a profound alarm.

And this shot was the last we were to see of Keaton's highly personal wariness of womankind. With the completion of *Steamboat Bill Jr.* in 1927, his mentor, Joe Schenck, informed him that he was through as an independent filmmaker. Henceforth he would be a Metro-Goldwyn-Mayer star, under studio supervision. The supervision would be friendly, he was assured, because it was under the partial control of Schenck's brother, Nick. All in the family again. Keaton was stunned but submitted. Though he had not always directed his films—he directed four on his own, co-directed four, and gave sole directing credit to others on the remaining two independent productions—he had been in over-all control, the man who made the decisions. Now he would be very much subject to the interference of men who were not so much interested in idiosyncrasy as in standardization.

It almost seemed like a good idea with *The Cameraman*, the first film made under the new arrangement, though Keaton was immediately robbed of certain of his oddities, his ambiguous estimate of "the girl" among them. *The Cameraman* is a fine comedy, carefully tooled, crowded with gags that are unmistakably Keaton's: Buster overexcitedly yanks the telephone from the wall on getting a call from his girl and promptly races miles through the city streets to arrive at her house before she has hung up; Buster climbs from the top deck of an overcrowded bus to sit on an outside fender so that he can chat casually with the girl at a lower window; Buster, photographing a Tong war, remains astride a high platform that has lost its supports and so glides ominously toward the ground as though he were doing nothing more than skiing in rather dangerous territory.

The girl, this time, is a Metro-Goldwyn-Mayer girl, the pretty Marceline Day. She is sweet, she is devoted to Buster, and she is directly helpful to Buster—as studio heroines were duty-bound to be. The change, this once, is acceptable. A loving interplay develops that is surprisingly believable: we sense that it will be from the moment that Buster, brushed against Miss Day in a crowd, finds his nose in her hair and rapturously keeps it there. Keaton *could* play the comedy's romantic scenes as though there were no bear trap lying in wait.

Opposite, above: Keaton's girls had a habit of strangling him while being rescued. *Steamboat Bill Jr.*

Below: Newsreel photographer Buster dutifully covers a Tong War in *The Cameraman*.

What is being chipped away, though, is more apparent in *Spite Marriage*, the second studio film and Keaton's last silent feature. If his character is being guided toward a sympathy he'd always refused to ask for—here a stuffed dog with a tear-drop eye becomes Buster's alter ego for a time—his confidence in what was peculiar about him is being even more relentlessly undermined. "Too many cooks," Keaton told Herbert Feinstein, "and they warp your judgment." Suddenly he is doing gags everyone had always done, would always do: knocking over the scenery during a stage performance, gluing on a false beard messily, burning trousers while he presses them. Worse, he has been given a girl who is wrong for another kind of reason.

Dorothy Sebastian is the girl, a sophisticate with flashing eyes and a hint of talons, and, since she marries Buster only to ditch him, she is called upon to behave badly indeed. Tearing up flowers in her rages, making appalling scenes in night clubs, getting so drunk that Buster must heave her over his shoulder in his vain efforts to deposit her on a bed, she is, from first to last, a handful. Buster, of course, was used to handfuls, but not handfuls of this kind. No matter what discomforts his own girls had caused him, no matter how suspiciously he might have regarded the whirrings inside their heads, no matter how dolefully he had looked into the future, his own girls had always been nice.

26. Two Epics

The silent screen produced just two comic epics: Chaplin's *The Gold Rush* in 1925 and Keaton's *The General* in 1926. What is surprising is not that there are so few but that there are any at all. For there had been no such form until these two men saw a way to it. A comedian's qualities are not at all what an epic wants. An epic wants an event of great scale and significance, one rooted in a historical moment, a moment so representative that it takes on mythological status. And it wants a hero at its center who certainly need not be perfect but whose high aspirations are matched by his capabilities. It is an elevated form, the epic as such, and it is a deeply serious one. But comedy's business had always been to reduce pretension, to mock deep seriousness, to ask what could be so lofty about a man whose shirttail was hanging out. Epic quality vanishes under the assault of the clown.

The stage, as a result, had never known the combination. For all the scale Aristophanes appropriates—there is nothing to keep him from either heaven or hell—and for all the soaring lyricism of his choruses, no one had ever chosen to call his fantasies "epics": they are too iconoclastic, too relentlessly reductive, for that. Nor did Shakespeare's vast range and serious verse—often most profound at its lightest—ever tempt anyone into describing *The Tempest*, say, as epic. Prospero's island is not Troy.

There *had* been an alternative open to the writer who wished to be funny at the expense of greatness and still keep something of greatness implied in his work. That was the "mock" epic, Don Quixote sallying forth to do majestic battle with windmills, Don Juan sallying forth to conquer exactly one half of the known world, the half that appealed to him. But when Byron writes, "My poem's epic," he is letting us know by the chatty contraction of his apostrophe 's' that it is nothing of the sort. Pope's *The Rape of the Lock* does its comic work brilliantly; but the earth-shattering event that sets "epic" shock waves into motion is actually the theft of a lock of hair. The very scale that makes an epic an epic is being jovially, maliciously inverted. The "mock" epic upends history, myth, and the serious-event-as-serious; the possibility of sober elevation disappears.

Naturally I am not suggesting that Chaplin and Keaton were somehow superior to those who had gone before them in arriving at a form that placed comedy squarely at its center without wrecking an epic reality of background in the process. I am simply saying that in the time of their lives and in the course of their careers they did arrive at it, and that what they arrived at was entirely new. It was new, and it was made possible, because of something the camera gave them: an authenticity inside which they could continue to be funny.

"It's got to be so authentic it hurts," Blesh reports Keaton saying to his staff as he set about constructing exact replicas of Civil War locomotives, preparing four thousand military uniforms, searching out virgin forests for *The General*. Keaton was turning to history for material, and to history that had already acquired mythological standing. Similarly, the opening sequence of *The Gold Rush* could be taken both as the opening of a documentary film and as a massive race-memory: hundreds of men make an antlike trail between snow-capped mountains, climb to the Chilkoot Pass exhausted. The footage is harsh, clean, factual.

Both films had their origins not only in general historical backgrounds but in specific historical fact. The fact, further, was angry fact, unpalatable fact. Chaplin had been reading about the Donner Party, trapped in impassable snowfields, reduced to cannibalism. Significantly, both the film's persuasive surrounded-by-snow atmosphere and much of its apparently improvised comedy—Charlie eating a shoe, Charlie being mistaken for a giant chicken by a partner who wants to eat *him*—come directly from this source. Keaton's base was an actual theft of a Southern train, *The General*, by Northern spies at a water-stop in Georgia. By stealing the train and destroying track and bridges behind them as they fled, the raiders would cut off supplies for a Southern army. As it happens, the spies came within minutes of safety, then were overtaken; those that were not shot down on the run were caught and hanged. History real, and history rough.

Mythological expansion of the backgrounds was ready-made. The Alaskan gold rush was virtually the climax, hence an ultimate symbol, of a country's discovery and mastery of its natural resources; a "mountain of gold" was the equivalent of every immigrant's dream of "streets paved with gold." And the Civil War, of course, had been traumatic for North and South alike: in the martyrdom of Lincoln on the one hand, in the loss of a way of life on the other. The power of legend lay on the side of the South: almost all successful plays, novels, and films have cast their sympathies there, acting on an intuition Keaton shared. "It's awful hard," he told Herbert Feinstein, "to make heroes out of the Northerners." It was not the dream that had survived but the dream that had vanished that lingered on as myth. The old South *was* Troy.

Epic scale was available to both films, then: history, fact, seriousness, and an overlay of legend were legitimately on tap. The reality of the camera guaranteed that the backgrounds would not be "mock," not stylized. Both men used subtitles, Chaplin more than Keaton, to keep echoes of size and of specificity reverberating: the Chilkoot Pass is "a test of man's endurance," "The Hand of the Law" reaches even into the vast Northern wastes, "The North" is "a law unto itself." Keaton's fewer titles were replaced in part by recurring, charismatic place names, sometimes photographed over railway depots: Marietta, Georgia; Big Shanty; The Rock River Bridge; Chattanooga. But associative words are constantly there. Buster himself is called Johnny Grey, his girl Annabelle Lee. Two doors open simultaneously, dramatically, as a son enters from the street, a father from an interior room. "Fort Sumter has been fired upon" is the son's message.

Above: Chaplin did not discard intimacy or the tight focus on himself in chancing the epic *Gold Rush*, as the celebrated boiled-shoe dinner and bun-dance testify. But the background in which he managed to fit himself expanded enormously—to the proportions, overleaf, of the Chilkoot Pass.

GENERAL STORE

SALOON

The problem, of course, was to keep the scale from killing the comedy. Scale is normally the enemy of humor, if only because the little man becomes difficult to find in so much mass; scale is the enemy of intimacy, even of personality. Douglas Fairbanks had planned the towering castles for *Robin Hood* and gone to Europe while they were being constructed. When he returned to find them built he was suddenly appalled, ready to call the whole project off. He was certain he'd be overwhelmed by the sheer spectacle, and had to be persuaded that there were ways of taming it. Chaplin himself visited the set one day and tamed it with a few seconds' thought: he had the great drawbridge of King Richard's castle lowered, shuffled out on it alone, picked up the milk and the Sunday papers, and shuffled back in again, the drawbridge rising behind him.

But that was simple playfulness, and it *was* mockery. The Great North was by no means to be diminished so cavalierly in *The Gold Rush*: men were to drop under the weight of their sleds at the top of the pass, murder in cold blood was to be done, a man was to be buried alive under an avalanche of ice. Chaplin's problem was doubly acute in that he was not so much a domestic comedian as he was an enclosed one. Though he had often enough taken to the streets in his Sennett days, and to the fields for his own *Sunnyside*, he was essentially a man who liked being bound to a tight frame, with shadows rather than naked light behind him. The narrow courtyard of *The Kid* was good enough; an attic room was better. As Chaplin's effects grew subtler, he wanted less and less potential distraction about. He wanted to be with us at close quarters so that we should miss nothing, however infinitesimal the detail might now be.

In point of fact, *all* of the comedian's most celebrated comic turns in *The Gold Rush* take place not in the snow fields but in extremely constricted enclosures: in cabins. A "lone prospector," he wanders into a "lone cabin" during a storm, sharing it with a man who is wanted for murder and a burlier man who has just uncovered a rich claim. It is here that he cooks a Thanksgiving dinner of boiled shoe. It is here that a starving companion begins to fancy him as fresh chicken. When he is forced to abandon this first cabin, he promptly adopts another one, serving as caretaker for a fellow who must leave to inspect his mines. In the second cabin he dreams of the festive party he is giving for his adored Georgia Hale and her friends, entertaining them by plunging forks into two buns and dancing an admirably accomplished Oceana Roll. Chaplin, in short, is running entirely true to form: when he wants us to laugh immoderately, and to feel a little something for him behind the laughter, he takes us indoors, holding the camera perfectly still.

What has happened to the epic, then? It is there, elemental and uncompromising, blowing a gale of such force that snow flurries will slip through any cabin's chinks and create whistling eddies along the floor. The epic is in the rhythm of the film, and is not for a moment forgotten. *We* may forget it, long after the fact, remembering only the bun dance and boiled shoe, the bits and pieces that gave us such pleasure. Chaplin did not.

He built his film like a giant bellows, blowing out, sucking in. We see the panorama of Chilkoot, straggling men scaling monstrous peaks. We are then permitted to see Charlie jauntily negotiating a cliff path, unaware that he is being followed by a bear. We see Big Jim McKay driving a stake into the frozen ground, falling to his knees in the stunned realization that he has discovered "a mountain of gold." We then see Charlie giving himself a free ride down a snowy slope. We see Black Larsen, hard eyes glittering, burn the police notice that says he is "Wanted"; he is already inside the cabin, alone, which means that the cabin is established as serious before it can serve to house comedy. We then see Charlie reach the safety of the cabin in a storm, only to be blown out a moment later.

The contrasts continue, sharp and calculated, throughout the first half of the film: outdoor, indoor; large, small; savage, friendly; sober, light. The most abrupt swing of the pendulum occurs where it would seem least likely. The Thanksgiving Dinner is a cherished memory for all of us; Chaplin may never have done anything more delicately hilarious. Does anyone recall that it directly follows Black Larsen's brutal murder of two territorial policemen? First a straightforward gunning-down out in the open; then the droll fancy of basting a shoe so that its sauces shall not be lost, sucking on its nails for the savor of chicken bones, twirling its laces about a fork in the approved manner of eating spaghetti, nodding a judicious "Not bad, hm?" to a companion chewing leather.

Against the business of maddened Big Jim's pursuit of chicken-Charlie around the cabin is set Black Larsen's greedy relish of his stolen food over a campfire on the tundra. Against the superb business of Charlie opportunely shooting a bear and instantly laying out dinnerware for two is set the fierce struggle between Big Jim and Black Larsen over Jim's claim, with Jim left for dead and Larsen going to his own death as a crevice opens beneath his feet.

If these things—scale and intimacy, melodrama and a skipping fancifulness—had merely been alternated, the film would have ended up a teeter-totter, without secure footing anywhere. But, from the outset, Chaplin is too shrewd for that. Almost at once he begins to make a weave of scale, seriousness, and comedy by letting one thread cross another and become hopelessly entangled with it. As we've seen, the cabin is first established as serious: Black Larsen, carrying the film's burden of melodrama, is in possession of it. Charlie is blown in, blown out, blown in again. Larsen *can't* get him to leave because the wind is stronger than Larsen is: comedy has been forced to remain with melodrama; the elements won't have it otherwise. Big Jim, a mountainous man in Mack Swain's fine performance and also the man with a "mountain of gold," brings the sweep of the gold rush itself, the thrust of history, with him as he is forced by the storm to join them. The three live together for some days, binding the film's fabric tight. When it is clear that one must go out for food, and Larsen is chosen by lot, Jim and Charlie are left to become companions of a sort: the big and the little in harness. Once Larsen has been lost to the film, his "straight" function is taken over by Big Jim. Jim, rising from the blow Larsen has dealt him with a shovel, has lost his memory and can now only wander in endless Odyssey, searching for the little man who may remember where the cabin is.

Ultimately all forces converge again in the film's spectacular, spectacularly funny, climax. Jim has found Charlie, Charlie has found the cabin, tomorrow they will set out for Jim's mine. During the night one more storm—even greater in scale—blows up, carrying the cabin to the edge of a precipice. It is dangling there, held only by a rope caught in the cleft of a rock, when the two men awake, unaware of their plight. The comedy, framed for the last time by the cabin, begins. Charlie plucks icicles from the rafters to boil down for morning coffee. Soon, though, the cabin is tilting under the weight of its inmates, the rope is slipping, both men are trapped on the downslide, unable to crawl to a door higher than their heads. The weave is now complete. Comedy *and* coming death inside the cabin; outside, the edge of the precipice slowly crumbling away, the silent, majestic skies looking on with indifference. Inside and outside are all one now; even the comedy is inextricably bound to the scale. As Charlie makes his leap for freedom, the cabin goes over. But Charlie and Jim are at last standing on Jim's "mountain of gold," deposited there by cosmic chance. Fate, that constant interloper in the serious epic, is just as willing to play its tricks here.

The film ends with both men millionaires, and with Charlie getting his

Merging the comedy with the melodrama. Above, the confrontation between Black Larsen and Big Jim is perfectly straightforward. Below, a moment later, as the two men struggle fiercely over a rifle, the rifle somehow or other keeps training itself on Charlie.

Georgia on a responsible basis—an eventuality he would never repeat. Chaplin *tried* to avoid wealth and marriage here: an earlier, more characteristic, ending was shot and scrapped. The film, built as it was, could not tolerate Charlie being diminished again at its close: the forces he'd unleashed were too serious and too powerful for that, had simply caught him up in an epic logic of their own.

The logic is there in all of the earlier love scenes, which are psychologically serious. Here there is no playful baiting of Edna Purviance even as he steals furtive glances at her, no flirting while plainly intending to move on. Edna herself is gone. Before beginning production of *The Gold Rush*, Chaplin had taken time to direct Miss Purviance in *A Woman of Paris*, hoping to establish her as a mature leading woman and star in her own right. After thirty-four films together, it was a farewell gesture; Chaplin turned his attention to girls more nearly ingenues, though Miss Purviance remained on the studio payroll until her death.

The Gold Rush is more than a third over by the time Georgia Hale, the brunette dance-hall girl, appears; when she does, Charlie, having endured Black Larsen and survived the hungers of Big Jim, is already deeply rooted in the relatively grave progress of the narrative. He is prepared to be grave with Georgia. The old comedy pops out, inevitably, emphatically. Opening the door of his shack to find the dazzling Georgia on his threshold, Charlie is promptly hit in the face with a snowball. Deliriously cavorting about the cabin and hurling pillows every which way once Georgia, leaving, has agreed to come to his party, he finds himself an embarrassed mass of feathers when she returns to pick up a pair of gloves. But his responses when she is present are the responses of a realistically embarrassed, romantically awkward man. Simply being near her in the dance hall causes him to turn rigid as marble, eyes scanning the ceiling in fright. Playing host to Georgia's friends in the shack leaves him mute, self-conscious, at a loss for the kind of quick impersonation that has come so readily before. He is a whole man,

Above: Charlie and Mack Swain are still inside the cabin, but the cabin itself is at the mercy of the gods.

Opposite: Charlie is not playful in his wary longing for Georgia. *The Gold Rush* won't tolerate a love story that can be lightly brushed off.

this one time, with a whole man's lack of resourcefulness. Indeed, he carries his emotional involvement too far. When the girls do *not* appear for the New Year's Eve supper he has planned, he stands in the doorway listening sorrowfully to the revelry and the "Auld Lang Syne" that drift up from the dance hall, his face in something close to soft focus, his Adam's apple dipping in regret. This is, I think, the one truly sentimental shot in the Chaplin library, the only close-up or near-close-up in which self-pity predominates. But all of these things determine the film's fade-out. The very bellows that expand and contract to give the film its epic-comic life seem to take longer, deeper breaths during the whole Georgia-conscious center of *The Gold Rush*. Scenes are extended, somewhat slowed; the contrasts come at greater intervals. Charlie has been immersed in the momentous before he meets Georgia; his immersion dictates his response to her; the two fuse to become part of a last joyous inhalation that simply cannot be shrugged off with a little back-kick and a philosophical shuffle down the road. Play with vast forces and you may wind up cradled in their arms, as Buster Keaton well knew.

Keaton's structure for *The General* was simpler and much easier to come by. Keaton had always worked in scale: with ships, locomotives, hurricanes. He had wedded himself to huge inanimate objects before and careered across the landscape with them. Joining them had kept him from being overwhelmed by them; he'd become part of what was so overwhelming. The gravity of his own countenance permitted gravity about him: he could let Northern and Southern generals and spies play their scenes straightfaced without seeming to contradict them the moment he appeared. And, by some accident of metamorphosis, he looked perfectly at home in period costume. We had already seen him slip into the frock coat and gray top hat of *Our Hospitality* without a trace of anachronism; the fit was snug. Now he could adopt the Dutch bob of the Civil War, the celluloid collars and the foreshortened derbies, and seem instantly to have come out of a Brady

The General's comic scale and authenticity remain unsurpassed. Above, Buster racing his locomotive past two entire armies without noticing. Opposite: Left: the second Union army advancing upon the Rock River Bridge; Right, Buster alerting Southern troops to the danger at the bridge, and Buster overhearing the entire plan in Northern headquarters.

photograph. *The General*, as a film, has the peculiar quality of not dating at all: we quite forget that we are looking at work done in the 1920's and tend to identify the pictures we are watching with the period of the narrative. This is only in part due to the fact that it was a costume film to begin with; many costume films of the 1920's are transparently sham today. It is more nearly due to Keaton's integral relationship with his background. Both Keaton and Chaplin had developed personal images iconographic enough to be timeless. Chaplin simply held onto his—baggy trousers, mustache, cane, derby—resolutely, carrying it with him wherever he went. Keaton, more naked, had made a virtue—even a philosophical fetish—of his very adaptability; he could swap one costume for another and continue to ride with its outlines. He was wedded to matter, and no matter that the matter changed shape.

Neither was his architectural problem as formidable as Chaplin's. For one thing, the story he had hit upon took maximum advantage of one of silent film comedy's most venerable tools. It was one long chase. Or, rather, *two* long chases, back to back: from South to North, from North to South, using the same track both ways. And there had always been another side, a geometric side, to Keaton's sense of narrative form. Along with his taste for rambling improvisation—the loose-as-a-lazy-lariat films—had gone a compulsive drive toward progressive constriction, a liking for being boxed in by inanimate forces, by the days of the week or by the haunting prevalence of identical billboards. He had learned, particularly with *The Navigator*, how to achieve this constriction *inside* expansion—so that he could extend his films to feature length and even greater scale while at the same time tightening the noose about his neck. *The Navigator* is extraordinarily constricted: in effect he has scaled the cast down to two, himself and the girl, and confined their activities to a locale that functions as a trap. They cannot leave the drifting liner that locks them in. But, simultaneously, the horizon is opening wide. The liner is a very large one, so large that they can lose one another on it. The ocean on which it drifts is larger still. "In" and "out" do not alternate; they are identical with one another.

The General uses the same geometric pattern, intensifying both the constriction and the expansion. For a good half of the chase, Keaton has scaled the com-

pany down to one: he is alone on the locomotive that is racing headlong into enemy territory in pursuit of his stolen *General*. But the range, laterally, is infinite: so long as there is track ahead of him, he can go on and on and on. Then, once he has caught up with the beloved stolen engine, the film turns in on itself in another way, reducing possibilities. He must take it back over the very same route he has traveled, repeating along the way *every bit of business* that has been done on the way out. On the way out the Northern spies have dumped railroad ties, crates, boxcars in his path, burning wooden bridges he must pass through. Once he has leapt into the *General*'s cab and headed it for home again with two Northern trains hot on his heels, he will do all of the same things, with interesting variations. The film folds over, becomes its own mirror image, limiting itself to the first premises of a theorem. And yet the homeward track is infinitely open too: the highest of speeds cannot exhaust its endless invitation.

If Chaplin's structure resembles a bellows, Keaton's resembles a boomerang. *The General* is a great parabola flung against the skyline, lifting on a first long curve that seems destined to go on forever, then gently and ominously curling in space to retrace its passage until it lands without loss of force in the hand that has set it in motion. Call it the Keaton Curve magnified to embrace the two halves of a continent, if you will. It is a controlled and challenging design for an epic film.

The sense of epic in *The General* does not end with the spectacular shape of the film. The epic feeling permeates—with its authenticity—the weatherbeaten clapboards of wayside houses, the close-to-peeling pillars of the girl's colonial "mansion," the dusty roads of smallish towns and teeming military encampments, the very weeds that push through gravel to wrap themselves about railroad ties. We do not seem to be looking at "sets" at all, but at a mythic past in its tangible life recovered whole after a hundred years. The scene in which *The General* is stolen is singularly beautiful in its proportions because it is so palpably fact. In a long-shot the train rolls into Big Shanty. The passengers debark for lunch, in the broken rhythms of a tide washing over a beach, moving across a vast trampled field to the station house. Buster, before eating, soaps his hands at a basin provided for the purpose against an outside wall. The spies saunter from their cars, elaborately casual, waiting for their opportunity to strike. We watch most of what is

happening—one group of people disintegrating, another easing firmly into place—with the detached eyes of a mountaineer coming down a hillside for his own spot of lunch. It is a clear day, in an open place, with life going on so normally that it is difficult to imagine any untoward event taking place.

Once the chase has begun—Buster begins on a handcar that is derailed by freshly broken track, literally flies onto a wooden two-wheel bicycle that will not support him long, then corrals an army locomotive with no more than a tender attached to it—the rolling landscape is with us, late and soon. Everything Keaton does by way of massive comedy, to massive purpose, is done with the skyline, the swiftly vanishing fir trees, the rippling mountainsides full in our eyes. Buster may anchor a snub-nosed cannon to the tender, load it and light its fuse, only to find its snout joggled lower and lower by the roadbed until it is pointing directly at *him*, the while his foot is caught in a chain that anchors him helplessly as target. He may be riding the cow-catcher, snatching up one log dumped directly into his path and using it as a hurled missile to dislodge the next log ahead of him with Euclidean grace. He may be chopping firewood on the tender while an entire retreating Southern army and then an entire advancing Northern army pass him by without his noticing. Whatever he is doing, the magnificently factual world of V-shaped valleys and whipped-away pines is with him, behind him, racing past his preoccupied figure to certify the universe he stands astride.

It is a country made for giants, peopled—except for the trouble-prone yet masterful Buster—by fire-breathing monsters. We see the monsters eye one another, preparing to do battle. The stolen *General* roars through a ground-level opening in a towering five-story trestle made of timbering, and circles around the mountain to arrive at the top of the trestle just as Buster, in his army locomotive, steams through the lower passage: two flights cross in space, the ogres take each other's measure and seem to snort. On the return journey, we see three locomotives converging: one is reversing rapidly, the other two charging forward. They must meet, and all will be over. They don't. The reversing train plunges into the area at the precise moment the other two are sent shooting up an inclined spur, the second ramming into the first, creating overall a visual tangle of steel quite worthy of an earthquake.

As *The General* must be the most insistently *moving* picture ever made, so its climax is surely the most stunning visual event ever arranged for a film comedy, perhaps for a film of any kind. Nearing home in the final chase, Buster, girl, and *General* are crossing the high Rock River bridge. Buster knows that two Northern armies—on rail and on foot—are massing behind him; to gain just enough time to warn a nearby Southern army of the impending attack, he must set fire to the bridge. Leaping from tender to trestle, he swiftly builds a pyre out of firewood, then covers it with kerosene. A burning brand rests on the tender's edge to start the holocaust when Buster is ready. Before he is ready, and while he is on the far side of the pyre, the girl, performing her usual function, inadvertently knocks the blazing brand onto the pyre. Flames leap up between Buster and the train. Doing the only thing he can do, he makes a desperate dive toward the train through the spreading fire. Unfortunately, the girl has chosen the same moment to set the train in motion, so that Buster plunges through the bridge into the waters far below. Struggling to the bank and hurriedly catching up with the train, Buster makes it to the Southern encampment, and sounds the alert; now horses, cannon, windstorms of military equipment thunder past him on the road in their race to the river, covering him with dust and indifferent about running him down.

In the meantime, the Northern armies have joined at the burning bridge. A general, heavy-jawed, stern-eyed, showing only the least trace of fatuousness,

It scarcely matters what the inanimate object is. Buster fits it. And shortly it will prove not so inanimate after all. On the outward chase in *The General*.

decides that the bridge is not yet sufficiently damaged to prevent crossing; he orders his supply train to proceed while his cavalry descends the bank to ford the river beneath. In a breath-taking long-shot, the train moves forward onto the bridge while the foreground begins to fill with men and horses advancing below. Then, as the train is halfway across, the bridge palpably weakens. With all forces moving and the panorama embracing river, steep slopes, and endless forest, the train's belly begins to droop through the burned gap in the bridge, the gap splinters wide, the understructure pulls away as the great beast seems to claw at it, and in a serpentine curve that is as beautiful as it is horrifying the train goes down to the water with its smokestack vomiting steam, a dragon breathing fire even in death. By this time the Southern army has raced into place on the opposite bank and opened fire with its cannon: smoke belches from both sides of the river to fuse with the angry geyser of the slain locomotive. It is as though the sacrifice of the beast has instantly unleashed the holocaust.

The awe of the moment is real: we are present at *some* kind of history, if only the history of four or five minutes on a day when an actual locomotive, a true burning bridge, masses of breathing men, a verifiable landscape, and a cameraman were present. For years visitors to Cottage Grove, Oregon, where the shot was made, were able to see the fallen locomotive; today, I am told, its reality is obscured by natural undergrowth. Chaplin, in *The Gold Rush*, might move without a qualm from the documentary snows of the Pass to the obvious studio-made cliff along which Charlie himself saunters; cinematically the clash is garish, but Chaplin's animated presence is enough to quiet questions. But there are no miniatures, there is little paint, in the climax or in any other part of *The General*.

The fidelity itself is epic, the film beautiful simply as photography.

Keaton is at home not only in the costumes but on the overgrown roadbeds of a country out of time. Above: The odd, near-mythic conjunction of locomotive, timber, and Buster will, in a moment, produce one of *The General*'s most satisfying laughs; Overleaf: Incident at the Rock River Bridge.

W.&A.R.R.

Yet the climax is at the same time funny. Even as the train is going down, we remember that it is Buster who has set the fire, that the train is an *enemy* train, and that the man who has sent it forward is a fool. The film now cuts back to this man's face, without direct ridicule. The general is still astride his horse, still looking on without obvious grimace, stolid, stunned, almost incapable of believing what he sees. There is just a faint queasiness about those rock-hard outlines of his jaw now, an abashed glaze beginning to steal over his eyes. The shot invariably creates one of the film's loudest laughs, and that without emphasis of any sort. Keaton lets us make our own connections, lets us provide the man with what we know he is feeling. Keaton was, in fact, extremely fond of just such sustained "reaction" shots, the comedy coming from the fact that the face that has just looked upon unforeseen and unprecedented disaster displays no reaction at all.

For all that is unique about *The General*, the film is nonetheless crammed with the comedian's favorite ploys. The Curve is there, again and again: when the stubby cannon whose barrel is aimed directly at Buster finally does go off, it goes off precisely as the roadbed swerves to the left, sending its ball not into the tender but across the now open fields to hit the rear of the train Buster is chasing, a good half-mile away. The familiar stance is there: Buster climbs to the roof of the cab, leans forward as though he were still wearing vaudeville slapshoes to keep his slanted form in balance, shades his eyes with his hand to inspect the unknown ahead. The silence is there: as a captive Northerner who has been knocked unconscious begins to revive on the tender's floor, a block of wood flies in from nowhere to put him out again; Buster leaps into the frame from above and we conclude that he has done the job, though he hasn't told us.

He did, however, break his silence about the girl, this one time. Keaton liked to begin his films slowly, maintaining a gentle rhythm for as long as was feasible. He opens *The General* by walking methodically to the girl's house, trailed methodically by two worshipping small boys. It so happens that the girl is returning from the local library, unnoticed; she falls into step behind the small boys. A foursome parading to see the girl, who is its fourth member. Arriving at her house, Buster raps on the door, stands waiting. So, behind him, does she. What she is waiting for, just whom she expects will open the door, we shall never know. When Buster discovers that she has been present the whole time, there is no reproof in his glance, just modest worship. It is modest because he loves her but loves his locomotive more.

Neither does he register any doubt of her intelligence while he is rescuing her from the Northern camp. When she assumes that he has gone to all this trouble to rescue *her* rather than his locomotive, he shrugs, spiritually, and lets her assume what she will. He *does* treat her as mere material object more than any other of his heroines; somehow she invites it. To stow her aboard *The General* for its return flight, he must cram her into a gunnysack stolen from a supply depot; he pushes her head down into it as though he were packaging melons. Carrying the sack on his back and joining a line of Northern soldiers tossing supplies into a boxcar, he tosses *his* sack routinely, watches while barrels and crates are flung in on top of her. Let it be said that he winces. Stealing the train on the run, he hacks out a wall of the boxcar to get to her; inside the boxcar he tramps over everything stored there searching for the sack, and finds it by stepping on *her*.

Freed, she will be as helpful as possible. While Buster pauses to gather firewood, she cunningly thinks how to delay the pursuit train. Buster finds her stretching a piece of rope across the tracks, tying it to pine trees on either side. He does not comment, except to stand for a moment with his hands on his hips and then to test the flimsiness of the rope with his fingers. Rather, he is now at his

most elaborately polite and devoted, kneeling and offering her his open palms to step on as she climbs into the cab. She bypasses his palms and hikes herself upward efficiently, leaving him with his gentlemanliness unrewarded and forcing him to scramble aboard through the window of the cab.

The upshot is ambiguous. The pursuit train naturally plows straight through the rope. But it does pick up the two pine trees, which are now caught in the train's wheels and revolving like great furry antennae. The train must stop to dislodge them. She is being otherwise helpful, pitching firewood into the boiler. She comes across one substantial piece of wood that has a knothole in it, however; filled with distaste by this defect, she throws it overboard. Buster merely stares. Shortly thereafter she feels it is time to tidy up. As the train rushes across the countryside she is seen busy with a broom, sweeping up the floor of the cab. This time Buster removes the broom from her hands and suggests she stoke the fire further. She picks up a piece of wood no bigger than her hand and ever so carefully refuels the boiler with it. Buster, watching, is clearly approaching crisis. He picks up an even smaller splinter and tosses it in after, eyes solemn in wild irony. Then his two arms leap forward to her shoulders and, for no more than a second or two, he shakes the living daylights out of her. This done, he kisses her.

He has spoken.

Buster saw to the girl's silence, briefly, in *The General*, but then, though even more briefly, broke his own.

27. Who Was Harry Langdon?

I am going to reminisce. When I was about twelve, a friend and I began showing films on Friday nights in the auditorium of the school we attended. I suppose we really wanted to see the films again for ourselves—naturally, we weren't allowed to book current features but had to wait six or eight months until they had exhausted their commercial runs—or perhaps we just enjoyed playing the role of exhibitor. Certainly we enjoyed participating in one minor transgression of booking ethics: occasionally, with the cheerful connivance of a local theater operator, we "bicycled" film. That is to say, we sent a runner posthaste to the friendly commercial house, had him pick up the Felix the Cat cartoon the theater was then showing, ran it as part of our own program, and then sped it back so that it could appear at the scheduled time on the theater's bill. Of course we paid regular rentals for our features; but this practice did help out a bit with the short subjects.

As it happened, the over-all project was quite successful, and not entirely because of our sometime chicanery: at the end of a year and a half we had earned six hundred dollars for the school, or just enough to equip the auditorium with splendid new seats. And, as it happened, the project took its impetus from the work of a single man: the comedian Harry Langdon. Langdon was enormously popular at the time, having risen rapidly during two years of making short comedies for Mack Sennett and then going into independent production on features under the releasing aegis of First National. We made our debut as showmen with Langdon's initial feature, *Tramp, Tramp, Tramp*, in 1926, and included his subsequent films on our programs as rapidly as we could get our hands on them. He proved, for as long as we needed him, a solid foundation.

I have a reason for reminiscing. In the course of learning how to rent features along Chicago's Film Row, I became acquainted with the bookers in the various exchanges. It is astonishing, by the way, how considerate busy men can be with children. Though I must have been taking up valuable time, and though the rental fees charged schools brought only minimal returns to the exchanges, the bookers were always willing to chat, and if anyone loved talking film "shop," it was I. Whereupon I got another of my youthful shocks.

I had gone into First National one day to book Langdon's third successful feature, and, the paperwork done, I asked—out of personal interest—when his next might be appearing in the theaters. "Oh, I don't know," the booker said casually, "we'll be dumping the little son-of-a-bitch soon."

I probably reeled a little, and not because I was unaware of the fact that glamorous performers could be less than fondly regarded, or behave unglamorously, apart from their work. What stunned me was the notion that Langdon could be in trouble at all. Each of his first three features had been both critically and financially successful. In the second he had been compared to Chaplin: *Photoplay* magazine had warned Charlie that a real rival was gaining ground. Now, at the crest, he was being dismissed out of hand—and by the very men who had been tucking away profits for two exhilarating years. How was such a turnabout possible, without a single box-office failure having cast its shadow? No doubt my bewilderment was compounded by a sense of instant personal loss: like most adults of the period, certainly like most youngsters of the period, I loved Langdon.

The prognosis was correct, though. With his fourth feature Langdon slipped ominously, with his fifth he embraced disaster, with his sixth he closed out forever his career as an important star. No other major comedian was major for so short a time: if the rise was rapid, the descent was dizzying.

Fate dogs him still. With the strong revival of interest in the work of the period, Langdon's name now reappears more often, certain of his films make their ways into the programs of film societies. But you cannot really "sell" him. A Keaton retrospective is easy to manage: simple exposure to the man will retrain an audience to silence quite rapidly, provoke exactly the response Keaton intended. Try a Langdon retrospective and you are apt to meet with utter bafflement. Twenty years ago—with silent film already more than twenty years dead—I ran a university film series and included Keaton's *The General* and Langdon's *The Strong Man* as samples of comedy. *The General* was greeted with constant astonished laughter. *The Strong Man*—Langdon's best film—was stared at in stony silence.

End of the story? I don't think so. There was too much that was unique, and something that was superlative, in Langdon for that. But before we can tackle the task of finding eyes for him again, we have somehow got to contend with two delicate questions: what happened then, and what happens now?

When we look at Langdon today we expect him to do what any major figure must presumably do: assert himself on acquaintance, take over the screen, take over the audience, dictate response without reference to anything outside himself. But Langdon cannot do that for a somewhat peculiar reason. He existed only *in reference to* the work of other comedians. He could never have invented the form, as Chaplin virtually did; he was too small, too peripheral for that. The form had to be there first, its syntax wholly developed, its more extravagant convolutions deeply known. With the form at hand—a sentence completely spelled out—Langdon could come along and, glancing demurely over his shoulder to make sure no one was looking, furtively brush in a comma.

He was called a baby, though he was scarcely ever that. But his function—and the whole of his originality—was to serve as little more than a breath, an unlooked-for hesitation in the hurry of silent comedy style. Coming late to films—he didn't begin work until 1924—Langdon could only look over the skillfully articulated, at some points already exhausted, comic design, study it for unlikely caesuras, put up a stubby finger, draw in his inconclusive personal punctuation,

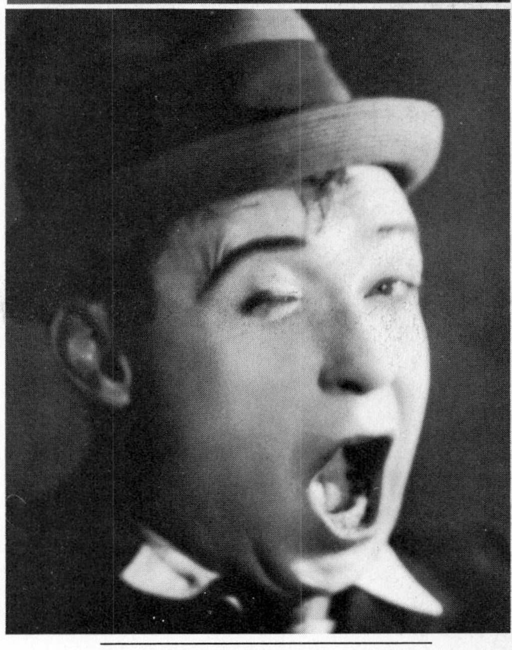

Harry in three moods: wary, warier, and more than usually sleepy.

and shy away before something hit him.

It was an ingenious bid for legitimate novelty and, on the instant, audiences understood it. They understood it because they had been living within the developed tradition of silent film comedy for quite a long time, were intimately and almost tactilely familiar with its grammar. In fact, Keaton and Lloyd were now becoming almost *too* familiar; their films of 1926 and 1927 simultaneously show traces of matter-of-factness about the edges and a determined casting-about for fresh tactics. Chaplin escaped the threat of familiarity by producing less often; but in 1927 he was in agonies over his inability to transcend himself in *The Circus*. Audiences knew the structures, even with the sliest variations, all too well. They didn't particularly want new ones: the old were safe coin in the pocket, still immensely jolly. What an audience probably wanted was a comment on them, a visual inflection that would slightly threaten their stability, an unanticipated tremor that would shake them up without bringing them down. Langdon, with his *luftpause* gently but constantly surprising the music, provided that.

How does one function as a comma? This way. Harry is standing in the middle of a very busy street. Traffic is bearing down on him. From the beginning of film comedy clowns had known what to do next. They could start running for dear life, straight down the street at an accelerating speed with an onrushing car, engine steaming, hot on their heels; the zigzag, and the near-death, could go on for miles. Or they could let themselves be hit by the car in the first place, to go looping the loop high in air. The patterns were established. What did Harry do? Nothing, more or less. He stood there, really too simple to quite comprehend the danger, one cheek tucked up into a chipmunk bulge, one half of a sweet smile skidding upward from puckered lips. A car whizzed by and missed him entirely. But a fraction of a second *after* the car had gone, Harry jumped a little jump, as though to get out of its way. A rather profitless jump—optional, as commas often are. Aftermath. Yet notice how it changes the rhythm of the sentence. And it is, in its sublimely unfunctional yet thoughtful way, funny.

For years comedians had been accidentally spilling kerosene or various other indigestibles into restaurant soup tureens and confidently serving the malodorous brew to customers. Comedy was made first of the fact that the comedian didn't know what he had done and then of the explosive reaction of the ravaged customer, chase included. Harry did it another way. He began by noticing what had happened: the soup was lethal. He then did his earnest best to talk the customer out of ordering it. With the customer adamant, he would provide the potion, constantly rushing steins of beer and urging him to take regular sips that might intercept and minimize the outburst to come. He would wipe the customer's lips for him too, lest the kerosene chap them. Langdon was forever trying to *prevent* the comedy other men made.

He liked being helpful in small ways, without being good at it. Say that someone—it was usually Vernon Dent, his beefy sidekick—had dropped something, a hammer or perhaps a king's crown. Harry always instantly stooped to help, putting out pudgy hands in a shapeless grope. Before his spread knees had quite lowered him to the object, the man who had dropped it had already retrieved it. That left Harry with his hands to cope with, willing, empty, spiritually unsatisfied. He usually balanced them for a little while, as though some other object might appear magically in midair and find a use for them. This failing, he would probably make a large loop with his elbows to bring the hands spinsterishly together, clasped in a highly approving attitude as if to say, "Well done!" Once the thing is done, though he hasn't done it, Harry is pleased.

The trick was to do nothing—or *almost* nothing—in a form that had always done everything, and done it fast. The minimal things he does do are not really gags. The gags are built around him, rush past him, sweep over him. He lives in their backwash, eyes wary with wondering friendliness, one palm ever ready to flip upward from a tight elbow and flop open in tentative greeting. There was a dent in his hat that suggested a dent in his brain; but he was a nice fellow and if, riding in the rumble seat of a car, he decided to blow kisses through the rear window to the girls up front, he would probably add a kiss for the driver, Mr. Dent. He wasn't, please understand, homosexual. He didn't make such choices, and women always appropriated him first in any case. It was just that when his hands started doing a certain thing, they tended to keep on doing it, in boundless generosity. He didn't discriminate.

He could, in fact, scarcely keep awake. His eye-blink, if it had ever been medically charted, would surely have been the slowest in recorded history. Once he had grasped an idea and seen it to its unpromising conclusion, his eyelids would start down like an asbestos theater curtain. When they had finally retracted, and we could begin to read him again, it would be apparent that his mind had been washed clean by the operation and was ready for a new thought. His thoughts came one at a time, with intermissions.

When he was badly treated, there was no time wasted on resentment. Hit him and he might seem grateful for the timely blow. With an uppercut to the chin he would stiffen almost imperceptibly, eyes misting. Then a seraphic smile might steal over his face as sleepiness descended. He would very likely lower himself onto the nearest object available, without bothering to see if it was there, turn up his coat collar to shield him from night winds, lock his arms together in gentle repose, and sit in serene contemplation, eyes wide, pasty face composed, one ear cocked slightly so as not to miss the music playing somewhere. Arnold Toynbee speaks of the re-energizing process of withdrawal and return. Whenever Langdon does return, something of the withdrawal still clings to him. He had found a way to renew the energies of silent film comedy by acting out their absence. Definition by denial.

What he did was by no means lost on his contemporaries. If you watch *College* closely, you can see Buster Keaton on a ballfield halfway between first and second base—Langdon was always halfway between here and there—stealing looks out of the corners of his eyes that are unmistakably Langdon-inspired. Keaton is not imitating Langdon; he is unconsciously absorbing him. A few years later Chaplin would appropriate Langdon's blind heroine of *The Strong Man* for *City Lights*. When Langdon left Sennett to make his own features, Sennett promptly—and horrendously—tried to turn an able young moon-faced comic named Eddie Quillan *into* Langdon, borrowing not only his mannerisms but entire sequences and even camera-angles from *The Strong Man*. For a very few years Langdon was simply in the comic air; his reflexes—the reflexes of a wind-up toy whose springs are beginning to run down—were so authentically what they were, whatever they were, that they prompted sympathetic reflexes all about him.

But Langdon's special position as a piece of not quite necessary punctuation inserted into a long-since memorized sentence means that he remains, today, dependent on our memory of the sentence. It is not even enough to *know* the sentence. We must inhabit it, live in its syntax in the way we daily take in air, share its expectations because they are what *we* expect, if we are to grasp—and take delight in—the nuance that was Langdon. You would have to soak yourself in silent film comedy to the point where Lloyd seemed a neighbor again, Chaplin a constant visitor, Keaton so omnipresent that he could be treated as commonplace, and the form's structure as necessary as the roof over your head in order to join

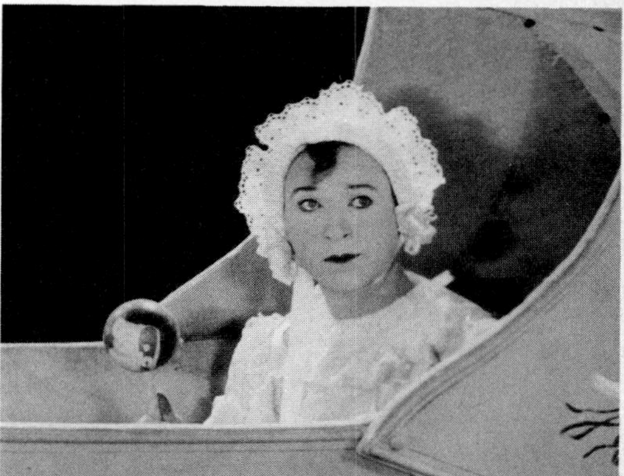

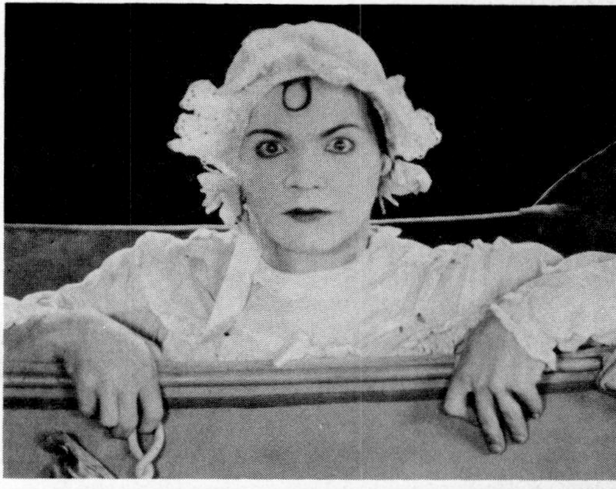

Langdon's new style was so pervasive that it provoked outright imitation. The top two shots, faraway and near, are of Harry himself in one of his rare appearances as an actual infant. *His First Flame*. The lower two, near and faraway, are of Eddie Quillan, an able young comedian whom Mack Sennett attempted to turn *into* Langdon when Langdon left him. *For Sale, A Bungalow*.

Streetcleaner Harry has been assigned Chinatown just after one of those Tong Wars. *Feet of Mud.*

Opposite: Having proved a profitable source of income to a junk dealer, Harry happily joins the firm, imitating his elders as always. *Fiddlesticks.*

hands with Langdon once more and go swinging, fingers childishly interlocked, down the street. That sort of immersion can never really take place again, except perhaps among archivists, and we shall all no doubt continue to have our troubles with Langdon. It seems likely, however, that our reacquaintance with silent film comedy is going to develop a good deal beyond what it is now; the closer we come to feeling reasonably at home in it, the larger will Langdon's decorative work—all miniature—loom.

I have been trying to explain why Langdon does not speak to us as immediately as his colleagues do. But what of his contemporaries, who loved him in summertime and abruptly discarded him in fall? Why did *they* turn on him? More important still: why had they loved him? What was there about this nearly forty-year-old man, face heavily covered with something close to clown white, running with his legs apart as though he just possibly still wore diapers, to endear him so readily to the sophisticated 1920's?

It would be tempting, but a bit too pat, to say that it was precisely his innocence that appealed to a highly sophisticated time, a time that may well have been tiring of the eternal need to seem knowing. Reversals of this sort are common social phenomena. But some degree of innocence is indispensable to any comedian, and winsomeness alone could not have accounted for Langdon's popularity. An air of innocence in comedians is essentially a protective tactic meant to cover for

them during their more outrageous assaults. Innocence served wholesale could only become cloying. In fact, some of Langdon's most delectable effects come when the eyes in that immature face narrow evilly, promising an altogether improbable malice.

What I think won Langdon his first audience, and held it mysteriously transfixed for a time, was his extraordinary complexity, a complexity so dense and unfathomable that it pushed silent screen fantasy to its farthest limits, threatening to unravel altogether the weave of real and unreal that formed its texture. Threatening, and then stopping just short. The figure on the screen, however likeable he might be, was flatly impossible. Yet there he stood, an unchallengeable *fait accompli*. Langdon was the most ambiguous of all silent film clowns, and his survival depended on his maintaining that ambiguity, explaining himself not at all.

Look at him. His motor responses, and to some degree his cerebral responses, are approximately those of a five-year-old. Call him and he doesn't know whether to come or not. Children are uncertain about how to respond properly; they have difficulty in reading the social message that is being imparted. When a parent beckons, it may be for a hug or it may be for a spanking. Which? The five-year-old hesitates, drawn to the parent, fearful of the parent's power. A child can stand paralyzed between choices.

Thus Harry—unsure of the verbal and visual structures that the adults about him seem to use with such ease. He may try to resolve the issue by flapping his hands inconclusively in a hopeful gesture of "Scat!" He may back away in a little slip-slide, pretending to be about to disappear himself. He hovers, attempting to look as resolute as possible. His feet, locked at the ankles, turn both ways.

When the omens are favorable and he feels among friends, he will happily accompany man or woman along a street, skipping sideways to keep up. Every now and again, still skipping, he will bend over to peer up into his companion's face, checking the emotional weather. If his companion is smiling, Harry will stop abruptly to laugh, smothering his mouth with splayed fingers, closing his eyes tight in hilarity. If his companion is displeased with anything or anybody, Harry will second the displeasure. Vernon Dent, in wrath, kicks a telephone pole. Harry, loyal, gives the pole a severe dressing-down.

He takes his cues from his elders, and he has learned a gesture or two. One asserts oneself strongly by pumping one's arm straight up and down, index finger directed at the floor. Since no other part of the body is engaged, the gesture is not entirely convincing. Slap his hand away and he will very probably slap back, usually with both hands and in a splatter of what might be sparrows' wings. He has a repertory of false fierce scowls borrowed from others; for the most part he employs them when he is alone. He is endlessly rehearsing the act of growing up.

His clothes are telltale. The trousers, overlong and ballooning at the cuffs, would seem to have been handed down from an older brother. Draping over the locked ankles, they sometimes make him seem a statue. His tie is never tied quite tightly at the neck, nor is it properly centered; some other kid has been tugging at it. His too-small jacket is fastened high by a single enormous button, its tails flaring behind in seagull sweep. He uses his hat-brim as ballast; let the least wind stir and both hands fly to its edge, finding security in the firmness with which it rides his brow. One forelock slips beneath it. A five-year-old not gaining much on six.

But. He is past puberty—not safely past, but past. He is sexually aware. Let a girl in a lumber camp approach him and he will retreat as his mother has told him to do. Let her pucker her lips and he will lean forward with great interest to study them. Let her take one step nearer and he will raise an axe straight up in the air to defend his virtue. He knows what these creatures are after.

Indeed, he is extraordinarily sensitive about the matter. He is happy to be with a girl on his Saturday afternoon off, ever so chatty as they swing hands along the sidewalk. Then the girl, quite thoughtlessly, fingers the strap of his overalls. He jumps his circumscribed jump, turns to stone on the spot, stares at her with the rueful wisdom of the ages in his eyes. It is as though she had stripped him.

When a girl does kiss him, he likes it. True, his reaction may be somewhat out of the ordinary. First the dazed, well-fed smile. Then a topple backward, rigid, out a window. Then a sleepy pawing of the ground and an ecstatic attempt to nuzzle the stone wall of the house, as though he could cuddle his way through it. His romance with the wall, and his attempt at metamorphosis, goes on for quite a while. But he does blink his way back to what is for him clarity, and he promptly returns to the girl for more. He is an apprehensive twelve-year-old experimenting for the first time with rapture.

But. He is a fully grown man, capable of holding down any sort of job, marriageable and very often married—in one short film the father of three children. True, his connubial interests are somewhat confused. In *Soldier Man*, a late Sennett, he is a substitute King—in the *Prisoner of Zenda* manner—whose Queen has called him to her boudoir. Entering the chamber, he passes a tray of tea sandwiches. On the instant he is transfixed, torn between the alluring summons from the bridal couch and the even more alluring sandwiches. The first round is won by the sandwiches. He makes constant feints toward the bed, but they coil in on themselves and bring him back to the tea tray. He stuffs as much as he can into his mouth against a possibly sandwichless romance. Eventually locked into the Queen's embrace, he is still munching, swallowing hard in an effort to get on with his next responsibility. He is very considerate. He defers the Queen's kiss—an unconscionable number of times—while he carefully de-crumbs his lips and garment, brushing off his hands for good measure. Then he goes back for another sandwich. There is, in due time and after all, a kiss. It is so powerful that the Queen faints dead away, permitting him to return to the tray. He is plainly possessed of a man's capacities, if only he can be distracted from other pursuits.

There is a waiver, then another. The sequence with the Queen proves to be a dream—he has not overwhelmed her after all—and he is being wakened for work by his wife. Langdon, being waked, invariably leapt to the floor and started off in three directions; then he woke up. Remembering his dream, and eyeing his wife with a conquering fondness, he attempts to reproduce the embrace, hoping to reproduce its remarkable effect. His wife shoos him off, impatient as she would be with the five-year-old. But she *is* his wife, and we can conclude that they've been married long enough for her to resist fun and games at odd hours.

A five-year-old and not a five-year-old. A twelve-year-old and not a twelve-year-old. A full-grown functioning male and not a full-grown functioning male. Langdon was and was not all three at once, with nary a seam showing. There was no nailing him, no naming him, no insisting that he settle down and be this or that. He was called "the baby" for convenience, but "baby" doesn't precisely describe the remaining two thirds of the incredibly imagined contradiction. As an idea, he would be monstrous. But he has escaped thought and become existential fact. He is up there on the screen an incontestable whole—not a collection of mismatched gags but an organic impulse charting its own unthinkable flight; and the fact that we cannot define him, pigeonhole him, teach him to see reason, becomes his tantalizing hold on us. He is, at his best, an enchanting unknowable, following his own inhibited toe-dance without apology for its peculiarities.

In fact, define him and you will kill him. It was his status as something that could not be, but was, that gave his audience its first, greatest pleasure.

Opposite: Just how old *was* this creature?

28. Langdon: Creating an Ambiguity

The ambiguity known as "the baby" had three midwives, Mack Sennett not really among them. Sennett did indeed discover Langdon, plucking him from a second-rate vaudeville act in which he had been tangling with a new and intractable automobile for close to twenty years. Even after Langdon left him, Sennett was extravagant in praise of his find. There is a 1928 interview with Sennett written by, of all people, Theodore Dreiser—preserved now in George C. Pratt's *Spellbound in Darkness*—in which Sennett calls Langdon "the greatest of them all." The remark obviously startled Dreiser. "Yes, greater than Chaplin," Sennett went on. "He's terribly funny to me. On the other hand, Langdon knows less about stories and motion picture technique than perhaps any other screen star. If he isn't a big success on the screen, it will not be because he isn't funny, but because he doesn't understand the many sides to picture production. He wants to do a monologue all the time. . . ."

Yet when he first hired Langdon, Sennett hadn't the faintest notion of what to do with him. He had a hunch, he was stubborn about it, and he then washed his hands of it, assigning to his staff the task of turning an already aging, essentially slow-moving, thoroughly un-Sennettish wool-gatherer into some sort of film comedian. The staff balked. Capra recalls going into the screening room to see a filmed record of Langdon's vaudeville act. He saw a man who already worked in a retarded rhythm: "Harry got out to survey the steaming, panting new car. Slowly—very slowly—like a child trying to calm a cranky pet, he patted it gently on the radiator. The ornery tin can roared, popped, and lunged at him. Harry turned and ran for his life, holding the brim of his hat in both hands. . . .[He] came back sheepish and wary." How was anyone to adapt this butterfly flutter to the breakneck requirements of the studio's stock fare?

Capra's memory, by the way, is probably doing what memory so often does: superimposing late images on earlier ones. Photographs of the vaudeville act show Harry dressed in chauffeur's uniform, with a cap that has a peak but no brim to grasp. And as a trio was gradually formed—director Harry Edwards, Capra, and companion gag-man Arthur Ripley—to develop the new employee's career, there is no indication that Langdon was immediately seen as "different" from any other racing zany in the lot's stable. He is at once engaged in regulation Sennett business: throwing beach balls at bathing girls, sliding on a shoe-store ladder toward and through a window until he winds up frantically straddling a flagpole, putting his head under a photographer's hood only to discover that a pestiferous child has put a skunk under it first.

In *Picking Peaches*, the first short film, the comedian is not even really baby-faced. His face is oval and rather abnormally white, but no more so, say, than Bobby Vernon's was. His mouth glides upward at the corners to make a demure "V," but somewhat less emphatically than Billy Dooley's did. Langdon seems, if anything, a cross between the two men. Strictly speaking, his mouth is a standard vaudeville mouth, two wings flown upward from a pucker; Eddie Foy had the most extravagant of these. Langdon is nattily dressed, sporting straw hat, cane, and carnation; his hair is sleeked down with a sharp part in the middle. His eyes are wide enough but not yet the least sleepy. If there is a slight bulge to the left cheek, it is not from baby fat; it more nearly suggests a chap who has spent a sinful youth chewing tobacco. His flirtations with girls at the beach are accomplished, the critical look in his eyes as he surveys a fashion parade is altogether sophisticated, and the energy with which he batters down a door to get at an oversized fellow who may have compromised his wife is Sennett energy *un*compromised.

There are just two faint suggestions of the Langdon to come. Having successfully flirted with a girl under a beach umbrella, Harry curls up in her lap, rather as though what he'd really been looking for was a motherly cuddle. The flicker of oddity breaks stride with the routine gagging. Later, when someone happens to tickle his nose with a feathered fan, he instantly puts palm and all five fingers to it, in a directionless spasm, as though his motor control weren't secure enough to guide him to any one particular itch. Again we are slightly surprised; we almost seem to see jam on his face.

These are oddities in passing, not yet distinctive character traits. I find even fewer in his second film, *Smile, Please*: here Harry is almost completely involved in vigorous brawls with children and with Sennett trickery that blows a vast rug up off the floor when he happens to sneeze. But I mention those oddities I can find because I suspect they were precisely the first flashes of illumination that were granted the men guiding him.

Capra is given principal credit, correctly, I'm sure, for ultimately shaping Langdon's style. Yet the image that was arrived at after only six or seven more films cannot have been entirely imposed. Langdon, at maturity, is too deeply imbedded in what he does to have been directly instructed in his unaccountable behavior—too dependent on aberrant and aborted impulses that come out of him not as gags but as imprisoning idiosyncrasy. What Capra and associates did, I think, was to watch him intensely for the least trace of distinctive and identifying mannerism, and then to lure him on, encouraging him to expand what had scarcely been conscious, to formalize what had popped out at random. It was a matter of teasing a man *into* himself, coaxing and editing and taking care *not* to impose too much—until a hidden nature, an undeveloped intuition, could flower into preposterous expression. Capra says that Langdon never did understand the character that was drawn out of him. Certainly the films Langdon made under his own direction, without the team, bear Capra out.

By the tenth short film, *All Night Long*, the daring composite was cutting its teeth. Harry begins the film as married man and father, conventionally dressed. He

There is little to distinguish Harry in this early Sennett from the equally pop-eyed and just as well-armed rival comedians on the lot.

still wears a straw hat; the characteristic Langdon hat, which looks like a popover that is beginning to deflate, is yet to come. But in a flashback to World War I, we meet the complex and contrary Harry. Sergeant Vernon Dent has been asked to dinner with a French family and told to bring a companion; he can't find another doughboy who hasn't a date. Harry hasn't a date and would like very much to go, but Dent ignores him as one would ignore a child in the circumstances. Though Harry is sidling casually past him, back and forth, back and forth, then strutting wistfully to call attention to his presence, Dent simply can't *see* him. Harry first adopts a sitting position, then finds something to sit on, directly under Dent's indifferent nose. *Nothing* will bring him within range of Dent's consciousness. A first principle has been established: if Langdon is to be believable when behaving like an infant, other people must treat, and dismiss, him as one.

In the end, Harry begs, and Dent gives in. As the French family settles to dinner, its oldest member nods in slumber. The nod is mistaken as a signal for grace, and all heads bow. The "grace" proves a long one. Harry, hungry, furtively plucks at one of the dishes ready for serving. Dent, lifting his eyes long enough to see what Harry is up to, slaps his hand. Harry contritely reverts to solemnity, then can stand it no longer. As stubby fingers reach out toward a casserole, he shields one eye with his free hand—if *he* can't see what he is doing, no one else can, either. His tactics prove immature, and he is slapped again.

Yet this is the film in which the daughter of the family gives him a kiss so devastating that it drops him, in glorious daze, through a window. And, as we leave the flashback, we learn that it is he, and not Dent, who has won the girl. The three ages of Harry are subtly fusing.

The development is erratic. In a comedy made immediately afterward—Sennett never did mind titles like *The Sea Squawk*—the carefully nursed impossibility is almost completely discarded, and Harry is seen in kilts and tam when he is not cavorting about in crinolined drag. The matter of female impersonation is instructive. I have come across a film rental catalogue which suggests that Langdon, in hoop skirts and pantalettes, looks rather like Lillian Gish. He doesn't. He looks like flattened dough, encased by frills, ready to be baked into a gingerbread man. His actual sex is never more evident than in bonnet and curls; the effect is coarse and unattractive. There is, however, a curious kinship with Miss Gish. Take any of his characteristic films and follow it directly with, say, *Broken Blossoms* and you are apt to be somewhat startled. The insecure, unfinished, plaintively bewildered gestures that Miss Gish managed to make so touching are in fact very like Langdon's comic repertoire. One cannot help suspecting that, however unconscious the adaptation may have been, the comedian at one time or another incorporated certain of the actress's grace-notes into his own burgeoning incongruity.

The incongruity was wholly established, as secure as it ever would be, before Langdon left Sennett—certainly with one of the last short films, the three-reel and quite perfect *Saturday Afternoon*. Dent has talked the married Harry into accompanying him on a joy ride with two girls, though Harry is due home with his weekly paycheck. Before going home, Harry pauses, mesmerized, to watch Dent kiss his date over a garden fence, studying the process as raptly as though he himself weren't thoroughly married. Then he does go home to his wife—has he never kissed her?—with some hope of escaping later on. His entrance, with the scold waiting impatiently, is true Langdon. He comes into the room, but barely, not advancing toward his waiting wife. He smiles his twinkling smile of welcome, which is unreciprocated. He wavers. He tries the door, testing it firmly to make sure he has closed it behind him. He has. There is a chair beside it. He sits, looking up

Harry begins, with his fingers, to register his own kind of alarm, but he is still a natty boulevardier with little of the "baby" about him.

Opposite: Harry doing his Sennett-duty with the bathing girls—and without much character of his own to guide him.

at his wife. He waves to her, pleasantly. He attempts to drape himself on the chair nonchalantly but has difficulty crooking his arm over its back. He rises to adjust a picture on the wall beside the chair, then sits again, slapping his knees as if to say, "Well, how *are* you?" There is a long pause. Then he rises and offers to shake hands.

He is working very, very slowly now; conveying his rhythm in words is like trying to construct a musical line out of rests. But another principle has been established. If Langdon is to take so long, while doing so little, a tension must be arranged around him. Here the tension is provided by the sustained and unresponsive, hence forbidding, presence of his wife. At its simplest, it is a matter of tying a lighted stick of dynamite to a man incapable of making a decisive move; with the fuse growing shorter, hesitation is funny. But the tension, the pressures inside which he is hopelessly suspended, must be there; otherwise, as occasionally happens in a Langdon film, the light goes out and we find ourselves staring at an immobility—a flaccid immobility—that amuses us not at all.

Even Langdon must move at last if a comedy is to have a climax. But to move he must be freed of his inhibitions; he is never freed of his charming awkwardness. Freeing him is normally done by stunning him, by one or a series of consciousness-shattering blows. James Agee has written evocatively of the habits of silent film comedians under the impact of blows. Pointing out that, in talking films, the most a stunned clown does is to look sleepy, he goes on to say that "when a silent comedian got hit on the head he seldom let it go so flatly. . . . he might make a cadenza of it—look vague, smile like an angel, roll up his eyes, lace his fingers, thrust his hands palms downward as far as they would go, hunch his shoulders, rise on tiptoe, prance ecstatically in narrowing circles until, with tallow knees, he sank down the vortex of his dizziness to the floor, and there signified nirvana by kicking his heels twice, like a swimming frog." The passage describes almost exactly Langdon's conduct once he finally enters the fray in *Saturday Afternoon*, rushing futilely to Dent's aid when two thugs try to take their girl friends from them. Once Harry has been sublimely dispensed with and has crawled away between two parked cars, he curls himself up on the running-board of one, his knees resting peacefully on the other. Naturally, both cars are started, racing each other through city streets, with an unaware Harry serving as the hyphen between them. Notice that the film is now moving, though Harry isn't.

Moving Langdon through feature-length films ought to have proved more of a problem than it did. The shift to major status was made in 1926 with *Tramp, Tramp, Tramp*, and *Tramp, Tramp, Tramp* cannily takes care of that particular matter with its episodic, automatically on-the-go format. The film is built around a race, a walking race from somewhere in the east to California, and no matter where we may pick Harry up—wandering lost in a sheepfold, caught stealing chickens with his face a smear of blackberries, doing time in a prison camp, entering a deserted town unaware that a cyclone is on the way—we are conscious of the fact that steep hills have had to be negotiated, watermelon patches explored, deserts crossed. What is to me the film's most satisfying gag grows directly from the need to move Langdon without his consent. He is escaping, along with his fellow convicts, from the prison camp, and, as all race to a passing freight train, Harry is naturally last to arrive, ball and chain still cradled in his arms. He skips sideways to keep pace with the moving car, hoping to hop in; the door slides shut in his face. But just ahead there is a low-slung coal car. He hoists the heavy ball into it, preparing to climb in after. At this point the car comes uncoupled from the rest of the train and speeds on alone, Harry running alongside in a game effort to keep up, literally chained to a world in motion.

Forty miles later, as a title tells us, the car glides at last to a stop; Harry is able to retrieve the ball and sit on a rock to rest his burning feet. As it happens, the chain is now draped over the rail just in front of the rear wheels. When the car begins to glide away again, it cuts the chain cleanly. Harry, however, hasn't noticed this, hasn't even noticed that the car has moved; he is too preoccupied with his feet. The first thing he does notice is his principal rival, the world champion walker, striding confidently up a hillside ahead. In an instant, Harry has gathered up the ball and is racing up the hill after him, carrying with him matter-of-factly the now unnecessary burden he is so accustomed to.

More familiar, because it is his variant on Lloyd, is the business of climbing a high fence to escape a sheepfold and then snagging his bulky wool walking-sweater on a nail once he is on the other side. Naturally he fusses to free the sweater. Then, in a decidedly delayed double-take, he notices that below him is a sheer drop; he is suspended by a thread over a precipice, with heavy traffic far below. He does not try to regain the top of the fence, as Lloyd surely would have done. Instead he immediately begins wrapping more threads of the sweater about the nail. It does not occur to him to make a stab at getting out of there; his instinct, always, is to fix himself firmly in place, any place. He can be relatively ingenious about this. Taking a hammer from his pocket, he begins drawing nails from the corner-join of the fence and hammering them *into* his sweater, one after another. Unfortunately, the practice eventually loosens the corner-join altogether, so that Harry finds himself fastened to a stretch of fencing that is flapping freely in the wind and steadily uprooting itself. We have here no permanent kingdom. I am sorry to say that at this point the film cheats, and Harry, with his segment of fence serving as surfboard, goes sliding down an incline that simply wasn't there earlier.

Still more interesting is what happens when Harry is confronted with a kind of leading lady he hasn't had before, the young Joan Crawford, then new to films. In his short comedies the women had helped to protect Langdon's ambiguity by being in some way beyond him: the wives were shrewish or motherly, the queens wicked, the Frenchwomen arbitrarily aggressive. The actual sexual role of his women tended to be as puzzling as his own, the relationship between parties left unstated.

With Miss Crawford, however, he was given a wholly plausible leading woman who might have done for Harold Lloyd and who could scarcely have been expected to fall plausibly in love with Harry. Curiously, the ambiguity holds. Harry falls in love with her face on billboards, spectacularly reveals his love on meeting her, wins her as he wins the race. The film's final shot is of the two of them, married, staring through a garden window at their first-born in a cradle. The first-born is also played by Harry.

Apparently this particular "happy" ending had not been originally planned for the film; the decision to let Harry win Miss Crawford seems to have been made during production. And the relationship must seem unthinkable now. If it could be cheerfully accepted at the time, it was because Langdon had reached a stage in his development at which he was so confidently the master of his mannerisms, so authoritatively at home in his three-layered construct, that he could dominate a

The fully developed, three-level Harry acquires a ball and chain he finds hard to part with. *Tramp, Tramp, Tramp.*

In *The Strong Man*, Harry found his perfect love: a girl who couldn't see him.

leading lady as firmly as he could dictate what we were to watch. His presence was stronger than hers; the best she could do was be nice and tag along.

Director Edwards and staff were exceedingly careful. There is a very long, incredibly accomplished pantomime sequence in which Harry meets his true love for the first time. He has adored her image from afar, has nailed her pictures by the dozens to his walls, has even tucked one under his blanket. At the moment, he is sitting on a park bench, mooning. She approaches, he looks up casually, does his double-take. She is there. He leaps into the air. The dawn of a smile is erased in terror. His knees give but he is able to jelly them straight again. He shivers. A grip on the hat brim calms him. Ineffectually affecting nonchalance, he strolls away, eyes peering back over his shoulder, hands locked behind him. His saunter done, he puts his spine against a tree for support and stares. He places his hands on his hips, as if to say, "Now what are *you* doing here?" in a most sociable way. He comes closer, bending, gets down on hands and knees to peer up into her face. Swiftly retreating, he sits on the bench, convivial host at a party, stricken child forbidden the party. His knees are apart and he spreads his hands over them, chin tilted in pleasant inquiry. The fact is that he would *never* speak if she didn't finally seat herself on the bench, assume that he can be made attentive, and seriously begin telling him how he may enter the walking race. He is attentive, though scarcely to her words; his eyes, or what can be got into the corners of them, are on her face, in tentative gratitude and mortal disbelief.

Edwards shot the entire scene from *behind* Miss Crawford, so that we should never see her reactions at all. Langdon is performing, really, for us, and so long as we are being entertained she will simply have to take care of herself. She does, pleasantly, straightforwardly, throughout the film. For most of it, she sees very little of Harry. She is usually waiting for him to complete a lap of the journey, while he is making comedy along the road. The one kiss they exchange is fleeting indeed: we happen to see it because the front of a house is blown away by a cyclone and, given the circumstances, the two disengage swiftly. If Langdon is in command of his improbable identity, that identity is also being shielded from possibly hazardous romantic prying.

The issue was even more successfully met in his next film, *The Strong Man*. This time the girl is blind. Harry is a Belgian soldier-boy in World War I who has been receiving letters from an American girl, though the girl, protecting the secret of her blindness, has never given him her address. When Harry is literally hauled to America after the Armistice, appropriated by a muscular showman to assist in a vaudeville act known as Zandow the Great, he devotedly begins his search for the girl who has been so kind to him. He begins it, characteristically, by sitting on a street corner in New York and comparing every girl who passes with the sadly creased photograph he holds in his hands. He does try a bit harder, stopping possible candidates to ask, "Are you Mary Brown?"; but this practice makes him a public nuisance, and he retires to his roost. In due time the vaudeville act plays a small town named Cloverdale, where Mary is the minister's daughter, engaged with her father in a losing battle against the Prohibition-era bootleggers who have thoroughly corrupted the once idyllic community. Mary and Harry *will* meet, and Harry will, single-handedly and in spite of himself, rout the bootleggers.

Harry Edwards had departed, breaking up the team that had guided Langdon through nearly twenty-four short comedies and a first successful feature. With *The Strong Man*, Frank Capra took over as both director and principal writer, and the young Capra's gifts are immediately apparent. *The Strong Man* is structurally sounder than anything in which Langdon had previously appeared. Good and evil are simplified in the somewhat sentimental Capra manner—a title tells us that

"justice and decency have fled" before a new law, "money"—but the gradual interweaving of the two lovers' stories has a cat's cradle inevitability that still leaves ample open space, geometrically arranged, for the comedy. The comedy itself acquires a new visual gloss and scale: entering a waiting room on Ellis Island, Harry inadvertently tips forward the last of a series of curved benches; each topples the one before it with nightmare regularity, so that we seem suddenly in a world of liquid dominoes, poor Harry running just behind the moving crest, arms outstretched to halt the unhaltable dissolution.

Capra, obviously entranced by his star, gives him extraordinary "monologue" room, holding the camera on him and letting him improvise while guarding him against monotony by the growing narrative pressures of the fable. Harry can use up as much footage as he likes, in long-shot, trying to shoo away an adventuress who is bent on luring him into her apartment building. She is pretending to be Mary Brown; the pretense keeps the story alive while Harry flinches, stamps an uncertain foot, flaps his paws, ponders and ponders.

There is a close-up sequence on a bus that runs for nearly eight minutes—eight minutes in which Harry does little more than medicate himself for a bad cold and fail to prevent himself from sneezing on the other passengers. The sequence is prime Langdon: once Harry has been angrily rebuked by a male passenger for removing a mustard plaster in public—interestingly, there is no attempt to disguise the manly hair on Langdon's chest—the comedian summons up all the resentment that is in him, which is very little, narrows his eyes dangerously, doubles the fist that seems glued to his sides, and debates indefinitely whether he will slaughter the fellow. We are free to laugh at the mock murder in his eyes, sustained so long; we know that the bus is coming into Cloverdale.

But the happiest inspiration of all is the girl's blindness. Chaplin used the device in *City Lights* to disguise his poverty. Here it is used to disguise Langdon's

A newcomer to films, Joan Crawford, finally calms the adoring Harry in *Tramp, Tramp, Tramp.*

identity. When the leading lady can't *see* the leading man, he can be anything, even Harry Langdon. Romance is home free, no questions asked. Add to this the fact that the girl herself is in part incapacitated, and the marriage of charmed misfits is without impediment. The perfect answer had been found—an answer that could only be given once—to any and all questions that might be raised about Harry's human standing.

The meeting of the two is beautifully handled. Harry is backstage, going about his chores. He needs water and is told by a stagehand that there is a well in the churchyard beyond. "Ask Mary Brown," the stagehand says. Harry goes rigid, spectacularly so. Who? The name is repeated. Harry shakes himself to life, tiptoes to the back door, peeps out. There, in the garden, is Mary. He shuts the door, and his heart seems to take leave of him, his senses following directly: he darts in five directions, slides down a wall to a sitting position on the floor, leaps for his jacket, leaps for his pail, races toward the door. Two steps from it, and without visible transition, the jackrabbit scamper turns to an effortless stroll. I don't think even Chaplin ever shifted rhythm more absolutely, more mysteriously.

Harry enters the garden, standing at some distance from the girl. She hears him speak, turns her head toward him. Supposing that she can see, Harry now presents himself for approval, displaying his worldliness by jauntily striding in review, skipping a little to express his elation, smiling benignly and offering himself whole. Is she perhaps interested in the merchandise? Something in her face halts him. Then she has turned away and gone to sit by a tree, silent. Harry's head tilts. Has he been rejected, after all this?

Capra elides what might have been mawkish in the situation by a dissolve that finds the two of them seated by the tree, laughing happily now that the truth of her blindness is known and of no matter. Having found the girl he wanted, Harry is neither retiring nor ignorant; he knows what he wants to do, and, allowing for reflexes that aren't entirely coordinated, means to do it. He runs his finger along the line of her arm, half an inch away, would like to put his hand to her face; he doesn't quite dare that. Her hand is on the bench. On an inspired impulse, he puts his hat over it. Then, after a suitable social interval, he puts his hand under the hat, too, and there they hold hands.

It is because of an insult to Mary that the film's climactic action begins—a wildly inventive fracas in the town saloon—and Harry is, as he always must be, lured into action. He will wind up swinging wildly on a trapeze over the heads of rioting thugs, yanking an act-curtain loose from the stage on one of his great arcs so that it covers the embattled throng, walking on the curtain that is now a sea of covered, bobbing heads, and at last blowing the saloon's four walls apart with his vaudeville cannon.

But his greatness must be thrust upon him. He has shaken a finger at Mary's detractors and been knocked down twice. It is only when he is picked up bodily by a looter to be thrown like a missile at the mob that he is put within reach of the trapeze; suddenly he is off. He remains a man who needs a boost.

He needs more than that. At the end of the film he is the village policeman, kissing Mary behind a tree and sending her home while he goes his rounds. Mary would much prefer to accompany him, but that doesn't strike him as seemly. Mary pouts. He gives in. Together, arm in arm, they start off on official patrol. He promptly falls off the sidewalk. Blind Mary has to help him up and lead the way.

The Strong Man, with its trace of sentiment and its sometime irony, was Langdon's most successful film. But 1927 was coming, and with it a strange halt to the development. *Long Pants*, the next film, was popular, though one can sense in it intimations of danger. *Three's a Crowd* was the heartbreaker.

At the mercy of a rioting mob in *The Strong Man*, Harry is about to take off on a trapeze.

Below: He ends the turmoil by creating a bigger one of his own, blowing out the saloon walls with a vaudeville cannon.

29. Langdon: The Ambiguity Dissolves

After an astonishing rise and three successful features, Harry Langdon failed because he let the ambiguity come apart. The destruction of an ambiguity is almost as subtle a process as its creation. But let's try to be simple about it: an ambiguity courts destruction whenever any one of the contrary elements that make it up becomes too literally defined, too specific. Let Langdon *really* become a "baby," *really* a five-year-old, *really* a twelve-year-old, *really* a full-grown man, and the tantalizing composite collapses, leaving one strain dominant and that strain either implausible or unattractive.

Warning might have been taken from the final shot of *Tramp, Tramp, Tramp*, that in which Langdon appears as an infant in a crib. Capra and his associates had all along been careful to keep the adult in Langdon in plain view; to do anything else would have been to defy reason, since the man was a man and there was no mistaking the fact. In a late two-reeler, *Fiddlesticks*, Harry might sit waiflike on a curbstone playing his bass viol for coins, only to have whole apartment houses turn on him and hurl pots and pans at his head. He might then innocently be taken into partnership with a junk dealer, who is well able to use the pots and pans with Harry serving as lure. Having been taught to weigh the thrown objects on the junk dealer's scale, Harry, with boyish ardor, immediately weighs everything in sight, including a steamroller. But when Harry, at last rich, returns home, he is wearing a top hat, smoking a cigar, carrying a cane, and sporting three wristwatches. His age remains an instant variable—and his secret.

But seeing him in a crib draws the line too firmly, abandons the secret for a momentary certainty. Having so often heard Langdon called "the baby," the team about him no doubt thought it would be fun to accommodate the popular label and display him as one, briefly. The display, however, is merely grotesque. Ironically, Langdon seems less a baby here than he ever has. As he rocks in his oversized cradle, twiddling his fingers over an elongated nipple he can't quite get hold of, bouncing a rubber ball off the nearest wall only to have it return with a thump to his bonneted head, he is no longer an undefinable yet *present* apparition, he is a heavily made-up vaudevillian doing a "stunt" turn. This is not fantasy, it is direct impersonation. The creature in the cradle is an impostor.

It didn't matter at the time, in part because the film was riding home on its residual laughter, in part because the business was offered as no more than a quick gag, in part because another aspect of the character—the mature Harry—was to be seen looking on through a window. In this last there is a faint indication of a split between two Harrys, but it isn't marked enough to do real damage.

With *Long Pants*, however, the move toward undue definition takes another turn. We first see Harry's hand removing a cheap romantic novel from the shelves of the Oak Grove Public Library. We follow his progress, by hand only, as he returns home, closing the garden gate behind him, cautiously opening the front door, stealing up the attic stairs and locking himself in. Finally we see him whole as he reads and dreams of the spectacular love affairs he is one day going to have. He is in short pants, he wears a bow tie, the boyish forelock on his brow is emphatically in evidence. He hears girls laughing on the street outside. He goes to the window, moons after them, regrets that his mother and father have not yet permitted him to come of age, nerves himself to whistle at the girls and is scoffed at for his presumption. But not long after, the great day comes: he is given his first long trousers.

There is good comedy to be got out of pinning Langdon to this just-past-puberty stage. When a limousine breaks down outside his house, Harry is quick to notice the woman seated in it, impatiently waiting for her chauffeur to make repairs. She is precisely what Harry has dreamed of: the city siren of lurid fiction, infinitely knowing, infinitely desirable. Harry walks his bicycle out to the lane and stands draped against it to display his badge of maturity—the trousers—for the jeweled Circe in the car. He must woo her. He woos her by stunting on his bicycle, around and around the car, one foot high in the air. He rides the handlebars for her, doubling his speed when she gives him a conventionally approving glance; he has talents, and passion may come of them. The sequence is marred by having been shot against a badly painted studio backdrop, but it has its points.

Yet we are aware that Langdon *is* being pinned down; I think that audiences sensed it at the time and were puzzled, put off a bit by a bare-kneed Harry at the window proclaiming himself a stated age. The age was definite: at that time boys got their first long trousers at twelve or thirteen, depending on the stubbornness of their parents. I had my own troubles. It wasn't until a younger child had come up to me on a street corner one day and asked, "Are you a boy or a man?" that I developed the courage—it wasn't courage, it was rage—to charge home and demand my release from knickerbockers. I was thirteen.

In *Long Pants*, then, Langdon is thirteen—and, for a time, nothing else. But that takes something of the comedy away, for what was funny was a man behaving like a thirteen-year-old, not a thirteen-year-old behaving like one. Belief in the image is diminished as well, for what we see is still a man, pretending. The drift toward explicitness—generally a drift toward defining Langdon as child rather than man—is risky; what had intrigued us, and had resisted our initial itch for an explanation, was now yielding to literalness, letting the composite crack.

The film saved itself with its audiences, I think, by a bit of sleight-of-hand. Suddenly, after having firmly established Harry as thirteen, it proposes that he is *also* old enough to be married, and right away. Harry's parents are determined that he shall marry a local girl, while Harry wishes to pursue the mysterious lady of the limousine.

The transition is not accounted for; it is simply made. With it, the ambiguity is restored—late, but restored. Now Harry is free to confound us again with his

impenetrability. On the day of his wedding to the local miss, and with his head still full of the Graustarkian romances he has been reading, he decides to take his bride-to-be for a stroll through the forest, there to shoot her. He must nerve himself to a studied ferocity even to think of it, but he does think of it and he does persuade the girl to go. In the forest, there are difficulties. For one thing, there are signs tacked to trees here and there saying "No shooting." Harry doesn't want to do anything illegal. He also has trouble keeping the prepared revolver hooked properly, killer-style, into his belt. It keeps slipping down into his trousers, which makes it difficult for him to walk. He remains considerate. When he has talked the girl into playing a game of hide-and-seek so that she will turn her face to a tree-trunk while he slips ten paces away to draw a bead on her back, he first pauses to make a bed of leaves where she is likely to fall. Between the pause and his tendency to let the pistol slip out of his hands there is quite enough time for the girl to complete the count agreed on, turn from the tree, and happily catch him. Discovering the pistol, she is delighted; the spirit of the game is still upon her. The sequence ends with her firing steadily away, engaged in target practice, while Harry sits ruefully contemplating the ruin of his dreams.

The sequence, like the film, is filled out with gags that are no more than gags—Harry brushes into barbed wire, catches his foot in a bear trap—though much of *Long Pants* makes imaginative use of his near-immobilized face. Langdon was normally not photographed from behind or in profile. Catching him from behind, with neck and jaw-line exposed, overaccented his actual age. In profile, he simply disappears and a most ordinary-looking creature, with blunted nose and low forehead, takes his place: there is a moment in *Tramp, Tramp, Tramp* when Harry turns sideways to tack a poster to a wall that is apt to bring a gasp from anyone schooled in Langdon, so little does this nonentity seem to resemble him. The familiar face was a flat one, all of its complexity contained in two dimensions, and it had to be recorded head-on for full effect.

It was during the filming of *Long Pants* that relations between Langdon and Capra became strained. "Our nuzzling days were few and far between," Capra reports: Langdon had been unprepared for the scale of his success, had been reading his favorable notices too ardently, had more or less decided that if he could be compared to Chaplin he could *become* Chaplin. Capra's recollection:

"'Pathos,' he'd scream at me, 'I want to do more pathos.'

"'Harry, the pathos is in your *comedy*. If you deliberately *try* for pathos, it'll be silly, believe me.'

"'I believe the New York writers. You know more'n they do?'"

Capra fought to preserve the style he had himself done so much to develop, as well as to maintain some authority as director, and was fired. Henceforth Langdon, who had become increasingly unmanageable on the set in any case, would direct his own films. The "little son of a bitch" was proving troublesome, and *could* he direct?

He could not. He was indecisive with a camera, clumsy as an editor, without any real grasp of the narrative pressures that had to encase him if his small solo flights were to be cheerfully tolerated. Yet *Three's a Crowd*, the first film that lists him as director, is very nearly an extraordinary film. It was and is a failure: it doesn't seize the pathos it all too obviously reaches for. But certain of its sequences are so bizarrely imagined, certain of its gags so architecturally solid, that one is bound to suspect that Capra had left Langdon a legacy: a partially prepared shooting script. I have asked Capra about this and he reports that he doesn't remember. "But I can tell you," he adds, "that in the previous Langdon features . . . it was customary to have our story and gag-men working on the next film before

Harry is bent on seduction, his bicycle his principal weapon. *Long Pants*.

we had finished with the ongoing one."

Seeing the film today makes the inference all but irresistible. I can think of nothing comparable to its "framing" gag, a long and quietly atmospheric opening sequence that merely sets the stage for the joke the film will end on, seventy minutes later. The camera looks down on a very ordinary city block, so early in the morning that the street lights are still glowing. A milk truck enters the deserted street; bottles are sleepily deposited at various stoops. As daylight increases and the milkman finishes his chores, the street lights go out. With a new day thus begun, we cut to Harry waking up in his attic room. As the film moves along, Harry will discover a woman—pregnant and abandoned—in the snow, stoop over her like a puppy, carry her to his room and care for her until the baby can be born. Toward the end of the film, without Harry knowing it, the woman's repentant husband will find wife and child and spirit them away. Harry wakes once more, this time to find them gone. Dismayed he rushes into the still-dark streets in his nightgown, searching vainly for his charges, a kerosene lamp held high in his hand to show the way. At last, his pace slowing forlornly, he wanders into the street we have seen at the beginning. Dawn is breaking, the pursuit hopeless. Harry stops. Surrendering to his loss, and noticing that it is now dawn, he blows out the lamp in his hand. At the same instant the street lights go out. Harry looks up, terrified. *He* has blown out the street lights and will surely be arrested. He runs from us in panic, nightgown flapping about his heels.

That is a most striking kind of architecture—not narrative architecture precisely but gag architecture so patiently planned and so extensive in scope that it holds the entire narrative firmly in place between the "plant" and the "payoff" of a single gentle jest. A joke wraps the film in its arms. There is a strong sense of visual architecture about *Three's a Crowd* as well—as in the startling, unsupported diagonal made by Harry's attic staircase against an utterly undecorated outside wall. The line is a single pencil-stroke against blank white paper, more bizarre in its patent reality and patent impossibility than anything out of *The Cabinet of Dr. Caligari*. It is functional, not mere paint; it looks best when the weather is snowy; it is the sort of staircase a child imagines when he first hears about heaven—not ethereal but practical, and resolutely straight up.

Surreal and solid at once, it is no accident of design. It leads to an attic and also to a sequence as odd as it is mysteriously authentic. Harry has grown fond of the woman and her infant; perhaps he will inherit both when the woman is well enough to leave her bed. But there is a husband, the father of that child, somewhere about. There *must* be, though Harry has never seen him. Worries of that sort disturb a man's sleep. When Harry sleeps—he has put himself to sleep in the process of trying to get the baby to doze off—the window curtains take to blowing wildly while the attic door flaps open and shut. A lamppost appears beside the mother's bed; it too is blown about by the wind. There is a face at the window, the face of a villain from melodrama, the father. The room becomes a vast boxing ring, the mother's bed one of its corners. The villain enters. The mother rises avidly, confesses her love for Harry, begs him not to let the father spoil their idyll. A single oversized boxing glove his only weapon, Harry meets the villain in the ring. With the lamppost dipping and swaying, the mother crying, the curtains billowing, Harry is counted out. Dream sequences were among the most common of silent film comedy's devices, but they were normally no more than easy transitions to transport the comedian to another place or time—where the action would seem exactly as real as it had in a waking state. This one dares a great deal more, creating subtle and startlingly *natural* nightmare out of mismatched commonplaces, binding together the varied substitutions that the subconscious makes with

Above, Harry arrives with rifle and drum for the new baby born in his attic.

Opposite: Harry is about to inherit the only family he will ever have. *Three's A Crowd.*

ease and a frightening rectitude. We look at the unstable juxtapositions and find them a persuasive whole. Someone's intuitions were telling him true.

The comedy is less secure. Langdon always had difficulty in finishing gags; without Capra to help snatch a finish out of the busy world around him, the comedian mires himself in a long "thrill" passage—he is hanging onto a blanket, several stories up, that is slowly slipping through a trapdoor—from which he can find no escape except to let himself drop. The thump is double.

Nor were Langdon's instincts any match for Chaplin's. In *City Lights* Chaplin is also caring for a girl who is both impoverished and ill. But Chaplin does not make the mistake of spending the lion's share of his time with the girl. Most of his time is spent trying to earn the money that will help her, which means that each new job he takes on can become a full-scale comedy routine. The comedy is up front, the pathos protected. Langdon, less canny, ties himself down to crib and bedside; there is less room for saving laughter there.

To be sure, while Harry is at work inside the domesticated room, he is capable of pleasant small mistakes. It is wintertime and the baby's diapers, taken off the clothesline outside, are quite frozen. To thaw one out, Harry places it on the kitchen table and begins to beat it flat with the blade of a small hatchet, much as a housewife might soften up the dough for a pie crust. Because Harry is chatting amiably with the bedded mother all the while, he continues his work routinely: he adds flour, adds filling, trims the crust. He ends up, to his absentminded dismay, with a perfectly splendid diaper pie.

But the film has two fatal defects: it means to wear its heart on its sleeve, always a dangerous proposition in comedy; and, to compound the difficulty, there is a hole in the sleeve where the heart should be. The hole is once again the result of ambiguity destroyed. The earlier and secure Langdon, the Langdon of three-ages-in-one, had often toyed with the notion of having children. "I'll soon be pushing a baby buggy around myself," he volunteers to a mother in *His First Flame*; however improbably, he then went ahead and had children.

In *Three's a Crowd* matters are different. From the outset Harry is not hopeful but wistful, noticeably downcast, among children. His boss's wife wants to cheer him up. Giving him an encouraging pat, she tells him to stop worrying, insisting that "There's a wife and child for every man." There is a two-way implication here. The boss's wife is clearly saying that Harry is the world's least likely candidate for marriage and fatherhood; she is urging him to count on a miracle. And Harry's response is plainly disbelieving. He knows better, knows—as he smiles plaintively—that he is doomed to go through life yearning and unsatisfied.

The ambiguity, with its various and cheerful options, is not only being rejected but is being rejected in a new way. The adult in Harry is explicitly scuttled; he is incapable of functioning as a man. But this reduction in his complexity does not really fasten him to either of his two other roles: the five-year-old or the twelve-year-old. A five-year-old would not be aware of the problem; a twelve-year-old, at puberty, would remain confident that sooner or later maturity would be his. Harry is being fixed—"fixed" is the appallingly right word—at yet another level.

What does the situation suggest? The only reasonable inference that can be drawn is that Harry is either impotent or sexually undeveloped, probably the latter. The figure that has so mystified us—delighting us in passing with sex-play that was simultaneously infantile and able—mystifies us no longer. Harry is in some sense a cripple, incomplete; the baby has never grown up, is never going to. But that leaves us with an image that is worse than literal: it is essentially disturbing. Yet the narrative depends absolutely upon the premise: Harry inherits another man's wife and child because he can only have a family by proxy.

Obviously this impalement of Harry to a butterfly-board came about as a result of his determination to be wept for. There had *seemed* to be a sort of pathos in his relationship with the blind girl in *The Strong Man*; critics had spoken of it. And so *Three's a Crowd* pulled out the stops. There is a rag doll in the film. Early on, Harry finds it in a trashcan, playfully tosses it in the air as a symbol of the child he will never have. Later, while Harry is finding and caring for his borrowed brood, the doll is seen lost in a gutter, battered by snow and rain. The doll is intercut, quite gratuitously, with Harry's progress as foster-father and his sense of impending loss. A dog gets the doll between his teeth, savaging it. It winds up above the street, caught in telephone wires. We can identify it with Harry's dream of fatherhood or with Harry himself; or with both. However we regard it, we recognize it as a plain case of begging.

Perhaps the doll would not recur so often if we were being more moved by Harry. We aren't, and not only because we are put off rather than touched by what has narrowed down to simple sexual incapacity. There is some question in my mind whether the Langdon character could ever have been a suitable object for the curious emotion we call pathos. Pathos is to be distinguished from pity. Pity is what we feel when confronted with disability or serious misfortune, and it moves us to try to help the victim; it is an active emotion. Pathos is a much more relaxed, meditative, and even contented state, essentially passive. Webster's quotes Coventry Patmore to the effect that pathos "is the luxury of grief; and when it ceases to be other than a keen-edged pleasure, it ceases to be *pathos*."

But this means that pathos is of necessity an adult emotion, not one felt by a child or normally for a child. We look at Chaplin, the experienced adult, philosophically; we see that he is in tatters but understand that he has come by the tatters logically, even by choice. Chaplin is no cripple. He has been everywhere, done everything. In mid-life he sighs: he has made himself what he is, the boats he has missed are the boats most of us have missed, the future is not likely to be different from the past, and aren't our mutual fates, mutual disappointments, odd? Nothing to be done about them but smile a knowing smile, shrug, and, with that little kick-step, go on. Pathos comes of a mature knowledge of life; it gives amused assent; it is an agreeable sadness. And it was probably ruled quite out of bounds for Langdon the day he first developed the inexperienced responses of a near-infant. We can't share wisdom with *him*.

Langdon can *only* be an object of amusement, really—he is altogether too unlikely to demand that we identify ourselves with him. The ambiguity in full sail was amusement enough; we hadn't asked him for anything more. By trying to give us more, he broke the ambiguity without being able to achieve the highly specific effect he had aimed at; the limited segment of his personality that he now stressed was all wrong for it. *Three's a Crowd* proved a commercial and critical failure—the disintegration of the character is cruelly hinted at in the *New York Times* reviewer's remark that certain sequences had "all the humor of Babe Ruth playing Peter Pan"—and Langdon panicked.

In a rush to retrieve his reputation as a comedian, and as no more than that, he tried reverting to straight gagging, modeling *The Chaser* all too closely on the Sennett three-reeler *Saturday Afternoon*—long after the earlier inspiration, and the companions who helped provide it, had departed. Once again there is a nagging wife, this time seconded by a nagging mother-in-law; once again Harry attempts to cope with his wife's shrill nagging on the telephone by inconclusively juggling the receiver at arm's length and even putting it in his pocket, where it burns him; once again he takes off with a crony—Bud Jamison standing in for Vernon Dent—to pick up some girls on a beach. Where he borrows from his bet-

The bid for pathos. Harry, in apron, uncomplainingly doing the dishes in *The Chaser*.

Below: Harry with the much-abused doll that becomes his alter ego in *Three's A Crowd*.

ter films, as he does from *Tramp, Tramp, Tramp*, he borrows what was worst in them: an automobile teeters on the brink of a sheer drop, goes over, plunges into a long bumpy ride down a nonexistent incline. Borrowing from Chaplin, he kills the joke. In *Sunnyside* Charlie, preparing his farm breakfast, placed a live chicken directly onto the frying pan, where it promptly laid the morning's egg. All dispatch. Harry, doing the same business, virtually strangles the prop chicken as he labors to press an egg from its innards.

Fundamentally, Langdon has now leapt to the other of his possible extremes, to the mature man who is exclusively that. He *is* a chaser, stealing out of the house nights to find women in local speak-easies. On the beach, he is devastating. He stands, in his lodge regalia, eyeing a girl until, apparently mesmerized, she comes to him. He kisses her, so manfully that she at once goes limp, one arm dangling loose; he puts the loose arm in his pocket. When he releases her from the kiss, she drops in a swoon. Turning to other prey, he selects a schoolmarm type—why?—and proves as fatal to her; she is left in a heap on the picnic grounds. There are no waivers here, no dreams to awake from. It is all happening, and we are to believe Harry sexually irresistible. Of course the complexity that had once made us laugh is shattered.

There is a forlorn attempt to reinstate it—though at the *Three's a Crowd* level—halfway through the film. Harry is doing the housework, in apron and dust-skirt, when a bill collector comes. Apparently a baby-crib has never been paid for. Harry decides that, rather than pay for it, it had best be returned. He runs upstairs and brings it down, still wrapped. It has never even been opened. Presumably Harry and his wife have been married for several years; the implication, however, is that they have never had sex. The moment would be maudlin in any context. Here it further serves to sever one aspect of Harry—the sexually incapable aspect, worrisomely developed in the previous film—from the new Lothario that unmistakably dominates the balance of this film.

The weave that went to make up Harry Langdon has now come unraveled everywhere, leaving only single strands to be doggedly, unamusingly, pursued. In the absence of a unified personality, desperation rules the gags: Harry sits on an egg, the pots and pans on a stove jump up and down when the gas is lighted, a chamber pot lands exactly over the bill collector's head with the trick-film precision always so disillusioning in Sennett. Langdon's insensitivity as his own director-editor can perhaps best be indicated by a single instance. Harry has decided to commit suicide, has assembled a variety of poisons from the shelf, has then inadvertently taken castor oil instead. Preparing to die, he stretches on the kitchen floor, covers himself with a sheet. The joke here—a very possible joke—involves keeping the camera immobile for Harry's long wait. We are to hold and hold and hold and hold until at last the surprised Harry is forced to rise again, not dead but in urgent need of a bathroom. But the comedian hasn't the courage of the gag or its necessary camera-work. Halfway through the shot, perhaps in fear that no audience would be able to endure so long a delay, he cuts from long-shot to medium-range, though there is still nothing more to see than Harry's draped form. Then he returns to the long-shot, as arbitrarily as he left it. But the joke is entirely dependent on the sustained delay; we can't even start laughing until the shot has been held beyond all reason. The cut kills the one thing that is essential to the comedy. The man making it is of two minds, or of none; he has clearly grown insecure.

My own memory and a small legend that has grown up both insist that the comedian made a partial recovery with his sixth and last feature, *Heart Trouble*. Alas, there is no way of knowing; the film—for the moment, at least—has disappeared. Partial recovery or not, Langdon's career had lost its momentum. The

Harry the demon lover of *The Chaser*, leaving the victims of his kisses where they fall.

Opposite: Back to the bathing beauties as he tries to recapture the Sennett formula for *The Chaser*.

releasing contract with First National had ended; after three commercial failures no major studio was ready to take him on as a star; sound-film was in any case well under way. Langdon lived on for another sixteen years, doing two-reelers for Hal Roach and lesser studios, appearing as support in other men's starring films, finally working in near-anonymity as a gag-man.

Something uniquely valuable had, at the very top, been clumsily aborted. Langdon at his best, and in the hands of men who understood better than he the indefinable impulse that moved him, was a genuine original, strangest by far of all the fantasists who walked real city streets. He must be looked at selectively today, with some sympathy for the lost language on which his furtive whisper depended. But even his minor films can catch the skeptical unawares. *Soldier Man*, a late three-reel Sennett, is a minor film, certainly not a film with which to begin one's acquaintance with Langdon. Still, there is a brief surprise in it that could have come from no other clown. Harry, newly made King for reasons that are entirely confusing to him, is asked if he has any orders to give. Eager to cooperate, and with the daze in his eyes giving way to a sneaky appreciation of his new powers, he suggests that it would be nice if a fellow who has been pestering him could have his head cut off. As his prime minister departs, ostensibly to do his bidding, Harry cocks his head slightly in deep contemplation, blinking slowly once or twice. Then the sweet smile forms. Suddenly, hands gripping the arms of the throne and feet shooting high in air, he is rocking wildly back and forth, whistling, infant monarch on his hobby-horse, a picture-book creature off to Banbury Cross with the highest of hearts. I never knew a child who didn't delight in decapitation.

30. The Demiclowns

In a 1921 feature-length comedy, *The Home Stretch*, Douglas MacLean sees that a little girl, no more than a tot, has strayed onto a racetrack, directly in the path of galloping horses. Leaping onto his own mount, he cuts across the field to scoop the child up in his arms before she can be trampled to death, taking a spill in the process. In another feature comedy of the same year, *Burn 'Em Up Barnes*, Johnny Hines is riding the rods of a freight train and sees that a child of three or four has wandered onto the railroad tracks, with locomotives bearing down in both directions. He stretches out from his perch directly above the racing wheels to snatch the child to safety as the great engines pass each other. There has been no prior relationship between child and comedian; nor does either film envision the developing companionship of *The Kid*. The successful catch is straight thrill, straight sympathy; no comic fillip adds a laugh to the rescue.

What kind of comedians are these? Their kind was legion throughout the twenties: performers who appeared in "comedies" but were only demiclowns themselves. What both men are doing in the instances above is the theatrical equivalent of "patting a dog" to establish themselves as virtuous, hence likeable. They had to if they were to survive, because, in most cases, their specifically comic talents weren't sufficiently outsized to command the sympathy of laughter on sight. Not for them the gratuitous cruelties of Chaplin, the emotional indifference of Keaton; they weren't free to patrol the universe as visitors from Grimm's Fairy Tales, answerable only to laws they had created for themselves, amoral as dreams. They had to function as the heroes of melodrama function, establishing their claims honorably, rescuing girls from buzz saws without so much as a thought for themselves and then nobly declining marriage if the girl should happen to have money. I notice that the American Film Institute's catalogue of films produced prior to 1930 describes their individual films, as often as not, as "melodramatic farces." MacLean himself, quoted in a *Photoplay* interview unearthed by Kevin Brownlow, offered his own formula: "Make it a bit of human drama—or humor—

that is going on before their eyes. I don't try to make my pictures comic. I try to make them entertaining."

I have called these men demiclowns not to suggest that their films were half as popular as those of the major fools—most had an impressive series of box-office successes—or even that they were half as talented, though of course that was the case. What drops them to second rank, or lower, really, is the fact that they only half understood, and half used, the medium into which they had so fortuitously stumbled. They were silent comedians who might have functioned equally well with sound, or on a stage. Their work is not distinctively, indelibly *silent*.

Very often their story materials were taken directly from the stage. Very often the laughter they got was heavily indebted to titles. For the most part they were good-looking, well-dressed performers who might *almost* have passed for straight leading men and women if there weren't—somewhere, somehow—something romantically lacking. Occasionally one or another would shuttle back and forth between drama and comedy. And, as a rule, they were studio products.

As the major studios came into being, committing themselves to the release of as many as fifty-two feature films per year *each*, there was an obvious need for the kind of comedian whose inspiration did not require nursing for unpredictable lengths of time, just as there was a need for the kind of comedian who did not arrogate too much authority to himself. A balanced yearly output wanted comedies, and wanted them on time. When the studios could temporarily capture one of the great clowns—letting him make his films independently and then simply serving as releasing agent—they did so. First National had snared Chaplin, losing him when United Artists was formed; Metro had always had an itch to get and keep Keaton; Lloyd, once he began producing on his own, released his films through Paramount. But these few men, even when they were not straying into United Artists as Keaton temporarily did, could scarcely keep the vast assembly line rolling, and the studios were forced to manufacture, or import from the theater, manageable stars of their own.

The Douglas MacLean mold—clean-cut, nattily derbied, flashing the white smile of a musical-comedy man—proved a staple, with Universal's Reginald Denny and, later, Metro-Goldwyn-Mayer's William Haines repeating its appeal. If MacLean had used racing cars, so would Denny, and William Haines would continue the sporting tradition by winning the football games of *Brown at Harvard* and the baseball games of *Slide, Kelly, Slide*. If these men bore any conceivable relationship to one of the major clowns, it was to Lloyd, who had done his own time in difficult dress suits and on football fields. But the owlish stamp of the glasses, isolating the awkward romantic from his breezily confident fellow men, together with the prolonged extravagance of the stunting, is conspicuously missing. There is nothing to prevent the demiclowns from winning the girl in reel one—nothing intrinsic, that is to say. Denny is something of a fashion plate, perfectly knotted tie always firmly in place. If his perennial sunniness belongs anywhere, it is in the reserved sort of farce that shades into comedy of manners—the high comedy that lives on epigram—which would have to wait for sound films to assert itself.

Johnny Hines is a bit less conventional than Denny, thanks to a grin that seems to crack his crinkled face in two and a tantalizing dual resemblance to Eddie Cantor and George M. Cohan, with a soupçon of something Oriental left over. He had come from the stage, had knocked about in films supporting Marie Dressler and others, had appeared in a film version of Cohan's *Little Johnny Jones*, and had finally seemed ripe for stardom after a particularly successful series of *Torchy* short comedies. He never abandoned the Cohanesque brashness, abet-

The normally impeccable Douglas MacLean being attended to by shocked valet Raymond Hatton. *The Hottentot*. Reginald Denny, with Marian Nixon on his arm, remaining unruffled in *What Happened to Jones*. Johnny Hines being winning over pancakes in *The Crackerjack* and with a contented infant in *Doggone Torchy*. Monty Banks acquiring a mail sack in *Play Safe*.

ted by a cheerily aggressive jaw and eccentric footwork that suggested, to the end, musical comedy. The plots were the go-getter stage patterns of the period: *Get-Rich-Quick Wallingford* done over and over again.

Hines did have a certain appetite for the whimsically improbable. In *The Speed Spook* a town is terrorized by a driverless car. The driver is Johnny, curled up where the engine should be; the film does not precisely say where the engine is *now*. In *The Crackerjack* he is a pickle salesman who discovers that his merchandise is being filled with bullets and shipped across the Mexican border; substituting cheese for the bullets, he becomes entangled in a revolution, battling his way up staircases and leaping from balconies like a minor-league Fairbanks.

A flash of visual invention interrupts the busy plotting now and again. Because Johnny is needed to drive the car in the big race, his father tries to get him out of jail. He can't: the jail is locked—even the sheriff has gone off to the track. In disgust, Johnny's father kicks the welcome mat before the jailhouse door. The key is under the mat. That's better than Reginald Denny's father getting *him* out of jail for the big race by straight bribery.

But Hines is all mainly "push, pluck, and providence," with incorrigibly punning titles left to carry the intended comedy. One speaks of "girls in their nicoteens"; another informs us that a chap is "rich enough to extend a cordial welcome and a welcome cordial." If Hines still seems an agreeable enough fellow, his films no longer provoke anything like laughter. They weren't built for gags, good or bad ones; they were built for speed. During the climactic auto race in *Burn 'Em Up Barnes*, even the normally static titles keep the action moving: behind the lettering we see painted automobiles whose wheels continue to spin frantically. In their own time the headlong rush of the films, together with the manufactured sympathy the leading figure had bestowed on himself, established a certain quasi-comic excitement. Perhaps it was comic only in the sense that it wasn't meant to be taken seriously.

No comedienne ever became a truly important silent film clown for many of the same reasons. Comediennes, from Mabel Normand all the way to Marion Davies, labored under an instant handicap: they had to be pretty. Constance Talmadge, Dorothy Gish, and Colleen Moore all were. The girl was expected to function as a *girl*, no matter what incidental nonsense she might be capable of; grotesques need not apply, except for supporting roles. Studios liked having people about who could be glamorous for Cecil B. De Mille in January and acrobatically amusing for, say, Clarence Badger, in March: Bebe Daniels provided Paramount with just such a "swing" performer. So far as I know Miss Daniels's *Senorita*, directed by Mr. Badger, is lost, but it is a film that I should very much like to find—with my fingers crossed. Crossed fingers are advisable in returning to youthful memories of the now-and-again clowns, the clowns-by-courtesy. Marion Davies's mentor, William Randolph Hearst, is known to have protested whenever a *too* comic role was proposed for his star, and this has given rise to a legend that Miss Davies was a superb comedienne wasting her time in romantic trash. Reacquaintance with King Vidor's *Show People*, the film in which Mr. Hearst refused to permit Miss Davies to take a pie in the face but finally and reluctantly allowed her to be doused with seltzer-water, does little to bear out what, I am afraid, is wishful thinking. Forcing a genuinely pretty face into the extravagances of silent mime produces mugging: one must look like Chaplin or Langdon to work small. *Show People* is actually stolen from the too-hard-working Miss Davies by comedy-juvenile William Haines, characteristically underplaying and making certain we feel for him. The vehicles of most comediennes were adaptations from the stage: if Constance Talmadge could make *Dulcy*, Miss Davies could make *The*

Comediennes might be talented, but they also had to be pretty. Above: Constance Talmadge in an all-purpose portrait.

Opposite: Dorothy Gish in *Susan Rocks the Boat*.

Comediennes at work. Colleen Moore with a stern Milton Sills in *Flaming Youth.* Marion Davies with an enraged Marie Dressler in *The Patsy.*

Opposite: Syd Chaplin finally became a feature film star in his own right, with female impersonation a recurring though not exclusive trademark. *Oh, What a Nurse!*

Patsy, once more with the wit imbedded in the printed words between shots.

Melodrama took up the slack with women as it had with men. Mabel Normand's most successful feature, the early *Mickey*, was felt, on completion, to be too much of a stylistic muddle and was withheld from the market, escaping the shelf when it was accidentally shipped to a theater in place of another film that had been booked. Then the miracle happened: by midafternoon there were lines in the street outside the lucky house; *Mickey* went on to become so popular with theater owners that it was dubbed "the mortgage-lifter." Audiences did not care what it *was*; they simply liked it. Technically a comedy because it permits the playful Miss Normand to struggle with a toppling grandfather clock and to skate about the highly polished floors she ought to be dusting, *Mickey* does not in the least mind including—it is forced to include—a steeplechase in which Miss Normand is thrown from her horse short of the finish-line and a raging hero-villain battle in an attic while the actress dangles perilously from the roof-edge outside. Perhaps I should add, without malice, that silence itself was no woman's *métier*; the suitably archetypal Marie Dressler was actually a failure in silent films and a thundering success the moment she could speak. There are no women clowns in circuses.

It is possible that an important comedian can always be recognized by what is now called his *shtick* and what the Italians would once have called his *lazzi*: the highly personal, physically improbable tricks and turns that would identify him even if he were masked. Chaplin's shuffle and cane-flip, Keaton's instantly reversible walking and running rhythms, Langdon's palm jackknifed open in welcome are all mannerisms that have been endlessly imitated because they summon up the whole man so rapidly, asserting his uniqueness even in his absence.

The comedians—and comediennes—of whom we have been speaking were marked by no such telltale idiosyncrasies, habits of eye, hand, and spine that might recur in any situation and be funny because they were inappropriate to all. It is almost impossible now to describe a once-popular comedian like Monte Banks by speaking of his mannerisms; he doesn't seem to have any. He is short, on the plump side, possessed of a miniature mustache that would seem suave on a head waiter but is somehow a badge of apprehension on him. He is likeable. But, after a long and rigorous training at Warner Brothers and elsewhere, when he came to make features independently he took refuge in "thrill" comedies that owed a great deal to Harold Lloyd. Let it be said that he made these legitimately: in *Play Safe* he lowers himself by a rope from the roof of a runaway train toward the open door of a boxcar, letting the girl climb first on him and then up the rope while he sways precariously over embankments, bridges, and mountainside drops that are unmistakably authentic. The stunting is impeccable, worth keeping in film anthologies; but we cannot quite remember the man.

Neither did Sydney Chaplin, Charlie's brother, really own an identifying repertoire of "turns," unless a knack for female impersonation qualified him as outsider and irrepressible zany. After working with Charlie during the First National contract, Sydney—ultimately shortened by the public to Syd—marked time for a while in supporting roles that no longer called for the coffee-dipped "mo" he had once pasted on his upper lip, then suddenly found himself in demand after appearing in a minor studio's version of the already venerable stage farce, *Charley's Aunt*. He had been known for his devastating takeoffs of prominent film actresses at Hollywood parties; perhaps the habit had something to do with his getting the lucky part.

Warner Brothers quickly assigned him to the payroll, gave him another old Chaplin hand—Charles Reisner—as director, and kept him, for a time at least, in skirts. *The Man on the Box* finds him posing as a maid in a household that is

about to be robbed by enemy agents of its secret plans for manufacturing helicopters; *Oh, What a Nurse!* presents him as an Advice to the Lovelorn columnist who keeps the heroine from marrying the wrong man by his constant presence as unofficial duenna. Audiences of the period looked at female impersonation in an uncomplicated way: it was a talent, not a hint that the performer was a probable transvestite. The attitude is made most explicit in Keaton's *Seven Chances*: Buster, looking for someone to marry in a hurry, passes a stage door decorated by a photograph of what seems a female star; a wardrobe trunk conveniently conceals the performer's name. Buster slips through the door to make his instant proposal, and as he does so the trunk is moved to display the name of Julian Eltinge, a well-known female impersonator of the period. Buster emerges, very shortly, with a blackened eye.

Syd Chaplin was an accomplished farceur, male enough not to look too probable in ringlets and rose-crusted bonnets, possessed of a trowel-shaped nose between his marked dimples that turned him into a character-woman eccentric rather than a displaced ingenue. He had long since learned his trade, could drop a bottle and catch it without looking as well as Langdon or Laurel could, was quick on his feet and adept at flapping friends away with his skirts. What is funny about *Charley's Aunt*, however, is what had always been funny about *Charley's Aunt*: the elementary but foolproof situations Brandon Thomas had created for the stage. If Syd's male garter falls loose beneath his skirts and the elderly swain who has been pursuing him mistakes it for his own, swiftly fixing it to *his* leg, the subsequent business is amusing: each time one crosses his leg as they sit side by side

on a sofa, the other must too. But the business is impersonal, mechanically dictated; any competent performer could have done it.

As Syd's popularity increased, Warner Brothers permitted him a wider range of roles. The "mo," indeed the whole appearance of the Syd of *Shoulder Arms*, came back for *The Better 'Ole* because the Bruce Bairnsfather cartoons on which the original stage play had been based called for a World War I Cockney with just such an endowed, wryly twitchable upper lip. In other films, *The Missing Link* among them, Syd is free to appear as himself throughout, cheeks puckered slightly as though they were permanently storing apple rinds, hair parted in the middle and combed severely forward into side-bangs, musical-comedy teeth as white as Douglas MacLean's and, it often seemed, twice as big. For these more conventional flings, he had a pleasant assortment of grossly injured looks and an apparent fascination with bananas: in one film he is a soda jerk so offended at being asked for a banana split that he upends the ice-cream glass, breaks a banana sharply over it, and simply hurls the results at his customer; in another he means to smoke a cigar but first patiently peels it as though it *were* a banana. In the latter instance, he is lying on a sofa, waiting for the girl to come by. When she does, there is no trace of his cigar; but he is noticeably smoking at nose and ears. The girl concludes that he is burning up with fever and promptly mothers him, which is what he has had in mind. So it went with Syd Chaplin: adroitness in playing out small absurdities of plotting, very little left over to claim as his own. He had been self-effacing when working with his brother, serving Charlie loyally; when it came time to make his own starring films, he simply switched to serving his plots. The readily cooperative probably do not make major clowns.

Interestingly, the exception to all rules governing the studio demiclowns is W. C. Fields, who made a regular series of program films for Paramount in the latter half of the 1920's. Fields, of course, was no true demiclown but the real thing: bulbous nose, fastidious fingers forever twiddling in air, the stroll of a somnambulist, equally matter-of-fact about pleasing a woman or mauling a child. The very air parted about him as he walked. But he was a major comedian under wraps. Today it is virtually unthinkable that Fields should ever have been a *silent* comedian: we remember him first as something heard, then something seen. People who have grown up on his sound-film and radio appearances are much surprised, even now, to learn that he had a considerable screen career long before his oracular nasalities could be put to their normal use. Mustn't the titles have had to do *all* his work for him?

The titles play their part, to be sure. "Night spreads its sable wings o'er a fair countryside" are the first words we read in the 1926 *It's the Old Army Game*. Seeing the film today, we immediately supply those words with the high and wheezing pretensions to literacy that are still fresh in our ears, making them funnier than they can have been to audiences who knew him by sight alone. Later in the film, he is cagey about the men who enter his drugstore to make surreptitious requests for liquor. He has the Prohibition "hootch" under the counter, all right, but is less than eager to make the mistake of selling a bottle to a Federal agent. To establish a customer's identity, he casually fiddles an electric fan into place on the counter so that it will gently blow open the visitor's lapels. No badge under the lapel, okay. That, by the way, is visual comedy. When a badge does turn up, however, Fields explodes into printed language. "Would you have me break the laws of our glorious country to satisfy your depraved taste?" he wants to know. There is already comedy, characteristically Fieldsian comedy, in the rhythm and choice of words. But the comedian could not become whole—or a star of the first magnitude—until the visual and the verbal in him stopped inter-

Opposite: Charlie helps Syd promote *Charley's Aunt*—and stardom for his half-brother.

Above: W. C. Fields with Chester Conklin in the thoroughly silent *Fools for Luck*.

rupting each other, ceased occupying separate frames.

Even so, Fields is funnier in his best silent features than a notoriously loquacious man had any right to be. Coming from the stage, he had established himself in films by way of the stage: when D. W. Griffith decided that he wanted to turn Fields' legitimate theater vehicle *Poppy* into *Sally of the Sawdust* it seemed fairly reasonable to bring Fields along. Not that Griffith, with his indifference to comedy, was truly interested in Fields; he was interested in reshaping the piece into a sentimental melodrama centering on the girl, an actress named Carol Dempster whom he had long tried to make a star. For goodly portions of the film Fields is relegated to "insert" shots, in which he must pretty much fend for himself. While we are following the girl's blossoming romance with the young Alfred Lunt or watching her turn spitfire in her own defense in a courtroom, Fields is elsewhere, no doubt inventing his own business. One "insert" finds him hawking peanuts on a fairground to a surprisingly eager line of males. What the men are really bargaining for is forbidden liquor, stashed away in Mr. Fields's vending cart. Fields is selling more than liquor, however; he is selling atmosphere. With each purchase, a tiny bar rail, not more than a foot and a half long, is propped under the buyer's foot to provide ambiance, while Fields sprinkles a soupçon of sawdust round about it for good measure.

Fields had appeared in films earlier, in support of Marion Davies in *Janice Meredith*; as Griffith managed things here, this was still a supporting role. But it was a bigger one; perhaps the sight of him scurrying down a city street in full Indian regalia suggested to Paramount that a viable series-star was at hand. In any case, Fields took up residence at the studio, turning out at least seven feature films before the sound watershed of 1928.

What is truly surprising is that the films are as fully Fieldsian as they are, so much so that one prolonged sequence from *It's the Old Army Game* could be reproduced, virtually intact, in a later sound film, *It's a Gift*. Moreover, it is approximately as funny in the original. Fields is having some difficulty taking a well-deserved nap on a second-story porch. A tot is at hand, bawling unmercifully. Fields carefully gauges the next time the child's mouth will open and promptly pops a gag into it. The child is persistent. Fields gives it a hammer and mirror to play with. Ultimately desperate, Fields is about to drop the little one through a convenient opening in the second-floor railing but is unfeelingly prevented. He has found the child none too easy to pick up due to the fact that he is standing on the child's hand. Child gone and snooze begun, a vegetable vendor comes by to hawk his wares. Fields, aroused, reaches for a rifle and would unquestionably shoot if the rifle weren't hopelessly entangled in the chains of a porch swing. The vendor is moving along. Fields—in the passage's only necessary title—begs him not to go away until he can free the weapon. At the end he is pacing the porch, rifle slung on his shoulder, standing guard over the nap he is never going to get.

Because we do hear Fields now, we quite forget how many open spaces there were in his work, to be filled in sound-films with no more than incoherent, *sotto voce* rumblings and grumblings. The latter are not really missed; they are implied in the thoroughly intelligible visual image.

Several of Fields' films of the period had scripts credited to the popular humorist J. P. McEvoy. Whether Fields took something of his madness from McEvoy, or whether McEvoy simply abetted Fields in doing what he wanted to do, the gag structures are already typical: the world of a sane man who merely wants to run his drugstore or get some sleep is invaded by patent lunatics, ultimately trying the patience of the most alcoholic of saints. After night has spread her sable wings o'er the fair countryside, we see a car being recklessly driven, even

For a man denied the carnival barker's voice by which we all remember him, W. C. Fields had a surprisingly substantial silent film career.

Opposite: The expansive gesture in the courtroom, top, is from *Sally of the Sawdust*, as is the gallantry shown Carol Dempster on a sideshow platform at bottom. Between them, Fields, on his best behavior, takes daughter Mary Brian motoring.

racing a train, in the dark. The driver, a woman, pulls up outside Mr. Fields's drugstore in panic, arousing him and forcing him to reopen the store. As always, he is obliging. The woman wants to buy a postage stamp. Having purchased it—Fields has made no move to kill her—she deposits her letter in the fire-alarm box outside. This naturally brings the town's fire truck, with full personnel, to Fields' door. Apologizing for the inconvenience, he feels it necessary to treat them all to free sodas. Still sleepy and fearful of further invasions of his stock, he tricks them into leaving by sounding another alarm. As the fire truck pulls away, it spews cinders, one of which sets Fields' drugstore on fire.

A day off is no better. He is sentenced to spending it with his family, most members of which he does not greatly cherish. True to his fatherly calling, he takes the brood picnicking on the lawn of a private estate, to the considerable damage of that estate. Watching his wife beat their small son with a stick, he courteously provides her with an axe. He is happy, at last, to lock the lot of them in jail. Fields' views on domesticity were established long before *The Bank Dick*.

The matrix was there, all but complete. The fact that it remained somewhat incomplete for the time being is indicated both by Fields' failure to expand his comic imagery to the proportions permitted by the form's fantasy—the material continues to be domestic and relatively enclosed—and by an obvious need for more and more title-gags the longer a film runs. Long after the plotting has got under way in *It's the Old Army Game*, yet another customer comes to the drugstore for a two-cent postage stamp. "Could I interest you in a Special Delivery?" Fields inquires in print. The customer is determined to have a clean stamp, so selects one from the middle of the sheet. "Shall I send it?" Fields asks, still accommodating the world's madmen and still dependent on placards.

The last matter would soon be rectified. In the meantime, the comedian had indicated that his resources were sufficient to survive the absence of his mellifluous whine. We believe what we see—and only see—when he somehow gets one finger into the sandwich he is eating.

31. The Unexpected Raymond Griffith

In 1926 Robert E. Sherwood wrote in *Life* that "at this particular moment . . . Raymond Griffith leads all comedians in point of ingenuity, imaginativeness, and originality. Since he became a star he has appeared in three consecutive pictures—*Paths to Paradise, A Regular Fellow*, and *Hands Up!* . . . They have all been funny, and they have all been progressive. . . . Raymond Griffith deserves enthusiastic encouragement. He is flying in the face of movie tradition and getting away with it beautifully."

Mr. Sherwood could and did go too far. A year later, when Keaton's *The General* was released, he wrote: "*The General* is not nearly so good as Raymond Griffith's Civil War comedy, *Hands Up!*" In the Stanley Kauffmann–Bruce Henstell anthology, *American Film Criticism*, the editors quite properly spank Mr. Sherwood for his relative myopia. "Even Keaton's admirers could falter," they scold in a note commenting on the passage, going on to say that "In an international poll of critics in 1972, *The General* was voted one of the ten best films of all time. *Hands Up!* is deservedly forgotten."

But now *they* have gone too far. *The General* is what they say it is: a masterpiece. But "deservedly forgotten" is surely the wrong phrase for what has happened to *Hands Up!* "Ignobly forgotten" might be better. For, without laying claim to anything like the scale, the pictorial beauty, or the ingeniously balanced structure of Keaton's film, *Hands Up!* contains some work that is daring—for its period, certainly—and some that is masterfully delicate, the work of an inventive, unaggressive, amiably iconoclastic intelligence.

One reason for the neglect of Griffith's films today is that so little of his output is available. Of the nine or ten starring films he made between 1925 and the end of the silent period, only four can be seen at the moment; and the most recently discovered, *You'd Be Surprised*, is self-indulgently unrepresentative. It is difficult to develop a new audience for a man who is more than half invisible; and critical judgments must be somewhat reserved, given such piecemeal evidence. I feel no reserve of my own: Griffith seems to me to occupy a handsome fifth place—after Chaplin, Keaton, Lloyd, and Langdon—in the silent comedy pantheon, a place that is his by right of his refusal to ape his contemporaries and his insistence on following the devious curve of an entirely idiosyncratic eye. But, admittedly, I have only two whimsical impertinences to go on: *Hands Up!* and *Paths to Paradise*; the remaining available, and earlyish, comedy, *The Night Club*, is markedly inferior to both. Yet sometimes enough is enough.

Raymond Griffith, looking quite as though the jewels belonged to him. They don't, in *Paths to Paradise*.

As it happens, the odds were—from the beginning—somewhat against Raymond Griffith ever emerging as a star of the first rank. He is no memorable grotesque, made instantly indelible by his outline. Rather, he is slight, trim, neatly mustached, most often equipped with opera cape and top hat. At a glance he belongs to the Max Linder tradition, too much the habitué of drawing rooms and boudoirs ever to escape the polite formulas of boulevard farce. Some of his vehicles *were* adaptations from the stage; he is enough of a "manners" man to have gone the way of Adolphe Menjou or even Reginald Denny, sufficiently domesticated in his deportment to fill in as a faintly upper-class Charley Chase. While he was building his following by appearing in supporting roles at Paramount—there were nineteen or twenty such—he seemed the debonair supporting player par excellence, as handy as Edward Everett Horton would be through the coming years of sound. Always welcome, always amusing, always content with his lot.

And when Paramount did advance him to stardom, he became a studio comedian, inheriting the hazards of the breed. Where Keaton might take six months to make a film, Lloyd a year, and Chaplin three years if he chose, Griffith was forced to turn out as many as four in a season, inexpensively and most often within the confines of the studio lot. Too conventional in appearance for myth-making, too hurried at work for major inspiration, he might well have helped fill booking schedules—charmingly, routinely—and deserved no remembering at all.

Except for the fact that he was wittier than his own training, a rebel who had mastered all the gag-formulas ever devised and was eager to toss the lot of them over his shoulder, brushing off his cape in passing and trusting himself to pluck something better—something outrageously better, if need be—from the blue. His training had been basic Sennett. After a boyhood in the theater that included tours of America and Europe with a company of French pantomimists, he was provisionally taken on by Sennett as an actor. In a short Sennett comedy called *The Surf Girl* he can be seen doing the necessary Sennett things: struggling with a live ostrich to retrieve a locket it has swallowed, leaping from the top of a Ferris wheel only to sail serenely groundward courtesy of the open umbrella in his hand.

But he is already the natty, lithe, bland, and unmugging figure of his later films, insufficiently exaggerated at any point to survive as a Sennett clown. He was retired but not fired: retired to the upstairs conference room, where he swiftly developed a reputation as one of the most fertile gag-men on an already crowded lot. In due time he became story editor and very much top dog among the studio's "brains," endlessly hatching and then cross-breeding routines for other men. Herbert Howe, a press agent of the period and himself something of a wit, summed up Griffith's standing in 1925 for *Photoplay*: "When he left Sennett a few years later, he was a master mechanic of comedy. He could gag. He could time his business to a second. He knew to an inch how much footage a scene should have to get the biggest laugh. In addition to being an actor, he was qualified as a director and a scenario writer. His attitude toward the art of screen comedy is that of the mathematician. There is no emotion about it, he will tell you; it is pure mathematics."

In 1923, Griffith was taken on as a gag-man by Douglas MacLean and allowed to write that comedian's first risky venture into independent production. The film, *Going Up*, proved a considerable success. During the same year, having had a taste of working on feature-length films, Griffith returned to acting, playing supporting roles for Samuel Goldwyn and at Universal. He was noticed, and Paramount put him under contract in 1924, a contract that was to hold until sound ended his career.

Almost immediately he developed a knack for stealing films from presumably more important fools: no matter what the impassioned principals might be doing—dashing through one another's bedrooms, furiously demanding the return of jewels, flying into fits of jealousy during bicycle races in Parisian circuses—he would sit stolid in armchairs or sleep curled up on stairwells until emotion blew over. He was entirely amiable in his detachment, never resentful; he simply wished to present himself as infinitely adaptable and comfortably out of it all. Each time the editor of a Bebe Daniels starring film, *Miss Bluebeard*, cuts from the frantic impostures and bigamous liaisons of the plotting to find Griffith, banished to the hallways, curled up in slumber like an ever-so-flexible cat, the film perceptibly brightens. It's not simply that his snugness increases with each new shot, suggesting a sublime contentment in inverse proportion to what is going on around him. Rather, his rule of thumb for valid gagging—"no emotion"—has been incorporated into, and become a prime key to, his personality. He inched his way to stardom, over a two-year apprenticeship, by refusing to participate.

Of course, he was required to exert himself from time to time. If he could meet the requirement in pantomime, without bothering to dislodge his smile—at once bold and shy—he would do it that way: explaining a broken saucer by momentarily turning himself into a cat, making an assignation with one woman while dancing with another by indicating—in perfect silence—"call me." And his principle of "no emotion" did not mean that he was callous; it meant that he was logical. On hearing that a friend is not really married after all, the first thing Griffith does is to retrieve the wedding presents he has given him. The act is not an unsocial one; it merely—and quite genially—takes cognizance of the facts. He looks as though he is courteously saving his friend the terrible trouble of returning the gifts. Of such bits—bits of instant *sense* in otherwise giddily busy and very often quite bad films—was Griffith's reputation made.

As the studio eased him into stardom, it also temporarily threw him off stride. Studio stardom in the 1920's was rarely a matter of sudden executive fiat, with a halo descending on the performer and his name swiftly leaping above the title. More often than not cautious studios tried trial-flights: a few co-starring films with the companion star protecting the investment, a few films unmistakably centered on the performer without insisting that the audience come to see *him*. Even as late as *Paths to Paradise*, unmistakably a Griffith film, the comedian's name appears below the title and *after* Betty Compson's. As a result, it is difficult to be exact about the number of Griffith's "starring" films, particularly with the early *Forty Winks* and *A Regular Fellow* missing.

If, however, we are to take *The Night Club* as a film meant to test the comedian's capacities for going it alone, we see at once that there were initial difficulties. Griffith had two things to reconcile: the urbane noninvolvement of his successful supporting roles and the total, tumbling involvement of his thorough Sennett training. How much of Sennett might he have to reach for in order to sustain a sixty-minute film? He couldn't play possum, as he had lately been doing, for that long a time, couldn't be indifferent to the requirements of suspense and climactic chase. Could the two be made to blend?

They couldn't, not in *The Night Club*. The insouciant, easy-come-easier-go

Griffith is present and accounted for, certainly at the beginning. He is discovered at the altar, in the process of marrying a statuesque beauty much taller than he. At the height of the ceremony there is an interruption. In the doorway of the church stands another man, calling out to his love, who also happens to be Griffith's love and near-bride. The bride flies to the newcomer's arms. He is no newcomer: he is her long-lost fiancé, thought shipwrecked. Griffith is more than decent about the matter. With a pooh-poohing gesture he accepts it all as though he had really only come to give the bride away. Every day brings its mishaps, why not this one? And isn't it admirable how devoted these two are to each other? The man who hasn't a heart to break is most gentlemanly about his irretrievable loss.

The sequence is actually a framing device, pointing toward the end of the film. At the end of the film Griffith is once more at the altar, this time with a girl he is *determined* to marry. He will inherit a million dollars when he does, and, besides, she's a very nice sort. At the height of the ceremony there is another man in the church doorway, another cry of "Halt!" This is a bit much for Griffith, all things considered, but he is spared the necessity of evicting the fellow. The poor chap has simply come to the wrong church.

Raymond Griffith takes leave of Marian Nixon with undying devotion in *Hands Up!* He will do as much for her sister, just as sincerely, thirty seconds later.

Elsewhere in *The Night Club* Griffith keeps his engaging peace, and we are able to recognize the man we watched grow during the Bebe Daniels–Jetta Goudal–anybody-at-Paramount romps. But we also see, rather alarmingly, the Sennett shoddy that Paramount made shoddier by shooting everything against flimsy mock-ups that could be knocked down the next day and on streets that were—for want of hired extras—curiously empty. It is as though Griffith and his few colleagues had been permitted the use of a back lot on everybody's day off.

And once we are into the perpetual misunderstandings of the plot, the Sennett substitutions take over too readily. Much of the chase footage is filmed against obviously painted dioramas, though Griffith does manage one lovely sprint as a runaway car chases him beneath an exotic archway and up an enormous flight of stone steps. When, attempting suicide, he makes use of the Sennett–Semon buzz saw, tying himself to its moving track only to have it hurl blocks of wood at him, the flying wedges are plainly coming from the prop man. He is freed from the buzz saw too readily: the saw cuts the rope with which he has bound himself. Other gags are the gags we expect. He puts a revolver to his head. No bullets. He hangs himself from a chandelier. The ceiling comes down. When he jumps from a second-story window, a dummy takes the dive. We are forced to cling, in the end, to the dexterity with which Griffith vaults a corridor chair as he rushes to his girl and then tumbles over the same chair on his discouraged return, or to a light-hearted skip into a hotel lobby, complete with tap-dance to the elevator. *The Night Club* was successful enough on a block-booking basis, which guaranteed showings in houses controlled by the studio. It does not suggest an important original in the making.

Fortunately, Griffith was tough, tough enough to force his way through the assembly-line haste and economies of the company that employed him, tough enough to discard along the way the "easy outs" of his earlier heritage. In fact, it is his stubbornness—even his vanity—that comes most strongly through the interviews Mr. Brownlow assembled while talking with men who had worked with Griffith. "He doesn't even play the game to the extent of differing with his director in privacy," columnist Adela Rogers St. John is quoted as grumbling, "but openly asserts his authority, as I have seen myself." A writer on *Hands Up!* adds: "I've met a few stubborn people in my life, but he was about the tops."

This last leads to a story I should like to reprint from Brownlow in detail because it is, I think, too quickly misread. For *Hands Up!*, Mack Swain, the old

Sennett comedian and just recently Chaplin's cabin companion in *The Gold Rush*, had been cast as the father of the two ingenues. Writer Monte Brice and director Clarence Badger were with Griffith on the set of what was supposed to be—and finally looked as though it might be—Fort Laramie, Wyoming. "Right off the bat," Brice remembers, "we had a big row about Mack Swain. We were out on location and Mack's supposed to come rushing out of this store. Someone's stolen his horse. I remember the title—'Nobody ever steals my horse and lives to warm the saddle!' All the townspeople standing around gave Mack a big laugh. Griff was standing against a fence, watching the thing, and chewing his fingers.

"'Hey,' he said to me. 'Get rid of him.'

"'Get rid of Mack Swain?'

"'Get rid of him.'

"'Jesus, I don't hire and fire people. You can do it. What's the matter with him, anyway?'

"'Too goddam funny!'

"So now we call it off. Mack doesn't know what the hell's happened. We all go back to the hotel.

"'You can't tell from one little scene,' I said. 'The guy comes out, he's a funny man—they recognize him from the Chaplin pictures and that's why he gets the laugh.'

"'Don't want him. . . .'

"Finally I pin Ray down to the fact that what made Mack so funny was his big floppy hat. We have to send to the studio for another hat, so he can play it straighter. Well, that's a whole day gone. . . .

"Griff was a great gag man, but boy, he was stubborn. We had a lot of fun, though. *Hands Up!* was a hell of a funny picture."

The immediate and obvious reading of the episode makes Griffith unattractive, apparently jealous of a fellow worker and determined that only *he* get laughs. But, I submit, that isn't quite what the story tells us. Griffith, making a comedy, surely wasn't objecting to the fact that a supporting player—one with a long reputation as a comedian—was truly funny. He was objecting to the fact that Swain was funny-funny, using an extreme bit of costuming to play into a too easy laugh that would violate the film's style. "Play it straighter" are the key words here. Once the offending hat was replaced, Swain stayed; he is in the film and, as matters now stand, entirely in keeping with its not "too goddam funny" tone.

A glance at the opening sequence of *Hands Up!* may clarify the point. The sequence—in which neither Swain nor Griffith appears—is a downright miracle of understatement. In it, Griffith achieves not so much the impossible as—one might have thought—the unacceptable. He makes Abraham Lincoln funny. And he does it by not being "funny" at all. Lincoln is meeting with members of his cabinet: a financial crisis has developed during the war and unless the North can avail itself of the resources of an important new gold strike before the South does, all will be lost. The assembled cabinet makes a tableau, very much in the D. W. Griffith manner, very much in the manner of any photograph or drawing of the Civil War period. All is sober, all is somber. Lincoln himself is downcast, though his deep spirituality remains evident. His shoulders are bowed but his eyes stray ever so slightly upward; the glance is ever so slightly moist. From the first frame, mysteriously, we sense that we are in a comedy. Is the tableau *too* perfect? Is this the time we have seen it once too often? Is Lincoln posing for a five-dollar bill? Nothing is accented. The scene flows as straight drama: a Pinkerton man arrives to report that he is sending a man west to the mine, that the gold will surely be theirs. Lincoln grasps the man's shoulders in quick gratitude. Is the grip one

Hands Up! Though staff and headquarters are vanishing about them, spy Raymond Griffith and commander Robert E. Lee find themselves able to continue an important conversation.

Hands Up! Abraham Lincoln and his cabinet, opposite, wrestle soulfully with their problems.

thousandth of a beat too quick, one thousandth of an erg too firm? The Pinkerton man goes; Lincoln returns to his rocker, where, quite characteristically, he rocks. We see one leg comfortably lapped over the other, swinging up and down in a new contentment.

"No emotion." We have attended to three or four emotions, of a sort we readily recognize, and we have recognized them so swiftly that they have come out just minimally spurious. The scene is not only funny, it is *very* funny in a reserved, subliminally shocking way. We are somewhat appalled that we should find ourselves secretly amused. We also sense by this time that we are not going to be rooting for the North in this film.

Dissolve to Robert E. Lee's crossed legs, one also jogging up and down, this time in impatience. Lee hasn't Lincoln's sweet serenity. Nothing is done to make him sympathetic, but we're on his side, in his hurry. So, immediately, is Raymond Griffith, who rides up outside Lee's mere shack of a headquarters in a swirling cloud of dust. Griffith is in Confederate uniform—no top hat for the moment—and he is reporting for duty as a spy, duty being a matter of getting to the gold first. The cloud of dust in which he brings his steed to a stop is funny. Why? I suppose because, in the exterior shot, it is so authentic, so exactly like a reining-up in *The Covered Wagon* or *Hell's Hinges* that we are delighted to find such a bland and diminutive figure as Griffith—no J. Warren Kerrigan or William S. Hart he—disturbing the landscape as mightily as stronger, if no more silent, men had done. Entering the shack behind battle lines, he salutes smartly, though bullets are piercing the cabin walls to sing directly over his and Lee's unheeding heads. He is given instructions while grapeshot blows away the window frames. His mission accepted, he and Lee shake hands: a cannon ball is rolling under the foundations. In an exterior shot we see the whole headquarters go up. As the smoke and debris clear, the two men are completing their handshake on a now open plain. Salute, and go.

The comedy has here opened up to its proper—its fantastically proper—proportions, but we have known this was coming from the outset. What Griffith has done is to make the *picture* adopt his detached habits of mind. The film itself will remain outside its own displayed events and emotions, recording them without participating in the jumpy nerves, dilating blood vessels, and dubious moral judgments that normally accompany them. The world blows up. And so it does, did you notice? No comment, just a stiff upper smile and on to the next disaster, which will be survived. Brush your teeth every day.

We make a mistake when we think *heartless* means *cruel*. In a way, the word really outlaws cruelty. If we take the absence of "heart" to indicate a lack of sympathy or sentiment, we are on sound enough ground. But what we are really saying is that the heartless man lacks emotion of any sort—which means that he also lacks all the nastier urges of the organ: jealousy, spite, greed, malice, the lot. An unfeeling man can scarcely feel vindictive. He is more likely to feel neutral in the face of all empathic demands made on him. And a neutral man can be a very cheerful man: he is unfussed, unconfused by those cantankerous contentions at the core that beset the rest of us. Unruffled himself, he is apt to wear ruffles on his sleeves, which is where Griffith puts them.

But a truly heartless figure must be fantasy—no such human animal has been known to exist—and the world in which he appears must be fantasy to contain him. Example. When next we see Griffith in *Hands Up!* he has so far failed in his mission as to have been recognized as a spy, captured by Northern troops and placed against a wall before a firing squad. He is a spy because he is not in his proper Confederate uniform: he is in opera cape and silk hat. The silk sleeves of his white shirt are ruffled. Facing the firing squad, he is as agreeable as ever. He does ask for a handkerchief. He wishes to dust his patent-leather shoes. Not even the fact that his execution is momentarily stayed by the need to measure him for his grave perturbs him; he is gracious to the men who take his fit. When his execution is interrupted a second time, by an elderly woman carrying a hamper of dishes, he is the soul of courtesy. The poor woman, realizing that she has strayed into the middle of an execution, quite naturally throws up her hands in horror—these emotional people do carry on so!—and runs, leaving her basket behind. Griffith at once sets off in pursuit, to return the basket. Since he might also like to escape, he is hauled back, the basket torn from his arms. Rifles are aimed now, the end in sight. At the cry of "Fire!" Griffith jauntily tosses a dinner plate he has filched from the basket into the air, rather as though he were conducting a trapshooting contest. Inevitably all rifles swing with the plate and, firing, bring it down. Griffith applauds the men's marksmanship, is really very pleased with them. Their commander is less pleased, hurries them through a second countdown. Another plate, to the left rather than the right this time—and a smaller plate, to see if they can hit *that*. True to instinct and superb training, they do. It is becoming very difficult to kill Griffith. Ultimately the plates become so small that the marksmen object, complaining to their commander that no one could be

expected to hit so minuscule a flying object. Griffith will have none of that. Of *course* a small plate can be hit. He will show them, and is already borrowing one of the rifles when the commanding officer realizes that perhaps he had best be intercepted. Griffith is still shaking his head in gentle reproof as he is returned to the wall.

I won't go into further detail. But what Griffith has done in the sequence is to free himself from the domestic-boulevard limitations of a debonair appearance and lift himself into the capriciously absurd world of the unfettered clowns. Looking plausible no longer demands that he *be* plausible. Out of a sublime coolness he has contrived an escape hatch: not only from firing squads but from the realism of "stage" deportment. He is now as flexible as his improbable medium.

This airiness that soared into fantasy proved a stumbling block to some of the men who worked with him. Brownlow quotes director Eddie Sutherland, one of Griffith's closest friends, as complaining that "he would never be the butt of any joke. Now the success of almost all great comedians comes from being the butt of jokes. Griff was too vain for this. He would get himself into a problem, and then he'd want to think himself out of it."

But Griffith *couldn't* be the butt of jokes. He had no feelings. To be the butt of a joke one must be emotionally vulnerable, capable of being hurt; even Keaton, that nearly invulnerable man, could be momentarily crushed—and no need to speak of Chaplin. Griffith's originality, and the *essence* of his comedy, lay in his

Though Mack Swain and daughters are about to be burned at the stake, Griffith remains cheerfully resourceful. *Hands Up!*

perfectly honest, undemanding, unregretted, eternally grinning iconoclasm.

The iconoclasm becomes the bone-marrow of *Hands Up!* Griffith meets the two ingenues, Marian Nixon and Virginia Lee Corbin. Both become enamored of him, and he of them—equally. This is not emotion speaking now, just everyman's natural, pleasant, undiscriminating sensual appetite. There is also gentlemanliness in it: who would wish to be impolite to either girl? Throughout the film all of the "romantic" scenes are played on the double: one girl makes overtures, Griffith responds happily; the other girl makes the same overtures, Griffith responds happily. Cruelty would consist in choosing. He could not do that. Some scenes are played with a girl on each shoulder, Griffith being careful to divide his kind attentions evenly. Others are played serially. Griffith has a stagecoach loaded with gold and is about to drive off with it. Miss Nixon appears, terrified he will be killed. "Aren't you sweet?" he says. "I love you," she says. "Would you marry me?" he asks. Not *will* you, but the more distantly hypothetical, though interested, *would* you. "I'll have to ask papa," she says and runs off. Before he can mount the coach, Miss Corbin scurries in, hoop skirts billowing. She is terrified that he will be killed. "Aren't you sweet?" he says. And so forth, the entire sequence being tenderly repeated with identical subtitles. "I'll have to ask papa."

At long last the stylization comes to its inevitable crunch. Griffith has been caught stealing gold for the South and is about to be hanged by mine owner and paterfamilias Mack Swain. The noose, a very thick one, is about his neck. Miss Nixon slips a ring onto her finger and rushes into the crowd, proclaiming that Griffith is her husband. The news gives Swain pause. Before he has paused long, Miss Corbin appears, just as breathlessly, to announce that Griffith is *her* husband. Now the girls have rather overdone things. Swain will hang him not for treason but for bigamy. Several events interfere with the hanging: a wild escape by Griffith in which, racing through the rooms of a mansion and onto its rooftops, he takes desperate leave of both his loves on the run, again identically; and the news that the Civil War happens to be over.

In the end Griffith is left a free man, except that he has two equal claimants to his eternal adoration on his hands. The three are quite disturbed. What to do? Miss Nixon offers to surrender him to Miss Corbin. Miss Corbin offers to surrender him to Miss Nixon. Soon the two girls are quarreling heatedly over which of them will give him up. Griffith makes peace by swearing his absolute love for them both. Peace, but no resolution: each girl reclines on one of his shoulders, and the three make a pretty, perplexed trio. A new carriage drives up in the dust of the road. A bearded man, descending, recognizes the girls as old friends. He introduces his wife, Anna, as she descends from the carriage. He introduces his wife, Grace, as she descends from the carriage. He introduces his wife, Jane—and Helen, and several more—as his true loves multiply. He is Brigham Young, and a gratifying end to all perplexities. The final shot of the film finds Griffith and female companions bucketing off in a carriage, "To Salt Lake City" writ large on its rear. It is possible for an entire film, and a very funny one, to rise above heart.

There are minor flaws in the film: When Griffith teaches a hostile band of Indians to substitute the Charleston for their war dance, there is no problem in absorbing the characteristically cavalier anachronism; Griffith, in top hat, is as much out of time as he is emotionally out of touch. But it's an awfully convenient way to free Mack Swain from being burned at the stake. Also, if you look hard enough, you can find a bit of Sennett cheating in a sort of village-wide one-man chariot race during which Griffith has a firm grip on the reins but, unfortunately, no chariot. But *Hands Up!* is its own film, as Griffith, sometimes to the annoyance of those who worked more conventionally, was his own man. For sweet,

simple, effortless impudence, I know of nothing precisely like it.

Griffith's detachment, his emotional isolation from the situations in which he participated, was not at all like Chaplin's. For one thing, Chaplin *felt* his isolation; he simply could do nothing about it. He was an emotional and psychological outsider. Griffith is an unemotional insider. He is perfectly at home wherever he is—in high society, in an opium den—with no wish to leave, unless forced. He is satisfied to remain where he is and win, with his wits, whatever contest may be going on. In a sense, he is even more a chameleon than Chaplin, for he *truly* adapts to the circumstances in which he finds himself; he holds no other self in reserve, keeps no nest in a vacant lot to retire to. He can never be an outsider because he is not critical of the milieu he inhabits. Chaplin may look faintly scandalized that a church elder—Mack Swain again—should carry a bottle of whiskey on his hip; *he* should carry the whiskey, not Swain, an attitude that rather justifies his purloining it. Griffith judges no one, is never scandalized. With emotion waived, life becomes pure game; Griffith is exclusively addicted to the turn of the cards, the roll of the dice, the spin of the wheel, and cannot be got out of the casino. He is dressed to last the evening.

He cannot really understand Betty Compson's desire, in *Paths to Paradise*, to "go straight." Miss Compson is a professional swindler and potential jewel thief. Mr. Griffith is whatever he chooses to be at the moment: sucker, detective, con man, jewel thief, confidant of the wealthy. Each time he is introduced to someone in the film he affably gives his name. Each time it is different: McIntosh, Dusenberry, Cedarbrook, Callahan. It is his habit, in hotel lobbies, to answer all paged calls: there is no knowing what fun may be had out of accepting identity by chance.

In the course of the film, he first competes with Miss Compson, during a fashionable wedding party, to see which can filch from a safe the diamond necklace intended for the bride; as the going becomes trickier, the two join forces. Griffith's fantasy is lightly and delightfully explored at both stages. While going it alone, he makes endless deft trips to the safe between bouts of white-tie socializing, always to be interrupted. At long last we lose him for a second or two and pick up two burly detectives returning from a tour of the mansion to stand guard over its most precious cache. We notice instantly that the safe itself is gone; the detectives, of course, do not. One of them, needing very much to light his pipe, tucks his flashlight under his arm. Its circle of light instantly picks out Griffith, frozen in midflight in an alcove, the entire safe tucked under *his* arm. By the time the detective has sensed something amiss and refocused his flashlight on the alcove, the space is empty. When the household dog gets the detective's flashlight between his teeth and struggles to keep it, the insane parabolas of light catch Griffith here, there, and everywhere, engaged in a nightmare dance to escape its beam, safe still cradled in his arms.

Once Compson and Griffith have together purloined the treasure, a superb chase to the Mexican border includes a piece of business that at last legitimizes Sennett. The comedy of the chase is made of sheer numbers and imaginative visual design. Hundreds on hundreds of motorcycle police are called out along the way, spilling from mountainous side roads to join the main stream of pursuit. Overhead shots make the Griffith–Compson car seem to be leading a motorized snake-dance through figure-eights wrapped around valleys. But Griffith's front tire is shot out along the way. Griffith and Compson leap from the car, he to remove the front wheel, she to whip out the spare, each rolling a wheel to the other so that wheels pass in dizzying eclipse; both are back in the car and on their way before the onrushing motorcade—in plain view throughout—can quite overtake

A dubious Raymond Griffith kneels to a spurious Betty Compson in *Paths to Paradise*.

them. The business is flatly impossible, as much a gleeful seizing on silent-comedy permissiveness as Griffith's frantic ballet with a safe that ought to have weight to it. Fortunately, we *see* it, see the perfectly real posse racing over perfectly real terrain in the same frame that contains the switched wheels, see the pursuers come within inches of the pursued before the repaired car can be off again. Griffith's planning eye has told him precisely what camera angles are needed to validate the gag while reveling in its preposterousness. We revel in the contradiction too: we *like* looking on at the brazenly implausible so long as it is plainly not being faked, only happily conceived and shot.

I said that Griffith could not understand Miss Compson's flickering urges toward reform. Every so often during the chase, in which she wholeheartedly cooperates, it occurs to her that they may not be "doing right," that she might conceivably prefer being an honest woman. At these moments Griffith simply stares at her, not in disbelief but curiosity. He gives no thought to such considerations: you play the game you're playing. But apparently some people are given to fretting. How interesting! He is not allowed to dwell long on her curious introspection, for he is doing one hundred miles an hour and just now bumping across the border into Mexico—and safety.

At this point the film, as we now have it, ends abruptly. The last reel is missing. But we know from reviews and press releases of the period what happens in it and can only grind our teeth for not having it. Now that he has brought us through a funny, hair-raising, visually gratifying climactic chase, Griffith is prepared to reverse gears and give us *another* complete chase all the way back. The reversal in itself is freshly funny as an idea. Miss Compson, securely inside Mexico after all that trouble, decides that this isn't what she wants at all; she wants to live within the law. Which means that she will have to get back to the mansion before the police do in order to return the jewelry voluntarily. Well and good. We don't need the final reel to know Griffith's reaction. He will instantly turn the car around and play *that* game. He doesn't have to understand or share the motive. The exhilaration is in the doing, not in the unfathomable reasons people give. His head will tilt slightly, his wide eyes turn opaquely relective as though measuring exactly *what* must be done, his cooperative but slightly formalized smile remain in place. And he will take her back as he has brought her, with complete concentration and a disarming neutrality. Be accommodating, always.

It should be clear that, for all his rumored vanity, Griffith was no camera hog. His image and comic attitude forbade it. The image was not extravagant enough in its mannerisms to justify lingering close-ups, a camera fastened to his "turn" until its finish. The only "turn" was in his head, and the only way to project that was through the effrontery of the narrative taken as a whole. Thus, he had to insist upon dictating the texture of a film, its playing, its pacing, its inherent impertinence—in spite of the fact that he did not nominally direct himself. The films are his because they reflect the gleam in his eye—amoral, inquisitive, unjudging, ready for anything—and because, as Mr. Brownlow's interviews have shown, he did take full responsibility for them. But there is another side to this business of assuming responsibility: it is not all arrogance. When John Grierson came from England in 1926 for an extended stay in Hollywood he reported, regretfully, that "it is bad manners in Hollywood to discuss a picture's weaknesses in the presence of its director or its star." He made a single exception: "In all my stay in Hollywood I met but one person (Raymond Griffith), who was humble enough in his art (and great enough) to curse his bad work to his own face."

It is to be hoped that the balance of his work, good or bad, will be recovered.

32. Missing Film

A word about missing film. You may have noticed that as we move deeper into the 1920's, we have had to speak more often of important titles that are unavailable: Harry Langdon's last feature, *Heart Trouble*; half of Raymond Griffith's starring films. This is odd. One might readily expect early and primitive work to be lost; but by the mid-1920's the studios were firmly organized and presumably prepared to protect both their copyrights and their prints. Even Laurel and Hardy, of whose work we must speak next and whose highly original doodlings constitute the final fresh flourish of the form before sound destroyed silence, lack a few of their subjects. Their omnipresence, thanks to television, makes us continue to think of them as virtual contemporaries; but, recent as they are, they have not quite escaped the blight. We can see Chaplin's very first film from 1914, as well as the film in which he first adopted what became his representative costume; but of Bebe Daniels's 1927 *Senorita* there is not a trace.

Precisely why more important late films should have vanished than early ones is a puzzle. The probable answer lies with sound itself. When sound-film came in, panic came with it. The studios turned their rattled—and exclusive—attention to microphones, alternate recording devices, cameras that did not whirr, actors without unintelligible accents. Overnight an entire library—the silent film library that had accumulated in studio vaults—was obsolete. Because audiences now wanted speech and nothing else, there was no longer any profit to be taken from the exhibition—or, for that matter, maintenance—of outdated materials. Most probably these were left to languish, untended, while they rotted. The studios had second thoughts on the matter later, as we shall see. For the moment, nothing was neglected as silent film was neglected, and the films that had been produced closest to the silent-sound deadline were the films that, ironically, suffered most. Earlier titles had already been given some care and renovation. Why waste money on the later ones when the form had suddenly died?

It is much less difficult to explain the survival of important early films, includ-

Harry Myers, in oval opposite Mark Twain, is remembered today for his work as the drunken millionaire in Chaplin's *City Lights*. But in 1921 he was playing the lead in an obviously lavish Fox production of *A Connecticut Yankee in King Arthur's Court*, inventing a medieval Model-T Ford rather than be hoisted onto horseback again. Of the original eight reels, only reels two, four, and seven are known to exist.

ing, so far as I know, the entire Chaplin canon. The major silent comedians were so inordinately popular that, in order to meet the demand for their films, many more prints were struck off than was customary for lesser lights. The sheer number of prints that were rushed to market favored the preservation of some: most would be damaged and ultimately worn to ribbons in the constant rerunning, but a few would inevitably escape, perhaps back into the studio vaults, perhaps into the hands of collectors.

Furthermore, popular films were not retired from circulation as rapidly as they are today. Exhibitors often needed "Saturday features," especially for the matinee trade; they often needed revivals as boosters on double bills; they often came upon dead spots in a week when an old but established Chaplin or Fairbanks film might tide them over for a night or two. Exchanges kept prints available for just such secondary bookings for years after first release; and when *these* prints wore out they were promptly replaced, because the maintenance of a kind of library backlog was profitable. The backlog was necessarily limited, but it did keep many of the historically significant films on the working shelves, where they were protected by regular inspection.

Deliberate re-release on a large scale was another piece of good fortune, though sometimes a scarred one. Chaplin's Mutual shorts, which Chaplin himself did not own, were sent around as a series again and again, offered as regularly scheduled bookings rather than casual pickups. Thus, films made in 1916 were being reprinted and shown, with insensitive soundtracks added, deep into the 1930's. With each reissue, however, alterations might be made, in theory to "sophisticate" the film for more knowing contemporary audiences. If anything, these mutilations destroyed the innate sophistication of the originals: the cuts were not so bad, and could for the most part be restored later; but the additions—mainly titles—were appalling. Chaplin's titles had been few and terse; during the 1920's his early two-reelers suddenly exploded with the bad puns and labored wisecracks of the period, as title-writers put their minds to the problem of making Chaplin "funnier." Today, when a firm catering to collectors of old film—Blackhawk

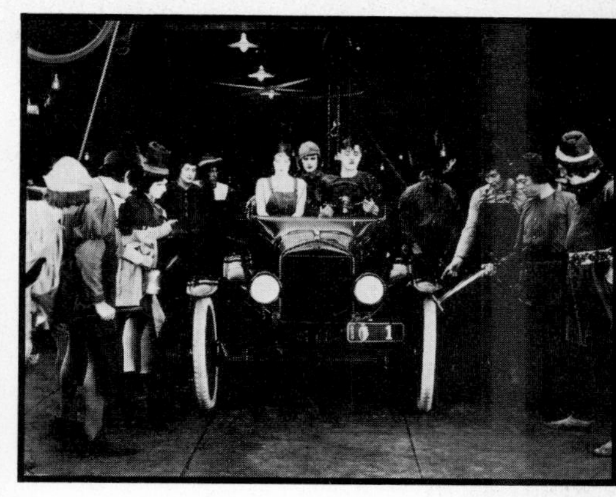

Films, say—can announce that it has finally succeeded in compiling a print with the original titles reinstated, it does so with considerable pride. The detective work may have been long and arduous; but we can again see the film Chaplin *made*.

Thus, there are no serious gaps in the early work of the major clowns. A few gaps do exist: one of Buster Keaton's short comedies, *Hard Luck*, seems to have disappeared altogether, and half of another, *Convict 13*, is lost. *Hard Luck*, it so happens, was Keaton's own favorite among his short films, which whets one's appetite for its recovery; it may still turn up. If there are a greater number of hard-to-find titles from the still earlier period of Keaton's association with Arbuckle, the cause of the difficulty is clear enough: at the time of Arbuckle's enforced retirement from the screen, showings of his films were banned, and the reprinting that would normally have been commonplace with such popular materials came to an abrupt end. No one has yet attempted to assemble in a single library *all* the films Harold Lloyd made during his long apprenticeship: the task would be formidable, though probably not impossible. But with his maturity, Lloyd became in effect his own archivist, carefully preserving all his significant work. We are at no real loss for evidence when we attempt to establish the relative standing of the men at the top.

Even so, there were enemies at work, and the films of secondary stars—who might, conceivably, seem less secondary if all their films were at hand—are in no such ample supply. What, for instance, of the talented Harry Myers, who was to prove such a superb foil for Chaplin as the besotted millionaire of *City Lights*? Myers made the first screen version of *A Connecticut Yankee in King Arthur's Court* in 1921; he appeared in six other films during the same year. After prolonged inquiry, I have been able to turn up only a fragmented version of *A Connecticut Yankee*; it would be valuable to know more of the background of the man who could match Chaplin cigar for cigar, purloined chair for purloined chair.

What were the enemies? Fire was one, neglect another—with neglect the more important of the two. Laboratory fires were commonplace and probably un-

Harold Lloyd's early partner, Bebe Daniels, reverted to comic form for a Zorro-like romp called *Senorita*. Whereabouts unknown.

preventable: at one time several of Keaton's most important films were thought to have been lost forever because their negatives had gone up in a blaze; much of Lloyd Hamilton's work is still regarded as unrecoverable for the same reason.

But negatives were not the whole story. Both negatives *and* positive prints were stored in studio vaults, and one could always hope that, even with a negative gone, a positive—from which a new if less satisfactory negative could always be made—might survive. Unfortunately, film of the period was printed on nitrate stock, which was not only highly flammable but readily deteriorated—it literally turned to dust—when neglected. Of course the studios took care of subjects that remained in any way profitable, but most films played out their little day and joined in limbo the hundreds of others made in a given year—the limbo of vaults no one ever bothered to go into. There was really no thought in the twenties of preserving the record of film as such, of establishing a permanent library for future reference. To many producers the product was simply perishable merchandise, approximately as delicious and as durable as popcorn. There was a disarming lack of vanity in the attitude: posterity couldn't possibly care for the money-making trinkets of the moment. And costs might be sizable if serious maintenance were attempted on a long backlog: better to sell worn prints to junk dealers for the silver that could be extracted from them.

Thus the vaults became very much a hit-or-miss repository of past creative work. A few years ago a studio official offered to help me find a print of a long-forgotten film produced by his company. He went into the vaults and came away with a silvery powder on his hands. Decomposition had been total. More and more often, now that film history has begun to interest a greater number of people, studios are turning over what they have to university libraries and to the American Film Institute. But what they have, in many cases, is pitiful. Warner Brothers has generously deposited a cache at the University of Wisconsin for student research; there are no more than four or five silent films in the entire group. Sydney Chaplin's *The Better 'Ole* is one of the four or five; it lacks a reel, who knows why?

No doubt everything in the studios' possession will sooner or later make its way to one or another institution capable of caring for old materials. But the materials in the studios' possession offer nothing like a satisfactory accounting of the silent period. Is what they have lost, or let go, forever lost, then? Not necessarily.

There are, and always have been, private collectors about—fifty thousand of them, by one recent estimate. Some of these are simply thieves. Perhaps they have rented a film and then reported it lost in transit or destroyed during projection. The film has ended up in a basement or attic, tucked away for personal pleasure or future profit. Some are in effect quit-claim operators, men who in one way or another acquire legal title to the films in their possession; they may then rent them out to interested parties, keep them in hand for "retrospectives," husband them so fiercely that museums are denied the right to show them. Some specialize in collecting and duplicating films on which the copyright has lapsed, doing a lively trade with newcomers to collecting: it is surprising how many popular stars—Douglas Fairbanks among them—failed to exercise their right of copyright renewal on important films. Some devote their lives to preserving old film for the special pleasure of introducing youngsters—usually students in university classes—to an unfamiliar, though strongly defined, form.

Some—most—are enthusiasts and no more than that: they love the films and want to be able to look at them when and as they please. Where do the merely ardent, who are not thieves, find their prints? From the beginning, prints have slipped out of the studios' hands in dozens of ways. Many were given to stars or producers for their home libraries. When the stars or producers died, the prints went somewhere—rarely back to the studio. James Mason once rented what had been Buster Keaton's home: in a sunken vault in the yard he came upon reel after reel of preserved Keaton material, which he promptly turned over to the Motion Picture Academy. How many others, similarly discovered, were never turned over to any academy?

The junk dealers who bought prints for the silver that could be reclaimed from them did not always immediately reclaim the silver; sometimes they had the films copied first, selling off the duplicates. For a time in the 1920's a collector could come by treasures readily, openly. With the development of sixteen-millimeter film, Eastman Kodak was empowered to reproduce and rent to laymen, for home or school use, a goodly portion of the Hollywood catalogue. Sixteen-millimeter film, slightly less than half the size of that used in theatrical projection, was easy to handle, took up minimal storage space, could be less expensively manufactured and marketed; printed on safety stock rather than nitrate, it was much more durable and not at all dangerous in an amateur's hands. The films themselves were somewhat truncated in their so-called Kodascope versions: seven-reel features might be condensed to five, two-reelers to one-reelers. This reduction always did some damage—occasionally serious damage—to the rhythm of a film. The pictorial quality, however, was superb, and the collector who today owns an original Kodascope print is normally the envy of his colleagues, most of whom must make

Raymond Griffith wholly comfortable astride a cabinet in *Forty Winks*. The film is missing.

do with second- or third-generation reproductions made from stray positives. "Dupes" made from positives are progressively fuzzier in outline, lacking in tonal values.

How did collectors come to "own" Kodascopes rather than simply lease and return them? The issue was always somewhat ambiguous. Certainly the friends of my youth who ran Kodascope two-reelers on their home projectors were in permanent possession of the prints, however the contract by which they had acquired them had been worded. And with the advent of sound, silent prints were sold without reservation; silence had become an anachronism, and the old stock had to be liquidated. The preoccupied studios did not protest at the time.

Film exchanges, charged with leasing and repairing film to be shown in their respective territories around the country, did not always return prints to the California studios. Shelves were overburdened, prints damaged, personnel careless or just easygoing. As a child I could wander Wabash Avenue in Chicago, visiting exchange after exchange, begging for throwaway film to be put through my hand-crank Keystone projector. I don't think I ever came away empty-handed. I might have nothing but newsreels and trailers, or portions of unrepairable longer films, for my pains, but I did have film and I came by it honestly. I traded film with friends who had got it God knows where. Everywhere there were loopholes in the system.

Europe most of all. During the silent period there was no language barrier to limit the popularity of American stars. All work was done for an international market, and it was common practice to edit an entirely separate negative to be shipped abroad for reproduction there. Interestingly, these negatives were not necessarily identical with the negatives used here; I once closely examined three different prints of *The Gold Rush*—two of which must have come from abroad—to discover that in several sequences Chaplin had used alternate "takes." The chase through the Alaskan saloon, with Big Jim McKay trying to get his great paws on Charlie, exists in variant patterns, each so funny that it is virtually impossible to choose among them.

But the existence of negatives abroad meant that the prints struck from them could not be as rigidly controlled as they were in the United States and that the return of all such prints to home base was a decidedly "iffish" matter. Uncounted numbers slipped away, with the result that a museum director of the 1970's who is hunting for a "lost" film is much more likely to turn his attention to Prague or Brussels than he is to Hollywood; he may even write to Moscow, which seems to have an astonishingly large, stubbornly-held library of rare American film.

In any event, the search need not be thought over. Scattered about the world, in uncertain quantities, are prints that somehow eluded the studio vaults. We don't yet know where all of these are or what gaps they may fill. When I asked Buster Keaton in 1949 whether *The Three Ages* still existed, he morosely thought not; one print has since been unearthed in Czechoslovakia, another—as recently as 1972—in Japan. For what the studios could not, or did not, take care of, we are now indebted—and may yet be further indebted—to private hands. We are lucky to have the films that were so furtively preserved and must be grateful to the men who saved them, whether we approve of their tactics or not.

The studios did not approve. From the beginning their legal departments waged war on the "illicit" possession of prints. Their claims of ownership, and the contracts they drew with exhibitors, were clear enough: they held the copyrights, and they leased but did not sell films for commercial showing. *All* prints were to be returned to the studio vaults, a premise that in retrospect may well cause historians to shudder. Once the transition to sound was firmly accomplished, the mo-

mentarily neglected silent materials were discovered to have a degree of value, after all. Because it was possible to remake certain silent properties as sound films—as, for instance, W. C. Fields and Laurel and Hardy did—the copyrights could be said to have a continuing commercial value. Thus, the pursuit of escaped prints was vigorously renewed. Even now, a collector of silent film may be harried: several years ago a man was sent to jail for duplicating and selling to other collectors the 1926 Lillian Gish version of *The Scarlet Letter*. This despite the fact that the version had no commercial prospects at the time and its "remake" value was nil, the source materials having been in the public domain to begin with.

Obviously a man who duplicates and sells materials to which he has no title is a pirate. Just as obviously, if there had been no pirates, we should be without a number of the films we prize most highly. The ethics of the situation remain ambiguous. Recently the courts have shown a tendency to be more lenient with collectors who merely possess, rather than copy and sell, film to which they have no formal title. It is, after all, virtually impossible to say where any one print in hand has come from. In any event, such legalities are soon likely to be academic. For the day of the collector is nearly done, the long and rather foolish battle almost over. With the formation of national, municipal, and university libraries to house film for the purposes of research, the flow of film is all one way. Studios are submitting what is left of their now uncommercial backlog; collectors are as ready to surrender the more precious items in their grab bags so that the record can be filled in and the prints themselves better cared for.

Raymond Griffith back to back with William Powell in *Time to Love*. Also missing.

Care is not yet absolute. Having gathered good evidence that a print of Raymond Griffith's *Wedding Bills* had been in the vaults of a distinguished museum five or six years ago, though it was no longer listed in the files, I made something of a nuisance of myself pressing inquiry. I was at last reluctantly told that the print had indeed been there but had, alas, been allowed to disintegrate before it could be copied. This is not quite the same thing as studio indifference. The museum authorities were by no means indifferent to the fate of the film; they simply hadn't the money to recopy rapidly enough everything currently in their possession.

Funds remain a problem. One recent Christmas week a friend who was then an archivist for a national institution called me in despair: Did I know any way to raise a great deal of money *fast*? It seems that Fox Film, or its present ownership, had agreed to give the institution's library everything stored in its New Jersey vaults. My friend had made a trip out to the vaults, sequestered—because of the hazard of fire—in unsettled woodland. There were masses of aged film for the taking. But the walls of the building had long since cracked, portions of the roof had caved in, snakes were slithering about in the interior undergrowth, foxes were eating the Fox Film. He didn't get enough money fast enough to save everything.

In London I was graciously allowed to go through the vast card-index of films belonging to an equally distinguished institution. The cards showed an extensive collection of early Max Linder material, and a day's showing was arranged. On the day before the planned showing, I received a telephone call informing me that not one of the films was in "projectable condition." The financial position of museums will undoubtedly improve under the increasing pressure from scholars: interest in film history is growing phenomenally among the young. But the situation is not good enough yet.

At the same time remarkable things are being done. A Mary Pickford feature was believed irretrievably gone. One of the possible sources for vanished film is the laboratories in which they were first printed. In the course of its restless searching, the American Film Institute came upon patches of film hanging from such a laboratory's tinting-racks. The process of tinting silent film—blue for night, amber for out of doors, deep red for fires—had to be done sequence by sequence. The film was therefore dismantled, its segments separately treated. And here were the pieces, entirely out of continuity, of Miss Pickford's feature. There were, of course, no titles. A further search unearthed the original title-cards, still stacked, again out of sequence, in the shop that had photographed them. It was now the Institute's exhausting, if pleasurable, task to study the fragments until a cohesive narrative could be established. The film was not so much found as recreated. Something of the same sort has been underway in England with an early and important John Barrymore film. No matter the quality of the reclaimed film: the American Film Institute's recreation turns out to be decidedly lesser Pickford, and the Barrymore may disappoint us too. The point is that there is no discussing quality at all until we have something to look at.

The day of the collector is not *quite* done. In Paris I sat with Henri Langlois of the Cinémathèque Française running down a list of thirty or more films I thought might have found their way into his vast archives. Not one had. It is still necessary to cross one's fingers and look everywhere: in closets in Amsterdam, garages in Terre Haute, projection booths in Berlin suburbs, the basements of nearby neighbors. The Museum of Modern Art occasionally publishes lists of "lost" films. The list must constantly be revised because the very advertisement that certain films are "lost" tends to flush them out.

But it is very late. Given the vulnerability of film, we must either find what we need soon or reluctantly surrender the dream of a reasonably complete record.

Part Four— The Twilight Dance

33. Laurel and Hardy: The First Turnaround

When Stan Laurel and Oliver Hardy were finally teamed in 1927, silent film comedy had less than two years of life left to it. No one knew this at the time, of course, and the sunny emergence of these two overgrown playmates as stars simply seemed additional evidence of silent comedy's apparently inexhaustible capacity for renewing itself. Certainly it was in no one's head in 1927 and 1928 that Laurel and Hardy, those most gentle of violent men, were to be the last of their line, writing—with a bold flourish—*finis* to the form that gave them birth.

Yet in a sense they were doing just that—putting an end to a style. For Laurel and Hardy, no doubt quite unconsciously, were to alter silent film comedy in a way that made it possible for them, alone among their contemporaries, to pass over into sound film with scarcely a hitch of their philosophical shoulders, and to become even more popular than they had been before. What had they done to make themselves instantly adaptable to what would be an entirely different, decidedly inimical, comic rhythm and rationale? In approximately twenty silent two-reelers—the number must be approximate because in some films they appeared together without truly being teamed, because a few early "team" films are lost, and because a handful of late films were made in both sound and silent versions—the imperturbable partners turned silent film comedy completely around.

But before they could do that they had to turn themselves around. Neither man was naturally geared to the role he would play once the two became spiritually inseparable, so inseparable that it seemed no more than just for them to end a film turning a corner in perfect stride, lifting their derbies in harmonious farewell to us, both tucked snugly into Hardy's admittedly ample trousers. For most of their earlier film careers—before the mating, Hardy had been in films for thirteen years, Laurel for ten—each of the two clowns had been working in what proved to be a "wrong" direction. What a happy thing hindsight is!

At least nominally, Laurel was a star from the beginning. As a star, he was a bantam cock, pushy, agitated, agile: if he wanted to follow a girl out of a restaurant—and he did, desperately—he took the shortest route between corner and door, directly across the tabletops. He had come to America as Chaplin's understudy in the Fred Karno revue imported for a vaudeville tour from the British music halls. When the Karno troupe went back to England, Laurel elected to stay on, developing his own vaudeville act. The manager of one house booking his act, deciding to take a flier in films, financed him in a single short comedy, *Nuts in May*, a comedy just successful enough to win him a contract at Universal.

But contracts were less than permanent for Laurel. Though audiences recognized him quickly enough, and rather liked him, no growing cult ever seemed to demand more of him. He was out of Universal and back in vaudeville after three or four films, and this hiring-firing pattern persisted during his ten years as star-apprentice. He worked for Broncho Billy Anderson, where he just happened to play a brief sequence with Oliver Hardy in a film called *Lucky Dog*. He worked for Larry Semon, where he was reportedly tied to a tree to keep him from outracing and outmugging Mr. Semon. Hal Roach signed him on no fewer than three times, but by the time of the last contract in 1926 Laurel was quite willing to abandon his efforts to establish himself as an important comedian and agree to turn his talents to writing and direction. Within the year, the miracle happened.

During these earlier films Laurel neither looks nor behaves like the dissolving snowflake he was to become. You *can* see him begin to cry in some of them, though his toothy mouth is apt to remain open rather than twist into an improbably elongated rubber-band and the earthquake-like convulsion of his face does not yet make his eyes vanish without a trace. You can also see him demurely turn on his heel and walk away from a mess he has made, as though he had plainly been elsewhere the whole time.

But the intimations of an unaggressive Laurel are rare. Stars were people who took charge, led the assault, skipped across mountain-ridges and skylights, frightened off enemies by doing Lupino Lane scissors-jumps, stomped their feet at ocean waves to beat them into retreat. Laurel might borrow an occasional grace note from Keaton: sitting in a steadily sinking rowboat, he continues to play solitaire though the cards are now floating on water. He might appropriate a virtually copyrighted gag of Lloyd's: knowing that one straw hat is to be snatched away from him, he has a second ready for wear behind his back. But he was obviously happiest—and perhaps most successful with exhibitors—when he could engage in uninhibited, often roughhouse, parody of serious silent films. For *The Soilers* he is more than eager to improve on the celebrated William Farnum–Tom Santschi fight in *The Spoilers*, tearing both a saloon and James Finlayson apart while a homosexual cowhand strolls in now and again to counterpoint, and call sufficient attention to, the havoc. In the last of the solo starring series he made before surrendering to Roach, his name is not only above the title, as usual, but is repeated in a border drawn about each of the dialogue captions—with his photograph in the lower left-hand corner. In the photograph he is grinning brightly at us, using a traditional clown's smile to the end. He was, and wished to be, a comedian like any other—hair sleeked down from a part in the middle, bow tie, laughing to help us laugh, his whole demeanor a promise of lightning reflexes. But that was the problem. He was still a comedian like any other comedian, rather too much like his countryman from the music halls, Lupino Lane, for comfort or firm identification. He was not only capable of driving a film before him; he seemed sometimes on the verge of hysteria.

Oliver Hardy had come to films as an amateur three years earlier than Laurel. Steadily employed thereafter, he was forever second man, or third man, a huffing and puffing also-ran. Cherub at birth and cherub to the end, he was a Southern "fat boy"—he is said to have weighed two hundred and fifty pounds

Top: The young Oliver Hardy supporting Larry Semon and Dorothy Dwan in *The Wizard of Oz*. Center: The first chance meeting of Laurel and Hardy for a brief sequence in Essanay's *Lucky Dog*. Below: The team as it came to be, much later.

Laurel and Hardy: The First Turnaround

Left to right: Laurel in a knockabout parody of Valentino's *Blood and Sand*. A toothy grin became his early trademark, leading to a habit of laughing at his own jokes. He learned, in due time, that tears were more nearly his forte. Meantime, Oliver Hardy is slipping into mock-villain roles, unrecognizably.

Far right: A cheerful Charley Chase, whose sponge-padded tights have suffered from exposure to lawn sprinklers.

at the age of fourteen—who first fled home when he was eight and who had a sufficiently prepossessing singing voice to be taken on by traveling minstrel troupes. It was while he was watching a film being made at the Lubin studios in 1913, a mere bystander, that he was dragooned into doing a bit and then allowed to stay on in almost any capacity, lugging props when he wasn't taking falls.

On the screen, he seemed self-effacing, a backgrounder little worried by his relegation to the shadows, willing workhorse and compliant support. He supported the Chaplin imitator Billy West—and when Billy West wasn't available a chap named Harry Mann would imitate Billy West imitating Chaplin—and it was never necessary to tie him to a tree when he worked in support of Larry Semon. Though his roles were theoretically more prominent in the Semon comedies, prominence was a decidedly relative matter where Semon was concerned; not only did the star make certain he dominated the footage but he seems to have held a notion that if one fat man was funny, two would be funnier. Thus Hardy is often the *other* fat comic in Semon films and, pound for pound, the lesser. Indeed, more than his outlines were blurred. His function was made ambiguous: he was part comic, part villain. He might begin a film as Semon's principal rival for the girl's hand. In due time, however, another and more menacing villain would probably turn up, so that Hardy became the *other* villain as well.

Gradually he seemed to resign himself to mock-villain roles in comic melodramas—heavily mustached, whipping about him the opera cape he was to put to such different uses later—and it was for just these purposes that Roach sent for him in 1924. According to John McCabe's affectionate and intimate *Mr. Laurel and Mr. Hardy*, he was playing a plug-ugly in support of Theda Bara when a horse he was riding buckled under his weight on a sand dune. The incident struck the assembled crew as so funny that Hardy was permitted to revert to outright comedy, mainly in support of such Roach regulars as Charley Chase and the ailing Mabel Normand. Though he was still no more than a backup man, he was at least on the lot when Laurel arrived as a writer-director.

The accident that threw them together, though not yet as partners, was an act of desperation called the Hal Roach Comedy All-Stars. All-Stars meant then just what it does today: no stars. Ever since Harold Lloyd's departure from the studio, Roach had been looking for a performer who might one day equal Lloyd's importance and popularity—without success. His Our Gang children's comedies were still chugging along at a secure though unspectacular level, and Charley Chase could be counted on to fill out a release schedule with a steady supply of more

than acceptable two-reelers. But there was no pushing Chase beyond a sprightly domestic base, or toward features: his trim face and manner had no fairy-tale excess in them, no line to invite a caricaturist's ballooning, no mystery to be wrestled with. He would always be at his best as a faintly fussed Mr. Normal, condemned—in his best comedy, *Movie Night*—to hustling his children to the bathroom across the resisting knees of rows of patrons trying to watch the screen. At his less than best he would manufacture gags too transparent for surprise: having padded his thighs with sponge because he is going to play Romeo in tights, he carelessly—and really inexplicably—walks across a lawn covered with revolving sprinklers; as we expect, and as he ought to have expected, the sponge inflates wildly, providing him with the legs of an overfed frog. Chase was a craftsman and would often be of help, behind the camera, to others on the lot, Laurel and Hardy included; but he was trapped between the arbitrary gagging of his Sennett origins and the sheer, not unattractive, ordinariness of his appearance.

But there were any number of trained slapstick clowns on the lot, either under contract or regularly available, and Roach decided to toss them all together into a kind of revolving stock company to see what, if anything, might happen. Something did, but with an almost stubborn slowness. The people on tap included James Finlayson, Max Davidson, Clyde Cook, Eugene Palette, Edgar Kennedy, Noah Young, Oliver Hardy, Mae Busch, and an exceptionally withering, unjustly forgotten comedienne named Anita Garvin; Stan Laurel was dragged from his directorial duties to join the troupe.

If it took a while for Laurel and Hardy to emerge from the melees concocted for the Comedy All-Stars, it was only partly because of Roach's surprising obtuseness. Almost everyone who has written about the team has expressed astonishment at the producer's sluggishness in pairing them. It was rather quickly apparent that audiences and exhibitors had singled out the two men as the most likeable of the lot; Roach knew that. And there, before his eyes, was the precise formula he had long proclaimed for greatness: important visual comedians, he had always said, "essentially imitate children." Certainly he saw Oliver Hardy, roly-poly as an infant, already lowering his head in shame so that all of his double chins would show, twiddling his string tie in pleased embarrassment as though he'd been unaccountably praised before the class by teacher; certainly he noticed that Stan Laurel was given to crying.

Furthermore, there was no need at the time to wait for a *single* star to assert himself and ascend the throne. Teams were a commonplace, often great box-office

Laurel and Hardy: The First Turnaround

assets, of the 1920's. Films had been hospitable to such couplings from the beginning, and by the mid-twenties it seemed as though the studios, with their casting pools and guaranteed exhibition outlets, could create profitable comedy teams virtually at will. Paramount tied burly Wallace Beery and raisin-like Raymond Hatton together for a series of service comedies—*Behind the Front, We're in the Navy Now*—that are mechanical and unamusing now but were rapturously welcomed then. Metro followed suit by putting tall and gangling Karl Dane in tandem with doormouse-sized George K. Arthur, very nearly making the Beery–Hatton films over again. During the same years George Sidney and Charlie Murray were sustaining a series of Cohen and Kelly comedies at Universal.

It was all there, and Roach hesitated. When, in response to obvious audience interest, he did turn a film like *Sailors Beware* over to the pair for their virtually exclusive use, he seemed to take pains to keep the two men apart. *Sailors Beware* is a Laurel and Hardy film, all right; but half of it is Hardy's, the other half Laurel's. Hardy is the purser of a cruise ship, and we follow him as he graciously welcomes women aboard and worries about the exploits of a jewel thief. Laurel is a cab driver whose cab is accidentally roped and hauled aboard; we follow *him* while he loses at dice to a midget and takes a fist straight in the eye from adventuress Anita Garvin. In effect, the two comedians have by this time brushed the competition aside and earned all the footage; but they have very little footage together. As late as their seventh or eighth film together, and with their names "featured" on the title-card, the split continues: *Flying Elephants* is yet one more stone-age parody, material Chaplin and Keaton had pretty well exhausted, but a parody in which the presumed partners do their respective clubbing and wooing in separate frames. Why the long standoff?

They hadn't found the secret yet, which lay in a reversal of functions. Laurel is still the Laurel of his solo films, busy, headlong, unmistakably the man out front. He bustles into a room with briefcase and pince-nez, slapping butler Hardy away firmly as butler Hardy attempts to remove his hat. In *Sailors Beware* he pushes a girl into a swimming pool simply for being haughty to him, then pushes in every male who dares disapprove his behavior. Kibitzing a woman who is playing bridge and playing her hand badly, he snatches the cards from her and thumps them furiously onto the table. When he does have a rare moment with purser Hardy, he claps him hard on the shoulders and orders him to return the ship to harbor, rattling off apparent epithets at linotype speed.

Even as the men begin to share scenes more noticeably, as in *Do Detectives Think?*, Laurel remains the jackrabbit of all occasions: each time a revolver is fired he leaps piggyback onto the shoulders of the person next to him, including those of the woman of the house. Hardy, meanwhile, is in the beginning left sidelined and virtually unrecognizable: a Dutch-comic "mo" obliterates his face during his very few moments in *Love 'em and Weep*. As the two are gradually given scenes together, Hardy seems at first to be trying to keep up with Laurel on Laurel's terms: in *Do Detectives Think?* he winds up for a quick kick at Laurel's posterior before Laurel can fire off one of his own. But that is no solution: two kickers, working at the same fierce speed, simply cancel each other out. Hardy was really too gentlemanly by nature for that sort of thing, which meant that, unless he wished to engage in unpersuasive flailing, he had to let Laurel charge on alone. But so long as Laurel was such a feverish distance ahead of him, the two could not merge.

It all changed the moment that the officious yet courteous Mr. Hardy politely tapped his finger on Mr. Laurel's shoulder and, when Laurel turned to face him, ordered him to the rear with a gracious wave of his hand. "Let me do it" was the

silken, rather sweet, command, and, possibly much to his own surprise, Laurel obeyed. Standing in reserve and blinking his frowsy eyelashes at the camera, Laurel could now wait for the glory, or disaster, or glorious disaster, that might ensue. Laurel had been put in his place, *second* place, and told to calm down. He would be much funnier there, *re*acting to pyramiding horrors rather than racing to perpetrate them. There was a smooth strategist up front who would do all this sort of thing for him at last.

I cannot pinpoint this moment for you in any one film. Perhaps it occurred in a piece of film that has been lost; perhaps it occurred in a piece of film that was never used but simply served as inspiration for an entirely new relationship; perhaps it is there in a complete film shot out of sequence so that we see its results before we see *it*. However that may be, the turnabout—with Hardy as discreet but firm aggressor and Laurel as deferential, if stunned, tag-along—is very nearly complete in what William K. Everson calls the team's first "official" starring vehicle, *Putting Pants on Philip. Putting Pants on Philip* was held back in release, while Roach was finally abandoning independent status to join Metro-Goldwyn-Mayer, so that several films shown earlier display a more firmly sealed compact between the clowns than *Philip* does. But *Philip* lets you see the switch in process.

The two comedians are not buddies from the first frame. The corpulent and confident Hardy, in straw hat rather than the later mandatory derby, is at dockside, awaiting the arrival of his nephew, Laurel. Laurel, upon arrival, is plainly fresh from Scotland, complete with kilts, tam, and crooked stick. Hardy, here and hereafter a most fastidious man, cannot bear the sight of Laurel's kilts, especially when they are blown waist-high passing over air vents, and decides that he must

Opposite: Among the comedy teams readily formed and easily exploited during the 1920's: Karl Dane and George K. Arthur in *Detectives*; Raymond Hatton and Wallace Beery in *Behind the Front*; Charlie Murray and George Sidney in *The Cohens and the Kellys*.

Above: Stan Laurel is still playing aggressive front man in *Sailors Beware*, though Oliver Hardy is somewhere in the film, tagging along.

at once be equipped with socially acceptable trousers. He *commands* Laurel to head for the nearest haberdashery, taking care to keep step a few paces behind so as not to be too closely associated with this living and breathing embarrassment. The march to the tailor's is interrupted each time Laurel passes an attractive girl: in an echo of his earlier energies, Laurel instantly does a scissors-jump and takes off in hot pursuit of the frightened damsel. Both the music-hall acrobatics and the interest in girls would vanish within a film or two. Meantime, Hardy has collared him again and guided him on.

At the tailor's Laurel must be measured. In an exceptionally subtle, original, and funny sequence, the new Laurel establishes himself definitively. Deeply virginal, immensely shy of the tailor's attentions as the measuring-tape is applied to his leg, Laurel recoils, near tears, with each overture. Alert as he is to the tailor's unthinkable intentions, his eyes are sleepier now, glazed with injury; his hair, no longer sleeked down, stands on end like a field of alfalfa, hinting fright. Without any help from titles—what titles could decently do the work?—he makes plain to us his fears. This man is going to rape him. Flinching demurely, then desperately, from each new advance upon ankle and thigh, he makes the tailor's task quite impossible. Hardy asserts himself once more; he and the tailor must wrestle Laurel to the floor, at some length and in an eel's-nest tangle, to get the job done.

Previous page: Escaping from prison by tunneling directly into the warden's office would confuse anybody. *The Second Hundred Years.*

Above: When pants must be put on kilted Stan Laurel, Oliver Hardy takes over, politely but ruthlessly.

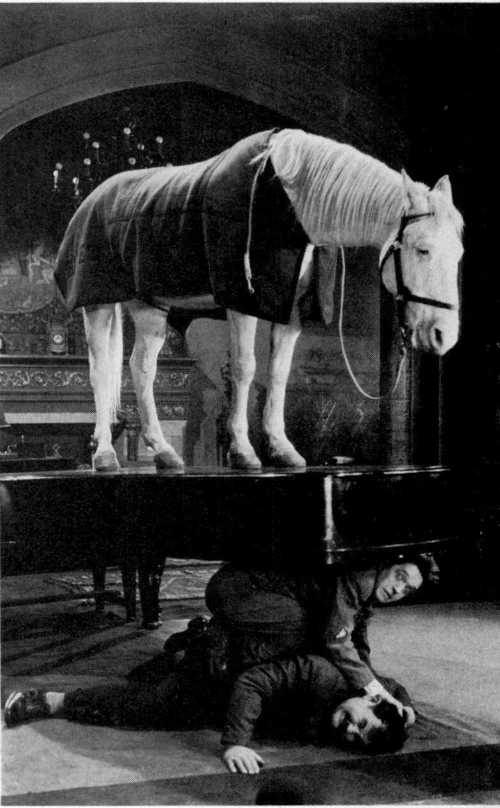

When 'tis done, 'tis done. We are now given what seems an infinitely sustained reaction shot—the first of many for Laurel—in which contending emotions, here the Seven Stages of Humiliation, make a playing field of his face. The assault upon him has been conclusive: he is sullied forever. Ravished, crushed, head hung in eternal shame, eyes filled with the pain of "How could you?", he holds back disintegration as long as he can. But there is no evading the truth, he has been robbed of a pearl of great price, a deflowered man is a ruined man—and the sobs come. The fact that the assault is taken as homosexual and Laurel doesn't even know what homosexuality *is* is simply an indication that the once knowing and aggressive Laurel is becoming as childlike as Roach envisioned and Hardy already looked. Laurel the victim, Laurel the put-upon, Laurel the go-stand-in-the-corner booby is well on the way to being born.

This does not mean that he is necessarily less bright than his lofty mentor. There are often indications that he is brighter. When, for instance, he sees Hardy elegantly approaching a dinner table with an enormous cake and also sees a banana peel directly in his path, he knows perfectly well what is apt to happen. He tells us so with his expectantly resigned glance. Or when the two men are instructed to bring a horse into a house and mount it on a grand piano—perhaps we'll be able to explain *that* situation later—it is Laurel who finds the instructions unlikely and a little disturbing, Hardy who is all affable, idiot compliance. The new relationship simply means that, no matter what he knows, Laurel is to hold his peace. In the matter of the cake, he does. Maintaining the silence that is expected of him, Laurel simply shields his eyes with his hands so he won't have to observe the debacle. He goes along with the installation of the horse as well, with no more than a quizzical intimation to us that something is surely amiss; in fact, it is *he* who ultimately succeeds in placing the horse, named Blue Boy, on the baby grand. No doubt I have indicated the plot by this time; they are supposed to be returning a stolen painting, not a stolen horse. If Hardy rarely questions instructions but hops to with a will, Laurel questions them to no avail; it is understood that he

In *Wrong Again*, Stanley and Oliver are required to establish a horse upon a piano. But it's not the horse that is the problem.

The ineffably patient Oliver Hardy waits for Stan Laurel to straighten up as he also waits for him to surrender the wheel of the condensed auto-streetcar Stanley seems to be driving.

is follower, not leader, which is why his finger is so often slapped away from doorbells.

Neither does the relationship mean that Hardy is unfeeling in his new leadership. He is officious, to be sure, and not to be interfered with by underlings. But nobility obligates, as the phrase has it; Hardy is ineffably gracious toward those who must serve. It will be noticed, in film after film, that if a difficult cooperative effort must be undertaken—perhaps a wall must be scaled, an upper berth reached—it is invariably Hardy who first assigns himself the hard work. Faced with wall *or* upper berth, Hardy is the man who instantly drops to his knees so that Laurel can use him as footstool. It is only when Laurel fails to top the wall that Hardy assigns *him* the kneeling position so that he, Hardy, can start from ten paces back and use Laurel for a flying springboard, collapsing the entire wall inward as he hits it with his ample weight. In the matter of the upper berth, Hardy is extraordinarily obliging, long-suffering even. Hardy kneels in the aisle of the train. Laurel steps on his back to approach the height of their sleeping quarters. While standing on Hardy's back, however, Laurel realizes that he has not removed his overcoat and that unbuckling it may prove awkward in the narrow confines of the berth. In a fit of sublime absentmindedness, he pauses where he is to undo the elaborate buckling, casually disrobing while still astride his partner's back. It is some time before Hardy's pique begins to show.

Nor are we to conclude from Hardy's assumption of full authority in all weathers—taking over dinner checks that can't be paid, forcibly assuming the wheel of an automobile that he will promptly run up a telephone pole, determining the direction of a prison tunnel that will bring the two escapees directly into the warden's office—that Hardy is the funnier man of the pair, the principal comedian. Certainly Hardy is funny in his own right, staring at us ruefully from mud puddles that come up to his chins—though not his bangs—but I would guess that most people have always found Laurel the more amusing genie of the two, have been happy to watch the camera lens pass from Hardy's delightfully florid sashays into holocaust to Laurel's furrowed-brow hope that the worst will not be worse than last time. Laurel's reputation as a gag-man was high; his was the inventive mind behind the series, keeping him working on the lot late at night to construct improbabilities for the morrow while Hardy—a nine-to-five homebody who liked to spend his spare time golfing—contented himself with learning his lines and conserving his energies for the next drop down a manhole. Laurel had at last found his genuine stardom—you will notice that his name comes first in the billing—but had found it by taking lead position behind the scenes, back seat on the screen.

It just worked better that way.

34. Laurel and Hardy: The Saving Turnaround

Having inverted roles and temperaments, the two clowns proceeded to invert the methods of silent film comedy as well. The entertainer-musician Max Morath has explained how, in the late nineteenth and early twentieth centuries, the stately quadrille was transformed into ragtime. Silent film comedy may be said to have begun as ragtime. Laurel and Hardy turned it back into a stately quadrille.

Once again, rather unexpectedly, it was the lesser of the two zanies, the courtly and formerly upstaged Oliver Hardy, who was most responsible. For it was he—composed, like a child's drawing, almost entirely of circles—who seemed always to be escorting his entourage, including the now pliant Mr. Laurel, through a world become a ballroom, counting his steps punctiliously and insisting on an elegant, even a rather dainty, beat. He led the grand march deferentially, but nonetheless *led* it, ready to lower his eyes and his graceful balding head in a condescending bow on the very last note and to indicate—with the fingers of one hand spread open on his breast, the fingers of the other curling in a genteel "come hither"—that refreshments were to be served in the next room.

It was Hardy's personal rhythm, a rhythm that has been recognized as that of a "Southern gentleman," that determined the new pace at which both men were to work and to which silent comedy would be forced to accommodate itself. In taking over from Laurel as go-getter, as initiator of all catastrophe, Hardy could not behave as the impetuous Laurel had behaved in the role, or as virtually all two-reel runaway clowns had eagerly behaved before him. *They* had sprinted from square one, as though in response to a starter's gun; there would be further gunshots along the way to make them go faster and faster. Hardy heard music instead, the soothing guidance of a steady 2/4 beat, the mellifluous promptings of a chastely tuned pianoforte. Whether he was opening a door in doorman's greatcoat and braided cap or escorting a damsel to a curb where yet another devilishly deep puddle lay in wait, he moved to a tune, all obsequious grace and grand manner. Nor was anyone to interfere, displaying vulgar hurry, unsuitable urgency; a chap's

Laurel and Hardy: The Saving Turnaround

Oliver Hardy: The tie-twiddle.

Opposite: Situations of this sort do not call for passion but for patience. Stanley is the most patient.

hands could get soundly slapped for that. This front-man's deportment was deliberate, most fashionably controlled; and if the front-man was slowed down by the delicacy of his nature, the second-man, Laurel, had to be slowed further still, rendered all but inanimate as he waited for his master's cue. How, then, were the gags to be performed? They were to be performed by dispensing with both passion and surprise.

They did not change the gags. They did exactly what other silent comedians had always done, and when they had finished repeating other comedians they repeated themselves: they threw pies, stepped on tacks, slipped on banana peels, went to the dentist, backed out of parking places to crash into other cars, visited graveyards at midnight to run in terror from men wearing sheets. Substantively, they invented almost nothing.

Instead, they did something almost as venturesome, perhaps even more daring. Like two little children caught with their hands in the cookie jar, they confessed. They confessed to the joke. It was, they sheepishly and rather winsomely admitted, the same old joke. Hardy might pluck embarrassedly at the folds of his voluminous nightgown as he looked demurely into the camera to say so. But, they went on to ask, who's kidding who? Everyone knows *all* the jokes by this time, has seen them a hundred thousand times. How could we possibly fool anyone into thinking them new?

And so instead of trying to fool anyone with the joke, they *showed* everyone the joke, explained it most carefully, anatomized it. Here, you see, is Mr. Hardy climbing out of bed to get a hot water bottle for Mr. Laurel, who has a toothache. Here, on the floor between the bed and the bathroom, is a tack. Here comes Mr. Hardy, stately in his kindliness and blind to his peril. Here is Mr. Hardy *stepping* on the tack, howling in pain and plucking it from his bare foot. Here is Mr. Hardy throwing the tack away with infinite disgust. Here is Mr. Hardy in the bathroom, filling the hot water bottle, and returning to the bedroom. Here, once again, is the tack on the floor, exactly where Mr. Hardy has thrown it. Here is Mr. Hardy stepping on the tack a second time, howling a second time, plucking it loose a second time. You see how it is done? Inevitable, ineffable.

Comedians before them had elided as much as possible, concealing the tack or the ditch or the loose brick that lay in wait. It was a point of honor, and a proper one, for earlier clowns to avoid the close-up that would display the tack, to see to it that its presence was either implied or inadvertent or possibly forgotten. No such deviousness for Laurel and Hardy. The syntax would be laid out now, frame by frame, sedately entered and endured. The joke was no longer a jack-in-the-box to be sprung on the unwary. It was a ritual through which the well-informed were courteously conducted, a ceremonious tour of well-marked terrain.

The agenda allowed for small exceptions, to be sure: if Laurel and Hardy, photographed at waist-height, were to be seen strolling side by side down a street, Laurel might suddenly simply disappear from the frame, the camera continuing to pull back to let us see that he has gone down a manhole. In such cases, however, the pair were apt to repeat the gag *exactly* a little later in the same film so that we should this time thoroughly grasp the comic machinery and know where to look for its victim.

Having more or less got rid of surprise, Laurel and Hardy went on to dismiss the passions that normally drove the uncautious into its treacherous arms, even to dismiss the passion that might follow upon affront. As their relationship became firmer, they were seen to be extraordinarily passionless creatures. They had, for instance, virtually lost their interest in women, the one motive that would most surely drive comedians to unseemly excess. A few of their most celebrated gags

are indeed sexual: running from their wives, one of whom has a rifle, in *We Faw Down*, they scamper through an alleyway between two apartment buildings; as the rifle blazes away at their fleeing forms, trouserless men instantly leap from *every* window in the adjacent buildings. The alley is alive with errant husbands. But that, as it happens, is a joke about other men's sexuality. It is not about Laurel and Hardy's. For, though they have in fact spent the afternoon in the apartment of two damsels to whose aid they have catastrophically come, they are wholly innocent. One of the damsels, on the pudgy side and given to flirtation, may have invited Laurel to "play" with her. But Laurel's notions of "play" do not extend beyond giving her several happy, increasingly hearty shoves, the most exuberant of which quite topples her from her chair. Mr. Hardy is most often married; Mr. Laurel is occasionally henpecked. But they are overgrown lads who have arrived at some neutral ground on which they stand loyal to, but romantically uninterested in, their wives, while other women inspire in them no more than gallantry, with pushes.

If emotion has given way to form where women are concerned, it is under majestic control in all other relationships—including battle to the death. Hypothetically, such genteel and/or anesthetized types should have produced a kind of comedy in which mayhem would be minimal. Actually, Laurel and Hardy were the most destructive of all comedians, hurling more pies in *The Battle of the Century* than the Sennett lot had ever baked, tearing more clothes apart in *You're*

Darn Tootin' than the Roach lot could likely afford, turning a long line of stalled cars in *Two Tars* into an automobile graveyard of apocalyptic proportions.

But they did it methodically, experimentally, really without malice. They were objective, detached about such damage as might be done. If another man stepped up to Mr. Hardy, or for that matter to Mr. Laurel, and slowly and firmly ripped the lapel from his jacket, Mr. Hardy—or, for that matter, Mr. Laurel—would not promptly fly into a rage and do immediate violence in return. He would stare into the camera for a very long time, considering that God's universe has come to this. He might then turn his benumbed attention to the ripper, wondering what further project he might conceivably be contemplating. The ripper, having done a little waiting of his own, would now just as carefully strip away Hardy's—or Laurel's—*other* lapel. Now, the victim would ask us silently while staring once more into the camera, isn't that exactly what you'd expect?

Laurel and Hardy were not made of stone. They would, in their own very good time, retaliate. Perhaps Hardy, if it was he who'd been shorn, would turn to face his tormentor regally for a moment or two and then do some work on *his* jacket. Or he might, after a pause, go into a little one-two-three seizure, beginning with his ankle and ending with clawed fingers, showing at last a trace of fury—about three minutes after the fact. *Or* Mr. Laurel might do the job for him, without the twitch, simply stepping forward in noncommittal efficiency—and with his mouth compressed into a fathomless straight line—to carefully remove from the aggressor one or two lapels on a fair-is-fair basis. Mr. Laurel, having acquired a leader, had become very loyal to him. He *liked* him, would assist him in any sufficiently delayed emergency. John McCabe has sent me a scrap from Stan Laurel's notebook, a first jotting for a gag which he and Oliver "Babe" Hardy might use:

Babe: Please, teacher, may I leave the room?
Teacher: Certainly not.
Stan: *(Puts hand up)*
Teacher: What do you want?
Stan: Please let him!!

Perhaps the double exclamation point at the end of the last sentence suggests that Stan was fearful of some impending accident, even one that might discomfort *him*. The two, in their sexless boyishness, did make use of bathroom gags and just-past-puberty embarrassments: when the hot water bottle that has been provided for Stan's toothache begins to leak in the bed they share, it is clear from the expression on Oliver's face that he thinks quite another sort of mishap is underway; attempting to exchange trousers because they have inadvertently got each other's on, they are constantly flushed out of alleyway corners and telephone booths with their flies open and shirttails out. Most likely, though, the fragment I've quoted illustrates Stan's deep devotion to his companion and to his companion's needs. He would always step forward, resolute in the same retarded rhythm, to shatter an oppressor's windshield or scissor the belt from his trousers.

The waiting game being so solemnly played spread to embrace not only the two principals but all their supporting players, including—so uncharacteristically—policemen. If Edgar Kennedy had sloshed a bucket of water into Oliver Hardy's face and Oliver Hardy were now on the way to a faucet for a refill, Kennedy would not—as any reasonable man or any other comedian would have done—take to his heels. He would stand his dry ground until Hardy had returned to make it wet. After that, it was someone else's turn. The rules held: Do not react, except to show a degree of resignation; hold for the next slosh, the next rip, the next blow, and then count ten before deciding on the form of reply. The victim, whoever he might be, would remain available.

Confidence on the one hand, serenity on the other. Or is it vice versa? *The Finishing Touch*. Unruly gum-ball machines are the least of it in *Two Tars*, not yet risen to its apocalyptic proportions.

Thus the *comedy* of Laurel and Hardy came to consist of the pauses between the effronteries. The comedy of the effronteries themselves, the acts of violence, we had had before, endlessly. What is distinctively funny about these two men is the time-lag, the unemotional patience, even dignity, with which the unthinkable is accepted, allowed to play itself out. They were still insisting that we fully anticipate the next joke, as they themselves were so plainly anticipating it, and it took a great deal of stolidity, some trace of hauteur, to do that. They *chose* to be emotionally uninvolved while in all other respects being horrendously involved: it was a matter of temperament, of comic philosophy, of personal honor. The choice is also, of course, their form of fantasy. Normal men, real men, have much shorter tempers. Theirs is a violence governed by Euclid, maybe Mozart.

Such a rhythm, as I've suggested, can have come only from Hardy; Laurel had to be reduced to it. Just how and when everyone else at the Roach studio decided that it would be wise, or perhaps just consistent, to follow suit, I don't know. But during their reign on the Roach lot the style became so infectious that it was perfectly possible to make a Laurel and Hardy comedy without Laurel and Hardy: *A Pair of Tights* is a delightfully strict echoing of the method with Edgar Kennedy, Anita Garvin, Stuart Erwin, and Marion Byron wreaking most of the stubborn havoc outside an ice-cream parlor. By the time of the 1929 *Big Business,* in my opinion the funniest of all their films and—after *Two Tars*—no doubt the most destructive, the formula is tooled to such a fineness that Laurel and Hardy can make a shambles of James Finlayson's home at the same time that Mr. Finlayson is reducing their curbside automobile to shards of tin—without either party to the contest making the least effort to protect what is his own. As Laurel hurls lampstands through plate-glass windows and pitches vases for Hardy to bat at as though he were trying for three-baggers, Mr. Finlayson watches from the lawn, his fierce Scot's countenance screwed up into ever-rubberier contortions but his body rooted in space until the orgiastic impulse of the moment has spent itself. Then he marches to the car, Laurel and Hardy just behind, so that they can attend while Finlayson conducts its disembowelment, yanking out headlights to throw through the windshield, stripping away fenders, casting loose the Christmas trees Laurel and Hardy have been trying to sell, putting a match to the gas tank. No interference, either way. Just a stately procession from crumbling car to splintering home—the chimney is now coming down—as though honestly engaged men were working toward an ultimate tie score. A neighborhood crowd that gathers simply follows the contestants from lawn to curb, like spectators at a golf match, deeply interested. A policeman drives by and stops; he sits in his car, permitting a moderately disapproving scowl to come to full rest on his face, observing the antiphonal devastation. All are present at a ceremony and behave, between

The mayhem in *Big Business* is methodical, mannerly, and dispassionate—up to a point.

assaults on inanimate objects, with the utmost circumspection.

Finlayson, incorrigibly a mugger and overheating too quickly to quite adopt Edgar Kennedy's "slow burn," does show passion betweentimes. Having demolished the car beyond even miraculous redemption, he takes to wrestling a Christmas tree on the ground, most savagely. But he never attacks the gentlemen who have now tumbled his piano onto the lawn and are taking an axe to it, nor do they care to lay a finger on him. Oh, perhaps it has all begun with a bit of fingerwork: Mr. Finlayson has used a lawn shears to snip off Mr. Hardy's tie and shirttails, Mr. Hardy has appropriated them to remove the few fronds of hair left on Mr. Finlayson's glossy head. But the hostilities have almost at once become quite impersonal, and only dormant objects suffer. The pavane is a rite, not a fight.

The mainly even-tempered formality with which the comedians conducted their depradations snugly fit their images as Roach's long-sought "children." Children are destructive, but they are—for the most part—destructive in Laurel and Hardy's way. Children build Tinkertoy structures and then knock them down. But they build them as much *for the pleasure* of knocking them down as they do out of any sense of achievement. They are young yet, not concerned with permanence. They like patterns, and broken things make new patterns, surprising ones. A child who topples *another* child's structure too soon may stir up a bit of pique; but it is thoroughly understood that the other child now has a right of rejoinder, which he may deliberately—and without interference—exercise. Chances are the two children will be giggling, like Laurel and Hardy, over the whole thing two minutes later. The children are at "play."

So are Laurel and Hardy, always, from the moment they escape prison in *The Second Hundred Years* to skip through the town with paint buckets, daubing every store front, lamppost, and unwary woman within reach. Laurel is Hardy's valet in *Early to Bed*, and his whole problem is to get his master tucked away for the night while his master, who has been out on the town and is a bit tiddly, insists, "I don't want to go to bed, I want to play." Though they would eventually be a shade too literal about it all—in a sound-film called *Brats*, playing their own children—there was never any real conflict between the big-boyishness that increasingly wrapped itself about them and the stubborn deliberateness that had become their identifying pace.

It was the ceremonious pacing—the admission that we all knew the joke and might just as well wait for it, it would come—that altered silent film comedy. The two comedians did not do the work alone, of course: with a cameraman like George Stevens and an editor-director like Leo McCarey in training on the Roach lot, and with fellow comedians who were fabled for their willingness to help, their curious accomplishment was a collaborative achievement. But the focus on screen was on two faces, two forms: it was Laurel and Hardy who did not kick back instantly when kicked but who bided their time in sheepish close-ups until we'd been given an opportunity not only to catch up with the joke but to get well, well ahead of it.

Their work was in some senses limited; it always would be. The absence of passion, for women or for other goals, would deny them the extended narrative base on which feature films generally depend. Forced into features by the economic depression that soon followed the coming of sound—double features became an almost universal practice, eliminating much of the market for short comedies—they at first appeared in supporting roles and then in features of their own that would do well enough as one half of a dual bill but that might, like their much-admired *Sons of the Desert*, seem no more than thinnish extensions of their twenty-minute improvisations. The features tended to be on the insubstantial side,

and Laurel, late in life, thought they ought never to have gone into them at all.

Being essentially men who stood their ground, they were not really interested in the farther reaches of silent film fantasy, those reaches that lifted agile men above street level to flirt with the horizon, or in the kind of camera-work that would give the magnified landscape authenticity. When Laurel is atop a ladder that will not reach the second-story window he is trying to enter and Hardy obligingly, but perspiringly, hoists the ladder itself into the air, we see—in alternate shots—Laurel weaving wildly about on his unstable perch, Hardy, below, manfully trying to keep swaying ladder aloft. But we never see the master shot, the complete image all at once, which, by Lloyd's or Keaton's standards, is unforgivable filmmaking. This is simply not Laurel and Hardy territory, any more than the naked girders of *Liberty* are: no doubt sent to climb them by Roach, who had had such success with Lloyd at these heights, the comedians are constantly photographed from angles that suggest secure flooring just a few inches away. A splendid comic *idea* in one of their later sound features is often cited as an example of silent film's continuing influence: Laurel and Hardy are trying to move a piano across a suspension bridge, above a deep chasm, when they meet, at the halfway mark, a gorilla; but the idea, enchanting as it is, is quite spoiled in the shooting by the fact that the two men are obviously working, in complete safety, against a "process" background. The pair are indeed zanies, but they are not acrobats. And where, in any case, would there be room on girders or suspension bridges or untrustworthy ladders for them to display the all but embalmed fortitude of their most characteristic responses?

The degree of fantasy they possessed was in *them*, in the passers-by and mundane gumball machines they could most readily lay inept hand to, not in their mating with the universe's more treacherous, vaster wiles. It was a fantasy of physical, if not mental, retardation, of nobly refusing to be hurried into anything at all by anything at all, of waiting out the jest until it had completed its own point-by-point exegesis. Thus equipped, they could amble into the world of sound self-contained, a private zaniness intact, an idiosyncratic rhythm unaltered.

Sound-film, with its naturalistic rate and consequently subdued deportment, couldn't slow them down. They had got there first.

This posed shot, presumably for *Big Business*, is uncharacteristic of the mature Stanley and does not appear in the completed film. A shade unseemly, no doubt.

35. The Transition, After and Just Before: A Self-conscious Chaplin

Chaplin was the holdout. As it became apparent, in late 1928 and early 1929, that sound had irrevocably won the contest with silence, Hollywood stars tumbled over themselves in their eagerness to prove that they could survive the change. Chaplin's fellow comedians, or at least those among them who continued to command loyal audiences and were physically capable of making the transition, joined the rush, scarcely glancing back to see what they might be leaving behind them. A few were blocked: Harry Langdon's career as a star of features had so disintegrated by 1928 that no one was going to bother to discover whether or not he could speak, and he did what he could to keep alive by making catch-as-catch-can two-reelers and occasionally appearing as minor support in other men's full-length films; Raymond Griffith had seriously damaged his vocal cords as a young man and could summon up no more than a husky whisper, which meant he had to abandon his career as a performer forthwith and turn his talents—successfully enough—to writing and producing.

But Harold Lloyd was so determined not to be even a few months behind the times that he took an already completed silent film, *Welcome Danger*, and remade it as a talkie before releasing it. The move was an expensive one; but it theoretically kept him in the vanguard. Keaton had no decision of his own to make, now that he was completely in the hands of Metro-Goldwyn-Mayer. The studio promptly put him into its all-star musical showcase, *The Hollywood Revue of 1929*, where he mournfully held an umbrella during the original "Singin' in the Rain" number, and hurried with preparations for his next singing and dancing vehicle, *Free and Easy*. Both Lloyd's *Welcome Danger* and Keaton's *Free and Easy* were financial successes. And we have already watched Laurel and Hardy stroll imperturbably from one form to the other.

The general impression is that virtually all silent film stars were dethroned by sound, replaced on the instant by well-spoken, better-trained importations from the Broadway stage. That is not at all the case. There were indeed disasters:

confronted with the necessity of following up what was already being acknowledged as a "masterpiece." Having decided upon *The Circus*, his last film to be released during the silent period as such, he was quickly beset with difficulties. Some of these were personal rather than professional: more marital problems, more threats of attachment of completed or uncompleted film. Halfway through the project, he stopped work altogether and escaped to Europe, obviously hoping through rest to resolve some canker at the film's heart. Returning, he pushed it through to completion, settling for craftmanship rather than the inspiration that hadn't come. In fact, it was all he could do.

The Circus is not a poor film, it is simply the workaday product of a comic genius at odds with himself. Neither the problem Chaplin faced nor the response he made to it is an unfamiliar one. With his stature elevated to near-Olympian heights by *The Gold Rush*, he had grown self-conscious *as a comedian*. In order to cope with the problem, he decided to dramatize it. He would make a comedy about the consciousness of being funny.

Other writer-directors have attempted to confront vast success, or perhaps circumvent it, by following the same course. Fellini did it with *8½*. But a comedian runs a risk with this tactic that a director of more serious films does not. He must create laughter and dramatize the process of creating laughter at one and the same time, a near-impossibility. And to tease a feature film out of it Chaplin had to probe the subject in some depth, displaying the *failure* to provoke laughter as well as success in provoking it; he then had to account in some way for the difference. Almost at once he was embroiled in a lie, one I'm sure accounted for some of his discomfort in making the film. The narrative premise of *The Circus*—once it is isolated from the perfunctory love story and some anachronistic melodrama—is really this: comedy is created by accident, not intention.

A circus that has temporarily taken up residence in an amusement park is in dire trouble: its professional clowns are getting no laughs at all; the audiences at the circus yawn and read newspapers while the clowns lamely dance about on a turntable. Charlie, broke and running from a policeman, bursts through the tent-flaps and onto the turntable, the policeman hot on his heels, both weaving in and about among the bewildered professionals. At once the circus audience breaks into gales of laughter, laughter quite in excess of the chase we are looking at. Still trying to evade the policeman as a magician introduces his act, Charlie keeps popping up in boxes and draped chairs where the magician's "disappearing" girl assistant should be, eventually unleashes the whole of the magician's paraphernalia in a swoop, reaping the whirlwind. At this point what Chaplin is doing *is* funny, and we are laughing. But the hysteria and applause of the circus audience is so much greater a response than our own that *our* laughter is sharply tempered. We seem not to have been giving this accidental clown his full due. The lie has been compounded: humor is an accident, it creates effects more immediate and intense than we are able to recognize.

The difficulty grows increasingly complex, dogs the film like a toothache. Once Charlie has eluded the policeman and fled the tent, the professional clowns are to be seen half-heartedly disporting themselves in ways that not even they could possibly consider amusing. The circus audience is booing, furiously. Their cry goes up in a caption: "Where's the funny man?" But the caption cannot be taken at face value, as mere reference to a character in a film who did not mean to be funny at all. If Chaplin himself had been known as anything during his already long and fabled career it was as "the funny man." The phrase was reserved for him. Thus the title is making double, and disturbing, reference. It refers to the inept little vagrant of the narrative; and it refers to the highly professional, inter-

Charlie thoughtfully assimilating one of the circus magician's tricks. *The Circus*.

The Transition, After and Just Before: A Self-conscious Chaplin

Above, Charlie being chased into the circus—and into inadvertent laughter. Below, apple on head, Charlie trying to be funny about *not* being funny.

Opposite, above: The Funny Man. Opposite, below: Success in the ring—though Charlie, somehow, is unaware of it.

nationally acclaimed man who is playing him. Our eyes begin to cross. *How* are we to take this figure, as booby or as skilled entertainer?

Our perplexity is not in the least resolved by the next title and shot. The circus audience has clamored for "the funny man." Laconic title: "The Funny Man." Iris open to Charlie sound asleep on wisps of straw in an idle circus chariot, altogether unaware of what has happened. This bit of aftermath is of course meant to be ironic. It is also meant to build sympathy for the shabby stranger who has no sense of his accomplishment. Chaplin is downgrading himself as a clown, hinting that fame is not merely elusive but unrecognizable and that a man on whom it has unpredictably, even unfairly, descended is not likely to find himself at once on a bed of roses. Much as we love this figure, and suggestively mythic as the shot itself is, we are aware that the image is a cheat. It is Chaplin himself who has here called attention to his inadvertent function as a "funny man." But Chaplin, as a "funny man," is the very man we know to have been instantly rewarded with adulation, the very man who has been so painstaking about his conscious craft that he hasn't hesitated to spend two or three years making certain that his next film would be "funny."

Chaplin's dilemma in deciding to discuss his craft with us has now been established and must be pursued, almost ruthlessly. Discovered by the circus manager—a mustached villain who uses his ringmaster's whip on his daughter whenever her bareback riding isn't up to snuff—Charlie is invited to join the circus and learn his trade as a clown. At rehearsal next morning, the manager's command to Charlie to "Go ahead and be funny" is, for us, close to blood-curdling. *We* expect Chaplin to be funny, have always known him to be. The scene, however, demands that he not be. The "character" he is playing has only earned laughter by happenstance, has no equipment for doing it on demand. Thus, as he steps into the ring to do a low vaudeville waddle and hoist himself higher with the help of his cane, he is not funny. To us this can only be disappointing. Told that what he has done is terrible, he is ordered to watch the regular clowns go through a William Tell routine in which the arrow is never let fly because the target clown keeps removing the apple from his head to take bites out of it, then through a barber-shop routine in which buckets of lather are sloshed every which way. These routines too must be inadequate: the circus has been failing because of them. But Charlie, the novice on the sidelines, is doubled up with laughter by them, clapping his hand over his mouth in a Harry Langdonish effort to control himself. Whatever he is telling us about this "character," we know better, know that *he* knows better.

Now, sent into the ring to repeat the routines, Chaplin is in an ultimate bind. The narrative demands that he fail at both of them, that he not be funny. But the film's *rhythmic* structure, our psychological expectation, demands that he be funny to us while bungling the routines. He must be funny while being unfunny, and what way is there out of that? His solutions are weak indeed: finding a worm in the half-eaten apple, he substitutes a banana on his head; flailing about with the paint brushes used for lathering, he is willing to give but not take, flinching whenever the suds approach him. But there was never any way out of the dilemma, and the sequence stands heartsick at the center of the film.

How could it do otherwise? Chaplin has contradicted his basic character. The infinitely adaptable Charlie has always been good at everything he has undertaken. He is now asking us to believe that he cannot be good as a clown!

Helplessly, the film pursues its way through the maze of self-contradiction. Charlie is fired, then rehired as a mere property man when the circus's unpaid backstage staff goes on strike. While he has his arms piled high with a rippling tower of

As Charlie stands in the demolished ring he couldn't master, the wagons roll.

Opposite: Clown Henry Bergman tries to cheer a Charlie who didn't get a laugh. A more successful Charlie keeps the ringmaster's whip at bay. The girl is Merna Kennedy.

dishes intended for some other entertainer's act, a hostile mule spies him and gives chase, driving him once more into the arena itself, tumbling him over the ring and sending spirals of dishware into the air about him.

At once the circus audience is cheering again, anticipating and overwhelming our own response to a brief incident that is in fact reasonably amusing. In all probability a theater or film audience should *never* be shown, or even told, that what it is watching is proving irresistible to others; passing such judgment is our prerogative, and we do not care to be bullied.

The result of the new clamor, however, is that Charlie is given the mule-and-dishes mishap as his regular routine at each performance, a move which quickly makes the circus immensely profitable. Charlie, however, does not seem to understand that he is continuing as anything more than a property man. As one of the manager's titles puts it, "He's a sensation but doesn't know it." The situation continues, apparently, for some months. But for the fourth or fifth time, we are baffled. Fleeing from the mule at each performance, hasn't he heard the laughter?

Eventually the girl tells him that he is really "the hit of the show" and, with a quick swagger and a snap of his fingers, he says "I knew it!" But the humor of the moment stems from the fact that he *hasn't* known it and is now pretending to shrug off his prominence as inevitable.

When he learns that the girl he has fallen in love with has herself fallen in love with a new tightrope walker, he is crushed. Returning from the ring and the mule after the next performance, the manager-bully is waiting for him, demanding to know what's gone wrong. "You hardly got a laugh," he snarls. Is comedy, then, not an accident after all? Has it, at the very least, something to do with the entertainer's high or low spirits, his ability to transcend himself and provoke laughter by calculated control? The film's premise is flypaper; no matter in which direction Charlie—or is it Chaplin?—moves, his nimble feet are mired.

That is so, however, only so long as *The Circus* is directly attending to its thematic business. The premise does make the love story a cursory affair, for the simple reason that the love story has nothing to do with its problems. The figure of the tightrope walker is roughed in at the last minute, much too late for the pathos Chaplin strives for as the girl rides away with her new husband in a circus van while Charlie stands waving and alone beside the dusty tumble of gaudy, curlicued wagons on the move. We are forced to settle for the visual beauty of the shot as "shot"; it is in fact very beautiful.

But the conundrum at the core of the film does not exclude incidental improvisation. And the incidental improvisation is often Chaplin at his finest: turning himself into a mechanized woodcarving on the deck of a Noah's Ark, indistinguishable from the rest of the bobbing gallery; stealing a baby's hot dog, bite by bite, while giving it sweetly avuncular headshakes and then considerately wiping *its* lips; dodging both a policeman and a pickpocket in a house of mirrors, choreographing the cross-eyed images so precisely that two men stealing away from each other bump headlong; giving the hungry girl a severe motherly scolding for stealing half his piece of bread, then mocking the appalling way she wolfs it down, which just happens to be the way he once wolfed down brother Sydney's muffins in *A Dog's Life*; stunting dangerously but with great aplomb on a high-wire, his cameras at last placed as cleverly—and nearly as authentically—as Lloyd's.

There is just enough brilliance all along the outer edges of *The Circus* to compensate for the troubled preoccupation at its center. The film was a respectable financial success, and it did serve the purpose of exorcising such private demons as *The Gold Rush* had unleashed. But *The Circus* was released in 1928, and since Chaplin was now in the habit of taking several years to complete a film, sound had to be faced. Chaplin chose to face it down.

36. Chaplin Confronts Himself

When Chaplin finally did decide to speak on the screen—in 1940, with *The Great Dictator*—the fate that had overtaken his fellow clowns so many years earlier also and inevitably overtook him. He knew that it would. Once he had finished *Modern Times* and was debating his next step, he told himself, according to his autobiography, "If I talked I would become like any other comedian." Eventually he reconciled himself to what he believed a compromise. In *The Great Dictator* he would play two roles, a parodied Adolf Hitler and a guileless Jewish barber dressed pretty much as the Chaplin figure had always been dressed: "As Hitler I could harangue the crowds in jargon and talk all I wanted to. And as the tramp I could remain more or less silent."

As it happens, the "tramp"—actually not a tramp at all, let it be noted, but a marvelously expert barber who owns his own shop—is by no means silent in the completed film. He speaks often, in a tight, clipped, plaintively husbanded voice that quite clearly displays Chaplin's regret at reducing the mythic outline to an identifiable individual with a specific, specifically British, life history. But the "compromise" did leave the door open to at least two enchanting, if brief, silent passages: in one, having been hit on the head with a heavy frying pan, Charlie dances in great loops along the sidewalk as though he were a bird half-grounded by a slightly out-of-kilter wing; in the other he shaves a customer, most precisely, to the rapidly shifting rhythms of Brahms's "Hungarian Dance No. 5." The episodes are almost damaging to the film in their exquisite lightness and triumphant élan, reminding us as they do of what had been. The moments directly alongside them must seem leaden.

Otherwise the damage is approximately what Chaplin had expected, against which he now tried intelligently to protect himself. He understood, for instance, that the essential joke had changed. In *The Great Dictator* an enthusiastic inventor comes to the dictator proudly wearing a new bullet-proof vest, inviting immediate testing. The dictator fires a shot and the inventor drops. Another inventor appears with an instantaneously opening parachute, happily leaps from a window to demonstrate its virtues. The dictator and his colleagues watch his fall, turn away with a sigh. In silent film the joke had always been that the man downed by gunfire or dropped from a window promptly got up and ran away. But the reality of sound-film had dashed this pleasant fantasy. Chaplin would therefore make his new joke out of the "real" thing that happens in such circumstances: death. As a visual joke, death may not be so exhilarating as its predecessor had been—after all, there are now bodies to be disposed of, which invites cutting away discreetly before the jest can be extended or topped—but the adjustment was necessary, and Chaplin made it as efficiently as he could.

Curiously, he did not fully anticipate how many time-honored bits of business would no longer be effective at the sound-camera's naturalistic rate. In *The Great Dictator* he permits himself a tumble down a flight of stone steps, photographed at the slower, more detailed speed. The fall is lumbering, awkward, without line, unfunny. Some years later he would allow three of his early silent films to be combined and reissued as *The Chaplin Revue* in "stretch-printed" form, with many frames repeated in order to accommodate the original visual rhythm to sound-trained eyes. The cadence of all three films, and of Chaplin's work in them, is utterly destroyed. Let no newcomer to the form begin acquaintance with Chaplin on such terms; only the originals will do. In any event, Chaplin retired the familiar "tramp" figure altogether after *The Great Dictator*, going on to play roles that could not—in their echoes—further diminish the silent image he had labored so conscientiously to perfect.

But there was still a good bit of time before 1940 and *The Great Dictator*, time enough to turn out—against all odds—yet another silent "masterpiece," together with a successor very nearly as good. "*City Lights* and *The Gold Rush* and *The Navigator* and *The General* are the four great comedies, aren't they?" Woody Allen asked Penelope Gilliatt when she interviewed him for *The New Yorker*. And yes, I guess they are. But what is it that makes one film incontestably great while another, almost its equal, is begrudged the accolade?

I'm not going to attempt to define the word *masterpiece*. But I do suppose that any work to which the label sticks and sticks and sticks contains at least two things: an accounting, in perfect balance, of the materials it chooses to embrace; and an accounting, so complete that it amounts to a summary, of the artist's own creative method. The content of the work must fall into place without forcing, with simple rectitude. And its creator must expose himself in the content as wholly as it is possible for mortal man to do.

City Lights meets these requirements as if they were not requirements but afterthoughts, virtues that had slipped in while a conscientious entertainer was doing nothing more than taking care to be entertaining.

Superficially, the film may seem a summary of all the gags that silent film was preparing itself to abandon, as though Chaplin, in defying the prevailing enthusiasm for sound-film, had determined to gather in one great bundle the routines that had first defined and then disinguished a form. There is a prizefighting sequence, one so precisely danced that Chaplin can slip away from his opponent to leave opponent and referee continuing the time-step face to face. It is a brilliant passage, one of the funniest Chaplin ever filmed, but it might easily be taken as a reminder of Chaplin's brief appearance as a referee in a Sennett-Arbuckle film of 1914. There is a street-sweeping sequence, with Charlie as white-wing confronted first with a parade of circus ponies, then with an elephant; everyone up to and after Harry Langdon had done it. There is a substitution of a bar of soap for the cheese in a laborer's sandwich, with bubbles floating from the poor man's mouth as he

New uses for old routines: The superb prizefighting sequence, the street-cleaning sequence. Below: all refinement, Charlie simply refreshes himself.

dresses down his careless companion; it might as readily have appeared in *Pay Day*. There is a jail door, with Charlie being yanked toward it, flipping his cigarette over his shoulder so that he can give it a last kick with his jaunty foot.

But simply to have submitted a record of past tactics, however joyously improved, would have satisfied neither Chaplin nor audiences that were now three years deep into sound. Chaplin did not care to wax nostalgic about the form but to display its continuing viability. He knew that he would have to, for he was being warned on all sides during production that he was pursuing a lost cause and, as he approached release date, told that no first-run theaters would be open to him. In fact, he had to rent his own New York house, an out-of-the-mainstream legitimate theater that had fallen into disuse, in order to establish the film's drawing power and command any sort of rental fees in subsequent runs. He did so, and added mightily to his fortune.

City Lights may also be read as a structural exercise, with great satisfaction. It is the most ingeniously formed, immaculately interlocked of Chaplin's experiments in combining comedy with pathos. The comedy and the love story depend utterly on each other; neither can move until the other requires it to do so. If there is a prizefighting sequence, hilarious in itself, or a street-sweeping sequence or a soap-sandwich sequence, it is only because Charlie *must* attempt these things in order to find money for the blind girl he loves. No gag is gratuitous; it grows directly out of the need of a helpless girl and her knight unvaliant.

In reverse, no love scene is played without functioning simultaneously as humor, which means that a potentially sentimental situation has been scrubbed clean with the sturdy brush of irony. Adoring the blind girl mutely as she changes the water for her flowers, he gets the dirty water directly in his face; after all, she cannot see him and that sadness must be made funny. Yearning under her window after he has escorted her home—to a courtyard that is once again unmistakably Londonish—he is hit by a falling flowerpot, toppled into a rain barrel. Spending an afternoon with her in her room and telling her of the wonderful things he is about to do for her, he is inadvertently stripped of his underclothes: the girl has asked him to hold the skein of yarn she is raveling up, and she has got hold of a loose thread that has strayed from beneath his vest. He continues to talk with her

Charlie buys a single flower and is mistaken for a millionaire; then, with the real millionaire's money, he buys a whole basket of flowers. Later he keeps up the imposture by visiting the girl at home, bringing largesse. The girl: Virginia Cherrill.

Opposite: Living it up in the millionaire's mansion. *City Lights*.

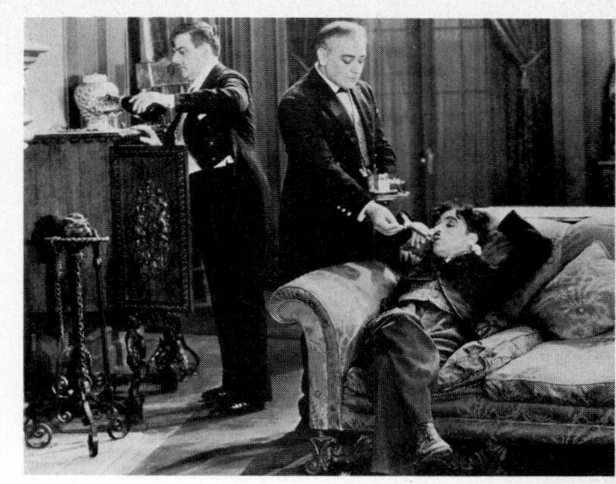

eagerly and encouragingly while he writhes under the threads that are slithering and knotting against his skin. There is a title, just after he has informed her that a Viennese doctor can cure her blindness, in which she exclaims, "Wonderful! Then I'll be able to see you!" Chaplin gives us a quick look, leaping through the lens as confidingly as he has always done, and we know what it means: it means that she had better *not* see him. The look is one of alarm, is meant to be disturbing. It is plainly preparation for the ending of the film, still so far away. But there is no bob of the Adam's apple in it, no quiver, no hint that we might pity him. It is simply knowing, as funny as it is ominous. And he is instantly wriggling under the unraveling again. The two poles, the positive of comedy, the negative of sympathy, are locked in.

The love story is just as locked into his encounters with a now cheerfully drunken, now satanically sober millionaire, which I have chosen to mention last though they are normally mentioned first. *City Lights* is most often described, in synopsis, as the film in which Charlie is befriended by a millionaire whenever that millionaire is in his cups and instantly cast off the moment the man is himself again. The description suits our predilections: we like to think that Chaplin is saying something about money, about an unjust social order, about the capricious gulf that exists between the haves and have-nots. And, in a way, no doubt he is. But it is a most peculiar way. For it is the millionaire's money that saves the impoverished girl. The film is neither a thundering "*J' accuse*!" nor simplistic social criticism; in fact, we grow almost as fond of the millionaire as we do of Charlie and his girl. Something much more intricate is at stake.

What is finally at stake is Chaplin's archetypal ambivalence, his delightful/disastrous duality, brought at last to ultimate confrontation. Ever since Chaplin arrived at his complex identity, he has been two things at once: he has been nobody and everybody, and he has been nobody *because* he can be everybody. But what does that mean, apart from the pain it occasionally gives him when he realizes he can sustain no one role for long? It means that the problem is not exclusively personal, though it is acutely personal for him. The problem would *have* to be universal or Charlie could not get away with his pretenses at all.

That is to say, it is not Charlie alone who has found his position in the universe unstable because he can adopt any posture in a twinkling, fool anybody—at least temporarily—into thinking him the real thing. If he can, on the spur of the moment, supplant a count or a clergyman or, for that matter, a millionaire in any society he chooses to enter, and be instantly accepted in his adopted guise, then there must also be a terrible instability in those who accept him. They have no norms, or they would detect his spuriousness on sight. They are, in fact, as uncertain of who they are and what kind of society they inhabit as he is; they also are poseurs, in some degree frauds, insecure in their own identities. The only difference between them and Charlie is that he is aware of the situation and they are not. The awareness is what makes him an outcast; they, in their own kind of blindness, can remain comfortably "in." *All* appearances are deceiving.

I have often wondered why Chaplin chose "City *Lights*," with its explicit emphasis on urban life, for his title, the metropolis for his background. He had often shown us street-and-gutter life at its meanest. But why mansion-life at its most glittering? I suspect that he wanted these extremes, extremes in close juxtaposition, because the metropolis offers us society at its most highly organized, its most firmly structured. And, whether consciously or unconsciously, he was about to embark on his most exhaustive exploration of the instability of the very concept of structure, private or public.

Even the incidental sight-gags work over the theme of "instability" obsessive-

ly throughout the film. Charlie is standing before the display window of an antique store, *pretending* to give judicious attention to a dozen *objets d'art*, actually stealing glances at a nude. He steps back a bit for a better view and the sidewalk on which he steps isn't there. A descending freight elevator has left a great gap in it, and, after he has narrowly missed the gap two or three times, he half plunges into it, scrambling back for safety as the elevator rides up bearing a man who comes to Charlie's waistline. Charlie, from his obvious advantage, scolds the man for his carelessness. The elevator rides higher and the man is seen to be twice as big as Charlie. Charlie tips his hat and leaves. What's stable?

Charlie is offered a deal by a prizefighter: Charlie is not to be hurt but will obligingly lose the match, splitting the purse fifty-fifty. At ring-time an entirely different fighter takes his opponent's place. Terrified, Charlie watches a nearby Negro boxer kiss his rabbit's foot and rub it behind his ears for luck. Charlie does the same. Moments later the Negro boxer is carried from *his* bout, unconscious. Charlie's eagerness to remove any vestige of rabbit from behind his own ears is now frantic. Neither deals nor charms hold.

A man may be toasting you with a wine glass, spilling the contents of a martini pitcher down your trousers at the same time. You may actually light a cigar in your mouth three times; it is always someone else's cigar. Reproving his drunken companion for driving so wildly through the early-morning streets, Charlie gets his answer: "Am I driving?" What is fortunate is unfortunate. During the boxing match, the bell-rope becomes wrapped about Charlie's torso. Each time he is hit, his stagger rings the bell, luckily, for the end of the round. Each time he gratefully turns to his corner, the movement rings the bell again to start the next round.

Hank Mann, as the prizefighter with whom Charlie does not have a prior understanding, is decidedly alarmed by Charlie's friendly overtures.

It is possible to become so caught up in the eternal instability that you quite forget to take advantage of it. Charlie is desperately arguing his case with a policeman, unaware that it is a forgotten gun in his hand that is actually keeping the policeman at bay. Suddenly noticing the revolver, Chaplin immediately, dutifully, gives it to the policeman, restoring the natural order of things. The policeman promptly covers him with the gun, arrests him. Charlie snaps his fingers, disgusted with himself. *What* natural order of things, and why hadn't he made the most of the loophole? Over-all, nothing animal, vegetable, or mineral is to be trusted.

Least of all human beings. It is as we approach the millionaire, flawlessly played by Harry Myers, that vertigo begins to overtake us. For Chaplin has not been satisfied this time with his own duality: he has duplicated it, nearly as a mirror-image, in the second principal comedian with whom he shares much of the film. Millionaire Myers is two men, at the very least. He is a scowling, arrogant, high-handed, and quite heartless scion of wealth; his wealth is apparently inherited, we never see him do any work. Informed that his wife has left him, he hurls her photograph from his dresser-top roughly; discovering himself in bed with Charlie on the morning after an all-night revel, he ruthlessly orders his butler to rid him of this nonentity, instantly and without breakfast. He is also the most demonstrative of boon companions, when drunk, embracing Charlie with open arms, kissing him with delight on both cheeks; he gives Charlie money to buy flowers from the girl and even enough to send her to Vienna to cure her blindness as genially and generously as he offers him his Rolls Royce the moment Charlie expresses admiration for the car. Which is the real man? Both, interchangeably; but never to fuse. And the expansive, congenial drunk is divided yet once again. He is sometimes a frolicsome *bon vivant*, thoroughly relishing the prospect of "burning up the town." At other times, unpredictably, he is suicidal; a revolver is always close at hand. It is Charlie who must carry the burden of uplift throughout the film, persuading both the millionaire and the girl that life is worth living.

Charlie has his own two personalities. He is the homeless nobody, wandering the litter of the streets while callous newsboys mock him, pepper him with peashooters, rip his undershorts loose from a rent in his trousers. And he has his adopted role, as usual. What role? That of millionaire. He has been mistaken for a millionaire by the blind girl: selling flowers near a busy intersection, she has heard him descend from a limousine, slam its door behind him. Actually, he has simply slipped through it, from one door to the other, to avoid a policeman. But once he has purchased a flower from her—staring in rapture the while—and she hears the door of the departing limousine slam shut again before she can offer proper change, she concludes that he is both wealthy and kind. Charlie, naturally, has not departed in the limousine; its owner has. He is still standing in worshipful awe of her, committed now to a pretense that will be difficult to keep up.

Thus there are three, if not four, millionaires in the film, constantly shifting identities. Millionaire Charlie must hurry to drunken-happy millionaire Myers to get money only to find that drunken-happy millionaire Myers does not now exist and that scowling millionaire Myers is prepared to throw him out. It is hard being a millionaire either way. It is even harder to know when a millionaire is a millionaire, when a friend is an enemy, when a posture is supportable or insupportable.

These philosophical instabilities are not belabored in the film; they simply exist like the multiple, maze-like, imprisoning refractions of Charlie's fun house in *The Circus* have existed. All those repeated, reversed images, and no way out. In fact, we may look at them in their most complex interrelationship and burst into laughter at what seems simply a stunning gag. Myers, drunk, has told Charlie that the Rolls Royce is now his. Myers, sober, has had him turned from his townhouse

This unstable universe: The generosity of the drunken millionaire; the yearning for a cigar butt of a man who's been given a Rolls Royce; the casual cruelty of newsboys.

door. Charlie, bewildered, deflated, but accepting such eventualities as routine, searches for a cigarette. He has none, and people are passing him on the street puffing the most delicious and tormenting aromas his way. One passer-by is enjoying a cigar that is nearing its end. The Rolls Royce is at the curb. Charlie, inspired, leaps into it and keeps pace down the street with the cigar-smoker. The cigar-smoker finally abandons the butt, and, as he does so, a bum on a street corner spies it and heads for it. Charlie instantly brakes, leaps from the car, and beats the bum to the butt. Puffing away in deep content, he returns to the Rolls Royce and drives away. The bum stares after him in prolonged bafflement, as well he might.

We have been treated to as good a joke as a camera ever filmed. But within the joke are the layers upon layers of the film's content. In fact, the joke is made of those very layers, could not exist without them. The rich man who is not a rich man drives a car that is his and not his to snatch from the gutter what he should not, but does desperately, need. The bum staring after the departing car can, after this, believe *anything*, the rules of the game and the meaning of appearances having been so entirely, so overwhelmingly, negated.

Ultimately, Charlie must get from his friend the thousand dollars he needs to cure the girl's blindness: all plot-threads are now intertwined and ready for resolution. Charlie does not even have to ask for the money; the millionaire, conveniently and joyously in his cups, has simply pressed it upon Charlie once he has heard of the girl's plight. Before Charlie can leave the mansion, however, burglars who have been hiding in it and have caught a glimpse of the cash knock out the millionaire with a blackjack. There is a chase in which Charlie outwits the burglars readily enough, but not the millionaire's butler. The butler appears on the scene, summons the police as the burglars vanish, detains Charlie, to whom he has ever been

Charlie has no midnight rendezvous with anyone, but the day has already brought him a flower from a blind girl and a suicidal millionaire is coming his way soon. Lonely, he is never precisely alone.

hostile, and accuses him of having stolen the money. Charlie explains what his bountiful friend has done, tries to wake him to support his story. When millionaire Myers at last comes to and is questioned by the police, he stares blankly at Charlie and snarls, "Who is this man?" Charlie knows that he is in the soup now and that there is nothing else for it: he grabs the money, which has been passing from hand to hand, and runs.

On the town with Harry Myers, his unpredictable friend.

That is to say, he steals what has been freely given him by a friend who is not a friend in order to pose as the millionaire he is not.

There are those who have objected to the film's final close-up as sentimental, even monstrous. I refuse to count myself among them. It is possible to find fault with the editing of the closing sequence: there are several shots of Charlie clinging to a rose and raising his fingers to his teeth that are not precisely matched. But the concluding image itself is more than commanding in its usurpation of the entire frame, in the sympathy it unquestionably generates. It is the showdown, the last and absolute confrontation of Chaplin with the world he has created and the world that has created him. It takes Chaplin's meaning to its ultimate limits and then stops, transfixed in space.

The girl has now recovered her sight and is running a prosperous flower shop. Charlie, having been convicted for his "theft" and just now freed from a term in prison, is ambling dispiritedly toward a familiar street corner. The shot, incidentally, is the most harrowing Chaplin has ever permitted himself: Charlie is as filthy as the gutter beside him, he has made no effort to pretend that his ragged clothing is somehow the work of a superb tailor. Worse, there is a lag in his walk, one that has never been there before. Charlie, source of everyone else's hope in the film, is now without hope himself. When the corner newsboys who have always tormented him begin to torment him again, he does not engage them in deft byplay: his eyes take on the aggrieved look of a bullied child, there is a hurt and impotent "You just watch out" air to his unsuccessful evasions. In the midst of this mean-spirited badgering, he notices a flower in the gutter, stoops to pick it up. When he has finally released himself from the newsboys, he turns to go on, then sees the face of the girl through the shop window he has nearly passed. He stares in almost unbelieving delight at the miracle that has been wrought. The grin on his face is so melting, so overwhelmingly gratified, that it is, in the strict sense, a silly grin. The girl is certainly amused by it, turning to her grandmother inside the shop to suppress her laughter and to murmur, in an ironic aside, "I've made a conquest." Charlie simply continues to stare, the smile frozen on his face, the petals of his reclaimed flower falling away. It is only when the girl, through the shop window, mimes offering him a fresh flower to replace the wilting one in his hand that he alerts himself to the danger of the situation and begins hastily to move along the street. But the girl follows him, determined in her benevolence, brings him to a halt on the sidewalk. Touching his hand glancingly as she gives him the new rose, she is suddenly puzzled. She places her hand over his, more firmly. Her own face turns grave. The hand is familiar. She reaches to touch his shoulder, then, lightly, his face. Stunned, she can only ask "You?" Charlie's nod of assent is very slight, as tentative as the embarrassed fingers he has lifted to his lips. He can think of only one thing to say, one unnecessary thing to say: "You can see now?" The girl nods her head, slowly, solemnly, first tears beginning to form in her eyes. Cut to Charlie in giant close-up, smiling expectantly, hopelessly, gratefully, unreachably. *City Lights* ends with the close-up.

What else can it do, what else can Charlie do, what else can Chaplin do—ever? His meaning has arrived at stalemate, *is* stalemate. The truth is out and the truth is a stone wall. Nothing more can be said, no further gesture made. Which of these two can move, toward or away from the other? The girl is every bit as paralyzed, as imprisoned, as he. He has even helped create her prison, made her inaccessible. That is what we do to one another at the precise moment we make contact.

Once their social roles were those of benevolent millionaire and impoverished cripple. Now their social roles are those of derelict vagabond and prosperous beauty. Tides of fortune can reverse themselves, identities can be turned inside out, but there is no secure center at which they can meet, stabilize themselves. Think a moment. Strictly speaking, there has not in the beginning been any real personal or social gulf between Charlie and this girl. Both were poor, both were lonely, each was attracted to the other. But she was blind and he was an impersonator. Strictly speaking, and supposing a universe with stable norms, there need be no gulf between them now. There is nothing to prevent the girl from hiring him, dressing him, making a florist of him. He will be exactly as good a florist as he has been everything else. There is nothing, these things accomplished, to prevent her making a husband of him. Except, of course, that it is unthinkable for this lovely and able child to set such a process in motion: her identity, as she now conceives it, as it now *exists*, prohibits the misalliance. And, imagining for the moment an insane impulse that would sweep all such prohibitions aside, Charlie would not in the end be able to sustain for long any role offered him. He would only be playing at florist, playing at husband as he had—so briefly, so long ago—in *Police*. For he does not believe in the possible permanence, the uncompromised commitment, of either. He yearns to believe but he understands sham too deeply, too sweepingly, for that. There is a terrible ache in knowing too much, seeing too much. "You can see now?" are the cruelest words of all, severing pretended bonds, pretended unions, forever. The end is isolation, face to face, smiling through ice.

City Lights is an utterly stable film about total instability. Its pieces come together in perfect harmony, shutting its people out. Without the least loss of laughter, Chaplin has remade the world in his own despairing, but unyielding, image.

The closeup.

37. The End Without an Ending: Chaplin Defines the Road

Modern Times was to be Chaplin's last silent film, quite consciously so; and, since it was made and released long after everyone else had abandoned the form, it would also put an end to an entire tradition. Much later, that tradition might be self-consciously revived by one or another star with something offbeat in mind: Ray Milland would make what was called a "silent" film though it was of course photographed at sound speed; so would Jerry Lewis. And one can still catch directors and cameramen yearning after certain of the profitable elisions that silence had made possible. In a single week while working on this book I have come across two such instances. In George Roy Hill's *The Sting* Robert Redford hikes himself into a barber's chair for a shave, haircut, and manicure that will transform him from seedy con man into big-league gambler; suddenly time and speech are bypassed while the rapid miracle is wrought, though Redford is speaking, unheard, to the manicurist throughout. Less fleeting, and much more important, is a passage in Ingmar Bergman's *Cries and Whispers*: when it is time for two estranged women to effect a passionate reconciliation, Bergman hurls us into a series of silent, watery dissolves in which the two women urgently exchange all the words left unsaid over the years without any of their tumbling dialogue being reproduced on the soundtrack. Silent film had its efficiencies, its swift visual mysteries capable in certain circumstances of evoking more than the tortured snail's pace of speech, and something of these can occasionally be recovered when a confident hand asserts its right to an open form.

But Chaplin's awareness that he was bidding farewell to silent film as such is clear from his intermittent use of speaking voices in *Modern Times. City Lights* had not used speech of any kind. It had had a musical score, composed by Chaplin, to support its images. It had had a parodistic gabble of not quite human sounds to mock the rhetoric of city officials assembled for the unveiling of a statue and to mock the concept of talking pictures as well. It had contained only one sequence in which a sound-effect was indispensable to the comedy: that in which

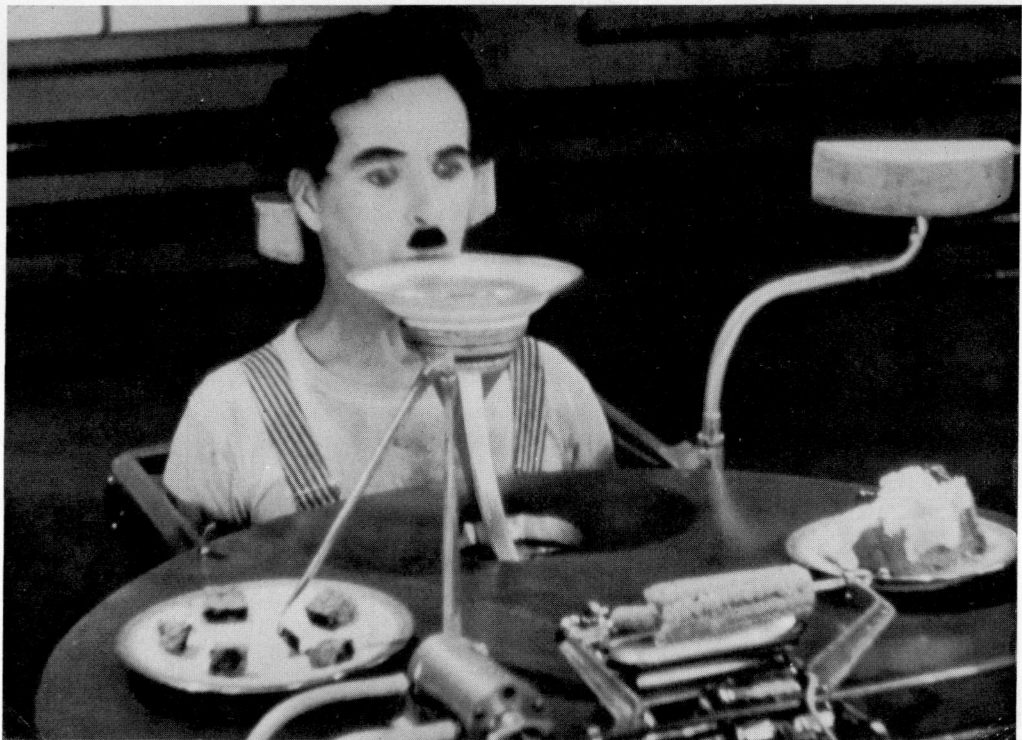

Charlie, at a party thrown by his millionaire friend, swallows a whistle which sends forth interruptive bleats each time he hiccoughs during a baritone's emotional solo. The gag does not work well, gives the film its weakest moment. We hear the whistle but hear nothing of the gay party that is going on, nothing of the baritone's song, and the realism of the whistle's wholly isolated sound gives the lie to the familiar, bustling fantasy that surrounds it.

Modern Times takes a decisive step toward speech, without altering its status as a true silent film. When the chief executive of an industrial firm puts away his jigsaw puzzle to snap on the closed-circuit television that will enable him to inspect the assembly line and even the bathrooms of the plant he supervises, the orders he gives over the system are spoken orders, not titles. When an inventor brings him a new machine that will automatically feed workers without requiring them to leave their jobs, he uses a phonograph record to describe the time-saving virtues of his device. We hear the phonograph record. We also hear news bulletins and commercials on a radio in the office of a prison warden. And, very late in the film, we at last hear Chaplin's voice, though only in a song composed entirely, and deliberately, of nonsense syllables. *Modern Times* is not so much a transitional film as a preparatory one. We know when it is finished that henceforth we shall hear as well as see Chaplin. But, the nonsense-song excepted, we do not hear him in this one. It is a silent comedy, filmed almost entirely at silent speed.

Interestingly, the two speeds—silent and sound—appear simultaneously in certain sequences of the film without causing any sense of dislocation. Charlie leaves his assembly line, hands still jerking from the endlessly repetitive twisting of wrenches, to go to the bathroom, punching the time clock in and out on his journey. He really wants to sneak a cigarette, if he can calm his hands long enough to get one lighted. He has no sooner begun to relax against a washbowl and savor the first drag than the television screen in the bathroom leaps to life, the executive's face appears scowling at truant Charlie. The executive orders him, vocally, to return to work, on film that must be shot at sound-speed. Charlie immediately flips away the cigarette and scurries back to his toil, in frames that go by more swiftly because they are shot at the old speed. Why is there no clash, no real visual disharmony, between the two? I suppose because, from the outset, the film has established itself as fundamentally silent and because the executive's voice is unmistakably an alien force in the sequence, an intrusion carefully framed on the wall

Above: Lunch hour in *Modern Times*; Charlie feeds Chester Conklin, caught among the cogwheels, and Charlie himself is force-fed by a temporarily obliging machine.

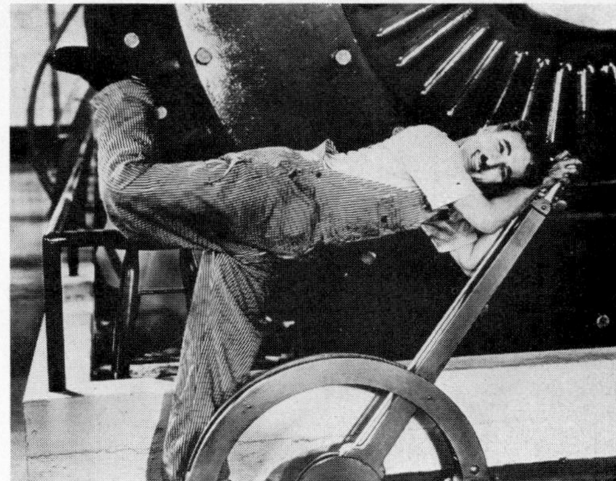

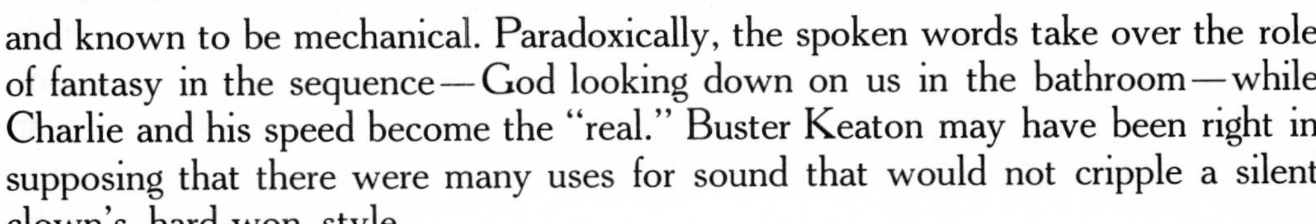

and known to be mechanical. Paradoxically, the spoken words take over the role of fantasy in the sequence—God looking down on us in the bathroom—while Charlie and his speed become the "real." Buster Keaton may have been right in supposing that there were many uses for sound that would not cripple a silent clown's hard-won style.

Not quite so readily assimilated is a conjunction of silence and sound that occurs very late in the film. The girl, Paulette Goddard, has managed to get Charlie a job as a singing waiter in a waterfront café, and he is frantically rehearsing the little song he is going to sing. Just ahead of him on the bill is a quartet. We have seen *and heard* the quartet march onto the floor and begin its number. As we cut to the dressing room where Paulette is encouraging Charlie and helping him memorize his lines, we continue to hear the song from the floor—firmly fixed at sound-speed. But Charlie and the girl are not only bobbing about in a much livelier silent rhythm, they are conversing in titles. Here sound has been allowed to proclaim itself dominant; we know that Charlie is going to join it in a moment. The titles surprise us, set against the singing voices. Two worlds do not quite mate; we are going to have to choose very soon.

But everywhere else that Charlie appears in the film he appears as the Charlie we first met in 1914, moved by a camera that helps him make the magic, mute. And because *Modern Times* is a silent film, it is no doubt going to say something more about that iconographic Charlie who confronted himself and his world so totally in *City Lights*.

What else was there to say? Not very much, it is true, and Chaplin faced—late in the day and with no competing clowns to spur him on—the risk of repetition, of following a masterpiece with the superfluous. To guard against the overly familiar, Chaplin moved himself forward in time, surrendering his yearning for those Dickensian courtyards that had somehow survived even into the metropolitan *City Lights*, and took his place among fellow mechanics in an industrialized world. *Modern Times* would *keep* him modern, keep him abreast not only of the routinized labor that could drive a contemporary factory hand close to breakdown but of the Depression and its labor unrest that could imperil even so inhuman a life. More, it might begin to satisfy those of his critics who wanted political or social comment from him.

Four stages in a nervous breakdown, danced among the dynamos.

Characteristically, in meeting this last demand Chaplin would insert careful political and social waivers, announcing himself no Communist, siding with the authorities as much as with the poor. One well-remembered sequence places Charlie on a street corner just as a truck rumbles by, hitting a pothole and dislodging the red "danger" flag attached to its rear. Charlie, ever helpful, promptly snatches up the flag and hurries after the truck, hoping to call the driver's attention to his loss. Just as he does so a formation of Communist demonstrators comes marching around the corner behind him, so that he is, in the eyes of the onrushing police, its flag-waving leader. Naturally, he is arrested as principal revolutionary. Chaplin's disavowal of any such role could scarcely be more explicit.

And, when a riot breaks out in the prison he has been sent to, it is he who frees the warden and guards from the cells in which they have been locked, he who knocks out his rebellious fellow inmates one by one with the aid of a swinging iron door. True, he is doped at the time; an addict next to him at the lunch table has, as inspection approaches, hastily ditched his "nose powder" by funneling it into the saltshaker; and Charlie has lavishly helped himself to the salt. But the pattern is familiar, drug or no drug. Charlie instinctively attempts to set right *whatever* is wrong, asking himself few ideological questions in the impulsive ingenuity of the moment.

Perhaps Chaplin's fundamental ambivalence where party-line social struggle is concerned is most evident when he finally does seem to ask himself a question. The factory, having been shut down by the Depression for a very long time, is finally reopened; hordes of men battle one another at the gates for any jobs that may be available. Charlie, slipperiest of broken-field runners, squeaks through and is set to work with Chester Conklin repairing the rusted machinery. Conklin, by the way, is this film's instance of Chaplin's generous remembrance of things past. Just as he would not part with Edna Purviance without attempting to secure her future, so he was constantly employing veterans of the early two-reel days, whether they had worked with him before or not: Mack Swain, Hank Mann, Harry Myers, and Henry Bergman turn up in the films—some very often. Bergman, a squat, balding man who rarely played more than bits, had been with Chaplin since his Mutual period and leapt to Chaplin's call the moment it came, if only to appear in two minutes of film. Bergman worshipped Chaplin. "He'd have kissed me if I'd let him," Chaplin said. Jackie Coogan, Mack Swain, and Harry Myers had virtually divided films with Chaplin, under his direction, along the way. No doubt the acid test came when Chaplin shared the climactic comic sequence of *Limelight*, the last talking film he made in the United States, with Buster Keaton. It must have been apparent from the first preview that Keaton had stolen the sequence, topped the master; the sequence, which might have been heavily trimmed in Chaplin's favor, remained Keaton's.

In *Modern Times* he and Conklin have had their mishaps while oiling and otherwise rejuvenating the plant's giant pistons and treadles. Unfortunately, the lunch-whistle has sounded at the very moment that Conklin, trapped in the machinery and rotating with it, has popped no more than his head from between imprisoning cogwheels. Since the machinery cannot be started again until the noon-hour is over, Charlie considerately feeds Conklin while Conklin is upside down. It is possible, after all, to ease an entire hard-boiled egg into a man's open mouth, to channel his tea through the carcass of a chicken. Once the machinery is on again and Conklin released, the two men are prepared to resume their chores. They are immediately halted by the arrival of a labor representative who tells them, in a title, "Get your coats, we're on strike"—this on the very day they have clamored to return to work. Charlie and Chester look at one another, scratching their heads. Charlie looks at us. What insanity is this? he plainly wants to know,

Buster Keaton and Charlie Chaplin in the dressing room of *Limelight*, a few moments before performing their only comic routine together.

even as he is already accepting the situation philosophically.

Ambiguities apart, Chaplin did find in *Modern Times* at least two dazzling opportunities for ironic social comment that would not compromise him personally. The first comes when he is strapped down inside the inventor's feeding-machine, a turntable on which plates of soup, meat, and pie revolve while levers escort the assorted delicacies to his mouth. A cob of corn is suspended on a slowly spinning skewer, an everlastingly accommodating mouth-wiper is prepared to swing forward regularly and daintily massage his lips.

Charlie's eyes are dubious, if not alarmed, as he is locked into his dinner, but he will meet the challenge primly, as ever. No more need to behave badly than when eating boiled shoe. And Chaplin, the knowing comedian, is careful to show us at once that the machine works. Morsels of beef are nudged his way seductively, the corn rotates at a suitable rate for chewing, the mouth-wiper makes certain that no unsightly traces of the feast linger. He is becoming quite accustomed to being so royally served while remaining firmly planted at his workbench when a short circuit interrupts the repast. In the uncontrollable catastrophe that follows—the viciously speeded-up corncob seems to be shedding Charlie's teeth rather than kernels, bolts instead of beef are rammed into his flinching mouth, soup is emptied into his lap and pie firmly pressed to his face—one majestic symbol keeps doing its duty. No matter what is happening, the mouth-wiper returns on schedule. The sequence is convulsingly funny even as predictable slapstick; its richness is in the mouth-wiper and the placidly impersonal insult it conveys. Industrial society may not feed a man; but it will teach him to be mannerly.

The second brilliant flight of fancy—and it is literally that—occurs after Charlie has returned to work, and the order has come for a speed-up. The racing belt of nuts and bolts over which Charlie slaves first threatens to elude his wrenches, then sucks him into its chute. And down he goes through the cogwheels to the sound of carousel music; out he comes as the deranged Pan that is the only Pan the twentieth-century can know. He is a sprite in his crack-up, a faun of the fan-belts, a dancing genie with dynamos to provide the puffs of smoke he rides on.

Generally I dislike references to Chaplin as Pan; the term sentimentalizes his normal role and attributes something of his inspiration to a coyly borrowed mythology when in fact he has invented his own. Here, however, he is no longer normal; a nervous collapse has set him loose among imagined Elysian Fields, fields composed of turbines, cranes, steel catwalks, magical levers. He fancies his wrenches as either earrings or the drooping ears of a hound, waggles them wild-eyed as he darts at his oppressors and then at any women in sight, eludes foreman and all foes by skipping gaily with a spurting oilcan to bestow black benediction upon rows and rows of workers, lifts one foot high in the air as he plays lovingly with control-sticks that will blow up every machine in the place—echoing the ballet stance of *Behind the Screen* as he does so—and then takes to the air, soaring over his disrupted kingdom on a gliding pulley like the disoriented but deliriously happy *deus ex machina* he is. The maddened solo, with the local Furies in hot pursuit, is enchanting; it could not take its shape at any other than silent-speed; it makes its "comment" on the pressures of the assembly line; and it promptly puts Charlie into a hastily summoned ambulance.

The last is important, because it is actually the beginning structure of the film. Until now *Modern Times* has seemed to deal principally with industrialization and its effects on the working man, material patently derived from René Clair's early satirical sound-film *À Nous la Liberté*. Because the borrowing from Clair is so transparent, it becomes a compliment rather than a theft: all Chaplin has to do is show that he can make the content his own, fill it with fresh inspiration—which he does. But in fact not more than one fourth of Chaplin's film takes place in the factory or is much concerned with it. Chaplin's true theme lies elsewhere and is much more personal; we get our first taste of it as he is popped into the ambulance, sirens roar, and he is hospitalized.

Charlie has been whisked into a vehicle and temporarily lodged somewhere. He will be again, and again and again, as *Modern Times* feels its way, often improvisationally, to its meaning. Indeed, vehicles and temporary lodging places become the governing rhythm of the film, provide it with the recurring beats that give it form. First the ambulance and hospital. Then, the very moment he is released and told to avoid excitement in future, he falls into the clash between Communists and police. He is hurled into a new vehicle, a police van, temporarily lodged in a new place, a jail cell. He becomes so comfortable in these quarters, with chintz curtains, flowers on the barred windows, and a pin-up of Abraham Lincoln on the wall, that he is loath to leave them. When, after foiling the prison break, he is told that he is pardoned and free, he is in utter dismay. Turned onto the street, he is determined to go back to jail: when he sees that the girl, Paulette, is about to be arrested for the theft of a loaf of bread, he promptly takes the blame and is as promptly deposited in the police van—where he is subsequently joined by Paulette, who has been identified by an eyewitness as the true culprit. Later in the film, having made a considerable mess of his first stint as night watchman in a department store, he is once more hustled into the patrol wagon, hurriedly summoned by the store's manager. And later still, leaving the strikebound factory dispiritedly and inadvertently stepping on a plank that catapults a brick in a cop's direction, he invites the van again. If the film has a formal principle of control, a distinctive cadence, it is composed of the van and Charlie's readiness to enter it.

City Lights had left one question unanswered: where does nobody live when he is at home? In it, we had seen Charlie in the millionaire's home, in the girl's home, but never in his own—not even in the kind of garret that the plot of *The Kid* had imposed on him. The presumption is simply that he has no home, that he lives on the streets he walks. But that is a presumption, and it does not confront the issue head-on. *Modern Times* will at last, and as exhaustively as it can, confront the issue of "home" for a man psychologically incapable of integrating himself into society.

What had been a presumption becomes explicit. Though other men, including Paulette's unemployed father, seem to have at least shanties in which to shelter themselves and their broods, Charlie exists only in passing. Because, as a character, Charlie cannot put down roots anywhere, it becomes improper to imagine him as having arranged anything so stable as living quarters. And so we learn that he has none, learn it from the bliss that overtakes him once he has so cozily domesticated his jail cell. This is his "home," the only kind available to him. Just so long as he can "play" at making a home of something that is not, he is on safe ground; he would hang neither chintz nor pin-up in a real one. Pretense is all, and for just so long as the pretense is forced on him in inappropriate circumstances, he is happy as can be. Small wonder that approaching sirens should prove, for him, a tolerable sound.

The toe protruding from Charlie's shoe suggests that there is something funny about the road ahead. The tiredness in Charlie's face suggests there is not.

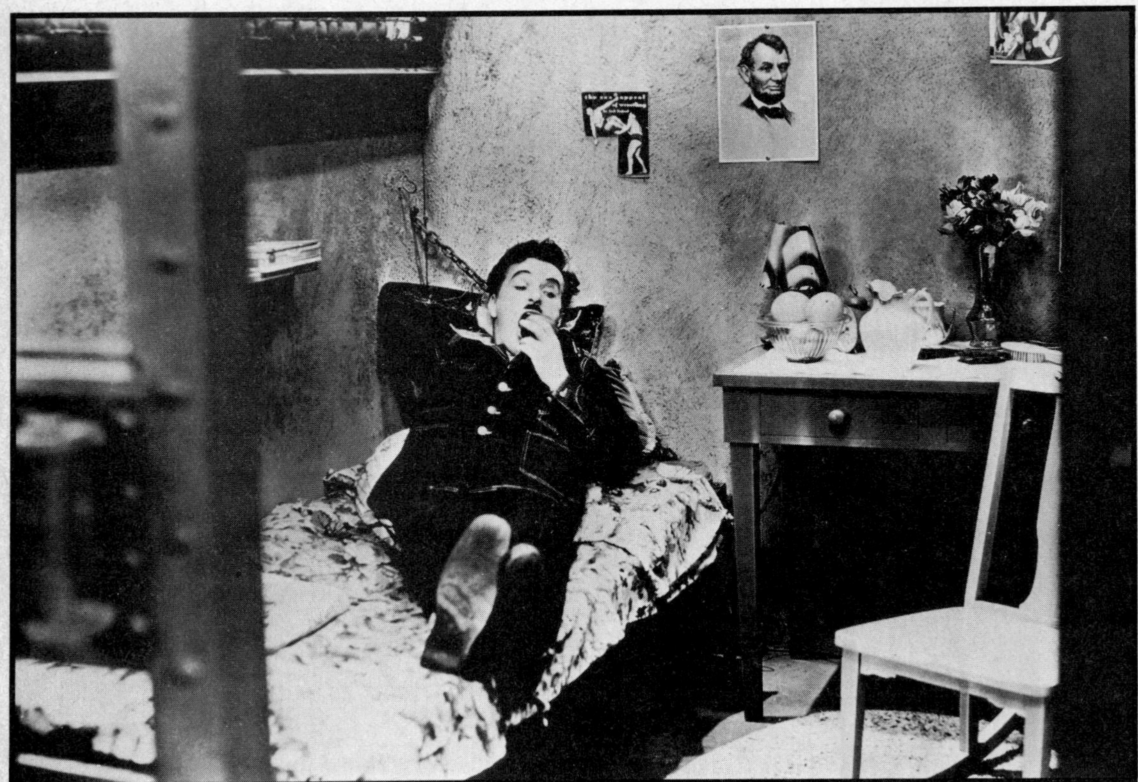

The issue is pressed further. Paulette too, the waterfront child with torn skirts and smudged cheeks, loses her home when her father is killed in a street demonstration. Her two younger sisters, for whom she has stolen bread, are assigned by the authorities to an orphanage; Paulette, older though still under-age, eludes officialdom to slip away from the shanty and wander homeless on the streets. In doing so, she becomes Charlie's double—the mirror-image so necessary to a self-confrontation—in the film. From this moment forward they are two of a kind.

With a slight difference. She, impossibly, would *like* to have a home, while Charlie has long since resigned himself to "pretend" resting-places. The two meet in the theft-of-bread episode. When Paulette joins Charlie in the police van, he recognizes her, tips his hat, and offers his seat. But Paulette—she is listed simply as "The Gamin" in the opening titles—doesn't in the least share Charlie's longing for the imagined domesticity of a cell. She is the other half of his nature: the *yearning* for stability, even when stability must be disbelieved in. And so she tries to bolt from the wagon, tussling with the guard at its door. Charlie leaps to assist her, not because he wishes to escape himself but because he is above all a gentleman, and a sharp turn by the speeding van tumbles all three—guard, Charlie, Paulette—into the street, dazed. Paulette is first to recover, leaping to her bare feet and swiftly disappearing around a corner. Charlie is quite prepared to return to the patrol wagon. Then Paulette, interested in this curious, kindly fellow, reappears around her corner just long enough to beckon him to join her in her escape. Charlie is torn, drawn by his yearning in her direction, by his eternal realism in the other. Then he decides. Whatever it means, he will go with her. He is off and running, hot on the heels of his alter ego.

The two move endlessly along pavements until both must sink exhausted on a curbstone to fan themselves and relieve aching feet. Where does Paulette *live*?, Charlie wants to know. "No place, anyplace," her title shrugs back. They are resting in a suburban area: a housewife nearby is leaping from the doorway after her departing spouse for a farewell kiss. Charlie's title-question is a mocking one: "Imagine us in a little house like that?"

He promptly imagines one. He is good at that. It is of course outlandish fantasy, never, never to be credited. In a spic-and-span cottage, while Paulette fusses over dinner, Charlie assuages his appetite by plucking an orange from an orange-

Three of Charlie's improvised homes in *Modern Times*: The entirely satisfactory jail cell, the idyllic kitchen he fantasizes for Paulette, the after-hours comfort of a department store.

tree that bends its boughs to the open window. Having carefully wiped his hands on the draperies—Charlie will not even fantasize without reminding us of his unsuitability in such surroundings—he summons a cow to the kitchen door, a cow which halts in precise position to provide them with a steaming pail of milk while Charlie, waiting for its bounty, nibbles at grapes that grow abundantly over the lintel.

Charlie laughs as he completes his absurd dream, hoping that he has at least entertained her. But Paulette is downcast. For one thing, she is hungry; for another, "home" is no idle joke. To cheer her, Charlie promises he will get a job so that the dream can come true.

As in *City Lights*, it is Charlie's need to help the girl that provokes the most developed of the film's comedy routines, first as he is taken on as night watchman in a department store and later as he becomes caught in a whirlpool of dancers and drunken football players while trying to serve a customer squab in a restaurant. The department store requires that Charlie punch time-clocks on every floor as he goes his midnight rounds of inspection: he does it on roller skates. Rollerskating naturally leads him into stunting, blindfolded, above an opening in the floor he doesn't know is there, repeating the arabesques of *The Rink* with risk added; it also leads into getting caught wearing the skates on an upgoing escalator while armed thieves are ordering him to come down, repeating the helpless ascensions and desperate descents of *The Floorwalker* with all movement doubled by the wheels.

But the comedy does not even temporarily go its own way to the neglect of what has become the film's theme. After Paulette has saved him from his solo flight above the drop and before he begins his floor-to-floor sweep through the building, he pauses to tuck her into bed for the night: into a luxurious queen-sized nest just right for the ermine cloak she has wrapped about herself. This is her "home" for the time being—if he can hold the job—and she will sleep well. What with the gunmen below, and the drunken revel that follows when Charlie discovers that the burglars are simply down-and-out old friends, he does not hold the job. Paulette slips away with the dawn, and Charlie is sent to jail again.

When he is released, there is a surprise for him. Paulette is waiting, arms spread-eagled against the walls of the prison in case there should be any need to scurry off, dressed in a new makeshift bonnet and full of news. She has found them a home.

It is a dilapidated shanty alongside the barges of the waterfront, and Paulette dances invitingly through its doorway, promising him, "It's a paradise!" Paradise, in the form of a ceiling beam, promptly drops on Charlie's head, the dinnertable he touches comes apart in his hands, the chair he sits on sinks through the floorboards, the wall he nonchalantly leans against gives way to toboggan him into the water beyond. But life may yet be tolerable there: after Charlie has spent the night sleeping in the shanty's lean-to while Paulette dreams inside—the film is constantly reminding us that this is not a sexual relationship and that Paulette is underage—Charlie emerges in the morning in a bathing-suit, prepared for a refreshing dip. The dip proves unfortunate since the water is rather shallow, but Paulette does have bread and ham ready for a sumptuous breakfast—if only the furniture will hold it up. The meal is not eaten. News arrives that the factory is reopening; Charlie is immediately off to prove himself the good provider he has proclaimed himself and is almost as quickly back in prison.

Alone, Paulette takes to street-dancing and so impresses café-proprietor Henry Bergman that he offers her work inside, even yields to her entreaties that her friend—when he arrives—be given a chance as a singing waiter. This time when Paulette greets Charlie on his release from prison—the shift from "pretend" home to dubious "home" becomes as regular as an anvil-strike—there is nothing makeshift about her clothing. In a small way, she is prospering. And Charlie does get the job.

But confrontation is at hand. Paulette's dancing is applauded, Charlie's song is successful. Supposing that both are to continue being employed, what will they do now, where will they live? Presumably something better than the shanty lies ahead, *possibly* Charlie will come to rest—if he can.

The questions go unanswered because the film gives them no time to be asked. Even as Paulette and Charlie are presumably staking out futures on the floor of the café, the officials the girl has earlier eluded are watching her closely from a ringside table. As Charlie and girl embrace happily in the dressing room after their triumph, authorities intervene: the girl's "home" in future will be the orphanage. There is only one thing for it: battle reflexes, instant flight. In a melee that Chaplin does not forget to make funny, the authorities are trapped among tumbled tabletops and Charlie and the girl escape, heading for the road.

And this is where the film has been going all the time. The "road" ending has been stock for Chaplin almost from the beginning. But this time it is definitive. In earlier films Charlie might simply have been going off to another adventure. In this one nobody is going nowhere. For the film has, for the first time, looked squarely at the problem of Charlie's origin and destination. It has investigated all possible "homes" for him—hospital beds, jail cells, fantasy cottages, well-furnished department stores, tumbledown shacks that do tumble down—and found none to offer him for more than a night or two. The film has been *about* Charlie's "road," about all those "road" endings, about their inevitability, their necessity. Alternatives have now been exhausted, and the ultimate command is clear: keep moving, nobody; keep moving.

This time, also for the first time and once again definitively, he does not move alone. He has a companion with him as he heads for the horizon. The companion is a girl. But she is not a viable woman, not a wife; at his side, she is the other side of himself, the side that hoped for permanence if only such a thing could be found. It has been honestly sought and it has not been found, which is exactly what he expected. Her hope and his knowledge cancel each other out, which is

The road.

the only way they can meet and merge in a single rejected, if indefatigable, image. Charlie the dreamer and Charlie the realist are one and the same, destined for a single fate.

If *City Lights* confronted, as fully as it could, the instability of personality in its human relationships, *Modern Times* forthrightly faces the question of how the unstable are ever to put down roots, call anywhere "home." That is not as large or complex a theme as the earlier one, and it makes for a slightly less substantial, necessarily more episodic film. Footloose by premise, it cannot erect quite so intricate or so strong a structure to embrace its gags. The gags themselves are mint Chaplin—several entire sequences must be included in any catalogue of Chaplin's richest—though there is one he might better have not bothered to borrow. Taking work in a shipyard and ordered to find an available wedge, he delightedly spies one that is tucked under a ship's stays, plucks it loose. The massive skeleton of the ship instantly slips down the runways, smooth as can be, and sinks. But it is 1936, and "process" shooting has been developed. We are entirely aware, as we watch the hull glide away from us and from Charlie, that Charlie has been photographed by one camera, the ship-sinking by another. Keaton had done the business earlier, on a smaller scale but more honestly. Here the camera's function as recorder of fact, the function that gave birth to the fantasy of fact that was Chaplin's own womb, has been so plainly compromised that we are unable to surrender ourselves to delight in the image.

But *Modern Times* is still an ebullient film, to be judged not by its lapses but by its light-hearted exploration of a fundamentally serious subject: rootlessness. The film's spirit is effervescent; in its despair, it stands on tiptoe. Charlie has never been more accomplished, in more assured control of the dead-certain uncertainties about him, than he is as he enters a cafeteria to help himself to an enormous meal. He has no money. He knows that he will be arrested. That is what he is doing it for. But if a man wants to go back to jail, and if he is more than happy to subject himself to the humiliation of arrest, what better way to arrange it than by enjoying a feast of feasts? He rises from the two full trays of food he has devoured like a gourmet deeply satisfied with a master-chef's cuisine, casually raps his knuckles against the restaurant window to summon a policeman as he strolls toward the cash register. At the register, he pantomimes that he cannot pay as though he were conducting a perfectly pleasant business transaction, then turns to the policeman who has answered his summons with infinite *politesse*. The entire situation is impeccably social; Charlie has organized the inequities of a world he thoroughly understands with unruffled dexterity, innate decency, easy aplomb. Ironies may be multiplied to the *nth* degree and still made sublimely cohesive. As he is handcuffed and taken exactly where he wants to go for doing something he has utterly enjoyed doing, he does not indulge in vulgar glee. With a matter-of-fact loftiness, he helps himself to a toothpick. An after-dinner probe is just the thing now. Can he possibly find himself a cigar?

He does. He finds everything he wants, except a permanent role and a place of rest.

At the end he and his yearnings must go down that road again. As they do, in *Modern Times*, they take silent film with them.

THE
END

Photo Sources

All photographs not specifically credited are from the Author's Collection.

Page 1: *Museum of Modern Art / Film Stills Archive*
Page 7: *Maurice H. Zouary / De Forest Phonofilm Collection, Library of Congress*
Page 11: *The Bettmann Archive*
Page 12: *Top, courtesy of Sy Hassan*
Page 14: *Museum of Modern Art / Film Stills Archive*
Page 16: *Academy of Motion Picture Arts and Sciences*
Page 17: *Top to bottom: Eastman House Archives; Academy of Motion Picture Arts and Sciences; Academy of Motion Picture Arts and Sciences; Academy of Motion Picture Arts and Sciences*
Page 19: *Top: Eastman House Archives; Bottom: Museum of Modern Art / Film Stills Archive*
Page 20: *John E. Allen Inc. Collection*
Page 21: *Eastman House Archives*
Page 23: *Below: Courtesy of Blackhawk Films*
Page 25: *Collection of The Institute of the American Musical, Inc.*
Page 27: *Top: Collection of The Institute of the American Musical, Inc.; Bottom: Gordon Berkow Collection*
Page 29: *Academy of Motion Picture Arts and Sciences*
Page 31: *Museum of Modern Art / Film Stills Archive*
Page 33: *Museum of Modern Art / Film Stills Archive*
Page 35: *Leonard Maltin Collection*
Page 37: *Courtesy of James Card, Eastman House*
Page 40: *Collection of The Institute of the American Musical, Inc.*
Page 41: *Eastman House Archives*
Pages 42–3: *Theatre Collection of the New York Public Library*
Page 45: *Top: Eastman House Archives; Bottom: Museum of Modern Art / Film Stills Archive*
Page 46: *Eastman House Archives*
Page 47: *Museum of Modern Art / Film Stills Archive*
Page 48: *Eastman House Archives*
Page 49: *Culver Pictures, Inc.*
Page 51: *Eastman House Archives*
Page 52: *Culver Pictures, Inc.*
Page 53: *Eastman House Archives*
Pages 54–5: *Museum of Modern Art / Film Stills Archive*
Page 56: *Museum of Modern Art / Film Stills Archive*
Page 57: *John E. Allen Inc. Collection*
Page 59: *Eastman House Archives*
Page 60: *Left: Cinemabilia; Right: John E. Allen Inc. Collection*
Page 63: *Top: Museum of Modern Art / Film Stills Archive; Bottom: Courtesy of Blackhawk Films*
Page 64: *Eastman House Archives*
Page 65: *John E. Allen Inc. Collection*
Pages 66–7: *Gordon Berkow Collection*
Page 68: *Left: Museum of Modern Art / Film Stills Archive; Right: Eastman House Archives*
Page 69: *Left: Eastman House Archives; Right, top: William K. Everson Collection; Right, bottom: Academy of Motion Picture Arts and Sciences*
Page 70: *John E. Allen Inc. Collection*
Page 72: *Top to bottom: Eastman House Archives; Academy of Motion Picture Arts and Sciences; Eastman House Archives; Mark Ricci's Memory Shop*
Page 73: *Top to bottom: Eastman House Archives; Eastman House Archives; William K. Everson Collection; Culver Pictures, Inc.*
Page 75: *Museum of Modern Art / Film Stills Archive*
Page 76: *Top: William K. Everson Collection; Bottom: John E. Allen Inc. Collection*
Page 77: *Museum of Modern Art / Film Stills Archive*
Page 79: *Top: William Kenly Collection; Bottom: Museum of Modern Art / Film Stills Archive*
Page 81: *Bottom: William K. Everson Collection*
Page 83: *Bottom: William Kenly Collection*
Page 85: *William K. Everson Collection*
Page 87: *Museum of Modern Art / Film Stills Archive*
Page 89: *John E. Allen Inc. Collection*
Page 90: *Top, left: William K. Everson Collection; Top, right: William K. Everson Collection; Middle, left: Leonard Maltin Collection; Middle, right: Museum of Modern Art / Film Stills Archive; Bottom, left: Museum of Modern Art / Film Stills Archive; Bottom, right: Museum of Modern Art / Film Stills Archive*
Page 91: *Top: Museum of Modern Art / Film Stills Archive; Bottom: William K. Everson Collection*
Page 93: *Museum of Modern Art / Film Stills Archive*
Page 94: *Bottom: Museum of Modern Art / Film Stills Archive*
Page 95: *William K. Everson Collection*
Page 97: *Top: John E. Allen Inc. Collection; Bottom: Theatre Collection of the New York Public Library*
Page 99: *Culver Pictures, Inc.*
Page 101: *Culver Pictures, Inc.*
Page 103: *Culver Pictures, Inc.*
Page 105: *Culver Pictures, Inc.*
Page 107: *Culver Pictures, Inc.*
Page 109: *Collection of The Institute of the American Musical, Inc.*
Page 111: *Collection of The Institute of the American Musical, Inc.*
Page 112: *Killiam Shows Inc. Collection*
Page 113: *Left: Eastman House Archives; Right: Theatre Collection of the New York Public Library*
Page 115: *Gordon Berkow Collection*
Page 116: *Top: Culver Pictures, Inc.; Middle: Museum of Modern Art / Film Stills Archive; Bottom: Museum of Modern Art / Film Stills Archive*
Page 119: *Museum of Modern Art / Film Stills Archive*
Page 121: *Top, left: Culver Pictures, Inc.; Top, right: John E. Allen Inc. Collection; Bottom: Culver Pictures, Inc.*
Page 123: *Culver Pictures, Inc.*
Page 125: *Top: William K. Everson Collection; Bottom: The Bettmann Archive*
Page 130: *Side panel, bottom: The Bettmann Archive*
Page 133: *Top: William K. Everson Collection; Bottom: Museum of Modern Art / Film Stills Archive*
Page 134: *Bottom: Movie Research Associates*
Page 137: *Right, top: Museum of Modern Art / Film Stills Archive*
Page 138: *Museum of Modern Art / Film Stills Archive*
Pages 146–7: *Springer / The Bettmann Archive*
Page 149: *William K. Everson Collection*
Page 153: *Top: Collection of The Institute of the American Musical, Inc.*
Page 155: *Top: John E. Allen Inc. Collection; Middle: Culver Pictures, Inc.; Bottom: Museum of Modern Art / Film Stills Archive*
Page 157: *Top: Academy of Motion Picture Arts and Sciences; Bottom: John E. Allen Inc. Collection*
Page 159: *Theatre Collection of the New York Public Library*
Page 161: *Museum of Modern Art / Film Stills Archive*
Page 165: *Gordon Berkow Collection*
Page 167: *Top: Collection of The Institute of the American Musical, Inc.; Bottom: Gordon Berkow Collection*
Page 168: *Top: Museum of Modern Art / Film Stills Archive; Bottom: William K. Everson Collection*
Page 169: *Top: William Kenly Collection; Middle: Museum of Modern Art / Film Stills Archive*
Page 172: *Eastman House Archives*
Page 173: *Left: Culver Pictures, Inc.; Right: Eastman House Archives*
Page 175: *Culver Pictures, Inc.*
Page 176: *Gordon Berkow Collection*
Page 177: *Top: Gordon Berkow Collection*
Page 180: *John E. Allen Collection*
Page 182: *Culver Pictures, Inc.*
Page 183: *Top: Gordon Berkow Collection; Middle: Gordon Berkow Collection*
Page 185: *Museum of Modern Art / Film Stills Archive*
Page 187: *Top: Museum of Modern Art / Film Stills Archive; Bottom: William K. Everson Collection*
Page 189: *Museum of Modern Art / Film Stills Archive*
Page 191: *John E. Allen Inc. Collection*
Page 193: *Museum of Modern Art / Film Stills Archive*
Page 197: *Eastman House Archives*
Page 198: *Top: Museum of Modern Art / Film Stills Archive; Middle: Eastman House Archives; Bottom: Culver Pictures, Inc.*
Page 199: *Museum of Modern Art / Film Stills Archive*
Page 201: *Mark Ricci's Memory Shop*
Page 202: *Eastman House Archives*
Page 204: *Museum of Modern Art / Film Stills Archive*
Page 205: *Museum of Modern Art / Film Stills Archive*
Page 206: *William Kenly Collection*
Page 207: *Left: Museum of Modern Art / Film Stills Archive; Right: William Kenly Collection*
Pages 208–9: *Counterclockwise: William Kenly Collection; William Kenly Collection; William Kenly Collection; Culver Pictures, Inc.; William Kenly*

Collection; Culver Pictures, Inc.; William Kenly Collection; William Kenly Collection; William Kenly Collection; John E. Allen Inc. Collection
Page 213: *Museum of Modern Art / Film Stills Archive*
Pages 214–5 *Eastman House Archives*
Page 216: *Left: Eastman House Archives; Right: Museum of Modern Art / Film Stills Archive*
Page 217: *Top: Museum of Modern Art / Film Stills Archive; Bottom: Eastman House Archives*
Page 218: *Mark Ricci's Memory Shop*
Page 223: *Leonard Maltin Collection*
Page 224: *Culver Pictures, Inc.*
Page 226: *Theatre Collection of the New York Public Library*
Page 227: *Museum of Modern Art / Film Stills Archive*
Page 228: *Left: Academy of Motion Picture Arts and Sciences; Right: Eastman House Archives*
Page 229: *Left: Museum of Modern Art / Film Stills Archive; Right: Eastman House Archives*
Page 230: *Museum of Modern Art / Film Stills Archive*
Page 231: *Top: Museum of Modern Art / Film Stills Archive; Bottom; The Bettmann Archive*
Page 233: *Eastman House Archives*
Page 235: *Top: Eastman House Archives; Bottom: David Bradley Collection*
Page 237: *Top: Museum of Modern Art / Film Stills Archive; Bottom: Theatre Collection of the New York Public Library*
Page 238: *Top to bottom: Museum of Modern Art / Film Stills Archive; David Bradley Collection; Theatre Collection of the New York Public Library; Museum of Modern Art / Film Stills Archive*
Page 239: *Top: Museum of Modern Art / Film Stills Archive; Bottom, left: David Bradley Collection; Bottom, right: Museum of Modern Art / Film Stills Archive*
Page 241: *Eastman House Archives*
Page 243: *Left: John E. Allen Inc. Collection; Right: Killiam Shows Inc.*
Page 245: *Top: John E. Allen Inc. Collection; Bottom: Eastman House Archives*
Page 247: *Top: John E. Allen Inc. Collection; Bottom: Eastman House Archives*
Pages 248–9: *William Kenly Collection*
Page 251: *Museum of Modern Art / Film Stills Archive*
Page 252: *Cinemabilia*
Page 253: *Museum of Modern Art / Film Stills Archive*
Page 254: *Museum of Modern Art / Film Stills Archive*
Page 255: *Left: Museum of Modern Art / Film Stills Archive; Right, bottom: William K. Everson Collection*
Page 256: *Bottom: Museum of Modern Art / Film Stills Archives*
Page 257: *Left: Movie Star News*
Page 261: *Collection of The Institute of the American Musical, Inc.*
Page 266: *The Bettmann Archive*
Page 267: *The Bettmann Archive*
Page 269: *Museum of Modern Art / Film Stills Archive*
Page 271: *Gordon Berkow Collection*
Page 272: *Culver Pictures, Inc.*
Page 273: *Culver Pictures, Inc.*
Page 275: *William Kenly Collection*
Page 276: *William Kenly Collection*
Page 277: *John E. Allen Inc. Collection*
Page 278: *Top: Museum of Modern Art / Film Stills Archive; Bottom: William Kenly Collection*
Page 281: *Museum of Modern Art / Film Stills Archive*
Page 282: *Museum of Modern Art / Film Stills Archive*
Page 283: *William Kenly Collection*
Page 285: *Bottom: Museum of Modern Art / Film Stills Archive*
Page 286: *Museum of Modern Art / Film Stills Archive*
Page 287: *William Kenly Collection*
Page 289: *Top to bottom: Museum of Modern Art / Film Stills Archive; Museum of Modern Art / Film Stills Archive; Museum of Modern Art / Film Stills Archive; John E. Allen Inc. Collection; Museum of Modern Art / Film Stills Archive*
Page 290: *John E. Allen Inc. Collection*
Page 291: *John E. Allen Inc. Collection*
Page 292: *Top: Museum of Modern Art / Film Stills Archive; Bottom: Eastman House Archives*
Page 293: *Museum of Modern Art / Film Stills Archive*
Page 294: *Culver Pictures, Inc.*
Page 295: *Museum of Modern Art / Film Stills Archive*
Page 296: *William Kenly Collection*
Page 297: *Middle: William Kenly Collection*
Page 299: *Eastman House Archives*
Page 301: *Jeb H. Perry Collection*
Page 302: *Museum of Modern Art / Film Stills Archive*
Page 303: *Museum of Modern Art / Film Stills Archive*
Page 305: *Museum of Modern Art / Film Stills Archive*
Page 307: *Eastman House Archives*
Page 310: *Theatre Collection of the New York Public Library*
Page 311: *Left: John E. Allen Inc. Collection; Right: Eastman House Archives*
Page 312: *Museum of Modern Art / Film Stills Archive*
Page 313: *Eastman House Archives*
Page 315: *Eastman House Archives*
Page 317: *William K. Everson Collection*
Page 319: *Top to bottom: Museum of Modern Art / Film Stills Archive; John E. Allen Inc. Collection; Killiam Shows Inc.*
Page 320: *Left: Cinemabilia; Right: Museum of Modern Art / Film Stills Archive*
Page 321: *Left: Museum of Modern Art / Film Stills Archive; Middle: Museum of Modern Art / Film Stills Archive; Right: Mark Ricci's Memory Shop*
Page 322: *Top to bottom: Museum of Modern Art / Film Stills Archive; Museum of Modern Art / Film Stills Archive; John Cocchi Collection*
Page 323: *The Bettmann Archive*
Page 324–5: *The American Cinematheque Collection*
Page 326: *Museum of Modern Art / Film Stills Archive*
Page 327: *Left: Museum of Modern Art / Film Stills Archive; Right: Culver Pictures, Inc.*
Page 328: *Left: Gordon Berkow Collection; Right: William Kenly Collection*
Page 330: *Museum of Modern Art / Film Stills Archive*
Page 331: *William Kenly Collection*
Page 333: *Left: Culver Pictures, Inc.*
Page 334: *John E. Allen Inc. Collection*
Page 335: *Gordon Berkow Collection*
Page 337: *Museum of Modern Art / Film Stills Archive*
Page 339: *Cinemabilia*
Page 340: *Top: Museum of Modern Art / Film Stills Archive; Bottom: Eastman House Archives*
Page 341: *Museum of Modern Art / Film Stills Archive*
Page 342: *Culver Pictures, Inc.*
Page 343: *Left: Cinemabilia; Right: William Kenly Collection*
Page 345: *Top: William Kenly Collection; Middle: William Kenly Collection*
Page 346: *Left, top: William Kenly Collection*
Page 349: *William Kenly Collection*
Page 352: *Culver Pictures, Inc.*
Page 354: *Right: Culver Pictures, Inc.*
Page 355: *Left: Museum of Modern Art / Film Stills Archive; Right, top: Museum of Modern Art / Film Stills Archive*
Page 357: *John E. Allen Inc. Collection*
Page 359: *Culver Pictures, Inc.*
Pages 360–1: *Left to right: Museum of Modern Art / Film Stills Archive; Eastman House Archives; Museum of Modern Art / Film Stills Archive*
Page 363: *Museum of Modern Art / Film Stills Archive*

Index

Graphic Credits

The text of this book was set in film in a typeface called Cheltenham. Bertram Grosvenor Goodhue specifically designed this typeface for Ingalls Kimball, Cheltenham Press of New York. The Cheltenham face appeared in 1902; it owes little or nothing to historical inspiration, and in that sense it is truly a twentieth-century type design. The display typeface has also been set in film in a typeface called Parsons, a period typeface which has recently reappeared in film.

The text type was photo-composed by Superior Printing, Champaign, Illinois. The display type was set in typositor by TypoGraphic Innovations, New York, New York.

Production and manufacturing coordination was handled by Marylea O'Reilly. Manuscript and proof coordination was handled by Lesley Krauss. Book design and graphics were styled by Janet Odgis. Design and graphics were directed by R.D. Scudellari.